MOUNTAINEERING

The Freedom of the Hills

MOUNTAINEERING
The Freedom of the Hills

EDITION 7

EDITED BY STEVEN M. COX AND KRIS FULSAAS

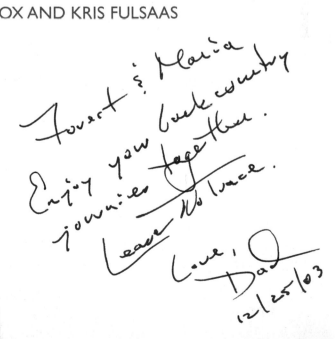

Forest & Maria

Enjoy your backcountry
journies together.

Leave No Trace.

Love,
Dad
12/25/03

THE MOUNTAINEERS

Published by
The Mountaineers Books
1001 SW Klickitat Way, Suite 201
Seattle, WA 98134

First edition 1960. Second edition 1967. Third edition 1974. Fourth edition 1982. Fifth edition 1992. Sixth edition 1997. Seventh edition: first printing 2003.

Book manufactured in Canada. Cover printed in the United States of America.

Project Editor: Christine Ummel Hosler
Developmental Editor: Kris Fulsaas
Copyeditor: Julie Van Pelt
Cover and book design: Ani Rucki
Layout: Jennifer LaRock Shontz
Illustrators: Jim Hays; Electronic Illustrators Group
Photographers: James Martin; Mark Kroese; Mike Burns; Scott Darsney

Front cover photograph: *Climbers on Bugaboo Spire*, British Columbia (Photo by James Martin)
Spine photograph: *Above Washburn's Thumb, Denali's West Buttress, Alaska* (Photo by Scott Darsney)
Back cover photograph: *Mixed climbing on Chair Peak's North Face, South Cascades, Washington* (Photo by Mark Kroese)
Frontispiece: *Climber on Liberty Bell, North Cascades, Washington* (Photo by James Martin)

Library of Congress Cataloging-in-Publication Data

Mountaineering : the freedom of the hills / editors, Steven M. Cox and Kris Fulsaas.— 7th ed.
    p.   cm.
Includes bibliographical references and index.
    ISBN 0-89886-827-0 (hardcover) — ISBN 0-89886-828-9 (pbk.)
1. Mountaineering. 2. Rock climbing. 3. Snow and ice climbing. I. Cox, Steven M., 1951- II. Fulsaas, Kris. III. Mountaineers (Society)
    GV200 .M688 2003
    796.52'2—dc21
                                    2002153642

A NOTE ABOUT SAFETY

Safety is an important concern in all outdoor activities. No book can alert you to every hazard or anticipate the limitations of every reader. The descriptions of techniques and procedures in this book are intended to provide general information. Nothing substitutes for formal instruction, routine practice, and plenty of experience. When you follow any of the procedures described here, you assume responsibility for your own safety. Use this book as a general guide to further information. Under normal conditions, excursions into the backcountry require attention to traffic, road and trail conditions, weather, terrain, the capabilities of your party, and other factors. Keeping informed on current conditions and exercising common sense are the keys to a safe, enjoyable outing.

— *The Mountaineers Books*

The Mountaineers Books is proud to be a corporate sponsor of Leave No Trace, whose mission is to promote and inspire responsible outdoor recreation through education, research, and partnerships. For more information, visit *www.lnt.org*, or call (800) 332-4100.

Contents

Preface

Mountaineering: The Freedom of the Hills is a leading text on mountaineering. It is used by recreational and professional climbers around the world and is translated into thirteen languages. It is intended as both an introductory and advanced text on mountaineering. Although it is a significant milestone, this seventh edition continues the tradition established by the previous six editions. Many contributors, all knowledgeable in mountaineering and especially knowledgeable in the area about which they wrote, prepared the content. It is this foundation, based on the experiences and collective wisdom of thousands of climbers from around the world, that makes this text the world's most accepted reference on mountaineering. A professional editor brought the various parts and chapters together to form a comprehensive and consistent text.

Each chapter from the sixth edition has been revised, rewritten, and, where necessary, expanded. New chapters on waterfall ice climbing and mixed climbing, stewardship and access, and physical conditioning have been added. These revisions reflect the rapid changes in mountaineering, including the development of new techniques and the introduction of new and improved equipment. This new edition emphasizes the responsibility we take as climbers to practice good stewardship of wild areas and to use minimum impact techniques in order to leave no trace of our passing.

SCOPE OF THE BOOK

As in previous editions, *Freedom* provides sound, clear, and current coverage of the concepts, techniques, and problems involved in the pursuit of mountain climbing and provides a fundamental understanding of each topic covered. In addition to presenting information for

the novice, much of the material in this book can help experienced climbers review and improve their skills. Individual topics, such as rock climbing or aid climbing, are detailed enough to be useful to readers with specific interests in those topics. *Freedom* is not intended, however, to be exhaustive or encyclopedic.

Sport climbing—making use of artificial climbing walls or fixed-protection routes at developed climbing areas—is increasingly popular. Although many techniques of sport climbing are interchangeable with those of mountain and rock climbing, there are differences. Those solely interested in sport climbing should also consult specialized texts.

Mountaineering cannot be learned just by studying a book. *Freedom* was originally written as a textbook for students and instructors participating in organized climbing courses. The environment of learning that is found in a climbing course taught by competent instructors is essential for beginning climbers.

Of necessity, climbing requires continual awareness of the situation and environment at hand. Varying conditions, routes, and individual abilities all mean that the techniques used and decisions made must be based on the particular circumstances. To any situation, the individual climber and climbing team must bring their knowledge, skills, and experience and then make their own judgments. To reflect this process, *Freedom* presents a variety of widely used techniques and practices and then outlines both their advantages and limitations. Material is presented not as dogma or the final word but as the basis for making sound judgments. To climb safely, climbers must view mountaineering as a problem-solving process and not as a rote application of techniques.

The type of climbing described in *Freedom* is frequently

Previous page: *Ice climber on the Aiguille du Midi, Chamonix, France* (Photo by James Martin)

experienced (and, most people would say, best experienced) in the wilderness. Wilderness mountaineers take responsibility for helping to preserve the wilderness environment for present and future generations.

ORIGINS OF THE BOOK

Freedom's direction and emphasis originated from the development of climbing in the Pacific Northwest. The wild and complex character of the mountains in this region, with their abundance of snow and glaciers throughout the year, furthered the mountaineering challenge. Access was inherently difficult. There were few roads, and the initial explorations were themselves expeditions, often with native guides.

When The Mountaineers Club was organized in 1906, one of its major purposes was to explore and study the mountains, forests, and watercourses of the Northwest. The journey to the mountain summit was a long and difficult one, and it required a variety of skills. With the knowledge of these skills, the competence that comes from their practice, and the experience gained through climbing mountains, more than a few gained the exhilarating freedom of the hills.

As interest in mountaineering in the region grew, so did a tradition of tutelage. Increasingly, experienced climbers took novices under their wings to pass on their knowledge and skills. The Mountaineers formalized that exchange by developing a series of climbing courses. This book grew out a century's worth of teaching mountaineering and conducting climbs in the Northwest and throughout the world.

LEGACY OF THE PRECEDING EDITIONS

Isaac Newton said, "If I have seen further than certain other men, it is by standing upon the shoulders of giants." The previous editions of *Freedom* represent a tradition of bringing together and sorting through the knowledge, techniques, opinions, and advice of a large number of practicing climbers. Students, both in training and on climbs, have been a pivotal source of information.

Prior to publication of the first edition of *Freedom* in 1960, The Mountaineers climbing courses had used European works, particularly Geoffrey Winthrop Young's classic *Mountain Craft,* as required reading. These works did not cover various subjects unique and important to American and Pacific Northwest mountaineering. To fill in the gaps, course lecturers prepared outlines, which they distributed to students. Eventually these outlines were fleshed out and gathered together as the *Climber's Notebook,* subsequently published, in 1948, as the *Mountaineers Handbook.* By 1955, tools and techniques had changed so drastically, and the courses had become so much more complex, that a new and more comprehensive textbook was needed.

Members of the first edition editorial committee were Harvey Manning (chairman), John R. Hazle, Carl Henrikson, Nancy Bickford Miller, Thomas Miller, Franz Mohling, Rowland Tabor, and Lesley Stark Tabor. A substantial portion of the then relatively small Puget Sound climbing community participated—some seventy-five were writers of preliminary, revised, advanced, semifinal, and final chapter drafts, and another one or two hundred were reviewers, planners, illustrators, typists, proofreaders, financiers, promoters, retailers, warehousemen, and shipping clerks. At the time, there were few Mountaineers climbers who did not have a hand in making or selling the book. Those donating their time were rewarded by their accomplishment, and those donating their money were repaid from the success of the book. *Freedom of the Hills* became the first title published by the now very successful Mountaineers Books.

Efforts leading to the publication of the second edition (in 1967) began in 1964. Members of the second edition editorial committee were John M. Davis (chairman), Tom Hallstaff, Max Hollenbeck, Jim Mitchell, Roger Neubauer, and Howard Stansbury. Even though much of the first edition was retained, the task force was, again, of impressive proportions, numbering several dozen writers, uncounted reviewers, and helpers. Survivors of the previous committee, notably John R. Hazle, Tom Miller, and Harvey Manning, provided continuity to the effort. As he had with the first edition, Harvey Manning once again edited the entire text and supervised production.

The third edition editorial committee was formed in

Porters at Urdukas looking out at the Trango Tower Group, Pakistan (Photo by Mike Burns)

1971 and headed by Sam Fry. Initially, a planning committee analyzed the previous edition and set guidelines for its revision. A steering committee, consisting of Sam Fry, Fred Hart, Sean Rice, Jim Sanford, and Howard Stansbury, directed the revision and had overall responsibility for the text. A large number of climbers contributed to individual chapters; the reviewing, revising, editing, and collation of chapters and sections was a true community effort. Peggy Ferber edited the entire book, which was published in 1974.

The fourth edition of *Freedom* (1982) involved a major revision and included complete rewrites of many chapters, most notably the entire section on ice and snow. A cast of hundreds was guided by a team of

technical editors: Ed Peters (chairman), Roger Andersen, Dave Anthony, Dave Enfield, Lee Helser, Robert Swanson, and John Young. A large number of climbers submitted comments to the committee. Small teams of writers prepared a series of drafts for review by the technical editors. In addition to the substantial contribution such writers made, many others provided valuable help through critiques of subsequent and final drafts not only for technical accuracy and consistency but also for readability and comprehension.

Efforts on the fifth edition began in late 1987. Chaired by Paul Gauthier and, later, Myrna Plum, the committee undertook another major revision. Content was brought up to date and the layout and illustrations were made more contemporary and readable. Editorial coordinator Ben Arp and section coordinators Marty Lentz, Margaret Miller, Judy Ramberg, and Craig Rowley worked with volunteer contributors to develop the book's content. A professional editor/writer, Don Graydon, blended the volunteers' efforts into a consistent and readable style for the edition published in 1992.

In the autumn of 1994, Kurt Hanson led the effort to write the sixth edition. Section coordinators were Jo Backus, Marcia Hanson, Tom Hodgman, Myrna Plum, and Myron Young, with Don Heck coordinating the illustrations. Don Graydon again edited the text. New sections were added on geology, the cycle of snow, and mountain weather.

THE SEVENTH EDITION

What sets *Freedom* apart from other climbing texts is the process by which its content is prepared. The contributors are all active climbers who regularly use and teach the information and techniques about which they write in this book. The collaborative effort distills the knowledge and experience of the many contributors into a whole. Although one individual has responsibility for preparing the initial draft of a chapter, the other contributors comment and share their opinions on the material.

Planning for the seventh edition began in autumn of 2000. The Mountaineers Board of Trustees chartered Steven M. Cox to lead an effort to develop a new edition. Comments and suggestions were then gathered from experienced climbers throughout the world, and the revision committee first met in mid-May 2001.

Part 1, Outdoor Fundamentals, was overseen by Cebe Wallace, with individual chapters written by Susan Wright Geiger, First Steps; Bill Deters, Clothing and Equipment; Margie Cashman and Cebe Wallace, Camping and Food; Courtenay Schurman, Physical Conditioning; Bob Burns, Navigation; Ron Sheats and Satu Muldrow, Wilderness Travel; Steve Payne, Leave No Trace; and Andy Fitz, Stewardship and Access.

Jeremy ("Jake") Larson oversaw the compilation of Part 2, Climbing Fundamentals. Individual chapters were written by Patrick Mullaney, Basic Safety System; Phil Kelley, Belaying; and Gene Yore, Rappelling.

Myrna Plum oversaw Part 3, Rock Climbing, and individual chapters were prepared by Lynda Hillman, Alpine Rock-Climbing Technique; Steve Firebaugh and Shirley Rogers, Rock Protection and Leading on Rock; and Chris Johns and Chuck Neudorf, Aid Climbing.

Part 4, Snow, Ice, and Alpine Climbing, was overseen by Ron Eng. Individual chapters were written by Bruce Greenstein, Mike Burns, Ron Eng, Satu Muldrow, and Paul Russell, Snow Travel and Climbing; Peter Clitherow, Glacier Travel and Crevasse Rescue; Mike Burns, Ron Eng, and Mike Maude, Alpine Ice Climbing, and Waterfall Ice and Mixed Climbing; and Grace Parker, Expedition Climbing.

John Wick oversaw Part 5, Emergency Prevention and Response, with individual chapters contributed by Don Goodman, Leadership; Don Schaechtel, Safety; Gretchen Lentz, M.D., and Dave Simpson, First Aid; and Dave Shema, Alpine Rescue.

Part 6, The Mountain Environment, was overseen by John Wickham. Individual chapters were written by Scott Babcock, Mountain Geology; Sue Ferguson, The Cycle of Snow; and Jeff Renner, Mountain Weather.

Illustrative material was overseen by Jeff Bowman and Debra Wick.

Tegan Wallace assisted the contributors of the chapters Aid Climbing and Expedition Climbing. Mike Burns, Glenn Eades, Steve Firebaugh, Kurt Hanson, and Myrna Plum provided additional valuable input. The staff of The Mountaineers Books also contributed their time and talents, particularly Graphic Project Manager Ani Rucki, Freelance Art Director Marge Mueller, freelance editors Kris Fulsaas and Julie Van Pelt, and Project Editor Christine Ummel Hosler.

THE MOUNTAINEERS

THE MOUNTAINEERS, founded in 1906, is a nonprofit outdoor activity and conservation club. Its purposes are:

- To explore, study, and enjoy the mountains, forests, and watercourses of the Northwest and beyond.
- To gather into permanent form the history and traditions of these regions and explorations.
- To preserve by example, teaching, and the encouragement of protective legislation or otherwise the beauty of the natural environment.

- To make expeditions and provide educational opportunities in fulfillment of the above purposes.
- To encourage a spirit of good fellowship among all lovers of outdoor life.
- To hold real estate and personal property and to receive, hire, purchase, occupy, and maintain and manage suitable buildings and quarters for the furtherance of the purposes of the association, and to hold in trust or otherwise funds, received by bequest or gift or otherwise, to be devoted to the purposes of said association.

Based in Seattle, Washington, the club is now the third largest such organization in the United States, with seven branches throughout Washington State.

The Mountaineers sponsors both classes and year-round outdoor activities, which include hiking, mountain climbing, ski-touring, snowshoeing, bicycling, camping, kayaking and canoeing, nature study, sailing, and adventure travel. The club's conservation division supports environmental causes by providing educational activities, sponsoring legislation, and presenting informational programs. All club activities are led by skilled, experienced volunteers, who are dedicated to promoting safe and responsible enjoyment and preservation of the outdoors.

If you would like to participate in these organized outdoor activities or the club's programs, consider a membership in The Mountaineers. For information and an application, write to The Mountaineers, Club Headquarters, 300 Third Avenue West, Seattle, WA 98119; phone (206) 284-6310; visit *www.mountaineers.org;* or e-mail *clubmail@mountaineers.org.*

The Mountaineers Books

The Mountaineers Books, an active, nonprofit publishing program of the club, produces guidebooks, instructional texts, historical works, natural history guides, and works on environmental conservation. Books produced by The Mountaineers are aimed at fulfilling the club's mission.

The Mountaineers Foundation

The Mountaineers Foundation is a public foundation established in 1968 to promote the study of mountains, forests, and streams, and to contribute to the preservation of natural beauty and ecological integrity. The Mountaineers Foundation fulfills its mission by stewardship of important preserves and by grant making. Grants are targeted for startup activities, important small-scale studies, and innovative initiatives. Flexible cooperation with the Trust for Public Lands, The Nature Conservancy of Washington, and other conservation agencies greatly extends the foundation's ability to preserve habitats, protect wilderness areas, and remove the threat of development from other significant lands. Contributions to The Mountaineers Foundation are tax deductible to the extent allowed by United States law. More information is available at *www.mountaineersfoundation.org* or through The Mountaineers.

Next page: *Hiker at Lago Pehoe in Torres del Paine National Park, Chile* (Photo by James Martin)

OUTDOOR FUNDAMENTALS

1
CHAPTER

First Steps

TECHNICAL KNOWLEDGE AND SKILLS ■ PHYSICAL PREPARATION ■ MENTAL
PREPARATION ■ JUDGMENT AND EXPERIENCE ■ CARING FOR THE
WILDERNESS—LEAVE NO TRACE ■ PRESERVING WILDERNESS ■
A CLIMBING CODE ■ GAINING THE FREEDOM OF THE HILLS

**Mountaineering is many things. It is climbing, panoramic views, and wilderness experience.
For many, it is the fulfillment of childhood dreams; for others, an opportunity to grow in
the face of difficulty. In the mountains await adventure and mystery and lifetime
bonds with climbing partners. The challenge of mountaineering offers you a
chance to learn about yourself outside the confines of the modern world.**

To be sure, you will also find risk and hardship, but despite the difficulties sometimes faced—or maybe because of them—mountaineering can provide a sense of tranquility and spiritual communion found nowhere else. In the words of British climber George Leigh Mallory, "What we get from this adventure is just sheer joy."

But before you find joy or freedom in the hills, you must prepare for the mountains by learning technical, physical, mental, and emotional skills. Just as you must take a first step in order to climb a mountain, you must also take first steps to become a mountaineer. And though becoming skilled in the mountains is a process that continues as long as you spend time there, you have to begin somewhere. This book can serve as your guide and reference in acquiring those skills and, as such, your passport to the freedom of the hills. This chapter starts you along the path to learning the techniques needed for safe and skilled mountain travel.

Technical Knowledge and Skills

To travel safely and enjoyably in the mountains, you need skills. You need to know what clothing, basic equipment, and food to bring into the backcountry, and how to overnight safely. You need to know how to cover long distances while relying on only what you carry in your pack, navigating without trails or signs. You need technical climbing skills, including belaying (the technique of securing your rope partner in case of a fall) and rappelling (using the rope to get down), to competently scale and descend the mountains you reach. And you must have the specific skills for the terrain you choose—whether it be rock, snow, ice, or glacier. Although mountaineers always strive to minimize risks to themselves and others, mountain travel can never be completely predictable. For that reason, every mountaineer should be trained in safety, wilderness first aid, and rescue.

Physical Preparation

Mountaineering is a physically demanding activity. Nearly every type of climbing has become increasingly athletic, especially at the higher levels of difficulty. Climbers today accomplish what was considered impossible only a few years ago. In rock, ice, and high-altitude climbing, standards are taken to new levels each year. Limits are being pushed not only on the way up peaks, but also on the way down. Steep routes once considered difficult or impossible to ascend are now also descended on skis and snowboards. Among the changes to the landscape of climbing, very notable are the advances and increasing popularity of steep ice

climbing and "mixed" climbs, those that include a combination of frozen water and rock. Although most people appreciate such extreme achievements from the sidelines, higher levels of performance are often reached by recreational climbers and mountaineers after these new standards are set.

Whatever your skill level and aspiration, good physical conditioning is important. The stronger you are, the wider your choice of mountains to climb. You will enjoy trips rather than endure them. More important, the safety of the whole party may hinge on the strength—or weakness—of one member. Chapter 4, Physical Conditioning, outlines the basic principles of how to train and stay conditioned for mountaineering.

Mental Preparation

Just as important as physical conditioning is mental attitude, which often determines success or failure in mountaineering. The ability to keep a clear, calm mind really helps in deciding whether to push through a difficult move or back off. Mountaineers need to be positive, realistic, and honest with themselves. A can-do attitude may turn into dangerous overconfidence if it is not tempered with a realistic appraisal of the circumstances and environment.

Many a veteran mountaineer says the greatest challenges are mental. Perhaps this is one of mountaineering's greatest appeals: While seeking the freedom of the hills, we come face to face with ourselves.

Judgment and Experience

As important as mental preparation and attitude is the ability to solve problems and make good decisions. Sound judgment, perhaps a mountaineer's most valued and prized skill, develops from integrating knowledge with experience. This book outlines mountaineering equipment and techniques ranging from the basic to the advanced, but the goal of every mountaineer is determining how best to use that learning to answer the sometimes unpredictable challenges of the mountains.

Much of what mountaineers need are coping skills and problem-solving skills—the ability to deal with external factors such as adverse weather, long hikes, and mountain accidents, as well as internal factors including fear, exhaustion, and desire. As climbers experience these situations, they become better decision-makers, gaining judgment and experience that can help them in the future.

However, mountaineering tends to provide many novel situations that require careful judgment rather than automatic responses. Although you may use past experience to make decisions in the mountains, you will almost certainly never face the same situation twice. To be sure, this creates the potential for tragedy, but this uncertainty also holds the allure and challenge of mountaineering.

The same can be said of many situations that involve risk, challenge, and accomplishment. As Helen Keller observed, "Security is mostly a superstition. It does not exist in nature, nor do the children of men as a whole experience it. Avoiding danger is no safer in the long run than outright exposure. Life is either a daring adventure or nothing at all."

Caring for the Wilderness— Leave No Trace

The mountaineering skills in this book are tools that allow you to visit remote areas of the world. If you use these skills to answer the call of wild vistas, remember that the beauty of wilderness frequently becomes its undoing by attracting visitors—leaving the landscape touched by human hands and eventually less than wild.

People are consuming wilderness at an alarming rate—using it, managing it, and changing it irreparably as they do so. For this reason, The Mountaineers and many other outdoor enthusiasts have adopted a set of principles referred to as Leave No Trace. These principles and ethics are explained in more detail in Chapter 7, Leave No Trace.

The mountains do not exist for our amusement. They owe us nothing and they ask for nothing from us. As fervently described by Hudson Stuck, a member of the first team to ascend Mount McKinley, the climbing party felt they had been granted "a privileged communion with the high places of the earth." As mountaineers traveling in the wilderness, our minimum charge for this privilege is to leave the hills as we found them, with no sign of our passing. We must study the places we visit and become sensitive to their vulnerability; we can then camp, climb, and travel in ways that truly leave no trace.

Preserving Wilderness

The privileges we enjoy in the mountains bring the responsibility not only to leave no trace, but also to help preserve these environments we love. The facts of mountaineering life today include permit systems that limit access to the backcountry, environmental restoration projects, legislative alerts, clashes of competing interest groups, and closures of roads, trails, and entire climbing areas. In addition to being vigilant in treading softly in the mountains, mountaineers must now speak loudly in support of wilderness preservation, access, and sensitive use of our wild lands. We can no longer assume that we will have access to explore the vertical realms of our planet. In addition to being mountaineers, climbers, and adventurers, we must be active wilderness advocates if we want to continue to enjoy what was once taken for granted.

A Climbing Code

Many years ago, The Mountaineers devised a set of guidelines to help people conduct themselves safely in the mountains. Based on careful observation of the habits of skilled climbers and a thoughtful analysis of accidents, those guidelines have served well not only for climbers but, with slight adaptation, for all wilderness travelers. This climbing code (see the sidebar) is not inflexible doctrine, but it has proven to be a sound guide to practices that minimize risk.

This climbing code is not meant to be a step-by-step formula for reaching summits or avoiding danger but, rather, a set of guidelines to safe mountaineering. It is recommended especially for beginners, who have not yet developed the necessary judgment that comes from years of experience. Experienced mountaineers often modify these guidelines in practice, making judgments based on an understanding of the risk and the skill to help control that risk.

Climbers sometimes question the need for such standards in a sport notable for the absence of formal rules. However, many serious accidents could have been avoided or minimized if these simple principles had

CLIMBING CODE

- Leave the trip itinerary with a responsible person.
- Carry the necessary clothing, food, and equipment at all times.
- A climbing party of three is the minimum, unless adequate prearranged support is available. On glaciers, a minimum of two rope teams is recommended.
- Rope up on all exposed places and for all glacier travel. Anchor all belays.
- Keep the party together, and obey the leader or majority rule.
- Never climb beyond your ability and knowledge.
- Never let judgment be overruled by desire when choosing the route or deciding whether to turn back.
- Follow the precepts of sound mountaineering as set forth in textbooks of recognized merit.
- Behave at all times in a manner that reflects favorably upon mountaineering, including adherence to Leave No Trace principles.

been followed. This climbing code is built on the premise that mountaineers want a high probability for safety and success, even in risk-filled or doubtful situations, and that they want an adequate margin of safety in case they have misjudged their circumstances.

Gaining the Freedom of the Hills

"Freedom of the hills" is a concept that combines the simple joy of being in the mountains with the skill, equipment, and strength to travel without harm to ourselves, others, or the environment. The hills do not offer this freedom inherently—only on trade. What must you offer in this trade? Training, preparation, and desire.

We live in an age in which a conscious choice is required in order to avoid civilization with all of its modern technologies and conveniences. Computers remind us where we need to be when and how to get there. With the right equipment, you can be no more than a phone call away anywhere on the planet. Although you do not have to leave these things behind to go to the mountains, for those who want to step out of—if only briefly—this mechanized, digitized world, the mountains beckon. They offer a place of richness and communion with our world that can be found in few places on earth.

Mountaineering takes place in an environment indifferent to human needs, and not everyone is willing to pay the price for its rich physical and spiritual rewards. But those who dream of climbing mountains can use this book to follow that dream. And if you learn to climb safely and skillfully, body and spirit in tune with the wilderness, you too can heed the inspiration of John Muir. "Climb the mountains," he told us, "and get their good tidings. Nature's peace will flow into you as sunshine flows into trees. The winds will blow their own freshness into you and the storms their energy, while cares will drop off like autumn leaves." As Muir wrote, "Walk quietly in any direction and taste the freedom of the mountaineer."

Clothing and Equipment

**CLOTHING ■ FOOTGEAR ■ PACKS ■ ESSENTIAL EQUIPMENT—
A SYSTEMS APPROACH ■ EQUIPMENT CHECKLIST ■
PREPARING FOR THE FREEDOM OF THE HILLS**

**Packing for a wilderness trip is a matter of take it or leave it. With thousands of choices
available in outdoor clothing and equipment, it is no longer a question of how to find
what is needed but, rather, of limiting the load to just the items that will keep you safe,
dry, and comfortable. The idea is to carry what is needed and leave the rest at
home. More clothing and equipment may make you more comfortable,
but the extra weight may also limit how far, fast, or high you can go.**

To strike a balance between too much and too little, monitor what you take on a trip. After each trip, determine what you used, what was genuinely needed for a margin of safety, and what items were unnecessary.

When buying equipment, go for lightweight, low-bulk alternatives if the reduction does not jeopardize the item's performance or durability.

If you are new to mountaineering, you will not have

the experience yet to know what will work best, so do not buy all the basic gear right away. Take it one trip at a time, one purchase at a time. New climbers tend to buy for extremes they seldom encounter. Wait until you have garnered enough experience to make intelligent decisions before spending money on clothing, boots, or packs. Rent, borrow, or improvise during early outings. Get advice by talking to seasoned climbers, by window-shopping at outdoor stores, and by reading mountaineering magazines. The "latest and greatest" is not always best overall. The best items for a person's intended use are not necessarily the most costly. However, the cheapest gear is often not the most economical; with experience, you might discover that certain gear features and attributes justify higher cost, and as a result replace cheaper gear with what you really want and need.

This chapter provides information on basic and essential wilderness gear. Additional gear for overnight trips, such as stoves, cookware, sleeping bags and pads, and tents, is covered in Chapter 3, Camping and Food. This chapter includes guidelines on what constitutes good equipment, and though it will not advise which brands to purchase, it will help you find high-quality items among the many choices.

CLOTHING

Clothing helps a person stay comfortable by creating a thin insulating layer of air next to the skin. The enemies of comfort—rain, wind, heat, and cold—work against this protective air layer.

"Comfort" is usually a relative term for mountaineers. Inclement weather often forces climbers to endure conditions that deteriorate far below most people's concept of comfort. In climbing, the key to maintaining relative comfort is to stay dry—or, when wet, to stay warm and get dry quickly.

Mountaineering clothing serves a much greater purpose than comfort. In the wilderness, safety is a primary concern. When venturing into remote territory, climbers lose the option of quickly dashing back to civilization to escape foul weather. Instead, they must deal with difficult conditions for however long those conditions last.

Prolonged periods of dampness, even in moderately cool temperatures, can cause the body's core temperature to fall. Failure to protect the body from wind leads to the effective drop in temperature known as wind chill factor (see Appendix B, Wind Chill Temperature Index). For many unfortunate individuals, substandard clothing has led to hypothermia—a dangerous, uncontrolled drop in body temperature that is a frequent cause of death in the mountains (see Chapter 23, First Aid, for more on hypothermia). Carefully select your clothing system to assure your survival during sustained exposure to the cold and wet.

Conversely, the clothing system must be able to protect you from overheating on hot days and to prevent excessive sweating, which can dampen clothing from within and lead to severe dehydration. Ventilation, breathability, and sun protection are key considerations.

At outdoor equipment stores, there is an overwhelming variety of garments, high-tech fabrics, features, and brand names, each proclaiming superior performance. With the dazzling matrix of high-tech gear vying for purchase, assembling a clothing system for the first time can be a daunting and confusing task. When shopping for clothing, ask questions and read tags to help make informed decisions. Evaluate garments for their functionality—will they work when wet? In addition to cost, consider durability, versatility, and reliability. Clothing for other active outdoor sports may be suitable for climbing also.

Keep in mind that no single garment or fabric is ideal for all climbers or all situations. One climber may select a clothing system markedly different from that chosen by another with a different body structure or metabolism. Nor will an individual climber always use exactly the same clothing system on every outing. Different clothing may be worn depending on the season and type of activity. Personal preference plays a significant role. The best way to select an outdoor wardrobe is to gain experience and judgment by trial and error, sticking with the clothing strategies that provide the most comfort.

If you are new to wilderness travel, it is probably best to start out carrying what seems like more than enough layers to keep warm and dry. Delete items from your pack only when there is no doubt that it is possible to survive without them, whatever the conditions. Try to minimize the weight of your clothing, but not at the expense of safety. Before heading out to the peaks, get a weather forecast and think ahead about what temperatures and conditions will be encountered, then pack accordingly.

Layering

Optimize the effectiveness and versatility of clothing by wearing it in a system of layers. Layering makes it easier to adapt to fluctuating temperatures and conditions in the mountains. The goal of layering is to keep body temperatures comfortable at all times, with the least weight and bulk possible. This often means frequent adjustments. Most experienced mountaineers eventually develop a basic system of a few very select garments of high functionality, which they use in combination, depending on conditions and personal preferences, for most of their mountaineering activities. The base layer may change, more or less insulation might be carried, perhaps a different outer garment, or something new to try out—but the basic layering system has withstood the test of time and the latest craze in high-tech sportswear. This basic outdoor clothing system consists of three types of layers: a layer next to the skin, insulating layers, and an outer shell layer.

Layer next to the skin: This should allow perspiration to pass away from your skin, keeping it dry. This "wicking" process can be vital to keeping you warm, because wet garments in contact with the skin can cause far more heat loss than dry ones.

Insulating layers: These should trap warm air next to your body. The thicker the layer of trapped air, the warmer you will be. Although not as efficient as a single, monolithic block of "dead" air (as in a down parka, for example), several light, loosely fitting layers can trap a lot of insulating air in and between each other, and such an arrangement is very adjustable.

Shell layer: The outer layer should provide protection from wind, rain, and sun.

Choosing Fabrics

Clothing suitable for the outdoors is made from a great variety of fabrics, each with its particular advantages and drawbacks. Various qualities of outdoor fabrics are detailed in the following sections and summarized in Table 2-1.

Natural Fibers

In the early days of mountaineering, natural-fiber clothing was all that was available. Although they can work well, most natural fibers readily absorb water. This is usually (but not always) a disadvantage.

Cotton: This is comfortable to wear when dry, but loses its insulating qualities when wet, absorbs many times its weight in water, and generally takes a long time to dry. Because of these characteristics, it is dangerous to rely on cotton for warmth. Cotton plays a common role in many hypothermia tragedies. In hot weather, however, cotton ventilates and cools well, and can provide good sun protection. Wear a wet cotton T-shirt on a hot day, and the evaporating water will cool you off.

Wool: This is far less absorbent than cotton, so it holds less water when wet and requires less heat to dry. When wet, wool does not collapse as much as cotton; thus it retains much of its dead-air space and works well as an insulating layer. This noncollapsing feature also makes wool a great material for socks. The main drawbacks of wool are its relatively heavy weight and its bulkiness. Wool garments vary in their processing— the lighter the processing (that is, the closer the wool resembles "raw" wool), the better the garment will shed water. Wool can feel scratchy, but some types (such as merino) are very soft and comfortable next to the skin. Wool's greater absorbency next to the skin is preferred over synthetics by some; it does not melt when exposed to heat from a stove; and it creates more friction than other fibers when the person wearing it is sliding on steep snow—a real plus for self-arrest.

Synthetic Fibers

Synthetic fibers and fabrics have largely replaced natural fibers in mountaineering clothing. Many synthetic fibers are hydrophobic, which means they tend not to absorb moisture. Garments made of synthetic fibers will absorb some moisture, but only in the spaces between the fibers rather than inside the individual fibers themselves. When such a garment is wet, most of this moisture can be wrung out; the rest evaporates quickly.

TABLE 2-1. FABRIC COMPARISONS

Fabric	Advantages	Disadvantages	Uses
Polyester/polypropylene	Most types absorb little water. Retains insulating qualities when wet. Lightweight.	Some types retain odors. Not wind resistant. Can be bulky. Melts with high heat.	Many different forms. Skin layers (underwear, T-shirts). Insulating layers (pile/fleece), hats, gloves, socks.
Wool	More abrasion- and wind-resistant than many synthetics. Retains insulating qualities when wet. High friction on snow/ice. Does not melt with high heat.	Heavier, absorbs more water, dries less quickly than most synthetics. Can be bulky.	Skin layers, insulating/outer layers (sweaters, shirts, pants), hats, gloves, socks.
Nylon	Strong, durable, lightweight. Good wind and abrasion resistance.	Fairly absorbent if not treated. May dry slowly. Slippery. Melts with high heat.	Outer garments (parkas, wind garments, rain pants, overmitts), hats, vapor-barrier socks.
Stretch/woven nylon blend	Versatile. Stretchy, durable, fairly insulative and wind resistant. Usually dries quickly. Wide comfort range.	Some types dry slowly. May snag. May be expensive.	Skin layers, light outer/midlayer garments (pants, shirts).
Cotton	Good in hot weather. Breathes well. Comfortable when dry.	Highly absorbent; dries slowly. Loses insulating qualities when wet.	Sun protection, bandannas, hats, T-shirts. Generally inappropriate for cool/wet conditions.

Polyester and polypropylene: These fabrics are good at wicking perspiration, so they are well suited for use next to the skin. They are not absorbent, however, so depending on how a garment made from them interacts with the next layer, it may not completely dry the skin. Polypropylene underwear performs well but is somewhat scratchy and tends to give off an offensive odor after being worn for a while. Polyester has largely replaced polypropylene for underwear, offering a softer feel against the skin and less odor retention.

The packaging for different types of synthetic underwear commonly displays fancy-sounding brand names. It is easy to become confused trying to compare them. Often, brand names merely refer to different fabric treatments, and different-looking garments may actually be quite similar. Reading the garment tags and consulting a salesperson can help you to sort through the confusion.

In addition to use against the skin, polypropylene and polyester work well as insulating layers. There are a number of different weights of long underwear. Or consider jackets and pants of different weaves, such as thick and fluffy polyester pile or fleece. Although generally lightweight, most of these garments, by themselves, offer only fair wind resistance, and some are bulky.

Nylon: This synthetic is manufactured in many, many forms, making it one of the world's most versatile materials. In outdoor clothing, nylon fabrics find their main uses in shell garments. Characteristics vary widely from one style of nylon to another. Some nylons provide good wind resistance, others feel slick or soft, but virtually all are known for strength and durability. One shortcoming is that, unless treated, many nylons absorb water and may dry fairly slowly.

When two or more fibers are blended together, the

2

resulting fabric's characteristics are somewhere in between those of the materials used. For example, underwear that is 80 percent polyester and 20 percent spandex provides more stretchiness but less wicking than plain polyester.

Waterproof/Breathable Fabrics

Rain parkas and rain pants are generally made of nylon or nylon blends. Nylon itself is not waterproof, so rain garments derive their waterproofness from a number of different fabrication methods and/or treatments applied to the fabric.

Waterproof/nonbreathable coating: The simplest method is to cover the nylon garment with a waterproof/nonbreathable coating, such as polyurethane. Such coatings are lightweight and relatively inexpensive, but not very resistant to abrasion or mildew. Although such coatings keep rain out, they also seal sweat and water vapor in. If you are working hard, the sweat generated can dampen the insulating layers. Think of a cup of hot coffee. If a lid is put on top, water from the coffee's steam will condense on the inside of the lid. In a way, your body is like that coffee: If your sweat does not have a way to escape through the clothing, you will get wet.

Waterproof/breathable coating: These coatings were designed to reduce the problem of sealing water in as well as out. Applied to the inside of a nylon shell, the coatings have billions of microscopic pores per square inch. Moisture vapor from the skin is emitted in the form of individual water molecules, which are much smaller than droplets of rain. The holes in the waterproof/breathable coating are large enough to let vapor escape but too small for raindrops to get in, so the coating breathes somewhat while staying waterproof. Unsurprisingly, high-tech coatings such as these are more expensive than regular coatings. Like much mountaineering equipment, waterproof/breathable coatings go by a variety of brand names, and often it is necessary to talk to a salesperson to understand what to purchase.

Laminated waterproof/breathable membrane: These membranes—Gore-Tex is the best known—are perforated with microscopic pores, like a waterproof/breathable coating. Membranes work on the same theory as such coatings but are instead fabricated as a separate layer inside the nylon shell. These garments typically are even more expensive than those with waterproof/breathable coatings. Both can have a long functional life if they are cared for properly (see below).

Although the waterproof/breathable fabrics are a marked improvement over old-style coated nylons, they are not perfect. When working hard, a person can exceed the garment's ability to blow off steam, and sweat will condense inside the shell. Once in liquid form, the sweat can no longer escape through the garment, and the original problem is back again. The water repellency of the outer fabric is also a factor; if rain does not "bead up," it coats the exterior, greatly reducing the fabric's ability to breathe. Most waterproof/breathable fabrics work reasonably well at being waterproof, but designs can vary considerably in their ventilation, depending on construction techniques and features such as zippers under the arms or in the torso. Extra ventilation often demands a higher price.

Care of waterproof/breathable fabrics: Waterproof/breathable shells—whether they have a coating or a laminated membrane—depend on relatively delicate components in order to function. Do not expect even the most-expensive rain parka to last for long if it is abused. Many experienced mountaineers use less-expensive wind shirts or shells for most activities, keeping their waterproof/breathable shells in the pack until they are really needed.

Dirt and sweat can clog and contaminate fabric pores, reducing breathability. Keeping the shell clean helps it to function at its full capability. Certain types of detergents can break down shell elements, so read the tags and follow the manufacturer's recommended washing and drying procedures.

It is usually not a good idea to toss a parka in the washer after every use. The churning motion of a washing machine will gradually remove the shell's water-repellent finish.

Water-repellent finishes are applied, as mentioned above, in order to make rainwater bead up on the shell surface. When water no longer beads on the surface, the shell can be restored somewhat by putting it through a gentle cycle in the dryer or by ironing it. Follow the manufacturer's instructions, especially before retreatment with a spray-on or wash-in agent.

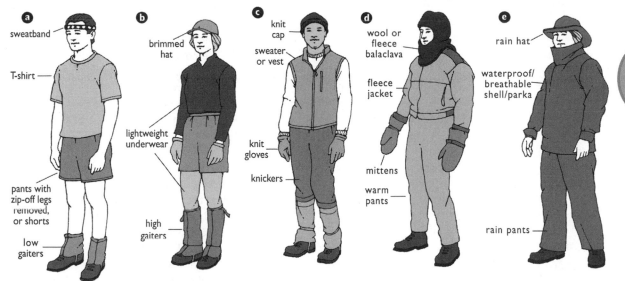

Fig. 2-1.

Typical examples of clothing layering systems: a, hiking in warm weather; b, hiking in cool weather; c, cool weather in camp; d, cold weather in camp; e, rainy or windy weather.

Insulating Fills

Down: High-quality goose down is the warmest insulating fill available by weight. It is also the most compressible, so it packs small yet quickly regains its loft—and therefore its warmth—when unpacked. These qualities make down very popular for cold-weather jackets and especially for sleeping bags. Good down is expensive, yet has a much longer useful life than other insulating fills. Unfortunately, down loses all its insulating value when wet and is almost impossible to dry in damp conditions. Down must be protected from moisture.

Synthetic fill: Unlike down, synthetic fills do not collapse when wet, so they provide more-reliable insulation in moist climates. Heavier and less compressible than down, they are also cheaper and more easily cleaned. Again, brand names for these fillings can be confusing, so read the tags to figure out what the product really is made of.

Putting the Clothing System Together

Armed with knowledge of outdoor fabric characteristics and the strategy of layering, you can assemble an effective mountaineering clothing system. Figure 2-1 shows typical examples of how the various articles in a complete clothing system can be mixed and matched to function over a wide spectrum of weather conditions. The exact items that are chosen will vary significantly from climber to climber. The goal is to make the system comprehensive and versatile. Following are some specific guidelines for each clothing layer.

Layer Next to the Skin

Long underwear: Protection from cold begins with appropriate long underwear. Wicking fabrics of polypropylene and polyester are very popular for this purpose; some climbers prefer wool. Dark-colored long underwear (fig. 2-1b) absorbs more heat and dries more quickly in sunlight. Light colors are better on hot days, when long underwear may be worn as protection from sunburn or insects.

For rock climbing, spandex-blended polyester tights are occasionally used instead of long underwear because their stretchiness permits fuller range of motion. They are generally not as warm as polyester underwear. Lightweight nylon or nylon/stretch pants or knickers are also used alone against the skin.

2

T-shirts and shorts: Although T-shirts, shorts, underwear, and sports bras do not in themselves constitute a "layer," they need to perform as part of the total clothing system (fig. 2-1a).

For hot weather, a cotton T-shirt or tank top may suffice, although long sleeves provide more sun protection. But for cooler mountain climates, cotton is a poor choice. On a moderately cool and breezy day, a cotton T-shirt can become soaked with sweat during an ascent of a steep hill and you can get a deep chill when stopping for a break. Less-absorbent fabrics are much better than cotton for most situations. Warm-weather shirts should be light-colored for coolness and moderately baggy for good ventilation.

Ventilation and durability are key requirements for shorts. A loose-fitting pair of nylon shorts, fitted with an integral mesh brief, usually work well. Cotton shorts are far less versatile. A popular clothing combination for mild conditions is lightweight polyester long underwear under a pair of nylon shorts. Lightweight nylon pants with zip-off legs that convert to shorts are also very popular and versatile.

Insulating Layers

For cold weather, more insulating layers are needed. Upper-body layers can include more long underwear, wool or synthetic shirts, fleece sweaters and jackets, or down- or synthetic-filled jackets (fig. 2-1c). For the legs, choose long underwear or pants made of wool, blends, stretch/woven nylon, or fleece. One-piece insulating garments are sometimes used in very cold weather. There are many choices; the main objective is retaining warmth when wet. Leave the cotton sweatshirts and jeans at home.

Shirts and sweaters: These should be long in the torso so they tuck into or pull over the waist of the pants. Gaps between the pants and upper-body layer(s) let valuable heat escape. Turtleneck underwear and sweaters can provide a significant warmth benefit with little extra penalty in weight.

Insulating pants: These should be loose fitting or stretchy for freedom of movement and made of a closely woven fabric with a hard finish for resistance to wind and abrasion (fig. 2-1d). Wool and wool/synthetic blends work well. Fleece pants, while lighter, are not

as abrasion- or wind-resistant by themselves. Look for pants with reinforced seats and knees and with full-length side zippers that make it possible to put the pants on while you are wearing crampons or skis.

Knickers: Some climbers prefer knee-length knickers and gaiters (see the "Footgear" section below) for freer movement and better ventilation, and to avoid saturating pant legs from contact with snow or dew.

Shell Layer

The ideal shell is uninsulated, windproof, completely waterproof, and completely breathable. There is no single garment that can achieve all these objectives, but there are various strategies that come close.

One strategy is to have a single, multifunctional, waterproof/breathable shell layer for both parka and pants. If this single shell layer provides sufficient breathability, it may be the best way to go.

Many climbers carry two shell layers: a light, breathable layer of wind gear and a light set of raingear, either breathable or (occasionally) not. With these systems, the wind gear is worn in cool, windy, and even lightly drizzling conditions, and for periods of heavy exertion, whereas the more expensive shell goes on for slower periods, or in heavier rain. This two-shell strategy can be cheaper, and the wind gear allows much better ventilation. But a nonbreathing layer (if used) will be more uncomfortable than waterproof/breathable raingear, and additional shell layers may carry a weight penalty.

Rain parkas: These come in different styles. Standard parkas feature full front zippers and are easier to ventilate; anoraks (pullover parkas without full front zippers) are preferred by some climbers as lighter, less bulky, and more windproof (fig. 2-1e). When shopping for a rain parka of either style, look for the same qualities whether or not the fabric breathes (see sidebar).

Rain pants: These should have full-length zippers so they can be added or removed over boots, crampons, skis, or snowshoes. Because rain pants tend to be worn less often than parkas (often a good set of gaiters is enough) and they can be ruined by bushwhacking through brush or glissading down snow, choosing a nonbreathable pair of rain pants can save money.

Some climbers, especially in cold conditions, use waterproof/breathable bib pants held up with suspenders

WHAT TO LOOK FOR IN A RAIN PARKA

- A size large enough to allow for additional layers of clothing underneath without compressing insulation or restricting movement
- A hood with a brim, neck flap, and good drawstrings to keep water from dribbling down your face and neck. The hood should be large enough to accommodate a climbing helmet but not impair vision when you glance to the sides.
- Adjustable openings at the front, waist, underarms, sides, and cuffs that can be opened up for ventilation or shut tight
- Zippers with large, durable teeth and good flaps that keep the zipper dry but still allow ventilation. Some zippers are waterproof.
- A design that does not interfere with a climbing harness or belaying
- Well-bonded, tape-sealed seams
- Pockets that are easily accessible with gloved hands and with a pack on. Pockets also need good rain flaps that keep water out.
- A length that extends well below the waistline of pants and a drawstring at the waist so the torso can be sealed off.
- Sleeves that cover the wrists. Snaps, elastic, or Velcro should keep the sleeve in place at the wrist.

as a lower-body shell layer. Some bibs contain insulating fills and are best suited to extreme-cold-weather expeditions. They are considerably warmer than rain pants because they cover much of the torso and keep snow from entering around your waistline, but they are too warm for most summer uses. One-piece suits are also used by some—they are the warmest but least-versatile option.

Headgear

The old adage says, "If your feet are cold, put on a hat." Without a hat, a person's head acts like a radiator and can account for more than half of the body's heat loss. As the body gets cold, it reduces blood flow to the arms and legs in an attempt to warm more vital areas, including the head. Putting on a hat helps reverse this effect.

Climbers often carry several different types of hats. A small arsenal of hats in a convenient pocket provides a quick method of adapting to changing temperatures. To prevent the misfortune of having a hat blow off and sail over a cliff, sew leashes (security cords) onto headgear.

Warm insulating caps come in wool, polypropylene, or polyester fleece. Balaclavas are versatile insulators because they can cover both your face and neck, or can be rolled up to allow ventilation of the collar area. Consider carrying two insulating hats; an extra hat provides almost as much warmth as an extra sweater while weighing much less. Sometimes a thin hat may be worn beneath a climbing helmet in cold weather.

A rain hat is useful, because it provides more ventilation and is often more comfortable than a parka hood. Some rain hats are available in waterproof/breathable fabrics, allowing further ventilation.

Sun-protection hats, with wide brims or protective shades draping over your neck and ears, are popular for glacier climbs. A baseball cap with a bandanna pinned on it can accomplish the same purpose. A bill helps shade your eyes and keep rain and snow off glasses.

Gloves and Mittens

Activities such as handling wet rope or scrambling on wet rock can saturate gloves or mittens, even in dry weather. Fingers are perhaps the most difficult part of the body to keep warm because of the body's tendency to sacrifice blood flow to the extremities when cold. Unfortunately, this altered blood flow can inhibit tasks that involve the fingers—such as pulling zippers and tying knots—which may slow a climbing party's progress at the very time when they need to move fast to find shelter from the cold.

It can take considerable experience to wisely select the mittens and gloves that work best for each individual. The decision usually entails a compromise between dexterity and warmth. In general, bulk means increased warmth and reduced dexterity. The more

25

technical a climb, the more significant the compromise.

The layering concept for clothing also applies to hands. The first layer may be a pair of gloves; additional layers are usually mittens. Mittens are warmer than gloves because they allow fingers to share warmth. A layered system of thin glove liners topped with mittens and overmitts usually works well, as long as it does not constrict circulation.

As with other insulating garments, mittens and gloves must be made of fabrics that retain warmth when wet. Suitable gloves and mittens come in synthetic, wool/synthetic blends, or all wool.

Overmitts are the shell layer for hands. A nonslip coating on the palm will improve your grip on snow and ice tools. The overmitt cuff should overlap the parka sleeve some 4 to 6 inches (10 to 15 centimeters), and elastic or Velcro closures can cinch the overmitt around your forearm.

Sew security cords onto mittens and overmitts. It is well worth the effort when you need to pull off your mittens to climb rock or apply sunscreen.

In camp, wearing thin glove liners or fingerless gloves inside mittens can permit good dexterity for delicate chores without exposing bare skin. Be aware that many synthetics can melt in the heat from a stove. Even so, in very cold temperatures—around 0 degrees Fahrenheit (minus 18 degrees Celsius)—it is important to keep fingers from freezing to metal, and glove liners are better for this than fingerless gloves. But when you are rock climbing in cold weather and it is not desirable to add a layer of fabric between your fingers and the rock, fingerless gloves are best. Some climbers carry several pairs of liners, changing when they become wet and cold.

Leather gloves are often worn for rope handling such as rappelling or belaying, providing a better grip and preventing rope burns in the event of a fall. They provide no insulation when wet, and dry slowly.

FOOTGEAR
Boots

Historically, mountaineering boots were made of heavy sewn leather. With efforts to reduce costs and improve performance came the advent of alternative materials

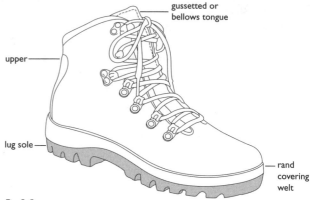

Fig. 2-2.
Classic leather mountaineering boot.

and construction methods. The "classic" leather boot is less common today, having been joined by new designs—boots with plastic shells, boots incorporating fabric panels, composites, and so on. Although boots themselves are changing, the many jobs they need to do have not.

Leather Boots

A major factor in mountaineers' enduring respect for classic leather boots is their versatility. A general mountaineering boot must strike a balance of being tough enough to withstand being scraped on rocks, stiff and solid enough for kicking steps in hard snow and wearing crampons, yet comfortable enough for the approach hike. In a single day of climbing, boots may have to contend with trails, mud, streams, gravel, brush, scree, hard snow, steep rock, and ice. The classic leather mountaineering boot (fig. 2-2) has most or all of the following features:

- High upper (5½ to 7½ inches / 14 to 19 centimeters) to support and protect the ankle in rough terrain
- Vibram-type lug sole for traction on slippery vegetation, mud, and snow
- Welt (the joint between the upper and the sole)
- Rubber rand sealing the sole to the upper, to aid in waterproofing and to simplify boot maintenance
- A fairly stiff shank (the metal or plastic stiffener built into the boot sole)
- A minimum number of seams, to minimize places water can leak through

- A gusseted or bellows tongue, to keep water from easily entering the boot
- Beefed-up toe and heel, with double- or triple-layered leather, for durability and protection
- Hard toe counter (interior stiffener) to protect the foot, reduce compression caused by crampon straps, and facilitate step-kicking in hard snow
- Heel counter (interior stiffener) to increase foot stability and facilitate plunge-stepping down steep snow slopes
- Top that opens wide so the boot can be put on easily even when it is wet or frozen

Leather/Fabric Boots

Advances in boot technology have led to boots that incorporate synthetic fabric panels that partially replace leather. Some (not all) may be suitable for climbing. Leather/fabric boots (fig. 2-3) provide a number of advantages over all-leather boots, including:

- Reduced weight
- Improved comfort and shorter break-in time
- Faster drying time
- Lower cost

However, leather/fabric boots may have significant drawbacks compared with all-leather boots:

- Less stability on difficult off-trail terrain
- Less waterproofness
- Less durability
- Insufficient weight/stiffness for step-kicking in firm snow or for wearing with crampons

Most (not all) of these boots are more suitable for trail walking. However, if you are considering leather/fabric boots for climbing, here are some things to look for: Check that the uppers are high and rigid enough for good ankle support, that stiff counters wrap the heel and toe, and that abrasion areas are reinforced. If the boot is very flexible, it will not edge well or be suitable for crampons. A distinct heel is desirable, especially on snow.

Some leather/fabric boots feature Gore-Tex liners, which can help keep feet drier in wet conditions. Gore-Tex is no panacea for boots, however: The membrane is hard to keep clean and can degrade from dirt and sweat. It also adds cost, and it may make feet more uncomfortable during hot weather.

Plastic Boots

Plastic boots (fig. 2-4) consist of hard plastic outer shells with inner insulating boots. They were originally designed for cold-weather expeditions and serious ice climbing, but have since found a much wider market among those interested in snow and glacier routes.

The plastic shells of these boots are generally very stiff, which makes them good for use with crampons

Fig. 2-3.
Lightweight leather and fabric boot.

Fig. 2-4.
Plastic mountaineering boot: a, waterproof shell; b, insulating inner boot.

or snowshoes, because they permit straps to be cinched tightly without impairing circulation in the feet. They provide solid support for edging and kicking steps.

Being truly waterproof, plastic boots are great in wet conditions. The inner insulating boot remains free of snow-melt and keeps feet warm. In camp, the inner boot can be removed, which helps in drying out perspiration. Unfortunately, the very factors that make plastic boots ideal for snow and ice (rigidity, waterproofness, and warmth) make them a poor choice for general trail use.

The Right Choice

A good alpine climbing boot is a compromise of performance in all conditions that are likely to be encountered during an outing: No single boot type or design will do everything well. For this reason, outdoor equipment stores typically carry a wide array of footwear, from trail shoes and cross-trainers to light- and heavy-duty backpacking boots to full-scale mountaineering boots. The degree of rigidity of the sole, the stiffness and support provided by the upper, and how the sole and upper interact in use are the characteristics that matter most. The best choice of boot depends on how it will be used and is generally a compromise between the boot's walking comfort and its technical capability.

For trails and easy snow or rock routes, boots with moderately stiff soles and uppers provide enough support while being acceptably flexible and comfortable. Both leather and leather/fabric boots can work well for these applications, provided their soles and uppers are reasonably firm.

For technical alpine rock climbing, a stiffer boot is desirable for its edging capabilities. Flexible boots (fig. 2-5b and d), while used by some, are a poor substitute for rock shoes. (For information on rock shoes, see Chapter 12, Alpine Rock-Climbing Technique.) Stiffer

Fig. 2-5.
The stiffness of a boot affects its technical capability—stiffer boots edge better, flexible boots "smear" better: a and c, stiff mountaineering boots edge well on small holds; b and d, flexible backpacking boots bend more, requiring more contact with a hold to give good support.

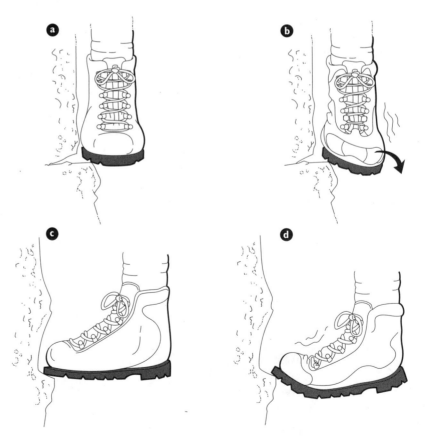

boots make walking somewhat harder, but they greatly reduce leg fatigue when a climber is standing on small rock nubbins. Look for boots stiff enough to permit edging on narrow rock ledges with the toe (fig. 2-5c) or with either side of the boot (fig. 2-5a).

For traveling on hard snow, a too-flexible boot is a disadvantage. Even with the most forgiving crampon bindings, it takes a stout boot to kick good steps or plunge-step with confidence.

Ice climbing demands an even higher level of boot support, and very stiff soles and uppers are desirable. Plastic boots or extremely stiff leather boots are generally best (see Chapter 18, Alpine Ice Climbing).

The Proper Fit

No matter what the boot's design, fit is critical. Try on several makes and styles. Some brands are available in multiple widths; others offer both men's and women's models—so shop around.

When heading to the stores to compare boots, take along socks similar to the ones you will wear on a climb, as well as any orthotic devices, custom insoles, or other inserts that you will use. Most people's feet swell during the course of the day, so consider shopping in the evening when your feet are at their largest.

After lacing up the boots in the store, try standing on a narrow edge or rocking side to side to test stability. Stand and walk in the boots for several minutes, with a heavy pack on if possible, to allow the boots and your feet to get used to each other. Then note whether the boots have any uncomfortable seams or creases or whether they pinch anywhere. In boots that fit properly, your heels will feel firmly anchored in place while your toes will have plenty of room to wiggle and will not jam against the toe box when you press your foot forward. Try standing on a downward incline for a critical test of toe space. Kick something solid—toes should not hit the front of the boot.

Boots that are too tight will constrict circulation, which causes cold feet and increases chance of frostbite. Either too-tight or excessively loose boots can cause blisters. Given the choice between boots that are a bit too big and ones that are a bit too small, go with the larger boots. The space can be filled somewhat with thicker socks or insoles.

Plastic boots need to fit well from the start because their rigid shell will not mold around your feet as much as the lining of a leather or leather/fabric boot will. Be especially careful that boots intended for use in extreme cold and/or high altitudes do not constrict your feet and impede circulation.

Boot Care

With proper care, good boots can last many years. Keep mildew and rot at bay by keeping the boots clean and dry when not in use. Avoid exposing boots to high temperatures, because heat can damage leather, linings, and sole adhesives. During an outing, water can seep into boots through the uppers and seams. Waterproofing agents can help limit the entry of water. Waterproofing is a process that needs to be repeated regularly.

Before waterproofing, boots must be clean and dry. Clean them with a mild soap, such as saddle soap, that will not damage the leather. Use a stiff brush to remove grit. It is difficult to remove every speck of dirt, so waterproofing usually does not last as long on used boots as on new. With plastic boots, remove the inner boots after use and allow them to dry. Shake and/or wipe out any debris in the plastic shells to prevent abrasion and excessive wear.

There are several types of boot waterproofing products. The appropriate type for a pair of boots depends on how the leather uppers were tanned, so follow the manufacturer's recommendations. Fabric panels in leather/fabric boots can be made more water-resistant by applying silicone-based sprays. Whatever product is appropriate for the boots, apply it frequently to keep your feet dry, following the manufacturer's instructions.

INSOLES

Adding insoles to the inside of boots provides extra insulation and cushioning. Synthetic insoles are nonabsorbent, do not become matted when damp, and have a loose structure that helps ventilate the foot. Insoles made of felt, leather, or lambskin all absorb moisture and must be removed when drying boots.

2

SPECIALIZED FOOTWEAR

Depending on the trip, a climber may wear one kind of boot for the approach hike, another type of footwear in camp, and yet another climbing. If additional footgear is affordable and the climber is willing to carry the extra weight, consider these options:

■ Lightweight, flexible trail shoes for easy approaches—they are less likely to cause blisters and are less fatiguing to wear than leather boots. However, these lightweight shoes may not provide the support needed when carrying a heavy pack, especially on rough ground or descents.

■ Running shoes, tennis shoes, sandals, or neoprene socks or booties for comfort in camp and to give boots and feet a chance to dry—they can also be used for stream crossings

■ Insulated booties and/or fleece socks for warmer lounging and sleeping

■ Rock-climbing shoes for technical rock (see Chapter 12, Alpine Rock-Climbing Technique)

■ Insulated overboots for extremely cold weather

Socks

Socks cushion and insulate the feet and reduce friction between the boot and the foot. Socks made of wool or synthetic materials can perform these functions; those made of cotton cannot. Cotton socks will saturate, collapse, and stick to the feet, softening the skin and leading to blisters.

Socks should absorb perspiration. Because boots do not breathe appreciably, the sweat generated by the feet collects and builds up until the boots are removed. Synthetic sock materials (including polyester, nylon, and acrylic) dry faster than wool.

Many climbers wear two pairs of socks. Next to the skin, a thin liner sock transports perspiration away from the foot and stays somewhat dry in the process. The outer sock is thicker and rougher in order to absorb the moisture passing through the inner sock and to cushion against the boot lining. Others prefer a single medium- or heavy-weight wool or synthetic sock.

Of course, there are many exceptions. A rock climber wants flexible rock shoes to fit like skin, and so wears no socks or one thin pair. A hiker using trail shoes on a warm day may keep feet cooler by wearing a single pair of socks, whereas a winter climber may wear three pairs of socks inside oversize boots. Whatever the strategy, keep your toes free enough to wiggle; an additional pair of socks will not improve warmth if they constrict circulation.

Before donning socks, consider protecting your feet at places prone to blisters, such as the back of the heel, with athletic tape, duct tape, or Moleskin (adhesive-backed, soft padding). This is especially valuable when breaking in new boots or early in the climbing season before your feet have toughened up. Another blister fighter is foot powder sprinkled on your feet, on socks, and in the boots.

Waterproof/breathable Gore-Tex socks can improve comfort in wet conditions. Worn over an inner pair of standard socks, the Gore-Tex socks function much like boots with Gore-Tex liners, while providing a higher and snugger cuff.

In very cold weather, a vapor-barrier sock may be worn between two main sock layers. Vapor-barrier socks are nonbreathing, which may seem at first to be contradictory to clothing strategies outlined earlier in this chapter. However, think of the example of the hot coffee in the cup: Although putting the lid on the cup keeps the moisture trapped inside, it also keeps the coffee hotter. Vapor-barrier socks apply the same principle to feet: Your feet get damp, but they stay warm. Vapor-barrier socks are best suited for extreme cold, where they reduce the danger of frostbite. However, if the internal moisture is allowed to continue for long, the serious condition of trench foot can develop (see Chapter 23, First Aid). If you use vapor-barrier socks, dry your feet thoroughly at least once each day.

Gaiters

During an outing, water, snow, and debris can get into boots over their cuff. Gaiters are used to seal the boundary between pant legs and boots. Climbers often carry gaiters in both summer and winter, because rain, dew,

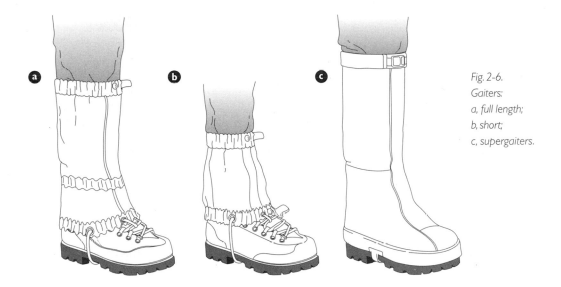

Fig. 2-6.
Gaiters:
a, full length;
b, short;
c, supergaiters.

mud, and snow provide year-round opportunities for water to saturate pant legs, socks, and boots.

Short gaiters (fig. 2-6b), extending 5 or 6 inches (12 or 15 centimeters) above the top of the boots, are adequate for keeping corn snow and debris out of boots in summer. The deep snows of winter, however, usually call for standard gaiters (fig. 2-6a) that extend up to the knee. Supergaiters (fig. 2-6c) completely cover the boot from the welt up, leaving the lug soles exposed. Insulation built into these gaiters covers the boots for added warmth.

The portion of any gaiter covering the boot should be made of a heavy-duty fabric coated with some type of water repellent. Higher-performance gaiters feature an additional waterproof membrane inside the heavy-duty fabric. The fabric covering your calf should be breathable or waterproof/breathable, to allow perspiration to escape.

Gaiters are usually held closed with Velcro, snaps, or zippers, with Velcro offering the easiest fastening in cold weather. If you select gaiters with zippers, be sure the teeth are heavy-duty. A flap that closes over the zipper with snaps or Velcro protects it from damage and can keep the gaiter closed and functional even if the zipper fails. A drawstring at the top of the gaiter keeps it from sliding down. A snug fit around the calf helps prevent crampon points from catching on the gaiters.

A close fit all around the boot is essential to prevent snow from entering under the gaiter, especially when plunge-stepping during descents. A cord, lace, strap, or shock cord runs under the foot to help the gaiter hug the boot. The part under the foot will wear out during the life of the gaiter, so look for designs allowing easy replacement. Neoprene straps work well in snow but wear quickly on rock, whereas cord survives rock better but can ball up with snow.

PACKS

Climbers usually own at least two packs: a day pack to hold enough for a single-day climb, and a full-size backpack to carry gear for camping in the backcountry. All packs should allow the weight to be carried close to your body and the load to be centered over your hips and legs (see Figure 2-8, below).

Internal-Frame versus External-Frame Packs

Internal-frame packs (fig. 2-7a and b) are by far the most popular packs among climbers and ski mountaineers. A rigid frame within the pack helps it maintain its shape and hug your back, assisting you in keeping balanced while climbing or skiing. When you wear such a pack, weight is carried relatively low on your body, a plus

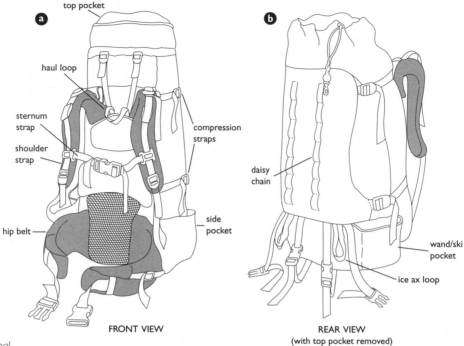

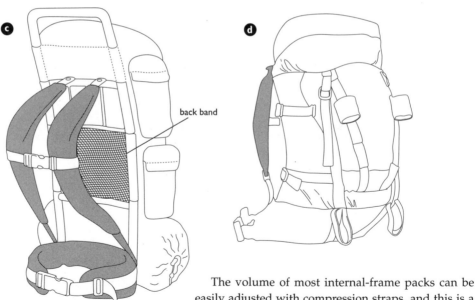

Fig. 2-7.
Typical packs:
a–b, large internal-
frame pack;
c, large external-
frame pack;
d, medium-size
day pack.

for maintaining balance. The body-hugging nature of internal-frame packs can make them somewhat uncomfortable in hot weather.

The volume of most internal-frame packs can be easily adjusted with compression straps, and this is a significant advantage for climbing. A full-size pack can be used on the approach and then emptied of tent and sleeping bag at camp and transformed into a compact summit pack. The clean, narrow profile of internal-frame packs allows them to be taken through heavy brush or hauled up rock pitches with a minimum of snags.

External-frame packs (fig. 2-7c), once the main type of pack in use, now see only limited service with mountaineers. The pack contents are suspended from a ladderlike frame, which is held away from your back by taut nylon back bands. External-frame packs provide some advantages with very heavy loads, and keep the wearer cooler. Some climbers use them for long, easy approaches, carrying a small day pack (fig. 2-7d) inside for the summit day. But external frames are mainly limited to open trail use. They tend to shift without warning on uneven terrain, and may catch on brush or in tight quarters. It is also difficult to glissade or self-arrest on snow while wearing an external-frame pack.

Buying an Internal-Frame Pack

Before shopping for a full-size internal-frame pack, decide what capacity is right for how it will be used. Overnight trips typically require packs of around 3,000 to 5,000 cubic inches (50 to 80 liters) capable of carrying 30 to 55 pounds (13 to 25 kilograms) or so, depending on the demands of the climb. Longer trips and winter climbs require more volume; expedition climbs can demand even more. (For special considerations in buying day packs, see the next section.)

The most important objective is to buy a pack that fits your body. The pack's adjustment range must be compatible with the length of your back. Some packs adjust to a wide range of sizes; others do not. Virtually no individual backpack provides a good fit for everyone, so do not place faith in endorsements from acquaintances or outdoor equipment magazines. Try on various packs and make your own decision.

Do not be in a hurry when fitting a pack. Load it up, as you would on an actual climb; bring personal gear to the store. Without a typical load, you cannot tell how the pack rides or if the adjustments provide a good fit.

Loosen all the adjustment straps before putting the pack on, and then tighten up the straps in the order recommended by the salesperson. Check in a mirror, or ask someone to check, to see if the frame correctly follows the curve of your back. If it does not, check whether the stays or frame can be bent to improve the fit. Some frames are made of composite materials that cannot be reshaped. The shoulder straps should attach to the pack about 2 or 3 inches (5 to 7.5 centimeters) below the crest of your shoulders and leave little or no gap behind your back.

Once the pack is adjusted well, check the head clearance. Is it possible to look up without hitting the back of your head against the pack? Is it possible to look up while wearing a helmet? Next, check for adequate padding wherever the pack touches your body. Pay particular attention to the thickness and quality of padding used in the shoulder straps and hip belt. The hip belt should be substantial; its padding should cover your hipbones by good margins. For proper load

QUESTIONS TO CONSIDER WHEN CHOOSING A PACK

- How is the suspension system designed? Does it look durable, or does it look as though it could fail at weak spots?
- How sturdy is the pack's stitching?
- Does the pack rely on zippers to retain the contents? If the zippers fail, can the pack still be used?
- How convenient is it to store, arrange, and access gear in the pack?
- Does the pack provide a means of carrying special items such as crampons, skis, snowshoes, shovels, and wands?
- Does the pack have haul loops and ice-ax loops?
- Are there compression straps to reduce the pack's volume and prevent the load from shifting during climbing or skiing?
- Is there a means of increasing the pack's capacity for extended trips, such as an expandable snow collar with a floating top pocket or separate side-pocket accessories?
- Does the pack have a sternum strap to help prevent the pack from shifting on difficult terrain?
- Does the pack have a smooth profile, or will it get tangled up during bushwhacks through heavy brush or get hung up during hauling up a steep face?

transfer to your hips, ensure that the hip belt wraps directly onto the top of your hipbones, not around the sides of your hipbones or around your waist.

Buying a Day Pack

Day packs for climbing (see Figure 2-7d, above) usually have volumes of between 1,800 and 2,500 cubic inches (30 to 40 liters), enough to carry 20 to 30 pounds (9 to 14 kilograms). There is a wide selection of day packs on the market, varying over a wide spectrum of sturdiness. Some are designed without rigid frames or padded hip belts and can be too flimsy for serious climbing. Keep in mind that climbers carry heavy items such as rope, helmet, climbing gear, and ice ax in or on a day pack. Seek a pack with a sturdy internal frame and a hip belt that is at least 2 inches (5 centimeters) wide at the buckle and 4 inches (10 centimeters) wide where it covers the hips. Eliminate day packs that lack climbing features such as ice-ax loops, haul loops, crampon carriers, or compression straps.

Most of the features that are considered in choosing a full-size pack are applicable to day packs. Does the pack offer a sternum strap, compression straps, sturdy stitching, convenient storage and access, and a smooth profile? Try on and compare day packs as thoroughly as you would a full-size backpack.

Tips on Packing

Strategically loading items in a pack can dramatically influence a climber's speed, endurance, and enjoyment of an outing. Generally, climbers will feel best if they can concentrate the load on their hips and avoid loading their back and shoulders.

Pack heavy items as close to your back as possible and centered in the pack to lower your center of gravity and allow you to more easily keep your balance (fig. 2-8).

Along with arranging items in the pack for optimum weight distribution, organize them for quick access. The gear that will be needed most often should be carried close at hand. Articles such as gloves, hats, sunglasses, maps, and insect repellent are ideally carried in side and top pockets, jacket pockets, or a fanny pack that is worn on the abdomen in combination with the main pack. Adjusting and readjusting the backpack during use will help reduce soreness and fatigue.

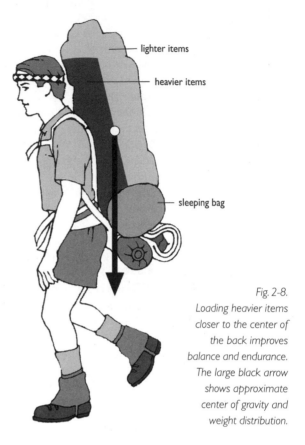

lighter items

heavier items

sleeping bag

Fig. 2-8. Loading heavier items closer to the center of the back improves balance and endurance. The large black arrow shows approximate center of gravity and weight distribution.

Determine a strategy to keep pack contents dry in rainy weather, because even packs constructed from waterproof materials are not necessarily waterproof. Water can leak through seams, zippers, pockets, the top opening, and places where the coating has worn off. Individual plastic bags or good stuff sacks can help protect pack contents, especially when it is necessary to set up or break camp in the rain. Waterproof pack covers are available as accessories. Some climbers use a large plastic trash bag as a waterproof liner inside their pack.

ESSENTIAL EQUIPMENT— A SYSTEMS APPROACH

There are certain systems that deserve space in every pack. A climber will not need every one of them on every trip, but they can be lifesavers in an emergency.

Exactly how much "insurance" should be carried is a matter of healthy debate. Some respected minimalists argue that weighing down a pack with such items causes people to climb slower, making it more likely they will get caught by a storm or nightfall and be forced to bivouac. "Go fast and light. Carry bivy gear, and you will bivy," they argue. The other side of this debate is that, even when climbers are not slowed by the extra weight of bivy gear, they still may be forced to bivouac. Will the party be safe?

The majority of climbers take along carefully selected items to survive the unexpected. They sacrifice some speed but argue that they will be around tomorrow to attempt again what they failed to climb today. The best-known list, first developed in the 1930s, became known as the Ten Essentials.

The Ten Essentials

The point of this list has always been to help answer two basic questions: First, can you respond positively to an accident or emergency? Second, can you safely spend a night—or more—out? The list has evolved over time from a list of individual items to a list of functional systems. As shown in Table 2-2, the classic list has been expanded in the systems approach to include hydration and emergency shelter. The systems are discussed in more detail below.

1. Navigation

Climbers must carry the tools and possess the skills required to know their location and how to get to their objective and back. Always carry a detailed topographic map of the area you are visiting, and place it in a protective case or plastic covering. Always carry a compass. Climbers may also choose to carry other navigational tools such as an altimeter or global positioning system (GPS) receiver; other aids include route markers, route descriptions, and other types of maps or photos. Know how to use map and compass and other navigation aids—refer to Chapter 5, Navigation, for more information. Route markers (such as glacier wands) should be removed after use to leave no trace.

2. Sun Protection

Carry and use sunglasses, sunscreen for the lips and skin, and clothing for sun protection.

Sunglasses: These are critical items in alpine country. The eyes are particularly vulnerable to radiation, and the corneas of unprotected eyes can be easily burned before any discomfort is felt, resulting in the excruciatingly painful condition known as snow blindness. Ultraviolet rays can penetrate cloud layers, so do not let cloudy conditions fool you into leaving your eyes unprotected. It is advisable to wear sunglasses whenever you would wear sunscreen, and both are especially necessary on snow, ice, and water, and at high altitudes.

Sunglasses should filter 95 to 100 percent of the ultraviolet light. They should also be tinted so that only a fraction of the visible light is transmitted through the

TABLE 2-2. THE TEN ESSENTIALS	
Ten Essential Systems	**Ten Essentials: The Classic List**
1. Navigation	1. Map
	2. Compass
2. Sun protection	3. Sunglasses and sunscreen
3. Insulation (extra clothing)	4. Extra clothing
4. Illumination	5. Headlamp/flashlight
5. First-aid supplies	6. First-aid supplies
6. Fire	7. Firestarter
	8. Matches
7. Repair kit and tools	9. Knife
8. Nutrition (extra food)	10. Extra food
9. Hydration (extra water)	
10. Emergency shelter	

2

lens to the eyes. For glacier glasses, a lens should allow 5 to 10 percent visible light transmission. Look in a mirror when trying on sunglasses: If your eyes can easily be seen, the lenses are too light. Lens tints should be gray or brown for the truest color, or yellow for better contrast in overcast or foggy conditions.

There is little proof that infrared rays (heat-carrying rays) harm your eyes unless you look directly at the sun, but any product that filters out a high percentage of infrared, as most sunglasses do, gives added eye insurance.

The frames of sunglasses should have side shields that reduce the light reaching your eyes, yet allow adequate ventilation to prevent fogging. Problems with fogging can be reduced by using an anti-fog lens-cleaning product.

Groups should carry at least one pair of spare sunglasses in case a pair is lost or forgotten. If no spare is available, eye protection can be improvised by cutting small slits in an eye cover made of cardboard or cloth.

Many climbers who need corrective lenses prefer using contact lenses instead of eyeglasses. Contacts may improve visual acuity, they do not slide down your nose, they do not get water spots, and they allow the use of nonprescription sunglasses. Contacts do have some problems, however. Blowing dust, sweat, and sunscreen can irritate your eyes. Backcountry conditions make it difficult to clean and maintain contacts. Eyeglasses protect your eyes better than contacts. Whether you choose contacts or eyeglasses, if you depend on corrective lenses, always carry a backup, such as a spare pair of normal glasses or prescription sunglasses or goggles.

Sunscreen: These skin treatments are also vital to climbers' well-being in the mountains. Although individuals vary widely in natural pigmentation and the amount of screening their skin requires, the penalty for underestimating the protection needed is so severe, including the possibility of skin cancer, that skin must always be protected.

While climbing, use a sunscreen that blocks both ultraviolet A (UVA) and ultraviolet B (UVB) rays (UVA rays are the primary preventable cause of skin cancer; UVB rays primarily cause sunburn). To protect skin from UV rays, use a sunscreen with a sun protection factor (SPF) of at least 15. The SPF number means that the sunscreen is formulated to permit you to stay in the sun that many times longer than if no protection was applied, with the same effect. For example, wearing sunscreen of SPF 15 allows you to stay in the sun fifteen times longer than possible if you are not wearing any sunscreen. To protect skin from UVA rays, use a sunscreen that contains zinc oxide, titanium dioxide, or avobenzone (sometimes listed as Parsol 1789).

All sunscreens are limited by their ability to remain on the skin while you are sweating. Some sunscreens are advertised as waterproof and will protect longer than regular products, but regardless of the claims on the label, reapply the sunscreen frequently.

Apply sunscreen to all exposed skin, including the undersides of your chin and nose and the insides of nostrils and ears. Even if you are wearing a hat, apply sunscreen to all exposed parts of your face and neck to protect against reflection from snow. Apply sunscreens half an hour before stepping out in the sun, because they usually take time to start working.

Zinc oxide paste (also called clown white) can be used on your nose as an alternative to regular sunscreens, because it ensures complete protection and will not wash off. One application lasts the entire climb, except where your fingers or equipment rub it off. These creams can be messy and difficult to remove, however.

Clothing offers more sun protection than sunscreen. Light-colored, breathable long underwear or wind garments are frequently worn on sunny glacier climbs. The discomfort of long underwear, even under blazing conditions, is often considered a minor nuisance compared to the hassle of regularly smearing on sunscreen.

Lips burn, too, and require protection to prevent peeling and blisters. Sunblocking products that resist washing, sweating, and licking are available. Reapply lip protection frequently, especially after eating or drinking.

Also see Chapter 23, First Aid, for information on sunburn and snow blindness.

3. Insulation (Extra Clothing)

How much extra clothing is necessary for an emergency? The garments used during the active portion of a climb and considered to be the basic climbing outfit include inner and outer socks, boots, underwear, pants, shirt, sweater or fleece jacket, hat, mittens or gloves, and raingear. The term "extra clothing" refers to additional layers that would be needed to survive the long, inactive hours of an unplanned bivouac. Extra clothing should be selected according to the season. Ask this question: What is needed to survive the worst conditions that could realistically be encountered on this trip?

An extra layer of underwear can have great warmth value while adding negligible weight to a pack. It is also wise to pack an extra hat or balaclava, because they provide more warmth for their weight than any other clothing article. For your feet, bring an extra pair of heavy socks; for your hands, an extra pair of polyester or fleece mitts. For winter and expedition climbing in severe conditions, bring more insulation for your torso as well as insulated overpants for your legs.

4. Illumination

Even if the climbing party plans to return to their cars before dark, it is essential to carry a headlamp or flashlight, just in case. Batteries and bulbs do not last forever, so carry spares of both at all times.

Lights vary greatly in their brightness. In general, brighter illumination consumes more battery power. The highest powered lights require more weight in batteries to last long enough for several hours of use. Some technological improvements have been made to make lights more efficient—xenon or halogen bulbs, for example. Light Emitting Diodes (LEDs) combine relatively bright light, durability, and long battery life. Although not the most powerful illumination available, their high efficiency to weight ratio makes them a popular alternative for those who do not need (or wish to carry) a spotlight.

Headlamps: These allow freedom of both hands, and are so much more convenient than flashlights that few climbers carry anything else. Lights are important enough and temperamental enough to make it worthwhile to invest in only quality equipment. At a minimum, get a light that is at least moisture-proof (designed to keep out rain). Waterproof lights often merit their extra expense, because they function reliably in any weather and the contacts or batteries will not corrode even if stored for months in a moist basement or garage.

All lights need durable switches that cannot turn on accidentally in the pack, a common and serious problem. Switches tucked away in a recessed cavity are excellent. So are rotating switches in which the body of the light must be twisted a half turn. If it looks as though a light switch could be tripped accidentally, guard against this danger by taping the switch closed, removing the bulb, or reversing the batteries.

Adjustable focus is an excellent feature available on some lights. Wide floodlighting is good for chores close at hand; concentrated spotlighting assists in viewing objects far away, making it possible to see farther than with a brighter light lacking this feature.

Make sure the spare bulbs and batteries you are carrying still work and fit the light.

Alkaline batteries: Of general-purpose batteries commonly available at mass merchandisers, these perform the best. They pack more energy than cheaper lead-zinc batteries. The major problems with alkalines are that voltage (hence brightness) drops significantly as they discharge and their life is drastically shortened by cold temperatures: They operate at only 10 to 20 percent efficiency at 0 degrees Fahrenheit (minus 18 degrees Celsius).

Nickel-cadmium batteries: Nicads are easier on landfills, can be recharged, will maintain their brightness throughout most of their discharge, and function well in the cold—about 70 percent efficient at 0 degrees Fahrenheit. However, they do not store as much energy as alkalines. For climbing, look for high-capacity nicads, which pack two to three times the charge of standard nicads and are worth the added expense and weight.

Lithium batteries: These offer higher performance at a higher price. The voltage remains almost constant over the life of a lithium battery, and its efficiency at 0 degrees Fahrenheit is nearly the same as at room temperature. Lithium batteries may have twice the voltage of their same-sized counterparts, so make sure they are compatible with the light you are using.

5. First-Aid Supplies

Carry and know how to use a first-aid kit, but do not let a first-aid kit give you a false sense of security. The best course of action is to always take the steps necessary to avoid injury or sickness in the first place.

Getting Mountain-Oriented First Aid (MOFA) training or Wilderness First Responder (WFR) training is very worthwhile. Most first-aid training is aimed at urban or industrial situations where trained personnel will respond quickly. In the mountains, trained response may be hours—even days—away.

The first-aid kit should be compact and sturdy, with the contents wrapped in waterproof packaging. Commercial first-aid kits are widely available, though most are inadequate. At a minimum, a first-aid kit should include gauze pads in various sizes, roller gauze, small adhesive bandages, butterfly bandages, triangular bandages, battle dressing (or Carlisle bandage), adhesive tape, scissors, cleansers or soap, latex gloves, and paper and pencil.

Carry enough bandages and gauze to absorb a significant quantity of blood. Consider the length and nature of a particular trip in deciding whether to add to the basics of the first-aid kit. If the party will be traveling on a glacier, for example, tree branches will not be available for improvised splints, so a wire ladder splint would be extremely valuable in the event of a fracture. For a climbing expedition, it may be necessary to consider appropriate prescription medicines. See Chapter 23, First Aid, for a more detailed listing of contents of a basic first-aid kit for one person.

6. Fire

Carry the means to start and sustain an emergency fire. Most climbers carry a butane lighter or two instead of matches in a waterproof container. Either must be absolutely reliable. Firestarters are indispensable for igniting wet wood quickly to make an emergency campfire. Common firestarters include candles, chemical heat tabs, and canned heat. On a high-altitude snow or glacier climb, where firewood is nonexistent, it is advisable to carry a stove as an additional emergency heat and water source (see Chapter 3, Camping and Food, for information concerning stoves).

7. Repair Kit and Tools

Knives are so useful in first aid, food preparation, repairs, and climbing that every party member needs to carry one. Leashes to prevent loss are common. Other tools (pliers, screwdriver, awl, scissors) can be part of a knife or a pocket tool, or carried separately—perhaps even as part of a group kit. Other useful repair items are shoelaces, safety pins, needle and thread, wire, duct tape, nylon fabric repair tape, cable ties, plastic buckles, cordage, webbing, and parts for equipment such as tent, stove, crampons, snowshoes, and skis.

8. Nutrition (Extra Food)

For shorter trips, a one-day supply of extra food is a reasonable emergency stockpile in case foul weather, faulty navigation, injury, or other reasons delay the planned return. An expedition or long trek may require more. The food should require no cooking, be easily digestible, and store well for long periods. A combination of jerky, nuts, candy, granola, and dried fruit works well. If a stove is carried, cocoa, dried soup, and tea can be added. There are many possibilities. Some climbers only half-jokingly point out that pemmican bars and U.S. Army Meals Ready to Eat (MRE) packs serve well as emergency rations because no one is tempted to eat them except in an emergency.

9. Hydration (Extra Water)

Carry extra water and have the skills and tools required for obtaining and purifying additional water. Always carry at least one water bottle or collapsible water sack. Widemouthed containers are easier to refill. An accessory pocket makes it possible to carry a water bottle on a pack hip-belt for easy access. Some water sacks are designed to be stored in the pack and feature a long plastic straw and valve that allow drinking without slowing your pace.

Before starting on the trail, fill water containers from a reliable source, such as from a tap at home. In most environments you need to have the ability to purify—by filtering, using purification chemicals, or boiling—additional water that is encountered. In cold environments, a stove, fuel, pot, and lighter are needed to melt snow for additional water.

Daily water consumption varies greatly. Two quarts (liters) daily is a reasonable minimum; in hot weather or at high altitudes, 6 quarts may not be enough. In dry environments, carry additional water. Plan for enough water to accommodate additional requirements due to heat, cold, altitude, exertion, or emergency. (See

"Water" in Chapter 3, Camping and Food, for more information.)

10. Emergency Shelter

If the climbing party is not carrying a tent (see Chapter 3, Camping and Food), carry some sort of extra shelter (in addition to a rain shell) from rain and wind, such as a plastic tube tent or a jumbo plastic trash bag. Another possibility is a reflective emergency blanket. It can be used in administering first aid to an injured or hypothermic person, or can double as a means of shelter.

Carry an insulated sleeping pad (see Chapter 3, Camping and Food) to reduce heat loss while sitting or lying on snow.

Even on day trips, some climbers carry a bivy sack as part of their survival gear, and partially compensate for the extra weight by going a little lighter on their insulating clothing layers. Others rely on their regular gear. A bivy sack protects insulating clothing layers from the weather, minimizes the effects of wind, and traps much of the heat escaping from your body inside its cocoon. (See "Shelter" in Chapter 3, Camping and Food, for details on bivy sacks.)

Other Important Items

There are, of course, many items in addition to the Ten Essentials that are useful for climbing. Every climber has a personal opinion about what items are necessary. With experience, all climbers develop their own preferences. However, regardless of the "essentials" an individual climber selects or does not select, it is always essential to engage the brain while mountain climbing. Think ahead. Take time periodically to envision scenarios of possible accidents and unexpected circumstances. What would you do in those situations? What equipment would be necessary in order to be prepared? What risks are you willing to accept?

Ice Ax

An ice ax is indispensable on snowfields and glaciers and is very useful on snow-covered alpine trails. An ice ax is a versatile tool, coming in handy for traveling in steep heather, scree, or brush; for crossing streams; and for digging sanitation holes. (For details on ice axes

and their uses, see Chapter 6, Wilderness Travel, and Chapter 16, Snow Travel and Climbing.)

Insect Repellent

The wilderness is an occasional home for people, but it is the permanent habitat of insects. Some of them—mosquitoes, biting flies, "no-see-um" gnats, blackflies, ticks, chiggers—want to feast on the human body. For winter trips or for snow climbs any time of year, insect repellent may be unnecessary; for a low-elevation summer approach, thwarting mosquitoes may be essential.

One way to protect yourself from voracious insects is with heavy clothing, including gloves and head nets in really buggy areas. In hot weather, long shirts and pants made of netting may prove worthwhile. If it is too hot to wear much clothing, insect repellents are a good alternative.

Repellents with N,N-diethyl-metatoluamide (DEET) claim to be effective against all the principal biting insects but really perform best against mosquitoes. One application of a repellent with a high concentration of DEET will keep mosquitoes from biting for several hours, though they will still hover about annoyingly. Mosquito repellents come in liquid, cream, spray, and stick form and are available in various strengths.

Be aware that DEET is a potent toxin. It also can dissolve plastics and synthetic fabrics. There are less-toxic repellents such as citronella, but test them out first and make sure they work for you. In many situations, DEET is the only effective compound.

DEET is not very effective at repelling biting flies. Products with ethyl-hexanediol and dimethyl phthalate are much more effective against blackflies, deer flies, and gnats. Unfortunately, fly repellents do not do much to ward off mosquitoes.

Ticks are a potential health hazard because they can carry Lyme disease or Rocky Mountain spotted fever. In tick country, especially when thrashing through brush, check your clothing and hair frequently during the day, and give your clothes and body a thorough inspection at night.

Signaling Devices

Whistles, radios, avalanche transceivers, and cell phones may be lifesavers in some situations but useless

TABLE 2-3. SAMPLE EQUIPMENT LIST

Items in brackets [ ] are optional, depending on personal preference and the nature of the trip. Items with an asterisk (∗) can be shared by the group. **Note:** See various other chapters for details on some of the gear on this list.

ALL TRIPS

Ten Essential Systems

1. Navigation

2. Sun Protection
3. Insulation (extra clothing)
4. Illumination
5. First-aid supplies
6. Fire

7. Repair kit and tools
8. Nutrition (extra food)
9. Hydration (extra water)
10. Emergency shelter

Ten Essentials: The Classic List

1. Map
2. Compass
3. Sunglasses and sunscreen
4. Extra clothing
5. Headlamp/flashlight
6. First-aid supplies
7. Fire starter
8. Matches
9. Knife
10. Extra food

Clothing

Boots	Rain parka	Mittens
Socks (inner and outer)	[Windbreaker]	Gloves
[T-shirt/tank top]	Rain pants	[Glove liners]
[Shorts]	[Wind pants]	[Overmitts]
Long underwear (top and bottom)	Insulating hats (synthetic or wool)	[Gaiters]
Insulating shirts, sweaters, or jackets	[Rain hat]	[Stream-crossing footwear]
(synthetic or wool)	[Sun-protection hat]	[Waterproof/breathable socks]
Insulating pants (synthetic or wool)	[Balaclava]	

Other

Day pack	[Cup]	[Binoculars]
Toilet paper	[Moleskin]	[Bandannas]
[Signaling device: whistle, wireless	[Nylon cord]	[Ice ax]
phone, etc.]	[Altimeter]	[Helmet]
[Insect repellent]	[GPS]	
[Spare eyeglasses]	[Camera and film]	

ADDITIONAL ITEMS FOR OVERNIGHT TRIPS

Internal- or external-frame pack	∗Repair kit	[Toiletries]
Sleeping bag and stuff sack	∗Stove, fuel, and accessories	[Alarm clock or alarm watch]
Sleeping pad	∗Pots (and cleaning pad)	[Camp clothing]
∗Tent, tarp, or bivy sack	Spoon	[Camp footwear]
∗Ground cloth	[Fork]	[Pack cover]
∗Food	[Bowl]	[Candle lantern]
∗Water container		

TABLE 2-3. Continued

ADDITIONAL GEAR FOR SNOW, GLACIER, OR WINTER CLIMBS

Ice ax	*Climbing rope	[Avalanche transceiver]
Crampons	*Spare sunglasses	*[Avalanche probe]
Carabiners	*Snow shovel	*[Flukes, pickets, ice screws]
Seat harness	*Group first-aid kit	*[Wands]
Chest sling or harness	[Plastic boots]	*[Snow saw]
Prusik slings	[Helmet]	[Handwarmer]
Rescue pulley	[Runners]	[Thermos bottle]
[Belay/rappel device]	[Supergaiters]	
Additional warm clothing, such as	[Snowshoes or skis]	
mittens, mitten shells, socks,		
balaclava, insulated parka,		
insulated bib pants, long		
underwear		

ADDITIONAL GEAR FOR ROCK CLIMBS

Helmet	Leather belay gloves	[Rock-climbing shoes]
Seat harness	Prusik slings	[Chalk]
Carabiners	*Climbing rope	[Daisy chain]
Runners	*Rack: chocks, stoppers, etc.	[Athletic tape]
Belay/rappel device	*Chock pick	

in others. Because all signal devices are unreliable or ineffectual under certain circumstances, they should never be carried with absolute faith that they will actually communicate an emergency message. Bring signaling devices on a climb if it is decided that they are worth the burden of carrying them, but never depend on them to get the party out of a jam. Successful climbers prepare for the wilderness and act safely to minimize the chance they will ever need to send an emergency signal.

Whistle: Though limited in its scope, a whistle is probably the most-reliable signaling device that can be carried. A whistle's shrill, penetrating blast greatly exceeds the range of the human voice and can serve as a crude means of communication in situations in which shouts for help cannot be heard—such as being trapped in a crevasse or becoming separated from the party in fog, darkness, or thick forest. Whistles prove much more useful if a climbing party designates certain signals before the trip, such as one sound of the whistle for "Where are you?"; two for "I'm here and OK"; and three for "Help!" Snow climbs, especially during winter, can require carrying an avalanche transceiver, used to locate a buried victim of a snow slide. (See Chapter 16, Snow Travel and Climbing, for detailed instructions on using avalanche transceivers.)

Handheld radio: This may be worth its weight on some climbs. On an expedition, radios can greatly ease communication between climbers or from climbers to base camp, and they could save critical hours in getting help for an injured person. Local ranger stations or logging trucks may monitor specific channels, although their policies vary from region to region. Radios are by no means foolproof; their range is limited, and in rugged terrain a peak or ridge can easily block transmission.

Wireless telephone (cell phone): The cell phone is becoming more popular among mountaineers as technology improves and weight and costs decline. Cell phones can dramatically shorten the time it takes to summon rescuers. They are also useful for telling the people back home that the party will be late but is not in trouble and, thus, can be used to avoid unnecessary rescue efforts. Understanding the limits of cell phones is as important as understanding their usefulness: The batteries can deplete, and they are unable to transmit or receive in many mountain locations. Cell phones should be viewed as an adjunct to, not a substitute for, self-reliance. No party should set out ill prepared, inadequately equipped, or attempting a route beyond the ability of its members with the notion that they will just call for help if needed. They will imperil themselves and the rescuers who may try to bail them out.

EQUIPMENT CHECKLIST

Whether you are experienced or not, it is easy to forget an important item in the rush to get ready for the next trip. Seasoned climbers have learned that using a checklist is the only sure way to avoid an oversight. The list in Table 2-3 is a good foundation for formulating a personal checklist. Add to or subtract from this list as necessary; then get in the habit of checking your own list before each trip.

PREPARING FOR THE FREEDOM OF THE HILLS

This chapter began with the idea that when you go into the wilderness, you should carry what you need and leave the rest at home. Achieving that balance takes knowledge and good judgment. Understanding the basics of clothing and equipment will help you decide what you really need to be safe and comfortable in the mountains. This is only the beginning of your discovery of the freedom of the hills. The next chapter, Camping and Food, will further expand your horizons.

Camping and Food

SHELTER ■ SELECTING THE CAMPSITE ■ SNOW AND WINTER CAMPING ■
THE SLEEPING SYSTEM ■ STOVES ■ WATER ■ FOOD ■ "IT'S JUST CAMPING"

Spending nights out in the beautiful alpine environment is one of the delights of mountaineering. The enjoyment is enhanced by mastery of the arts of camping and alpine cooking. Setting up a temporary home in the wilds ought to be quick work and provide cozy shelter, a warm bed, and good food. And it should be done with care so that you leave no trace of your passing.

SHELTER

Choosing a shelter depends on each climber's situation and preference.

Tents are the most common and versatile mountain shelter. They are relatively easy to set up, usually in 10 minutes or less; they provide privacy; they are rainproof and a refuge from wind or sun; they are usable in almost any terrain; and often they are roomy enough for both you and your gear. Tents usually are the first choice for shelter above timberline and for glacier camps, for winter camping, in moderate winds, and in bear and/or mosquito country.

Tarps are a lightweight alternative to tents, and can be used in conjunction with bivy sacks to provide

43

3

effective shelter from rain and sun. The term "bivy" comes from *bivouac*, a French word meaning "temporary encampment." Bivy sacks can be used as lightweight emergency shelters or can be carried as primary bare-minimum shelters for light traveling.

Tents

Tent selection is a calculation of trade-offs between protection (sturdiness), weight, comfort, and price. The choice is dictated by how and where the tent is to be used and by personal preferences.

Moisture Strategies

Tents must serve two competing functions in managing moisture. They need to keep out as much moisture as possible from the external environment, while at the same time venting as much moisture as possible from the interior. One person exhales a substantial amount of water overnight. If the tent were completely waterproof, this water vapor would drench sleeping bags and leave puddles on the floor. Therefore the tent must "breathe."

Tent floors are coated nylon, and most tents have what is called a sill. The sill is an extension of the floor up the sides of the walls. A higher sill gives more protection from rain blown in under the fly, but also reduces the amount of breathable fabric and can become an area of gathering condensation.

The floor and sill can be separate pieces connected by a bound seam or can be one continuous piece of fabric, commonly known as a bathtub floor. Bathtub floors give better protection from groundwater but are not easily replaced if the floor wears out before the upper part of the tent.

Many tents come with floors and flies seam-taped at the factory to keep the water from passing through.

If a tent is not factory taped, then a sealing compound must be applied to all exposed seams to prevent leakage.

Double-wall tents: The dilemma of a waterproof yet breathable tent is usually solved by using double-wall construction. The inner wall, suspended away from the outer wall, is breathable: It is not waterproof, so it allows exhaled moisture and perspiration to pass through to the outside. The outer layer is a detachable waterproof rain fly that keeps rain off the tent's inner wall and also collects the moisture from inside the tent, which then evaporates into the air flowing between the two layers. The rain fly must not touch the inner walls, because where it touches, water will leak through the inner wall. The fly of a mountaineering tent should come fairly close to the ground, covering the tent and entryway, shedding wind-driven rain.

Single-wall tents: These are made with just one layer of waterproof/breathable fabric. This fabric is usually made of three layers laminated together. An outer layer of nylon provides strength and protects the middle membrane layer. The membrane keeps water and rain out but allows warm vapors from inside to escape. The inner layer is a fuzzy, blotterlike facing that holds any excess moisture.

The great advantage of single-wall tents is their light weight, typically about 5 pounds (2.3 kilograms) for a two-person tent. They are also quieter in high winds because there is no outer fly to flap against the tent walls. The major disadvantages of single-wall tents are that they are quite expensive and they sometimes collect moisture on the inside during warm, wet weather. The membrane works best when outside temperatures are several degrees cooler than inside. This temperature differential pushes the moist air out through the breathable tent walls.

QUESTIONS TO CONSIDER WHEN CHOOSING A TENT

- Can it be set up easily and without help?
- Is it easy to get in and out of the door(s)?
- Is there enough head and foot room?
- How much of the occupants' gear will fit inside?
- Does it match the intended use? For example, three- versus four-season; room for two, three, or more climbers; etc.
- Is everything included that is needed to use the tent, such as stakes, poles, fly, seam sealer, instructions, and stuff sacks?

Winter and Nonwinter Tents

Tents used in mountaineering often are categorized as either three-season tents (nonwinter use) or four-season tents (for all situations including snow camping).

Three-season tents: These tend to be lighter in weight and construction. The side or top panels of many three-season tents are made with see-through netting, providing ventilation, bug protection, and light weight. However, blowing snow can come in through the netting. These tents often are quite adequate for mountaineering in a wide variety of conditions from late spring to early fall, and they can be ideal on weeklong traverses on which weight must be kept to a minimum.

Four-season tents: These are usually heavier, more costly, and built tougher to withstand winter conditions of high winds and snow loading. These tents have stronger poles (higher-strength aluminum or carbon fiber, rather than fiberglass) and more-durable reinforcing. The doors, windows, and vents have solid panels that can be zipped as near to closed as is wished (keeping ventilation requirements in mind), and the fly extends close to ground level all the way around. Four-season tents usually have at least three poles, and greater attention is paid to guylines (cords attached to the tent that can be staked out to brace it). Some manufacturers also supply an internal guyline kit to augment the external guylines, but climbers can set up their own internal guys as well. Usually the tent shape is some variation on the dome.

Tent Shapes

Designers shape tents to maximize usable interior space, load-bearing strength, and ability to withstand high winds, while at the same time minimizing their weight. A great tent must be easy to pitch and take down but very tenacious when storms attempt to take it down.

Dome: The freestanding dome (fig. 3-1a) has several poles crisscrossing over it, so it needs no stakes to hold its shape; it can be picked up and moved as a unit, but it still must be staked down and attached to guylines so it will not blow away. The possibility of the tent blowing away is a real danger in a heavy storm or when the tent is unoccupied. Dome tents are usually round or hexagonal in shape.

Wedge: The wedge tent (fig. 3-1b) uses two crisscrossed poles as a frame and is relatively freestanding. It is less rigid than the dome and so needs guylines to hold its shape in high winds.

Hoop: The two- or three-hoop tunnel tent (fig. 3-1c), usually not freestanding, offers efficient use of space and is good at shedding wind.

Comparing these designs, a freestanding tent is much easier to assemble and move to the best location

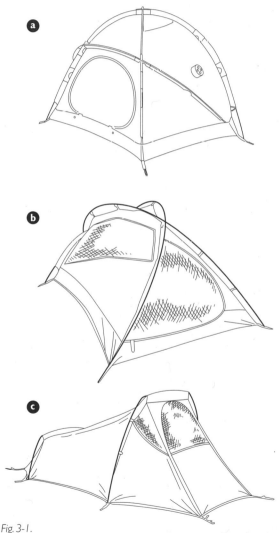

Fig. 3-1.

Tent designs (shown without rain flies): a, dome tent; b, wedge tent; c, hoop-style tent.

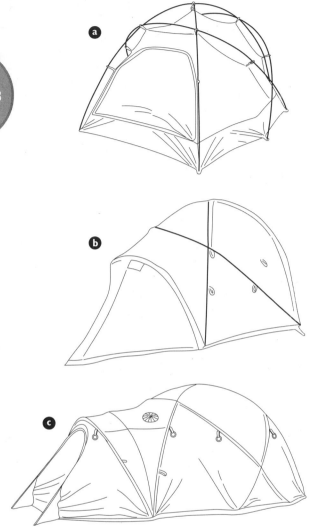

Fig. 3-2.
Dome tent rain fly and vestibule styles: a, tent with no rain fly;
b, tent with three-season rain fly and vestibule; c, tent with
four-season/mountaineering rain fly and tunnel-style vestibule.

than a tent that must be staked down before it will hold its shape. The hoop and wedge designs are typically lighter for a given volume.

Tent Size

Two-person: This size of tent is most popular for mountaineering because it offers the greatest flexibil-

ity in weight and choice of campsite. For a group, it is generally more versatile; for example, bringing two two-person tents rather than one four-person tent offers more options. Many two-person tents handle three people in a pinch, yet are light enough to be used by one person. However, the tent will be warmer if there is more than one occupant.

Larger: Some three- and four-person tents are light enough to be carried by two people who crave luxurious living (or two large people who crave adequate space). Larger tents, especially those high enough to stand in, are big morale boosters during an expedition or long storm but are major burdens to carry. On the approach, the weight can be distributed among the party by dividing the tent into parts.

Features

A good mountaineering tent is designed to keep out most of the rain and snow as climbers get in and out. Manufacturers offer many different features, such as zip doors, interior pockets and gear loops, tunnels, alcoves, vestibules, and hoods. Of course, most extra features add weight and cost. That nice extra door or vestibule must be paid for and then carried all the way to high camp before it can be enjoyed.

Vestibules: Four-season tents, and some three-season models, commonly include a floorless, protruding, protected area known as a vestibule (fig. 3-2b). Some expedition rain flies come with their own poles for extending the vestibule area farther (fig. 3-2c). Vestibules can be helpful as a way to shelter the entrance and provide more room for storing gear and boots, dressing, and cooking. In foul weather, cooking in the tent vestibule is an art to be appreciated (but be *very* careful—see the stove safety section later in this chapter). In better four-season tents, two vestibules are provided, allowing some specialization of vestibule use (i.e., cooking in one, boot storage in the other).

Vents: A tent needs vents up toward the ceiling that can be opened to allow warm, moist air (which rises) to escape. Mosquito netting allows air to flow freely when the doors are unzipped, and will keep out rodents and reptiles as well as flies and mosquitoes.

Color: Tent color is a matter of personal taste. Warm tent colors such as yellow, orange, and red are cheerier if the party is stuck inside, and they make it easier to spot camp on the way back from a summit. On the other hand, more subdued hues blend into the landscape. One is an eyesore; the other may be camouflaged only too well when the party is having a little trouble finding camp.

Anchoring the Tent

Tent stakes that come with the tent when it is purchased may be inadequate. Consider the terrain where the tent will be used, and bring stakes designed for the job. In forest duff, short plastic or wire stakes such as those that come with most tents are just fine. In rocky alpine terrain, metal skewer-type stakes (fig. 3-3a) or sturdier plastic T-shaped stakes (fig. 3-3b) may be required. In sand or snow, a broader surface area on the stake will help (fig. 3-3c).

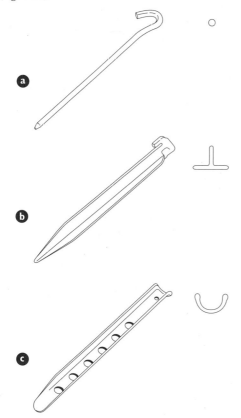

Fig. 3-3.
Tent stakes: a, skewer; b, T-shaped ; c, snow/sand stake.

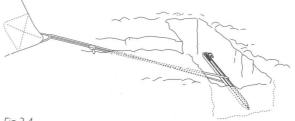

Fig. 3-4.

Deadman anchor: Dig a T-shaped trench about 12 inches deep, with the long leg of the T facing the tent. Then put the tent's guyline around the anchor—stake, stuff sack, rock, whatever— and place it in the trench in the crossbar of the T. Pull the line taut to tension the tent. Backfill the trench and stomp to compact the snow.

Anchoring a tent in snow requires a few special techniques. Stakes simply driven into the snow in the normal fashion will pull out in heavy wind and melt out during the day. Snowshoes, ice axes, skis, and ski poles also make solid anchors, but of course cannot be used for anything else while they are holding down the tent. For extra security, tie the tent to a tree if there is one nearby.

It is better to use deadman anchors (fig. 3-4). These can be stakes, stuff sacks packed with snow, metal plates called flukes made specifically for this purpose (see "Snow Anchors" in Chapter 16, Snow Travel and Climbing), or even rocks. First tie the deadman to the tent guyline, or form a loop in the line and slip the deadman into it. Dig a T-shaped trench at least 12 inches (30 centimeters) deep, with the long leg of the T facing the tent. Put the deadman into the trench in the crossbar of the T, then pull the line taut, backfill the trench, and stamp down the snow.

To keep the guylines taut, there are a couple of tensioning methods. One way is to buy small plastic or metal tensioners that slide up and down the line to make adjustments (fig. 3-5a and b). Another is to use a tautline hitch (fig. 3-5c).

Tent Setup, Care, and Cleaning

When setting up or taking down a tent, push poles through the tent sleeves rather than pulling them. Pulling leads to separation of the pole sections and snagging of sleeve fabric on the section ends. A tent goes up

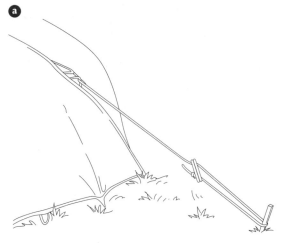

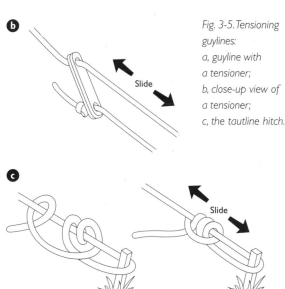

Fig. 3-5. Tensioning
guylines:
a, guyline with
a tensioner;
b, close-up view of
a tensioner;
c, the tautline hitch.

cloth does not channel in rainwater). Some manufacturers offer a tent "footprint" ground cloth shaped exactly for the tent.

A tent gives more years of good service if it is carefully air-dried after each trip. To clean a tent, hose it off or wash it with mild soap and water. Scrub stains with a sponge. Spot-clean any tree sap. Do not put the tent in a washer or dryer.

High temperatures and prolonged exposure to sun are damaging to tent material, so do not leave the tent set up for unnecessary periods of time in the sun. The damage from ultraviolet light can utterly ruin a rain fly in a single season of prolonged exposure. Do not touch tent fabric just after applying insect repellent to yourself; the chemicals can ruin fabric coatings.

Tarps

A tarp is lightweight and low cost, and may offer adequate shelter from all but extreme weather in lowland forests and among subalpine trees. Compared to a tent, a tarp gives less protection from heat loss and wind, and none at all from insects or rodents, and requires ingenuity and some cooperation from the landscape to set up (fig. 3-6a and b). It may be a poor choice above timberline unless poles, such as ice axes or ski poles, are brought along (fig. 3-6c and d). A tarp shelter can be very helpful as a cooking and dining area in camp during inclement weather. Do not wrap yourself (with or without a sleeping bag) in a tarp as if it were a blanket, because perspiration will condense inside the waterproof material.

Plastic tarps do not hold up very well but are inexpensive. Coated nylon tarps are stronger and usually very lightweight. Many come with reinforced grommets on the sides and corners for easy rigging. If a tarp lacks grommets, sew on loops of fabric, such as nylon or twill tape. Alternatively, just tie off each corner around a small cone or pebble from the campsite (fig. 3-6e). Take along some lightweight cord to string the tarp, and perhaps a few light stakes.

Some manufacturers offer lightweight, floorless nylon tents. They are shaped, not simply flat sheets, and usually have at least one pole. Similarly, the rain fly of some double-wall tents can be set up without the tent, serving as a freestanding, lightweight shelter.

quickly and easily if two or three members of the party know exactly who does what: who holds the tent to keep it from blowing away, who threads poles through the sleeves, and who pushes the poles toward the threader.

Discourage wearing boots inside the tent, to protect the tent floor from water, dirt, and abrasion. A small whisk broom and a camp towel or sponge help keep the floor clean. When not on an ultralightweight trip, bring a tarp to set underneath the tent to protect the floor from abrasion (tuck in the sides so the ground

Bivy Sacks

The bivy sack is a lightweight alternative to a tent, although appreciation of the bivy sack is an acquired taste. The sack is designed for one person, two in an emergency. It is a large fabric envelope with a zipper entrance at one end, sometimes with a zippered mosquito netting. Bivy sacks should provide the moisture-management functions of a tent—keeping out external moisture while venting internal water vapor. The bottom is usually made of waterproof coated nylon; the upper is of a waterproof/breathable material. Styles vary from spartan sacks (fig. 3-7a) weighing scarcely 1 pound (about 0.4 kilogram) to mini-tents that may be staked out and have a hoop to keep the fabric off the sleeper's face (fig. 3-7b).

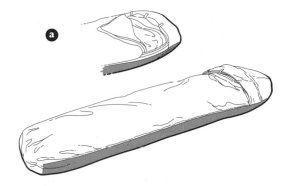

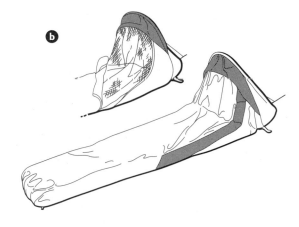

Fig. 3-7.
Bivy sacks: a, lightweight; b, hoop style.

Fig. 3-6.
Improvised tarp shelters: a, using two trees and two sticks; b, A-frame using two trees; c, shaped tarp with two short poles; d, using two ice axes; e, tying off corners on a tarp that has no grommets or tie-off loops.

3

A bivy sack can be used by itself, and is sometimes carried as an emergency shelter. But the common practice is to put a sleeping bag inside and an insulating pad beneath. A bivy sack increases the insulation provided by a sleeping bag, making it a nice addition in snow shelters. In very cold conditions, the bivy sack must be large enough to allow the sleeping bag to loft fully. In mild conditions, a bivy sack, in combination with a tarp set up over it, offers good protection at less weight than most tents. In wet conditions, a bivy sack inside a tent will keep the sleeping bag dry no matter how damp the tent gets. As with a tent, make sure all seams are sealed before taking the bivy sack out on an adventure.

SELECTING THE CAMPSITE

The ideal campsite is comfortable, with plenty of flat space for tents and cooking, great views, and a nearby water source. Some places have it all, but usually selecting a campsite involves making trade-offs. Climbers may walk right past an idyllic spot in the forest in favor of a cramped mountain ledge because that puts them closer to the summit.

Wind is a big consideration in choosing a campsite, and mountaineers learn to think about windbreak shelter. A ridgetop camp will be very exposed should a strong wind develop. A notch or low point on a ridge is the windiest of all. In most areas, prevailing winds tend to come from some particular direction. Alpine breezes are capricious. An afternoon breeze blowing upslope may reverse at night as heavy, chilled air rolls downslope from the snowfields above. Cold air, heavier than warm air, flows downward during settled weather,

following valleys and collecting in depressions. Thus, often there is a chill breeze down a creek or dry wash and a pool of cold air in a basin. Night air is often several degrees cooler near a river or lake than on the knolls above.

Consider wind direction when pitching a tent. Often it is best to pitch camp on the lee (downwind) side of a clump of trees or rocks. In good weather, facing the tent door into the wind will distend the tent, minimizing flapping. In stormy conditions, pitch the tent with the rear toward the wind so rain and snow will not be blown inside whenever the door is unzipped.

Consider how changes in temperature or weather may affect the campsite. For example, avoid camping in gullies or creekbeds, which could be swept by a flash flood if a thunderstorm hits. Consider the potential for significant rises in water level if you are camping near a river or stream. The braided rivers in the Alaskan interior, for example, often rise considerably during the day due to increased runoff from glaciers as the day warms up. In winter or in the high country, make sure the tent is well clear of any potential avalanche path.

Leave No Trace

One paramount factor in campsite selection is environmental impact. The more human traffic there is and the more fragile the setting, the more careful you must be. Read Chapter 7, Leave No Trace, which discusses campsite selection in detail. Here briefly are campsite options, listed from best to worst in terms of minimizing damage to the environment:

Best choice: Established, fully impacted campsite
Snow

A FEW CARDINAL RULES FOR CLEAN CAMPING

1. Camp in established campsites whenever possible.
2. Dispose properly of human waste away from water, trails, and campsites (see Chapter 7, Leave No Trace).
3. Use a camp stove instead of building a fire.
4. Wash well away from camps and water sources.
5. Leave flowers, rocks, and other natural features undisturbed.
6. Keep wildlife healthy and self-reliant by not feeding them and not increasing the likelihood of encounters between wild animals and humans.
7. Pack out all of the party's garbage, plus any litter left by others.

Good choice: Rock slab
      Sandy, gravelly, or dirt flat
      Duff in deep forest
Poor choice: Grass-covered meadow
      Plant-covered meadow above
      timberline
Worst choice: Waterfront along lakes and streams

In Bear Country

Learn to recognize the "game trails"—which look like faint trails through the terrain—that large animals are most likely to amble on, and never set up camp on a game trail. Sleep in a tent rather than out in the open. Large animals such as bears and cougars are not known to attack parties of four or more persons, so this may be a useful minimum group size for extended trips in wilder areas—if everyone stays together.

In treeless bear country, set up camp in a triangle configuration (fig. 3-8) that is at least 100 yards (90 meters) on each side: One point of the triangle that has *good visibility in all directions* is the cooking and dining area; at another point of the triangle, set up storage of food, camp kitchen items (stove, pots, pans, scrubber, and so

on), and any other items with an aroma (such as toothpaste, deodorant, lotions, and used feminine-hygiene products); at the third point of the triangle, upwind from the other two points, establish the tent site.

SNOW AND WINTER CAMPING

For winter camping, it is essential to have a good shelter, insulation, and the skills to stay dry. For changing weather conditions with temperatures near the freezing point, low amounts of snow, short trips, or circumstances in which camp must be set up quickly, tents are

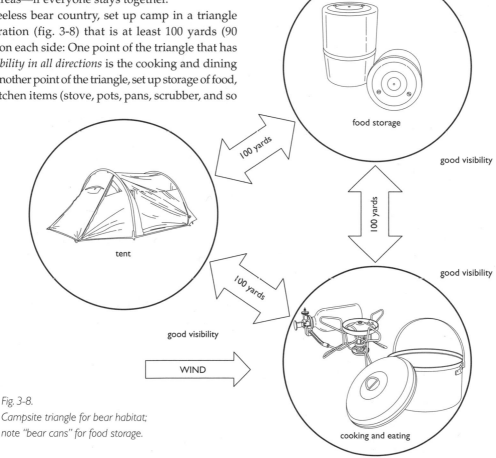

Fig. 3-8.
Campsite triangle for bear habitat;
note "bear cans" for food storage.

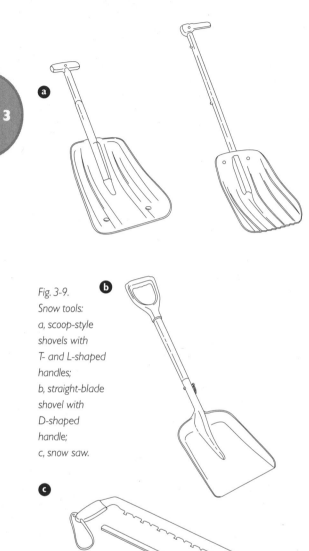

Fig. 3-9.
Snow tools:
a, scoop-style
shovels with
T- and L-shaped
handles;
b, straight-blade
shovel with
D-shaped
handle;
c, snow saw.

blade guard

Tools

A snow shovel is essential for preparing tent platforms, digging emergency shelters, excavating climbers from avalanche debris, and sometimes even clearing climbing routes. In winter, every member of the party should carry a shovel. For summer snow camping, take one shovel per rope team or tent, with a minimum of two per party.

Look for a lightweight shovel with a compact sectional or telescoping handle and a sturdy blade. Blades are made of metal (aluminum is most common) or a strong plastic. Some mountaineers prefer the metal blade because it is better at chopping into icy snow. The blade may be scoop-shaped (fig. 3-9a), which makes it easier to move large volumes of snow, or relatively straight-bladed (fig. 3-9b), which makes cutting easier. A D-shaped handle (fig. 3-9b) or L- or T-shaped handle (fig. 3-9a) can provide leverage and a firm grip on the shovel.

A snow saw (fig. 3-9c) is the best tool for cutting blocks to make an igloo, a snow trench, or a wind-blocking snow wall around your tent (as shown in Figure 3-10, below).

Tents in Winter

Locate a winter camp away from hazards such as crevasses, avalanche paths, and cornices. Observe the local wind patterns: A rock-hard or sculpted snow surface indicates frequent wind, whereas an area with loose, powdery snow indicates a lee slope where wind-transported snow is deposited. An area deep in powdery snow may be protected from wind, but the tent might have to be cleared of snow frequently.

Select a spot that is as nearly flat as possible. Establish a tent platform by compacting an area large enough to hold the tent and allow movement around it to check guylines or clear snow. Flatten and smooth the tent platform thoroughly to keep occupants from sliding downslope during the night, and to get rid of any uncomfortable lumps. This is especially important when you will be staying in one location for several nights because the platform becomes rock hard after the first night, and all features will be cast in ice. A square-bladed shovel works well to flatten the tent site. Tromping around on it with snowshoes will compact

obviously the preferred choice. If it is midday and the sun is out, the inside of a tent can be 40 or 50 degrees Fahrenheit (22 to 28 degrees Celsius) warmer than the outside air, making it a great place for drying out sleeping bags and clothing. More exotic snow shelters such as snow caves and igloos require more time, effort, and skill, but may be stronger, more spacious, and even warmer in very cold weather.

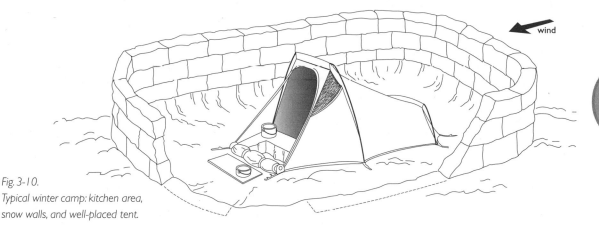

Fig. 3-10.
Typical winter camp: kitchen area,
snow walls, and well-placed tent.

the surface. A ski does a great job of grading it. If the site is slightly off level, sleep with your head toward the high side. Use deadman anchors (as shown in Figure 3-4, above) attached to long guylines to secure the tent in snow.

After erecting the tent, dig a pit about 1 foot (30 centimeters) deep in front of the tent door (fig. 3-10). Climbers can sit comfortably in the doorway of the tent with their feet in this pit while putting on boots and gaiters. Put the cook stove on the snow directly across from the pit. In bad weather, the pit is a convenient wind-protected location for the stove, allowing climbers to wiggle forward in their sleeping bags and just reach out to do the cooking. The tent vestibule can be erected over the pit.

Build snow walls around the tent if the site is exposed to winds as shown in Figure 3-10. The walls can be anywhere from about 3 to 6 feet (1 to 2 meters) high to deflect some of the wind away from the tent. Keep the walls as far away from the tent as they are high: a 3-foot-high wall, for example, should be 3 feet away from the tent, because wind will deposit snow on the leeward side of the wall and fill this area quickly. Blocks cut by a snow saw or straight-bladed snow shovel make the easiest, quickest walls. The wall can also be made by simply shoveling snow into a pile but the pile, being rounded, is less effective as a windbreak.

During a storm, party members periodically will have to get out and clear snow away from the tent. In most storms, the problem is not the snow falling from the sky but, rather, the snow carried in by the wind.

Snow is deposited on the leeward side of tents and snow walls. Even a partially buried tent poses the risk of asphyxiation, especially if someone is cooking inside. In addition, snow can pile up and load the tent with enough weight to break the poles and bring the whole structure down. Regularly shake the tent walls and shovel out around the tent, taking care to remove snow from below the lower edge of the fly so air can move between the fly and tent. Be careful not to cut the tent with the shovel; nylon slices easily when tensioned by a snow load. In a severe or prolonged storm, a tent may begin to disappear into the hole created by neighboring snowdrifts. Eventually it may become necessary to move the tent up on top of the new snow surface.

A number of special tent items are useful for winter camping. Each tent should have a small whisk broom to sweep snow from boots, packs, clothing, and the tent. A sponge is nice for cleaning up food and water spills and removing condensation from the inside walls. A cheery addition, especially during long nights near the winter solstice, is a candle lantern. For a larger community tent, the party might even consider a gas lantern, which can repay its price in weight and bother by adding tremendous brightness and warmth to the tent.

Some house rules can help make the tent-bound hours more pleasant. For example, with a small tent, packs may have to be kept outside. Most four-season tents have vestibules where gear can be stored under cover. If the tent is large enough and packs are brought inside, snow should be thoroughly brushed off first. It often helps to have one person enter the tent first to lay sleeping pads and organize gear before others enter. House rules may also dictate that boots be taken off outside, brushed free of snow, and placed in a waterproof boot bag inside the tent. Boots can bring in snow, and they also can cut or tear holes in the tent floor. Plastic boots are best for winter camping, because the shells can be left covered outside or in the vestibule while the liners can be brought inside to keep them from freezing. Use stuff sacks or a large tent sack to help organize and protect personal gear and keep it out of the way of tent mates. Put next day's dry clothing inside your sleeping bag or in a waterproof plastic sack so it does not get wet from tent condensation.

The warmth of the sleeping bag offers not only comfort but also an opportunity to dry out some gear, such as gloves and socks. Put boot liners in the bag before you go to sleep, and they will be dry and warm in the morning. Do not, however, attempt to dry large items of clothing by wearing them to bed; they will just make the bag wet and cold. In extreme cold, put boots inside an oversize stuff sack and place them inside or next to the sleeping bag to prevent them from freezing. A water bottle—tightly sealed—will be kept from freezing overnight if it is placed inside the sleeping bag.

Snow Shelters

When the temperature drops or winter storms bring strong winds and heavy snowfall, seasoned mountaineers often prefer to sleep in a snow shelter rather than a tent. A snow cave or an igloo takes more time to build, but is more secure than a tent and in cold weather is warmer. Newcomers to snow camping are surprised at what a warm, comfortable, and beautiful experience a snow shelter can be. The interior of a properly built snow cave will be at least 32 degrees Fahrenheit (0 degrees Celsius) no matter what is going on outside, and when a few warm climbers pile in, it gets warmer than that. In a storm, as the snow accumulates the snow shelter becomes even more sturdy, whereas a tent must be continually cleared of snow to protect the structure and its occupants. Snow shelters make sense especially on extended winter trips, where the construction time can be offset by staying in it for several nights.

Construction time and effort are the major drawbacks of snow shelters. Of the different types, snow trenches are relatively quick to complete; snow caves take more time to build, and igloos require the most time. Snow shelters require no special equipment other than a mountaineering snow shovel and perhaps a snow saw to cut blocks, but they do require skill. Practice before committing to a trip that depends on snow shelters.

Dripping water is a potential problem in any snow shelter. Air warmed by the occupants' body heat rises to the ceiling, which causes some melting. If the ceiling is smooth, most of the meltwater will be absorbed back into the snow. But little spikes and bumps in the ceiling will become dripping points, so the inner walls should be carefully smoothed. Finally, do not cook inside the snow shelter itself; the ventilation may not be adequate and there is a risk of carbon monoxide poisoning.

Snow Trench

A snow trench can be constructed in a half hour, making it suitable for bivouac use as well as for spartan one- or two-person quarters. It is the simplest structure that can be built of snow blocks sawed with a snow saw. Unlike a snow cave, a trench does not require particular terrain features; it can be built either on the flats or on an avalanche-safe slope, and snow depth must be sufficient so that the completed trench floor still sits in snow.

Establish an initial cut line 6 to 7 feet (about 2 meters) long with either a straight-blade shovel or a snow saw (fig. 3-11a). Dig a narrow trench along this cut line by using the snow saw or shovel to quarry snow blocks about 1 to 1½ feet (40 centimeters) thick by 2 feet (60 centimeters) wide by 3 feet (90 centimeters) high (fig. 3-11b). The blocks can be created as part of the process of removing snow for the trench, or they can be quarried nearby. Set each snow block aside carefully when it is removed from the quarry—they will form the roof of the trench.

Once the trench area is large enough—3 feet deep by 2 feet wide by 6½ feet (2 meters) long for one person—roof the trench, A-frame style, with the snow blocks (fig. 3-11c). Close off the back with another snow block. When the A-frame roof is in place, crawl underneath it into the trench and enlarge the interior down and out to accommodate the intended number of occupants. Build steps leading down into the trench. Provide a ventilation hole in the roof. Use loose snow to caulk any gaps between roof blocks and around the

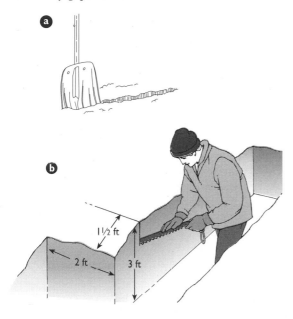

back; smooth out any bumps or irregularities in the ceiling so meltwater will run down the blocks to the sides rather than dripping on the occupants. Cover most of the entrance with a pack covered by a plastic bag, but leave some space for ventilation. Cook outside of the trench.

A more-basic, emergency snow-trench shelter can be built by digging a trench some 4 to 6 feet (1.2 to 2 meters) deep and large enough for the party to sleep in. Stretch a tarp over the top and weigh the edges down with snow (fig. 3-12). On a flat site, provide some slope to the tarp by building up the snow on one side of the trench. This quick shelter works moderately well in wind or rain, but a heavy snowfall can collapse the roof. As with all snow shelters, the smaller the trench, the easier it is to keep warm.

Snow Cave

Snow caves are best suited to locations where climbers can burrow into a snow-covered hillside. A strong and stable cave requires somewhat firm (consolidated) snow. The snow must also be deep enough to leave about 2 feet (60 centimeters) of ceiling thickness.

Several people can shelter in one snow cave. A well-built cave dug in firm snow is a very secure structure. However, if the outside temperature is warming toward freezing, a tent or tree shelter may be a better choice. The weight of a collapsed snow-cave roof could cause serious injury to people underneath.

Find a short—7 feet (2.1 meters) minimum—30- to 40-degree slope or snowdrift that is clear of any potential

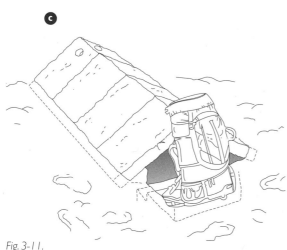

Fig. 3-11.
Building a snow trench: a, establish initial cut line with straight-blade shovel; b, quarry snow blocks 1 to 1½ feet thick by 2 feet wide by 3 feet high; c, build A-frame roof with snow blocks, enlarge interior, and provide ventilation holes in roof.

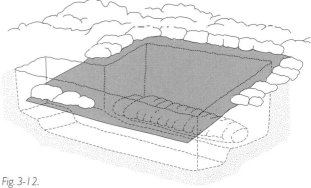

Fig. 3-12.
Snow trench roofed with a tarp.

avalanche hazard (fig. 3-13a). It is easier to dig the cave into a steep slope than a gentle slope. The snow must be deep enough that you will not hit ground before you finish excavating the entire cave. Dig an entry that is 1½ feet (0.5 meter) wide and 5 feet (1.5 meters) high (fig. 3-13b), and dig it into the slope about 3 feet (1 meter). Then create a construction-debris exit slot by digging a waist-high platform centered on the entryway, forming a T that is 4 feet (1.2 meters) wide by 1½ feet high (fig. 3-13c). Develop this platform so that it forms a horizontal slot extending into the slope, providing a temporary exitway for all the snow being shoveled out as the interior of the cave is excavated. Excavate so that the cave floor is about 6 inches (15 centimeters) higher than the bottom level of the horizontal slot.

Create the main room of the cave by digging inward from the entry and expanding the room to the front, sides, and upward—all directions except down (fig. 3-13d). Shovel snow out through the horizontal slot; a second person, working outside, can clear the snow away and trade places with the excavator working inside. Keep digging until all the snow within easy reach has been excavated. Extend the original entry hallway another 2 feet (60 centimeters) into the slope (fig. 3-13e), permitting the excavator to get farther into the cave to continue excavating outward and upward. Now it should be nearly possible to stand inside. Continue to excavate, now out of the wind; when enough snow has been cleared to allow the excavator to sit up on the main cave floor, another person can enter and help continue to expand the cave in all directions except downward.

Excavate until the inside dimensions are about 5 feet (1.5 meters) from front to back by 7 feet (2.1 meters) wide and 3½ feet (1 meter) high, a comfortable minimum for two people. Make the cave larger for more

3

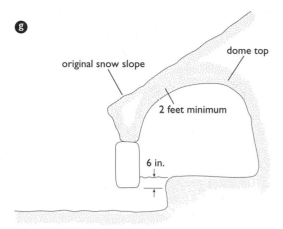

g

original snow slope

dome top

2 feet minimum

6 in.

CUTAWAY SIDE VIEW

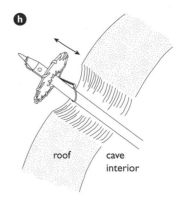

h

roof

cave interior

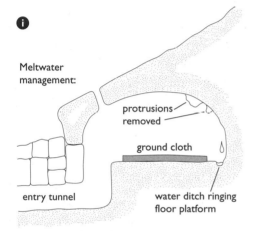

i

Meltwater management:

protrusions removed

ground cloth

entry tunnel

water ditch ringing floor platform

CUTAWAY SIDE VIEW

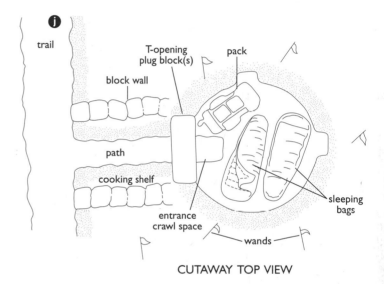

j

trail

T-opening plug block(s)

pack

block wall

path

cooking shelf

entrance crawl space

sleeping bags

wands

CUTAWAY TOP VIEW

Fig. 3-13.

Building a snow cave:
a, choose the location;
b, dig the entry;
c, dig a T-shaped slot;
d, dig inward, expanding up, left, and right;
e, expand to desired size;
f, fill in T-shaped slot;
g, snow cave cross-section;
h, create ventilation holes;
i, smooth ceiling and dig water ditch;
j, mark cave perimeter, erect wind blocks, and create cooking area;
k, create storage alcoves and deepen entryway.

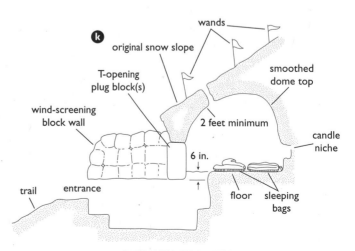

k

wands

original snow slope

T-opening plug block(s)

smoothed dome top

wind-screening block wall

2 feet minimum

candle niche

6 in.

trail

entrance

floor

sleeping bags

CUTAWAY SIDE VIEW

occupants, but remember that a small cave is warmer than a large one. Keep a minimum of 2 feet (60 centimeters) of firm snow on the slope above the cave ceiling to provide enough strength to keep the roof from collapsing. Avoid building a flat ceiling. The more dome-shaped the ceiling contour, the stronger it will be and the less it will sag.

Fill in the temporary horizontal slot with snow blocks (fig. 3-13f); one large block or two smaller blocks leaning against each other may be sufficient to close the slot. Caulk any spaces around the blocks with snow. The top of the completed entrance tunnel should be at least 6 inches (15 centimeters) lower than the cave floor, keeping warm air in the cave and cold drafts out (fig. 3-13g). Use snow blocks to build a wind-screening wall on either side of the entry path. Poke a pair of ski-pole-basket-sized ventilation holes through the ceiling of the cave from the inside out (fig. 3-13h); this is important to prevent asphyxiation of the snow-cave occupants. If it gets too warm inside the cave, enlarge these holes. Remember to not use a camp stove inside the cave—cook outside at the entrance, in open air.

Smooth the domed ceiling of the cave's interior so that it is free of any bumps or protrusions (fig. 3-13i); this way, melting water will flow down the walls of the cave instead of dripping from bumps onto the occupants. Scratch a small ditch all around the base of the wall to channel any meltwater away from the floor. Place a ground sheet on the floor to help keep things dry and prevent loss of equipment in the snow. Keep stormy weather out by putting a small tarp or a pack (inside a plastic bag) over the entrance, but leave some opening for ventilation air to flow in. To ensure that no uninvited guests drop in, mark the area around the cave with bamboo wands (fig. 3-13j), so that someone does not inadvertently walk onto the roof of the snow cave.

Customize the inside of the cave by digging small alcoves into the walls to store boots, stove, and cooking utensils or to hold candles for illuminating the cave at night (fig. 3-13k). Digging the entry tunnel deeper under the snow blocks will make entry easier. Entrance-area seats, a cooking platform, and other personal touches make the cave a snow home. When you are finished using the cave, collapse it so that it does not present a hazard later on for others.

Igloo

Igloo construction takes more time and skill than the other types of snow shelters. Temperatures must be reliably frigid, around 28 degrees Fahrenheit (minus 2 degrees Celsius) or below, for this shelter to be practical. Any warmer, and it is likely to melt and collapse. But igloos are undeniably fun to build and use.

Begin by finding a good location for the igloo, well clear of any potential avalanche path. The chief requirement is close proximity to a good "quarry" area for sawing snow blocks. Wind-packed snow is easiest to work with; if the snow seems too loose and powdery, tromp the quarry area down and let it set up (consolidate) for 30 minutes before beginning to saw. Use a snow saw; a straight-bladed snow shovel will also work, though not as well. Saw blocks about 2½ feet (75 centimeters) long by 1½ feet (45 centimeters) wide by 1 foot (30 centimeters) thick (fig. 3-14a). Heavier snow requires smaller blocks.

Note: If the snow quality of the blocks is not adequate and the snow blocks fall apart when moved, abandon plans for building an igloo and construct a different type of shelter.

Compact the igloo's base by walking over the area

EMERGENCY SNOW SHELTERS

Winter travelers should know how to build quick snow shelters for emergency situations, such as being caught out overnight on what was planned to be a day trip without tents. With a little improvisation, natural features can be converted into snow hideaways for an unplanned bivouac. Such shelters occur under logs, along riverbanks, or in the pits formed when snow has been deflected away from large conifer trees by their limbs. For a tree-pit shelter, enlarge the natural hole around the trunk and roof it with any available covering, such as ice blocks, tree limbs, an emergency space blanket, or a tarp. Boughs and bark can provide insulation and support (but do not cut live boughs unless it is a life-or-death emergency).

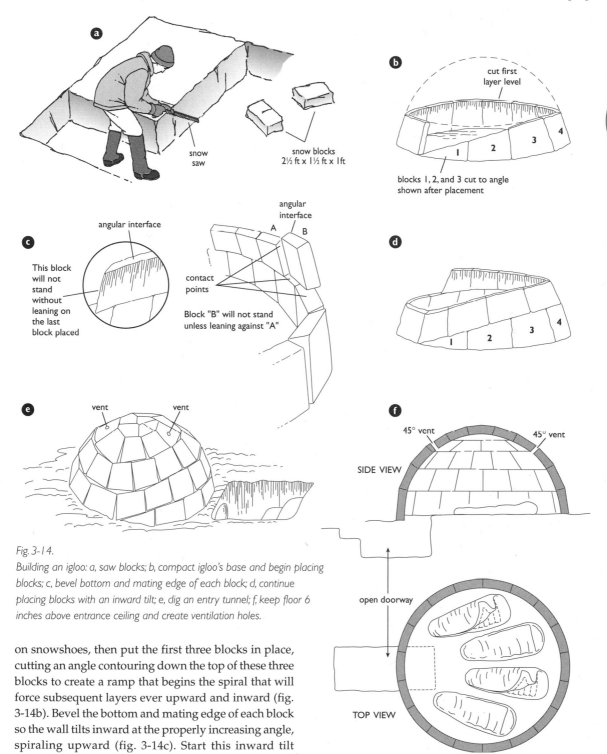

Fig. 3-14.

Building an igloo: a, saw blocks; b, compact igloo's base and begin placing blocks; c, bevel bottom and mating edge of each block; d, continue placing blocks with an inward tilt; e, dig an entry tunnel; f, keep floor 6 inches above entrance ceiling and create ventilation holes.

on snowshoes, then put the first three blocks in place, cutting an angle contouring down the top of these three blocks to create a ramp that begins the spiral that will force subsequent layers ever upward and inward (fig. 3-14b). Bevel the bottom and mating edge of each block so the wall tilts inward at the properly increasing angle, spiraling upward (fig. 3-14c). Start this inward tilt immediately, so that the igloo does not get so tall that the top cannot be reached to cap it.

Set each block firmly and hold it in place while it is installed and until the next block in the spiral is set and the cracks caulked with loose snow. One person works inside, shaping and setting the blocks and caulking. Others work outside, sawing and carrying blocks and caulking the outside. Although the igloo in Figure 3-13d shows alternating vertical seams between blocks, the seams may be either staggered or aligned.

Cap the igloo's apex, then excavate into the floor from outside, digging down below the igloo wall and inward to create a tunnel entrance for the igloo (fig. 3-14e). As with a snow cave, the igloo's entrance ceiling should be at least 6 inches (15 centimeters) below the level of the floor (fig. 3-14f). Place ventilation holes at 45-degree angles in at least two spots in the igloo roof.

THE SLEEPING SYSTEM
Sleeping Bags

For most climbers, a sleeping bag is the critical component to their outdoor sleeping system. A good sleeping bag fits your body, retains body heat, and is light and compressible. For mountaineering, nothing beats the efficient design of the mummy bag.

The warmth of a sleeping bag is provided by fill material that traps an insulating layer of air between the climber's warm body and the cooler world beyond the sleeping bag. How efficient a particular bag is at keeping you warm depends on the type and amount of this insulating fill, the thickness (loft) of the fill, the bag's size (its fit to your body), and the bag's style.

Insulation

There are two types of insulation for mountaineering sleeping bags: goose down and synthetic fibers. Each type has its own advantages and disadvantages.

Goose down: High-quality goose down (described as having 700 to 800 loft) expands to fill 700 or 800 cubic inches of volume per ounce (405 to 462 cubic centimeters per gram) of down. Down is the warmest, lightest, most compressible, and most luxurious insulation available. Disadvantages of down are its high cost and its loss of insulative value when thoroughly wet. Most stuff sacks are not completely waterproof, so in wet conditions, wrap the stuffed sleeping bag in a plastic bag before putting it into the pack.

Synthetic fibers: Synthetic-fiber bags are far less expensive than down bags and retain some of their insulative properties when wet—although sleeping in a wet bag, whether it is a down or a synthetic bag, is a miserable experience. The disadvantages of synthetic fill are that it is less compressible than down and it is relatively heavier than down for a given degree of insulating capacity. Further, a synthetic bag cannot withstand as many compression cycles (stuffing and unstuffing) as a down bag and therefore will lose its loft, thus its insulative properties, more quickly.

Cover Materials

Several types of cover materials are commonly used to make the outside shells of mountaineering sleeping bags. The most popular are laminates and breathable coated fabrics, microfibers, and nylons.

Laminated and waterproof/breathable-coated fabrics: These will keep water out while allowing moisture vapor to escape. These fabrics are expensive but advantageous in damp environments such as the inside of a snow cave, tent, or bivouac sack. They are especially desirable with a down bag. The laminate process is complex and occasionally the fabric will delaminate or wear excessively over time and extended use.

Microfibers: These shells are constructed of very tightly woven nylons or polyesters with a very high thread count. These shells offer water repellency with greater breathability than that of coated or laminated fabrics. Some microfiber fabrics are further treated with polymers such as silicone, which increase their water resistance and durability. Microfibers are lighter and are more compressible than coated and laminated fabrics.

Nylon: Sleeping-bag shells made of nylon are the very lightest, most compressible, and most breathable fabrics available. Unfortunately, they offer the least protection against condensation in the tent and moisture in the outside environment.

Features and Components

The features and components of a sleeping bag improve efficiency and ventilation. A good hood (fig. 3-15) surrounds your head, retaining precious heat, while leaving your face uncovered for respiration. A collar is designed to seal around your neck to further retain heat inside the main body of the bag. Long zippers make it easy to get in and out of the bag and help ventilate excess heat if it gets too warm inside. Some designs offer complementary left- and right-hand zippers so that two bags can be zipped together. A half- or three-quarter-length zipper saves weight and bulk, but some flexibility in ventilation is lost. A draft tube on the inside of the bag running along the length of the zipper helps to seal out cold air.

Accessories

Some manufacturers make washable sleeping-bag liners, which add a few degrees of warmth by trapping heat close to the body. A liner also keeps body oils from soiling the bag's interior and insulation. A liner is especially handy while you are on extended trips where it may be difficult or impractical to wash the sleeping bag. Bag liners add several ounces, however, and make the bag a bit bulkier when stuffed.

Vapor barrier liners (VBLs) are constructed of a nonbreathable, totally waterproof coated nylon; you sleep inside the VBL inside the sleeping bag. They make the bag warmer by reducing evaporative heat loss. VBLs also reduce the amount of moisture introduced into the insulation; in arctic environments, this cuts down ice buildup within the sleeping bag's insulation. Despite the advantages of VBLs, many climbers find them awkward and uncomfortably clammy. Try one out first before committing to using one on a big climbing trip.

Most sleeping bags come with a stuff sack and a breathable storage sack. If lost, they are available separately.

Fit

It is important that your sleeping bag fit your body. Too wide, and it will be drafty, cold, and unnecessarily heavy. If the bag is too tight, you will be uncomfortably snug and your body will compress the insulation from the inside, making the bag colder. If the bag is too short, the insulation in the footbox and hood will be compressed, making the bag colder.

Sleeping bags come in a variety of widths and lengths, designed for different body shapes, so get the size that fits you the best. Size the bag a little longer for winter camping or expedition use; the extra room can be used for drying small items such as wet gloves, socks, and boot liners.

Rating Systems

Manufacturers give their bags a minimum temperature rating or comfort range. Rating systems should be used only as rough guidelines. The ratings mean different things to different companies, and they are not meant to compare bags from different companies.

Many factors dictate how warm or cold you will be in a particular bag. Personal metabolism, level of hydration or fatigue, ambient air temperature, and ground insulation, among other factors, all affect warmth (see the "Tips on Staying Warm" sidebar at the end of this chapter). Remember that a sleeping bag does not warm the person who is inside it; you warm the bag with your body heat. The insulation and cover material only help to reduce radiated heat loss.

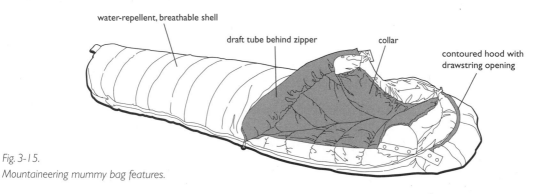

Fig. 3-15.
Mountaineering mummy bag features.

water-repellent, breathable shell

draft tube behind zipper

collar

contoured hood with drawstring opening

Specialty Bags

Some climbers prefer to go as light as possible, sacrificing a little comfort to gain a lightweight advantage. Half- or three-quarter-length bags are available, and when used in conjunction with an insulating jacket, they can be adequate for temperatures down to just below freezing.

Care and Cleaning

A sleeping bag is a serious investment, and with a little care it will last for many years. Always follow the manufacturer's recommendations. The company that made the bag will know the best way to care for it. That said, here are a few techniques to make that bag last a long time.

Storage: Always store the bag fully lofted. Only keep the bag in a compression stuff sack for a short period of time, such as while it is in the pack or during travel.

Protection from soiling: Consider using a removable liner to protect the bag's interior from body oils.

Cleaning: Spot-clean soiled areas with soap specified by the manufacturer. Over time, any bag will need to be laundered. Never have a sleeping bag dry-cleaned. Wash the bag using mild soap on the gentle cycle in a large washing machine. Run the bag through the rinse cycle several times to be sure that all the soap has been removed. Dry the bag in a large clothes dryer under medium heat. Remove the bag occasionally and break up clumps of down, or throw in a tennis ball during the last few drying cycles. Make sure the bag is completely dry by squeezing the insulation and feeling for moisture. Washing and drying a bag takes several hours. Alternatively, there are outdoor repair shops that specialize in laundering sleeping bags.

Ground Insulation

The foundation for a comfortable night in the outdoors is a good piece of insulation under the sleeping bag. In summer or in winter, whether you are in a tent or out under the stars, a sleeping pad reduces the amount of heat you lose to the ground or snow. If you are forced to sleep without a pad, use extra clothing, your pack, the climbing rope, or your boots for padding and insulation.

Materials

Closed-cell foam: A thin pad of closed-cell foam provides good lightweight insulation. Textured designs in closed-cell pads give them a softer sleeping surface, lower weight, and an increased ability to trap air, resulting in greater thermal efficiency.

Air mattress: By itself, an air mattress is comfortably soft but provides no insulation. In fact, the air in the mattress convects heat away from the body by internal air circulation—not a good choice for climbers.

Open-cell foam: Also avoid uncovered pads of open-cell foam; these are bulky and they absorb water just like the sponges they are.

Self-inflating pad: These are made of open-cell foam enclosed in an airtight, waterproof envelope. This type of pad combines the insulation of foam with the softness of an air mattress, which is very popular and effective.

Size

Insulation pads come in a variety of lengths, but the 4-foot (1.2-meter) length is usually adequate for general mountaineering; you can use a sit pad or items of gear to pad and insulate feet and legs. When camping on snow or in winter or arctic environments, use a 4-foot self-inflating pad on top of a full-length closed-cell foam pad for greater insulation.

STOVES

Stoves are better than campfires for backcountry travel because they are faster, cleaner, and more convenient; they will operate under almost any conditions; and they have minimal impact on the environment. In choosing a stove for mountaineering use, consider its weight (very important), the altitude and temperature where it will be used, fuel availability, ease of operation, and reliability. The stove should be easy to operate and maintain and should work even in cold, wet, windy conditions. It must have a high heat output to melt snow quickly and stability to avoid tipping. For travel in remote areas, choose a stove that accepts a variety of fuels. Read the operating instructions before buying, and ask questions.

Types

In mountaineering stoves, fuel must be pressurized so that it can flow at a sufficient rate to support a hot flame at the burner. Some stoves use a fuel cartridge; others use a refillable liquid-fuel reservoir. Different fuels are suited to these two types of stove (see "Stove Fuels" and Table 3-1 later in this chapter for a summary of each fuel's advantages and disadvantages).

Fuel cartridge: This is already fully pressurized (fig. 3-16a and f). In the cartridge stove, no pumping is required to maintian pressure during stove operation, but when the cartridge is nearly empty, the pressure becomes too low for adequate heat output. This causes a brief gap in cooking as the stove must cool before the cartridge is disconnected from the burner and discarded (for carrying out with the trash) and then replaced with a new cartridge. Cartridge stoves use pressurized butane, propane, isobutane gas, or a blend of these fuels.

Refillable liquid-fuel reservoir: This can be either a tank under the burner (fig. 3-16b and c) or a separate fuel bottle connected to the burner by a rigid pipe or flexible hose (fig. 3-16d and e). You must pump the reservoir up to operating pressure each time the stove is used. You must maintain the operating pressure by periodically pumping by hand to regain full heat output. Stoves with refillable liquid-fuel reservoirs typically use white gas or kerosene.

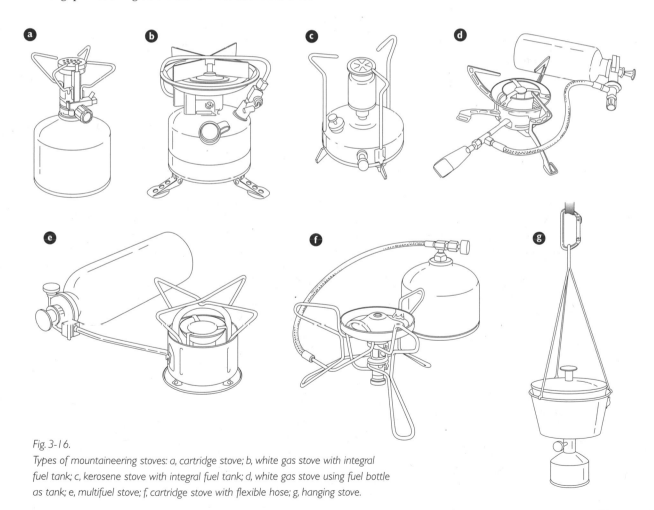

Fig. 3-16.

Types of mountaineering stoves: a, cartridge stove; b, white gas stove with integral fuel tank; c, kerosene stove with integral fuel tank; d, white gas stove using fuel bottle as tank; e, multifuel stove; f, cartridge stove with flexible hose; g, hanging stove.

Weight

Mountaineering stoves typically weigh 1 to 1½ pounds (about 0.4 to 0.5 kilogram); for a short trip, there is little weight difference between using a cartridge stove and using a stove with a refillable tank or bottle. For long trips, liquid fuel stoves are better. The fuel can be purchased and carried in bulk, and there are no empty cartridges to carry out.

Stability

Stoves that are constructed with the fuel cartridge or tank directly beneath and attached to the burner assembly (fig. 3-16a, b, and c) tend to be more vulnerable to tipping over than stoves with a fuel cartridge or bottle set out to the side of the burner assembly (fig. 3-16d, e, and f). The exception to this general rule is a specialized type of mountaineering stove, the hanging stove, in which the entire stove hangs as an integral unit from a chain or wire (fig. 3-16g). Hanging stoves usually use pressurized fuel cartridges. They are used in big-wall climbing and some expeditions.

Operation

A stove is ignited (or started) by a spark or flame applied to vaporized fuel at the burner. Some stoves have an integrated ignition device as a convenience; with most stoves, you must use matches or a lighter. With fuel cartridge stoves, the fuel already is vaporized, so starting the stove is a simple matter of turning the regulating valve and lighting the released fuel. In contrast, a stove with a refillable liquid-fuel reservoir must be primed to convert the released liquid fuel to a vapor before the stove will operate efficiently.

A common method of priming is to preheat the stove by burning a small amount of liquid fuel in a priming cup to heat the region surrounding the supply line's jet. When the flame from the priming process wanes but is not quite gone, open the fuel regulator valve to start fuel vaporizing at the supply line's jet, which ignites from the residual priming-cup flame. This is a simple process, but it must be perfected at home.

In windy, dusty conditions, a common reason for unexpected stove failure is that debris has clogged the jet. Learn how to clean the jet, following the manufacturer's instructions. To assure trouble-free operation, clean the stove regularly and rebuild it periodically, replacing seals and any pump leathers. Read the manufacturer's instructions and learn how to make emergency field repairs on your stove.

Accessories

Mountaineering stoves typically burn about an hour on 8 ounces (250 milliliters) of fuel, and will boil 1 quart (liter) of water in 4 to 8 minutes at sea level. Wind can increase that time to as much as 25 minutes, or even prevent boiling altogether. For fuel efficiency, keep a lid on the cook pot and use a windscreen to shield the flame and to prevent heat from being blown away. Some stoves come with a windscreen made of a flexible sheet of aluminum, which is placed around the burner like a curtain, to block wind (fig 3-17a). However, this type of screen should not be used with stoves that have integral fuel tanks because too much heat will be reflected back onto the fuel tank, dangerously overheating it. With any type of stove, it is safe to improvise a windscreen using pot lids, metal plates, or small rock walls.

A heat exchanger (fig. 3-17b) keeps even more heat around the stove and pot. These devices can be heavy, but on longer trips they may save enough fuel to repay their weight.

Some stoves have a flame-control valve designed to allow simmering. Stoves that boil water fast often do not simmer well. To reduce heat for slower cooking on any stove, put a metal lid or plate between the pot and burner.

For snow camping, bring along a small, foil-wrapped platform of thin plywood, Masonite, or even cardboard to support the stove and keep it off the snow.

COMMON PRIMING MISTAKES

- Using too much fuel initially in the priming cup, which prolongs the process and wastes fuel
- Opening the regulator valve too soon, causing a potentially dangerous flare-up
- Opening the regulator valve too late, leaving the stove to sputter out

Fig. 3-17.
Stove accessories:
a, windscreen;
b, heat exchanger.

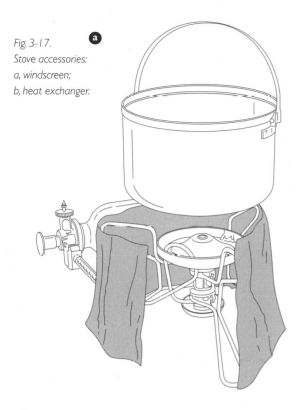

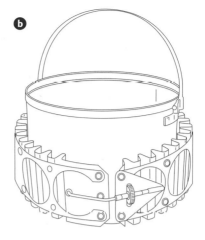

If using white gas (as is likely in cold conditions), slip the fuel bottle into a thick sock to insulate it for better fuel performance.

Stove Fuels

Fuel consumption depends on the conditions of the trip, how the party plans to cook, and water supplies. For instance, cup-cooking (see "Food" later in this chapter) takes less fuel than cooking meals on a stove. Melting snow takes at least twice as much fuel as simply heating water. Keep notes on fuel consumption under various circumstances; experience will provide guidelines on how much fuel is needed for various types of trips. A minimum is 4 ounces (125 milliliters) per person per day, if the party is neither melting snow nor doing elaborate cooking. If two people are using a stove, they will want at least 8 ounces (250 milliliters) of fuel for an overnight trip. Consider taking an extra fuel reserve on extended trips in remote areas. Table 3-1 below summarizes the pros and cons of common stove fuels.

White gas: This is the most popular mountaineering stove fuel in North America. It burns hotter than butane and is excellent for melting large amounts of snow, boiling water, or heating food quickly. Unlike kerosene, white gas can be used as its own priming agent. Use only refined or white gasoline prepared for pressurized stoves; do not use automotive gasoline, whether leaded or unleaded. The correct fuel is safer and is less likely to clog jets, build up excess pressure, or emit toxic fumes. Spilled white gas evaporates readily, with little odor, but is very flammable.

Kerosene: This is less volatile than white gas and therefore safer to transport and store. Because the fuel does not burn hot enough to prime the burner, kerosene stoves must be primed with white gas, alcohol, lighter fluid, or priming paste. If not adequately primed, the stove will burn with a sooty yellow flame, giving off smoke and carbon. But when it burns efficiently, a kerosene stove has a high heat output, at least equal to that of white gas.

Butane: Butane or butane/propane cartridge stoves are the most convenient—easy to light, good flame control, immediate maximum heat output, and no chance of fuel spills. Pressure in the canister forces fuel out as the valve is opened, eliminating both priming and pumping. Standard butane stoves do not function well at temperatures below freezing. The disposable cartridges cannot be refilled. There is no way to tell how much is left in a partially used cartridge, so owners of these stoves often carry a spare cartridge just in case.

3

TABLE 3-1. COMPARISON OF STOVE FUELS

Fuel	Advantages	Disadvantages	Best For
Liquid Fuels			
White gas	High heat output. Spilled fuel evaporates quickly. Readily available in North America. Can use the stove fuel for priming.	Priming required. Spilled fuel very flammable. Self-pressurized models must be insulated from cold or snow.	Cooking in any conditions, temperature, or altitude.
Kerosene	High heat output. Spilled fuel will not ignite readily. Available throughout the world.	Requires priming with another fuel. Spilled fuel does not evaporate readily, leaving a residue. Does not burn clean; jet must be cleaned periodically.	International expeditions on which fuel availability is unknown.
Alcohol	None.	Lowest heat output (slow cooking time).	Sometimes used in small emergency stoves. Poor choice for mountaineering.
Compressed-Gas Canister Fuels			
Butane	No priming or pumping required. Immediate maximum heat output. Full flame control, down to simmer. Maintenance-free. Stove units are superlightweight. No-spill fuel container. Readily available in North America and Europe.	Lower heat output than white gas or kerosene. Disposable canister must be packed out. Fuel cartridges expensive. Fuel must be kept above freezing for efficient burning. No way to know amount of fuel remaining in canister.	Short, light trips in temperatures above freezing. Good at high altitude if temperatures are above freezing.
Blended fuels (butane/ propane, sometimes with isobutane added)	Somewhat better cold-weather performance than straight butane.	Lower heat output than white gas or kerosene.	Same as butane.
Isobutane	All the advantages of butane. Works well below freezing.	Lower heat output than white gas or kerosene. On long trips, pressurized fuel cartridges heavier and bulkier than liquid fuels. Fuel not as widely available as white gas and kerosene.	Short trips under any conditions.

Some cartridges cannot be changed until they are completely empty. Never change a cartridge in the tent or near any flame because residual fuel in spent canisters can be a fire hazard.

Isobutane: This comes in canisters like butane fuel and shares all the conveniences and inconveniences of butane, but performs better at high altitude and sub-freezing temperatures.

Solid fuels: These include candles and canned heat that serve primarily as firestarters. They are lightweight and cheap, but provide only limited heat. They may be carried for emergency use, along with a metal cup for heating small amounts of water.

Stove and Fuel Storage

Carry extra white gas or kerosene in a metal bottle specifically designed for fuel storage, with a screw top and rubber gasket. Plainly mark the fuel container to distinguish it from other containers such as water bottles, and stow it in a place where a little leakage, if it occurs, will not contaminate any food.

Leave about 1 inch (2–3 centimeters) of air space in the stove's fuel reservoir, rather than filling it to the brim, to prevent excessive pressure buildup. At the end of the season, put the stove into storage and remember to empty the fuel bottle. After storage, test the stove at home before using it again in the field.

Safety

Tents have been blown up, equipment burned, and people injured by careless stove use. Let the stove cool completely before changing cartridges or adding liquid fuel. Change pressurized fuel cartridges, and fill and start liquid-fuel stoves, outside the tent and away from other open flames. Before lighting a stove, check fuel lines, valves, and connections for leaks.

Do not cook inside the tent unless it is so windy that the stove will not operate outside or so cold that the cook risks hypothermia. The risks range from the relatively minor one of spilling pots onto sleeping bags to the deadly dangers of tent fires or carbon monoxide poisoning.

If it is absolutely necessary to cook inside a tent, follow these safety rules:

1. Light the stove outside or near a tent opening so it can be tossed away from the tent if it flares; bring the stove inside only after it is running smoothly.
2. Cook near the tent door or in the vestibule, for better ventilation and so the stove can be thrown outside quickly in an emergency.
3. Provide plenty of ventilation. This is critical because carbon monoxide is colorless and odorless; humans cannot detect it. Better to err on the conservative side by cooling off the tent with too large a ventilation hole, rather than risk carbon monoxide poisoning with too small an opening.

WATER

During the sedentary activities of everyday life, mild dehydration simply causes thirst. With the sustained exertion of mountaineering, however, fluid loss may cause fatigue, disorientation, and headaches. Dehydration becomes debilitating more quickly than you might expect. It is a factor in a number of mountain maladies, including acute mountain sickness. (See Chapter 23, First Aid, for more information on dehydration, acute mountain sickness, and other health hazards.)

Drink more water than usual, perhaps 2 to 3 extra quarts (liters), during the 24-hour period before a climb to boost your strength and endurance. Additionally, it is wise to drink a generous quantity of water, more than feels necessary, immediately before beginning the climb. Your skin and lungs can release large amounts of moisture into cold, dry, high-altitude mountain air without your being aware of it. *Do not wait until you are thirsty to drink;* thirst is a sign that dehydration is already in progress. A better indicator of adequate hydration is lightly colored or colorless urine. At high elevations, dehydration can contribute to nausea that, ironically, reduces the desire to gulp down fluids.

Keep water handy. Have a bottle within easy reach inside your pack or in a pouch on the hip belt. Some climbers use a bladder device carried in the pack, with a tube clipped to the shoulder strap for an instant sip whenever desired.

A well-balanced diet replaces most electrolytes that are lost during heavy sweating. In hot weather or on extended heavy-exertion trips, however, climbers may need to pay specific attention to electrolyte replacement.

Sports drinks may be useful, but not everyone can tolerate them. Diluting sports drinks or drinking additional water afterward makes them easier to digest. Try them at home before relying on them in the mountains.

Water Sources

Water can be scarce in the mountains. Some climbs have abundant streams and snowfields to replenish water supplies, but often the high peaks are bone dry or frozen solid, and the only water available is what the climbers carry with them.

On one-day climbs, the usual source is simply the water tap at home. For most people, 1½ to 3 quarts (liters) of water is enough. Take more than what you think will be needed. During a tough three-day climb, each person might drink 6 quarts while hiking and climbing and an additional 5 quarts in camp. That is too much to carry, so supplies must be replenished from lakes, streams, and snow.

Snow can be melted for drinking by carrying it packed inside a water bottle. Start with a bit of water already in the bottle in order to hasten the melting time; stow the bottle on the sunny side of your pack. When there is both sun and enough time, set out pots of snow to melt. Try catching the drips from overhanging eaves of snow that are melting. Or find a tongue of snow that is slowly melting into a trickle, dredge a depression below, let the water clear, and channel the resulting puddle into a container.

When there is snow but no liquid water near camp, the best way to get water is to melt snow in a pot on the stove, though this takes time and uses up cooking fuel. Get the snow from a "drinking-snow" pit, well away from the designated toilet and cleaning areas. Always have a little water already in the pot when starting to melt snow. Oddly, the pot can "burn" if it contains only dry snow. Just before bedtime, melt enough to fill all water bottles and cooking pots so that there is enough to rehydrate during the night and refill bottles again in the morning. Collect the snow in small, pot-size chunks rather than as loose snow in order to make stoking the melting pot simpler and neater. If you are cooking in the tent vestibule, collect snow in a sack before bringing it inside.

Pathogens in Water

In the old days, there were few joys as supreme as drinking pure, refreshing alpine water right from the source. Nowadays, even in remote areas, water may be contaminated by animal or human waste. Even melted snow is suspect. Fresh-fallen snow is as pure as pure can be, but human and animal waste may contaminate snow, and microscopic organisms can survive freezing temperatures. The tainted snow melts, trickling and percolating its way to cross-contaminate other snow a long distance away. So you should purify melted snow just as if it were any other water source.

Treat water to guard against the three types of waterborne pathogens: viruses, bacteria, and large parasites.

Viruses: These most often are present in tropical waters. Hepatitis A (infectious hepatitis) is an example of a virus-caused disease that can be contracted by drinking contaminated water. Although wilderness waters in North America are usually free of viruses, it never hurts to treat against them. Viruses are easily killed with chemical treatment but are too tiny to be removed by most filters. Boiling kills viruses.

Bacteria: These are present in mountain waters in a wide range of types and sizes. Common harmful waterborne bacteria include *Salmonella* (incubation period 12–36 hours), *Campylobacter jejuni* (incubation three to five days), and *Escherichia coli* (incubation 24–72 hours). In some parts of the world, water may contain bacteria that cause severe illnesses such as cholera, dysentery, and typhoid. Like viruses, most bacteria can be effectively killed with chemicals. Bacteria are larger than viruses, and so can be removed with the proper filters. Boiling kills all bacteria.

Parasites: Larger parasites are protozoa, amoebas, tapeworms, and flatworms. The protozoa *Giardia lamblia* and *Cryptosporidium parvum* (crypto) are major health concerns for alpine travelers. Both are common in backcountry waters worldwide, including all of North America. The illnesses caused by these parasites—giardiasis and cryptosporidiosis, respectively—take two to twenty days to manifest themselves, with symptoms that include intense nausea, diarrhea, stomach cramps, fever, headaches, flatulence, and belches that reek like rotten eggs. Some of these parasites have tough cell walls that are resistant to chemical treatment. But because of their larger size, they can be filtered out, and boiling kills them.

A very small parasite, *Cyclosporum* species, commonly contaminates surface water in Nepal during spring and summer, and is found increasingly in other areas, including North America. It is not killed by halogen chemicals such as chlorine or iodine, but can be removed by a filter with a small-enough pore size (see the next section) or killed by boiling.

Water Purification

The principal methods of water purification are boiling, chemical treatment (iodine or chlorine), and filtering. No single method is the best for every situation, and the only guaranteed method is boiling. See the summary in Table 3-2. Water containing a lot of sediment should be strained through a cloth, paper coffee filter, or paper towel before proceeding with disinfection or pumping through a water filter.

TABLE 3-2. WATER TREATMENT METHODS

Method	Effectiveness	Advantages	Disadvantages
Boiling	Very effective against all pathogens.	Most effective method.	Slow and inconvenient. Requires additional fuel, which adds weight to pack. Leaves flat taste to water.
Iodine	Very effective against bacteria and viruses. Effective against *Giardia,* but requires soak time. Not effective against *Cyclosporum.*	Lightweight and compact. Can be combined with filtration to protect against all pathogens. Inexpensive.	Slow (1 hour for cold water or water cloudy with sediment). Disagreeable taste unless cleared afterward with vitamin C. Not to be used by persons with allergy to iodine or active thyroid disease. Not to be used as the sole method of purification.
Chlorine	Very effective against bacteria and viruses. Effective against *Giardia,* but requires soak time. Not effective against *Cryptosporidium* or *Cyclosporum.*	Lightweight and compact. Can be combined with filtration to protect against all pathogens. Inexpensive.	Waiting time. Disagreeable taste. Not to be used as the sole method of purification.
Chlorine dioxide	Effective against parasites, as well as bacteria and viruses.	Lightweight and compact. Can be combined with filtration to protect against all pathogens. Taste of water not altered significantly.	Waiting time.
Filtering	Very effective against large parasites. Effectiveness varies against bacteria, depending on filter's pore size. Not effective against viruses.	Quick. Taste of water not altered significantly.	Expensive. May be bulky or heavy. May clog or break. (River water carrying glacial silt definitely will clog the filter.) Not to be used as the sole method of purification.

Boiling

Boiling is the surefire method of water purification. Boiling kills all waterborne pathogens. Simply bring the water to a rolling boil and maintain the boil for 1 minute, regardless of elevation.

Chemical Disinfecting

Iodine: Treatment with iodine is effective against most bacteria and all likely viruses, but is not reliable as the sole method of purification. It does not work against the parasites *Cryptosporidium* or *Cyclosporum,* which are highly resistant to halogens such as iodine and chlorine. Iodine is effective against *Giardia lamblia,* although a soak time is required for penetrating the parasite's cyst walls. The time can be as much as 1 hour for frigid water from a glacial stream. The usual procedure is to drop iodine tablets or solution into the water in a bottle. Avoid dipping the drinking bottle directly into a stream because the threaded top may become contaminated. Do slosh a bit of the treated water onto the threads around the bottle's top and the cap. Iodine imparts a mildly disagreeable taste to the water. Adding vitamin C (50 milligrams per quart/liter), in tablet

form or in powdered drink mix, eliminates the iodine taste. It will also stop iodine's germicidal action, so wait until after the soak time is complete.

Chlorine: This is a common disinfectant, but perhaps not the best choice for climbers. It may not kill *Giardia* cysts, and it definitely is unreliable for attacking *Cryptosporidium.* Chlorine gives water an unpleasant taste and odor, though most of it can be eliminated by adding peroxide after disinfection is complete.

Chlorine dioxide: Water-treatment kits using this chemical are another choice. The chlorine dioxide is mixed with phosphoric acid 5 minutes before use, and oxygen is released to produce the disinfectant effect. There is a 15- to 30-minute wait period before the treated water is ready for use. The product (called Aquamira) appears to be effective against *Cryptosporidium* and *Giardia* as well as against other pathogens.

Filtering

Water filters work wonderfully well against protozoa and bacteria, but are not effective against viruses. Removal of bacteria depends on the filter's pore size and rating. Manufacturers describe filter pore size in various

Fig. 3-18.
Water filter.

ways. Look for information on the package stating that the "absolute" pore size is 0.4 micron or less.

Water filters (fig. 3-18), although expensive, are relatively quick and easy to use compared with other purification methods. To guard against viruses, treat the water with iodine before pumping it through the filter. Some filters feature an integral iodine chamber designed to do this for you. Others come with an integral charcoal element that removes iodine and its taste. Whichever special features may be offered, look for a compact, lightweight filter that is easy to use, clean, and maintain. Specifically, make sure that it can be "field-maintained," including cleaning a clogged filter in the field.

Sanitation

Use only purified water for dishwashing and toothbrushing. Always wash your hands well before preparing or handling food. If it is impractical to wash your hands, clean up with waterless hand-sanitizer gel (which kills germs by dehydrating them) or unscented antibacterial baby wipes.

FOOD

A well-rested, well-hydrated, and well-fed climber is less likely to experience difficulties from exertion, heat, cold, or illness. Mountaineering is a strenuous and demanding activity, so your body needs a variety of foods to provide sufficient carbohydrates, protein, and fats. With planning, it is possible to choose foods that keep well, are lightweight, and meet all nutritional needs. The longer the mountaineering trip, the more the menu must provide variety and complexity. And the food must taste good or it simply will not be eaten. If fueling your body quickly and simply is the first aim of alpine cuisine, the enjoyment of doing so is a worthy secondary goal.

Energy expenditure on a climb can go as high as 6,000 calories per day, possibly even higher for larger folks. To put this in perspective, most people require only about 1,500 to 2,500 calories per day when living a sedentary life. Adequate caloric intake is essential. Determine what food intake plan is best, depending on the strenuousness of the trip and your own size, weight,

metabolic rate, and level of conditioning. Never engage in calorie restriction ("being on a diet") during a mountaineering trip, because this can interfere with performance and stamina. Put the weight-loss diet on hold until the trip is over.

Composition of Foods

Each of the three basic food components—carbohydrates (sugars and starches), proteins, and fats—provides energy, and each must be supplied in approximately the right proportion for the human body to function well. For general mountaineering, try to consume total calories in roughly the proportions shown in Table 3-3 (compare with Table 20-1 in Chapter 20, Expedition Climbing).

TABLE 3-3. CALORIC PROPORTIONS FOR GENERAL MOUNTAINEERING	
Food Source	**Percentage of Daily Calories**
Carbohydrates	50 to 70 percent
Fats	20 to 30 percent
Proteins	20 to 30 percent

Carbohydrates: These are the easiest food for the body to convert into energy, so they should constitute most of the calories. Think of carbohydrates as the main "fuel food" to keep your body functioning most efficiently. Good sources of carbohydrate starches include whole grains, rice, potatoes, cereals, pasta, bread, crackers, and granola bars. Sugars can be supplied not only by honey or granulated sugar but also by fruits (fresh or dried), jam, hot cocoa, sport gels, and drink mixes.

Proteins: These are also important, and the daily requirement is nearly constant regardless of type or level of activity. The body cannot store proteins, so once the protein requirement is met, the excess is either converted to energy or stored as fat. High-protein foods include cheese, peanut butter, nuts, dried meat, canned or vacuum-packed meats and fish, beans, tofu, powdered milk and eggs, and foil-packaged meals containing meat or cheese.

Fats: These are an important energy source because they pack more than twice as many calories per gram as proteins or carbohydrates. Fats are digested more slowly than carbohydrates or proteins, so they help keep you satisfied longer. This is useful, for example, on cold nights as part of staying warm. Fats occur naturally in small amounts in vegetables, grains, and beans, and when these are combined with fish, red meat, or poultry, the body's requirements for fat are easily met. High-fat foods include butter, margarine, peanut butter, nuts, canned bacon, salami, beef jerky, sardines, oils, meat, eggs, seeds, and cheese.

The better a climber's condition, the more efficiently food and water will provide energy during heavy exercise. Many people find that foods high in fat are more difficult to digest during the day while they are exercising strenuously. Eat mainly carbohydrates during the day; replenish calorie stores by adding fats and proteins to the evening meal. Cold-weather mountaineers stay warmer at night if they have a bedtime snack high in slower-burning food fuel.

To fuel working muscles, maintain a steady all-day carbohydrate and water intake beginning 1 to 2 hours into the climb. The carbohydrate source can be solid food or a prepared beverage. Some climbers like to use a "high-performance" sports drink, an option for replacing water, carbohydrates, and electrolytes simultaneously. Try these preparations at home, however, before relying on them in the mountains. Some people react to particular brands with bloating. They are easier to digest if diluted or taken with additional water.

Food Planning

As a rough guideline, provide 2 pounds (0.7 kilogram) of food per person per day.

On very short trips, climbers can carry homemade sandwiches, fresh fruits and vegetables, and just about anything else. Taking only cold, ready-to-eat food saves the weight of stove, fuel, and cook pots, and is a good idea for lightweight bivies. In nasty weather, this approach allows you to bundle directly into the tent without the hassle of cooking. Using firm bread, rolls, or bagels for the sandwich keeps it unsquished. Leave out mayonnaise and other ingredients that spoil readily.

For trips of two or three days—or longer if base camp is close to the road—any food from the grocery store is fair game.

For longer trips, food planning becomes more complicated and food weight more critical. Freeze-dried food is compact, lightweight, and easy to prepare, but relatively expensive. Outdoor stores carry a large selection of freeze-dried foods including main courses, potatoes, vegetables, soups, breakfasts, and desserts. Some require little or no cooking; just add hot water, let it soak for a while, and eat from the package. Others are less easily reconstituted and require cooking in a pot.

With access to a food dehydrator, climbers can enjoy a more-varied menu and at substantial savings. Simple and nutritious mountaineering foods can be made from dried fruits, vegetables, and meat. Dehydrate thin slices of fruits and vegetables—some of the particularly tasty choices are bell peppers, carrots, summer squash, apples, pears, oranges, steamed yams, and blueberries. The dehydrated produce can be eaten as is or added as an ingredient to a cooked dish. Fruit leather is easy to prepare with a dehydrator. Dry a good spaghetti sauce to serve with angel-hair pasta (which cooks very quickly because it is so thin). Many dehydrated foods can be cooked simply by soaking.

With vacuum sealing, even more-complex meals can be packed. Dehydrate the food first, then seal it. This process removes all air from inside the food package, greatly reducing spoilage. Vacuum-sealing machines are expensive, but the results can be worthwhile, especially for extended trips.

For a Group

Because meals are social events, groups often plan all food together. A good menu boosts morale. A common, carefully planned menu can reduce the overall food weight carried by each person.

Another common arrangement is to leave breakfast and lunch to each individual, with only dinner, the most complicated meal of the day, as a group effort.

Group meals can be planned by the group or by a chosen individual. The usual process is:
1. Canvass the group members for food preferences and dislikes; one person may be a vegetarian, and another might refuse to eat freeze-dried entrees.
2. Write down a menu.
3. Discuss the menu with the group.
4. Compile an ingredients list.
5. Go shopping.

6. Package the food (see the next section) for back-packing it in to camp.

The ideal number of people in a cooking group is two to three per stove, four maximum. Beyond that, group efficiency is outweighed by the complexities of large pots, small stoves, and increased cooking times.

For High Altitudes

High-camp cooking is more difficult because conditions can be harsh and cooking times are longer. At higher altitudes, the atmospheric pressure decreases, and water—in its liquid form—does not keep getting hotter once it has reached its boiling point. Consequently, water boils at lower and lower temperatures (as shown in Table 3-4), and cooking takes longer at higher altitudes. For every decrease of about 10 degrees Fahrenheit (5 degrees Celsius) in boiling temperature, cooking time is doubled. The most suitable foods are those that require only warming, such as canned chicken and instant rice. The weight of fuel required for long cooking times is another argument for simple menus and precooked foods.

The rigors of rapid ascent to higher altitudes also require special attention to the choice of food. Many climbers fall victim to symptoms of mountain sickness, ranging from a slight malaise to vomiting and severe headaches. Under these conditions, food becomes more difficult to digest because the stomach and lungs are competing for the same blood supply. Climbers must continue to eat and drink, whatever the effort, because the loss of energy from a lack of food or water will only reinforce the debilitating effects of reduced oxygen.

Keeping well hydrated is essential. To cope with this aversion to food, eat light and eat often; and emphasize carbohydrate foods, which are easiest to digest. Fatty foods can be particularly unappealing to some climbers at altitude. Spicy foods also are sometimes unappetizing. Bring foods that have proven themselves appealing to you at high altitude. Trial and error will determine what foods your body can tolerate.

Packaging the Food

Most grocery-store food packages are too bulky and heavy for wilderness trips, and the entire contents may be more than needed. A small kitchen scale is useful for precise planning and packaging. Food can be repacked in resealable plastic bags, sealable plastic packets, or other containers. Enclose identifying labels and cooking instructions, or write this information on the outside with a permanent marker. Ingredient or meal packages can be placed inside larger ones labeled in broad categories, such as "breakfast," "dinner," or "drinks."

Menu Suggestions

Try out various menu items and food combinations on day hikes or short outings before taking them on an extended trip in the mountains.

Breakfasts

For many people, breakfast is the worst meal of the day for culinary adventures, so emphasize comforting and familiar foods.

For a fast start, prepackage a standard meal before the trip. A single bag can contain a prepared cold cereal

TABLE 3-4. BOILING POINT OF WATER				
Elevation		Temperature		Cooking Time Increase (relative to sea level = 1)
in feet	*in meters*	*°Celsius*	*°Fahrenheit*	
sea level	0	100°	212°	1.0
5,000	1,525	95°	203°	1.9
10,000	3,050	90°	194°	3.8
15,000	4,575	85°	185°	7.2
20,000	7,000	80°	176°	13.0

such as granola, with raisins or other fruit, and powdered milk. Stir in water—cold or hot—and breakfast is ready. Other quick breakfast options are instant or quick-cooking oatmeal, with some powdered milk added—just add hot water later; toaster pastries; bakery items; dried fruits and meat; nuts; fruit bars and energy bars; and dehydrated applesauce. Try to include some protein content along with the carbohydrates.

Hot drinks are a pleasant addition to a breakfast. Common choices are instant cocoa, coffee, malted milk, mocha, tea, powdered eggnog, and instant breakfast drinks. Fruit-flavored drinks include instant hot cider and flavored gelatin.

On a rest day, when an early start is not required, prepare a full-scale breakfast, with such items as hash browns, omelets, scrambled eggs, bacon bits, or pancakes with syrup (the latter can made by adding hot water to brown sugar or syrup crystals). Bring a small plastic container of vegetable oil when planning this type of cooking.

Lunches and Snacks

During a climb, lunch begins shortly after breakfast and continues throughout the day. Eat small amounts and eat often. At least half of a climber's daily food allotment should be for lunch and snacks. A good munching staple is GORP (originally, "good old raisins and peanuts"), a mixture that can contain peanuts, small candies such as chocolate chips, raisins, and other dehydrated fruits. One handful makes a snack; several make a meal. Granola is another option, with its mixture of grains, honey or sugar, and perhaps some bits of fruit and nuts. GORP and granola are available premixed at many food stores, or make your own. Other popular snack items are fruit leather, candy bars, energy bars, and dried fruits.

To encourage rehydration, mountaineers often enjoy mixing up a flavored beverage such as lemonade or fruit punch at lunch. In cold weather, fill a light thermos with hot water at breakfast, and enjoy a cup of instant soup at lunch. A basic lunch can include any of the following:

Proteins: Sources include canned meats and fish, beef jerky, dry salami, meat spreads, hummus (available in powdered form and reconstituted with cold water), cheese, nuts, and seeds (sunflower and others). Because these foods also contain fats, they are more suited for extended lunch breaks rather than brief rest stops. On trips longer than a weekend, any cheese should be firm and relatively low in water content. By the second half of a weeklong trip, most cheeses will have transformed into a messy, rubbery mass oozing oil.

Starches: These include whole-grain breads, bagels, pita bread, granola and other cereals, firm crackers, brown-rice cakes, chips or pretzels, and granola bars.

Sweets: Some are cookies, chocolate, candy bars, hard candy, muffins, pastries, jam, and honey.

Fruits: Sources include fresh fruit, fruit leather, and dried fruits such as raisins, figs, and apples.

Vegetables: These include fresh carrot or celery sticks, sliced sweet pepper, etc., or dehydrated vegetables.

Dinners

The evening meal should have it all: It should be nourishing and delicious, yet easily and quickly prepared. To supplement liquid intake, include some items that take a lot of water, such as soup, hot cider, tea, fruit drink, cocoa, or hot fruit-flavored gelatin. A cup of soup makes a quick and satisfying first course while the main course is being prepared. A hearty soup can also serve as the main course. Good choices include minestrone, bean, beef barley, lentil, chili, or chicken. Add instant potatoes, rice, crackers, cheese, or bread, and the meal is complete.

One-pot meals with a carbohydrate base of pasta, rice, beans, potatoes, or grains are easy and nutritious. To ensure adequate protein, fat, and flavor, add other ingredients such as canned or dried chicken, beef, or fish; sausage; freeze-dried vegetables or fruits; margarine; or a dehydrated soup or sauce mix. Outdoor stores carry a variety of freeze-dried entrees that are nutritionally balanced and easy to prepare, but rather costly. Prepackaged dishes from the grocery store—such as spaghetti, noodle dishes, rice mixes, ramen noodles, and instant salads—can be relatively quick and easy to fix.

Freeze-dried vegetables add variety to the meal. They can be prepared as side dishes or added to soups or stews. Freeze-dried cooked beans or processed soy products in powdered or textured forms (texturized vegetable protein, or TVP) are excellent, low-cost protein additions. Natural food stores often have a wide selection of these ingredients.

Margarine, which keeps better than butter on long trips, improves the flavor of many foods and is available in liquid form or in small tubs. For seasonings, try salt, pepper, herbs, garlic, chili powder, bacon bits, curry powder, dehydrated onions, grated Parmesan cheese, hot sauce, or soy sauce.

Dessert choices include cookies, candy, no-bake cheesecake, applesauce, cooked dried fruit, instant pudding, and freeze-dried ice cream. Dessert time, accompanied by a cup of hot tea, can provide a pleasant backdrop to group talk about the next day's itinerary and a decision on who will provide the morning wake-up call.

Cup-cooking: This works well for the evening meal and simplifies cleanup. Cup-cooking is particularly nice in winter or foul-weather camping when cleanup is a nasty chore. Use the cook pot only to boil water. Take food that requires no cooking—only the addition of boiling water—and reconstitute it in a drinking cup. Be sure to select items that do not need a long soak time, or the meal will be cold before it is ready to eat. Start with some instant soup. The main course can be based on a starchy food (instant mashed potatoes, instant rice, or couscous) with added protein, vegetables, and condiments. Or use a freeze-dried entree that can be rehydrated in its own packaging. Follow with a dessert of instant applesauce or instant pudding, and end with tea or hot cider. The only items to wash up are the spoon and cup; the cook pot remains clean.

Protecting Food from Animals

Bears, rodents, raccoons, ravens, and other animals can smell food and will tear or gnaw through plastic bags, stuff sacks, and even packs to get at it. At night and when leaving camp for an extended period, be careful not to leave food inside the tent. Ravens and jays can peck through mesh tent windows, weasels can fiddle with zippers skillfully enough to enter the tent, and other animals will simply rip or chew through the fabric, taking food, making a mess, and damaging a costly tent.

The traditional solution is to hang a nylon stuff sack or pack from a tree limb that is 12 feet (3–4 meters) off the ground, with the food bag at least 4 feet (1.2 meters) from the tree trunk. Attach a small, heavy object (such as a fist-sized rock) to a long cord and, holding on to the free end of the cord, toss the rock over the tree limb. Attach a food bag to one end of this cord and raise the food bag as high as possible, then secure the haul line to the tree trunk. Two food bags connected by a short cord can be counterbalanced on either side of the limb.

An improved version is the "bear wire," suspending the food bag(s) on a tight line strung 12 feet from the ground between two trees that are at least 8 feet apart, but this is difficult to rig. Land managers may set up steel-wire high lines or poles in popular camping areas. Be sure to use them if they are provided, because they are sure signs that local wildlife is adept at getting into campers' food.

Whatever method you use, begin food-storage preparations well before nightfall, so you have plenty of visibility for getting the system set up safely.

Animals have become clever at outwitting campers' efforts to keep food off-limits. They will sometimes gnaw through the cord suspending a food bag, dropping it to the ground. Dextrous critters such as bears and raccoons have actually been observed perched on a tree limb, hauling a food bag up "hand over hand."

Managers of numerous wilderness areas in the western United States are finding that use of special bear-resistant, unbreakable plastic food containers (as shown in Figure 3-8, earlier in this chapter) is a more effective technique than the traditional hanging food bag. The containers are bulky, however, and are heavier than nylon or plastic sacks. In places with significant bear populations, land managers often provide these containers, perhaps for a small fee. In some areas they are even required. In treeless terrain, it is necessary to triple-bag anything with odor attractive to bears and then pack it into a bear-resistant container.

Hiding a food cache in the wilderness generally is poor practice and in some areas is not permitted. Animals can get into an improperly protected cache and leave a big mess, which will only draw more animals, which then get in the habit of seeking people out for food. In the case of large predators such as bears and cougars, if the animal becomes habituated to people as a food source, this eventually leads to the animal being designated a nuisance and then a dangerous "problem" animal that has to be destroyed.

When storing food to protect it from animals, include such odorous items as toothbrushes and toothpaste, sweet-smelling lotions, and the like. Garbage, including used feminine-hygiene products, should be packaged separately and stored with food to avoid animals getting into it.

Food Handling in Bear Country

For meal preparation, go to the food storage site and collect just the items to be used at that meal, packing away other items immediately; then bring the collected items to the cooking and dining site. During cooking and dining, maintain a lookout; have a small pair of binoculars handy for checking suspect bear sightings in the distance. If a bear is seen ambling toward the group, quickly pack up the food.

At the end of the meal, wash up well (do not use scented soap) to remove food odors from people, clothes, and equipment. Dispose of cleaning water downwind from the campsite and well away from water sources (see Chapter 7, Leave No Trace). Then return all cooking equipment and leftover food to the storage site and pack these away again. Do not keep any food in the tent, and avoid bringing clothes with food stains or odors from cooking back into the tent. Do not sleep in a shelter that smells like food.

Utensils for Cooking and Eating

On a superlight trip with only cold food, fingers are the only utensils needed. (Wash hands before preparing food or eating, or at least use a hand-sanitizing gel.) Making dinner with the cup-cooking method described

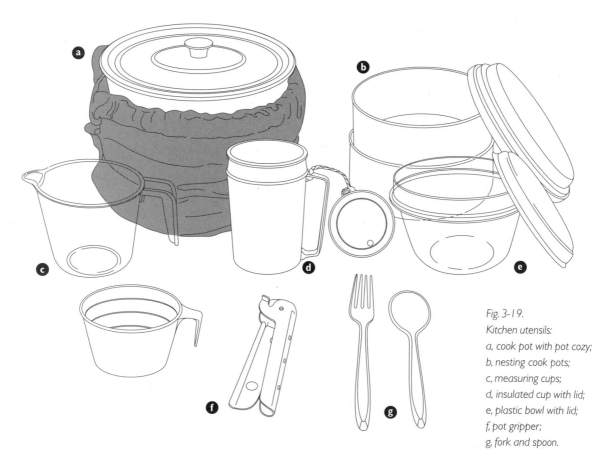

Fig. 3-19.
Kitchen utensils:
a, cook pot with pot cozy;
b, nesting cook pots;
c, measuring cups;
d, insulated cup with lid;
e, plastic bowl with lid;
f, pot gripper;
g, fork and spoon.

TIPS ON STAYING WARM

- Eat well and stay hydrated; this boosts metabolism.
- Use proper ground insulation to separate your body from the cold earth and snow.
- Dress and undress inside the sleeping bag. Sleep in a next-to-skin layer. Avoid wearing tight clothing that may reduce circulation and prevent radiated heat from entering the bag's insulation.
- Keep a hat or balaclava handy, and wear dry socks to bed.
- It is possible with some down bags to shift the fill around to the top side, increasing the loft on top. Augment loft by placing an insulated jacket on top of the sleeping bag.
- Place a leak-proof bottle of hot liquid in the bag.
- If you wake up cold, increase metabolism by drinking and eating.
- Use a pee bottle so that you can remain in the warm tent when nature calls.

earlier in this chapter requires only a cup and spoon per person, plus one cook pot for each group of three or four.

On less-spartan trips, bring one pot for cooking, another for boiling water, and light, unbreakable bowls for eating out of. Alpine cook sets come in aluminum, stainless steel, and titanium (fig. 3-19a and b). Aluminum is the most common, being light and relatively inexpensive. Stainless steel is strong and easy to clean but heavy. Titanium is light and strong but very expensive. A very large water pot is useful when snow is to be melted. A wide pot is more stable than a tall, narrow one, and also more efficient because it catches all of the stove's flame. Be sure all pots have bails or handles, or bring a small metal pot lifter (fig. 3-19f). Tight-fitting pot lids conserve heat.

Insulated cups (fig. 3-19d) are popular; a sipping lid keeps the contents warm and prevents spills. Cups, spoons, and bowls (fig. 3-19e and g) come in the same materials as cook sets and also in strong and light polycarbonate plastic. Some cooking pans have a nonstick coating for easy cleaning, but must be used with plastic utensils to avoid scratching the coating. Bring a small

plastic scrubbing pad and a synthetic-fabric pack towel for kitchen cleanup.

Many specialized pieces of kitchenware are available for camp cooking, such as bake ovens, Dutch ovens, pressure cookers, and espresso makers. These generally do not accompany mountaineers on a climb; they make their appearance on car camping, kayaking, or other expeditions when their added weight is less of a hindrance.

"IT'S JUST CAMPING"

That was what pioneer American alpinist Paul Petzoldt said in an interview about climbing in the Himalaya and Karakoram. His point was that technical climbing skills were less important than the ability to survive, and even be at home and comfortable, in the high mountains.

Camping skills are the platform upon which all the more-technical mountaineering skills rest. Once these skills are developed and honed, climbers will feel at home in the mountains on any adventure, and they truly will have the freedom of the hills.

Physical Conditioning

IDENTIFY CLIMBING GOALS ■ COMPONENTS OF A WELL-ROUNDED CONDITIONING
PROGRAM ■ RECOVERY AND INJURY PREVENTION ■ "CLIMB ON!"

Optimal physical fitness forms a strong foundation for the wide variety of activities involved in mountaineering: alpine, rock, and ice climbing and glacier travel. To succeed in different types of climbing, you need a well-rounded conditioning program that includes four basic fitness components: cardiovascular endurance, muscular strength, flexibility, and adequate recovery.

Many climbers dedicate 1 to 2 hours a day to conditioning, reserving weekends for longer outings in the mountains. By far the best way to train for any activity is to do the activity itself.

IDENTIFY CLIMBING GOALS

The first step in developing a solid conditioning program is to look closely at your climbing goals, in order to determine where to focus time and energy.

For instance, if rock or ice climbing is your goal, include several weekly sessions at an indoor climbing gym or at the local crags. To enhance technique and to progress to harder routes, take climbing lessons, add an upper-body strength program, or attend a yoga course to increase your flexibility.

If an objective is to climb Denali or Aconcagua, try developing a systematic six-month training program. Include some multiple-day winter climbs to see how you handle pulling a loaded sled. Add interval training to prepare your cardiovascular system for the anaerobic challenges of exertion at altitude.

To excel at climbing remote, glaciated volcanoes, your strength program might focus on your legs, lower back, and shoulders. Include weekend conditioning trips in the mountains with a fully loaded backpack.

COMPONENTS OF A WELL-ROUNDED CONDITIONING PROGRAM
Cardiovascular Endurance

Cardiovascular endurance refers to the body's ability to perform any repetitive activity over long periods of time, requiring use of large-muscle groups in addition to the heart and lungs. Examples include running, bicycling, and swimming. Your maximum heart rate can be roughly calculated as your age multiplied by 0.7 subtracted from 207, although this number varies widely with each person's age, exercise experience, and relative fitness level.

There are many effective training options available, which makes it much easier to establish a regular exercise program that you can stick to during the week, rain or shine. When first beginning cardiovascular training, try to slowly build a solid foundation of aerobic endurance by gradually increasing the length of the sessions until you can sustain your activity for 45 minutes or longer. If you enjoy running, increase your mileage by no more than 10 percent a week to avoid overuse injuries from repetitive impact. Or, if you like to swim, supplement that activity with a more-specific weight-bearing option such as those listed in the next section, in order to properly condition your leg muscles to begin carrying loads.

As you progress with your training, add about 5 pounds (2 to 3 kilograms) to your pack every other week until you can carry up to one-third of your body weight and comfortably gain roughly 1,200 to 1,500 feet (365 to 450 meters) an hour in hiking boots over moderate terrain. Allow a minimum of four to six months of consistent training before embarking on any major climbing expedition.

Aerobic Exercise

Aerobic exercise is cardiovascular activity requiring lots of oxygen; it is performed at a submaximal level, or 60 to 85 percent of your maximum heart rate. When choosing an appropriate training activity, try to make it as close as possible to the actual activity you intend to do. The following suggestions are listed in order from those with the most similarity to climbing to the least.

Walking with a pack or trail-running without a pack: Walking on nearby hiking trails, hills, or stairs can provide an excellent cardiovascular workout for mountaineers in-season. Trail running without a pack is another in-season option.

Snowshoeing, cross-country skiing, and telemark skiing: In the winter, these activities on those same trails are great training options.

Jogging, stair-climbing, inline skating, and cycling: These are excellent fair-weather, in-city activities.

Indoor options: To maintain aerobic fitness when the weather gets nasty, try elliptical cross-trainers, stair machines, treadmills, stationary bikes, rowing machines, and aerobic or step classes.

Anaerobic Exercise

Anaerobic exercise is near-maximal cardiovascular training that takes you to and just beyond the upper levels of your training zone. In anaerobic training, the body incurs an oxygen debt, using more oxygen than is breathed in. Most people can only tolerate work in the anaerobic zone for short periods of time, perhaps a minute or less.

Interval training: Using repeated hill climbing is one example of anaerobic training that is useful preparation for high-altitude climbers. Find a steep hill or several flights of stairs that will take roughly 2 or 3 minutes to ascend. Once a week, load a backpack and warm up by walking to the hill; walk up to the top as quickly as possible, then turn right around and descend. Repeat for the desired time interval. Start with 20 minutes and a light weight, then increase your speed or add weight in subsequent workouts so you can reach the upper levels of your training zone as you get stronger. This helps you get used to working at a higher heart rate than would be sustained in aerobic sessions, much as would be experienced at higher elevation.

Intervals can also be done by sprinting on flat ground, climbing hills on a bike, or increasing the intensity on any aerobic machine, and then allowing time to recover at a base pace before starting another high-intensity interval.

Muscular Strength

The second vital component of physical conditioning is building muscular strength. Strength is needed for nearly every climbing task, including controlling and balancing heavy loads; hoisting yourself, your pack, and team gear up the mountain; preparing and setting up camp; and even assisting with victim rescue. Training with free weights (as opposed to strength machines) directly prepares you to apply your strength in three-dimensional natural settings outdoors—such as traveling over uneven terrain or climbing challenging alpine routes that throw you off balance.

Rock or ice climbers may choose to include strengthening exercises such as pull-ups, triceps dips, calf raises, hanging leg raises, and additional grip training in order to be able to climb harder routes. It is also a good idea to add several exercises that work the muscle groups that oppose the climbing muscles in the arms and back—such as shoulder presses, push-ups, reverse wrist curls, and seated rowing—in order to maintain muscle balance and help prevent overuse injuries.

Glacier enthusiasts should include lower-body exercises such as squats, deadlifts, lunges, or step-ups; lower-back and abdominal exercises; and shrugs or upright rowing to develop the pack-carrying upper-body muscles. One common complaint among this group is painful knees on descents. Take full advantage of plunge-stepping and glissading whenever possible, once you have completely mastered the techniques discussed in Chapter 16, Snow Travel and Climbing. Add

several suitable activity-specific leg exercises such as step-downs or step-ups in order to strengthen the quadriceps, particularly the vastus medialis obliquus (VMO), or inner teardrop-shaped muscle near the knee. Use of trekking poles may help take some of the pressure off your knees, but remember that if they are relied on too heavily, the moment the poles are forgotten at home, you may find that you lack the balance and confidence to successfully navigate scree, talus, or snowfields.

Upper-body strength helps in nearly all climbing activities, ranging from hoisting a pack onto your back to shoveling snow. Try some of these creative strengthening tricks outside the gym:

- On weekend hikes or weekday conditioning sessions, carry filled gallon jugs in a backpack and dump the water at the top. This provides the training benefit of carrying additional weight on the way up, without the added stresses of heavy loads on the knees on the way back down.
- Instead of driving to the store, walk, taking a backpack along and loading it up with groceries for the return walk home.
- Use a loaded pack to do exercises at home such as squats, lunges, calf raises, shrugs, deadlifts, and step-ups.
- Install a chin-up bar in a doorway and do a few repetitions each time you pass by it. If you cannot do a chin-up, hang by the bar to develop grip strength, or jump up until your chin is above the bar and then slowly lower your body to the ground a few times to increase back, forearm, finger, and biceps strength.
- If a children's play area is nearby, try jungle-gym hand walks for grip, finger, and forearm strength.

Flexibility Training

Immediately following any strenuous climb or hike, take a few minutes to stretch muscles before crawling into your sleeping bag or collapsing into the car for the ride home. Stretching may help prevent or reduce muscle soreness over the next few days. At home, try taking a martial arts, yoga, or dance class to increase balance and flexibility and provide additional cross-training benefits.

By stretching, rock and ice climbers benefit from

KEEP A RECORD OF PROGRESS

Consider keeping a log that includes your reactions to all of your climbing adventures, cardiovascular sessions, strength training workouts, and stretches, so that you can learn what works best for you in terms of training, rest, and recovery.

increased range of motion in their hips and shoulders in order to use holds that would otherwise be beyond their reach, such as stem or mantel moves. Stretching also helps your fingers and forearms relax and recover after a challenging vertical pitch.

Glacier enthusiasts benefit from stretching calves that cramp during uphill travel, or hips that tighten under the load of a heavy backpack. Pay particular attention to the muscles in your legs and shoulders that get stressed during glacier travel, including your quadriceps, hips, hamstrings, calves, and lower- and upper-back muscles.

RECOVERY AND INJURY PREVENTION

The more active you are, the more important it is for you to get adequate rest; this includes taking days off from activity and getting quality sleep. Plan to take a day off following any strenuous outings in the mountains, and perhaps even the day before, to allow your body some time to recover and to help prevent overuse injury. When you create a physical conditioning program, make sure to schedule strength sessions or demanding rock or ice climbs at least 48 hours apart so that the targeted muscles, tendons, and ligaments can recover before they are stressed again. Keep in mind that tendons and ligaments take longer than muscles to adjust to increased workloads. They also take an infuriating amount of time to heal once they are injured.

To prevent injury, pay very close attention to your body at all times. During a warm-up, if you feel like you are still tired or sore from a previous workout or climb, do a lighter workout than planned or take a few days off. If your finger or elbow tendons are tender to the touch for several days following a hard rock climb, reduce the intensity of subsequent workouts or take a week off. Although it is very difficult for most climbers to take time off from a favorite activity, it is better to let the body heal completely before resuming; otherwise, a minor irritation may turn into a full-blown injury that requires much longer time away from the activity.

"CLIMB ON!"

Paying attention to conditioning from the outset of your climbing career is a crucial part of gaining the freedom of the hills. Experiment with the tips in this chapter in order to include plenty of variety in your training. When you feel strong and fit, climbing is a whole lot more enjoyable and ultimately is safer as well for you and your climbing partners.

CHAPTER 5

Navigation

TRIP PREPARATION ■ THE MAP ■ THE COMPASS ■ THE CLINOMETER ■ THE ALTIMETER ■ THE GLOBAL POSITIONING SYSTEM ■ ORIENTATION BY INSTRUMENT ■ NAVIGATION BY INSTRUMENT ■ LOST ■ FINDING THE FREEDOM OF THE HILLS

"Where am I?" "How far is it to the summit?" "How can I find my way back?" These are three of the most frequently asked questions in mountaineering, and this chapter shows you how to find the answers.

First, a few definitions: *Orientation* is the science of determining your exact position on the Earth. It requires mastery of map and compass, plus the ability to use an altimeter and perhaps a global positioning system (GPS) receiver.

Navigation is the science of determining the location of your objective and of staying pointed in the right direction all the way from the starting point to this destination. Like orientation, navigation requires use of a map and compass as well as other instruments and techniques. Navigation is a required skill for all wilderness travelers.

Routefinding is the art of selecting and following the best path appropriate for the abilities and equipment of the climbing party. In selecting the best path to your objective, you may travel on trails partway and cross-country where trails do not lead to where you want to go. The latter, wilderness routefinding, is covered in more detail in Chapter 6, Wilderness Travel, but understanding it requires a solid foundation in the routefinding, orientation, and navigation skills described in this chapter.

TRIP PREPARATION

Routefinding—selecting the best path to your objective—begins at home. Consult guidebooks for critical information and seek out other climbers who have made the trip. Useful details are also packed into maps of all sorts. See "Gather Route Information" in Chapter 6, Wilderness Travel, for suggestions on researching a route.

Before even shouldering a pack, have a mental image of the route to the planned climb. Using the information gained from guidebooks or other climbers, plot the route out on the topographic map for the climb. Drawing on your experience, and from all the sources of information about the climb, make the terrain work in your favor.

To avoid brush, try not to follow watercourses or drainages; select ridges rather than hillsides and gullies. Clear-cuts are also often full of slash or brushy second-growth trees. A rock-slide area can be a feasible route—providing the climber watches carefully for new rockfall. One problem in planning the route, however, is that a rock-slide area may look the same on a map as an avalanche gully, which can be an avalanche hazard in winter and spring and choked with brush in summer and fall. If information sources are not helpful, only a firsthand look can clear up this question.

The most straightforward return route is often the same as the route going in. If the plan is to come back a different way, that route also needs careful advance preparation.

THE MAP

No mountaineer should travel without a map or the skill to interpret its shorthand into information about details on the route. A number of different types of maps are available:

Relief maps: These attempt to show terrain in three dimensions by using various shades of green, gray, and brown, plus terrain sketching and raised surfaces. They help in visualizing the ups and downs of the landscape and have some value in trip planning.

Land management and recreation maps: These are updated frequently and thus are very useful for current details on roads, trails, ranger stations, and other human constructions. They usually show only a two-dimensional (flat) relationship of natural features, without the contour lines that indicate the shape of the land. These maps, published by the U.S. Forest Service and other government agencies and by timber companies, are suitable for trip planning.

Climbers' sketch maps: Often called climbers' topos, these are not topographic maps but are generally crudely drawn, two-dimensional sketches that usually make up in specialized route detail what they lack in draftsmanship. Such drawings can be effective supplements to other map and guidebook information.

Guidebook maps: These vary greatly in quality. Some are merely sketches, whereas others are accurate interpretations of topographic maps. They generally contain useful details on roads, trails, and climbing routes.

Topographic maps: Essential to off-trail travel, topos are the best of all for climbers. They depict topography—the shape of the Earth's surface—by showing contour lines that represent constant elevations above sea level. These maps are produced in many countries. Some are produced by government agencies; others are printed by private companies, with special emphasis on trails and other recreational features. Perhaps the most familiar of topographic maps in the United States are those produced by the U.S. Geological Survey (USGS). In some areas of the United States, private companies produce maps based on USGS topographic maps, but they are updated with more recent trail and road details and sometimes combine sections of USGS maps. These maps are often useful supplements to standard topographic maps.

How to Read a Topographic Map

Latitude and Longitude

Because the Earth is a sphere, the distance around it—whether from east to west or from north to south—can be divided into 360 units called degrees (the same as for a circle—remember high school geometry?). A measurement east or west around the globe is called longitude; a measurement north or south is called latitude. Longitude is measured 180 degrees east and 180 degrees west, starting at the north–south line (meridian) that goes through Greenwich, England. Latitude is measured 90 degrees north and 90 degrees south, starting from the equator. This system allows each place on the planet to have a unique set of coordinates. For example, New York City is situated at 74 degrees west longitude and 41 degrees north latitude.

Each degree is divided into 60 units called minutes, and each minute is further subdivided into 60 seconds—just as for units of time. On a map, a latitude of 47 degrees, 52 minutes, 30 seconds north would be written like this: 47°52'30"N.

Another way of identifying a point on a map is with the Universal Transverse Mercator (UTM) coordinate system. This system, very useful when using a global positioning system (GPS) receiver, is discussed in "Orientation Using GPS" near the end of this chapter.

One type of USGS topographic map commonly used by mountaineers covers an area of 7.5 minutes (that is, ⅛ degree) of latitude by 7.5 minutes of longitude. These maps are known as the 7.5-minute series. An older type of USGS map covers an area of 15 minutes (that is, ¼ degree) of latitude by 15 minutes of longitude. These maps are part of what is called the 15-minute series.

Scale

The scale of a map is a ratio between measurements on the map and measurements in the real world. A common way to state the scale is to compare a map measurement with a ground measurement (for example, 1 inch equals 1 mile) or to give a specific mathematical ratio (for example, 1:24,000, where any one unit of measure on the map equals 24,000 units of the same measure on the Earth). The scale is usually shown graphically at the bottom of a map (see Figure 5-2, below).

In the USGS 7.5-minute series, the scale is 1:24,000, or roughly 2½ inches to the mile (4.2 centimeters to the kilometer), and each map covers an area of approximately 6 by 9 miles (9 by 14 kilometers). In the 15-minute series, the scale is 1:62,500, or about 1 inch to the mile (1.6 centimeters to the kilometer), and each map covers an area of about 12 by 18 miles (20 by 28 kilometers). Mountaineers prefer the 7.5-minute maps because of the greater detail.

The 7.5-minute map is now the standard for the United States, except for Alaska. The 15-minute maps are no longer in production for the other forty-nine states. For Alaska only, the standard scale is 1:63,360, or exactly one inch to the mile. These cover an area of 7.5 by 15 minutes. The different number of minutes covered for the east–west and north–south dimensions is due to the fact that the lines of longitude converge as they get closer to the North Pole.

Each topographic map is referred to as a quadrangle (or quad) and covers an area bounded on the north and south by latitude lines that differ by an amount equal to the map series (such as 7.5 minutes or 15 minutes) and on the east and west by longitude lines that differ by the same amount. Each quadrangle is given the name of a prominent topographic or human feature of the area; for example, USGS Glacier Peak East.

What the Colors Mean

Most topographic maps use colors to differentiate features. On a USGS topographic map, colors have very specific meanings:

Red: Major roads and survey information, such as section lines; sections are 1-square-mile (2.6-square-kilometer) areas.

Blue: Rivers, lakes, springs, waterfalls, and other water-related features.

Black: Minor roads, trails, railroads, buildings, benchmarks, latitude and longitude lines, UTM coordinates and lines, and other features not part of the natural environment.

Green: Areas of heavy forest. Solid green indicates a forested area; mottled green indicates scrub vegetation. A lack of green does not mean that an area is devoid of vegetation, but simply that any growth is too small or scattered to show on the map. Do not be surprised if a small, narrow gully with no green color on the map turns out to be an avalanche gully choked with impassable brush in the summer and fall, with significant avalanche hazard in the winter and spring.

White: The color of the paper on which the map is printed; it can have a variety of meanings, depending on the terrain.

White with blue contour lines: A glacier or permanent snowfield. The contour lines and edges of glaciers and permanent snowfields are in solid blue.

White with brown contour lines: Any "dry" area without substantial forest, such as a high alpine area, a clear-cut, a rock slide, an avalanche gully, or a meadow. Study the map for other clues.

Brown: Contour lines and elevations, everywhere except on glaciers and permanent snowfields.

Purple: Partial revision of an existing map.

Contour Lines

The heart of a topographic map is its overlay of contour lines, each line indicating a constant elevation as it follows the shape of the landscape. A map's contour interval is the difference in elevation between two adjacent contour lines. In mountainous areas, this interval is often 40 feet on 7.5-minute maps, and 80 feet on 15-minute maps. Every fifth contour line is printed darker than the other lines and is labeled periodically with the elevation. On metric maps, a contour interval of 5, 10, or 20 meters is usually used.

One of the most important bits of information a topographic map reveals is whether the route will be uphill or downhill. If the route crosses lines of increasingly higher elevation, it is going uphill. If it crosses lines of decreasing elevation, the route is downhill. Flat or sidehill travel is indicated by a route that crosses no lines, remaining within a single contour interval.

This is only the start of the picture that contour lines paint of an actual route. They also show cliffs, summits, passes, and other features (fig. 5-1). Climbers get better and better at interpreting these lines by comparing actual terrain with its representation on the map (fig. 5-2). The goal is that someday you will be able to glance at a topographic map and have a sharp mental image

of just what the actual place will look like. The following gives the main features depicted by contour lines:

Flat areas: No contour lines at all, or contour lines very far apart (fig. 5-1a).

Gentle slopes: Widely spaced contour lines (fig. 5-1b and 5-2a).

Steep slopes: Closely spaced contour lines (fig. 5-1c and 5-2k).

Cliffs: Contour lines extremely close together or touching (fig. 5-1d and 5-2h).

Valleys, ravines, gullies, and couloirs: Contour lines in a pattern of Us for gentle, rounded valleys or gullies, and Vs for sharp valleys or gullies (fig. 5-1e and 5-2f). The Us or Vs point uphill, in the direction of higher elevation.

Ridges or spurs: Contour lines in a pattern of Us for gentle, rounded ridges, and Vs for sharp ridges (fig. 5-1f and 5-2j). The Us or Vs point downhill, in the direction of lower elevation.

Peaks or summits: Concentric patterns of contour lines, with the summit being the innermost and highest ring (fig. 5-1g, 5-2d, and 5-2i). Peaks may also be indicated by Xs, elevations, benchmarks (BMs), or a triangle symbol.

Cirques or bowls: Patterns of contour lines forming a semicircle, rising from a low spot in the center of the partial circle to form a natural amphitheater at the head of a valley (fig. 5-1h).

Saddles, passes, or cols: An hourglass shape, with higher contour lines on each side, indicating a low point on a ridge (fig. 5-1i and 5-2g).

Other Map Information

The margin of a USGS topographic map holds important information, such as date of publication and revision, names of maps of adjacent areas, the contour interval, and the map scale. The margin also gives the area's magnetic declination (discussed later in this chapter), which is the difference between true north and magnetic north.

Topographic maps do have certain limitations. They do not show all the terrain features that you actually see on a route because there is a limit to what can be jammed onto a map without reducing it to an unreadable clutter. If a feature is not at least as high as the

5

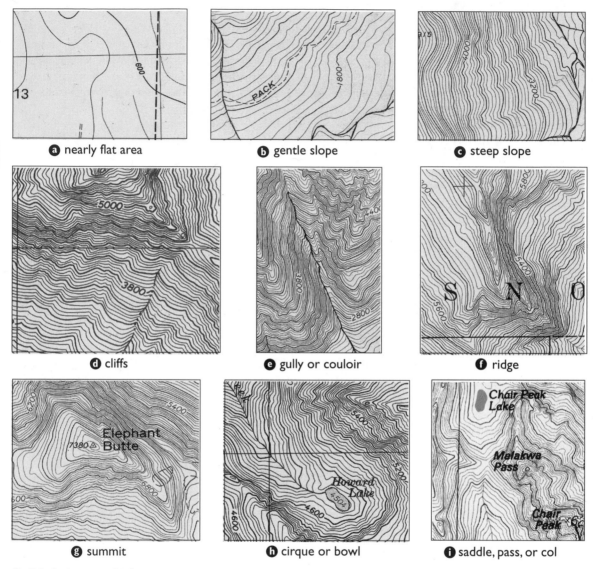

a nearly flat area b gentle slope c steep slope

d cliffs e gully or couloir f ridge

g summit h cirque or bowl i saddle, pass, or col

Fig. 5-1. Basic topographic features.

contour interval, it may not be shown, so a 30-foot cliff may come as a surprise to you if you are navigating with a map that has a 40-foot contour interval.

Check the date of the map, because topographic maps are not revised very often and information on forests, declination, roads, and other features could be out of date. A forest may have been logged or a road either extended or closed since the last map revision. Although topographic maps are essential to wilderness

travel, they must be supplemented with information from visitors to the area, Forest Service or Park Service rangers, guidebooks, and other maps. Note changes on the map as they are encountered.

Sometimes a trip runs through portions of two or more maps. You can fold adjoining maps at the edges and bring them together, or you can create a customized map by cutting out the pertinent areas and splicing them with tape. Include plenty of territory so that there is a good overview of the entire trip, including the surrounding area. There are computer programs for creating customized maps, but keep in mind that these maps are limited by printer quality and paper size.

As the precious objects they are, maps deserve tender care in the wilds. A map can be kept in a plastic bag or map case. On the trip, carry the map in a pocket or some other easily accessible place so you do not have to take off your pack to reach it.

Routefinding with a Map

Before the Trip

Most orientation, navigation, and routefinding is done by simply looking at the surroundings and comparing them with the map. This process is often aided by making some navigational preparations before the trip, such as identifying handrails, base lines, and possible routefinding problems.

A handrail, any linear feature on a map that parallels the direction of travel, helps you to stay on route. The handrail should be within frequent sight of the route, so it can serve as an aid to navigation. Features that can be used as handrails from time to time during a trip include roads, trails, powerlines, railroad tracks, fences, borders of fields and meadows, valleys, streams, cliff bands, ridges, lakeshores, and the edges of marshes.

A base line—a long, unmistakable line that always lies in the same direction from you, no matter where you are during your trip—provides another map technique that can help you find the way home if you have gone off track. During trip planning, pick out a base line on the map. It does not have to be something visible during the trip; you just have to know that it is there, in a consistent direction from you. A base line (sometimes called a catch line) can be a road, the shore of a large lake, a river, a trail, a powerline, or any other feature that is at least as long as the climbing area. If the shore of a large, distant lake always lies west of the climbing area, heading west at any time will be sure to get you to this identifiable landmark. Heading toward this base line may not be the fastest way to travel to the destination, but it may save you from being truly lost.

Before the trip, also anticipate specific routefinding problems. For example, if the route traverses a glacier or any large, featureless area such as a snowfield, consider carrying route-marking wands. (Chapter 16, Snow Travel and Climbing, explains the construction and use of wands.) Identify any escape routes that can be used in case of sudden bad weather or other setbacks.

During the Trip

Get off on the right foot by making sure that everyone in the climbing party understands the route. Gather the party around the map and take time to discuss the route and make contingency plans in case the party gets separated. On the map, point out where the party is, and correlate your surroundings with what is shown on the piece of paper in front of everyone.

Relate surroundings to the map: Along the way, everyone needs to keep relating the terrain to the map. Ignorance is definitely not bliss for any daydreaming climber who does not pay attention to the territory and then gets separated from the party. Whenever a new landmark appears, connect it with the map. At every chance—at a pass, at a clearing, or through a break in the clouds—update your fix on the group's exact position. Keeping track of position this way makes it easy to plan each succeeding leg of the trip, and will help to prevent climbers from getting lost. It also may turn climbers into expert map interpreters because they will know what a specific valley or ridge looks like compared with its representation on the map.

Look ahead to the return trip: The route always looks amazingly different on the way back. Avoid surprises and confusion by glancing back over your shoulder from time to time on the way in to see what the route should look like on the return. If you cannot keep track of it all, jot down times, elevations, landmarks, and so on in a notebook. A few cryptic words—"7,600, hit ridge"—can save a lot of grief on the descent. It will remind you that when the party has dropped to 7,600 feet, it is time to leave the ridge and start down the snow slope.

Think about the route: Your brain is your most valuable navigational tool. As the party heads upward, ask yourself questions. "How will we recognize this important spot on our return?" "What will we do if the climb leader is injured?" "Would we be able to find our way out in a whiteout or if snow covered our tracks?"

Fig. 5-2.
Photograph of a mountainous area; keyed features are represented on the accompanying topographic map.

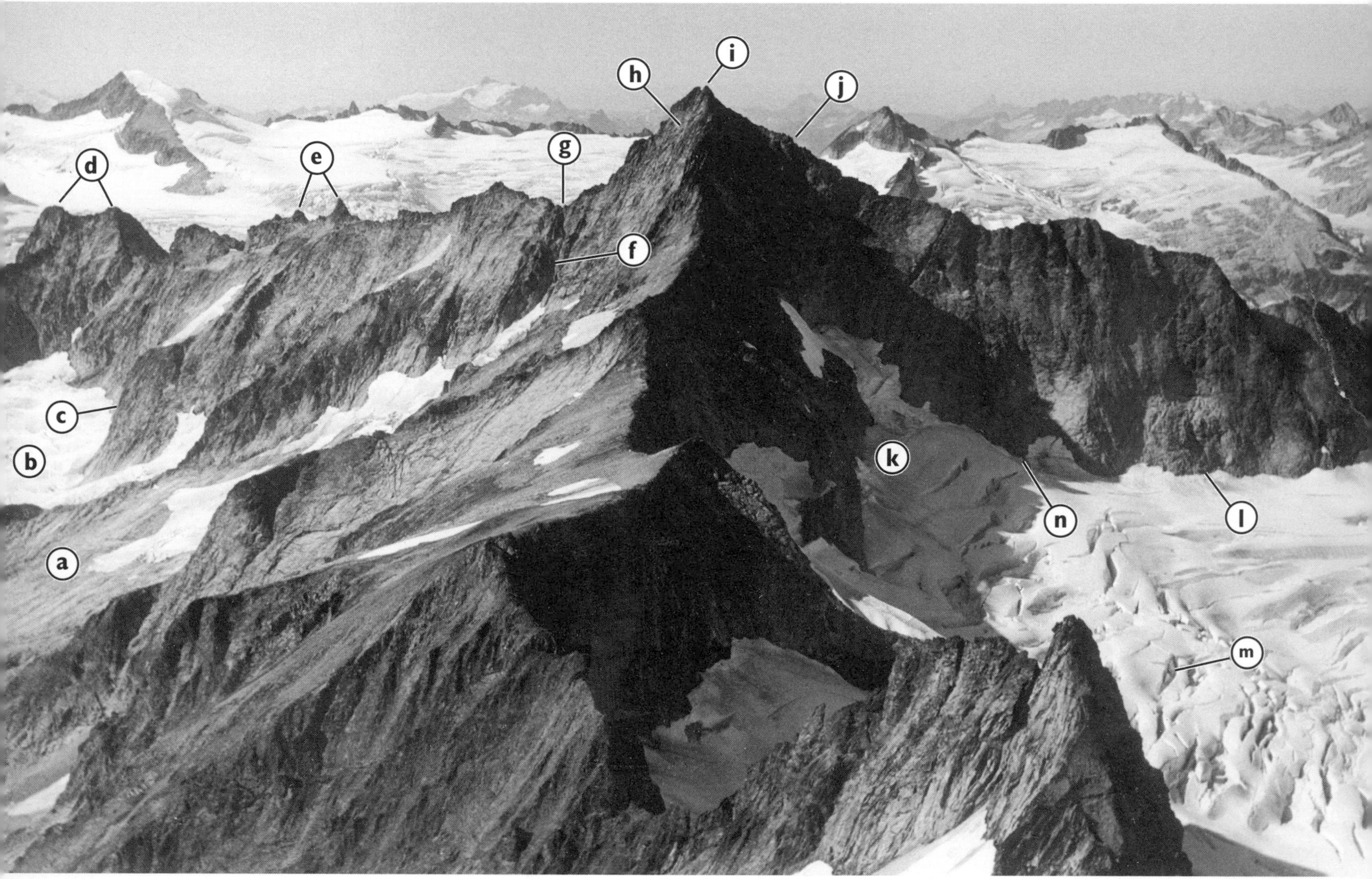

5

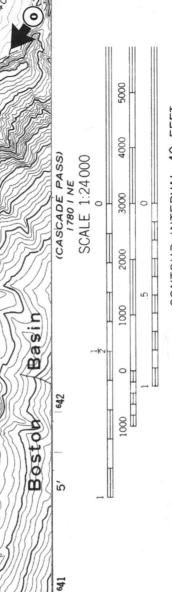

KEY

a. Basin: moderate slope, camp spots

b. Snow or ice line: dashed line ends on cliffs, rock

c. Buttress: change in features of wall may provide approach to ridge

d. Twin summits

e. Gendarmes, aiguilles, or pinnacles

f. Gully or couloir

g. Saddle, pass, or col

h. Rock face

i. Summit: highest point on map

j. Ridge or arete

k. East slope: note shadows and ice accumulation

l. Moat

m. Crevasses: indicated by irregular contours, not smooth as near buttress, c, above

n. Bergschrund: not seen on map but possibility inferred when rock and snow are steep

o. Photo taken from above this spot, looking in direction of arrow

(CASCADE PASS)
1780 I NE
SCALE 1:24 000

CONTOUR INTERVAL 40 FEET
DOTTED LINES REPRESENT 20-FOOT CONTOURS
DATUM IS MEAN SEA LEVEL

Forbidden Peak

Boston Basin

Mount Torment

"Should we be using wands or other route-marking methods right now?" Ask the questions as you go and act on the answers. Each person in the party should know the route, the route plan, and how to get back.

Mark the route if necessary: There are times when it may be best to mark the route going in so that it can be found again on the way out. This situation can come up when the route is over snowfields or glaciers during changeable weather, when the route is in heavy forest, or when fog or nightfall threatens to hide landmarks. On snow, climbers use wands to mark the path. In the forest, plastic surveyors' tape is sometimes tied to branches to show the route, but its use is discouraged due to its neon blight and permanence. From an ecological standpoint, unbleached toilet paper is the best marker, because it will disintegrate during the next rainfall. Use toilet paper if good weather is assured. If not, use crepe paper in thin rolls. It will survive the next storm, but will disintegrate over the winter.

One commandment here: *Remove your markers.* Markers are litter, and mountaineers never, ever litter. If there is any chance you will not come back the same way and will not be able to remove the markers, be especially sure to use paper markers.

Cairns—piles of rocks used as markers—appear here and there, sometimes dotting an entire route and at other times signaling the point where a route changes direction. These heaps of rock are another imposition on the landscape, and they can create confusion for any traveler but the one who put them together—so do not build them. If there comes a time when you must build a cairn, then tear it down on your way out. The rule is different for existing cairns. Let them be, on the assumption that someone, perhaps even land managers, may be depending on them.

Keep oriented: As the trip goes on, it may be helpful to mark the party's progress on the map. Keep yourself oriented so that at any time, you can point out your actual position to within 0.5 mile (about 1 kilometer) on the map.

Monitor rate of travel: Part of navigation is having a sense of the party's speed. Given all the variables, will it take the party 1 hour to travel 2 miles (3 kilometers), or will it take 2 hours to travel 1 mile (1.6 kilometers)? The answer is rather important if it is 3:00 P.M. and base camp is still 5 miles (8 kilometers) away. After enough trips into the wilds, climbers are good at estimating wilderness speeds (see sidebar "Typical Speeds for an Average Party," noting that there will be much variation).

In heavy brush, the rate of travel can drop to a third or even a quarter of what it would be on a good trail. At high altitudes, the rate of travel will also greatly decrease, perhaps down to as little as 100 feet (30 meters) of elevation gain per hour.

With a watch and a notebook (or a good memory), monitor the rate of progress on any outing. Always make sure to note the time of starting from the trailhead. Also note the times at which important streams, ridges, trail junctions, and other points along the route are reached.

Experienced climbers regularly assess their party's progress and compare it with trip plans. Make estimates—and re-estimates—of what time the party will reach the summit or other destination, and what time the party will get back to base camp or the trailhead. If it begins to look as though the party could become trapped in tricky terrain after dark, the group may decide to change its plans and bivouac in a safe place or to call it a day and return home.

On Technical Portions of the Climb

When the going gets tough, the tough forget about navigation and start worrying about the next foothold—but you should keep the map and other route information

---

TYPICAL SPEEDS FOR AN AVERAGE PARTY

- On a gentle trail, with a day pack: 2 to 3 miles per hour (3 to 5 kilometers per hour)
- Up a steep trail, with a full overnight pack: 1 to 2 miles per hour (2 to 3 kilometers per hour)
- Traveling cross-country up a moderate slope, with a day pack: 1,000 feet (300 meters) of elevation gain per hour
- Traveling cross-country up a moderate slope, with a full overnight pack: 500 feet (150 meters) of elevation gain per hour

handy for use during occasional rests. On rock climbs, do not let the mechanics of technical climbing overwhelm your need to stay on route.

On the Summit

Here is a golden opportunity to rest, relax, and enjoy—and to learn more about the area and about map reading by comparing the actual view with the way it looks on the map.

The summit is the place to make final plans for the descent, which often leads to many more routefinding errors than on the ascent. Repeat the trailhead get-together by discussing the route and emergency strategies with everyone. Stress the importance of keeping the party together on the descent, when some climbers will want to race ahead while others lag behind.

During the Descent

The descent is a time for extra caution while climbers fight to keep fatigue and inattention at bay. As on the ascent, everyone needs to maintain a good sense of the route and how it relates to the map. Stay together, do not rush, and be even more careful if the party is taking a descent route that is different from the ascent route.

Intentional offset: Imagine that your climbing team is almost back to the car after a tough 12-hour climb. The party follows a compass bearing directly back to the logging road, but cannot see the car because the group is off route by a few degrees. The car is either to the left or the right, so you may have to guess which way to go. It is a bad ending to a good day if the car is about 0.5 mile (about 1 kilometer) to the right and the party goes left. It will be even worse if the car is parked at the end of the road and a routefinding error takes the party beyond that point and on and on through the woods (fig. 5-3a).

The intentional offset (also called "aiming off") was invented for this situation (fig. 5-3b). If you fear you might get into this kind of trouble, just travel in a direction that is intentionally offset some amount (say, 20 to 30 degrees) to the right or the left of where you really want to be. When you hit the road (or the river, the ridge, or whatever), there will be no doubt about which way to turn.

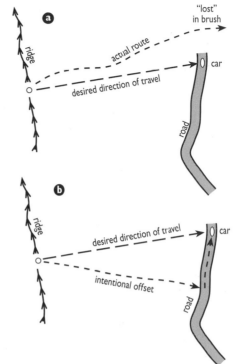

Fig. 5-3. Navigating to a specific point on a line: a, inevitable minor errors can sometimes have disastrous consequences; b, to avoid such problems, follow a course with an intentional offset.

After the Climb

Back home, write a description of the route and of any problems, mistakes, or unusual features, and do it while the details are fresh in your mind. Imagine what you would like to know if you were about to make the climb for the first time, so you will be ready with the right answers when another climber asks about it. If a guidebook was confusing or wrong, take time to write to the publisher.

THE COMPASS

A compass is essentially a magnetized needle that responds to the Earth's magnetic field. Compass makers have added a few things to this basic unit in order to make it easier to use. But stripped to the core, there is just that needle, aligned with the Earth's magnetism, and from that you can figure out any direction. These are the basic features (fig. 5-4a) of a mountaineering compass:

■ A freely rotating magnetic needle—one end is a different color from the other so it is easy to tell which end is pointing north.

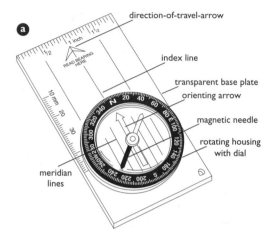

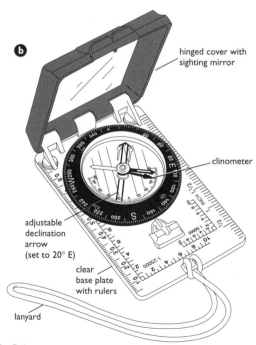

Fig. 5-4.

Features of mountaineering compasses: a, essential features; b, useful optional features.

■ A circular rotating housing for the needle—this is filled with a fluid that dampens (reduces) the vibrations of the needle, making readings more accurate.

■ A dial around the circumference of the housing—the dial is graduated clockwise in degrees from 0 to 360.

■ An orienting arrow and a set of parallel meridian lines—these are located beneath the needle.

■ An index line—read bearings here.

■ A transparent, rectangular base plate for the entire unit—this includes a direction-of-travel line (sometimes with an arrow at one end) to point toward the objective. The longer the base plate, the easier it is to get an accurate reading.

The following are optional features (fig. 5-4b) available on some mountaineering compasses:

■ An adjustable declination arrow—it is well worth the added cost because it is such an easy, dependable way to correct for magnetic declination.

■ A sighting mirror—this provides another way to improve accuracy.

■ A ruler—this is calibrated in inches or millimeters. Use it for measuring distances on a map.

■ A clinometer—use it to measure the angle of a slope. It can help resolve arguments over the steepness of slopes, and it can determine whether you are on the higher of two summits.

■ A magnifying glass—use it to help read closely spaced contour lines.

Some compasses have an adjustable declination arrow but no mirror. Such compasses are midway in price between the basic compass of Figure 5-4a and the full-featured compass of Figure 5-4b. These compasses offer a good compromise for someone who prefers the adjustable declination feature but does not want to pay for the added cost of the mirror.

Most compasses have a lanyard—a piece of string a foot or so long for attaching the compass to a belt, jacket, or pack. It is not a good idea to put the lanyard around your neck; this can be an unsafe practice, particularly when you are doing any technical climbing.

Small, round, cheap compasses without base plates are not suitable for mountaineering, because they cannot be used for precise work with a map.

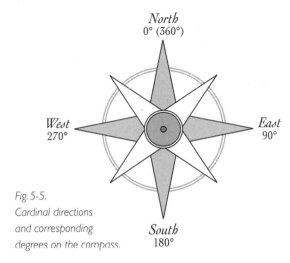

Fig. 5-5.
Cardinal directions and corresponding degrees on the compass.

Bearings

A bearing is the direction from one place to another, measured in degrees of angle with respect to an accepted reference line. This reference is the line to true north.

The round dial of a compass is divided into 360 degrees. North is at 0 degrees (the same as 360 degrees), East is at 90 degrees, South is at 180 degrees, and West is at 270 degrees (fig. 5.5).

The compass is used for two basic tasks regarding bearings:

1. The compass is used for taking bearings (also called measuring bearings). Taking a bearing means measuring the direction from one point to another, either on a map or on the ground.
2. The compass is used for plotting bearings (also called following bearings). Plotting a bearing means setting a specified bearing on the compass and then plotting out, or following, where that bearing points, either on a map or on the ground.

Bearings on the Map

The compass is used as a protractor to both measure and plot bearings on a map. Magnetic north and magnetic declination have nothing to do with these calculations. Therefore, never make any use of the magnetic needle when you are taking or plotting bearings on a map. (The only time the magnetic needle is used on the map is whenever you choose to orient the map to true north, which is explained in "Orientation by Instrument,"

later in this chapter. But there is no need to orient the map to measure or plot bearings.)

Taking (measuring) a bearing on the map: Place the compass on the map with one long edge of the base plate running directly between two points of interest. While measuring the bearing from Point A to Point B, see that the direction-of-travel line is pointing in the same direction as from A to B. Then turn the rotating housing until its set of meridian lines is parallel to the north–south lines on the map. (Be sure the orienting arrow that turns with the meridian lines is pointing to the top of the map, to north. If the arrow is pointed toward the bottom, the reading will be 180 degrees off.)

Now read the number that is at the index line. This is the bearing from Point A to Point B.

In the example shown in Figure 5-6, the bearing from Point A, Panic Peak, to Point B, Deception Dome, is 34

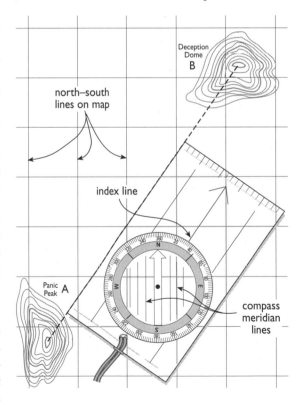

Fig. 5-6.
Taking a bearing on a map with the compass as a protractor (magnetic needle omitted for clarity).

degrees. (In this figure, the magnetic needle has been omitted to provide a better view of the meridian lines.)

If the map does not have north–south lines, just draw some in, parallel to the edge of the map and at intervals of 1 or 2 inches (3 to 5 centimeters).

Plotting (following) a bearing on the map: This case starts with a known bearing. Where does that bearing come from? From an actual landscape compass reading. In another hypothetical example (fig. 5-7), a friend returns from a trip, disgusted at himself for having left his camera somewhere along the trail. During a rest stop, he had taken some pictures of Mount Magnificent. At the same time, he had taken a bearing on Mount Magnificent and found it to be 130 degrees. That is all you need to know. You are heading into that same area next week, so get out the Magnificent quadrangle, and here is what you do.

First set the bearing of 130 degrees at the compass index line. Place the compass on the map, one long edge of the base plate touching the summit of Mount Magnificent. Rotate the entire compass (not just the housing) until the meridian lines are parallel with the map's north–south lines, and make sure the edge of the base plate is still touching the summit. Remember, be sure that the orienting arrow points to the top of the map, toward north. Follow the line made by the edge of the base plate, heading in the opposite direction from the direction-of-travel line because the original bearing was measured *toward* the mountain. Where the line crosses the trail is exactly where your friend's camera is (or was).

Bearings in the Field

Now the magnetic needle gets to do its job. All bearings in the field are based on where the needle points. These first two examples, for the sake of simplicity, ignore the effects of magnetic declination, which is covered in the next section. Imagine you are taking the bearings in Mississippi, where declination is not important.

Taking (measuring) a bearing in the field: Hold the compass in front of you and point the direction-of-travel line at the object whose bearing you want to find. Rotate the compass housing until the pointed end of the orienting arrow is aligned with the north-seeking end of the magnetic needle. Read the bearing at the index line—270 degrees in Figure 5-8. That is all there is to it.

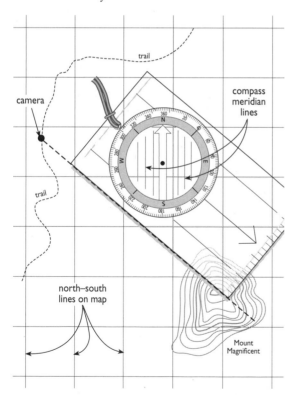

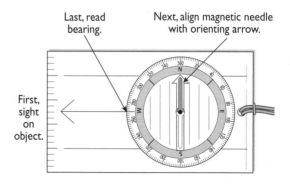

Fig. 5-7.
Plotting a bearing on a map with the compass as a protractor (magnetic needle omitted for clarity).

Fig. 5-8.
Taking a compass bearing in the field in an area with zero declination.

If the compass has no sighting mirror, hold it at or near arm's length and at or near waist level. With a sighting mirror, fold the mirror back at about a 45-degree angle and hold the compass at eye level with the sight pointing at the object. Observe the magnetic needle and the orienting arrow in the mirror while rotating the housing to align the needle and the arrow. In either case, hold the compass level. Keep it away from ferrous metal objects, which can easily deflect the magnetic needle.

Plotting (following) a bearing in the field: Simply reverse the process used to take a bearing. Start by rotating the compass housing until a desired bearing, say 270 degrees (due west), is set at the index line (see Figure 5-8, above). Hold the compass level in front of you and then turn your entire body (including your feet) until the north-seeking end of the magnetic needle is aligned with the pointed end of the orienting arrow. The direction-of-travel line is now pointing due west. That is all there is to that.

Magnetic Declination

A compass needle is attracted to magnetic north, whereas most maps are oriented to a different point on the Earth, the geographic North Pole (true north). This difference between the direction to true north and the direction to magnetic north, measured in degrees, is called magnetic declination. A simple compass adjustment or modification is necessary to correct for magnetic declination.

The line connecting all points where true north aligns with magnetic north is called the line of zero declination. In the United States, this runs from northern Minnesota to Louisiana (fig. 5-9). In areas west of the line of zero declination, the magnetic needle points somewhere to the east (to the right) of true north, so these areas are said to have east declination. It works just the opposite on the other side of the line of zero declination, where the magnetic needle points somewhere to the west (left) of true north; these areas have west declination.

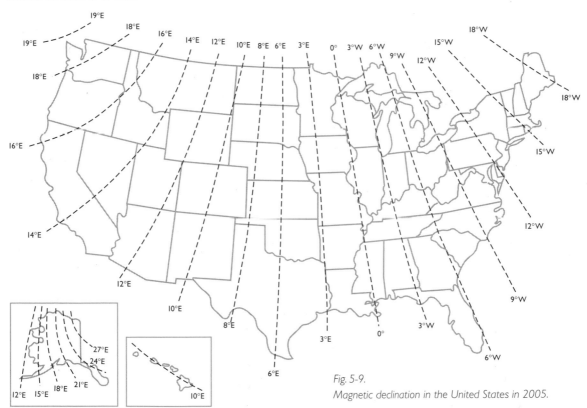

Fig. 5-9.
Magnetic declination in the United States in 2005.

95

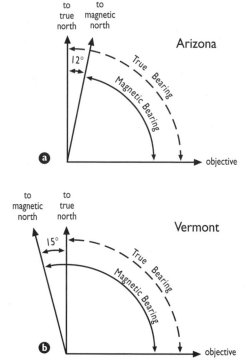

Fig. 5-10.

Magnetic and true bearings: a, in Arizona (east declination);
b, in Vermont (west declination).

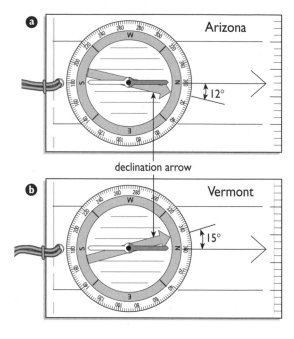

Fig. 5-11.

Compass declination corrections: a, for an area west of the zero-
declination line; b, for an area east of the zero-declination line.

Consider a traveler in Phoenix, Arizona, where the declination is 12 degrees east (fig. 5-10a). The true bearing is a measurement of the angle between the line to true north and the line to the objective. The magnetic needle, however, is pulled toward magnetic north, not true north. So instead it measures the angle between the line to magnetic north and the line to the objective. This "magnetic bearing" is 12 degrees less than the true bearing. To get the true bearing, it is possible to add 12 degrees to the magnetic bearing (though easier ways are described later in this section).

Travelers in all areas west of the zero declination line, as in the Arizona example above, could add the declination to the magnetic bearing. In Colorado, for example, about 10 degrees would be added. In central Washington State, it is about 18 degrees.

East of the zero-declination line, the declination can be subtracted from the magnetic bearing. In southern Vermont, for example, the magnetic bearing is 15 degrees greater than the true bearing (fig. 5-10b). Subtracting the declination of 15 degrees gives a wilderness traveler in Vermont the true bearing.

This is all very simple in theory, but can be confusing in practice, and the wilderness is no place for mental arithmetic that can have potentially serious consequences. A more practical way to handle the minor complication of declination is to pay somewhat more for a compass and get one with an adjustable declination arrow (as shown in Figure 5-4b, above) instead of a fixed orienting arrow (as shown in Figure 5-4a, above). The declination arrow can easily be set for any declination by following the instructions supplied with the compass. Then the bearing at the index line will automatically be the true bearing, and there will be no need for concern about a declination error.

On compasses without adjustable declination arrows, the same effect can be achieved by sticking a thin strip of tape to the top or (preferably) the bottom of the rotating housing to serve as a customized declination arrow. Trim the tape to a point, with the point aimed directly at the specific declination for the intended climbing area.

In Arizona, the taped declination arrow must point at 12 degrees east (clockwise) from the 360-degree point (marked N for north) on the rotating compass dial (fig. 5-11a). In Vermont, the declination arrow must point at 15 degrees west (counterclockwise) from the 360-degree point on the dial (fig. 5-11b). In central Washington State, the declination arrow must point at 18 degrees east (clockwise) from 360 degrees.

To take or to follow a bearing in the field, follow exactly the same procedure used in the earlier examples from Mississippi, where the declination is zero. The only difference is that you align the magnetic needle with the declination arrow instead of with the orienting arrow.

Note: From here on in this chapter, it is assumed you are using a compass with a declination arrow—either an adjustable arrow or a taped arrow that has been added. For all bearings in the field, align the needle with this declination arrow. Unless otherwise stated, all bearings referred to are true bearings, not magnetic.

Declination changes with time, by as much as 0.1 degree per year in some parts of the United States (this is because the molten magnetic material in the Earth's core is continually moving). The map in Figure 5-9 above shows the declination for the year 2005, and is valid for the period from 2000 to 2010. If the information in Figure 5-9 is not adequate for your purposes, you can buy a copy of a map called the "Magnetic Field of the U.S. Declination Chart" from the USGS (see Appendix C, Supplementary Reading, at the back of this book). There are also some Internet sites where declination information is available; one is the Canadian Geomagnetic Reference Field (see Appendix C).

Dip

The magnetic needle of the compass is not only affected by the horizontal direction of the Earth's magnetic field, but also by its vertical pull. The closer you get to the magnetic north pole, the more the north-seeking end of the needle tends to point *downward*. At the magnetic equator, the needle is level; at the south magnetic pole, the north-seeking end of the needle tries to point *upward*. This phenomenon is referred to as the compass dip.

To compensate for this effect, most compass manufacturers purposely introduce a slight imbalance to the magnetic needles of their compasses, so that their dip is negligible for the geographic area where they will be used. However, if you buy a compass in the northern hemisphere, say, in North America or Europe, and then try to use it in the southern hemisphere, say, in New Zealand or Chile, the difference in dip may be enough to introduce errors in compass readings, or even make it impossible to use. For this reason, if you bring your compass to a faraway place, as soon as you get to the country you are visiting, first try out your compass in an urban area to make sure it works properly *before* you head out into the wilderness. If your compass is adversely affected by dip, you may have to buy a new compass in the general area where you are traveling. Most compasses sold anywhere in the world are compensated for dip in that particular zone.

Some compass manufacturers produce compasses that are not affected by dip. Some such compasses have the term "Global" in their names, or a notation on the package that the compass is corrected for dip anywhere in the world. If you intend to go on worldwide climbing expeditions, you might consider such a compass.

Another way of ensuring that dip will not be a problem is to buy a compass ahead of time that is properly compensated for dip in the area you intend to visit. Some retail stores and mail-order companies have or can order compasses compensated for whatever zone you will be visiting. Doing this in advance of a visit ensures that you will not have a problem with compass dip on your climb.

Practicing with the Compass

Before counting on your compass skills in the wilderness, test them where you live. The best place to practice is someplace where you already know all the answers, such as a street intersection where the roads run north–south and east–west.

Take a bearing in a direction you know to be east. When the direction-of-travel line or arrow is pointed at something that you know is due east of you, and the declination arrow is lined up with the magnetic needle,

---

A MAP AND COMPASS CHECKLIST

Do you have the hang of using map and compass? Run through the whole procedure once more. Check off each step as you do it. And remember the following:

■ Never use the magnetic needle or the declination arrow when measuring or plotting bearings on the map.

■ When taking or following a bearing in the field, always align the pointed end of the declination arrow with the north-seeking end of the magnetic needle.

Taking (Measuring) a Bearing on a Map

1. Place the compass on the map, with the edge of the base plate joining the two points of interest.
2. Rotate the housing to align the compass meridian lines with the north–south lines on the map.
3. Read the bearing at the index line.

Plotting (Following) a Bearing on a Map

1. Set the desired bearing at the index line.
2. Place the compass on the map, with the edge of the base plate on the feature from which you wish to plot a bearing.
3. Turn the entire compass to align the meridian lines with the map's north–south lines. The edge of the base plate is the bearing line.

Taking (Measuring) a Bearing in the Field

1. Hold the compass level in front of you and point the direction-of-travel line at the desired object.
2. Rotate the housing to align the declination arrow with the magnetic needle.
3. Read the bearing at the index line.

Plotting (Following) a Bearing in the Field

1. Set the desired bearing at the index line.
2. Hold the compass level in front of you and turn your entire body until the magnetic needle is aligned with the declination arrow.
3. Travel in the direction shown by the direction-of-travel line.

---

the number at the index line should be within a few degrees of 90. Repeat for the other cardinal directions: south, west, and north.

Then do the reverse: Pretend you do not know which way is west. Set 270 degrees (west) at the index line and hold the compass in front of you as you turn your entire body until the needle is again aligned with the declination arrow. The direction-of-travel line should now point west. Does it? Repeat for the other cardinal directions. This set of exercises will help develop skill and self-confidence at compass reading and also is a way to check the accuracy of the compass.

Look for chances to practice in the mountains. A good place is any known location—such as a summit or a lakeshore—from which you can see identifiable landmarks. Take bearings as time permits, plot them on the map, and see how close the result is to your actual location.

Cautions about Compass Use

It should be evident by now that there is a big difference between using a compass for working with a map and using a compass for field work. When measuring and plotting bearings on a map, ignore the compass needle. Just align the meridian lines on the compass housing with the north–south lines on the map. In the field, however, you must use the magnetic needle.

It is true that metal can interfere with a compass reading. Ferrous objects—iron, steel, and other materials with magnetic properties—will deflect the magnetic needle and produce false readings, as will a battery-powered watch that is within a few inches of a compass.

Keep the compass away from belt buckles, ice axes, and other metal objects. If a compass reading does not seem to make sense, check whether it is being sabotaged by nearby metal.

Keep your wits about you when you are pointing the declination arrow and the direction-of-travel line. If either is pointed backward—an easy thing to do—the reading will be 180 degrees off. If the bearing is north, the compass will say it is south. Remember that the north-seeking end of the magnetic needle must be aligned with the pointed end of the declination arrow and that the direction-of-travel line must point from you to the objective, not the reverse.

There is yet another way to introduce a 180-degree error in a compass reading: by aligning the compass meridian lines with the north–south lines on a map but pointing the rotating housing backward. The way to avoid this is to check that "N" on the compass dial is pointing to north on the map.

If you are in doubt, trust the compass. The compass, correctly used, is almost always right, whereas your contrary judgment may be clouded by fatigue, confusion, or hurry. If you get a nonsensical reading, check to see that you are not making one of those 180-degree errors. If not, and if there is no metal in sight, verify the reading with other members of the party. If they get the same answer, trust the compass over hunches, blind guesses, and intuition.

THE CLINOMETER

The clinometer is a tool used to measure angles; it is a feature of some compasses (see Figure 5-4b above). The clinometer consists of a small needle (not the magnetic needle) that points downward due to gravity and a numbered scale along the inside of the compass housing (which may also be the scale used for declination adjustment). To use the clinometer, rotate the compass housing to either 90 degrees or 270 degrees at the index line. Then hold the compass on edge so that the clinometer needle swings free and points down toward the numbered scale. With the compass held level in this way (i.e., with the direction of travel line held level), the clinometer should read zero. Tilting the compass up or down will cause the clinometer needle to point

to the number of degrees upward or downward.

There are two ways to use a clinometer. The first is to measure the angle of a distant object. For example, suppose you are at the summit of a peak; you see another peak of nearly the same elevation, and you wonder if you are on the higher of the two summits. To find out, hold the compass on its side, with its long edge pointing toward the other peak. Then sight along the long edge of the base plate toward the other peak. Steady the compass on a rock or other stable object if possible. Tap the compass lightly to overcome any friction in the mechanism, and ask a companion to look at the clinometer needle to see if it indicates an upward or a downward angle toward the other peak. If the angle is upward, then the other peak is higher than you are.

The clinometer can also be used to find the angle of a slope. Set the compass to 90 degrees or 270 degrees at the index line, and lay the long edge of the compass on the slope. Then read the angle of slope on the clinometer scale. Due to variations in a slope over small distances, it is best to place an ice ax, ski pole, or other long object along the slope, and then place the long edge of the compass along this object to get a better idea of the average slope. The presence of metal, such as an ice ax or ski pole shaft, will affect the magnetic needle, but not the clinometer needle, which is affected by gravity.

THE ALTIMETER

An altimeter (fig. 5-12), like a compass, provides one simple piece of information that forms the basis for a tremendous amount of vital detail. The compass points the direction to magnetic north; the altimeter gives the elevation. By monitoring the elevation and checking it against the topographic map, mountaineers keep track of their progress, pinpoint their location, and find the way to critical junctions in the route. Every climbing party should have an altimeter.

An altimeter is basically a modified barometer. Both instruments measure air pressure (the weight of air). A barometer indicates air pressure, whereas an altimeter reads in feet or meters above sea level—which is made possible because air pressure decreases at a known rate with increasing altitude.

The most popular mountaineering altimeter is the

Fig. 5-12.
Typical
altimeters:
a–b, digital
wristwatch
types;
c, analog
pocket type.

digital type (fig. 5-12a and b), usually combined with a watch and worn on the wrist. The digital wristwatch altimeter has a number of advantages over the analog type (fig. 5-12c). Some digital altimeters display additional information, such as the temperature and the rate of change in altitude gain or loss. Because most climbers wish to wear a watch anyway, this type of altimeter is helpful because it combines two functions in one piece of equipment. The altimeter worn on the wrist is more convenient to use than one kept in a pocket or pack, and therefore will be used more frequently.

A disadvantage of the digital type is that it requires a battery—which can die. In addition, the liquid-crystal display (LCD) usually goes blank at temperatures below about 0 degrees Fahrenheit (minus 18 degrees Celsius), making it essential to keep the instrument relatively warm. To keep your altimeter watch from getting banged up on the rock when you are starting a technical pitch, it is a good idea to remove it from your wrist and attach it to a pack strap or put it in a pocket or your pack.

The analog altimeter has the advantages of being a simpler instrument than a digital one, requiring no battery, and working at temperatures well below zero. To read an analog altimeter, hold it level in the palm of one hand. Look directly down on the needle, your eyes at least a foot (30 centimeters) above it, to reduce errors due to viewing angle. Tap it lightly several times to overcome any slight friction in the mechanism, and then take an average of several readings.

The accuracy of an altimeter depends on the weather, because a change in weather is generally accompanied by a change in air pressure, which can cause an error in the altimeter reading. A change in barometric pressure of 1 inch of mercury corresponds to a change in altitude reading of roughly 1,000 feet (10 millibars of pressure corresponds to 100 meters of altitude). If a climber is in camp during a day in which the air pressure increases by 0.2 inch (7 millibars)—for example, from 30 to 30.2 inches (1,016 to 1,023 millibars), the altimeter will show a reading about 200 feet (60 meters) less than it did at the beginning of the day, even though the climber has remained at the same place. If the climber had gone out on a climb during that same day, the elevation readings would likewise be about 200 feet too low. During periods of unstable weather, the indicated elevation may change by as much as 500 feet (150 meters) in one day even though the actual elevation has remained the same. Even during apparently stable conditions, an erroneous indicated change in elevation of 100 feet (30 meters) per day is not uncommon.

Because of the strong influence of weather on an altimeter's accuracy, do not trust the instrument until it is first set at a location of known elevation. Then it is important while traveling to check the reading whenever another point of known elevation is reached so you can reset it if necessary, or at least be aware of the error.

How Altimeters Aid Mountaineers
Calculating Rate of Ascent
The altimeter helps mountaineers decide whether to continue a climb or to turn back, by letting them calculate their rate of ascent. For example, during a climb a party has been keeping an hourly check on time and elevation. It has taken the party 4 hours to climb 3,000 feet (910 meters), an average of 750 feet (230 meters)

per hour. But the actual rate of ascent has been declining with each hour. In fact, the party gained only 500 feet (150 meters) in the past hour, compared with 1,000 feet (300 meters) the first hour. The summit is at an elevation of 8,400 feet (2,560 meters), and an altimeter reading shows the party is now at 6,400 feet (1,950 meters). So the climbers can predict that it will take roughly 4 more hours to reach the summit. Take that information, courtesy of the altimeter, combine it with a look at the weather, the time of day, and the condition of the party members, and the group has the data on which to base a sound decision on whether to proceed with the climb or turn back.

Navigating

An altimeter also can help determine exactly where you are. If you are climbing a ridge or hiking up a trail shown on the map, but you do not know your exact position along the ridge or trail, check the altimeter for the elevation. Your likely location is where the ridge or trail reaches that contour line on the map.

Another way to ask the altimeter where a climbing party is located is to start with a compass bearing to a summit or some other known feature. Find that peak on the map, and plot the bearing line from the mountain back toward the climbing party. The group now knows it must be somewhere along that line. But where? Take an altimeter reading and find out the elevation. The party's likely location is where the compass bearing line crosses a contour line at that elevation.

Navigation gets easier with the aid of an altimeter. If you top a convenient couloir at 9,400 feet (2,870 meters) and gain the summit ridge, make a note of that elevation. On the way back, descend the ridge to that elevation to easily find the couloir again.

Last but not least, an altimeter may reveal whether you are on the real summit when the visibility is too poor to be able to tell by looking around.

Predicting Weather

The altimeter can help in predicting weather. The readings on an altimeter and on a barometer operate in opposition to each other. When one goes up, the other goes down. An altimeter reading showing an increase in elevation when no actual elevation change has taken place (such as at camp overnight) means a falling barometer, which often predicts deteriorating weather. A decreasing altimeter reading, on the other hand, means increasing barometric pressure and improving weather. This is an oversimplification, of course, because weather forecasting is complicated by the wind, local weather peculiarities, and the rate of barometric pressure change. (See Chapter 27, Mountain Weather, for more information on interpreting barometric change.)

Some digital wristwatch altimeters can be adjusted to read barometric pressure instead of altitude, but keep in mind that changes in barometric pressure are useful in assessing the weather only when the readings are taken at a constant elevation (such as in camp). Using the altimeter as a barometer while climbing will give readings that are influenced not only by changes in the weather but also by changes in elevation while climbing. This will lead to erroneous conclusions regarding barometric pressure.

Cautions about Altimeter Use

Because even the most precise and costly altimeters are strongly affected by the weather, do not be misled into trusting them to accuracy greater than is possible. A typical high-quality altimeter may have a resolution (smallest marked division of an analog instrument, or smallest indicated change of a digital altimeter) of 20 feet (5 meters). This does not mean that the altimeter will always be that close to the truth; changes in weather could easily throw the reading off by hundreds of feet.

An altimeter expands and contracts due to variations in its temperature, causing changes in the indicated elevation. Try to keep the temperature of an altimeter as constant as possible. Body heat will usually accomplish this with a wristwatch altimeter, particularly if you wear it under a parka when the outside temperature is low. Keep the temperature of an analog altimeter relatively constant by carrying it in a pocket rather than in your pack.

In temperature-compensated altimeters, a bimetallic element adjusts for the effect of temperature when there is no actual change in elevation. The element counterbalances the effect on other parts of the instrument. When you are gaining or losing elevation, however, this adjustment sometimes is not enough, resulting in errors even in altimeters that are temperature-compensated.

Get to know your own altimeter, use it often, check it at every opportunity, and note differences of information between it and the map. You will soon know just what accuracy to expect, and your altimeter will then be a dependable aid to roving the wilds.

THE GLOBAL POSITIONING SYSTEM

The U.S. Department of Defense has placed twenty-four satellites in orbit around the Earth. Small, handheld global positioning system (GPS) receivers (fig. 5-13) can pick up the signals from these satellites and give the user's position and altitude to within about 50 feet (15 meters). Most GPS receivers cost from $100 to $400 and have a variety of features that allow them to store and later recall specific positions (called landmarks or waypoints), determine the compass bearing and the distance between waypoints, and plot out routes comprising a series of waypoints from one position to another.

What to Look for in a GPS Receiver

Before deciding which receiver to buy, talk to friends and acquaintances who already have GPS receivers to learn about their features, ease of operation, ability to work in challenging terrain, and other attributes. If possible, borrow a receiver and try it out to learn if it is the receiver for you. If you intend to use the receiver in

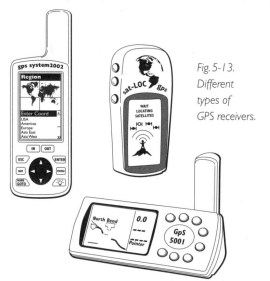

Fig. 5-13. Different types of GPS receivers.

a cold climate, pay particular attention to the operating temperature limitations stated in the specifications. Some receivers operate reliably down to only freezing; others work down to as low as about 0 degrees Fahrenheit (minus 18 degrees Celsius). Make sure your chosen GPS receiver can make use of the UTM coordinate system described in "Navigation by Instrument," later in this chapter.

To get the most benefit from a GPS receiver, be sure to read its instruction manual carefully and master all of its features. In addition, several good books are available that explain GPS in greater detail. See Appendix C, Supplementary Reading, at the back of this book.

Getting Started with GPS

Start by thoroughly reading the instruction manual and getting totally familiar with your receiver before using it in the wilderness. The first step is to initialize the receiver to establish your approximate position, using a menu-driven set of commands. Then select which units to use (miles or kilometers, feet or meters, magnetic or true bearings, etc.) and—very important—select the datum to agree with the datum for the topographic map of the area. Many GPS receivers use a default datum called "WGS84" (World Geodetic System 1984), whereas many U.S. topographic maps use the 1927 North American Datum (NAD27) for horizontal position. The difference in position between these two datums can be as much as 1,000 feet (several hundred meters), so it is essential to do this prior to trying to use a GPS receiver with a map. Try the GPS receiver out around home, in city parks, and on trail hikes before taking it on a climb.

Using a GPS Receiver in Mountaineering

This section is intended to give you a general understanding of how to apply GPS usage to mountaineering situations. Below is only one example of how a GPS receiver can help in mountaineering situations. Several more applications are given in "Orientation by Instrument" and "Navigation by Instrument," later in this chapter.

The first rule of GPS receiver usage is not to become dependent on it. The receiver is a delicate, battery-powered electronic device that can fail or whose batteries may give out. For this reason, you must also carry a topographic map and a magnetic compass. In addition, carry route-marking materials such as flagging and wands, regardless of whether you have a GPS receiver. Never rely solely on the GPS receiver.

A GPS receiver can be used along with a compass in order to be sure you can get back to your starting point. At the trailhead or campsite, or wherever your climb is started, turn the receiver on to establish your GPS position. This usually takes several minutes. Save this position as a waypoint, even giving it a unique name if desired. Then turn off the receiver to save battery power, and pack it away carefully to protect it from harm while you are climbing. At crucial locations along the route to the objective, again turn on the receiver and establish additional waypoints. Once you are at the destination or turnaround point, use the receiver to find the distance and compass bearing from one waypoint to another to get back to the starting point. Then turn off the receiver and use the compass to travel to the next waypoint.

Many GPS instruction manuals seem to assume that you are always traveling with the receiver turned on and in hand, constantly observing its display. Doing this wastes battery power and occupies a hand that might be better used for climbing or holding an ice ax or ski pole. In addition, it distracts you from observing the route and its hazards, as well as the scenery. Therefore it is better to use the GPS receiver only occasionally, and to travel by compass most of the time.

Limitations of GPS Receivers

Most GPS receivers cannot determine direction, so a compass is required to use the GPS in the wilderness. The GPS receiver can tell the straight-line route from one point to another, but has no way of knowing if there is a river, a lake, or a cliff along this route. For this reason, you still must have a topographic map along, even if you also have a GPS receiver. The GPS receiver is not a substitute for a map and compass or the ability to use them.

Most GPS receivers will not work at temperatures much below freezing, and battery life is limited to 15 to 30 hours, depending on the model.

GPS receivers must track signals from at least four

satellites to provide trustworthy position information. If the satellite signals are blocked by heavy forest cover, cliffs, or canyons, this is often not possible. When a GPS receiver is not able to pick up signals from the four satellites it needs in order to provide a three-dimensional position, it sacrifices altitude information in favor of horizontal position. Some receivers indicate that this is happening by displaying a "2D" message or icon to tell you that it is operating in a two-dimensional mode. Other receivers may merely display a "frozen" altitude display if this occurs. In either case, always note whether you are getting a two-dimensional position. If so, then be aware of the fact that the GPS receiver's horizontal position may be significantly in error as well, particularly if you are thousands of feet (meters) above sea level. Under such less-than-ideal conditions, horizontal position errors of 1,000 feet (hundreds of meters) are possible.

ORIENTATION BY INSTRUMENT

The goal of orientation is to determine that precise point on the Earth where you are standing. That position can then be represented by a mere dot on the map, which is known as the point position. There are two less-specific levels of orientation. One is called line position: The party knows it is along a certain line on a map—such as a river, a trail, or a bearing or elevation line—but does not know where it is along the line. The least specific is area position: The party knows the general area it is in, but that is about it.

Point Position

The primary objective of orientation is to find out your exact point position. Figuring out exactly where you are is usually relatively simple: Just look around and compare what you see with what is on the map. Sometimes this is not accurate enough, or there is just nothing much nearby to identify on the map. The usual solution then is to get out the compass and try to take bearings on some landscape features. This is an example of orientation by instrument.

With point position known, there is no question about where you are, and you can use that knowledge in identifying on the map any major feature visible on the landscape. You can also identify on the landscape any visible feature shown on the map.

For example, climbers on the summit of Forbidden Peak know their point position: at the top of Forbidden Peak. (Refer back to the topographic map in Figure 5-2.) The climbers see an unknown mountain and want to know what it is. They take a bearing and get 275 degrees. They plot 275 degrees from Forbidden Peak on their topographic map, and it passes through Mount Torment. They conclude that the unknown mountain is Mount Torment.

In reverse, if the climbers know from the map that they are in the vicinity of Mount Torment and want to identify which mountain it is from where they are atop Forbidden Peak, they must do the map work first. The climbers measure the bearing on the map from Forbidden to Mount Torment, and come up with 275 degrees. Keeping 275 at the index line on the compass, they turn the compass until the magnetic needle is aligned with the declination arrow. The direction-of-travel line then points to Mount Torment.

Line Position

With line position known, the goal is to determine point position. When climbers know they are on a trail, ridge, or some other identifiable line, they need only one more trustworthy piece of information. For example, they are on Unsavory Ridge (fig. 5-14)—but exactly where? Off in the distance to the southwest is Mount Majestic. A bearing on Majestic reads 220 degrees. Plot 220 degrees from Mount Majestic on the map. Run this line back

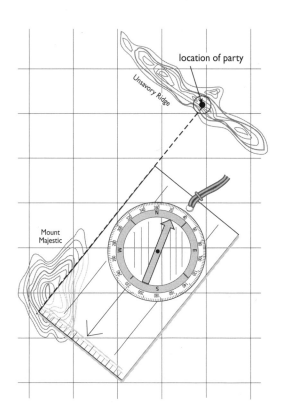

Fig. 5-14.
Orientation with line position known
(magnetic needle omitted for clarity).

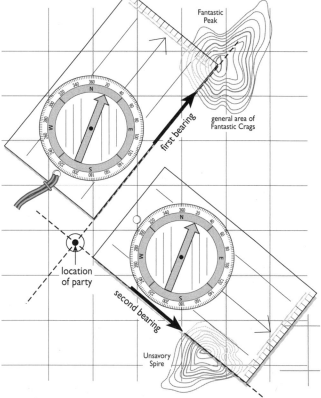

Fig. 5-15.
Orientation with area position known
(magnetic needle omitted for clarity).

toward Unsavory Ridge, and where it intersects the ridge is the point position where the climbers are.

Area Position

Suppose a climbing party knows only its area position: the general area of Fantastic Crags (fig. 5-15). They want to determine line position and then, from that, point position. To move from knowing area position to knowing point position, two trustworthy pieces of information are needed.

Climbers may be able to use bearings on two visible features. Suppose you take a bearing on Fantastic Peak and get a reading of 38 degrees. You plot a line on the map, through Fantastic Peak, at 38 degrees. You know you must be somewhere on that bearing line, so you now have line position. You can also see Unsavory Spire. A bearing on the spire shows 130 degrees. You plot a second line on the map, through Unsavory Spire, at 130 degrees. The two bearing lines intersect, and that shows your point position.

When the area position is known and there is just one visible feature to take a bearing on, the compass cannot provide anything more than line position. That can be a big help, though. If the climbers are in the general vicinity of Fantastic River, then they can plot a bearing line from the one feature to the river; they then know they are near where the bearing line intersects the river. Perhaps from a study of the map, the climbers can then figure out just exactly where they are. They can also read the altimeter and see on the map where the bearing line intersects the contour line for that elevation. The closer an angle of intersection is to 90 degrees, the more accurate the point position will be.

Use every scrap of information at your disposal, but be sure your conclusions agree with common sense. If you took bearings on Fantastic Peak and Unsavory Spire and find that the two lines on the map intersect in the river, but you are on a high point of land, something is wrong. Try again. Try to take a bearing on another landmark, and plot it. If lines intersect at a map location with no similarity to the terrain where you are, there might be some magnetic anomaly in the rocks, or you may have an inaccurate map. And who knows? Maybe those peaks are not really Fantastic and Unsavory in the first place.

Orienting a Map

During a trip it sometimes helps to hold the map open so that north on the map is pointed in the actual direction of true north. This is known as orienting the map, a good way to gain a better feel of the relationship between the map and the countryside.

It is a simple process (fig. 5-16). Set 0 or 360 degrees at the index line of the compass, and place the compass on the map near its lower-left corner. Put the edge of the base plate along the left edge of the map, with the direction-of-travel line pointing toward north on the map. Then turn the map and compass together until the north-seeking end of the compass needle is aligned with the pointed end of the declination arrow of the compass. The map is now oriented to the scene before you. (Map orientation can give a general feel for the area, but cannot replace the more precise methods of orientation covered in the preceding paragraphs.)

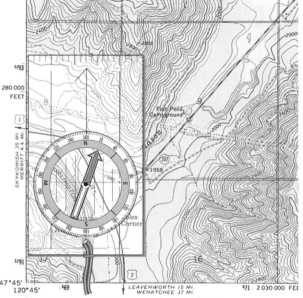

Fig. 5-16.

Using the compass to orient a map in western Washington State, declination 18 degrees east.

Orientation Using GPS

Suppose a climbing party wants to identify its point position on a map. Take out the GPS receiver, turn it on, and let it acquire a good, stable 3-D position. The receiver is probably reading latitude/longitude, the usual default coordinate system. (Most rescue and military agencies utilize the latitude/longitude coordinate system.) For mountaineering use, however, a much easier system to use is the Universal Transverse Mercator (UTM). The UTM system is a grid of north–south and east–west lines at intervals of 1,000 meters (3,281 feet or 0.62 mile). This is far more precise than the latitude/longitude system, because USGS maps only identify latitude and longitude coordinates every 2.5 minutes—approximately 2 to 3 miles (3 to 4 kilometers). Using the receiver's setup screen, the climbers should be able to change the coordinate system from latitude/longitude to UTM. They can then correlate the UTM numbers on the receiver's screen with the UTM grid on the map. Without using a scale or a ruler, climbers can usually eyeball their position to within about 100 meters (328 feet), which is often close enough to

get to within sight of an objective. If greater accuracy is desired, use the "meters" scale at the bottom of the map.

For example, suppose you are climbing Glacier Peak and clouds obscure all visibility. You reach a summit but are not sure whether it is Glacier Peak. You turn on your GPS receiver and let it acquire a position. The UTM numbers on the screen of your GPS receiver are as follows:

10 6 40 612E

53 29 491N

The top number is called the easting, which is the number of meters east of a reference point for your area. The "10" is the UTM zone number, which can be found in the lower-left corner of a USGS topographic map. The numbers "6 40 612E" indicate that your position is 640,612 meters east of a reference line for your area. In Figure 5-17, you can find the number "6 40 000mE" along the top edge of the map. This is the full easting (except for zone number). To the right of this is the number 6 41. This is a partial easting, with the "000" meters omitted. You can see that the number "10 6 40 612E" on the screen of the GPS receiver is approximately six-tenths of the way between 6 40 000 and 6 41 000. Your

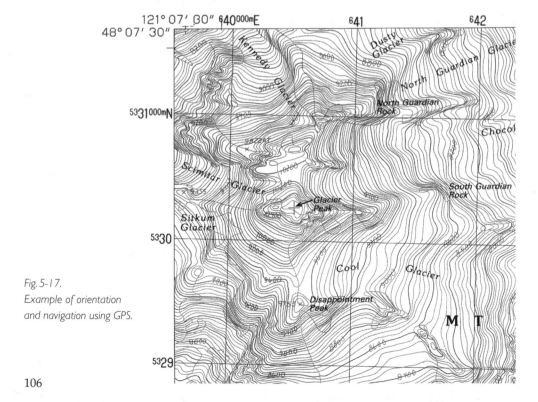

Fig. 5-17.
Example of orientation
and navigation using GPS.

east–west position is therefore about six-tenths of the way between the 6 40 000 and the 6 41 lines.

Along the left edge of the map is the number "53 31 000mN." This is the full northing, which indicates that this point is 5,331,000 meters north of the equator. Below this is a line labeled "53 30," and another labeled "53 29." These are partial northings, with the "000" meters omitted. The lower number displayed on the GPS receiver screen in this example is 53 29 491N. This is a horizontal line about halfway between 53 29 and 53 30. The point where the easting and northing lines intersect is your point position. Finding this point in Figure 5-17 shows that you are on Disappointment Peak.

NAVIGATION BY INSTRUMENT

Getting from here to there is usually just a matter of keeping an eye on the landscape and watching where you are going, helped by an occasional glance at the map. However, if your current objective is out of sight, take compass in hand, set a bearing, and follow the direction-of-travel line as it guides you to the goal. This is navigation by instrument.

Navigation by instrument is sometimes the only practical method for finding your way. It also serves as a supplement to other methods and as a way of verifying that you are on the right track. Again, use common sense and question a compass bearing that defies reason. (For example, is the declination arrow pointing the wrong way, sending you 180 degrees off course?)

Using Map and Compass

The most common situation requiring instrument navigation comes when the route is unclear because the topography is featureless or because landmarks are obscured by forest or fog. In this case, the climbers do know exactly where they are and where they want to go, and can identify on the map both their current position and their destination. Simply measure the bearing to the objective on the map and then follow that bearing.

Suppose you measure a bearing of 285 degrees on the map (fig. 5-18a). Read this bearing at the index line and leave it set there as is (fig. 5-18b). Then hold the

compass out in front of you as you rotate your body until the north-seeking end of the magnetic needle is aligned with the pointed end of the declination arrow. The direction-of-travel line now points to the objective (fig. 5-18c). Start walking in that direction.

Using Compass Alone

Navigators of air and ocean often travel by instrument alone; so can climbers. For example, if you are scrambling toward a pass and clouds begin to obscure it, take a quick compass bearing on the pass. Then follow the

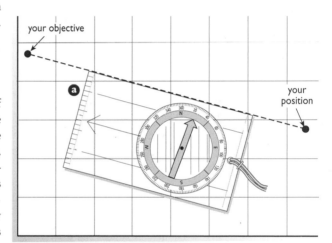

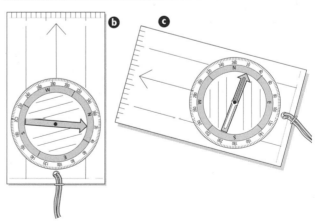

Fig. 5-18.

Navigation using the map and compass (on a and b, magnetic needle omitted for clarity): a, measuring the bearing on the map from your position to your destination; b, reading the bearing at the index line (leave the compass set); c, following the bearing.

bearing, compass in hand if desired. It is not even necessary to note the numerical bearing; just align the magnetic needle with the declination arrow and keep it aligned, and follow the direction-of-travel line.

Likewise, if you are heading into a valley where fog or forest will hide the mountain that is the goal, take a bearing on the peak before dropping into the valley (fig. 5-19). Then navigate by compass through the valley. This method becomes more reliable if several people travel together with compass in hand, checking one another's work.

Using Intermediate Objectives

The technique of intermediate objectives is handy for those frustrating times when you try to stay exactly on a compass bearing but keep getting diverted by obstructions such as cliffs, dense brush, or crevasses. Sight past the obstruction to a tree, a rock, or another object that is exactly on the bearing line between your position and the principal objective (fig. 5-20a). This is the intermediate objective. Now scramble over to the tree or rock by whatever route is easiest. When you get there, you can be confident that you are still on the correct route. The technique is useful even when there is no obstruction. Moving from intermediate objective to intermediate objective means it is possible put the compass away for those stretches, rather than having to check it every few steps.

Sometimes on snow, on glaciers, or in fog, there are no natural intermediate objectives, just an undifferentiated white landscape. A similar situation can occur in a forest, where all the trees may look the same. Then

another member of the party can serve as the intermediate objective (fig. 5-20b). Send that person out to near the limit of visibility or past the obstruction. Wave the party member left or right until the person is directly on the bearing line. That person can then improve the accuracy of the route by taking a back-bearing on you. (For a back-bearing, keep the same bearing set at the index line, but align the south-seeking end of the magnetic needle with the pointed end of the declination arrow.) The combination of a bearing and a back-bearing tends to counteract any compass error.

Using GPS

Suppose a climbing party can identify its desired destination on the map but cannot actually see it in the field. They can read the UTM position of the destination off the map and then enter it into the GPS receiver's memory as a waypoint.

Going back to the Glacier Peak example shown in Figure 5-17, above, suppose you wish to find the route to the summit of Glacier Peak. You can see that this point is about halfway between the eastings of 6 40 000 and 6 41 000, so you could estimate the easting as 10 6 40 500 (the zone number is 10 in this example). You can also see that the summit is about three-tenths of the way between the northings of 53 30 000 and 53 31 000, so you can estimate the full northing to be 53 30 300N. You can now enter these coordinates into the GPS receiver by simply turning it on and entering the UTM coordinates of 10 6 40 500E and 53 30 300N. You can then name the waypoint (for example, "GLPEAK") and save it.

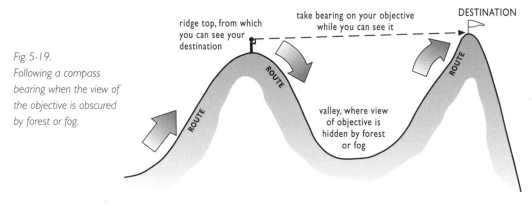

Fig. 5-19.
Following a compass bearing when the view of the objective is obscured by forest or fog.

ridge top, from which you can see your destination

take bearing on your objective while you can see it

DESTINATION

ROUTE

ROUTE

ROUTE

valley, where view of objective is hidden by forest or fog

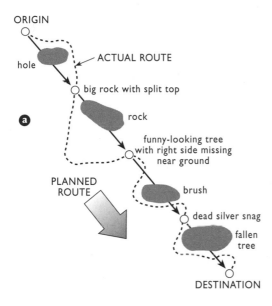

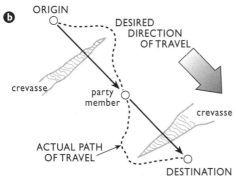

Fig. 5-20.
Use of intermediate objectives: a, in a forest; b, on a glacier.

Once you have entered your destination into the GPS receiver's memory, let it acquire a position. Then ask it to "Go To" the name of the new waypoint ("GLPEAK" in this example), and the receiver will tell you the distance and compass bearing from wherever you are to the summit of Glacier Peak. Then set this bearing on your magnetic compass, turn off the GPS receiver and put it away, and follow the compass bearing until you arrive at Glacier Peak.

What if you get off route due to a crevasse or other obstruction? After passing the obstruction, again turn on the GPS receiver, acquire a position, and again ask it to "Go To" the waypoint that is your destination. The receiver will then tell you the new distance and com-

pass bearing to your destination. Set the new bearing on your compass and follow it to your destination.

LOST

Why do people get lost? Some travel without a map because the route seems obvious. Some people trust their own instincts over the compass. Others do not bother with the map homework that can start them off with a good mental picture of the area. Some do not pay enough attention to the route on the way in to be able to find it on the way out. Some rely on the skill of their climbing partner, who may be in the process of getting them lost. Some do not take the time to think about where they are going because they are in a hurry. They miss junctions or wander off on game trails. They charge mindlessly ahead despite deteriorating weather and visibility, or fatigue.

Good navigators are never truly lost—but, having learned humility through years of experience, they always carry enough food, clothing, and bivouac gear to get them through a few days of temporary confusion.

What If Your Party Is Lost?

The first rule is to *stop*. Avoid the temptation to plunge hopefully on. Try to determine where the party is. If that does not work, figure out the last time when the party *did* know its exact location. If that spot is fairly close, within an hour or so, retrace your steps and get back on route. But if that spot is hours back, the party might instead decide to head toward the base line. If the party tires or darkness falls before finding its way out, bivouac for the night.

Groups of two or more rarely become dangerously lost, even if they have no wilderness experience. The real danger comes to an individual who is separated from the rest of the party. For this reason, always try to keep everyone together, and assign a rear guard to keep track of the stragglers.

What If You Are Lost Alone?

Again, the first rule is to *stop*. Look for other members of the party, shout, and listen for answering shouts. Blow your whistle. If the only answer is silence, sit down, regain your calm, and combat terror with reason.

Once you have calmed down, start doing the right things. Look at the map in an attempt to determine your location, and plan a route home in case you do not connect with the other climbers. Mark your location with a cairn or other objects, and then scout in all directions, each time returning to the marked position. Well before dark, prepare for the night by finding water and shelter. Go to an open area so that you can be seen from the air. Spread out some brightly colored clothing or other material to give searchers something to see. Staying busy will raise your spirits; try singing for something to do and to give searchers something to hear.

The odds are that you will be reunited with your group by morning. If not, fight panic. After a night alone, you may decide to hike out to a base-line feature picked out before the trip—a ridge, stream, or highway. If the terrain is too difficult for you to travel alone, it might be better to concentrate on letting yourself be found. It is easier for rescuers to find a lost climber who stays in one place in the open and shouts periodically than one who thrashes on in hysterical hope, one step ahead of the rescue party.

FINDING THE FREEDOM OF THE HILLS

The mountains await those who have learned the skills of orientation, navigation, and routefinding. In large part, navigation is the subject of this entire book because it is so essential to all off-trail adventure.

In medieval times, the greatest honor a visitor could receive was the rights of a citizen and the freedom of the city, sometimes even today symbolized by presenting a guest with the "keys to the city." For the modern alpine traveler, navigation is the key to wandering at will through valleys and meadows, up cliffs and over glaciers, earning the rights of a citizen in a magical land, a mountaineer with the freedom of the hills.

5

CHAPTER

Wilderness Travel

WILDERNESS ROUTEFINDING ■ APPROACH OBSERVATIONS ■
WALKING ■ TRAILFINDING ■ SHARING THE WILDERNESS WITH
ANIMALS ■ NEGOTIATING DIFFICULT TERRAIN ■ READY FOR THE WILDERNESS

**Climbing the mountain is one thing; getting from the trailhead to the mountain
is another. Wilderness travel is the art of getting there—along trails, around
brush, across rock, over snow, and across streams. If you learn the skills
of wilderness travel, you open the gateway to the summits.**

WILDERNESS ROUTEFINDING

Wilderness routefinding is the art of working out an efficient route from trailhead to summit that is within the abilities of the climbing party. Intuition and luck

play a role, but it takes skill and experience to surmount the hazards and hurdles between here and there. Aside from orientation and navigation skills described in Chapter 5, Navigation, climbers rely on their ability to interpret weather and snow conditions before and during the climb, to skillfully travel over different terrain, and to comprehend the clues that the wilderness offers as they go.

Gather Route Information

The more information you gather ahead of time, the better your judgment is later on. Take time to research the geology and climate of the area the party will be climbing in, especially if the party frequents the area. Each mountain range has its own peculiarities that affect routefinding. Mountaineers familiar with the Canadian Rockies, accustomed to broad valleys and open forests, will need to learn new rules to contend with the heavily vegetated, narrow canyons of British Columbia's Coast Range. The Pacific Northwest mountaineer used to deep snow at 4,000 feet (1,200 meters) in June will discover drastically different June conditions in the California Sierras.

Guidebooks offer detailed climb descriptions, including information on the climbing route, the estimated time necessary to complete it, elevation gain, distance, and so forth. But be aware that guidebooks become outdated; one bad winter can completely alter an approach. Make sure to have the latest edition, and take a look at two or three different guidebooks. Publications that cover other aspects of the area—its skiing, hiking, geology, and history—also will have something to offer as the party plans its trip.

Check online resources for weather forecasts, snow conditions, and Forest Service and Park Service information. Climbers who have made the trip can describe landmarks, hazards, and routefinding difficulties. Check climbers' message boards covering the area of the climb. (Exercise some judgment when using these types of computer sources, though; there is no accountability on the Internet, and it is difficult to gauge the credibility of those posting advice there.)

Useful details are packed into maps of all sorts: Forest Service maps, road maps, aerial maps, sketch maps, and topographic maps. For a trip into an area that is especially unfamiliar to you, more preparation is needed. This might include scouting into the area, observations from vantage points, or study of aerial photos. Forest Service or Park Service rangers can usually provide information on road and trail conditions. The most popular climbing areas may even have designated climbing rangers who are in the mountains regularly and can give informed and current reports.

Some of the best route details come out of conversations with locals. The person pouring coffee in the local cafe may be a veteran climber of the area. Ask about trails that do not appear on the maps, snow conditions, and the best places to ford streams.

Always consider the season and the amount of snowfall in a given year when preparing for a climb. Early in the season, avalanche danger may be high on steep slopes, especially if there is a heavy accumulation of snow from the winter before. Late in the season, or following a warm winter with low snowfall, a slope that is usually covered in snow may be exposed talus.

Finally, do not let outdated information ruin a trip. Check beforehand with the appropriate agencies about roads and trails, especially closures, and about climbing routes and regulations, permits, and camping requirements.

Learn from Experience

There is no substitute for firsthand experience. Climb with seasoned mountaineers, watch their techniques, and ask questions. The more familiar you are with the wilderness, the greater your freedom to find your own way.

APPROACH OBSERVATIONS

Climb with your eyes. Continually study the mountain for climbing routes. A distant view can reveal patterns of ridges, cliffs, snowfields, and glaciers, as well as the degree of incline. At closer range, details of fault lines, bands of cliffs, and crevasse fields appear. Look for clues of routes: ridges with lower incline than the faces they divide; cracks, ledges, and chimneys leading up or across the faces; snowfields or glaciers offering easy or predictable pitches. Look for climbable sections and link them together. With experience comes a good eye for what you know you can climb.

If the approach skirts the base of the mountain, try to view it from various perspectives. Even moderate slopes can appear steep when you look at them head on. A system of ledges indistinguishable against

6

background cliffs may show clearly from another angle or as shadows cross the mountain.

The presence of snow sometimes promises a modest angle and easy climbing, because snow does not last long on slopes of greater than 50 degrees. Snow and shrubs that appear on distant rock faces often turn out to be "sidewalks" with smaller ledges between. However, snow can be deceptive. What appear to be snowfields high on the mountain may be ice. Deep, high-angle couloirs often retain snow or ice year-round, especially when shaded.

Watch for Hazards

Stay alert to climbing hazards. Study snowfields and icefalls for avalanche danger and cliffs for signs of possible rockfall. Snowfields reveal recent rockfall by the appearance of dirty snow or rock-filled craters. If the route goes through avalanche and rockfall territory, travel in the cold hours of night or very early morning, before the sun melts the ice that bonds precariously perched boulders and ice towers. Move through such places quickly. Take rest breaks before or after danger zones, and when you enter them, try not to get caught behind slower parties. If possible, avoid these areas in heavy rain. Also watch for changing weather conditions (see Chapter 27, Mountain Weather).

Keep evaluating hazards and looking for continuous routes. If the route begins to look questionable, search for alternatives and make decisions as early as possible.

Think About the Return

Always consider the descent while making the approach. What is easy going up is not necessarily easy going down, nor is it easy to find. Look back frequently, take notes, take GPS and altimeter readings, and, if necessary, mark the route. (For additional information, see Chapter 5, Navigation, and Chapter 7, Leave No Trace.)

The approach is also a time for looking ahead to the end of the day. Consider where the party has to be by dark, and whether it will be safe to travel by headlamp if necessary. Keep an eye out for emergency campsites, water supplies, and anything else that might make the return trip easier and safer.

WALKING

Reaching the summit often involves more walking than climbing. Walking skill is as important as any other that climbers learn.

Before hitting the trail, stretch your legs, hips, back, and shoulders. Drink some water. Consider taping or putting Moleskin on areas prone to blisters. Take time to get a good fit of your pack and boots to avoid aches and pains—and frequent stops—later on.

Prepare for stops before starting. Use your pack's outside pockets for items that will be needed repeatedly throughout the day, such as snacks, water, jacket, hat, gloves, gaiters, sun/glacier glasses, and headlamp. Not only will it be easy for you to reach these items, but other members of the party can also reach them, without you needing to remove your pack or even reduce the pace. Strap your ice ax and trekking poles to the outside of your pack so they are readily available for rough terrain. The ice ax will be extremely useful, even before snow line.

Pace

Setting the right pace from the start ensures a happier, stronger day of climbing. The most common mistake is walking too fast, perhaps out of concern for the long miles ahead or from a desire to perform well with companions. Why get worn out on the first mile of a 10-mile (16-kilometer) approach if the whole day is available? You are going too fast if you cannot sustain your pace hour after hour, or if you cannot converse without losing your breath. Take your time and enjoy yourself.

The other mistake is walking too slowly. This only prolongs the hike and leaves less time to negotiate the more technical portions of the trip. If you are walking slowly due to fatigue, remember that the body has considerable reserves. Muscles may ache but still have 10 miles left in them. A degree of discomfort is inevitable; walking too fast or too slow only creates additional fatigue.

At the start, walk slowly to allow your body to warm up. Before you start to sweat, take a break and remove some clothing. Increase the pace, and accept the hurt as your body works harder to experience its second wind. Physiologically, your heartbeat and circulation increase, and muscles loosen. As endorphins kick in and the feelings of physical stress subside, you feel strong and happy.

Vary the pace depending on the trail. Plod slowly and methodically up steep hills. As the grade lessens, pick up the tempo. Eventually you will find a natural pace that adapts to pack weight, trail steepness, weather, and other conditions.

The pace will inevitably slow late in the day as fatigue sets in. Adrenaline may fuel short bursts of exertion, but there is no "third wind."

The Rest Step

Slow and steady gains the summit. On steep slopes, in snow, and at high altitudes, the rest step controls your pace and reduces fatigue. Use this technique instead of frequent rest stops whenever legs or lungs need to recuperate. The rest step is simple but subtle; practice it.

The essence of the technique is to end every step with a momentary but complete stop, giving your leg muscles a rest. Swing one foot forward for the next step. Stand upright and exhale while letting your rear leg support your entire body weight (fig. 6-1a). Straighten your rear leg so that you are supported by bone, not

muscle. Feel the weight sink into your bones and foot. Now completely relax and soften the muscles of your forward leg, especially the thigh. This momentary rest, no matter how brief, refreshes the muscle. Then take a breath and swing your rear foot forward for the next step (fig. 6-1b), and repeat the rest step for your other leg (fig. 6-1c).

Synchronize breathing with leg movements. Typically, take a new breath with each step. Inhale and take a step up; exhale while pausing and letting your front leg rest as your rear leg supports your weight. Keep repeating the sequence. Many experienced climbers find a tune they run over in their head to keep a comfortable rhythm. The number of breaths per step depends on the difficulty of the work and your level of fatigue. At high altitudes, climbers sometimes take three or four deep breaths before each step up.

The rest step requires patience. The monotony of the pace can undermine morale, especially when you are following another climber up a snowfield and there is no routefinding or step-kicking to occupy your thoughts. Play an upbeat tune in your head. Trust the technique to chew up the miles, even when the summit seems to recede.

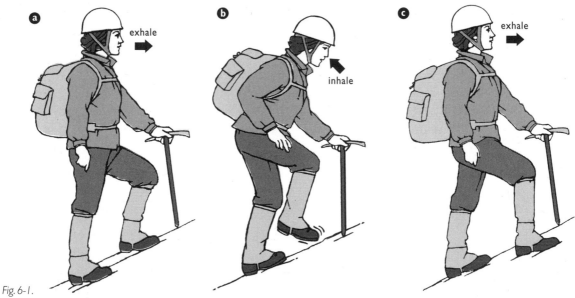

Fig. 6-1.
The rest step: a, stand with entire body weight on right leg and exhale, completely relaxing left leg; b, inhale and step forward with right leg, shifting weight to left leg; c, place entire body weight on left leg and exhale, completely relaxing right leg.

Rests

Rests allow your body to recover from strenuous activity and to maintain an efficient pace. Take rests only when necessary; otherwise, keep moving. Numerous unnecessary stops can turn a 10-hour day into a 15-hour day, affecting group morale, or even the team's chance of reaching a summit.

During the first half hour, stop to allow the group to readjust bootlaces and pack straps, and add or take off layers of clothing.

Take short breathers—say, once every 1 to 1½ hours—during the early part of the day, while bodies are fresh. Rest in a standing or semi-reclining position, leaning against a tree or hillside to remove pack weight from your shoulders. Take deep breaths, and have a bite to eat and something to drink. Stay hydrated—always drink at every stop.

Remember to declare regular party separations (toilet stops), especially out of courtesy to the person who may be too shy to express the need. However, in order to minimize your impact on the mountains, your first stop should be at the last available restroom facility found at or before the trailhead.

Later in the day, fatigue may demand more complete relaxation, and the party can take a full rest every 2 hours or so. Look for a place with advantages, such as water, convenient slopes for unslinging packs, and a view. Stretch muscles and put on additional clothing to avoid stiffness and chilling. Remove extra clothing before starting out again in order to prevent another stop minutes down the trail.

Downhill

Walking downhill is a mixed blessing. The pace quickens without increasing fatigue. However, climbers may feel pain long after the day is over. When you walk downhill, your body and pack weight drop abruptly on your legs, knees, and feet. Toes jam forward. Jolts travel up your spine and jar your entire body.

Avoid a host of injuries—including blisters, knee cartilage damage, sore toes, blackened nails, headaches, and back pain—just by using a few of the following tricks:

- Trim toenails close before starting out.
- Tighten laces—especially on the upper part of the boot—to reduce movement inside the boot and avoid jamming toes.
- Bend the knees with each step to cushion the shock.
- Place each foot lightly, as if it was already sore.
- Use ski/trekking poles to reduce the load on the knees and to provide additional stability.
- Maintain a measured pace that is slower than the one urged by gravity.
- Use an ice ax for balance or a brake when necessary. The ice ax self-arrest is not just for snow. It is also helpful in steep meadow, forest, and heather. (To learn the technique of self-arrest, see Chapter 16, Snow Travel and Climbing.)

Sidehill

The ups and downs of climbing are far preferable to the torments of sidehilling (traversing). Walking across the side of a slope twists your ankles, contorts your hips, and destroys balance. If possible, abandon a sidehill and drop down into a brush-free valley or go up onto a rounded ridge. If traversing is unavoidable, look for rocks, animal trails, and the ground just above clumps of grass or heather to provide flat spots of relief. Switchback often to avoid ankle strain.

TRAILFINDING

For a wilderness traveler, a trail is any visible route, no matter how ragged, that efficiently gets the party where they want to go. The goal is to find the easiest route using the tools at hand: awareness of the terrain, navigational skills, weather conditions, and tips from guidebooks and experts.

Even in popular areas with heavy foot traffic and signage, keep alert to find and stay on the trail. Missing a turnoff is easy when a sign is gone or where logging, erosion, or rockfall obliterates the trail. On an established forest trail in deep snow, saw-cut log ends peeking through may be the only indication of a trail's location.

Old blazes cut in tree trunks, or ribbon tied to branches, often mark the trail through a forest. Rock cairns may show the way above timberline. These pointers may be unreliable. A tiny cairn or a wisp of ribbon may indicate nothing more than a lost climber,

HIKING WITH THE GROUP

Walking with others involves certain considerations that help make travel more efficient and enjoyable.

- Set a pace that makes good time but does not burn out slower climbers. Adjust the party's pace so that slower climbers do not fall far behind. Do not allow anyone to travel alone, either last or first. Give the last person time to catch up with the party at rest stops—and time to rest once that person gets there.
- Try putting the slowest person in front to set the pace. This helps keep the group together, and may motivate a slow hiker to set a faster pace than usual.
- Redistribute group gear to people who are full of energy.
- Stay three to five paces behind the person ahead. Give the climber—as well as that person's ice ax—some space.
- Stay close to the group. Do not lose contact with other hikers or make them continually wait for you.
- When grabbing branches, mind the person behind you. Before releasing branches, look back and call out "Branch."
- When you stop, step aside.
- Ask permission to pass, and pick a good spot to do so.
- When meeting an oncoming party, be courteous. Traditionally, the party heading downhill steps aside to let the ascending climbers continue upward without breaking pace. However, in steep terrain or if the descending party is larger, the climbers moving uphill may step aside and take a few breaths. When meeting pack animals, move aside and stand on the downhill side of the trail; speak quietly and make no sudden movements. People on mountain bikes should always yield to those on foot.
- During long approaches and descents where routefinding is not a concern, select gathering points for the party. This allows party members to find their natural pace within smaller groups. Regroup at trail junctions and difficult stream crossings. Ask the most experienced members to take front and rear positions.
- Be cheerful and helpful. Be someone you would want to hike with.

a route to an alternate destination, or an old route since obstructed by rockfall.

The trick is to stay on the trail until the inevitable moment it disappears, or until it becomes necessary to head off trail in order to go in the right direction. Choose a course that a trail would follow if there were a trail. Trail builders look for the easiest way to go. Do as they do.

SHARING THE WILDERNESS WITH ANIMALS

Alpine wildlife is fascinating and often charming, but the birds and animals should be enjoyed from a distance and not disturbed. When you encounter animals on the route, move slowly and allow them plenty of time to drift away. Try to pass on their downhill side; typically they head uphill to escape. Give them plenty of elbow room. An animal rushing from a close encounter with a human is in danger of stress or injury; too many of these encounters, and it may feel forced to abandon its home grounds for poorer terrain.

Bears

In bear country, stay out of the "personal space" of bears. Try not to surprise them. Whenever possible, go around brushy ravines with poor visibility rather than through them, even if it makes the route considerably longer. Make plenty of noise in unavoidable, lower-visibility areas to warn animals of your approach.

If the climbing party surprises a bear or cougar, *do not turn and run*. Running away may elicit a chase-the-prey response in the large predator, and bears are surprisingly fast runners. Instead, stand your ground, face the animal, talk, and slowly edge away at a walk while still facing the animal. (See Appendix C, Supplementary Reading, for specific information about handling animal encounters.)

NEGOTIATING DIFFICULT TERRAIN

The biggest barriers on the way to a mountaintop often appear before snow line.

Brush

Brush thrives in young forests or in wet, low-altitude, subalpine areas that have few trees. A river that frequently changes course prevents large-tree growth and permits brush to thrive. In gullies swept by winter avalanches, the shrubs simply bend undamaged under the snow and flourish in spring and summer. The second-growth timber that springs up after a fire, windstorm, or logging is at its worst for brush when the young timber is about 20 feet (6 meters) high.

Brush can be a backcountry horror, making for difficult, dangerous travel. Downward-slanting vine maple and alder are slippery. Brush obscures the peril of cliffs, boulders, and ravines. Brush snares ropes and ice-ax picks. The best policy is to avoid brush. Try the following techniques for avoiding brush:

- Use trails as much as possible. Five miles (8 kilometers) of trail may be less work and take less time than 1 mile (1.6 kilometers) of brush.
- Travel when snow covers brush. Some valleys are easy going in the spring when it is possible to walk on snow, but they are almost impossible in summer when it is necessary to burrow through the brush.
- Avoid avalanche tracks. Avalanches are less frequent on southern or western slopes in the Northern Hemisphere. When you are climbing a valley wall, stay in the trees between avalanche tracks.
- Aim for the big trees, where brush is thinner. Mature forests block sunlight and stifle brush growth.
- Travel on talus, scree, or snow remnants, rather than in adjacent thickets.
- Look for game trails. Animals generally follow the path of least resistance. Take care not to startle large animals in heavy brush.

- Travel on ridges and ridge spurs. They may be dry and brushless, whereas creek bottoms and valley floors are often choked with vegetation.
- Scout both sides of a stream for the route with the least amount of bushwhacking.
- Consider going into the stream channel if the route parallels a stream. Wading may be necessary, but the streambed can be an easier tunnel through the brush. Dry streambeds are often ideal. Take care in deep canyons, where waterfalls and fallen trees interrupt a stream.
- Take a high route. Climb directly to timberline or a ridge top.
- Go up to the base of side bluffs. There is often an open, flattened corridor next to the rock.

Talus and Scree

Mountain peaks constantly crumble, dropping rock fragments that pile up below as talus and scree. Most of the rubble pours from gullies and spreads out in alluvial fans that often merge into one another, forming a broad band of broken rock between valley greenery and the peaks. These fans can alternate in vertical strips with forest. Talus consists of the larger fragments, usually big enough to step on individually. Scree is smaller—from the size of coarse sand up to a couple of inches across—and may flow a bit around your feet when you step on it.

Talus slopes build gradually over the ages. On the oldest slopes, soil fills the spaces between the rocks, locking them together to create smooth pathways. Talus can be loose on volcanoes and younger mountains, where vegetation has not filled in the spaces. Even large rocks can roll. Try for a route where the rock is lichen-

---

MINIMIZE BRUSH HASSLES

When a skirmish with brush is inevitable, here are some tips to deal with it:
- Choose the shortest route across the brushy area.
- Look for animal trails through the brush.
- Use fallen trees with long, straight trunks as elevated walkways.
- Push and pull the bushes apart, sometimes by stepping on lower limbs and lifting and clinging to higher ones to make a passageway.
- Use hardy shrubs as handholds on steep terrain.

covered, which indicates that the rock has remained in place for a long time.

Talus and scree slopes can either help or hinder a climber. Most offer handy, brush-free pathways to the mountains. Some are loose and dangerous, with sharp-edged rock that can cause injury.

Move nimbly on talus, ready to leap away if a rock shifts underfoot. Use your eyes and plan four or five steps ahead. Take care on wet talus.

Disturbing one key stone on a glacial moraine or a talus slope can set off a rock avalanche. Travel outside the fall line of climbers above and below you. If you are in a narrow gully where it is not possible to travel outside the fall line, tread gently and be ready to shout "Rock! Rock!" if a stone dislodges. Keep the party close together so a rock set off by one climber cannot gain dangerous momentum before reaching others. Consider permitting just one climber, or small groups keeping closely together, to move at a time while the rest remain in protected spots.

Facing the exposure while descending a talus or scree slope can be intimidating. Climbers may hesitate or move slowly. This can be dangerous. Move in short, quick steps, and know where the next step is, to be ready to quickly get off a moving rock and avoid injury. Trekking poles or an ice ax are helpful, as long as they are always in front of you.

Loose scree can make the uphill going a slow-motion torment, with each step lost as your foot settles in. Stepping on or just above a larger rock in scree can pry or wedge it out. However, descents can be fun. It may be possible to move down the scree in a sliding stride something like cross-country skiing or plunge-stepping down snow. Ice axes are helpful; the technique on scree is similar to that on snow. (See Chapter 16, Snow Travel and Climbing.) Nonetheless, be aware that scree can sometimes consist of only a thin, ball bearing–size cover over large rocks. If there is vegetation on the slope, avoid setting off scree slides that can damage the plants.

Although riding a scree slope can be fun, bits of rock can work their way into your boots and cause discomfort when you reach talus or a downward trail. Wear gaiters, even in the summer, just for scree.

Snow

Snow can be a blessing in wilderness travel, especially if climbers study weather and snow conditions before the climb. Many peaks are best climbed early in the season because consolidated snow covers talus, brush, and logging slash. Snow bridges provide easy access over streams. However, in a different season or with less-than-ideal snow conditions, snow can be a curse. Trails are lost under snow or are washed out by avalanche or heavy thaw. Thin snow is unstable. And, given the time of day, the pace, and changing weather conditions, a party may encounter different snow conditions on the approach, the climb, and the descent.

If there is snow on the approach, watch for visible terrain features, because they may indicate thin or melting snow. The snow next to logs and boulders often covers holes and soft spots called moats, which occur when the snow partially melts away from the wood and the rock. A moat is common around smaller trees where lower limbs keep the snow from filling in. Probe with an ice ax to avoid likely trouble spots, step wide off logs and rocks, and stay away from treetops poking above the snow. If the snow is thin on a talus slope, there can be large voids under the snow that are easy to punch through. Go slow on talus on the return trip if the snow is thin.

Streams will melt the underside of a snow bridge until it can no longer support your weight. To guard against a dunking, watch for depressions in the snow and variations in color or texture, and listen for sounds of running water. Water emerging at the foot of a snowfield indicates the existence, and perhaps the size, of a cavity beneath the snow. Probe for thin spots with your ice ax.

With experience, you will recognize both the advantages and dangers of snow and learn to use the medium to make wilderness travel easier and more enjoyable. See "Routefinding on Snow" in Chapter 16, Snow Travel and Climbing, and Chapter 26, The Cycle of Snow, for more information.

Streams

When your objective lies on the far side of a sizable river, crossing it is a major factor in route selection. Crossings can consume huge amounts of time and energy, and can be the most dangerous part of the trip.

Finding the Crossing

Try to get a distant, overall view of the river and scope out crossing possibilities. This can be more useful than a hundred close looks from the riverbank. When a distant view is impossible or unhelpful, the party may be stuck with either thrashing through the river-bottom brush looking for a way across or traversing the slopes high above the river in hopes of a sure crossing.

The surrounding landscape indicates the options. In a deep forest, there is a good chance of finding easy passage on a large log or logjam, even over wide rivers. Higher in the mountains, foot logs are harder to come by, especially if the river frequently changes course and prevents the growth of large trees near its channel.

If it is necessary to wade across, find the widest part of the river. The narrows may be the shortest way, but they are also the deepest, swiftest, and most dangerous. If snowmelt feeds a river, its flow is at a minimum in the early morning. Sometimes a party may camp overnight to take advantage of this morning low water.

Making the Crossing

Unfasten the hip belt and sternum straps of your pack before you try any stream crossing that may require swimming in case of a fall. It is necessary to be able to remove your pack in a hurry.

Logs: A foot log is a great way across. If the log is thin, slippery, or steeply inclined, use an ice ax, a stick, crampons, or a tightly stretched hand line (see below) to help with balance, traction, and support. Sit down and scoot across if that helps.

Boulder-hopping: Boulders offer another way across. Before you cross, mentally rehearse the entire sequence of leaps. Safety lies in smooth and steady progress over stones that may be too slippery and unsteady for you to stop for more than an instant. Use an ice ax or trekking pole for additional balance.

Wading: If you are wading, try to keep your gear dry. If the water is placid and the stones rounded, put your boots in your pack while you wade across. In tougher conditions, wear your boots, but put your socks and insoles in the pack; on the far side, drain your boots and replace the dry insoles and socks. In deeper crossings, consider removing your pants or other clothing. Loose clothing increases the drag from the water, but it also reduces chilling and may permit a longer crossing.

If you are trying to cross where the water is deep but not swift, cross with the least force against your body by angling downstream at about the same speed as the current. However, the best way to cross is to face upstream, lean into the current, and stab an ice ax or stout pole upstream for a third point of support. Your leading foot probes for solid placement on the shifting riverbottom, your following foot advances, and you thrust the ax or pole into a new position.

Swift water is easy to underestimate. With one false step, you can be pushed under and dashed against rocks and logs, or sent bouncing along in white water. Water is dangerous whenever it boils above your knee. A swift stream flowing only shin-deep can boil up against your knees. Knee-deep water may boil above your waist and give a disconcerting sensation of buoyancy. Frothy water, containing a great deal of air, is wet enough to drown in but may not be dense enough to float the human body. Streams fed by glaciers present an added difficulty because their bottoms are hidden by milky water from glacier-milled rock flour.

Team-crossing: Two or more travelers can cross together, taking turns securing each other as one person moves to a solid new stance. Team-crossing with a pole is another method. Team members enter the water, each grasping the pole, which is parallel to the flow of the stream. The upstream member breaks the force of the current. Anyone who slips hangs onto the pole while the others keep the pole steady.

Hand lines: A hand line for small streams can be helpful. Angle the line downstream so that if anyone loses their footing, they will be swept to shore. If all that is available is a nylon climbing rope, consider the rope stretch. Always use appropriate anchors (see Chapter 10, Belaying).

Using ropes for stream crossings in deep, swift water can be hazardous. If someone is belayed across the river, there is a possibility that the crossing person can be held by the belay but trapped under the water. Consider belaying the pack, however. If anyone falls, they can shed their pack and it will not get swept away.

Falling In

If you are swept downstream by a swift current, the safest position is on your back with your feet pointed downstream, backstroking to steer. This position vastly improves your chances for survival with minimal injuries. Be alert. If you approach a "strainer" (small dam or collection of debris), switch quickly to normal headfirst swimming. Swim furiously to stay high in the water and get on top of the debris. The strainer may be your route ashore.

If a fall off a log into the water seems imminent, try to fall off on the downstream side to avoid getting swept under the log.

If a member of the party falls in, those on shore can try to reach out with a pole, ice ax, or branch. It may be possible to throw out a floating object, such as an inflated water bag. Make a realistic evaluation of the danger to yourself before you decide to go into the stream to attempt a hands-on rescue.

READY FOR THE WILDERNESS

Traveling in the wilderness is like wandering in a foreign country. The unfamiliarity of a place is the attraction, yet it also limits the journey. Preparation is essential, and nothing rivals the knowledge gained from personal experience.

Immerse yourself in the wilderness again and again; study it like a new language. Use all five senses to master the "vocabulary" of the terrain. Some of your best moments will come when you discover your ability to respond well to what it asks of you.

With fluency comes the freedom to roam, and with that freedom comes responsibility. The next chapter discusses ways to keep the wild places wild for those who travel after us, so they too can experience the exhilaration of discovery.

Leave No Trace

PLANNING ACHIEVES MORE THAN A SUMMIT ■ TRAVEL AND CAMP ON DURABLE SURFACES ■ USE STOVES, NOT CAMPFIRES ■ DISPOSE OF WASTE PROPERLY ■ CLEANING UP ■ DO NOT DISTURB ■ RESPECTING THE FREEDOM OF THE HILLS

Mountaineers seek the uncharted way, the trail less traveled, and a summit to stand on. We recognize that the wilderness we seek is a resource that we must protect.

Most mountaineers have seen the consequences of overuse, carelessness, and thoughtlessness in the backcountry. Today's mountaineers need to be conscientious visitors who have developed the requisite knowledge and skills to preserve and protect the fragile natural resources they explore. Climbers not only set the example for appropriate wilderness behavior, but are frequently the educators who help other backcountry users accept individual responsibility.

Over the past forty years, there has been an ethical

121

evolution in climbing, beginning with the first chocks being used to replace rock-deforming pitons. Early educational efforts and publications emphasized basic messages, such as "leave only footprints" and "pack it in/pack it out." Through experience and research, mountaineers have expanded the skills and techniques that are applied in the backcountry so that all visitors can truly leave no trace of their visit.

In 1991, the National Outdoor Leadership School (NOLS) and the U.S. Forest Service partnered to develop cohesive guidelines regarding minimum-impact techniques; the Leave No Trace principles were born, consolidating a variety of tread-lightly messages from the previous twenty years. In 1994, Leave No Trace, Inc., was established as a nonprofit educational program with support from land management agencies, outdoor manufacturers and retailers, and NOLS and a variety of other outdoor education organizations.

This chapter's Leave No Trace guidelines can be applied to and adapted for any outdoor pursuit, location, and circumstance. They are as basic and essential to mountaineering as technical climbing skills, first aid, and navigation. Like any skill, Leave No Trace techniques do take practice, but with each trip, all mountaineers can enhance their knowledge and refine their skills so that their wilderness visits are neither seen nor felt by others.

PLANNING ACHIEVES MORE THAN A SUMMIT

If there is one common objective among backcountry visitors, it is to find solitude—a sense that you are alone—perhaps experiencing the perceived joy of being the first, even when this is not the case. This is a challenging objective, especially when you are visiting a popular destination. But visitors can achieve their small, personal space if they plan. If climbers cannot actually be alone, they can at least create the sense of being first or being alone in the wilderness, for themselves and others.

Be Realistic and Responsible

Start by defining the expectations and capabilities of the group. A party that stretches itself to the limit, and

perhaps gets into trouble, will no longer care about the principles of Leave No Trace. If rescuers must be called, safety comes first, regardless of environmental damage. Realistic planning can often prevent desperate situations in the first place.

Discuss trip expectations with party members so that everyone agrees to employ Leave No Trace techniques. Help them understand what that means for the area the group plans to visit.

If the party is new to Leave No Trace principles, use established trails and campsites at first. The group might encounter more people, but everyone gains valuable experience. Use hardened trails until the Leave No Trace techniques are mastered. Be willing to modify plans or the route if fragile conditions or sensitive circumstances are discovered. Books frequently direct people to the most popular summits, vistas, and crags. Consider the less-popular destinations, where visitor impacts can be spread out and visitors can find more solitude and wildlife.

Think Small

Limit the size of the group. Outdoor trips are often social events, but keeping groups smaller enhances the sense of solitude for the party and other visitors. If local land managers have a party size limit, consider making your group even smaller. Ask yourself, "What is the minimum group needed for safety?"

Consider Conditions

A little research goes a long way. Route descriptions from fellow climbers are a start, but dig deeper. Contact the land management agency responsible for the area you plan to visit so that the group can make decisions about when and where to go and the Leave No Trace techniques that should be applied. Inquire about:
- Permits and camping regulations
- Frequency of use
- Hiking or climbing difficulties or recommendations
- Waste disposal preferences—are backcountry outhouses or toilets available, or should the group pack out its wastes?
- Fragile or sensitive areas, including flora, fauna, or geology
- Soil conditions and moisture level

GEARING UP TO LEAVE NO TRACE

- Thoughtful selection of clothing and equipment is an important part of Leave No Trace. Stoves and adequate clothing eliminate the need for fires.
- A large, collapsible water container reduces the number of trips to water sources.
- A plastic scrubber eliminates the need to use sand or grass to clean cooking utensils.
- A small, lightweight trowel aids proper waste disposal.
- Waterproof footwear and gaiters make it possible to stay on the trail even where it is wet and muddy.
- Earth tones, instead of "hot" colors, for tents, packs, and clothing reduce the sense of overcrowding.
- Heavy, lug-soled boots are hard on soil and vegetation. Carry a pair of sandals or lightweight, soft-soled shoes to wear around camp.
- Use a sleeping pad. Cutting tree boughs for bedding is no longer acceptable.

When it is practical, schedule the trip when conditions will cause less impact, perhaps selecting a weekday rather than a weekend for popular destinations.

Eliminate Excess Packaging

The more packaging you carry, the greater the chance that something will be lost in the backcountry, such as that small, unnecessary wrapper around a favorite candy. Eliminate unnecessary food packages, wraps, and covers. This not only reduces the potential for littering, but also saves weight and space. Repackage food in reusable containers and resealable bags. Plan meals so you take only the amount of food necessary, except for emergency rations. Leftovers should be eaten later or carried out, not buried or burned.

TRAVEL AND CAMP ON DURABLE SURFACES

Whenever possible, stay on established trails and use established campsites. As climbers move off trail into pristine environments, Leave No Trace knowledge and skills become even more critical.

Trails are wilderness highways. Like the roads people drive on, trails that are designed properly can withstand high foot traffic, channel users through fragile areas, and prevent water flow and soil erosion. Trailside signs (fig. 7-1) urge hikers to stay on trails.

Trail Use

- Always use and stay on trails where they exist.
- Stay within the established tread, even if it is muddy

or rutted, to protect trailside vegetation and prevent unnecessary widening of trails. This usually means hiking in single file.
- Never cut switchbacks—doing so does not save a significant amount of time, but it does take more

Fig. 7-1.
Actual trailside sign at Mount Rainier National Park.

energy, increase chance of injury, kill plant roots, and create unsightly, eroded gullies.

- Travel on snow when possible. Take extra care when traveling through the fragile transition zone between dirt and snow where the soil is saturated with water, especially during spring and late fall.
- Keep a plastic bag in a pocket and pick up scraps of litter left by others. Carry a larger garbage bag to haul out larger materials, especially on the trip back out.
- Perform light and safe trail maintenance when storm debris or small rocks are encountered.
- Select resilient areas for rest breaks. Move off and away from the trail to remain unobtrusive to fellow hikers. If this is not possible due to fragile or dense vegetation, find a wide spot in the trail.
- Standard trail etiquette suggests stepping off the trail to yield to hikers coming uphill. Instead, take the initiative and set a better example by finding a durable spot and stepping aside, whether you are traveling up- or downhill. Otherwise, many hikers encountered will attempt to keep moving, thereby stepping off the trail and trampling the vegetation.
- Take care along streambanks to avoid erosion.

Off Trail

- Keep a slow enough pace to be aware of your surroundings and to plan a low-impact route.
- Unlike trail travel, for off-trail travel, spread the party out, each member taking a separate path, especially in fragile meadows. The exception is where there is an established climbers trail to use.
- Look for durable surfaces such as bare ground (patches between vegetation, wildlife trails), rock (bedrock, talus, scree, or stream gravel), and sedge grasses. Avoid tromping on woody or herbaceous vegetation, such as heather and partridge foot.
- During spring and late fall, take extra care in areas in transition between dirt and snow where the soil is water saturated.
- Leave trailless areas free of cairns and flagging unless those markers are already there. Never carve trees. Let the next party have its own routefinding adventure. If you need to mark the route, remove the markers on the way back down.

Campsites

Look for previously used, hardened sites. Resist the temptation to use a less-disturbed site because it has a better view or is closer to a water source. (See Table 7-1 for guidelines in choosing campsites.)

If a pristine site is all that is available, stay only a night or two and then find another location. If you have a choice between a pristine spot and a new, slightly impacted campsite, the better choice could be the pristine site if you carefully apply Leave No Trace guidelines. Although this may be contrary to first instinct, it allows a slightly impacted area to recover from use. In pristine sites, observe these recommendations:

- Avoid grouping tents together.
- A pristine area calls for dispersed toilet sites and varied walkways so that no single path gets so trampled that the vegetation cannot recover.
- Find a spot with a slight natural slope so that water will not pool beneath your tent and tempt you to dig a trench.
- Never level a site, remove leaves and needles, or dig trenches.

When selecting a campsite, apply the 200-foot rule (about seventy-five paces): Camp at least 200 feet (60 meters) away from water, trails, and people. Land managers may allow use of already hardened sites even though they are close to water. If so, go ahead and use them, but do not create a new site in the same vicinity. In a pristine area, enhance the sense of solitude for yourself and others by choosing an out-of-the-way site or one with good natural screening.

Try to use established mountaineering bivy sites or high camps. Moving alpine rocks may kill fragile plants that take many years to grow. Build new sites or improve existing ones only when absolutely necessary. Then select rocks that disturb the least possible amount of vegetation.

Keep track of gear and maintain a tidy camp so that equipment and food are not lost or forgotten. Leave the site in better condition than you found it. Pristine sites require a little extra effort; cover used areas with native materials, brushing out footprints and fluffing up matted grass.

TABLE 7-1. WILDERNESS CAMPSITE OPTIONS

Best to Worst	Campsite Option	Reasons to Select or Not Select This Campsite
1	Established, fully impacted campsite	A hardened site cannot be impacted further, as long as it is not enlarged or manipulated in any way. Use existing rocks and logs instead of moving more in.
2	Snow	Snow will melt and show no sign of use, but avoid the area if vegetation or soil is showing. Before leaving, break down snow structures and make the site as natural-looking as possible.
3	Rock slab	Solid rock resists most damaging effects except fire scars.
4	Sand, dirt, or gravelly flat	Most signs of human presence can be swept away.
5	Duff in deep forest	Duff and other decaying matter are only lightly impacted by campers' presence.
6	Grass-covered meadow	A meadow covered by tents for a week can have its entire growing season wiped out. Move a long-term camp every few days to reduce the harm to any one spot. The higher the meadow, the more sensitive it is to trampling.
7	Plant-covered meadow above timberline	Alpine plants grow very slowly, and woody plants are more sensitive to impact than grasses. Heather, for example, has only a couple of months to bloom, seed, and add a fraction of an inch of growth for the year. Alpine plants could take many years to recover from the damage of a brief encampment.
8	Waterfront along lakes and streams	Waterside plant life is delicate and water pollution is a growing problem as more people head into the backcountry.

USE STOVES, NOT CAMPFIRES

Today's climbers use lightweight stoves rather than campfires. Stoves do not consume wild materials and do not fill the mountain air with smoke. In addition, they are faster, cleaner, and more convenient and work in just about any weather conditions. There is a certain romance to campfires, but they result in trampled terrain, unwanted social trails, and denuded trees and shrubs, robbing an area of biological material and wildlife habitat. Campfire rings and blackened rocks and trees are blemishes that last for decades.

DISPOSE OF WASTE PROPERLY

Mountaineers generally travel in harsh environments—alpine, desert, and arctic—where waste breaks down slowly or not all. Improper waste disposal is unhealthy and creates unsightly and unpleasant discoveries. Whenever possible, use an outhouse or wait until returning from the backcountry. Granted, these are not always practical options, so go into the backcountry prepared for healthy, safe, and thoughtful waste disposal. Everyone's health is dependent on vigilant personal hygiene. Wash your hands frequently, away from camp and water sources, or use the new quick-dry liquid disinfectants.

The Fundamentals

Apply the 200-foot (60-meter) rule to take care of your business well away from watercourses, trails, campsites, and gathering areas. Urinate on bare ground or rocks—not on vegetation—in random locations. The salt in urine attracts animals that might damage plants. On snow or ice, concentrate urine at designated locations in camp or at rest stops, rather than creating a proliferation of pee holes. Cover yellow snow. On steep rock or ice faces, wait until you reach a place where urine can be streamed away from the climbing route. In tents or on long routes, some climbers use a pee bottle to collect urine for later disposal.

Instead of toilet paper, consider using natural materials such as river rock, conifer cones, broad leaves (being careful to recognize and use safe vegetation), or snow. If you use toilet paper, use neutral-colored and nonscented. Avoid the fire hazard of burning toilet paper; instead, pack it out.

There are two acceptable and time-tested approaches for ethical and safe waste disposal: cat-hole burial and packing it out.

Cat-Hole Burial

The cat hole is most suited to lower elevations where there is a deep layer of organic soil. Find a suitable, thoughtful location. A rule of thumb: If it is easy for you to reach, it will be easy for others, too. Challenge yourself to avoid concentrating waste. When you find a good location, use a trowel or ice ax to remove a top layer, or divot, about 4 to 6 inches (10 to 15 centimeters) in diameter, and set it aside. Dig the hole no more than 8 inches (20 centimeters) deep—deeper than forest litter and duff, but not deeper than the humus—for faster decomposition (fig. 7-2). After making your deposit, fill the hole with loose soil. Using a stick or trowel, mix the waste with some soil, then replace the divot. Tamp the soil and distribute area vegetation to create a natural appearance.

In thin mineral soil, on rocks of high alpine areas, or in desert canyon country—all places where the waste

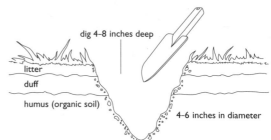

Fig. 7-2.
Cat-hole burial.

will not readily break down—burying solid waste is not recommended. Although it is possible to hide waste this way, its decomposition is doubtful. The cat hole is not suitable in snow, either, unless mineral soil can be found underneath it, possibly in a tree well.

Packing Waste and Materials Out

Mountaineers are already accustomed to packing out used toilet paper and personal hygiene products (bandages, sanitary napkins, tampons). Increasingly, climbers must be prepared to pack out feces as well. Packing out waste is the preferred practice on popular glacier routes, in alpine areas with thin mineral soils, in desert country, on steep rock and ice routes, on arctic tundra, and for winter travel.

Double-Bag

Two resealable plastic bags, stored in a stuff sack or a black garbage bag, work effectively and safely. In some wilderness areas, land managers hand out ready-made bag sets. Like a dog owner following a pet around the neighborhood, put the inner bag over your hand like a glove, then scoop up the solid waste. Then turn the bag inside out to envelop the waste, seal the bag, place it inside the second bag, and seal that. You can reduce odor in the first bag by placing a 2-inch-square (5-centimeter-square) sponge saturated with ammonia in it, or by adding some chlorinated lime or kitty litter to it. Using a lunch-sack paper bag for the inner bag permits easier, biodegradable disposal where possible (see below); then put the paper bag inside two sealed plastic bags.

At a few popular climbing routes, land managers

provide specially marked bins for human waste, but usually it will be up to you to dispose of waste properly after you have finished a climb. Do not simply put waste in a garbage can. Waste in paper bags may go into RV dump stations or front-country restrooms of the type that get pumped out. Paper bags should not go into pit toilets, flush toilets, or composting toilets. Waste in plastic bags should be emptied into a flush toilet; then the bag should be washed before it is thrown into the garbage. Be sure to wash your hands after handling waste.

The Poop Tube

The poop tube offers a good do-it-yourself way to pack out solid waste and can be cleaned and reused. Carry a supply of paper or resealable plastic bags, a sturdy plastic container with a tight-fitting lid, and something to control odor or moisture (ammonia sponge, kitty litter, or chlorinated lime). Defecate into a bag, add the odor control of choice, close up the bag, and put it into the plastic container. Using a paper bag permits easier, biodegradable disposal where possible (see paper-bag disposal options above).

Many types of light, durable, water-tight plastic containers can be used. Or construct a poop tube using commercially available 4-inch-diameter (10-centimeter-diameter) plastic polyvinyl chloride (PVC) pipe. Cut the tube to the desired length. Try a tube 6 to 10 inches (15 to 26 centimeters) long. The size you need depends on your personal habits, your diet, and the trip duration. Glue a solid cap at one end and a threaded fitting at the other. Tether the screw cap to the pipe with a cord. This is more rugged than a plastic bag, and offers a practical way to carry waste beneath big-wall haul bags or on backpacks. The downside is the guesswork on what size is needed for a given trip, which is not a concern with plastic bags.

After the climb, dispose of the waste properly in an RV dump station, an outhouse, a front-country restroom, or the toilet at home. In any of these cases, do not deposit the poop tube along with the waste. Also, do not deposit paper bags in pit toilets, flush toilets, or composting toilets. Be sure to wash your hands after handling waste.

Crevasse Burial in Remote Areas

For remote, expedition glacier travel, waste disposal in crevasses has been an accepted practice. Check with the responsible land management agency, if one exists. Where crevasse disposal is acceptable, feces are collected in a plastic garbage sack and then thrown into a deep crevasse, away from the climbing route, when the party breaks camp. This practice could be on the cusp of change as even distant routes gain popularity. The waste might not be ground up by the moving ice, as once was thought. Clean Mountain Can waste-management programs are becoming available in some areas; elsewhere, consider packing out your waste.

CLEANING UP
Garbage and Trash

If climbers can carry full food containers and packaging into the wilderness, they can carry them out empty—and maybe carry a little more out besides. In a pocket, carry a small resealable plastic bag to hold bits of litter you pick up from the trail. Take an extra heavy-duty plastic bag to carry out all your trash and anything else you find, no matter who left it. Never bury or burn garbage or dump it in outhouses.

Washing

For all types of cleaning and washing, always apply the 200-foot (60-meter) rule. Hot water cleans dishes just fine without soap. If you really want soap, use a biodegradable product and keep it off plants. Dispose of cleaning water downwind from the campsite and well away from water sources. Dig a small cat hole for waste water, straining food scraps out first; pack these out like other garbage. Or fling the waste water out in an arc with a fast, sweeping motion, which disperses the water in fine droplets. Carry out any leftover food.

Use different standards of cleanliness in the wilderness than at home—it is not practical to shower and wash your hair every day. If you do need to wash yourself or your clothing, either do without soap or use a biodegradable soap in very small quantities. Try new products that clean without water. Never wash directly in a water source. Take a pot of water 200 feet away from water sources, trails, campsites, etc.; wash, rinse, and dispose of the water 200 feet away as well. If you applied sunscreen or insect repellent, follow the 200-foot rule to wash yourself off before jumping into a lake or stream. These chemicals and oils can cause harm to aquatic plants and wildlife, and will leave an oily surface film.

DO NOT DISTURB
Leave What You Find

The Leave No Trace ethic goes beyond eliminating litter and waste. Learn to pass through the wilderness in a way that literally leaves no trace of your passage. Established campsites should be used and left as found, if not better. Do not bring saws, hatchets, and nails into the wilderness. Existing, legal fire rings can be left alone, rather than dismantled, because it is likely that someone will create a fire ring again and blacken more rocks. If a campsite has an excessive number of seats, tables, or fire rings, thoughtfully disperse logs and rocks.

Avoid disturbing vegetation or rocks on a climbing route. Look at, draw, or photograph wilderness flora rather than picking or collecting. Do not touch or remove fossils you may discover. Leave untouched any area with evidence of archaeological or historic artifacts, such as those left by prehistoric or native populations. Report findings to land managers. Do not climb, and never bolt, near indigenous rock artwork.

Respect Wildlife

Never feed wildlife. Animals will eat what is given to them or left behind, but a climber's food is not their natural diet and can threaten their health. Some animals will store human food for winter use, only to have it turn moldy and inedible. People do feed chipmunks and birds, but this makes them dependent on humans, and since you likely will not be around to feed them in winter, this could lead to their death. Clean up even the smallest specks of food at trail stops and campsites.

Watch for nesting birds, especially raptors, on rock routes so as not to disturb them. Check with land managers for nesting seasons and closures. If you do encounter nesting birds, back off or take another route.

Even the best-behaved pet can disturb wildlife. The mere presence of a dog can cause wild animals to flee, using up energy and exposing themselves to predators. This is especially harmful in winter when their energy reserves are low and must be carefully conserved. Consider leaving pets at home. If you do bring a pet into the wilderness, do so only where permitted. Pets must be leashed at all times. Use the 200-foot (60-meter) rule for dog waste, too, and bury it in a cat hole or pack it out in a poop bag.

Be Considerate of Other Visitors

Most people go into the wilderness to be alone or with just a few companions. Mountaineers can contribute to the wilderness experience of others by camping away from them, respecting their privacy, traveling through their space only if necessary, and keeping voices and other sounds to a minimum.

Enjoy the sounds of the wilderness. You will return to your daily routine, and the urban sounds that go with it, soon enough. Recorded music may be desired on long expeditions, but for most backcountry trips, personal radios, recorded music, and cell phones can be distracting and unpleasant. Check with trip companions before you take any of these along. If you do, wear headphones. If you insist on making a summit call, find a space away from others.

Minimize Climbing Impacts

- Use natural-color webbing at rappel points. Every time you place a rappel sling, remove and pack out at least one old sling, if not more. Remove all worn-out slings.
- On an alpine climb, try to adjust loose rocks to make them stable, rather than just pushing them off. (At popular sport-climbing crags, however, it is better to remove loose rocks because of the danger they pose in crowded areas.)
- Break down snow structures before you leave to reduce their visual impact and inadvertent safety hazards.
- Avoid setting up new, permanent fixed anchors and rappel points or reinforcing existing ones, unless it is necessary for safety.
- Never chip holds or alter the rock structure for climbing purposes. Use as little chalk as possible.

- Avoid using pitons or other types of hardware that mar or fracture the rock or that remain permanently in place. Hammerless nuts, cams, and other pieces of protection have largely eliminated the damaging practice of using pitons. Pitons are appropriate for winter climbing when cracks are filled with ice and for some aid climbing.
- Bolts should be considered only when no other protection is possible and when they are needed to provide a margin of safety. Because bolts are permanent, think carefully before deciding to place one.
- Follow the local practices and rules at climbing crags. In one area, the local climbers may use only camouflaged bolt hangers (painted so that they are not shiny); in another area, the bolting of new routes may be illegal.
- Cleaning new routes of vegetation should be done for safety, not aesthetic reasons.

- When you are traveling, learn about and respect the customs and culture of the area. Pack in stove fuel rather than despoiling these areas in the search for firewood. Just as you would at areas closer to home, pack your garbage out.

RESPECTING THE FREEDOM OF THE HILLS

As mountaineers we do our part to protect and preserve the wild country we explore by applying Leave No Trace principles, using good judgment, and educating others. There is no more positive way to help ensure continued access, unfettered by restrictions and excessive rules and regulations. When we enter the backcountry we are active stewards and contribute to the lasting protection of wild resources for ourselves and future generations.

7

Stewardship and Access

ACCESS PROBLEMS ■ PRESERVING ACCESS ■ THE FUTURE OF MOUNTAINEERING

Perhaps because of their unique relationship with the mountains, climbers have long been at the forefront of protecting wild places around the globe. John Muir, a leading conservationist in the nineteenth century, was a climber, as was David Brower, a leading conservationist of the twentieth century.

This tradition continues today. On every continent, climbers act as stewards of the mountains, taking on actions as small as packing out their own refuse and as large as fighting large-scale development that threatens the places mountaineers love.

As more and more people turn to the mountains, such stewardship becomes ever more important. The "freedom of the hills" is not absolute. To a great extent, outdoor exploration is subject to restriction by the persons or entities in control of the land where mountaineers climb. ·

Maintaining access to wild places depends on minimizing the actual and potential conflicts between mountaineering and the interests of those who control the land. Although practicing good stewardship should rightfully be considered the moral obligation of every climber, it is also the key to minimizing access conflicts.

ACCESS PROBLEMS
Environmental Impacts

Stewardship starts with the natural environments that attract mountaineers in the first place. Alpine ecosystems are typically fragile and highly affected by human impact. Vegetation is delicate and shallow rooted. Human waste is particularly slow to decompose in the ice and rock zone, and can become a problem on popular routes and at bivouac or camping areas. If a single climber fails to utilize Leave No Trace principles, the damage may be visible for months or years.

Cliff environments often have their own unique features. Cliffs may host nesting raptors, serve as home to bat colonies, and support highly specialized (and sometimes very rare) plant communities. Because cliffs may create their own microclimates and provide conditions that are either drier or wetter than the surrounding area, the tops and bases of cliffs may offer plant and wildlife concentrations unique to an area. Climber impacts can occur both on the cliff faces themselves (through wildlife disturbance and passive or active devegetation) and at cliff tops and bottoms (often in the form of erosion and ground-cover loss associated with concentrated foot travel and groups gathering).

In addition to affecting the environment, these impacts create access problems. This can result in access restrictions when these impacts conflict directly with laws intended to protect habitat for endangered species, create conflict with another user group, or reach a level that is unacceptable under the management mandate of the entity controlling the land. This "acceptable level" of impact may vary greatly depending on who manages the land. The same impacts that are accept-

able at a park that is being managed for recreation may be unacceptable on land managed specifically for habitat preservation.

To avoid such access problems, every climber should adhere to the principles discussed in Chapter 7, Leave No Trace. In practical terms, this means adjusting climbing practices in relation to whatever constitutes a "trace" where you are climbing. What constitutes a "trace" may be different at a popular roadside crag and at a remote alpine area. While climbers should strive to minimize their impacts everywhere, they should go to even greater lengths in wilderness and environmentally sensitive areas. Become familiar with who or what agency manages your climbing destinations and learn what rules govern those areas.

Cultural Impacts

In addition to environmental conflicts, cultural resource conflicts may also give rise to access concerns. Local cultural populations, including native and religious groups, have sought access restrictions for mountaineers, rock climbers, and trekkers in various locations around the world based on the religious or historic significance attached to natural features.

The issues are complex when climbing intersects with a religious significance attached to a climbing objective. Whether you choose to forego an ascent out of respect for another's religious considerations is a personal matter. However, at a minimum, you should inquire of the local customs, religious and otherwise, that may be impacted when you are climbing at an area

> I felt then that [this] was another special place. A place where climbers lived who cared for it, and knew it well enough to say that the yellow rock was more brittle than the red, or that there are hidden holds inside that crack, or that the number of condors is on the up, that the boulder in the next valley gives good shelter, or at what time exactly does the sun shine on that face of the mountain. Simple shared knowledge. That which we have of our home rocks.
> — *Paul Pritchard*, Deep Play (1997)

8

outside your own cultural background, and go forward with full knowledge of the consequences of your actions.

Good stewardship requires leaving artifacts and rock art (petroglyphs and pictographs) undisturbed and free from contact. (Oil from a human hand can adversely affect the pigments associated with rock art.)

Aesthetic Impacts

Certain climbing practices have led to access issues. The use of fixed gear such as bolts, in situ pitons, and rappel slings has been at the center of a number of conflicts. Some of this conflict is a matter of aesthetics: A high density of bolts on a cliff or rappel anchors that stand out from a distance can offend the sensibilities of certain climbers and nonclimbers alike. Some of this conflict can be traced to some people's philosophic opposition to the notion of drilling bolt holes or leaving slings on a cliff, even if the objective impact is minimal. The use of hand-drying chalk by rock climbers has also created some access issues, particularly where chalk residue on holds visually contrasts sharply with the surrounding rock or is not removed by weathering.

> We are entering a new era of climbing, an era that may well be characterized by incredible advances in equipment, by the overcoming of great difficulties, with even greater technological wizardry, and by the rendering of the mountains to a low, though democratic, mean.
>
> Or it could be the start of more spiritual climbing, where we assault the mountains with less equipment and with more awareness, more experience and more courage.
>
> — *Yvon Chouinard, "Coonyard Mouths Off,"* Ascent 1972

Fees and Restrictions

Restrictions and fees applicable to all recreational users can affect climbing access. For instance, one land management agency has established "solitude criteria" for designated wilderness areas. These criteria prescribe the number of human encounters a visitor should experience in a day in order to maintain a "wilderness experience." Such wilderness areas often include mountainous regions.

Access fees, climbing fees, and permit fees, particularly in Asia, create an economic barrier for some mountaineers. These fees are sometimes used for stewardship by land management agencies, and sometimes are simply governmental revenue devices.

PRESERVING ACCESS

As people who endeavor to enjoy the freedom of the hills, all climbers are at the center of at least some of these access issues.

Through Formal Channels

Certain issues, such as the appropriateness of solitude criteria and use fees, are purely legal or political questions. Regardless of whether you favor or oppose such measures, individual influence over such issues is largely obtained through a formal process rather than by how individual climbers conduct themselves while climbing. You are a stakeholder in the political process, and your influence will be proportional to your level of involvement in that process.

Through Stewardship

Each individual's conduct while climbing *can* make a profound difference regarding most other access problems. Maintaining access to wild places, as pointed out earlier in this chapter, depends on minimizing the actual and potential conflicts between climbing and the interests of those who control the land. To the extent that each person's climbing is in harmony with the management of an area, each mountaineer will help ensure access for all climbers. To accomplish this, you must constantly look to become an active steward of the places where you climb.

Stewardship can be as simple as picking up someone else's litter, decaying slings, and abandoned fixed lines. Taken to a greater length, stewardship can help transform an area through trail building and revegetation projects.

Through Active Membership

An easy way to influence access policies and practice stewardship is to support organizations and groups that are active in access issues. In North America, organizations such as The Mountaineers, the American Alpine Club, the Alpine Club of Canada, and particularly the Access Fund are active in access issues and stewardship projects. This includes work with agencies developing management plans for climbing, assistance in tailoring site-specific closures to protect critical re-

sources (such as seasonal restrictions for nesting raptors), and providing grants for land acquisition, trail building and trailhead maintenance, and other conservation projects, as well as scientific studies related to climbing impacts. Finally, local and regional climbing organizations have been formed at a number of areas to address access issues close to home.

THE FUTURE OF MOUNTAINEERING

Mountaineers, by their very nature, pursue unconfined exploration. This fact can pose challenges for those who control the land. As more people continue to join the climbing ranks, it is increasingly incumbent on all climbers to minimize their impacts and maximize their stewardship of the land and watercourses they travel. By doing so, they and the generations of mountaineers who follow can all continue to enjoy the freedom of the hills.

8

Next page: *Climber holding coiled rope atop the Rostrum, Yosemite* (Photo by James Martin)

CLIMBING FUNDAMENTALS

CHAPTER

Basic Safety System

ROPES ■ KNOTS ■ HELMETS ■ HARNESSES ■
RUNNERS ■ CARABINERS ■ KEEPING THE SAFETY NET STRONG

**The rope symbolizes climbing and the climber's dependence on another person. The
rope protects you when the difficulty of a pitch or an unexpected occurrence—
a broken hold or collapsing snow bridge—causes you to fall.**

However, the rope alone cannot safeguard you.
Instead, it is a critical component in a safety system
that includes knots for specialized tasks, the harness
that attaches you to the rope, the loops of webbing
(known as runners) used to connect the rope to rock or
snow, and the carabiners that join the various parts
of the climbing system. The mechanical components of
this safety system are the topics of this chapter.

ROPES

Originally, climbers used ropes made of natural fibers
(manila and sisal), but these ropes were not reliable for
holding severe falls. The development of nylon ropes
during World War II forever changed climbing. Nylon
climbing ropes are lightweight and very strong, capable
of bearing a load of more than 2 tons. They also have
the remarkable quality of elasticity, which is the critical
component in the rope's ability to protect a climber in a

Fig. 9-1.
Construction of a kernmantle rope.

fall. Rather than bringing a falling climber to an abrupt, jolting stop, nylon ropes stretch and dynamically dissipate much of the energy generated by the fall, thereby reducing the forces associated with the fall.

Early nylon ropes were of "laid" or "twisted" construction. They were composed of many tiny nylon filaments bunched into three or four major strands that were then twisted together to form the rope. Gradually, twisted nylon ropes were replaced by kernmantle ropes designed specifically for climbing. Today's kernmantle ropes (fig. 9-1) are composed of a core of braided or parallel nylon filaments encased in a smooth, woven sheath of nylon. Kernmantle rope maintains the advantages of nylon but minimizes the problems associated with twisted ropes—stiffness, friction, and excessive elasticity. Kernmantle ropes are now the only climbing ropes approved by the Union Internationale des Associations d'Alpinisme (UIAA), the internationally recognized authority in setting standards for climbing equipment, and the Comitée Européen de Normalisation (CEN), the European group responsible for creating and maintaining equipment standards.

Varieties of Climbing Rope

Climbing ropes are available in a great variety of diameters, lengths, and characteristics. All ropes designed for climbing are made of nylon and have a kernmantle contruction (see above). Any rope used for climbing should have the manufacturer's label, a UIAA or CEN rating, and specifications such as length, diameter, stretch/impact force, and fall rating. Because the rating organizations are both European, rope measurements universally use the metric system; in this book, English measurements (inches, feet, and so on) are occasionally given in parentheses as well.

Dynamic: Nylon ropes designed for climbing are termed dynamic ropes. Dynamic ropes achieve low-impact forces by stretching under the force of the fall. One of the most important considerations when looking at rope specifications is the impact force—generally, lower is better. Using a rope with a lower impact force means that a climber's fall will be stopped less abruptly (a "softer catch") and less force will be imparted onto the fallen climber, the belayer, and the anchor system.

A longtime standard for all-around recreational climbing has been a dynamic rope that is 11 millimeters in diameter and 50 meters (165 feet) long, with stretch of 8 or 7 percent. However, ropes in 60-meter (200-foot) and 70-meter (230-foot) lengths have become increasingly popular in recent years. Ropes are also offered in many other diameters, and which one a climber chooses depends on the intended uses for the rope. See Table 9-1, below.

TABLE 9-1. SOME TYPICAL ROPES AND THEIR COMMON USES

Diameter	Type	Common Use
8 mm	static	Fixed lines on expedition-style climbs and haul lines for aid climbing
8 mm	dynamic	As part of a twin-rope system for rock and ice climbing
9 mm	dynamic	As part of a double-rope system for rock and ice climbing or as a lightweight single rope for simple glacier travel
10 mm	dynamic	Lightweight single rope for rock and ice climbing and glacier travel
10.5 mm	dynamic	Moderate-weight single rope for rock and ice climbing and glacier travel
11 mm	dynamic	More durable single rope for rock and ice climbing and glacier travel
12 mm	static	Caving and rescue (not for climbing)

Smaller-diameter dynamic ropes (down to about 8 millimeters) are typically used in pairs as part of either a twin- or double-rope system (see Chapter 14, Leading on Rock). These small-diameter rope systems rely on the elastic properties of both ropes to protect the climber, and must be used as a pair.

Static: In contrast to dynamic ropes, static ropes, nylon slings, and cord do not stretch, and a fall of even a few feet can generate impact forces severe enough to cause failure of the anchor system or severe injury to the climber.

Climbers use no-stretch or very low-stretch ropes for purposes other than protecting the lead climber, including cave exploring or rescue work, as fixed line on expedition-style climbs, or as the haul line during aid climbing. Although static ropes often are sold at climbing stores, these ropes should never be used for lead climbing, which requires the impact-absorbing qualities of a dynamic rope.

Colors of Ropes

Ropes are manufactured with different patterns and colors woven into the sheath. Some ropes have a contrasting color at the midpoint to make it easy to find the middle of the rope. Others have distinctively colored ends so that it is easier for the climber to visually determine that the end of the rope is being reached while belaying or rappelling. If a climb calls for two ropes, it is useful to use different colors to assist in distinguishing between them when belaying or rappelling.

Water-Repellent Ropes

Wet ropes, in addition to being unpleasant to handle and heavy to carry, can freeze and become very difficult to manage. Equally important, studies show that wet ropes hold fewer falls and have about 30 percent less strength than the same ropes when they are dry.

Rope manufacturers treat some of their ropes with either a silicone-based coating or synthetic fluorine-containing resin coating (such as Teflon) to make them more water-repellent and therefore stronger in wet conditions. The "dry rope" treatment improves the abrasion resistance of the rope and also reduces friction of the rope as it runs through carabiners. Dry ropes usually cost about 15 percent more than untreated ropes.

Performance Tests

The UIAA and CEN test equipment to determine which gear meets their standards. Because climbing is a sport in which equipment failure can be fatal, it is wise to purchase equipment that has earned UIAA/CEN approval.

In its rope tests, the UIAA checks the strength of the single ropes used in most climbing—which generally measure between 9.7 and 11 millimeters in diameter—and also the thinner ropes used in double-rope climbing. To receive UIAA approval, a rope must survive a required minimum number of falls. The tests measure the impact force of the rope, which determines the stress of the fall on the climber's body and on the pieces of protection. The UIAA also applies static tension tests to determine how much the ropes elongate under load. Approved ropes do not stretch by more than a specified percentage.

Rope Care

A rope protects your life and must be treated with care.

Preventing Damage to the Rope

Stepping on a rope is a common form of abuse that grinds sharp particles into and through the sheath. Over time, the particles act like tiny knives that slice the rope's nylon filaments. When you are wearing crampons, you must be doubly careful about keeping off the rope, because a misstep could damage the rope. Crampons may damage the core of a rope without leaving any visible gash on the sheath. Protect the rope from contact with chemicals or other compounds that might damage the rope.

Washing and Drying

Follow the manufacturer's recommendations for care. Generally, a rope should be washed frequently with tepid water and a gentle soap, although some manufacturers recommend against using detergents on water-repellent ropes ("dry ropes"). The rope's water-repellent finish can also be replaced with after-market products made for that purpose. A rope can be washed by hand in a bathtub or in a front-loading washing machine (ropes can get caught under the agitator in a top-loading machine). Rinse the rope several times in fresh water and then hang it to dry, out of direct sunlight.

Storing

Before storing any rope, be sure it is completely dry. Remove all knots, coil the rope loosely, and store it in a cool, dry area away from sunlight, heat, chemicals, petroleum products, and acids.

Retiring a Rope

Examine your rope's sheath to get the best picture of the rope's overall condition. Inspect your ropes frequently, particularly after a fall, to ensure that the sheath is clean, that there are no abraded or soft spots in the rope, and that the ends are properly fused and not fraying or unraveling. If a crampon wound, excessive abrasion, rockfall, or a sharp edge leaves the sheath looking tattered, the rope's integrity should be seriously questioned.

It is harder to decide when to retire the rope if it does not contain any obvious soft spots or scars in the sheath. The rope's actual condition depends on many factors, including frequency of use, the care it has received, the number of falls it has endured, and how old it is.

After a severe fall, it may be wise to replace a rope, particularly if any segment of the rope feels mushy or flat. A new rope may be certified to take five UIAA falls, but in your decision whether to retire the rope, consider the rope's history and other factors affecting its condition. The guidelines for rope replacement assume that the rope is kept properly cleaned and stored.

Coiling the Rope

For carrying or storing, the rope is normally coiled, most commonly in the mountaineers coil or the butterfly coil. Most climbers prefer one coil or the other, but knowing both is useful.

Mountaineers coil: This coil is advantageous when the rope is carried over a pack. Coil the rope, leaving a couple of feet at one end and doubling back the other end, then bring the long end through the coil (fig. 9-2a). Wrap the coil several times, securing the doubled-back end (fig. 9-2b). Bring the long end down through the loop of the doubled-back end (fig. 9-2c), then tie the long end to the doubled-back end in a square knot (fig. 9-2d). See the next section for knot tying.

Butterfly coil: This coil is usually a little faster, does not kink the rope, and can be tied snugly to your body if you are not wearing a pack. Coil the rope, leaving both ends long, and bend the coil into a horseshoe shape (fig. 9-3a). Gather the two loose ends together and wrap them around the middle of the coil several times (fig. 9-3b). Bring a loop of the loose ends through the loop

Fig. 9-2.
Mountaineers coil:
a, bring an end
through coil near
doubled-back other
end; b, wrap coil
several times;
c, bring loose end
through loop of
doubled-back end;
d, tie square knot
to secure.

139

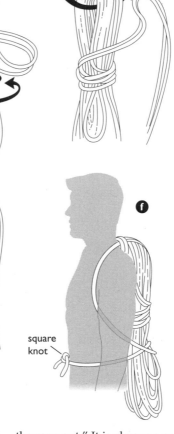

Fig. 9-3.
Butterfly coil:
a, form coil into horseshoe shape;
b, wrap both loose ends around the middle several times;
c, bring loop of loose ends through upper loop of coil;
d, bring loose ends through loop of loose ends;
e, bring loose ends all the way through and cinch;
f, put a loose end over each shoulder, around behind the back, and over the coiled rope, then bring each end forward around the waist and tie together with a square knot.

square knot

at the top of the coil (fig. 9-3c), pulling enough through to form a good-size loop. Then bring the rest of the loose ends through this good-size loop (fig. 9-3d), drawing the loose ends all the way through (fig. 9-3e). To tie the butterfly coil to your body, place the coil against your back and draw a loose end over each shoulder and around your back, crossing them over the coil and bringing them around your waist; tie them together in front (fig. 9-3f).

Flaking the rope out: Whatever coil method you choose, it is important to uncoil the rope carefully before you use it, to minimize the chance of coils balling up into a tangle. Do not just drop the coils and start pulling on one end, which may create a tangled mess. Untie the cinch knot and then uncoil the rope, one loop at a time, into a pile, a procedure known as "flaking

the rope out." It is always a good practice to flake out the rope before each belay to avoid the possibility of having a knot or tangle appear during the belay process.

Rope bags and tarps: These are alternatives to coiling the rope. Both can protect a rope during transport. The tarp, unfolded, also helps protect a rope from the ground. The bags and tarps add weight and cost, but for certain situations, such as sport climbing, they are worth it.

KNOTS

Knots allow you to use the rope for many special purposes. Knots let you tie in to the rope, anchor to the mountain, tie two ropes together for long rappels, use slings to climb the rope itself, and much more.

Climbers rely most heavily on a dozen or so basic knots and hitches. Practice these knots until tying them is second nature. In some cases, more than one knot can perform a particular task, and the knot chosen is a matter of personal preference. Some knots may be preferred over others because they have a smaller effect on the overall strength of the rope, as shown in Table 9-2. Others may be chosen because they are easier to tie or are less likely to come apart in use.

Regardless of the knot you use, there are some terms and techniques common to all knot-tying. The end of the rope that is not being actively used is called the standing end; the other end is called the loose end. A 180-degree bend or loop in the rope is called a bight. A hitch is a type of knot that must be wrapped around an object for it to function. A double knot is a knot tied in a pair of ropes or in a doubled portion of one rope.

Regardless of its type, tie a knot neatly, keeping the separate strands of the knot parallel and free of twists. Tightly cinch every knot, and tie off loose ends with an overhand knot. Always tie knots in perfect form so that it becomes easy to recognize a properly tied knot. It is also important to develop the habit of routinely inspecting your own knots and those of your climbing partners, particularly before beginning a pitch or a rappel.

TABLE 9-2. RELATIVE REDUCTION IN BREAKING STRENGTH OF SINGLE KERNMANTLE ROPE AT KNOT	
Knot	Reduction in Breaking Strength
None	None
Double fisherman's knot	15–30 percent
Clove hitch	15–20 percent
Fishermans knot	15–20 percent
Overhand knot	15–20 percent
Water knot (ring bend)	20–30 percent
Figure eight	20–25 percent
Bowline	25–30 percent
Source: *American Alpine Journal*	

Basic Knots

Basic knots are used to tie in to harnesses, to tie ropes together for rappel, and, in some instances, for anchoring and rescue procedures.

Overhand Knot

The overhand knot (fig. 9-4a) is frequently used to secure loose rope ends after another knot has been tied. For instance, the overhand knot can be used to secure rope ends after tying a square knot (fig. 9-4b) or a rewoven figure eight (fig. 9-4c). To tie the overhand knot, pass the loose end of the rope through a bight of rope.

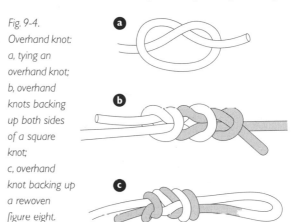

Fig. 9-4. Overhand knot: a, tying an overhand knot; b, overhand knots backing up both sides of a square knot; c, overhand knot backing up a rewoven figure eight.

Double Overhand Knot

The double overhand knot (fig. 9-5) is useful as a rappel knot in icy conditions or for rappels where the knot might catch when the rappel rope is retrieved. The basic overhand knot is tied using the loose ends of two ropes to set up a double-rope rappel.

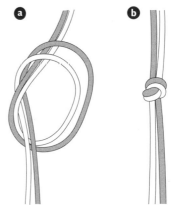

Fig. 9-5. Double overhand knot: a, tie an overhand knot in two strands of rope; b, pull all strands tight.

Overhand Loop

The overhand loop (fig. 9-6) is often used for creating leg loops in prusik slings or to make a loop in a doubled rope or a length of webbing. The basic overhand knot is tied using a bight in the rope instead of a loose end.

Fig. 9-6.
Overhand loop:
a, tie an overhand
knot in a bight
of rope; b, pull all
strands tight.

Water Knot/Ring Bend

The water knot (fig. 9-7), also known as the ring bend, is frequently used to tie a length of tubular webbing into a runner (see "Runners" later in this chapter). A water knot can work loose over time, so it is important to cinch the knot very tightly and to make the tails of the knot at least 2 to 3 inches (5 to 7.5 centimeters) long. Check water knots often and retie any that have worked loose or that have short tails.

Square Knot

The square knot (fig. 9-8) can be used as a rappel knot (finished with overhand knots on both rope ends), and it is often used to finish off a coil of rope.

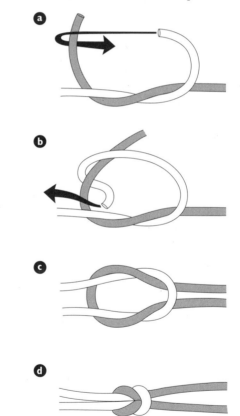

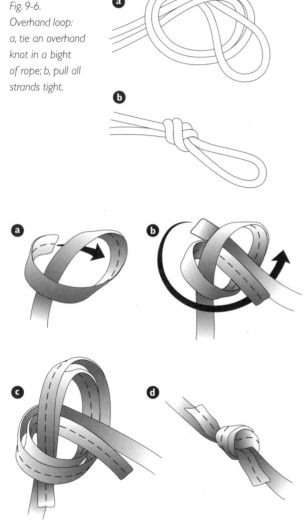

Fig. 9-7.
Water knot (also known as a ring bend): a, draw a loose end through a bight of webbing; b, bring other loose end through the bight, around the first end, and under itself; c, draw ends well through knot so 2–3 inches extend; d, pull tight.

Fig. 9-8. Square knot:
a, cross two loose ends over each other and bring one end up and around the other; b, bring this end through the loop formed; c, pull the pairs of ends in opposite directions to form the "square"; d, completed and dressed knot.

Fisherman's Knot

The fisherman's knot (fig. 9-9) is used to join two ropes together. Overlap a loose end of each rope and tie each end in an overhand knot around the other rope's standing end. For climbing purposes, however, this knot has been replaced to a large degree by the double fisherman's knot, and the fisherman's knot is shown here primarily to provide a clearer understanding of the double fisherman's knot.

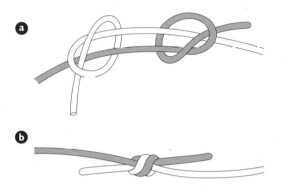

Fig. 9-9.
Fisherman's knot: a, overlay a loose end of each rope, and tie each end in an overhand knot around the other rope's standing end; b, pull the knot tight.

Double Fisherman's Knot

The double fisherman's knot (fig. 9-10), also known as the grapevine knot, is a very secure knot for tying the ends of two ropes together for a rappel. It is preferred over two rewoven figure-eight knots because it is less bulky and tends to hang up less often when the rope is being pulled down after a rappel. Start as for the fisherman's knot, but pass each loose end twice around the other rope's standing end before tying the overhand knot, pulling the ends through both their loops.

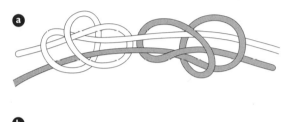

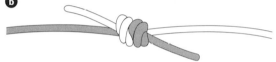

Fig. 9-10.
Double fisherman's knot: a, pass each loose end twice around the other rope's standing end and then tie an overhand knot; b, pull the knot tight.

EXAMPLES OF BASIC TIE-OFF LOOPS

A tie-off loop is a 3- to 5-foot length of 6- to 8-millimeter cord tied into a loop with a double fisherman's knot (fig. 9-11a), or ⁵⁄₁₆- to 1-inch webbing tied with a water knot (fig. 9-11b). A sewn single runner made from tubular nylon webbing can also be used as a tie-off loop. The size of the loop varies depending on its intended use—for example, for tying off a belay to effect a rescue (see "Tying Off a Belay" in Chapter 10, Belaying) or for self-belaying during a rappel (see "Self-Belay with a Prusik or Autoblock" in Chapter 11, Rappelling).

Fig. 9-11.
Tie-off loops:
a, double
fisherman's
knot in cord;
b, water knot
in webbing.

Figure Eight on a Bight

The figure eight on a bight (fig. 9-12) is a strong knot that can be readily untied after being under a load.

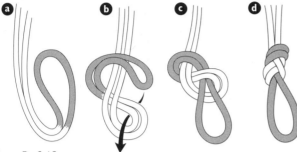

Fig. 9-12.

Figure eight on a bight: a, bring a bight back parallel to the standing ends; b, bring bight under and then over the ends, forming an "8", then bring the bight down through the bottom loop of the "8"; c, pull all four strands tight; d, completed and dressed knot.

Rewoven Figure Eight

The rewoven figure eight (fig. 9-13) is an excellent knot for tying into a seat harness at the end of the rope. The rewoven figure eight is finished off by tying an overhand knot in the loose end of the rope. This knot also can be used to connect a rope to an anchor.

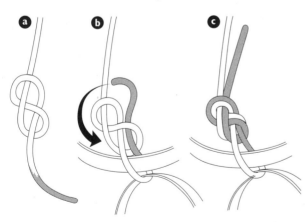

Fig. 9-13.

Rewoven figure eight: a, tie a figure eight; b, double the loose end back and retrace the "8" so the loose end is parallel to the standing end; c, pull both the ends and the end loop tight.

Single Bowline

The single bowline (fig. 9-14a) makes a loop at the end of the climbing rope that will not slip, and it can secure the rope around a tree or other anchor. The loose end of the rope should come out on the inside of the bowline's loop (fig. 9-14b) because the knot is much weaker if the loose end finishes on the outside of the loop. Tie off the loose end with an overhand knot (fig. 9-14c and d).

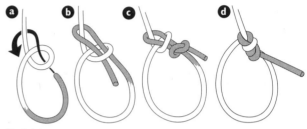

Fig. 9-14.

Single bowline: a, make a loop and pass the loose end of the rope under and through it, then around the back of the standing end; b, bring the loose end back through the loop; c, pull ends tight and tie an overhand knot; d, completed single bowline backed up with an overhand knot.

Double Bowline

The middle climber on a three-person rope can tie the double bowline (fig. 9-15a) to the seat harness. Secure the resulting end loop with an overhand knot or a locking carabiner (fig. 9-15b); the locking carabiner makes a cleaner finish and a smaller knot.

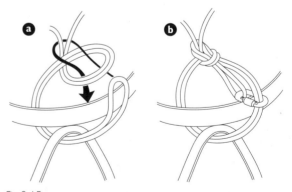

Fig. 9-15.

Double bowline: a, tie a bowline on a bight; b, secure end loop with a locking carabiner.

Single Bowline with a Yosemite Finish

The single bowline with a Yosemite finish is the same as a single bowline (fig. 9-16a), except that the loose end retraces the rope until it is parallel with the standing end (fig. 9-16b and c). This knot is easy to untie after it has been loaded, making it a good choice for a top-roping tie-in.

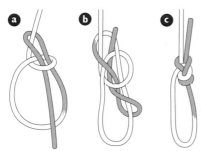

Fig. 9-16.
Single bowline with a Yosemite finish: a, tie a single bowline, keeping the knot loose; b, bring the loose end over and under the rope and under the entire knot, then up through the bowline's topmost loop; c, pull all strands tight.

Butterfly Knot

The useful characteristic of the butterfly knot (fig. 9-17) is that it can sustain a pull on either end of the rope or the loop and not come undone. A connection to this knot is made with a locking carabiner through the loop.

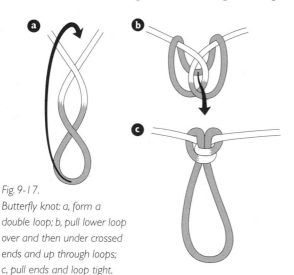

Fig. 9-17.
Butterfly knot: a, form a double loop; b, pull lower loop over and then under crossed ends and up through loops; c, pull ends and loop tight.

Clove Hitch

The clove hitch (fig. 9-18a and b) is a quick knot for clipping into a carabiner (fig. 9-18c) attached to an anchor (fig. 9-18d). The main advantage of the clove hitch is that the knot makes it easy to adjust the length of the rope between the belayer and the anchor without

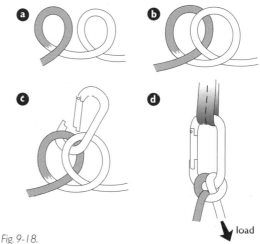

Fig. 9-18.
Clove hitch: a, form two loops side by side; b, bring left-hand loop behind the other; c, clip a carabiner through both loops; d, pull ends tight.

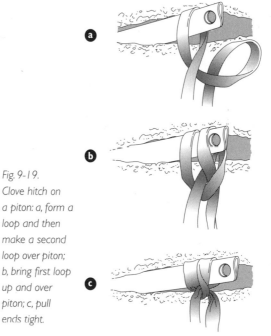

Fig. 9-19.
Clove hitch on a piton: a, form a loop and then make a second loop over piton; b, bring first loop up and over piton; c, pull ends tight.

145

unclipping the rope from the carabiner. The clove hitch is also a simple knot that can be used to tie off partially driven pitons (fig. 9-19).

Girth Hitch

The girth hitch (fig. 9-20a) is another simple knot that can serve a variety of purposes, such as attaching webbing to a packs haul loop (fig. 9-21b).

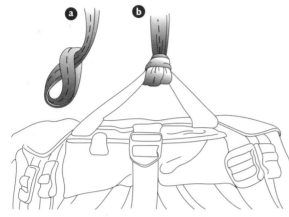

Fig. 9-20.
Girth hitch: a, pull both ends through a bight; b, girth hitch tied around a pack's haul loop.

Overhand Slipknot

The overhand slipknot (fig. 9-21a and b) is another simple knot used for tie-offs (fig. 9-21c).

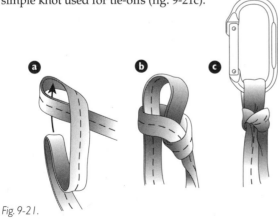

Fig. 9-21.
Overhand slip knot: a, make a loop, then bring a bight up through the loop; b, draw loop closed to tie off bight; c, clip bight into a carabiner and pull ends tight.

Friction Knots

Friction knots provide a quick and simple way to set up a system for ascending or descending a climbing rope. The knots grip the climbing rope when weight is placed on them, but are free to move when the weight is released. The best-known friction knot is the prusik, but others, such as the Bachmann and the Klemheist, are also useful.

Prusik Knot

The prusik knot requires a girth hitch (fig. 9-22a) and a few wraps of an accessory cord around the climbing rope (fig. 9-22b and c). The cord is usually a loop of 5- to 7-millimeter perlon, wrapped two (fig. 9-22d) or three (fig. 9-22e) times around the rope. Icy ropes or heavy loads require more wraps of the prusik knot to ensure sufficient friction to hold the load.

To create the necessary friction, the accessory cord must be smaller in diameter than the climbing rope;

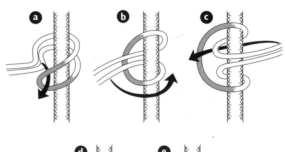

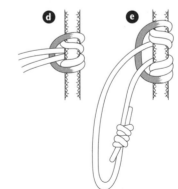

Fig. 9-22.
Prusik knot: a, girth-hitch cord around rope; b, bring loose ends under knot and rope; c, rotate knot 180 degrees and wrap loose ends around rope again; d, two-wrap prusik knot; e, three-wrap prusik knot.

the greater the difference in diameter, the better it grips. However, very small-diameter cords make the prusik knot harder to manipulate than do cords of larger diameter. Experiment to see which diameter of cord works best. Webbing is usually not used for prusik knots because it may not hold.

By attaching two slings to a climbing rope with prusik knots, you can ascend/descend the climbing rope. Chapter 17, Glacier Travel and Crevasse Rescue, explains the Texas Prusik method of ascending the rope using prusiks.

The prusik knot is also used as part of the rescue systems needed to raise and lower people and equipment during rescues.

Bachmann Knot

The Bachmann knot (fig. 9-23) is used for the same purposes as a prusik knot. The Bachmann knot is tied around a carabiner (fig. 9-23b and c), making it much easier to loosen and slide than a prusik. The Bachmann knot has the virtue of sometimes being "self-tending" (it will feed rope in the non–load bearing direction without requiring you to actively manipulate it) when the climbing rope is passing through it.

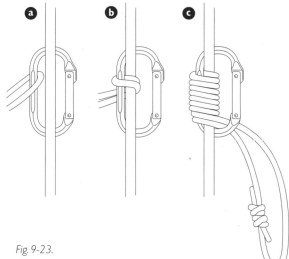

Fig. 9-23.
Bachmann knot: a, with a carabiner under the rope, clip a loop of cord into carabiner; b, bring cord up over and around rope and then under rope and carabiner; c, repeat between three and five times.

Klemheist Knot

The Klemheist knot is another alternative to the prusik, with the advantage that it can be made from either accessory cord or webbing, which may become important if you are caught with an ample supply of webbing but little cord.

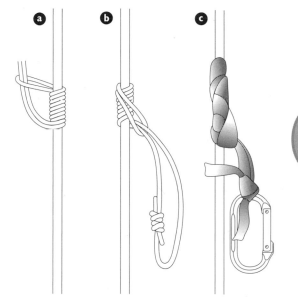

Fig. 9-24.
Klemheist knot:
a, wrap a loop of cord around the rope five times and draw loose ends through the end loop; b, pull ends down; c, Klemheist knot tied using webbing and clipped to a carabiner; d, Klemheist knot tied off—bring ends up, then under and over the loop, forming a new loop, and then down through this loop, pulling the ends tight; e, Klemheist tied around a carabiner.

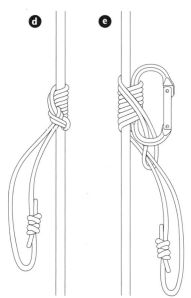

147

A circular piece of cord or webbing is wound around the main rope in a spiral and then threaded through the loop created by the top wrap of the circular cord or webbing (fig. 9-24a). Pull down to create the basic Klemheist (fig. 9-24b), which can be clipped to a carabiner (fig. 9-24c). The tied-off Klemheist (fig. 9-24d) is less likely to jam and easier to loosen and slide than the basic Klemheist. The Klemheist can also be tied around a carabiner (fig. 9-24e), which then provides a good handhold on the rope.

Autoblock Knot

The autoblock is similar to the Klemheist knot. One end of a loop of cord is secured to a carabiner. The cord is then wrapped three or more times around the rope to provide friction, and the free end of the loop is secured to the carabiner. The autoblock is often used as a self-belay device during rappels. One end of the cord is girth-hitched to the harness leg loop and the other end is attached to the leg loop with a carabiner. (See Figure 11-19 in Chapter 11, Rappelling.)

Münter Hitch

The Münter hitch is very easy to set up and use, but only feeds rope effectively if used on a large pear-shaped or HMS locking carabiner. The Münter is a simple hitch in the rope (fig. 9-25a) that is clipped into a carabiner (fig. 9-25b) to create friction (fig. 9-25c). It provides an excellent method of belaying a leader or lowering a climber because the hitch is reversible (the rope can be fed out of the carabiner or the rope can be pulled back in through the carabiner), and the knot provides sufficient friction for the belayer to stop a falling or lowering climber by holding the braking end of the rope. The Münter hitch can also provide the necessary rope friction for rappelling, though it puts more twist in the rope than other rappel methods. Even if you prefer to use a specialized belay device, this hitch is worth knowing as a backup if you lose or forget your belay device.

HELMETS

Climbing helmets help protect your head from rockfall and from gear dropped by climbers above you. Helmets also protect you from the many ways in which you can suddenly impact hard surfaces such as rock or ice: a fall to the ground, a leader fall that swings you into a wall, or a quick move upward against a sharp outcropping. However, keep in mind that no helmet can protect you from all possible impacts.

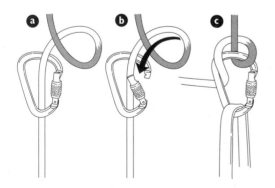

Fig. 9-25.

The Münter hitch: a, draw rope up through carabiner and form a bight; b, clip carabiner through bight; c, pull ends tight in opposite directions.

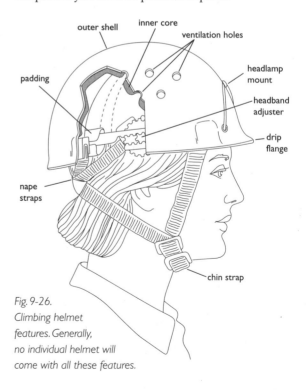

Fig. 9-26.

Climbing helmet features. Generally, no individual helmet will come with all these features.

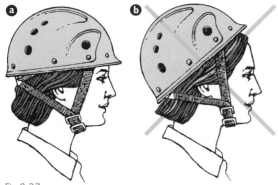

Fig. 9-27.
Wearing a helmet: a, proper; b, improper, leaving forehead exposed to rockfall and icefall.

head during impact, or a polystyrene core designed to shatter upon severe impact, absorbing force. This latter design must be replaced after an impact. It is recommended that any helmet be replaced as soon as possible after a significant impact.

Choose a helmet that fits well and can be adjusted to fit your bare head whether or not you are wearing a headband or balaclava. Fit is very individual because normal skull shapes and sizes vary. Make sure you wear the helmet so it is forward (fig. 9-27a), which helps protect your forehead and frontal lobe, rather than tipped back (fig. 9-27b). Make sure that a headlamp can be attached securely to the helmet.

Modern climbing helmets are lightweight, ventilated, and available in many designs (fig. 9-26). Buy a climbing helmet with the UIAA/CEN mark, which ensures minimum standards of impact resistance. Shell materials may be plastic, fiberglass, and/or carbon fiber. The suspension system may be a system of strapping that keeps the helmet shell from contacting your

HARNESSES

In the early days of climbing, the climbing rope was looped around a climber's waist several times and tied in to the rope with a bowline on a coil (fig. 9-28a through 9-28f for a climber on the end of the rope; fig. 9-28g and h for a climber on the middle of the rope). That practice is no longer considered safe because long falls

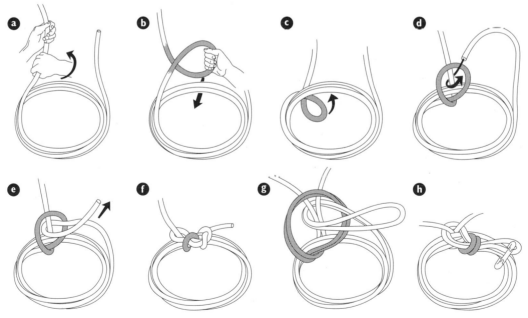

Fig. 9-28.
Bowline on a coil, to attach a rope around the waist of a climber who does not have a harness. It is not recommended that these knots be used around the body except in emergencies. A–f is for a climber at the end of a rope, g–h for a middle climber.

onto waist loops can severely injure a climber's back and ribs. Additionally, falls that left the climber hanging, such as a fall into a crevasse or over the lip of an overhang, could cause the rope to ride up and constrict the climber's diaphragm, leading to suffocation.

Today, climbers tie the rope into a harness designed to distribute the force of a fall over a larger percentage of the climber's body. A climber at either end of a climbing rope ties into the harness with a knot such as the rewoven figure eight (see Figure 9-13, above). A climber in the middle of a rope usually ties into the harness with a double rewoven figure eight or a double bowline (see Figure 9-15, above).

Harnesses deteriorate over time and should be inspected often and replaced with the same frequency as a climbing rope. The bowline on a coil remains an option for emergency use if no harness or harness material is available.

Seat Harnesses

With properly fitted leg loops, a seat harness rides snugly above your hip bones yet transfers the force of a fall over your entire pelvis. It also provides a comfortable seat during rappelling.

Manufactured Seat Harness

Several features are particularly desirable in a mountaineering seat harness (fig. 9-29). Adjustable leg loops maintain a snug fit no matter how few or how many layers of clothing you are wearing. A padded waist belt and leg loops can provide additional comfort, particularly in situations in which you will be hanging for any length of time. Leg loops that can be unbuckled permit toilet calls without your having to remove the harness or untie from the rope. Having the waist buckle located toward one side helps avoid conflict with the rope tie-in or with the locking carabiner that is attached to the harness for use in belaying and rappelling. Gear loops are desirable for carrying carabiners and other pieces of climbing gear.

Before buying a harness, try it on to be sure the harness fits properly over your climbing clothes. With the profusion of harness styles on the market, you should consult the manufacturer's instructions to learn how to safely wear and tie in to a particular harness. Printed

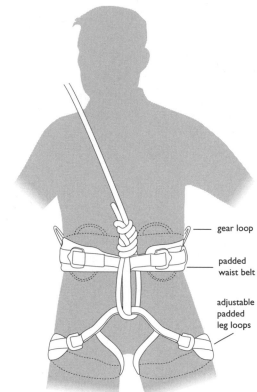

Fig. 9-29.
Seat harness with common features.

gear loop

padded waist belt

adjustable padded leg loops

instructions accompany any new harness, and they also are usually sewn inside the waist belt. For most harnesses, you must pass the waist strap back over and through the main buckle a second time for safety. Be sure at least 2 to 3 inches (5 to 7.5 centimeters) of strap extends beyond the buckle after you reweave the strap.

Swami Belt

A less-used variant on the manufactured seat harness is a waist band known as a swami belt, which is used in combination with leg loops. Just like a full seat harness, commercial swami belts are secured with a buckle, and they usually include padding and hardware loops. Typically a climber using a swami belt combines it with separate leg loops to complete a full seat-harness system. In the past, swami belts were used alone, without the addition of leg loops. This use is not recommended, because if you are left hanging, the belt can creep up and restrict your breathing. Leg loops keep the swami belt from creeping, and distribute the force of a fall to a larger area of your body.

Chest Harness

A chest harness helps keep you upright after a fall or while ascending a rope using prusiks or mechanical ascenders. Following a fall, you simply clip the climbing rope through the carabiner of the chest harness, which provides stability and assists you in staying upright. The chest harness will deliver some of the force of a fall to your chest, which is more easily injured than your pelvis (where the force is directed by a seat harness). Thus, a rope is not usually clipped into the chest harness during rock climbing or general mountaineering. The rope is sometimes clipped into the chest harness during glacier travel, though some climbers prefer to leave the rope unclipped until a crevasse fall actually occurs. (See Chapter 17, Glacier Travel and Crevasse Rescue).

A chest harness may be purchased or is readily improvised with a long loop of webbing (a long runner). One popular design depends on a carabiner to bring the ends of the harness together at your chest. To make a carabiner chest harness, start with 9½ feet (2.9 meters) of 1-inch tubular webbing. Tie it into a loop with a water knot. Adjust the size of the webbing loop to fit comfortably. Use a distinctive color for the webbing to distinguish the chest harness from other double-length runners (see the next section, on runners). Give the loop a half twist to create two temporary loops, and push one arm all the way through each loop. Lift the runner over your head and let it drop against your back, with the crossed portion at your back (fig. 9-30a); then pull the two sides together in front and clip with a carabiner at your chest (fig. 9-30b).

Body Harness

Full body harnesses, which incorporate both a chest and a seat harness, have a higher tie-in point (fig. 9-31). This reduces the chance of you flipping over backward during a fall. Because a body harness distributes the force of a fall throughout the trunk of your body, there may be less danger of lower-back injury.

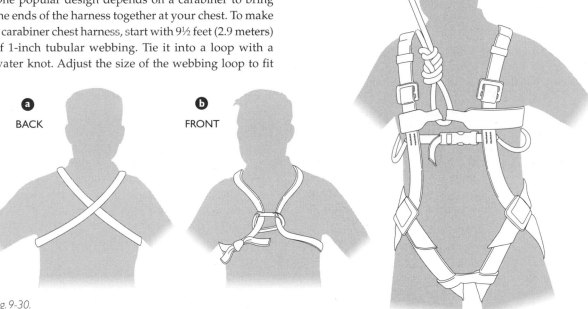

a BACK **b** FRONT

Fig. 9-30.
Carabiner chest harness: a, the two loops are formed by twisting a runner across the back; b, then clip the two loops together at the chest with a carabiner.

Fig. 9-31.
Full body harness.

9

Although in some circumstances body harnesses may be safer, they have not found popular favor in mountaineering. They are more expensive and restrictive and make it hard to add or remove clothing. Instead, most climbers use a seat harness and then improvise a chest harness when one is warranted, such as when climbing with a heavy pack, crossing glaciers, or aid-climbing under large overhangs. Full-body harnesses are necessary for children whose hips are not yet fully developed.

RUNNERS

Loops of tubular webbing or cord, called runners, are among the simplest pieces of climbing equipment and among the most useful. They are a critical link in climbing systems. Standard single runners require 5½ feet (1.7 meters) of webbing or cord. Double-length runners require 9½ feet (2.9 meters) of webbing or cord. Triple-length runners require 15 feet (4.6 meters) of webbing or cord. A beginning climber should own about six single runners, two doubles, and a triple.

To help you quickly identify the different lengths, it is useful to use single runners of one color of webbing, double runners of another color, and triple runners of a third color. For a tied webbing runner, it is useful to write your initials and the date the runner was made on one of the tails of the water knot. This helps identify the runner and its age for deciding when to retire it. Runners should be retired regularly, using the same considerations as for retiring a rope or harness.

It is very important to remember that webbing slings and accessory cords do not have dynamic characteristics. If they are used without a dynamic rope, a fall of even a few feet can impart catastrophic force onto the anchor system and climber.

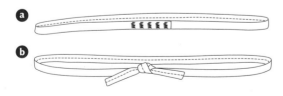

Fig. 9-32.
Runners made of webbing: a, sewn runner; b, tied runner.

Sewn: You can purchase high-strength, presewn runners (fig. 9-32a) at climbing stores. Sewn runners come in various lengths: 2-inch, 4-inch, 12-inch (half-lengths), and 24-inch (full-lengths). Some runners are specially sewn into preformed quickdraws, typically about 4 inches long, and have carabiners attached at each end. Runners also come in a variety of widths, with ⁹/₁₆-, ¹¹/₁₆-, and 1-inch widths being the most common. Runners made from Spectra (a high-performance fiber that is stronger, more durable, and less susceptible to ultraviolet deterioration than nylon) are usually made in ⁹/₁₆-inch webbing. Sewn runners are generally stronger, usually lighter, and less bulky than tied runners. Using a sewn runner also eliminates the possibility of the knot untying, which is a concern with tied runners.

Tied: Runners can also be made, by tying a loop in ⁹/₁₆- to 1-inch tubular nylon webbing or in 8- to 9-millimeter perlon accessory cord. A runner made of webbing is typically tied with a water knot to make the loop (fig. 9-32b). A cord runner is typically tied with either a double fisherman's knot (see Figure 9-10, above) or a triple fisherman's knot, required for Spectra or other aramid-fiber (Kevlar) cord. If the webbing or cord is cut to make the runner, the ends must be melted with a small flame to keep the ends from unraveling. Tied runners have several advantages over commercially sewn runners. The tied runners are inexpensive to make, can be untied and threaded around trees and natural chockstones (rocks firmly lodged in cracks), and can be untied and retied with another runner to create extralong runners.

CARABINERS

Carabiners are another versatile and indispensable climbing tool used for belaying, rappelling, prusiking, clipping into safety anchors, securing the rope to points of protection, and numerous other tasks.

Shapes and Styles

Carabiners come in many sizes and shapes. Ovals (fig. 9-33a) are very popular because their symmetry makes them good for many purposes. D carabiners (fig. 9-33b) also offer a good general-purpose shape and are stronger than ovals because more of the load is transferred

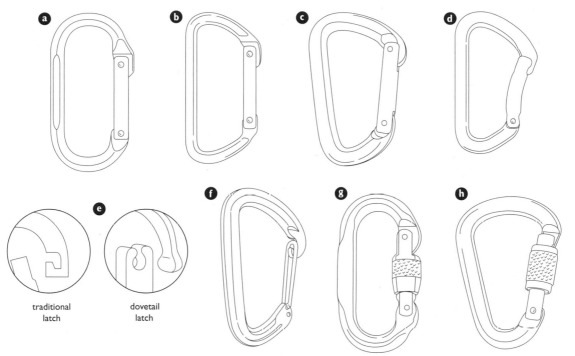

traditional
latch

dovetail
latch

Fig. 9-33.

*Carabiners: a, oval carabiner; b, standard D carabiner; c, offset D carabiner; d, bent-gate carabiner; e, two standard carabiner gate styles;
f, wire-gate carabiner; g, standard locking carabiner; h, pear shaped locking carabiner.*

to the long axis and away from the gate, the typical point of failure for a carabiner. Offset Ds (fig. 9-33c) have the strength advantage of standard Ds, but the gate on an offset D opens wider, making it easier to clip in awkward situations. Bent-gate carabiners (fig. 9-33d) are a specialty design most commonly used on difficult routes where it is important to quickly clip and unclip the carabiners from the feel of the gates alone. Bent-gate carabiners should always be used with a runner so that they are free to rotate.

Wire-gate carabiners (fig. 9-33f) provide a strong gate at a reduced weight. Some studies also indicate that wire-gate carabiners are less prone to gate fluttering, which can occur when a rope passes quickly through a carabiner.

Locking carabiners (fig. 9-33g), with a sleeve that screws over one end of the gate to minimize accidental opening, provide a wider margin of safety for rappelling, belaying, or clipping into anchors. Some

locking carabiners have a spring that automatically positions the sleeve whenever the gate is closed. Regardless of the carabiner's particular locking mechanism, you must always check to make sure that the carabiner is properly locked.

Pear-shaped locking carabiners (fig. 9-33h) are much larger at the gate-opening end than at the hinge end and are ideal for belaying with the Münter hitch (see Figure 9-25, above). They are also a good choice for use in conjunction with the seat harness. The extra cost and weight of pear-shaped locking carabiners is justified by the increased ease of loading and managing all the ropes, knots, cords, and runners that are used at the seat harness's anchor point.

Two regular carabiners can be substituted for a locking carabiner when they are used together with their gates on opposite sides (fig. 9-34). This configuration helps prevent the carabiners from being forced open and accidentally unclipping. You can check that the

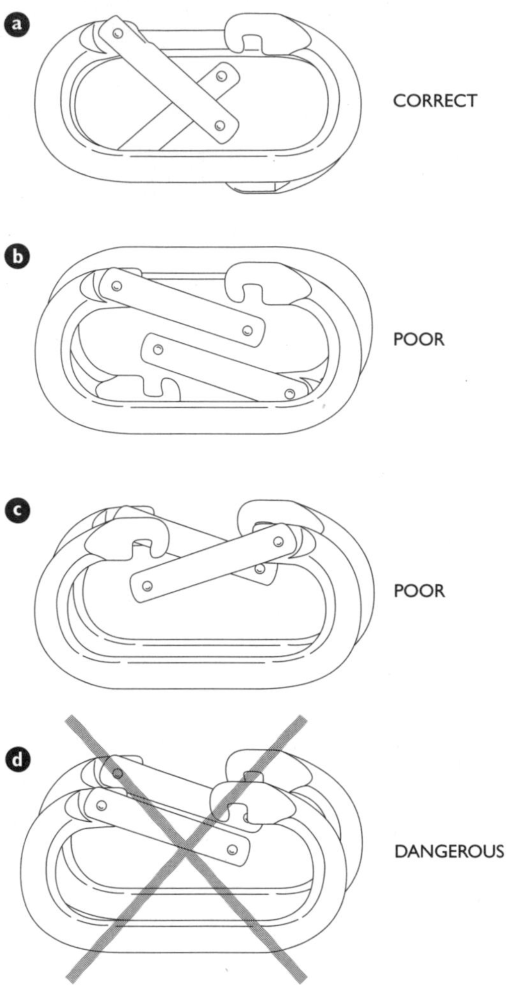

CORRECT

POOR

POOR

DANGEROUS

Fig. 9-34.
Substituting double oval carabiners for a locking carabiner:
a, gates are opposite and opposed (correct);
b, gates are opposite and parallel (poor);
c, gates are on the same side and opposed (poor);
d, gates are on the same side and parallel (dangerous).

carabiners are in the proper configuration by opening both gates at the same time; the gates should cross, forming an X.

Some carabiners are made from bars with cross sections that are oval, T-shaped or cross-shaped, or wedge-shaped—as opposed to round—in order to save weight.

Use and Care

A few basic rules apply to the use and care of all carabiners. Always make sure the force on a carabiner falls on the long axis, and be especially careful that the gate does not receive the load.

Check the carabiner gates occasionally. A gate should open easily, even when the carabiner is loaded, and the gate should have good side-to-side rigidity when open.

A dirty gate can be cleaned by applying a solvent or lubricant (lightweight oil, citrus solvent, or products such as WD-40) to the hinge, working the hinge until it operates smoothly again, and then dipping the carabiner in boiling water for about 20 seconds to remove the cleaning agent.

Finally, remember that a carabiner that has fallen off a cliff onto a hard surface may have suffered nonvisible damage and should be retired.

KEEPING THE SAFETY NET STRONG

In fact, you should avoid using any critical climbing equipment if its history is not personally known to you. Ropes, harnesses, runners, and carabiners, as well as protection pieces (see Chapter 13, Rock Protection) and belay devices (see Chapter 10, Belaying), are all vital links in your chain of protection. Secondhand equipment, whether found or passed along without an account of its use, increases the possibility of a weak link in the chain protecting the lives of you and your partner.

10
CHAPTER

Belaying

Belaying is a fundamental technique for climbing safely, a system of using a rope to stop a fall if one should occur. Belaying can safely control the enormous energy that a falling climber generates, but it takes practice to do well and requires an understanding of its underlying principles.

In its simplest form, a belay consists of nothing more than a rope that runs from a climber to another person, the belayer, who is ready to stop a fall. Three things make the system work:

1. A method of applying a stopping force to the rope
2. A stance with an anchor strong enough to resist the pull of the fall
3. A skilled belayer

155

There are many ways to apply this stopping force, a variety of stances, and many methods of setting up and tying into a belay anchor (the point on the mountain to which the rest of the system is attached). This chapter introduces the principal techniques and major options of belaying so that you can choose the methods that work best in your own climbing.

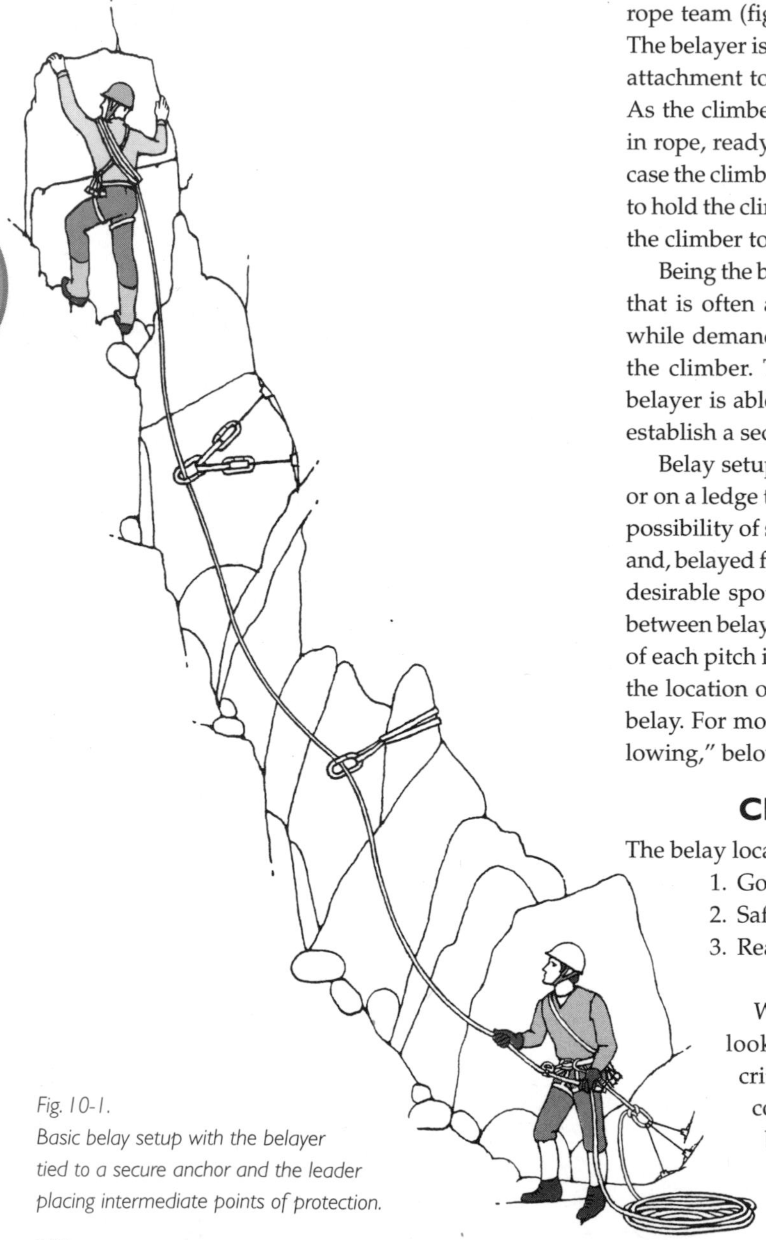

Fig. 10-1.
Basic belay setup with the belayer tied to a secure anchor and the leader placing intermediate points of protection.

HOW BELAYS ARE USED IN CLIMBING

Before explaining the details of belay setups and procedures, it is helpful to start with a general understanding of how belays are used on a climb. For simplicity, picture just the essentials of a belay. There are two climbers, each tied in to the end of a climbing rope, forming a rope team (fig. 10-1). As one climbs, the other belays. The belayer is connected to an anchor, a point of secure attachment to the terrain using rock or snow or trees. As the climber ascends, the belayer pays out or takes in rope, ready to apply a stopping force to the rope in case the climber falls. A belayer may also be called upon to hold the climber stationary under tension or to lower the climber to a ledge.

Being the belayer is a demanding and important task that is often awkward, of long duration, and boring while demanding constant vigilance for the safety of the climber. The belayer's job is much easier if the belayer is able to find a comfortable spot on which to establish a secure position.

Belay setups are usually established on the ground or on a ledge that provides reasonable comfort and the possibility of solid anchors. One climber takes the lead and, belayed from below, moves up the route to the next desirable spot and sets up a new belay. The distance between belays is known as a pitch or a lead. The length of each pitch is usually determined by rope length and the location of a convenient spot to establish the next belay. For more on this subject, see "Leading and Following," below.

Choosing a Belay Spot

The belay location should have three attributes:
1. Good placement for anchors
2. Safe position
3. Reasonable comfort

When choosing a belay position, always look for solid anchors. Solid anchors are critical to a safe belay and are of paramount concern. When selecting a belay location, be aware of the possibility of rockfall or icefall, and pick a stance that will provide some shelter if this seems a

10

156

likely hazard. If a belay location is exposed to imminent danger from rockfall or icefall, safety may require moving the belay to a location with less desirable anchors. Additionally, it is useful to find a position where climbing partners can see and/or communicate with each other.

Many factors ultimately determine the best choice for a belay spot. Longer leads are more efficient, so if several good belay ledges are available, climbers generally pick the highest one. However, the leader may decide to stop and set up the next belay early in order to mitigate the problem of rope drag (friction that impedes the rope's travel). A leader may also shorten a lead because a comfortable ledge at a half rope length is of greater advantage than pushing the lead as far as possible. Perhaps a difficult section may lie ahead, and the lead climber, feeling too tired or unsure of personal ability to lead, may want to end a pitch early so that the other climber can take over the lead.

Leading and Following

On multipitch routes, climbers commonly alternate or swing leads so that in turn they belay at the top of every pitch they lead, which allows a rest before following the next pitch. In other cases, climbers may lead in blocks, with one person taking four or more leads before trading off. This can be more efficient: less time is spent in changeovers, and one climber can become more immersed in the rhythm of leading. Also, if a team consists of climbers of different skill levels, one partner may assume all or most of the leading duties for increased safety or speed.

The climber belayed from above, known as the follower (or second), can climb aggressively, confident that any fall will be held easily by the belayer and will be very short, typically involving little more than stretching of the rope. It is a different matter for the leader of a pitch, who is belayed from below and will drop some distance before the rope begins to stop the fall.

To reduce the distance of a potential fall, the leader must rely on intermediate points of protection (see Chapter 14, Leading on Rock) that the leader sets in the rock or ice on the way up. The leader attaches the rope to the protection and continues the ascent. Now the length of a fall is limited to twice the distance that the leader is above the highest piece of protection, plus some rope stretch, belayer movement, rope slippage, and whatever slack was already in the rope. These factors are examined in detail later in this chapter, showing how the actions of the rope team influence each climber, as well as the possible implications in the event of a fall.

Holding the Fall

When considering the effects of a fall, climbers get used to thinking in terms of force, rather than weight, because force expresses not only a climber's weight, but also the energy that climbers and anchors are subjected to in the event of a fall. This notion of force should be a familiar one from experiences in everyday life.

Static force: Imagine that a 10-pound (4.5-kilogram) object is attached to a rope; then imagine grasping the rope a few feet (a meter or so) from the object in order to hold the object up off the floor. Gravity exerts a downward force on the object while you exert an equal and opposite force to hold it up. This force that gravity exerts on an object is commonly referred to as weight. The force you exert to hold the object up is a static force.

Impact force: Now imagine this variation. While holding your arm still and gripping the rope tightly, have someone lift up the object and then drop it. Gravity will cause the object to fall with an acceleration rate of 32 feet (9.8 meters) per second for every second it falls. When the rope you are holding arrests the object's fall, the sudden impact force generated will be much greater than the force of the object's weight when you were merely holding the object up against gravity. Catching the weight of this falling object obviously involves much higher forces than just holding a static weight because the amount of energy generated in a fall goes up dramatically as the falling object accelerates.

Impact forces are rated in kilonewtons (kN), a measure of force. One kilonewton of force is about equal to 225 pounds (102 kilograms) of static weight—remember, weight is a measure of force. The human body cannot withstand more than about 12 kN, which is equivalent to 2,700 pounds (1,200 kilograms)—or roughly fifteen times the weight of the human body—for a brief instant without risk of severe injury.

10

157

Length of fall: The force required to catch the object's weight also depends on how quickly its fall is arrested. It takes much more resistance to stop the weight quickly than if the rope is allowed to slip a bit. Similarly, holding the weight of a stationary climber involves relatively small forces, but a falling climber quickly generates much greater energy. Stopping a fall as quickly as possible may prevent the falling climber from hitting anything, such as a ledge; however, stopping a fall with a rope too suddenly would subject every component of the system—including the falling climber—to dangerously high impact forces. There needs to be some way to safely absorb the energy generated by the falling climber.

Benefits of dynamic rope: Modern dynamic climbing ropes prevent such dangerously high-impact forces by stretching to absorb energy. In the days of hemp ropes, the golden rule of belaying was "the rope must run." That was because the rope had neither the strength to withstand high impact forces nor the shock absorption to avoid injuring the climber. The only safe way to stop a fall was by making the belay dynamic, allowing some rope to slip through the belay to make a soft catch. This worked, but not without problems; it was difficult to learn, and the friction of the running rope could badly burn a belayer.

Because modern belay devices allow only limited rope slippage, something else must provide that soft catch. That *something* is rope stretch. For a rope to be safe for leading, in which falls are to be expected, it must be an approved dynamic climbing rope (see "The Standard Drop Test Fall" sidebar). Static ropes, webbing slings, and accessory cord, while fine for rappelling, constructing anchors, and other uses, do not stretch enough to safely catch a fall. Look at manufacturers' specifications for climbing ropes. They are not rated by strength, but by impact force. This is because the rope does more than simply not break under the impact of a falling climber; it also stretches to absorb that energy.

The beauty of dynamic climbing ropes is that they limit the impact force of a fall, thereby protecting the belay system: Less force is exerted on anchors, the falling leader receives a softer catch, and the belayer has an easier task holding the fall.

Fall factor: Impact forces generated by falls onto dynamic ropes are determined by both the length of the fall and how much dynamic rope is available to absorb the energy of that fall—together, these determine the fall factor, defined as the length of the fall divided by the length of rope fallen on. Fall factor, not length of fall, determines the impact force that will be generated in the event of a fall. This is written mathematically as:

length of fall ÷ length of rope fallen on = fall factor

In any normal climbing situation, a fall factor of 2 is the highest a climber could ever encounter, because this would mean falling exactly twice the length of the rope that the climber has run out. Assume that two climbers are on a smooth vertical face with no ledges or other hazards to hit in a fall. If the leader falls from 10 feet (3 meters) above the belay without any protection, there would have been 10 feet of rope played out. That climber would end up 10 feet below the belay stance, having fallen 20 feet (6 meters) on 10 feet of rope. Applying this example to the fall factor formula above:

20-foot fall ÷ 10 feet of rope = fall factor of 2

This would be a fall factor of 2, also stated as a factor 2 fall. Such a fall would generate the maximum impact on anchors and climbers, creating a hazardous situation. If there is any slack rope, intermediate points of protection, or dynamic action to the belay, the fall factor would always be less than 2. Once more rope is played out, falls of a similar length will generate much lower impact forces, putting less stress on the system. That same 20-foot fall on a 100-foot (30-meter) section of rope would still involve an exciting bit of air time, but the catch would be quite gentle by comparison:

20-foot fall ÷ 100 feet of rope = fall factor of 0.2

Lower fall factors always mean lower impact forces because there is more rope relative to the length of fall.

It is important to realize that any fall of the same factor will generate the same impact force. Take the 5-meter UIAA/CEN drop test fall described in the sidebar and multiply it by 5; now it is a 25-meter (82-foot) fall on 14 meters (46 feet) of rope, but the fall factor remains

THE STANDARD DROP TEST FALL

Typical maximum impact forces allowed for single dynamic ropes range between about 7 and 11 kN, and by UIAA/CEN standards may not exceed 12 kN (see Chapter 9, Basic Safety System). The 12 kN figure is derived from studies that showed the human body could briefly withstand fifteen times its weight when dropped.

In the standard drop test fall, the rope is rigidly fixed to a solid anchor and runs over only a 1-centimeter-diameter (⅜-inch-diameter) bar, so the rope absorbs virtually all of the impact force of the fall. Thus this drop test fall is, by design, quite severe—more severe than a fall experienced in a normal climbing situation. If a rope design passes this test, it is considered acceptable to manufacture and sell such ropes for climbing.

There are several reasons why the standard drop test fall is more severe than falls in a normal climbing situation. First, in most real-life situations, any belay is, to a certain extent, a dynamic belay. Rope slippage, belayer movement, and friction of the rope against the rock and through the carabiners all serve to dissipate force. The standard drop test fall is set up so that it is not a dynamic belay; the rope absorbs virtually all of the impact force of the fall. This tests the rope's strength to ensure that it will absorb the maximum impact force that would be generated by a fall in a normal climbing situation.

The second reason the standard drop test fall is so severe is because it is set up with a high fall factor. In the UIAA/CEN standard drop test, the fall factor is calculated like this (the maximum fall factor of 2 being replaced by the more technically accurate 1.78):

16-foot-5-inch fall ÷ 9 feet 2 inches of rope = fall factor of 1.78

5-meter fall ÷ 2.8 meters of rope = fall factor of 1.78

the same, 1.78. The fall is much longer (and clearly riskier for the falling climber), but because the amount of rope available to absorb shock is also greater, the amount of impact force that the belay system is subjected to remains the same.

Protecting the Leader

Understanding fall factor and how it determines impact forces is fundamental to safe leading. As described in "Leading and Following," above, the leader places intermediate points of protection to reduce potential fall length, and a leader fall is twice the distance between the climber and the last placement of protection. As described in "Holding the Fall," above, the impact forces are highest when a fall occurs on a relatively short section of rope. It is important to recognize that the most severe strain on the belay system and anchors may occur just as a leader starts up a pitch, should the leader happen to fall before any intermediate anchors have been placed to limit the distance of that fall.

Therefore, climbers should always establish a solid first placement as soon as possible after starting a new

lead. This not only will reduce the chance for a high-factor fall, but will establish the direction from which the force of a leader fall will come (see "Judging the Direction of Fall Forces" in Chapter 14, Leading on Rock). Chapter 14, Leading on Rock, goes into further detail about how these principles are applied; understanding the dynamics involved will help you make more sense of how belaying protects the leader.

APPLYING FRICTION TO THE ROPE

Climbing belays must be able to resist the large forces generated in a fall. With the dynamic climbing rope acting as the shock absorber in the system, the belayer's job is to quickly stop the rope from running. Any additional rope that runs through the belay system as the fall is caught has two related effects: softening the impact forces and lengthening the distance fallen. Occasionally the belayer may want to deliberately provide a more dynamic belay—for instance, if protection is suspected to be weak—but there is always the trade-off

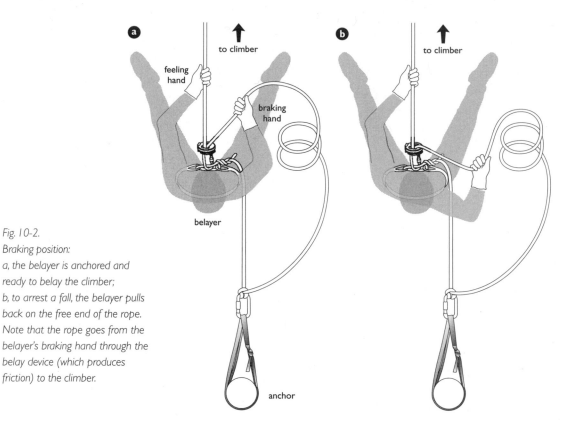

Fig. 10-2.
Braking position:
a, the belayer is anchored and
ready to belay the climber;
b, to arrest a fall, the belayer pulls
back on the free end of the rope.
Note that the rope goes from the
belayer's braking hand through the
belay device (which produces
friction) to the climber.

of a longer fall, with increased possibility of the lead climber hitting a ledge or other hazard.

In any belay method, the rope from the climber goes around or through some friction-producing element—such as the belayer's hips, a belay device, or a Münter hitch knot on a carabiner (see Chapter 9, Basic Safety System)—and then to the belayer's braking hand. Except for some self-locking devices (see "Types of Belay Devices" later in this chapter), the braking hand gripping the rope produces the initial force.

Because everything starts with the belayer's grip, it is important to consider what kind of force it can exert and how that affects braking ability. There is considerable variation in grip strength from one person to another, with average strength somewhere around 50 pounds (23 kilograms). The force that can be exerted by the belayer's grip is reduced when the belayer is using thinner ropes, wearing gloves, and substantially fatigued. In all cases, grip strength alone is not sufficient to stop a fall.

Knowing that hand grip strength alone cannot provide the required stopping force, climbers rely on a mechanical means of increasing this force. Arresting force is amplified by the friction-producing element, commonly a belay device, to stop the falling climber. This use of a device or method is essential: It is the means by which the limited force of the belayer's grip strength can control the large impact forces generated in a fall.

Stopping a fall is accomplished by gripping the rope tightly with the braking hand and assuming the braking (or arrest) position (fig. 10-2). This action must be practiced and learned well so that it becomes automatic; immediately going into arrest position as soon as a fall is sensed is the best way to stop a fall.

Wearing gloves while belaying is a matter of personal choice. Leather gloves protect your hands from friction burns in the case of rope slippage when you are arresting a fall, and it is probably a good idea for beginners to start out wearing them. Some climbers dislike the fact that gloves may interfere with dexterity and tend to leave their hands damp and soft, which is undesirable for climbing rock. Although there is some decrease in grip strength when you wear gloves, this should not be enough of a factor to be a problem.

The most important thing for all belayers to do is to perfect whichever belay method they use. Having one method that you can absolutely count on is the first priority; after that, learning other methods for versatility is valuable and quite worthwhile.

Belaying Technique

The belayer's hand that holds the rope coming from the climber, which is known as the feeling hand, is used to pay the rope in and out. The other hand, known as the braking hand, must never let go of its grip on the rope, remaining ready to catch a fall at any time. It is important to maintain the correct tension on the rope, preventing excess slack, anticipating the climber's movements and needs, letting out rope as the climber moves up or clips into protection, or taking rope in as needed.

With some practice, a belayer can learn to quickly take in or let out rope as required while never removing the braking hand from the rope. A specific sequence of hand motions is used to take in the rope. With both hands on the rope, start with the braking hand close to your body and the feeling hand extended (fig. 10-3a), then pull in the rope using both hands by moving the feeling hand toward your body and pulling away from your body with the braking hand (fig. 10-3b). Then slide the feeling hand forward beyond the braking hand and

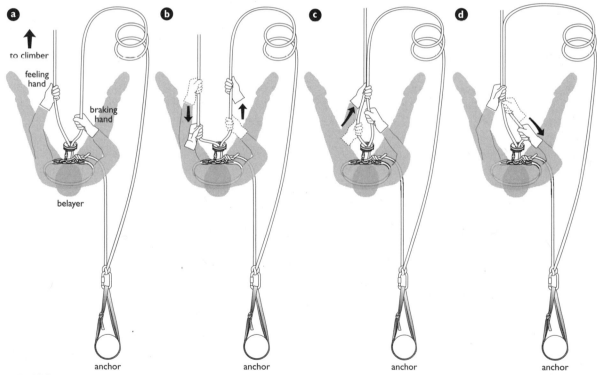

Fig. 10-3.

Hand motions for taking in rope, with the braking hand never leaving the rope: a, start with the feeling hand extended and the braking hand close to the body; b, pull in the rope with the feeling hand while pulling the rope through the belay device with the braking hand; c, extend the feeling hand past the braking hand and grasp both strands of the rope with the feeling hand; d, slide the braking hand toward the body and release the braking hand's strand of the rope from the feeling hand.

161

grasp both strands of rope with the feeling hand (fig. 10-3c). Finally, slide the braking hand back toward your body (fig. 10-3d); then let the feeling hand drop the braking-hand strand of the rope, and repeat the sequence of hand motions. The braking hand must never leave the rope.

Using Belay Devices

When properly used, most belay devices amplify the friction of the braking hand by passing the rope through an aperture, wrapping it around a post, and passing it back out through the aperture. This configuration provides wrap, or bend, in the rope to assist in producing a stopping force. The post is usually a locking carabiner or part of the device itself.

There is no automatic clamping effect with most belay devices. The belayer's braking hand is the initial, and critical, source of friction; without the braking hand on the rope, there is no belay. The total friction exerted on the rope during the arrest of a fall depends on (1) the strength of the belayer's grip, (2) the total number of friction-producing bends or wraps in the rope created by the belay device or method, and (3) the rope's internal resistance to bending and deforming. Fortunately, despite the variations in the strength of belayers' grips, modern belay devices work well enough that when they are properly used, adequate stopping force can be generated with even very modest grip strength.

To stop a fall, the belayer pulls back on the free end of the rope to create a difference in angle of at least 90 degrees between the rope entering the belay device (from the climber) and the rope leaving it (toward the free end). This angle of separation between the two strands of the rope is critical to the strength of the belay. The greater the degree of bend the rope is forced to make, the greater the stopping force that is generated. Figure 10-4 shows how the braking force is increased as the braking hand pulls the rope farther back to increase the angle of separation from 90 degrees to 180 degrees.

Nothing must be in the way of the belayer's braking hand or elbow when the belayer is carrying out the critical task of pulling back on the rope to create adequate separation of the rope ends; also, this critical task must not require an unnatural body twist or motion.

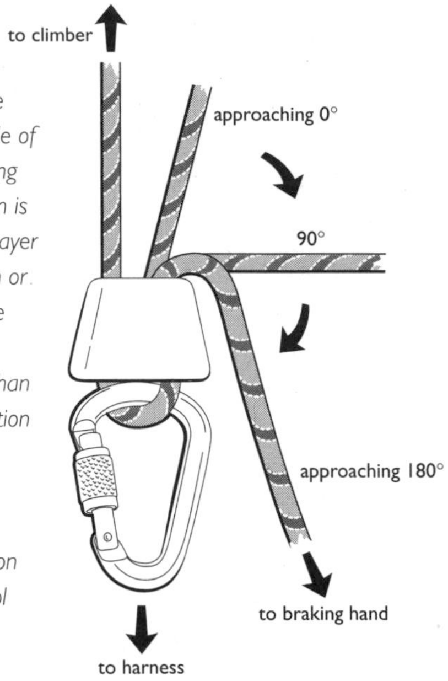

Fig. 10-4. *Angle of separation between the two rope strands. With the angle of separation approaching 0 degrees, little friction is produced and the belayer can easily pay rope in or out as required. As the angle of separation increases to greater than 90 degrees, more friction is generated. At the maximum angle of separation of 180 degrees, enough friction is generated to control the force of a fall.*

One of the simplest ways to do this conveniently in all situations is to clip the belay device into a locking carabiner on the seat harness (currently the most popular belay method in the United States) rather than directly to the anchor. This section describes the use of belay devices when they are attached to the seat harness. "Belay Position and Stance" later in this chapter addresses considerations for belaying off the seat harness versus belaying directly off the anchor.

Types of Belay Devices

There are many popular belay devices. When using any belay device, always read and follow the manufacturer's instructions carefully; be certain that you fully understand these instructions and that the device is properly rigged each time you use it.

Aperture devices: One general type of belay device may be called an aperture device: It simply provides an aperture through which a bight (loop) of rope is pushed and then clipped in to the locking carabiner on the seat harness. In one widely used version of this type, the aperture consists of a slot in a metal plate. (The original device of this type is the Sticht plate, shown in Figure 10-5a.) In another version, the aperture is a cone-shaped or somewhat square tube (the Lowe Tuber II, Black

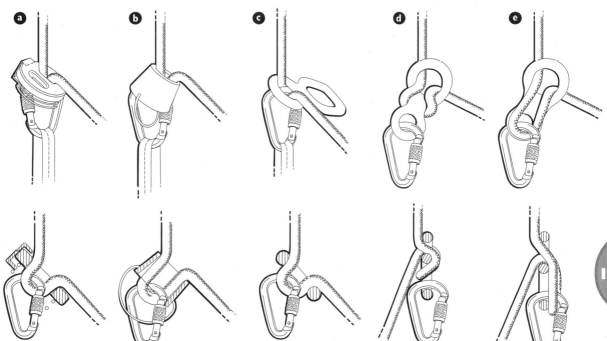

Fig. 10-5.
Aperture-type belay devices with the top illustrations showing the external view and the bottom illustrations showing a cutaway view to reveal the rope path: a, slot or plate; b, tube type; c, figure eight in aperture configuration; d, figure eight in rappel configuration; e, figure eight in "sport mode."

Diamond Air Traffic Controller—ATC, DMM Bug, Trango Pyramid, etc., are examples of such devices, shown in Figure 10-5b). Some aperture devices have two modes: a higher-force mode and a lower-force mode.

Plates and tubes must be attached to some sort of tether to keep them from sliding down the rope and out of reach. Some of these devices include a hole for attaching the tether; others include a wire loop (such as seen in Figure 10-5b) that is clipped in to the locking carabiner on the seat harness. A tether to the harness must be long enough so that it does not interfere with belaying in any direction.

Some aperture devices use a camming or "pinching" action to increase the stopping force. These are essentially a plate device with two configurations, one having a higher stopping force than the other, though the difference is quite small.

Figure-eight devices (not to be confused with the figure-eight knot described in Chapter 9, Basic Safety System) were originally designed for rappelling, not belaying, but some figure-eight devices can serve both functions. Figure eights may be used as belay devices in three different configurations. (1) If the hole in the small end of the figure eight is the size of the hole in a typical aperture device, the figure eight can be used similarly to a plate- or tube-type aperture device by feeding a bight of rope through this hole and through a locking carabiner (fig. 10-5c). This is the preferred method for using a figure eight as a belay device. (2) The standard rappel configuration may also be used for belaying (fig. 10-5d); a bight of rope is passed through the large end of the figure eight and wrapped around the back of the device. (3) Another method (the "sport mode") is set up by putting the bight of rope through the large hole and then clipping both the rope and the small hole into the locking carabiner (fig. 10-5e). The sport mode does not generate as much friction as other methods and is not recommended for situations in

163

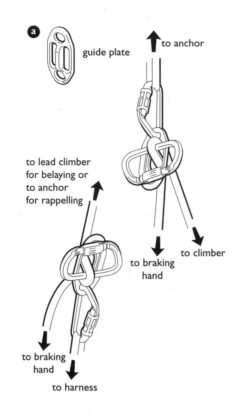

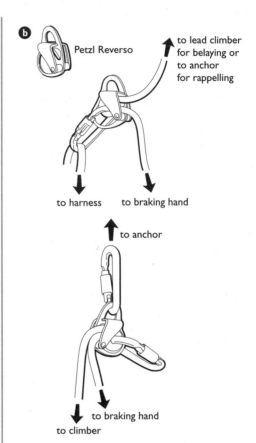

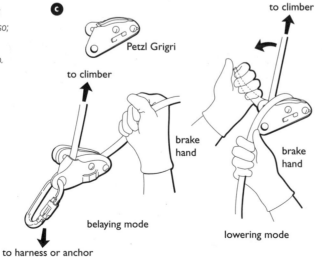

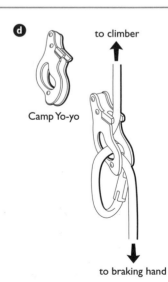

a
guide plate
to anchor
to lead climber
for belaying or
to anchor
for rappelling
to climber
to braking
hand
to braking
hand
to harness

b
Petzl Reverso
to lead climber
for belaying or
to anchor
for rappelling
to harness
to braking hand
to anchor
to braking hand
to climber

c
Petzl Grigri
to climber
to climber
to harness or anchor
belaying mode
brake
hand
brake
hand
lowering mode

d
Camp Yo-yo
to climber
to braking hand

Fig. 10-6.
Self-locking belay
devices with the
top illustrations
showing the
device by itself
and the bottom
illustrations
showing the
devices in use:
a, guide plate;
b, Petzl Reverso;
c, Petzl Grigri;
d, Camp Yo-yo.

10

which high-impact force falls may have to be held. Make certain that the figure-eight device is intended for belaying use by the manufacturer; many are not.

Self-locking belay devices: Several manufacturers also make belay devices that function differently from the common aperture-type devices in that they are self-locking or have a self-locking mode. There are currently four different types of self-locking devices available.

Two of the devices allow the rope to be run over itself in such a way that the rope can be easily pulled in by the belayer, but when a climber falls, the device locks off. These devices provide a very secure means of belaying the second directly off an anchor. One type of device, commonly referred to as a guide plate (fig. 10-6a) or plaquette, is simply a friction device with an elongated slot through which the bight of rope is fed and wrapped around a locking carabiner in such a way that a pull on the load strand of the rope clamps the rope down on itself, causing the device to lock off automatically. Another device (the Petzl Reverso; fig. 10-6b) looks similar to other aperture devices and may be used off the harness in the same way as a standard aperture device, but may also, by using a second locking carabiner, be rigged to belay directly off the anchor in a self-locking mode similar to guide plates.

These devices can be used to tend one rope or two ropes independently, making them especially useful for climbing using double-rope techniques (see Chapter 14, Leading on Rock, for a discussion of double-rope techniques). Self-locking belay devices allow the belayer using two ropes to easily and securely manage the separate ropes. However, pay particular attention if these devices are to be used with small-diameter ropes; the self-locking characteristics of these devices may not function in certain configurations or circumstances when used with ropes of less than 10 millimeters. Refer to the manufacturers' instructions before using self-locking belay devices on small-diameter ropes. Also be aware that, because these devices do lock up under load, they do not function as effective lowering devices, which is a drawback. Additionally, if the belayed climber falls and is unable to get back on the rock to take the load off the device, the belayer must rig a lifting system to unweight and thereby unlock the device.

The Petzl Grigri (fig. 10-6c) is a specialized belay device with an extremely useful feature: It does not require any stopping force at all from the belayer's hand. It works on the same principle as a car's seat belts. Rope feeds smoothly through this device as the belayer pays rope in or out, but the sudden acceleration of rope in a fall causes an internal cam to lock down on the rope, creating an automatic braking force. The Grigri has some tendency to lock up when the lead climber makes a sudden move up. The Grigri has become quite popular at climbing gyms and sport-climbing areas, and does provide increased security with less-experienced belayers. However, the self-locking mechanism can put high loads on anchors, and it works poorly or not at all with icy or wet ropes. These factors, together with its weight and bulk, make it largely unsuitable for mountaineering despite its other advantages. Note that those who have used the Grigri exclusively and have climbed only indoors may not be quite aware of the greater demands required of other belay methods and devices.

With another type of self-locking belay device—such as the Camp Yo-yo (shown in Figure 10-6d), Salewa Antz, and Wild Country Single Rope Controller (SRC)—sudden loads cause the device to rotate, locking the rope between the device's body and the anchor carabiner. These devices also incorporate slots that generate additional friction.

Special Considerations in Using Belay Devices

When a climber using a belay device is facing away from the belay anchor, the tie-in to the anchor should be on the braking-hand side. This way, body rotation under the force of a fall will assist, rather than hinder, the belayer. When facing toward the anchor (usually when belaying a leader), the belayer's braking hand should be opposite the side where the leader would likely drop in case of a fall before the first protection is put in place. For example, if the climber leads up and to the right, so that in an unprotected leader fall the climber would fall past the belayer on the right, the braking hand should be the belayer's left hand.

Another choice the belayer must make when using a belay device is whether to have the braking hand in the palm-up or the palm-down position. In the palm-down position (fig. 10-7a), the hand motions for taking

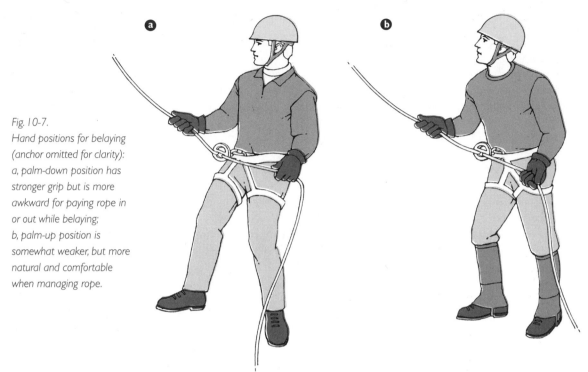

Fig. 10-7.
Hand positions for belaying
(anchor omitted for clarity):
a, palm-down position has
stronger grip but is more
awkward for paying rope in
or out while belaying;
b, palm-up position is
somewhat weaker, but more
natural and comfortable
when managing rope.

in rope are somewhat more awkward and put more strain on the upper arm. However, in the palm-down position, the grip on the rope in the braking position is more natural and grip strength is probably higher. But when the belayer in the palm-down position suddenly goes into the braking position, the tendency is to slap the closed hand up against the hip, possibly hitting the thumb knuckles against any equipment carried on the hardware loops of the seat harness. This can be a problem even when wearing gloves. The palm-up position (fig. 10-7b), although somewhat weaker than palm-down, usually makes rope management less awkward while still maintaining adequate grip strength. Beginning belayers should practice belaying and catching falls with both hand positions in order to decide which works best for them.

When taking in or letting out slack with an aperture device (whether a plate type or a tube type), keep the ropes strictly parallel; otherwise, the rope will pull the device up against the carabiner, and braking begins. Eventually the technique becomes automatic.

Like any piece of critical equipment made of metal, a belay device that is dropped a significant distance

should be retired because hidden damage may have occurred, weakening the device.

Performance Differences among Belay Devices

Belay devices vary significantly in the amount of friction they produce in routine rope handling and in arresting a fall. Occasionally a device or method that generates less friction is desirable in order for a party to travel more quickly, or for when a more dynamic belay is desired due to relatively weak anchors.

Belay devices also vary significantly in how easily they perform the tasks of holding the climber stationary under tension or lowering the climber to a ledge. Plate devices require the least force to hold the climber's weight, but are the least smooth in lowering the climber. There are some differences in how smoothly different tube devices work for lowering, but these are difficult to quantify and vary widely with different rope and device combinations.

Belay devices are frequently used for rappelling (see Chapter 11, Rappelling). Plates and tubes can produce a jerky ride that may put undesirable impact loads on the rappel anchor, a grave concern when circumstances do not allow for ideal rappel anchors. Figure eights are the smoothest for rappelling, but figure eights put twists in the rope, later producing snarls in the coils.

All belay devices come with manufacturer's instructions. Always read these carefully and follow them.

Using the Münter Hitch

The Münter hitch is a very effective method of belaying that uses only the rope, a carabiner, and a special knot to provide the friction necessary to stop a fall. The Münter hitch may be known by a variety of names, such as the friction hitch, Italian hitch, half ring bend, carabiner hitch, running R, half-mast belay, and UIAA method. It was introduced in Europe in 1973 as the *halbmastwurf sicherung* ("half clove-hitch belay"), now abbreviated as HMS. (Chapter 9, Basic Safety System, gives details on tying the Münter hitch.) When used with an HMS (pear-shaped) carabiner attached to an anchor or the front of the seat harness, the Münter hitch works as a very effective belay system.

Efficient belaying with a Münter hitch requires an HMS-type (pear-shaped) carabiner with an opening large enough to allow the hitch to feed through smoothly. As a result of its special configuration, the hitch amplifies the effect of the braking hand with friction created by the rope being wrapped on itself and around the HMS carabiner.

The Münter hitch is unique in that it is the only traditional belay method that provides sufficient friction regardless of the angle at which the braking end of the rope is held. With most belay devices, maximum friction is generated when the brake-hand strand of the rope is held at an angle of 180 degrees or more from the strand of rope attached to the climber. In contrast, the Münter hitch, because of the way it wraps around the HMS carabiner, actually generates more friction when both strands of the rope are aligned (fig. 10-8). Furthermore, in absolute terms, the Münter hitch often generates more friction than any other belay device regardless of the angle at which the braking strand of the rope is held. This higher friction can mean a quicker stop to a severe fall.

Because no special braking position is required, the Münter hitch has an advantage over most belay devices

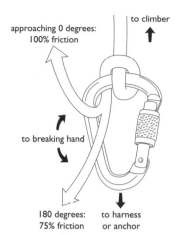

approaching 0 degrees: 100% friction

to climber

to breaking hand

180 degrees: 75% friction

to harness or anchor

Fig. 10-8. The Münter hitch provides sufficient friction for belaying regardless of the angle between the ropes entering and leaving it.

in that if a fall takes a belayer by surprise, the hitch will function even if the belayer does no more than firmly grip the rope. Rope handling with the Münter hitch is quick and easy, making it an ideal method when climbers are moving rapidly over easy ground. Finally, because no specialized equipment other than an HMS carabiner is required, the Münter hitch provides a ready backup belay method if a belay device is lost.

The Münter hitch has some drawbacks as well as advantages. It kinks the rope more than any other method, but this can be minimized by allowing the rope to feed freely until called upon to arrest a fall. To unkink the rope, shake it out while it is hanging free. After a big fall, the outermost layer of the sheath may be glazed—which, like the effect from the use of hard-anodized belay devices, is only cosmetic. The Münter hitch is not preferred for rappelling because it twists the rope.

Using the Hip Belay

The hip belay (also called the body belay) is a belay method in which the rope is wrapped around the belayer's body to generate enough friction to stop a climber's fall. The belayer connects to a solid anchor and assumes a stable stance facing the direction of an anticipated pull on the rope. The rope from the climber is passed around the belayer's back and sides just below the top of the hips (fig. 10-9a). To arrest a fall, grip the rope tightly with the braking hand and assume the braking (or arrest) position—braking arm pulled across the stomach (fig. 10-9b). This action must be practiced

167

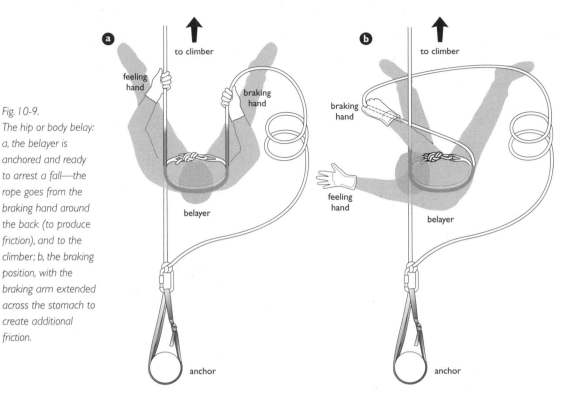

Fig. 10-9.
The hip or body belay:
a, the belayer is
anchored and ready
to arrest a fall—the
rope goes from the
braking hand around
the back (to produce
friction), and to the
climber; b, the braking
position, with the
braking arm extended
across the stomach to
create additional
friction.

and learned well so that it becomes automatic; immediately going into arrest position as soon as a fall is sensed is the best way to stop a fall. The braking position increases the amount of friction-producing wrap of the rope around the body, thereby increasing the stopping force.

The hip belay, once the standard for high-angle climbing, has significant disadvantages; therefore few climbers use it as their primary method of belaying.

Because the force of a fall is dissipated as friction against the belayer's body, a belayer stopping a severe fall can suffer from serious rope burns. Protective clothes are required to prevent this. Even fairly minor leader falls can melt and severely damage expensive synthetic garments. If a belayer is burned badly enough, the belayer could drop a falling climber. Because the belayer's hands provide a greater proportion of friction in the hip belay than in other methods, gloves are essential to protect the hands from burns. A tighter grip causes less-severe burns because slower rope velocity and less rope slippage generate less heat. Another problem with the hip belay is that if the climbing rope

runs over the anchor attachment during a fall, the anchor attachment may be burned.

Because the hip belay requires more time to attain braking position and generates less braking force than any other method, more rope slippage generally occurs and the climber usually falls farther. If the belay stance fails, it is much more likely that the belayer will lose control of the rope than with other methods.

Despite its drawbacks as a general-purpose belay method, the hip belay does have advantages that make it worth learning, if only for special purposes.

With the hip belay, the belayer can take in rope much faster than with other methods, and the hip belay can be set up quickly with a minimum of equipment. It is probably most useful when belaying a fast-moving partner from above. A common and efficient practice is to use a simple hip belay to bring a following climber up a relatively easy pitch and then switch to another method when this climber leads the next pitch. Assuming the belayer and climbing partner do not let slack develop and there is no possibility of a pendulum fall (in which the climber swings toward the fall line, creating larger forces), the hip belay method has little risk when belaying a second in this manner.

The hip belay can also be useful for belaying on snow, where it may be desirable to have a more dy-namic belay because anchors are often suspect. Also, if climbers have lost or forgotten their belay device and do not have the right kind of carabiner for a Münter hitch, there may be no choice but to use the hip belay.

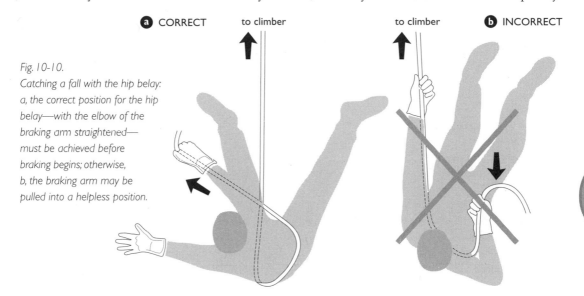

Fig. 10-10.
Catching a fall with the hip belay: a, the correct position for the hip belay—with the elbow of the braking arm straightened—must be achieved before braking begins; otherwise, b, the braking arm may be pulled into a helpless position.

a CORRECT   to climber   to climber   **b** INCORRECT

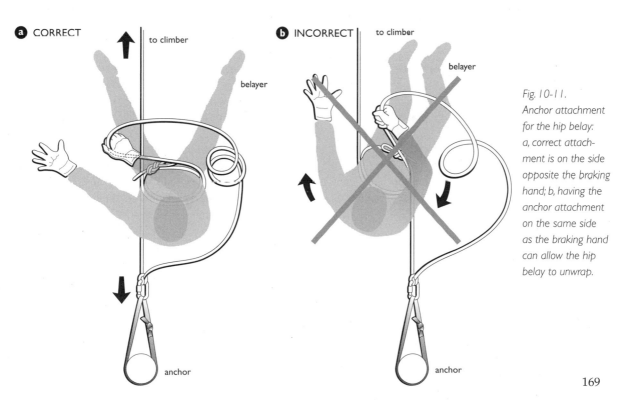

a CORRECT   to climber   **b** INCORRECT   to climber

belayer   belayer

anchor   anchor

Fig. 10-11.
Anchor attachment for the hip belay: a, correct attachment is on the side opposite the braking hand; b, having the anchor attachment on the same side as the braking hand can allow the hip belay to unwrap.

10

Special Considerations in Using the Hip Belay

When using the hip belay, you need to keep a number of special considerations in mind.

To catch a fall with this method, straighten the elbow of the braking arm before you begin to grip hard. Then bring the braking arm across in front of your body (fig. 10-10a), to increase the amount of wrap for maximum friction. The natural reaction is to grip the rope first, but this may pull the braking arm into a helpless position (fig. 10-10b), requiring you to let go and grasp the rope again. An optimal braking position can only be learned with practice, ideally with actual weights being dropped and held.

When you are attaching to the anchor, rig the connection to the side opposite the braking hand (fig. 10-11a). Note that this is different from tying in for belaying with a mechanical device. If the braking hand and anchor rope are on the same side of your body (fig. 10-11b), the force of a fall can partly unwrap the rope from around your body, decreasing both friction and stability.

Another precaution is to clip a control carabiner on your seat harness (fig. 10-12). The carabiner goes in front, or on the same side as the rope coming from the climber, but well forward of your hip bone. Clipping the rope into this carabiner keeps the rope where it is needed, at your hip, and also counteracts body rotation.

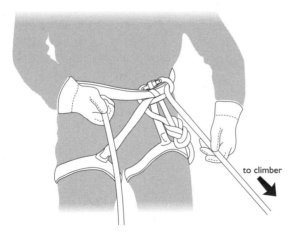

Fig. 10-12.
A control carabiner on the harness helps keep the hip belay from unwrapping.

If you are not using a control carabiner, take advantage of the anchor attachment to keep the climbing rope from being pulled overhead or under your seat. If the pull will come from below, put the rope above the anchor attachment. If the pull will come from above with no possibility of a downward pull, put the rope below the anchor line.

Choosing a Method

It might seem that the choice of a general-purpose belay method would be a simple matter of choosing the method that exerts the most stopping force. However, even if two belay methods differ significantly in the maximum stopping force that they can exert, there will be no practical difference at all between them for a very wide range of falls (almost all that a belayer will ever have to hold); the falls will be held statically because the force the belayer needs to exert with either method will not reach the level at which the rope will start to run.

When the difference between two belay methods matters is in the case of a high-factor fall on high-angle rock with little or nothing to produce friction other than the belay; in this situation, the belay method can mean the difference between the rope running and not running. Still, these types of falls are the critical ones, where things are most likely to go wrong.

If the rope starts to run while the belayer is holding a fall, the climber will fall that much farther than if the fall were held with no run-through. The extra fall is generally undesirable and occasionally disastrous. However, in any protected leader fall, it is important to consider that the maximum force on the top piece of protection is one and a half to two times as high as the maximum force on the climber—in a high-factor fall on vertical rock, the maximum force on the climber can easily be 1,500 pounds (6.7 kN). If the protection fails under this force, the climber will definitely fall farther. To reduce this force on the protection, some belayers choose a relatively weak method of belaying, one that will let the rope start to run at a lower force to lessen the likelihood of the protection failing.

Load-limiting runners: The leader can also effectively limit the maximum impact on individual protection placements by using a load-limiting device (such as the Yates Screamer). This consists of a sewn runner

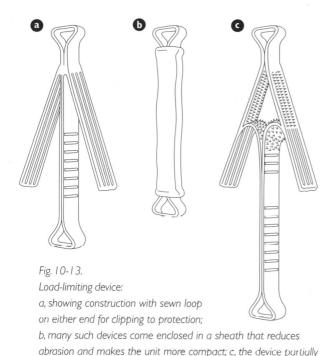

Fig. 10-13.
Load-limiting device:
a, showing construction with sewn loop on either end for clipping to protection;
b, many such devices come enclosed in a sheath that reduces abrasion and makes the unit more compact; c, the device partially deployed—even if all the bar-tacks fail, the runner still retains full strength.

with a series of weaker bar-tacks (fig. 10-13) that fail at a lower impact force and absorb high loads, while the runner retains full strength if fully deployed; load-limiting runners (also called energy-absorbing slings) are usually encased in a sheath (fig. 10-13b). The leader clips into a suspect placement with one of these devices without compromising overall belay strength. During a fall, a force greater than 2 kilonewtons (kN) will activate these runners, which can reduce by 3 to 8 kN the peak load that the fall imposes on the placement.

ANCHORS

Secure anchors are vital. Climbers should remind themselves, as they acquire more experience, that the moment when they will have to stop an extreme leader fall cannot be anticipated. And when it happens, the anchor must hold, or the climbers—leader and belayer both—will suffer a catastrophic fall.

Selecting an Anchor

This section gives a few tips on selecting good anchors for belays, but for full details on finding and using natural features, and on setting artificial anchors on rock, snow, and ice, study Chapter 13, Rock Protection; Chapter 14, Leading on Rock; Chapter 16, Snow Travel and Climbing; and Chapter 18, Alpine Ice Climbing. Also, see Appendix C, Supplementary Reading, at the back of this book.

When selecting belay anchors, always consider every possible direction from which a force may load the anchors. Belaying a follower usually results in a downward pull, but leader falls belayed from below generate substantial upward forces, and traversing pitches exert strong lateral loads. Make sure the belay anchors will withstand a pull from any conceivable fall.

Natural Anchors

A large natural feature, such as a live, good-sized, well-rooted tree or pillar of sound rock, can make an ideal anchor.

COMPARING BELAY DEVICES AND METHODS

When selecting a general-purpose belay device or method, research available performance information and consider the following factors:

■ Which device or method will hold a fall with minimum force exerted?
■ Which device or method allows for easy paying out and taking in of the rope?
■ Which device or method makes it easy to lower a climber?
■ Which device or method can most effectively double as a rappel device?

Occasionally figures are published that state the force at which a rope will start to run for certain belay devices or methods. In practice, any UIAA-approved belaying device or method provides adequate braking force if used correctly. Proficiency with a device or method is critical irrespective of the differing performance characteristics.

SRENE ANCHOR SYSTEMS

A simple yet highly effective set of principles to follow when evaluating anchor systems goes by the acronym SRENE. This means that any anchor system should be:

- **S**olid: Each individual component should be solid to the greatest extent feasible.
- **R**edundant: Always use redundant components in setting up an anchor. Two solid anchors are considered an absolute minimum, and then only if they are really bombproof. Three or more are preferable.
- **E**qualized: Use a rigging method that tries to equally distribute the load between the various individual anchors. This greatly increases the reliability of each part of the system.
- **N**o **E**xtension: Eliminate the possibility that failure of one of the anchors in the system will cause the anchor to suddenly extend, which would cause subsequent shock loading and generate dangerously high impact forces on the remaining anchors.

Trees and large bushes provide the most obvious anchors. Do not trust a tree or shrub that is loose or appears weak or brittle. Carefully evaluate tree anchors near or on cliff faces; these trees may be shallowly rooted and may not be as solid as they appear. Test all trees by pushing against them with one foot. Attaching to an unquestionably stout tree branch rather than low on the trunk helps limit the rope's contact with the ground, reducing abrasion on the rope and reducing the risk of rockfall. However, connecting to a branch rather than the trunk puts more leverage on the tree, increasing the danger that the tree could be uprooted. Be cautious about using a bush as an anchor. If you use one, consider placing an additional anchor or two for safety. Also be careful using trees and bushes in very cold weather, when they can become brittle.

Rock features—horns, columns, rock tunnels such as those formed by the contact point between two boulders, large and flat-bottomed boulders—are commonly used as anchors. Note that it is easy to overestimate the stability of large boulders. As important as size is the shape of the boulder's bottom, the shape of the socket it is sitting in or the angle of the slope it is on, and the ratio of its height to width. Imagine the hidden undersurface and the block's center of gravity: Will it pull over under a big load? Test it, gently at first so you do not send it over the edge. Occasionally climbers have to set up a belay at a jumble of large boulders, with some resting on others. A boulder underneath other large boulders might be quite solid but can be difficult to assess even with careful checking.

Any rock feature used as an anchor should be checked for fracture lines, which may be subtle and difficult to judge, such as at the base of a rock horn or near the edge of a crack. When using protection in a crack for an anchor, check to see whether one side of the crack may actually be a detachable block or movable flake; a crack has to widen only a fraction of an inch under the force of a fall for the protection to pull out.

Always evaluate the probable strength and stability of a rock feature or chockstone prior to using it as an anchor. If there is any question about a natural anchor, test it before gear is attached, never after the rope or the belayer is hooked in.

Artificial Anchors

The most common artificial (manufactured) anchors are bolts or pitons ("fixed pins"). On established routes, climbers may encounter previously placed bolts and pitons; in unknown alpine terrain, some climbers carry pitons and a hammer to set anchors. Bolts are permanent pieces of artificial protection, driven into a hole that has been drilled into the rock. Bolt hangers allow carabiners to be attached to bolts (see Figure 13-6 in Chapter 13, Rock Protection). Pitons are metal spikes pounded into cracks. The blade of the piton is driven into the crack; the eye is the point of attachment for a carabiner (see Figure 13-8 in Chapter 13, Rock Protection). Climbers may also encounter other fixed pieces, climbers' hardware known as chocks—nuts, hexes, and so forth, which are usually removable protection that became fixed when someone could not remove them. On rock-climbing topo maps, bolts and fixed pitons are often shown as "x" and "fp," respectively.

Fixed pins that have been left in place by previous climbers must be evaluated for safety. Bolts and fixed pitons are often solid if of recent vintage, but older placements are notoriously difficult to assess (see "Fixed Protection" in Chapter 13, Rock Protection). Old ¼-inch bolts, once considered adequate, have not been used regularly for decades and can never be considered trustworthy.

As a rule of thumb, when using artificial protection for anchors, it is better to use three or more and equalize the load between them. (See "Equalizing Multiple Anchors" later in this chapter.)

Tying In to the Anchor

The most common way for the belayer to tie in to the anchor is with the climbing rope itself, using the first few feet (a meter or so) of rope as it comes from its tie-in at the belayer's harness. The rest of the rope is available for use by the climber. Another way for a belayer to attach to an anchor is with runners from the anchor to the seat harness. Although this is often slower and uses up more equipment—especially when you must attach to multiple anchors—it is a good idea when the length of the next pitch is not known and the full length of the rope may be needed.

Several knots and methods are available for attaching to an anchor with the rope. Climbers commonly put a runner around or over the natural anchor and attach a carabiner to the runner, then use a clove hitch or figure-eight knot in the climbing rope to clip in to the carabiner. The figure eight is strong, stable, and easy to untie; the clove hitch has the advantage of being adjustable after it is tied and is the easiest way to back up a stance with a taut line from the belayer to the anchor.

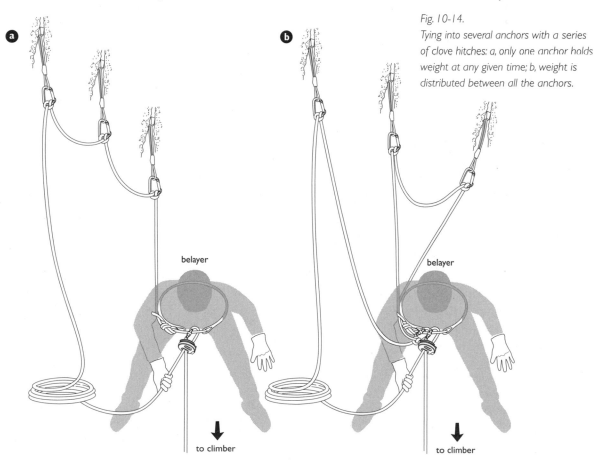

Fig. 10-14.
Tying into several anchors with a series of clove hitches: a, only one anchor holds weight at any given time; b, weight is distributed between all the anchors.

belayer

to climber

belayer

to climber

173

When connecting to an anchor, use one locking carabiner or two regular carabiners with the gates reversed and opposed (see Figure 9-34 in Chapter 9, Basic Safety System). Avoid chaining carabiners in succession, because they can twist, which weakens them and can open a gate.

Redundancy requires attaching to multiple anchors for belaying—commonly two or three that will hold a downward pull and one that will hold an upward pull. The upward-pull and downward-pull anchors are not necessarily separate: A multidirectional anchor (such as a bolt or a tree) may serve as one of the downward-pull anchors and also as the upward-pull anchor. When using protection such as chocks, a common arrangement is to create a multidirectional placement with at least one pair of opposing chocks (see "Opposition Placement" in Chapter 13, Rock Protection).

There are several different ways to rig multiple anchors, and a number of considerations affect the choice. One is to tie in separately, with the climbing rope, to a series of anchors, using clove hitches for their adjustability (fig. 10-14a). This method, although quick and simple, has several drawbacks. If a serious fall occurs, all the impact goes first to a single anchor. The other anchors come into play only if the first one fails. Although the force that goes to the second anchor may be less than that on the first (because some of the energy of the fall has been absorbed), it may still be considerable. And as each anchor fails, the belayer may suddenly drop some distance, dangerously shock-loading the remaining anchors with impact forces, and may lose control of the belay.

It is far preferable to use a method that equalizes the load among two or more anchors. Properly done, this distributes the load more or less equally between the various anchors, drastically reducing the load on any one and ensuring greater reliability for the belay. This could be done using a clove hitch to each anchor carabiner, as in the method described above, but running the rope back to a locking carabiner at the harness and tying in with a clove hitch after every other clove hitch at an anchor (fig. 10-14b). This results in a section of rope tied between the seat harness and each anchor carabiner. The belayer can then adjust the clove hitches to snug up the strand to each carabiner. Then if the an-

chor takes the force of a fall, the impact will be shared by the multiple placements, and if one fails, no drop results before the others come into play. Equalizing the load among the individual anchor placements is especially important in case one or more of the placements are suspected to be weak. However, this method uses a lot of rope and is somewhat cumbersome to set up; therefore, it is not often used. Preferred methods of equalizing the load among multiple anchors are discussed in the next section.

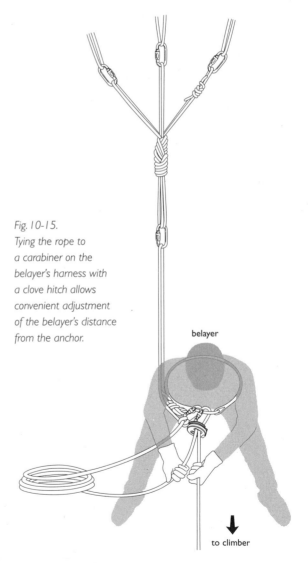

Fig. 10-15.
Tying the rope to
a carabiner on the
belayer's harness with
a clove hitch allows
convenient adjustment
of the belayer's distance
from the anchor.

belayer

to climber

Sometimes climbers will want to belay from a stance that is some distance from the anchors. Once the belayer is set in the stance, precise adjustment is impossible because the tie-in knot to the anchor is out of reach from the stance. A solution is to tie in with a knot on only the seat harness. Take the rope—after it has run from the harness and simply been clipped through the anchor carabiner—and tie it to the carabiner on the seat harness (fig. 10-15). Use a clove hitch so the tension on the rope between belayer and the anchor can easily be adjusted. This method avoids much fussing around and moving back and forth from anchor to stance, but does use up additional rope.

Equalizing Multiple Anchors

Most ways of equalizing the load on multiple anchors make use of runners or other loops, and can be roughly divided into two types: self-equalization and static equalization.

Self-Equalization

Self-equalization is intended to distribute any force equally among all the anchors.

Two-point equalizing, using two anchors, is the simplest example of self-equalization (fig. 10-16). Clip a runner into the anchor carabiners; then grasp the top part of the runner between the two anchors and put a

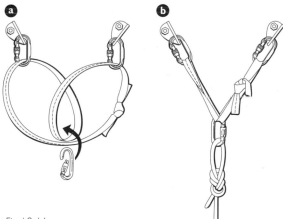

Fig. 10-16.

Two-point self-equalization: a, clip a single runner to the anchor carabiners and form a loop at top; b, then clip a carabiner into the loop and the bottom part of the runner.

half twist in it, forming a loop (fig. 10-16a). Then clip the loop and the bottom part of the runner together with a carabiner into which the rope is tied (fig. 10-16b). It is absolutely essential to put the loop in the runner rather than just clipping the top and bottom of the runner to the carabiner into which the rope is tied. Otherwise, if one anchor fails, the runner will simply slip through this carabiner, leaving the rope completely unanchored.

Two-point equalization has been much used in the past, on the theory that the carabiner attached to the rope can slide from side to side and self-equalize as the direction of pull changes. There are several problems with this system. Current test data indicate that in the event of severe loading, the system essentially locks; the carabiner fails to slide on the runner and does not accomplish the intended equalization of force, instead concentrating the load on one anchor and increasing the likelihood of failure of one component of the belay anchor. This method also violates the No Extension principle; in the event of one anchor failing, the other will be shock-loaded by extension of the runner as the load transfers to the one remaining anchor. This risks failure of the second anchor and potential loss of control of the belay.

Because of these problems, self-equalization is no longer recommended as a method of rigging belay anchors. Climbers may still see this system used, and it can be valuable in equalizing individual anchors as points of protection or components of a complete belay anchor system. However, be aware of the limitations described above. Currently, static equalization is the preferred method of rigging belay anchors.

Static Equalization

A very simple kind of static equalization uses two separate runners attached to two separate anchors, with the two ends clipped together at the bottom with a carabiner (fig. 10-17). This can distribute the load fairly well if the runners are of the right length, or if the belay can be aimed to even out the tension on the runners, but in practice this method will seldom achieve true equalization.

Another kind of static equalization, now quite popular, uses a cordelette, which is a long runner of about 18 feet (5.5 meters), usually made of 7- to 8-millimeter

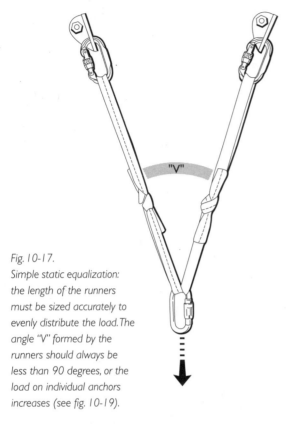

Fig. 10-17.
Simple static equalization: the length of the runners must be sized accurately to evenly distribute the load. The angle "V" formed by the runners should always be less than 90 degrees, or the load on individual anchors increases (see fig. 10-19).

perlon cord, or one of the new small-diameter high-strength cords made of a material such as Spectra.

The smaller-diameter cords are popular due to their low weight and bulk combined with high strength. Keep in mind that a triple fisherman's knot is required to tie many of these new materials due to their low friction qualities. These materials often have lower melting points, making it critical that they not be subjected to a loaded rope running over them. Additionally, recent test data show that with knotting and repeated flexing, some of these materials weaken much faster than nylon, which means that their strength in use is not actually much higher than that of the 8-millimeter perlon cordelettes. The smaller-diameter cords are more expensive than perlon, and may have to be replaced more frequently as they lose strength with use.

To equalize three anchors, clip the cordelette into all three anchors (fig. 10-18a), pull down the top segments between the anchors, and join them with the bottom part of the cordelette (fig. 10-18b). Then, while pulling in the predicted direction of force, tie all three segments together into an overhand or figure-eight knot and then clip a carabiner into the resulting end loop (fig. 10-18c). Either knot is acceptable; the overhand requires less cord, but it will be much harder to untie if it is heavily loaded. Of course, the cordelette can also be used on just two anchors.

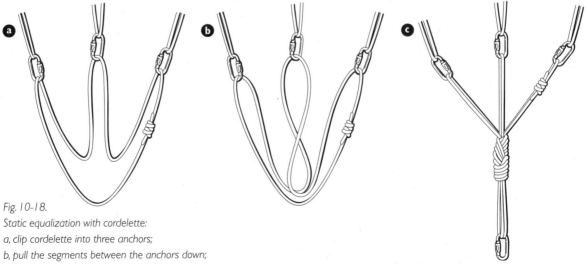

Fig. 10-18.
Static equalization with cordelette:
a, clip cordelette into three anchors;
b, pull the segments between the anchors down;
c, then grasp all three segments together, tie an overhand or figure-eight knot, and clip a carabiner into the loops.

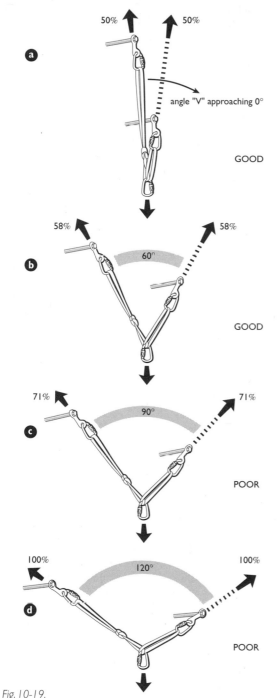

Fig. 10-19.

Two-point anchor equalized with tied runners: a, angle "V" where two runners meet approaches zero degrees; b and c, as the angle "V" increases, the load on each anchor component increases; d, load exceeds 100 percent on each anchor component as the angle becomes greater than 120 degrees.

Webbing cordelettes, called webolettes, are available as well; they are made of ⁹⁄₁₆-inch (14-millimeter) Spectra with a small carabiner loop sewn into each end. They are stronger and lighter than tied cordolettes. To equalize three anchors using a webolette, clip the sewn ends separately into two of the anchors, leaving the middle anchor free. Then take a bight from the middle of the webolette and clip it into the third (middle) anchor. Now take the two lengths of the webolette from between each of the three anchors and gather them into two equalized bights. Tie off the two equalized bights together and clip the anchor attachment into the loops formed below the tie-off knot in the same manner as a cordelette.

Choosing an Equalization Method

A common factor affecting both static equalization and self-equalization must be clearly understood. How well an equalization setup reduces the pull on each individual anchor depends on the angle formed by the runner or runners coming together (see Figures 10-16 and 10-17 above). The smaller the angle, the less force each anchor will be subjected to (fig. 10-19a). As the angle increases, each anchor experiences an increasing force (fig. 10-19b). For example, when the angle is 90 degrees in a two-anchor setup (fig. 10-19c), each anchor will take 71 percent of the force downward at the point of attachment (see Table 10-1). When the angle is greater than 120 degrees (fig. 10-19d), each of the two anchors will actually be subjected to a greater force than if equalization was not even used.

TABLE 10-1. FORCE ON EACH OF TWO EQUALIZED ANCHORS	
Angle	**Force on Each Anchor**
0°	50%
60°	58%
90°	71%
120°	100%
150°	193%
170°	573%

A rigging system sometimes used at bolt anchors consists of a single runner (or multiple runners all rigged this way) simply clipped in to both anchors and

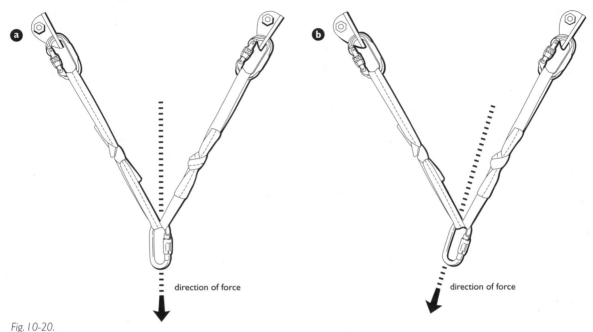

Fig. 10-20.
Static equalization: a, line representing direction of force bisects angle, thus load on the two anchors is equal; b, direction of force is to one side, thus load on the right-hand anchor is greater than on the left-hand anchor.

the carabiner into which the rope is tied. When loaded, the runner forms a triangle between the three points, apparently equalizing the load on both anchors. In fact, with this rigging system, forces on the bolt anchors are dangerously multiplied and may be many times more than the downward pull. Avoid using this rigging system. If you find such a configuration, it is best to replace it with a properly equalized configuration as shown in Figure 10-17.

Now consider a simple two-point static equalized anchor, as shown in Figure 10-17. If the vertical line representing the direction of force of a downward pull bisects the angle at the V, the load will be equalized (fig. 10-20a). If the vertical line representing the direction of force of a downward pull does not bisect the V but instead forms two unequal angles within the V, more of the load will be on the anchor that is closer to being parallel to the direction of force (fig. 10-20b), because the point of attachment does not move. Therefore, to get approximate equalization, two things must be done right. First, the direction of force must be accurately predicted. Second, the two runners must be sized just

right for an equal distribution of force. You can achieve static equalization without the need to tie or retie any runners if you use cordelette and can estimate the direction of pull correctly, tying the knot while pulling the rope in that direction.

The need to equalize the load and the need to have a relatively small angle at the V tend to work against each other. The smaller the angle, the more any wrong guess about the direction of force will load the anchors differently. A further difficulty is that the direction of force may not be known at all. For instance, if a climber is leading out on a traverse and falls before placing any protection, the fall may be downward, or it may be to the side if the rope runs over a block near the point of fall. When a belayer's guess on direction of force is so wrong that all the force of a fall initially goes onto one anchor, static "equalization" is no equalization at all; it is no different from simply tying separately into two anchors. In fact, many anchor arrangements that are intended to achieve equalization may fail to do so in an actual fall because it is difficult to predict the direction of force with the necessary precision. This practical limitation on the effectiveness of equalization underscores the importance of placing mutiple, solid, redundant anchors.

Intelligent use of equalization principles depends on finding suitable anchor placements close together. Anchor placements must be sufficiently close to each other to make equalization feasible without an unacceptably large angle at the V, which would magnify rather than reduce forces on the anchors. Inferior anchor placements should not be used in lieu of solid placements merely because the more solid placements cannot be equalized. You must always exercise judgment in determining the best anchor arrangement. Typically, the best arrangement involves equalized anchors—but not always.

BELAY POSITION AND STANCE

In the United States, most climbers belay by having their belay device or hitch attached to a carabiner on their seat harness. The alternative, more popular in Europe, is to belay from the anchor by attaching the device or hitch directly to the anchor (fig. 10-21). To use this method, you must be in a position to put a hand and arm in the correct braking position the instant a fall occurs, and you must be close to the anchor in a position to comfortably take in and pay out rope. Not surprisingly, in Europe, where belaying directly off the anchor is widely popular, the belay method of choice is the Münter hitch, which works well with the brake hand above or below the device. Additionally, the plaquette-type belay devices and the Petzl Reverso (see Figure 10-6, above) are designed to be used when rigged directly off the anchor. Be aware that many common belay devices may not work effectively when rigged directly off the anchor; aperture-type devices require that you be able to achieve a minimum of 90 degrees of separation between the load and braking strands of the rope, which often cannot be easily accomplished when you are belaying directly off the anchor.

An advantage of belaying from the anchor is that your body is not subject to the violent forces created by a serious fall, so you are less likely to be injured or lose control of the belay. Overall, there are many good arguments for belaying from the anchor, and this method probably deserves to be more popular in the United States. The issues of stance and position that are discussed in this section are hardly concerns at all when you are belaying from the anchor.

A small advantage of belaying from the body is that the movement of your body under the force of a fall introduces a dynamic element that somewhat reduces the forces on the protection and on the falling climber's body. Some believe that a significant advantage of belaying from the body is that you may be able to adopt

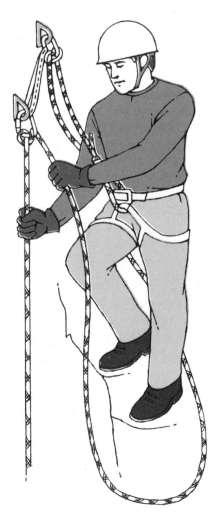

Fig. 10-21.
Belaying directly from the anchor with a Münter hitch.

179

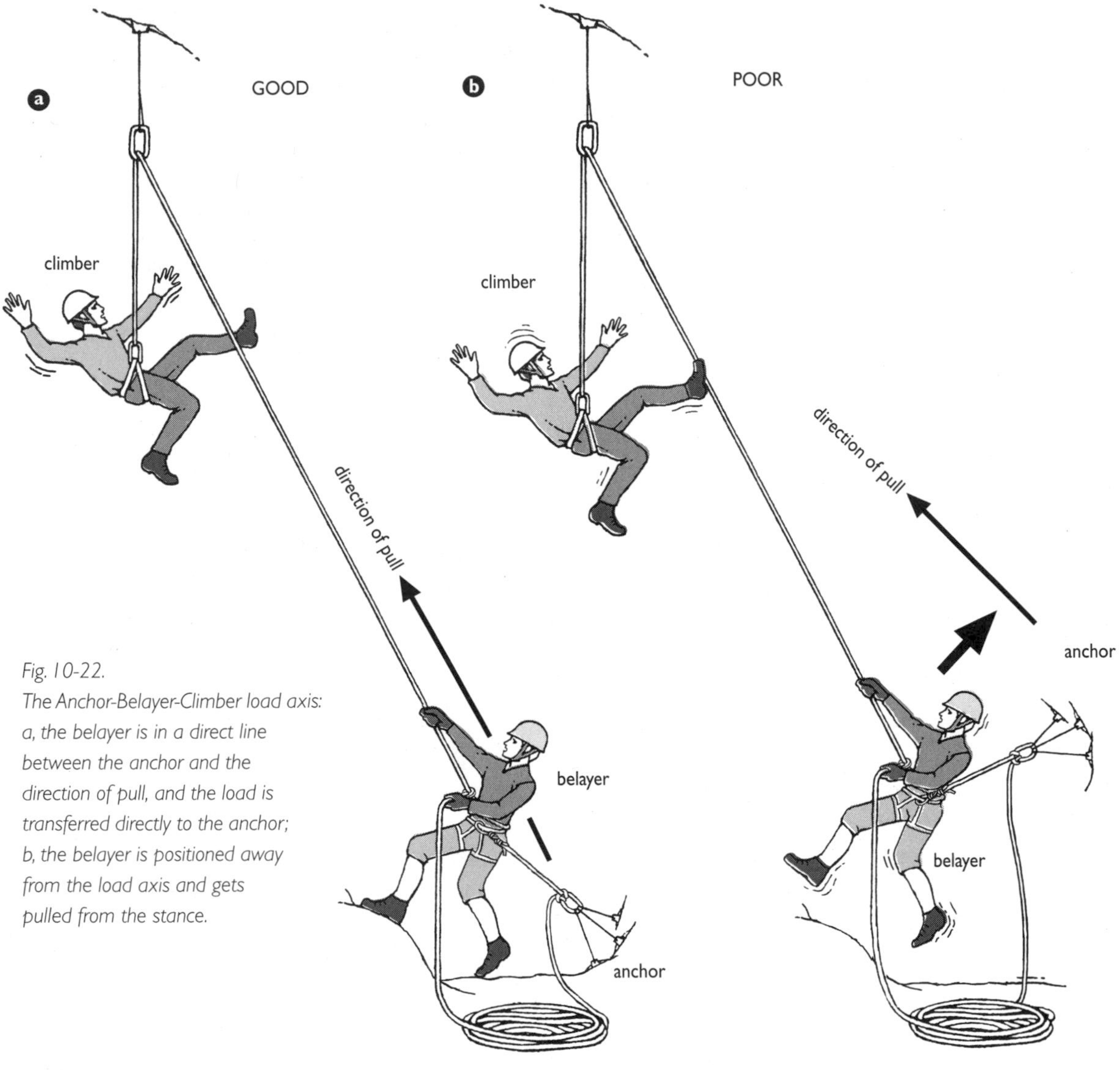

ⓐ   GOOD   ⓑ   POOR

climber

climber

direction of pull

direction of pull

belayer

anchor

belayer

Fig. 10-22.
The Anchor-Belayer-Climber load axis:
a, the belayer is in a direct line
between the anchor and the
direction of pull, and the load is
transferred directly to the anchor;
b, the belayer is positioned away
from the load axis and gets
pulled from the stance.

anchor

a stance so strong that little or no force goes onto the anchor—and the anchor essentially becomes a backup. This often makes sense when you are belaying a follower with little possibility of a serious pendulum fall or of significant slack in the rope; with a good stance, you may be able to prevent any force from going onto the anchor.

Although reducing loads on the anchor seems to make good sense, it is unreasonable to expect any stance to withstand the kind of force that would cause an ad-

equate belay anchor to fail. In any situation in which an extreme leader fall or a serious pendulum fall is a possibility, it is impossible for the belayer to protect the anchor by maintaining a stance; whatever force goes onto the belayer is likely to go largely undiminished onto the anchor.

Because any stance is unlikely to be able to withstand the force of a severe fall, belays should be set up with the assumption that in such a fall, the belayer will be pulled into a position in a direct line between the anchor and the first piece of protection placed by the fallen climber. One way to keep this in mind when setting up belays is to remember the ABCs: Severe forces will result in a pull in a direct line between the **A**nchor, **B**elayer, and **C**limber's line of travel (fig. 10-22a). If the belayer is in a position other than along this load axis, the belayer will be pulled, sometimes violently, in the direction of this axis (fig. 10-22b). Any significant belayer movement violates the No Extension principle discussed in "Selecting an Anchor" above, shock-loading the system and risking injury to the belayer or loss of control of the belay.

Earlier in this chapter, "Protecting the Leader," recommends that the lead climber place a secure point of protection soon after starting a new lead, to reduce the fall factor and establish a predictable direction from which the force of a leader fall will come. The importance of knowing the direction from which a shock load will come becomes apparent when you apply the ABC principles.

Facing In/Facing Out

When belaying a follower, it is common to face out, usually with the anchor at your back as you look down to watch for your climbing partner coming up.

An alternative that works especially well when in a hanging or semihanging stance on multipitch routes is to face in toward the anchor while you are hanging in the seat harness. Pass the rope through a directional carabiner (a carabiner acting to direct the rope) that is attached to the anchor and then to the climber below. In this setup, the force from a fall will always come from the directional carabiner rather than from the climber directly onto the belayer. If a separate piece of protection is used for the directional (see fig. 10-23), then a first solid placement is already established as the climber begins the next lead, ensuring the load direction and reducing the potential fall factor for the first moves. The components of the belay anchor should not be used as a first protection placement by the lead climber as this could subject the belay anchor component used to dangerous unequalized forces in the event of a high-impact force fall.

When belaying a leader, most belayers usually prefer to face in to the mountain. Facing in often allows you

to watch your partner climb, enabling you to anticipate movements and to pay out or take in rope more efficiently. It may also be possible to figure out how to get past some of the difficult sections when it is time for you to climb, by seeing where your partner had difficulty or found a good solution to a problem. You are better able to take cover from rockfall. And you are in the best position to see a leader fall start, brace, and go into the braking position. Being able to see a leader fall begin is a particular advantage when the first piece of protection is low and the force of the fall would tend to pull you into the rock.

These advantages of facing in are lost when you are belaying in an alcove with a small roof or bulge overhead that prevents you from watching your partner and when the first piece of protection is directly above you. In this situation, you are no worse off facing out when it comes to holding a protected leader fall, and you are probably in a much better position to hold an unprotected leader fall because you are not in danger of being spun around.

Position and Anchor

When belaying off the seat harness, the belayer's position relative to the anchor or anchors is a fairly straightforward matter: Tie in as closely as feasible to the anchors, with no slack, to avoid shock-loading the anchor system or being pulled off the stance by a severe fall. When belaying a follower, this tie-in needs to hold only a downward pull. But remember that in the event of a leader fall, you cannot be sure whether the force will be upward (most likely) or downward (unlikely but potentially dangerous).

Consider an upward pull first. In a severe fall, you may be jerked sharply upward for a couple of feet (a meter or so), especially if you are much lighter than your partner. This can cause you to lose control and can result in injury if you are yanked up against an obstruction. It can even result in the downward-pull anchors pulling out if they are not multidirectional, leaving you and your partner both hanging from the top piece of protection. Your sudden upward movement actually can reduce the force that is put on the top piece of protection—but it is still probably best to avoid such a surprising jolt by maintaining a fairly tight tie-in to

181

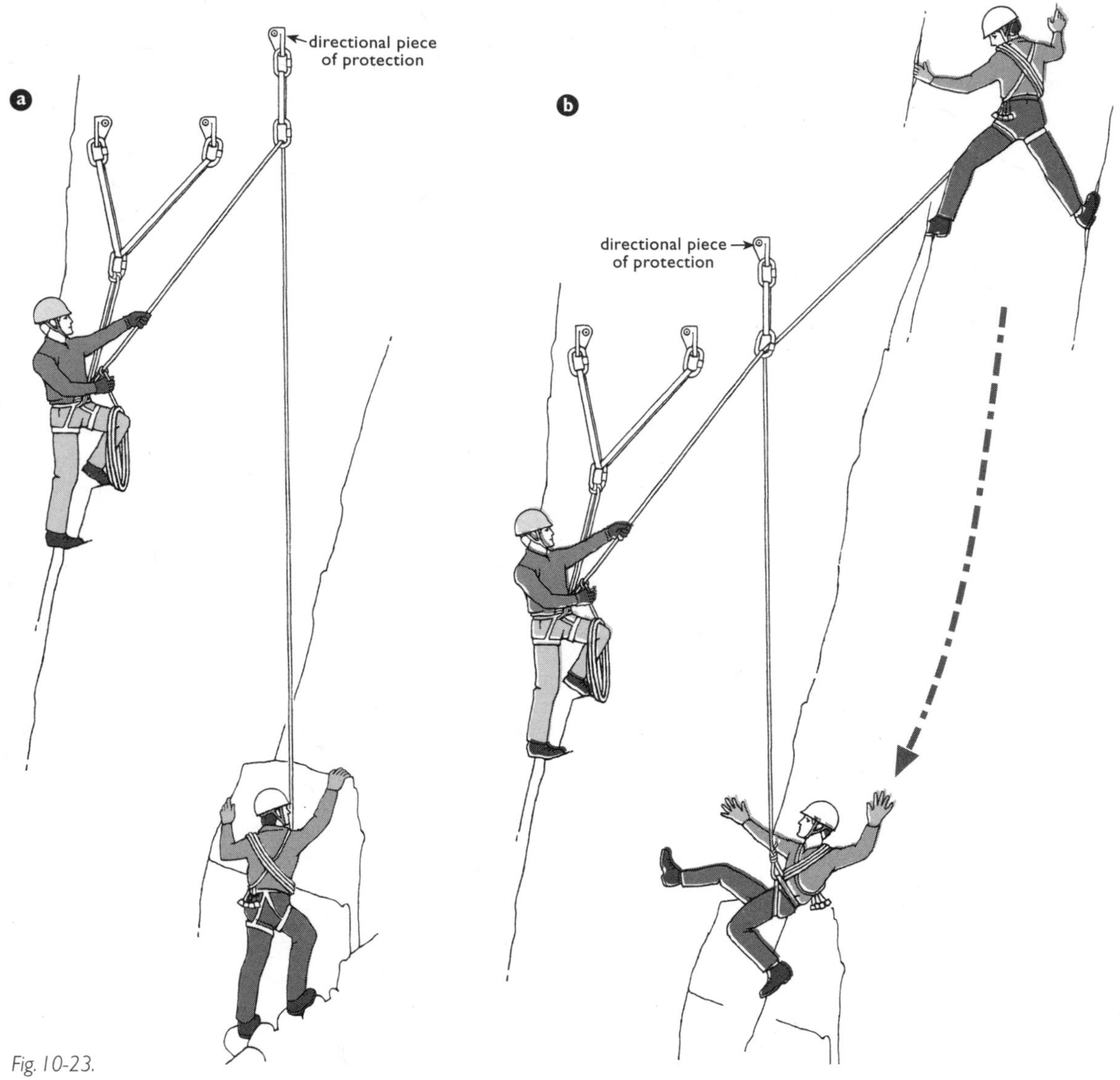

Fig. 10-23.

Use of a directional piece of protection in a semi-hanging stance: a, facing in while belaying the second up; b, the second leads off— with the first placement already established, fall factor is reduced and load direction is predictable.

an upward-pull anchor somewhat below your waist. A standing, rather than a sitting, position is best for this tie-in.

Now consider an unprotected leader fall where the force is downward. In a standing belay of a leader it is very common to see a belayer with a fairly long attachment to an anchor at about waist height or lower. This belayer is not prepared to stop an unprotected leader fall. If the belayer is standing on a ledge and the partner falls past the belayer, the downward force builds quickly beyond the point which the belay stance can hold. The belayer would then be pulled violently off the ledge or driven sharply down onto it, with almost certain loss of control of the belay and probable injuries. To prevent this possibility, you need to be tightly attached to anchors above your waist level so that you cannot be pulled down more than a few inches. (It might also be a good idea to adopt a sitting stance or to belay directly off the anchor in circumstances where solid anchors above waist level are not available.)

In deciding on a belay position in relation to the belay anchors, think through the possibilities of what could go wrong given varying positions and potential falls. Try to plan for worst-case scenarios and make sure that a bad fall would be caught by the belay anchor before you would be pulled off your stance, which entails the very real possibility of losing control of the belay.

ROPE HANDLING

When belaying the leader, never let the rope get taut, because that would impede the climber's next move. An alert belayer keeps just a hint of slack and responds immediately to the leader's advance by paying out more rope. Any friction applied by the belayer is multiplied, so if the leader tells you that rope drag is a problem, keep about a foot or so (half a meter) of slack in the rope and do everything possible to eliminate any pull. If the climber falls when there is a lot of friction in the system, you may actually be unsure whether a fall took place. If it is impossible to communicate with the climber, you can find out by letting out a few inches (centimeters) of rope. If the same tension remains, then you are probably holding the climber's weight.

Ideally, when belaying a follower there is no slack in the rope. At the same time, the rope should not be taut, which would hamper the climber's movement and balance.

An especially acute problem with slack can occur when you are belaying someone who is leading out on a traverse with a significant distance between you and the first piece of protection. Because of the weight of the rope, any attempt you make to keep only a little slack will exert a potentially dangerous pull on the climber, so it is natural to have quite a lot of slack. This extra slack cannot always be avoided, but it is important for both belayer and climber to realize that it can greatly increase the length of a fall. Only a few feet (a meter) beyond the last protection, the leader could be facing a fall of, say, 15 feet (4 to 5 meters) because of the slack.

When you are belaying a follower up to to the belay position, pile or drape the rope neatly. Do not let loops hang down the pitch. If the entire pile must be moved, it is tempting to pick it up, but this will produce snarls later. It is best to re-pile the entire rope twice, so that the leader's end is on top. If the follower is climbing rapidly, you can take in more rope with each pull by leaning forward or bending over.

Occasionally when you are belaying a follower, rope drag is so great that it is almost impossible to pull the rope in by hand in the usual way. Here is a technique that works when you are belaying in a sitting position, though it is extremely slow: Bend forward and simultaneously pull the rope through the belay device (this is easy, because you are not actually pulling the rope up yet). Then, gripping the rope tightly, in the braking position if necessary, lean back. This pulls the rope up a few inches; you are using your upper body, not your arms, to pull the rope. Then repeat the process. Once the climber is past the first few bends or obstructions, rope drag should decrease and you can revert to normal rope handling.

To minimize falling distance, leaders preparing to make difficult moves often place protection well above their harness tie-in and clip in before moving up. The leader will need some additional slack, and the direction of rope movement will reverse twice. While you are belaying the leader and letting out rope, you will suddenly be taking in slack as the climber moves up to the protection and then letting it out again as the climber moves past the protection and puts renewed pull on the rope. These switches call for extra attention, especially because this tends to happen at the most difficult spots.

COMMUNICATION

As climber and belayer get farther apart and begin to have difficulty hearing each other, stick exclusively to a set of short commands designed to express essential climbing communications (see Table 10-2). Prefacing these commands with explanations or justifications makes them harder to recognize and defeats their purpose. Use the commands alone. They have been chosen to produce a distinctive pattern. When the belayer

TABLE 10-2. BASIC VOICE COMMANDS USED BY CLIMBERS

Who Says It	Command	What It Means
Follower:	"That's me"	You have pulled up all the slack in the rope and are now tugging on my body; do not pull any more.
Climber:	"On belay?"	Do you have me on belay?
Belayer:	"Belay on"	I am belaying you.
Climber:	"Climbing"	I am, or will resume, moving up.
Belayer:	"Climb"	Response to "Climbing."
Climber:	"Slack"	Give me some slack in the rope and leave it out until I call "Climbing." (To indicate how much slack is needed, the command is "Slack X feet," with X being the amount.)
Climber:	"Up rope" (Usually to upper belayer.)	There is slack in the rope; pull it in.
Climber:	"Tension" (Usually to upper belayer.)	Take up all slack and hold my weight. (Should be used sparingly by beginners, to avoid overdependence on rope. Say "Watch me" instead.)
Climber:	"Falling!"	Assume your braking position and brace for a pull on the rope.
Belayer:	"Halfway"	About half of the rope remains.
Leader:	"How much rope?"	What length of rope remains?
Belayer:	"Feet . . . four . . . zero."	Forty feet of rope remains; find a belay soon (best used when 20 to 50 feet/6 to 15 meters remain).
Leader:	"Off belay"	I am secure and no longer need your belay. Take it apart and prepare to follow the pitch.
Anyone:	"OK"	I heard you.
Follower:	"Belay off" (After taking apart the belay.)	You may pull in all the slack and remaining coils when you are ready.
Anyone:	"Rock! Ice!" (Very loudly, immediately, and repeatedly until falling object stops; mandatory.)	Falling objects. Look up or take cover.
Anyone:	"Rope"	A rappel rope is about to be thrown down by another party. Look up or take cover.

Climbers also use some discretionary voice commands, depending on local custom or prior arrangement with a climbing partner. These are examples; many variations are used:

Leader:	"Pro in" or "Clipped in"	I have just clipped in to the first protection. (Or, I have clipped in to protection located above my harness tie-in, so the direction of rope movement will reverse twice as I move up through a difficult spot.)
Climber:	"Protection" or "Cleaning"	I am placing or cleaning protection and will not move up for a while.
Climber:	"Good belay" or "Watch me"	I anticipate a fall or difficult move.
Climber:	"On top"	I have passed the difficulty.

is a long way from the climbing partner, shout as loudly as possible and space out each syllable, using very big spaces if there are echoes. In a crowded area, preface commands with your partner's name.

Three problems are common at or near the end of each pitch, when hearing each other is most difficult. First, when you are calling out to tell the leader how much rope remains in the coils, the first syllable is often lost, and if normal word order is used, the leader hears only "—ty feet." Instead, invert the word order and pronounce each digit separately: "Feet: . . . three . . . zero" for 30 feet. The leader will pause upon the first word and have a better chance of understanding the remainder. Second, when the leader completes a pitch and calls "Off belay," do not respond with "Belay off" to indicate that you heard. Instead use "OK." "Belay off" means that you have taken apart the belay and the rope coils are ready to be pulled up, and you are not ready to shout that command for a while yet. Third, avoid the impatient question "On belay?" unless an inordinate amount of time has passed. Often the leader, at work setting up anchors, is out of earshot anyway.

If verbal communication becomes impossible because of wind or obstructions, commands are sometimes transmitted by rope pulls, but there is no universal system for this. Because of rope stretch at the end of long leads, it is necessary to greatly exaggerate the pulls. A simple tug will seldom be felt at the other end. Take in all slack and, for each signal, reach far out along the rope and pull the rope as taut as possible, holding it tight for a while before releasing the tension. If there is much friction, pulls may not be distinguishable from normal rope movements. The most common rope-pull commands correspond to the number of syllables in their verbal equivalents: One pull from the follower means "Slack," two means "Up rope," and three from the belayer above means "Belay on."

Whistle blasts may be used when rope tugs are ineffective, as often is the case with rope drag. Some climbers now use Family Radio System (FRS) radios to avoid this problem, but they are an additional piece of equipment to rely on. It is advised to have the basics of rope signals worked out as a backup in the case of a radio failure.

OTHER TECHNIQUES
Tying Off the Belay

There is at least one aspect of belaying that climbers hope they will never have to use: tying off the belay in order to help an injured partner. If a climbing partner is seriously injured and other climbers are nearby, it is usually best to let them help while you continue to belay. By staying there, you could also help in raising or lowering the victim, if necessary. But if two climbers are alone, it may be necessary to tie off the climbing rope to remove yourself from the belay system, so you can investigate, help your partner, or go for help.

If you are belaying directly off the anchor using a belay device or Münter hitch, you need only prevent the rope from sliding through the belay. Simply form a knot such as a clove hitch in the braking rope and clip it to another carabiner on the anchor. You can now take the braking hand off the rope and it will be held by the knot.

If you are using a belay device or Münter hitch attached to your seat harness, it is possible to tie off using one hand. However, it is easier and safer to wrap the rope a few times around one foot or leg. Then, while the leg wrap is doing the job of holding the belay rope, attach a tie-off loop or runner to the climbing rope with a friction knot (prusik or Klemheist). Clip the sling in to the anchor, chaining slings if necessary to make the connection long enough (fig. 10-24a). (If you cannot reach the anchor, create a new anchor, extended from the existing anchor, by tying a figure-eight knot in the slack part of the rope as close to the anchor as possible.) After first telling the climber to expect to be lowered a few inches, transfer tension from the belay to the anchor by undoing the leg wrap and letting the rope slip through the belay device. Once tension is on the anchor, get out of the belay and back up the arrangement by tying the climbing rope itself directly to the anchor, with a figure-eight knot on a separate carabiner (fig. 10-24b). If practicable, consider anchoring the rope before escaping the belay, leaving just enough slack to disassemble the belay.

Self-Belayed Solo Climbing

Self-belay devices, which allow roped solo climbing, have been available for some time. They are worn by

10

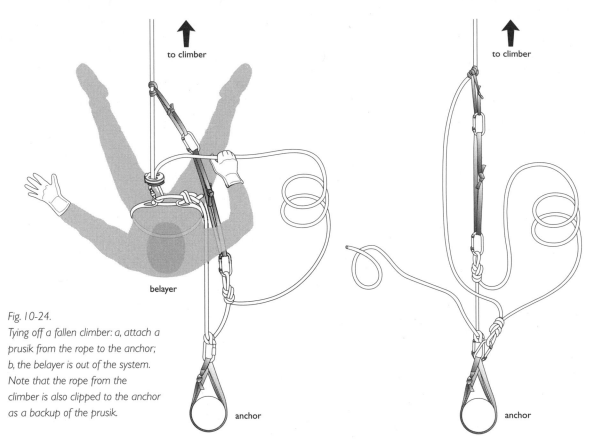

Fig. 10-24.
*Tying off a fallen climber: a, attach a
prusik from the rope to the anchor;
b, the belayer is out of the system.
Note that the rope from the
climber is also clipped to the anchor
as a backup of the prusik.*

the climber and work like a ratchet, sliding up the rope during the climb but not down it in a fall. To lead a pitch, the rope is first anchored at the bottom, and you place protection while ascending. Then you anchor the rope at the top and rappel. Finally, you remove the bottom anchor and climb the pitch a second time, retrieving the protection while ascending again.

This is not just another belaying alternative to be chosen on occasion. It is a different form of climbing, requiring a commitment to relearn many fundamentals. Compared to a belay by a live partner, shortcomings are inevitable. Read the manufacturer's literature critically, and practice in a safe situation. In evaluating the self-belay device, ask some questions: Is the belay static? Does it work if I fall in a horizontal or head-down position? When I am climbing, does the rope feed automatically, without producing extra slack or drag, especially at the top of a pitch or on a traverse? Can I clip in to protection above waist level without trouble?

Belaying in Sport Climbing

Much climbing today takes place on artificial rock and manufactured climbing walls, in gyms or outdoors, and on short routes in rock-climbing areas. Often sport climbs are top-roped; when led, they are usually protected by clipping in to bolts. Although in these instances the general principles of belaying are the same as in other climbing environments, there are some characteristic features and problems in sport climbing that are worth separate discussion.

The sport-climbing environment, which usually seems less threatening than that of longer, multipitch climbs, can induce complacency. It is important to keep in mind that the risk of serious injury always exists, and that a thorough understanding and application of safe climbing principles is the best way to prevent accidents.

Typically, when a sport pitch is being top-roped, the

belayer stands at the bottom, with the rope running up through a preplaced anchor and back down to the climber, who then ascends while the belayer takes in rope. At the top of the climb, the climber signals for the belayer to hold the climber by saying "Take." The belayer can then lower the climber to the ground. This technique is not typically used in alpine climbing. The belayer generally is not anchored; there is often nothing to anchor to, and even when there is, anchoring may seem too fussy and time-consuming.

Belaying without an anchor can cause problems. If you are belaying and standing well away from the rock or off to one side, the force of a fall—even a top-roped fall—can pull you sharply into or along the wall. You may be injured or lose control of the belay, and the climber's fall will certainly be lengthened—perhaps enough to allow the climber to hit a ledge or the ground. When considering what kind of force could have this effect, remember that the peak impact force, even with a top rope, is significantly greater than the climbing partner's weight; remember also that pendulum falls create even greater forces. If belaying without an anchor, it is usually best to be positioned as nearly as possible directly beneath the anchor. Even then, if you as the belayer are considerably lighter than your climbing partner, you could be lifted upward by the force of a fall. This movement is not always serious, but it does provide a reason to use a belay device, such as a Grigri, that is very unlikely to result in loss of control of the belay.

The problems of unanchored belaying can be even more serious when the pitch is being led instead of top-roped. If the bolts are in a straight line and a fall is taken low on the pitch—after the first or second bolt—the force on the belayer can be considerable. In this situation, stand as close as possible under the first bolt. If your climbing partner is much heavier than you, insist on being tightly anchored.

An occasional practice in top-roping areas is to run the rope through a runner on the anchor, rather than through carabiners, and then have several people take turns climbing the pitch. This is extremely dangerous because the friction generated by lowering a climber will weaken the runner very quickly, creating a risk of anchor failure.

A number of sport-climbing accidents have occurred when a climber was lowered from the top anchors on too short a rope. In multipitch climbing, the two climbers are typically tied in to either end of the rope, but in sport climbing, this is often not so. In this case, if the rope runs out while the climber is being lowered with the end unsecured, the result is a ground fall for the climber. Make sure that the rope is long enough to safely lower the climber all the way to the ground or, better yet, tie a figure-eight backup knot in the end of the rope.

Remember that even in seemingly benign climbing environments—with everyone having fun, pushing their limits, taking a lot of falls without getting a scratch—all the basic climbing hazards remain, requiring constant attention to safety.

SECURING THE FREEDOM OF THE HILLS

Belaying and anchor setup are the fundamental skills of the technical climber. Practice belaying often, with both your right hand and your left hand as the braking hand. Study and practice anchor techniques. There are many different ways of anchoring yourself, but ideally the anchor system should be SRENE: Solid, Redundant, and Equalized, and providing No Extension.

Being proficient with belay technique and anchor setup will help you become a good climbing partner. These methods are also related to skills required for rappelling; once you become proficient in them, you will have more confidence when it comes time to rappel. Overall, solid skills in belaying and anchor setup will help you secure the freedom of the hills.

10

11

Rappelling

THE RAPPEL SYSTEM ■ **RAPPEL ANCHORS** ■ **THE ROPE** ■
RAPPEL METHOD ■ **RAPPEL TECHNIQUE** ■ **MULTIPLE RAPPELS** ■
SAFETY BACKUPS ■ **RETRIEVING THE RAPPEL ROPE** ■
EXPERIENCING THE FREEDOM OF THE HILLS

Rappelling, the technique of descending a rope by using friction to safely control
the rate of descent, is indispensable to technical climbing in the mountains.
Unfortunately, rappelling is also one of the more dangerous techniques employed
by climbers because it is often so easy and routine that the inherent risks
may be forgotten or ignored. Proper rappelling technique, learned
thoroughly and employed carefully, allows for a safe descent of
almost any climbing pitch. In fact, rappelling is often
the only way to get down some faces of rock or ice.

When rappelling a steep cliff, you depend entirely on the strength of the anchors securing the rope, the rope itself, and proper technique. If any element of the rappel system fails, the result will likely be catastrophic. Unlike the belay system, which is called upon only if a fall occurs, the rappel system is necessarily called upon to absorb the forces exerted by the rappel each and every time it is used. Consequently, there is never room for error in the setup or use of the rappel system.

Coming down from a climb, you may have a choice between rappelling and down-climbing. Sometimes rappelling is the fastest and safest way to descend, but many times it is not. One of the hidden shortcomings of rappelling is that it can waste considerable time in the hands of the inexperienced. Think through the options available, considering the terrain, the weather, the time available, and the strength and experience of the party. If you elect to rappel, do it safely and efficiently.

THE RAPPEL SYSTEM

A rappel system has four basic elements: an anchor, a rope, a rappel method for applying friction to the rope, and the person rappelling (fig. 11-1). Each element is equally important. Always remember all four of the rappel elements—even when you are cold, tired, hungry, and racing to beat the darkness—and check and double-check that every element is in place, functioning properly, and connected together to make an integrated system. Each of these elements is briefly described below, followed by expanded sections in the rest of this chapter. The integrated rappelling system must be understood thoroughly and practiced properly at every rappel to ensure a safe descent.

Rappel anchor: The first element of the rappel system is the anchor, the point on the mountain to which the rest of the system is attached. The anchor must be carefully selected for strength and reliability. Once the rappel has begun, a safe descent depends entirely on the anchor, and returning to the anchor to make adjustments can be problematic, if not impossible.

Rope: The rope is the second element of the rappel system. The midpoint of the rope is looped through the anchor, with the two ends hanging down the descent route. You descend this doubled rope and retrieve it from below by pulling on one end.

Short rappels can be handled with just one rope. Longer rappels need the extra length of two ropes tied together, with a double fisherman's or double overhand knot. The knot joining the ropes should be placed near the anchor, with the two equal-length ends hanging down the route. Ropes of different diameters can be joined in a two rope-rappel, for example, mating an 11-millimeter rope with a 9-millimeter rope.

On rare occasions, you might use a single-strand rappel, in which the rope is simply tied at one end to the anchor.

Rappel method: The third element of the system is the method you use to apply friction to the rope to control your rate of descent while at the same time remaining firmly attached to the rope. There are two methods for applying this friction.

In mechanical rappel systems, the doubled rope passes through a friction device attached to your seat harness.

In nonmechanical systems, you wrap the rope around your body to provide the necessary friction.

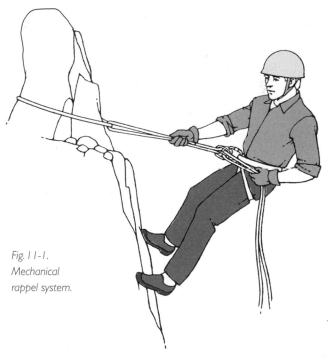

Fig. 11-1.
Mechanical
rappel system.

189

In either case, the braking hand grasps the rope to control the amount of friction and the rate of descent. Be vigilant regarding unaccustomed circumstances—such as a new, smaller-diameter, stiffer, or icy rope, heavier pack, etc.—because friction can vary greatly.

Rappeller: The rappeller is the final and most variable element in the rappel system. You must use proper technique both to attach into the rappel system and to descend safely. Individual circumstances such as your attitude, your level of fatigue and anxiety, poor weather, impending darkness, rockfall, icefall, and your level of skill and training potentially affect the safety of the rappel.

RAPPEL ANCHORS

A rappel anchor attaches the rappel system to the rock, snow, or ice that will be descended. The rappel anchor must be solid enough to support your full weight as well as absorb any additional forces that may occur, such as the dynamic force of a sudden stop during the rappel. Set up the anchor as near to the edge of the rappel route as possible while ensuring a solid and safe anchor. This affords the longest possible rappel. It also makes it easier to pull the rope down from below after the rappel and often reduces the danger of rockfall during retrieval of the rope.

When looking for an anchor, think about possible effects on the rope. Consider any sharp edges that might damage or sever the rope as it is loaded. Locate the anchor to minimize chances of the rope being pulled into a constricting slot or otherwise hanging up when it is retrieved from below. Check the position of the rope over the edge of the rappel route as the first rappeller finishes rappelling. If the rope moves near or into a slot on the surface that could cause it to jam upon retrieval, consider relocating the anchor. In winter conditions, be cautious of the rope cutting into snow or ice and freezing in place.

Either natural anchors or artificial (manufactured) anchors serve as suitable rappel anchors (see "Selecting an Anchor" in Chapter 10, Belaying). This chapter principally discusses anchors for use on rock. For information on anchors for use in snow and ice, see the sections on anchors in Chapter 16, Snow Travel and Climbing; Chapter 18, Alpine Ice Climbing; and Chapter 19, Waterfall Ice and Mixed Climbing.

On popular climbs, established rappel anchors have slings left behind from prior rappels. If the slings are not equipped with a rappel ring or carabiner, consider that they may no longer be safe because rappel ropes have been pulled through them on previous rappels, which generates friction that may have weakened the sling's nylon webbing. Nylon slings also suffer damage from ultraviolet light, and older slings will feel noticeably dry and less supple from UV damage. However, nylon may be seriously weakened by UV exposure without visible effects. Therefore, always carefully evaluate slings at a preexisting rappel anchor. Sometimes so many slings comprise an anchor that total failure of every sling is unlikely. Still, a prudent rappeller might cut out a few of the oldest slings and add a new one before attaching the rope. If using more than one sling, make them of equal length to help distribute the load. (And pack out the old slings.)

When using two anchors to support the rappel, the most common method is to run a separate sling from

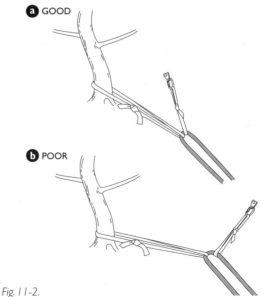

Fig. 11-2.
The most common method of attaching the rappel rope to multiple anchors, with a separate sling attached to each of two anchors and meeting at the rappel rope: a, a narrow angle between slings is best; b, the angle between slings is too wide.

each anchor, with the slings meeting at the rappel rope. Try to adjust the slings so the force is the same on each anchor. For the strongest setup, keep the angle between the two slings narrow (fig. 11-2).

Natural Anchors

Often the best natural anchor is a living, good-sized, well-rooted tree (see "Natural Anchors" in Chapter 10, Belaying). The rope usually goes through a runner attached to the anchor (fig. 11-3a). The rope could be looped directly around a tree without the use of a sling (fig. 11-3b), but this causes rope abrasion, soils the rope with tree resins, makes it harder to retrieve the rope, and, if done enough times, can kill the tree. Attaching a runner to an unquestionably stout tree branch rather than low on the trunk helps make it easier to retrieve and reduces the risk of rockfall. However, connecting to a branch rather than the trunk puts more leverage on the tree.

If there is any question about a natural anchor, test whether it can support the weight of the heaviest rappeller and still provide a large safety margin in case a rappeller puts extra force on the anchor by stopping quickly. Test the anchor before rappel gear is attached, never after the rope or the rappeller is hooked in.

If you are using a runner looped around a rock horn for an anchor (fig. 11-4a), take care to determine the angle of force on the horn. Guard against the dire possibility

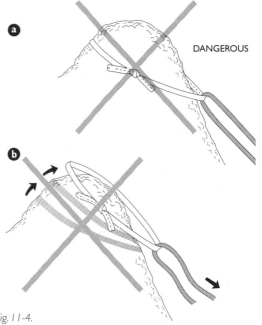

Fig. 11-4.
Runner looped around a rock horn: a, a dangerous rappel anchor; b, runner rides up and off rock horn.

that the runner could ride up and off the horn during a rappel (fig. 11-4b).

You might use a single anchor if it is an unquestionably solid, dependable natural anchor, but if you have any doubts, add another equalized anchor or two. (See "Equalizing Multiple Anchors" in Chapter 10, Belaying.)

Artificial Anchors

As a rule of thumb, when using artificial (manufactured) anchors, use two or more and equalize the load between them. (See "Equalizing Multiple Anchors" in Chapter 10, Belaying.)

In unknown alpine terrain, some climbers carry pitons and a hammer to set anchors. The most common artificial rappel anchors are bolts or pitons that have been left in place by previous climbers. These must be evaluated for safety just as they would if they were being used for belaying or for protection while climbing.

The climbers' hardware known as chocks—nuts, hexes, and so forth—are usually used only if no good alternative is available, but it is better to use and leave behind some equipment than to rely upon a shaky rock

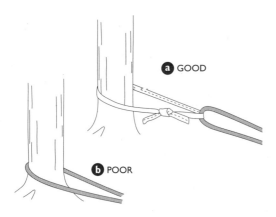

Fig. 11-3.
Rappel rope attached to tree: a, rappel rope through a sling tied around a tree (good); b, rappel rope directly around tree (poor).

horn. Be suspicious of chocks found already in place, perhaps left behind by climbers who were not able to work them loose. Also be aware of old slings attached to such chocks, which may no longer be safe. Sometimes an abandoned chock may be used like a natural chockstone—by looping a runner directly around it and making no use whatsoever of the sling attached to the old chock.

THE ROPE

Before setting up the rappel, run through the entire length of the rope to check that no cuts, fraying, or other damage occurred during the climb or a previous rappel.

Attaching the Rope to the Anchor

To prepare the rope for rappelling, attach it to the anchor, created from a natural feature or manufactured equipment. In the simplest case, suspend the midpoint of the rope from one or more runners or slings that have been attached to the anchor (as shown in Figures 11-1, 11-2a, and 11-3a, above). Some rappellers prefer to use two slings instead of one, for added security.

If you are using just one rope, put one end of the rope through the slings and pull it through until the midpoint is reached. Take care not to create friction between the rope and slings, because heat generated by friction may dangerously weaken the slings. As an alternative, tie the slings around the midpoint of the rope before attaching them to the anchor. If you are carrying sewn runners for climbing, bring along some ⁹⁄₁₆-inch webbing to use in tying rappel slings.

To eliminate the risk of damage from friction both when setting the rappel and when retrieving the rope, attach the rope to the anchor sling(s) with a rappel ring. Rappel or descending rings are simply continuous aluminum or titanium rings, about 1½ inches (3 centimeters) in diameter, made for rappelling. Thread the rappel sling(s) through the ring, and then thread the rope through the ring, to prevent direct contact between the rope and the anchor sling(s) and also the dangerous friction of a pulled rope on nylon slings (fig. 11-5a).

However, the descending ring does add another possible point of failure. Newer rings are continuous,

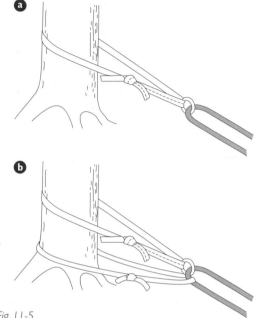

Fig. 11-5.
Rappel rope through descending ring: a, single ring; b, single ring with backup sling.

nonwelded designs, better than the welded type, which should not be trusted. Some climbers insist on two rings, even if both are nonwelded. An alternative is a single ring backed up by a non-weight-bearing sling from the anchor through the rope, ready to hold the rope in case the ring fails (fig. 11-5b).

For longer rappels, join two ropes together: Put one end of a rope through the slings and tie it to the other rope with a double fisherman's knot, backed up with overhand knots. Alternatively, join the ropes with a double overhand knot, leaving 12- to 16-inch (40- to 60-centimeter) tails (fig. 11-6a). This UIAA-approved method is popular because the double overhand knot is less likely to catch on edges (fig. 11-6b) and hang up during rope retrieval. It is dangerous to use a double figure-eight knot, instead of a double overhand knot, for this purpose; double figure-eight knots have been known to fail. You can back up the first double overhand knot with a second one.

If the anchor is a rock feature or bolts or pitons, always attach slings to the anchor, then run the rappel rope through the slings. Never put the rope directly

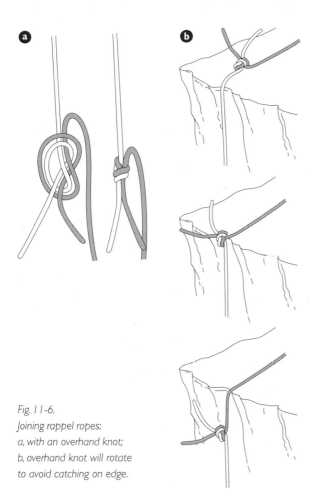

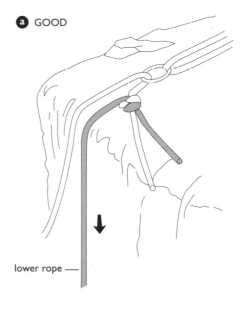

ⓐ GOOD

lower rope ——

Fig. 11-6.
Joining rappel ropes:
a, with an overhand knot;
b, overhand knot will rotate
to avoid catching on edge.

around the rock or through the eye of the bolt hanger or piton, because friction may make it impossible to pull the rope back down from below. When attaching the rope to the anchor, note which end of the rope will be pulled for retrieval. If the rope lies with one strand against the rock and the other strand on top of the first, friction will impede retrieval and it may be possible to pull only the strand closest to the rock. When using two ropes, place the knot joining them below the anchor, on the strand to be pulled (fig. 11-7a)—otherwise, the rope may pinch and retrieval may not be possible (fig. 11-7b).

Keep the point of connection between the rappel anchor sling and the rope away from the edge of the rock, snow, or ice of the rappel route to help prevent binding and abrasion (fig. 11-8).

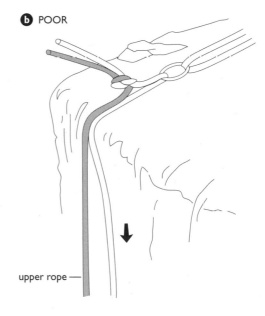

ⓑ POOR

upper rope ——

Fig. 11-7.
Keep knot on bottom rope to allow an easy pull and avoid
pinching: a, good; b, poor.

193

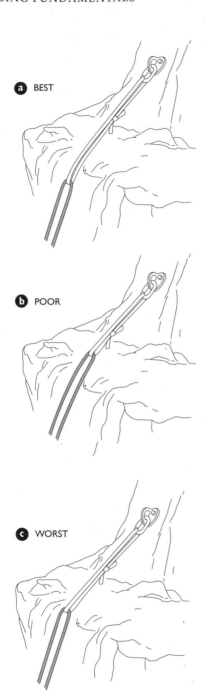

a BEST

b POOR

c WORST

Fig. 11-8.

The point of connection between the rappel sling and the rappel rope: a, rope free to move and clear of rock; b, rope doesn't bind but will still abrade; c, rope binds and abrades against rock.

Throwing Down the Rope

After looping the rappel rope at its midpoint through an anchor, prepare the rope for tossing it down the rappel route. The sequence described below reduces rope snags and tangling as well as the risk of losing the rope.

1. Tie backup knots at the ends of the rope if desired (see "Safety Backups" later in this chapter).
2. Beginning from the rappel sling, coil each half of the rope separately into two butterfly coils (see Chapter 9, Basic Safety System), creating a total of four butterfly coils, two on each side of the anchor.
3. Tie an overhand knot on a bight of rope near the midpoint and clip it to the anchor with a carabiner to prevent the disaster of losing the rope when the coils are tossed.
4. Be sure to attach yourself to an anchor before you stand at the edge of the route to toss the rope. Use a daisy chain or girth-hitch a long sling through your harness and secure it to the anchor, preferably with a locking carabiner.
5. Before making the toss, alert others below by shouting "Rope!" Some rappellers shout the word two times to give anyone below a little time to respond or to watch out for the rope. Others shout just once, but wait a moment for any response.
6. Evaluate the wind and terrain before throwing the coils out.
7. Start on one side of the anchor by tossing the coil nearest the anchor out and down the route, then the rope-end coil. Repeat for the other half of the rope (fig. 11-9).
8. After all four coils have been tossed, remove the carabiner and bight, leaving the rope in the anchor sling.

If the rope tangles or hangs up on the rappel route below, it is usually best to pull it back up, recoil it, and toss it again. Sometimes, however, it is possible to just free the rope during the rappel.

In some circumstances—for instance, in a high wind—it is hard to get a perfect toss. One of the more experienced rappellers in the party can rappel down to just above the first problem, stop, recoil the strands below that point, toss them again, and continue the rappel. ("Rappel Technique" later in this chapter explains how to stop in midrappel.)

In particularly adverse conditions, some experienced rappellers might carry the free ends of the rope with them on rappel, feeding it out of a pack or rope bag, for example, during the descent to avoid hang-ups.

Keeping Rope Lengths Equal

Both strands of the rappel rope must either touch the next stance or hang equally. If not, one end may pull through the rappel device before you reach a stance at the end of the rappel. Should this occur, you would fall out of the system. Watch for the potential problems discussed below. It may be essential to safeguard the rappel with backup knots at the ends of the rope (see "Safety Backups" later in this chapter).

When you are using two ropes of unequal diameters, take extra care to monitor the length of each strand during the rappel. The differing diameters and elastic characteristics of the ropes may cause one rope to advance through the rappel device more quickly than the other, thereby altering the relative lengths of the rope strands. It is also possible for the knot joining ropes of unequal diameter to "creep" away from the anchor, again resulting in differing lengths for the separate strands of rope. Place the knot on the side of the anchor most likely to slide; usually this is the smaller-diameter rope.

Also, ropes that are nominally of equal length, even from the same manufacturer, are often actually of different lengths.

RAPPEL METHOD

Once the rappel anchor and the rope are set up, you need a method of attaching into the rope and applying friction to it to control your rappel. Typically, a mechanical device provides a secure means of attachment, but methods of wrapping into the rope may also be used.

Mechanical Rappel Devices

Most rappellers use a system consisting of their climbing harness and a belay device as their principal rappelling method. All of the devices operate in essentially the same manner: by applying varying degrees of friction to the rope. (With some belay devices, the rope does not feed through the device smoothly on rappel. Some devices may also easily heat up. Before using any new device, closely read and follow the manufacturer's instructions.)

The two free strands of rope at the anchor are inserted into your rappel device, which is then clipped with a locking carabiner to your harness, in much the same way as for belaying. During the rappel, the bends

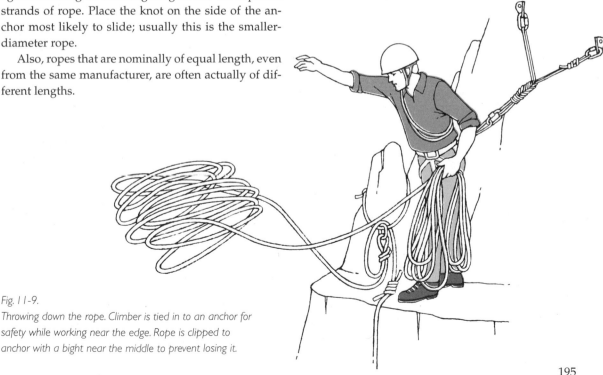

Fig. 11-9.
Throwing down the rope. Climber is tied in to an anchor for safety while working near the edge. Rope is clipped to anchor with a bight near the middle to prevent losing it.

195

in the rope through the device and around the locking carabiner apply friction, magnifying the force exerted by your braking hand. Your braking hand, which holds both strands of rope below the device (see Figure 11-1, above), provides a controlled descent through a combination of variations in grip and hand position. The rappel device and the braking hand together control the speed of descent, and allow you to completely halt the descent at any time.

At the top of the rappel, the weight of the rope hanging below the device adds friction, making it easier to control the rate of descent near the top of a rappel than at the bottom. This is especially so on very steep or overhanging rappels on which most of the rope hangs free. But no matter how little grip strength may be required to control the descent, the braking hand must never leave the rope. The other hand—the guiding, or uphill, hand—may slide freely along the rope to help maintain balance. With some setups, wrapping the rope partly around your back further increases friction.

Rappelling with a mechanical system requires a harness (see Chapter 9, Basic Safety System). Never rappel with just a waist loop, which is a simple loop of webbing tied around your waist—it can constrict your diaphragm enough to cause you to lose consciousness. In an emergency, an improvised diaper sling may be used for rappelling, even though it would not ordinarily be used for climbing.

The diaper sling takes about 10 feet (3 meters) of webbing tied in a large loop. With the loop behind your back, pull each end around your sides to your stomach

(fig. 11-10a). Bring one piece of the webbing loop down from behind your back and between your legs, and then up to your stomach to meet the other two loop ends (fig. 11-10b). Clip them together in front with doubled carabiners or a locking carabiner (fig. 11-10c). The diaper may also be clipped to a safety loop made of webbing tied around your waist.

Carabiner Brake Method

The carabiner brake method for rappelling is somewhat complex to set up but has the virtue of not requiring any special equipment—just carabiners. All climbers should know how to use the carabiner brake method, even if they normally use a specialized rappel device. It is a great backup if you forget or lose your rappel device. The carabiner brake system works best with oval carabiners and can also be managed with standard D-shaped carabiners (see Chapter 9, Basic Safety System).

To create the carabiner brake setup, start by attaching one locking or two regular carabiners to your seat harness. Because a harness carabiner could be subjected to a twisting or side load, two carabiners or a locking carabiner should be used. If you are using two regular carabiners, position the gates to keep them from being forced open and accidentally unclipping. The correct position is with the gates on opposing sides and reversed from each other, forming an X when they are opened at the same time (see Figure 9-34 in Chapter 9, Basic Safety System).

Next, clip another pair of carabiners—here, a pair is required and a single locking carabiner will not

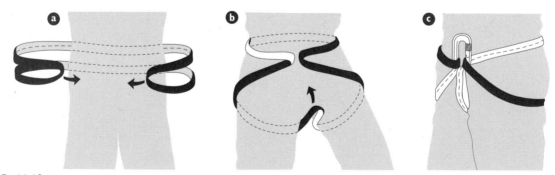

Fig. 11-10.
Diaper sling; a, bring large loop around waist from the back; b, bring one piece of loop behind back down through the legs and up; c, clip all three parts together.

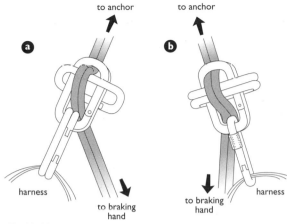

Fig. 11-11.

Carabiner brake system: a, with one carabiner clipped across the outer carabiner pair; b, with two carabiners clipped across the outer carabiner pair in order to give greater friction.

suffice—to the harness carabiner, with the gates opposed and reversed. Then face the anchor, if possible. Lift a bight of the rappel ropes through the outer carabiner pair, from the bottom. Take yet another carabiner and clip it across the outer carabiner pair, beneath the bight of rope, so its gate is facing away from the rope loop. The rope then runs across an outer edge (not the gate!) of this final carabiner, known as the braking carabiner (fig. 11-11a).

One braking carabiner provides enough friction for most rappels on ropes that are 10 to 11 millimeters in diameter. A second braking carabiner (fig. 11-11b) or even a third braking carabiner might be neeeded for thinner ropes, heavy climbers, heavy packs, or steep or overhanging rappels. The ropes must always run over the solid side of the braking carabiners, never across the gate.

There are a couple of things to watch for in setting up the carabiner brake system. First, it may not be convenient to face the anchor while you insert the bight of rappel rope into the carabiner brake; in this case, a possible mistake is to put the rope into the system backward, as if you are preparing to rappel "uphill" toward the anchor.

Second, the weight of the rope hanging down the cliff may make it very difficult to pull the bight of rope up through the outer pair of carabiners and hold it while clipping in the braking carabiner. It helps to get that weight off the system. Pulling up some slack rope and throwing a couple of wraps around your leg to take the weight solves this problem. Alternatively, pull the loop of rope through the carabiners but make it extra large and lay it over your shoulder while you are clipping in the braking carabiner. Then drop the downhill strands back through the system so the brake remains close to the anchor.

Other Mechanical Systems

Figure eight: This has been a popular special device for rappelling (fig. 11-12a). It is simpler to set up and requires less force to control than the carabiner brake method.

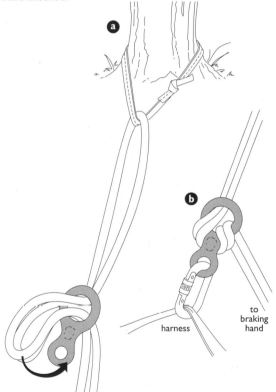

Fig. 11-12.

Attaching a figure-eight device for use in rappelling: a, pull a bight of the rappel rope through the larger aperture of the figure-eight device, then pull the bight down and over the device; b, clip the smaller aperture of the figure-eight device to the harness with a locking carabiner.

Fig. 11-13.
The dulfersitz.

Fig. 11-14.
The arm rappel.

Keep in mind its disadvantages. It means carrying an extra piece of equipment, and most figure eights are relatively heavy. If it is lost or forgotten, another rappel method must be used. Most figure eights require a locking carabiner to be attached to the harness (fig. 11-12b) and do not provide the option of using doubled carabiners. And the figure eight puts some twists in the rope. The figure eight was designed for rappelling, though some climbers use the device in one of several possible configurations for belaying (see Chapter 10, Belaying).

Münter hitch: The same hitch that is used for belaying can also be used for rappelling (see Chapter 10, Belaying). It is probably worthwhile to learn as insurance because it requires only a locking carabiner. Though it is easy to set up and very safe, it puts significantly more twists in the rope than do other methods.

Nonmechanical Methods

Two traditional rappel methods use no hardware whatsoever to create friction on the rope. Instead, the rope is simply wrapped around parts of your body.

Dulfersitz: This is a simple, all-purpose method that should be mastered by every rappeller in the event that carabiners or a harness are not available. Face the anchor and step into the dulfersitz by straddling the rope. Bring it from behind you and around one hip, up across your chest, over the opposite shoulder, and then down your back to be held by the braking hand (the downhill hand) on the same side as your wrapped hip (fig. 11-13). Your other hand is the guiding hand to hold the rope above and to assist you in staying upright.

The dulfersitz has a number of drawbacks compared with mechanical rappel systems. It can unwrap from your leg, especially on high-angle rappels, though it helps to keep your wrapped leg slightly lower than your other leg. Stay under careful control and try to pad your body underneath the path of the rope, because rope friction around your hip and across your shoulder can be painful, especially on steep rappels. Turning up your collar protects your neck. If you are wearing a pack, the dulfersitz is even more awkward. The dulfersitz is used in modern climbing only when there is no reasonable alternative or for short and easy, low-angle rappels to save the trouble of putting a seat harness back on.

Arm rappel: This is not used much, but it is occasionally helpful for quick descent of a low-angle slope. Lay the rappel rope behind your back, under your armpits, then wrap it once around each arm (fig. 11-14). Be sure the rope does not run over any exposed flesh; it will get surprisingly hot. Control the rate of descent by your hand grip. For an arm rappel with a pack, be sure the rope goes around your pack rather than on top of or underneath it.

RAPPEL TECHNIQUE

When a party reaches a rappel point, typically the first rappeller is one of the more-experienced members of the group. On the rappel, this first rappeller will usually fix any tangles or problems with the rope and clear the anchor area and route of debris that might be dislodged onto subsequent rappellers or others below.

Use the four elements of the rappel system—anchor, rope, rappel method, and rappeller—as a mental checklist to prepare for each rappel.

1. Anchor—Start by ensuring that the anchor is solid and dependable.
2. Rope—Ensure that the rope was inspected during the rappel setup for cuts, fraying, or other damage, which might have occurred during climbing or on prior rappels. Then check that the rope is properly threaded through the anchor, not tangled or knotted, and that it will not load dangerously over a sharp edge or suffer abrasion damage against the rock, snow, or ice. If you are using two ropes, check the knot joining them.
3. Rappel method—Then check your own attachment to the rope, through the rappelling device or other setup. Partners should also independently check each other's setups at each rappel. If a harness is involved (as it usually is), be sure it is fastened properly. Pay special attention to the brake system: Are both ropes threaded through the device and around the locking carabiner correctly? Is the locking carabiner attached to the harness properly and locked? Which hand will be the braking hand? Does the braking hand have a secure grasp on the rope? If you are using a carabiner brake system, are the gates of carabiner pairs correctly opposed and reversed?

Are the ropes threaded in the correct direction, so as not to "rappel uphill and jam the system"? Are any self-belay or safety backup methods properly set up and functioning?

4. Rappeller—Last, think through the entire rappel. Make a mind's-eye check of the setup, the descent, and the finish at the next stance. Check the backup knots; check that the rope will pull; ensure that both strands are properly attached through the device; check which rope to pull. Beginners should wear gloves. Look for and secure things that can get caught in the system, such as long hair, loose clothing, pack straps, or helmet chin straps. Be mentally prepared for a safe rappel and anticipate any challenges that might occur during the rappel.

When you are ready to go, face the anchor with your back to the descent route, firmly gripping the free-hanging strands of the rappel rope with the braking hand. With the nonbraking hand, detach your personal anchor sling from the anchor.

Getting Started

Just before descending, shout "On rappel!" to warn others that a rappel has begun.

Fig. 11-15. Starting rappel from a high anchor.

Now comes the most nerve-wracking part of many rappels. To gain stability, your legs must be nearly perpendicular to the slope. Therefore, at the very brink of a precipice, you must lean backward, out over the edge (fig. 11-15). In some cases you may ease the transition by down-climbing several feet (about a meter) before leaning out and weighting the rope to start the rappel (fig. 11-16).

With mechanical rappel systems, you may be able to sit on the edge of the rappel ledge (fig. 11-17a) and wiggle gently off (fig. 11-17b), simultaneously turning inward to face the slope (fig. 11-17c). This technique is particularly useful when you are starting the rappel above an overhang.

Making the Rappel

Position

While you are descending, your body position should be something like this: feet shoulder-width apart, knees flexed, body at a comfortable angle to the slope and facing a little toward the braking hand for a view of the route. Common beginners' mistakes include keeping your feet too close together and failing to lean back far enough. Some go to the other extreme and lean too far back, increasing their chance of tipping over. If anything should happen, such as tipping over or losing your footing, it is absolutely critical to remember to hold onto the rope with the braking hand. If the braking hand releases its grip, you will quickly accelerate out of control. Once the situation has stabilized, work on getting reestablished against the rock, in the basic position shown in Figure 11-17c, below.

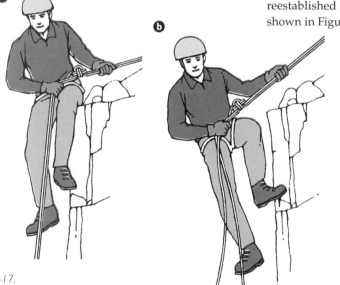

Fig. 11-16.
Climbing below a low anchor before starting rappel.

Fig. 11-17.
Starting a rappel from a steep ledge and a low anchor:
a, sitting down on a ledge; b, squirming off to get started; c, turning inward to face the slope.

POTENTIAL PROBLEMS WHEN RAPPELLING

Loose rock:

Use extreme caution when you are rappelling a face with loose or rotten rock. The danger here is that rock may be knocked loose and hit you or damage the rope.

Overhangs:

It is easy to end up swinging into the face below the overhang, smashing your hands and feet. There also is the risk of jamming the brake system on the lip of the overhang. A couple of methods assist in making the difficult transition from above the lip of an overhang to below it.

One method is to bend deeply at your knees with your feet at the uppermost edge of the overhang, then release enough braking tension to slip down 3 or 4 feet (1 to 1.2 meters) at once and then lock off the rappel with sudden braking action, which halts further acceleration once past the lip of the overhang. The abrupt halt and resulting bounce stress the rappel system, but this helps reduce both the chance of a swing into the face below and of jamming the brake system on the lip.

Another method is to place your feet on the lip of the overhang and then lower your waist down below your feet. Then "walk" your feet, while they are still above your waist, down the underside of the overhang until, once you are below the lip, the rope above makes contact with the rock face above.

Below an overhang, you will dangle free on the rope. Assume a sitting position, use the guiding hand to remain upright, and continue steadily downward. Often you will slowly spin as twists in the rope unwind. On very steep or free-hanging rappels, if you are using a tube-type rappel device, twists in the rope can be minimized by keeping the braking hand between your legs rather than outside your legs.

Pendulums:

Sometimes reaching the next rappel stance requires you to move at an angle to the fall line, walking down the face diagonally instead of moving straight down. If a slip occurs, you will swing on the rappel rope back toward the fall line in what could be a nasty pendulum fall. Also, after such a fall, it may be difficult to get reestablished on the proper rappel course without climbing back up the rope with prusik slings or mechanical devices. To avoid this potentially dangerous situation, try to rappel down the fall line as much as possible.

Loose ends:

Clothing, hair, pack straps, chin straps from a helmet, and just about anything else with a loose end all have the potential to get pulled into the braking system. Keep a knife handy to cut foreign material out of the system, but be extremely careful with a sharp knife around ropes.

Rope tangles:

If the rope gets tangled or jammed on the way down, the problem must be corrected before rappeling past it. Stop at the last convenient ledge above the area, or stop with a leg wrap (see the next section). Pull the rope up, correct the problem, then throw it down again. Sometimes there is a simple solution. For instance, when you are rappelling down blank slabs, tangles often may be shaken out as they are encountered.

Jammed rappel device:

If your rappel brake system jams on something (such as a shirttail) despite your precautions, it can most likely be freed by unweighting it. First, free your hands by using your backup autoblock, prusik, or leg wraps. Next, unweight the brake system by either standing on a ledge or tying a prusik knot above your brake system and chaining slings together until they are long enough to stand in. In the worst case you might even Texas prusik some distance up the rappel ropes (see Chapter 17, Glacier Travel and Crevasse Rescue, for information on the Texas prusik). Then, if you are able to free it, cut the jammed material away from the brake system, taking care not to nick the rope. A prusik tie-off loop, three or four slings, and a pocket knife should always be on hand.

Speed and Movement

Move slowly and steadily, with no bounces or leaps. Feed the rope slowly and steadily into the rappel system, avoiding stops and jerks. Higher rappel speeds put more heat and stress on the rappel system, and it is especially important to go slowly on any questionable anchor. A sudden stop during a rapid descent subjects the anchor to a dynamic load and a great deal of additional force.

Stopping in Midrappel

If you need to stop partway down a rappel, you can secure the rope in a couple of ways, described below. Some rappel or belay devices have other ways to stop the rope in the device; consult the manufacturer's instructions or obtain reliable instruction on their use.

Leg Wrap

The first method is to wrap the rope two or three times around one leg (fig. 11-18). The friction of the wrap, increased by the weight of the rope hanging below the wrap, is usually enough to halt further descent. Keep

Fig. 11-18.
Stopping in midrappel with the rope wrapped around the leg.

the braking hand on the rope until the wraps are completed and tested. If the wraps are not tight, you will slip a few feet (a meter or so) as the wraps tighten. To continue the descent, be sure to reestablish the brake hand before releasing the wraps. On steep rappels, simply remove your foot and leg from contact with the rock and shake the wraps off while holding the rope with the brake hand.

Prusik or Autoblock

A second method is to use a friction knot—either a prusik or an autoblock—below the rappel device (see "Self-Belay with a Prusik or Autoblock," later in this chapter).

Finishing the Rappel

Near the end of the rappel, it becomes much easier to feed rope through the rappel device because the extra friction caused by the weight of the rope below you is now considerably less.

The amount of rope stretch, particularly on a two-rope rappel, may be surprising. Be aware of this stretch factor as the rope is cleared from the rappel device after you complete the rappel. If you let go of the rappel rope, it could spring back to its normal length and suddenly be up out of reach. Better to end the rappel *near* the end of the rope rather than at the very end of it.

Near the end of the rope, be sure to find a good place to stop the rappel. Do not clear the rope from the device until after you establish a good stance and you are anchored in if necessary. In establishing a secure stance, consider the possibility of rockfall and icefall, and attempt to be out of the way of the next person coming down.

Shouting "Off rappel!" lets those above know that you have safely completed the rappel and the next person can begin the rappel.

MULTIPLE RAPPELS

A descent route often involves a series of rappels. These multiple rappels, especially in alpine terrain, present special problems and require maximum efficiency to keep the party on the move.

As a party moves through a series of rappels, the first person down each pitch usually carries gear to begin setting up the next rappel, after finding a secure stance, establishing an anchor, and attaching to it out of the path of icefall and rockfall. Gain more efficiency by moving ropes from preceding rappels down the current rappel as soon as practicable. With these ropes, prepare the next rappel while the remaining party members complete the current rappel. The more-experienced climbers in a party can take turns being first and last. It is best for beginners to be somewhere in the middle of the rotation so that assistance is available at each end of the rappel.

Unknown Terrain

The trickiest of multiple rappels is one into the unknown, down an unfamiliar route. Avoid this kind of multiple rappel if possible. If an unfamiliar rappel is necessary, take the time to check out the possible rappel lines as carefully as time and terrain permit. Sometimes it is possible before a climb to find a photo of the rappel route. Bring it along for reference. Keep in mind that the first couple of rappels down an unfamiliar route may commit the party to the route entirely, for better or worse.

If the bottom of an unfamiliar rappel pitch cannot be seen, the first person down must be prepared to climb back up in case the rappel hangs free at the end of the rope before there is a good stance. This rappeller should carry prusik slings or mechanical ascenders for ascending the rope.

Rappelling down unfamiliar terrain brings an increased risk of getting the rope hung up. Minimize the problem by down-climbing as much of the route as possible, instead of rappelling. Also, consider rappels using just one rope, even if two ropes are available. Although this increases the number of rappels and the time spent descending, one rope is easier to retrieve and is less likely to hang up than two. If the one rope does hang up, the second, unused rope is available to protect a climb back up to free the stuck rope. You may then carefully climb back down or establish an intermediate rappel where the hang-up occurred.

Although it is efficient to gain the maximum distance from each rappel, do not bypass a good rappel spot even well away from the end of the rope if there are doubts about finding a good place farther down.

SAFETY BACKUPS

Belay methods and backup knots at the end of rappel ropes can enhance the safety of a rappel. In addition, they add security to particularly risky or unnerving rappels and may save the life of a rappeller hit by rockfall. They also help beginners gain confidence in rappelling.

Self-Belay with a Prusik or Autoblock

Tying a friction knot (either a prusik or an autoblock) below the rappel device, clipped to a harness leg loop, enables you to stop without gripping the ropes. These self-belay knots will grip the rope and halt your descent anytime you do not actively tend them.

To make a self-belay knot, use a sewn runner of ⁹∕₁₆- or 1-inch webbing, or use 7-millimeter accessory cord for a nylon tie-off loop (see Chapter 9, Basic Safety System). Girth-hitch the runner or loop to the seat harness leg loop; wrap it around the rappel rope below the rappel device or carabiner brake; then clip the end of the runner or loop to the seat harness leg loop with a carabiner (fig. 11-19a).

If the brake hand releases the rope—for instance, as the result of rockfall—a self-belay friction knot can prevent you from accelerating out of control. Reestablish the brake hand and tend the self-belay knot by sliding it down along the rope to allow the descent to resume (fig. 11-19b).

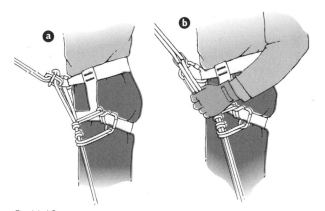

Fig. 11-19.

Autoblock self-belay on rappel: a, with a carabiner brake setup; b, rappelling with a rappel device.

*Fig. 11-20.
Rappel halted by a
climber below, who is
pulling down on the
ends of the rope.*

These knots require some testing and adjustment before each rappel in order to establish the proper length (so it does not hang up in the rappel device) and the proper amount of friction (adjusted by the number of wraps) to accommodate your weight, rappel device, comfort, and any other individual considerations. Some rappellers, concerned about the effects of friction, choose the more heat-resistant varieties of cord or webbing for self-belay knots.

Belay by a Partner Below

A person standing below a rappeller can easily control the rappeller's movement or stop it altogether—thus providing an effective belay—simply by pulling down on the rappel ropes, which puts friction on the brake system (fig. 11-20). To safeguard the rappeller with this method, the person at the bottom simply holds the rope strands loosely, ready to pull them tight the instant the rappeller has difficulty.

Backup Knots

Even very experienced rappellers have inadvertently rappelled off the end of their ropes with tragic results. When you use a rappel device, put a large knot, such as a figure eight, in the ends of the rope or tie the ends together to reduce this danger. If you add knots, do not rely blindly on them; knots might come untied, and in any case, you must keep an eye on the ends of the rope to plan where to stop. Knots may jam in the rappel device if you do not exercise care at the end of the rappel. Knots can also cause a problem before a rappel begins by jamming in the rock and hanging up when the ropes are tossed.

Top Belay

The rappeller can also be protected by a belay from above with a separate rope. If the belayer uses a separate anchor, the rappeller is safe from even a total failure of the rappel anchor. A top belay is recommended for all beginners, for climbers with minor injuries, and for the first person descending on a suspect anchor. The belays are too time-consuming for routine use because they drastically increase a party's descent time.

RETRIEVING THE RAPPEL ROPE
Final Precautions

Successfully retrieving the rope after a rappel depends on some important steps before the last rappeller starts down the rope. Just one frightening experience with a stuck rappel rope guarantees that these precautions will always be taken.

With two ropes joined at the anchor, it is critical to know which rope to pull on from below. Pull the wrong one, and the knot will jam in the rappel sling. In some parties, the last two rappellers say out loud which rope is to be pulled, as an aid to remembering which is which.

The last rappeller should take a good final look at the rope and the rappel sling to see that everything is in order and that the rope is not about to catch on the rock or the sling. Before the last person starts down, a person at the bottom should pull on the proper strand to check that it pulls freely. The rappeller above should confirm that the connecting knot in a two-rope rappel can be pulled free of the edge.

On a two-rope rappel, the last person who starts down may want to stop at the first convenient ledge and pull enough of the rope down so that the connecting knot is clear of the edge. This helps take some of the uncertainty out of the difficult business of recovering a long rappel rope. However, it also shortens one rope end, so be sure you still have enough rope to reach the next stance safely.

The last rappeller has the main responsibility for spotting any retrieval problems. This last person can get twists out of the rope by keeping one finger of the braking hand between the ropes throughout the descent. The same purpose is served by splitting the two ropes through a carabiner on your harness, just uphill of the braking hand.

Pulling the Rope Down

With the last rappeller down, it is time to retrieve the rope. First, take out any visible twists and remove any safety knots in the end of the rope. Then give the rope a slow, steady pull. Others should take shelter to stay out of the way of falling rope or rockfall. With proper preparation, the rope should pull free.

Rope Jams

A jammed rappel rope may be a serious problem, perhaps even stranding a party on a descent that requires further rappels. If the rope hangs up, either before or after the end clears the anchor, try flipping the rope with whipping and circular motions before attempting any extreme pulling. Often a change in angle, back from the face or to the right or left, can free the rope. Sometimes pulling on the other end of the rope (if it is still in reach) can free the rope. Be alert and cautious when pulling a stuck rope; as it springs free, it may be accompanied by rock- or icefall.

If both ends of the ropes are still in reach when the hang-up occurs, it is possible to safely prusik up both ropes (see "The Texas Prusik" in Chapter 17, Glacier Travel and Crevasse Rescue for one ascending method on a free-hanging rope), clear the jam, and rappel back down. Tie in to the rope at frequent intervals to back up the prusiks. If all else fails and only one rope end can be reached, it may be necessary to climb up and free the rope. If the route up is not too difficult to climb, several increasingly poor options are possible, depending on the situation:

1. If enough rope is available from the other strand, belay the climb up.
2. If not enough rope is available from the other strand, lead up the climb with a self-belay by anchoring the available rope and placing conventional protection in conjunction with a prusik ascent. If the rope suddenly pulls free from above, the hope is that the combination of the prusik attachment and the periodic protection and the anchor will limit the length of the fall.
3. If no belay is possible, and if the party cannot proceed without the rope, a final resort is to attempt the desperate and very dangerous tactic of ascending the stuck rope with prusik slings or mechanical ascenders. The extreme danger of climbing an unsecured rope must be weighed against the consequences of remaining stranded until another rope is available. Again, if it is possible to place protection during the ascent, attach the rope with clove hitches; perhaps the consequences of the rope pulling free from above might be mitigated.

EXPERIENCING THE FREEDOM OF THE HILLS

Rappelling is one of the activities central to climbing, and if you learn it thoroughly and employ it carefully, it is safe and works well. Take precautions to avoid complacency. Rappelling is one of the essential, specialized techniques that enables climbers to experience the freedom of the hills.

Next page: *Rock climbing in the Needles, Southern Sierra, California* (Photo by Mark Kroese)

ROCK CLIMBING

Alpine Rock-Climbing Technique

**TYPES OF ROCK CLIMBING ■ GEAR ■ CLIMBING EFFICIENTLY ■
FACE CLIMBING ■ CRACK CLIMBING ■ OTHER CLIMBING
TECHNIQUES ■ STYLE AND ETHICS**

**Alpine rock climbing can range from moderate routes only a few hours from
the trailhead to multiday climbs in remote settings. Rock climbing gives
you the kinesthetic pleasure of movement combined with the
challenge of solving a three-dimensional puzzle.**

This chapter focuses on the basic and intermediate-level rock-climbing skills you need in the mountains. For those interested in a sport-climbing emphasis, see Appendix C, Supplementary Reading, for several excellent texts on techniques more suited to that environment.

Note: When rock climbing on technical terrain, you should always be on belay. However, to more clearly show body positions involved in different climbing techniques, the illustrations in this chapter omit components of the basic safety system such as ropes, harnesses, and protection.

TYPES OF ROCK CLIMBING

Technical climbing begins when anchored belays are needed for the party's safety. *Free climbing* is simply climbing using your own physical ability to move over the rock via handholds and footholds, with the rope and protection used only for safety. *Aid climbing* involves the use of artificial means—protection placed in the rock—as hand- and footholds. Obviously, climbers use aid technique (see Chapter 15, Aid Climbing) when the rock does not offer enough natural features, or if the route is too hard for their skill level. *Big-wall climbing* means climbing on—what else?—a large, sheer wall, which usually requires extensive aid, but frequently these wall routes include sections of free climbing. Ascents of big walls typically take longer than one day, usually including either a hanging bivouac or ledge bivouac as well as sack hauling. *Solo climbing* is, of course, climbing by yourself, but it usually refers to unroped climbing, though you can also rope-solo a route, using gear, and so self-belay on a solo free or aid climb.

Nontechnical climbs, or scrambles, occur on second-, third-, or even fourth-class terrain (see Appendix A, Rating Systems, at the back of this book). Third-classing a section means to climb it unroped, and climbers will third-class not only third-class but also fourth- and some fifth-class terrain, depending on conditions and skill levels. Fifth-class rock is almost always steep and exposed enough to call for roped climbing. Although experienced climbers will occasionally solo a route, all unroped climbing is risky. The risk depends not only on how likely you are to fall, but what the consequences of a fall would be. Is the rock loose? Is it raining, which makes the rock slippery? Could you be hit by rockfall—or by a climber above you falling—and thereby be knocked off the holds? Is the ground 10 feet (3 meters) below or several hundred? Fatal falls have occurred on third-class terrain as well as on 5.12 routes.

Sport climbing and *crag climbing* refer to technical rock climbs close to roads and civilization that do not require alpine skills. They are usually in developed areas with detailed guidebooks, short routes—usually only one pitch—and bolts for belay and rappel anchors. If they are face climbs with little opportunity for protection placements, the routes themselves are bolted. If cracks are available for protection placements, the routes are usually not bolted. *Alpine rock climbing* refers to routes farther from civilization that require alpine routefinding or glacier-climbing skills and equipment. Of course, these categories have some overlap—there are long, technical rock climbs that start near a road, and multipitch bolted climbs that are in a somewhat remote area.

GEAR

Ropes and harnesses are covered in Chapter 9, Basic Safety System; protection hardware is covered in Chapter 13, Rock Protection.

Footwear

On climbs of moderate difficulty, the same mountain boots you wear on the approach generally work well for the actual climbing. (For more information on mountain boots, see Chapter 2, Clothing and Equipment.) When the climbing is more difficult, specialized footwear—rock shoes (fig. 12-1a, b, and c)—gives a significant advantage. Most rock shoes have flexible uppers, plus smooth, flexible soles and rands of sticky rubber. These soles create excellent friction when weighted on rock, allowing purchase on angles and nubbins that can amaze the beginning climber. Most alpine rock climbers use rock shoes if the technical difficulty is 5.6 or 5.7 on up.

On a climb that is a carryover—you will not go back to your starting point or base camp on the way down—using rock shoes on the route means climbing with the weight and bulk of your mountain boots in your pack. If the climbing includes patches of snow or ice between the rock sections, wearing mountain boots for the entire route avoids time-consuming breaks for changing footwear. Climbing often in mountain boots makes your footwork more precise, and you will have an advantage when you do use rock shoes.

Approach shoes (fig. 12-1d) are a compromise between mountain boots and rock shoes. These are useful when the approach is snow-free and can be worn on the climb itself if the route is of moderate difficulty.

When you are choosing an appropriate pair of rock shoes, the confusing array at outdoor stores can be daunting. Remember that your technique is far more

Fig. 12-1.
Rock shoes:
a, all-around shoe;
b, more specialized
edging shoe;
c, slipper;
d, approach shoe.

heel
rand

toe
rand

Good fit is paramount. Rock shoes should fit snugly, to give you dexterity and a good sense of the rock's features, yet not so tightly as to cause pain. Some makes are sized for wider or narrower feet than others; try on different styles to find what fits you. A thin pair of liner socks add comfort and a little warmth, because climbing often is done in chilly conditions. Some climbers have a pair of "alpine rock shoes" sized to fit over their mountain-boot socks. Unlike sport climbers at the local crag, alpine rock climbers do not have the leisure to take their shoes off after each 40-foot (12-meter) pitch. All rock shoes stretch somewhat, usually only a quarter to a half size in width and much less in length. Lined shoes stretch the least.

Rock-shoe rubber oxidizes and hardens over time; try a brisk scrubbing with a wire brush to expose a new, stickier layer.

Clothing

Alpine rock-climbing clothing must be comfortable, allow free range of movement, and handle changing weather conditions. For general information on alpine clothing, see Chapter 2, Clothing and Equipment.

Remove rings, braclets, and watches before you climb rock, because they will probably get scratched at the least, and at the worst may catch in a crack and damage your hands.

Tape

Athletic tape can be used to protect your hands from abrasive rock when you are crack climbing. Tape is advisable for those learning crack techniques or for those climbing more difficult cracks, especially on rock that has many sharp crystals. Some climbers feel that tape around their fingers helps protect finger tendons.

There are a number of different taping methods. See Figure 12-2 for one method. This method leaves your palm untaped, to ensure sensitivity during face holds. When taping your hands, flex them so that when you later make a fist or hand jam, the tape will not be too tight.

Chalk

Gymnastic chalk can improve your grip, especially in hot weather, by absorbing sweat. Chalk is available as loose powder and in crushable blocks, either of which

important than the shoes! That said, here are some useful guidelines on shoe selection.

Stiff-soled shoes are better at edging; flexible shoes are better at frictioning or smearing (see "Footholds," later in this chapter). Shoes with higher tops that cover your anklebones offer protection in deeper or wide cracks. If you are restricted to owning only one pair of rock shoes, a pair with all-around characteristics is best.

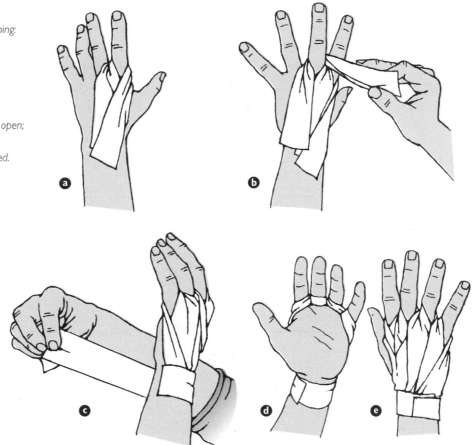

Fig. 12-2.
Hand taped for climbing:
a, wrap tape around
first finger;
b, wrap tape around
remaining fingers;
c, wrap wrist;
d, palm is mostly left open;
e, back of hand and
knuckles are protected.

is usually carried in a chalk bag. It is also available contained inside mesh balls that allow smaller amounts of chalk to sift out and thus minimize spillage.

Chalk marks tend to identify the holds that are used, thus making your moves obvious and minimizing the adventure for the next climber. Excess chalk on holds makes them slippery.

CLIMBING EFFICIENTLY

Efficient technique makes alpine climbing more enjoyable. It enables you to climb with as much speed as is reasonable, without exhaustion. You need to have enough strength for the approach and the climb itself, as well as the descent and the hike back out. Good technique combines balance, footwork, and handwork

with the minimum expense of strength necessary. This comes with time and practice.

Rock climbing may appear to require great arm strength. It is true that strength may get you up certain rock sections if you have no technique, but you will also burn out quickly. On some rock features, strength alone will not work; technique is necessary. The best of both worlds combines technique with strength and endurance. Following are some general guidelines that apply to climbing any type of rock, whether a face or a crack.

Focus on Speed and Safety

Speed is often an important part of safety on an alpine climb. Less time climbing means less time exposed to rockfall and changing weather, and more time to solve

211

routefinding problems, deal with injury, get off the mountain before dark, or handle any number of possible risks inherent in the alpine environment. However, reasonable caution must not be sacrificed to speed. Practice on shorter, easier routes and move to more difficult, longer routes as your efficiency improves.

Aim to move smoothly over the rock, set up belays, exchange gear, and manage the rope with a minimum of wasted time. Alpine climbing often necessitates carrying a pack. Pack enough gear to do the climb and survive unexpected situations, but be spartan.

The size of the climbing party and number of rope teams affect overall trip speed. The more rope teams there are, the longer it will take for the entire party to finish, all else being equal.

Climb with Your Eyes

Observe the rock. See where the holds are—the edges, the cracks—before even setting foot on the rock. Obviously you cannot visually memorize specifics of the entire pitch beforehand, but you can get an overall idea.

Look off to the side as well as up and down while climbing, to continually check where the holds are in relation to your hands and feet. Choices of holds are available on easy to moderate routes; do not let "tunnel vision" stop you from seeing them. Because the number of available holds decreases as the difficulty increases, a calm attitude helps on even more-difficult terrain.

Tune in to how your balance feels as you move in a deliberate, smooth, and fluid manner. Much of successful climbing involves a relaxed yet alert mind.

Use Footwork

Footwork and balance are the foundation of rock climbing. Good footwork gives you good balance and requires less exertion than handwork. Leg muscles are larger and stronger than arm muscles, and therefore provide the most efficient use of muscle power. That is why climbers are frequently told to climb with their feet.

Look for footholds that are comfortably spaced. Shorter steps take less energy than longer, higher steps, and you will stay in balance more easily. However, steps too close together take up more time per foot of upward progress.

Stand erect over your feet—this keeps your body weight centered over your feet, and the resulting downpressure helps keep your feet on the holds. Anxious climbers tend to "hug" or lean into the rock, but this just tends to push their feet off the rock because the pressure is out, not down.

Try to walk up the rock from foothold to foothold, as if you were going up a ladder—use your hands merely for balance. When you raise a foot toward the next foothold, eye the hold and aim precisely for it. Once your foot is set in place, commit to the hold and leave your foot there. Adjust your balance to the new position by shifting your hips over the new hold. Continue transferring your weight through your leg down to that foot. Complete the move: Stand up by using your leg muscles to push your body up.

Maintain Three Points of Contact

When you begin to learn rock climbing, keep three body points (any combination of hands and feet) weighted on the rock at all times (fig. 12-3). This can be two hands and one foot, or one hand and two feet. Keep your balance over your feet until you release a hold to move for the next one. This is an especially useful approach when you are testing a hold for looseness without weighting it because it allows you to balance securely on three holds while you test the new one.

Be aware of where your center of gravity is—directly over your feet is usually the most stable stance. Moving your center of gravity over a new foot- or handhold causes your weight to shift to that new hold.

On more difficult climbs, you cannot always keep three points in contact with the rock. There may be only one or two sound holds, and you will use your body position to maintain a delicate balance over those holds. Regardless of the number of points you do have in contact, however, the same principle of balance applies: Keep your weight over your holds.

Check for Loose Holds

Loose rock can be all too common in the mountains. Many loose holds are obvious, but be alert for those that are not. Look for fracture lines. Gently nudge any suspect hold, or give it a push with the heel of your hand. A hollow-sounding rock is usually loose. Make

12

Fig. 12-3.
Three-point suspension:
hands and right foot
provide secure stance
while left foot is moved
to a higher hold.

Fig. 12-4.
Face climbing.

sure your testing does not actually dislodge the rock! If loose rock cannot be avoided, move with extra care and deliberation. Sometimes a loose hand- or foothold can be used if you carefully push downward and in on it while weighting it—but be careful.

FACE CLIMBING

Face climbing is simply climbing by using the various features on the surface of a rock face, as contrasted with climbing the cracks that may split a face. A particular hold may be used in a variety of ways by your feet and hands as you move up the rock. Face climbing also includes the ascent of nearly featureless slabs, using friction and balance (fig. 12-4).

Handholds

You can use handholds for balance, to help raise yourself by pulling up on the hold, or to provide various forms of counterpressure. Handholds that are at about head height are best because they do not demand a tiring overreach.

Handholds offer maximum security when all your fingers are used. Keeping your fingers close together provides a stronger grip on the hold (fig. 12-5a). The most common handhold is the cling hold (fig. 12-5a and b). Large cling holds (fig. 12-5a) allow your entire hand to be cupped over the hold; smaller variations (fig. 12-5b) may allow room for only your fingertips. If the hold is not large enough for all your fingers to be placed on it, at least curl the other ones, which permits the fingers in use to get the most force from the muscle/tendon system (fig. 12-5c). When you are using cling holds, be careful not to overstress your fingers and cause injury by using holds that are too difficult or small for your technique level.

Because you depend mainly on your legs for upward progress, handholds are sometimes used only for balance. The pinch grip (fig. 12-5d) is a handhold that may allow you to maintain a balanced stance on good

213

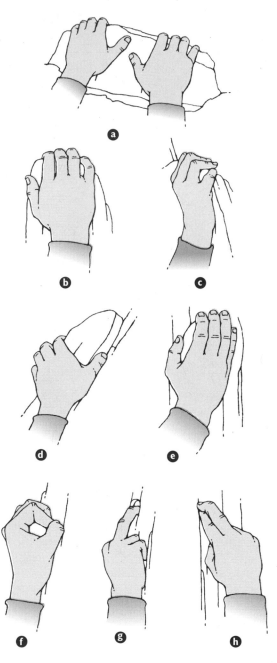

footholds long enough to shake out your free arm and to reach for a higher, more secure handhold or to place protection.

As holds become smaller, different techniques are needed. For example, with your fingers holding onto a tiny ledge, for additional strength you may use the thumb in opposition on a minor wrinkle (fig. 12-5e) or in a ring grip, where your thumb pressing against your index fingure adds strength (fig 12-5f). On a narrow hold or a small pocket in the rock you can use one or two fingers in a pocket grip (fig. 12-5g). On a very narrow hold, you can stack fingers on top of each other to increase pressure on the hold (fig. 12-5h).

Handholds that are at about head height are ideal if you need to hang straight-armed for a rest (fig. 12-6), which is less tiring than hanging from bent arms. You can lower your center of gravity by bending your knees or leaning out away from the rock. When you are able, hang an arm down and shake it out for a brief recovery before climbing again.

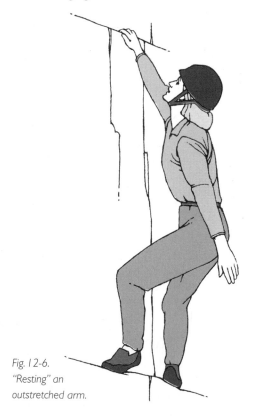

Fig. 12-5.
Handholds: a, large cling hold; b, smaller cling hold with an open grip; c, cling grip on a small hold (puts more stress on finger joints); d, pinch grip; e, thumb used in opposition to other fingers; f, ring grip; g, pocket grip; h, stacked fingers.

Fig. 12-6.
"Resting" an outstretched arm.

Footholds

Climbers use most footholds by employing one of two techniques: edging and smearing. On many holds, either technique will work, and the one to use depends on your own preference and the stiffness of your footwear. A third technique, foot-jamming, is covered in "Crack Climbing," later in this chapter.

When you are edging, you weight the edge of the shoe sole over the hold (fig. 12-7a). Either the inside or outside edge is used, but the inside is usually preferred for greater ease and security. The ideal point of contact may vary, but generally it is between the ball of your foot and the end of your big toe. Keeping your heel higher than your toes provides greater precision but is more tiring. Using the toe of your boot or rock shoe on a hold (toeing in) is also very tiring. With practice, you will become proficient using progressively smaller footholds.

In smearing, your foot points uphill, with the sole of your shoe "smeared" over the hold (fig. 12-7b). Smearing works best with rock shoes or flexible boots. On lower-angle rock, you may not need an actual hold, but only need to achieve enough friction between sole and rock. On steeper terrain, smear the front of your foot over a hold, and see how even tiny irregularities in the rock can provide significant friction and security.

In using footholds, make the best use of the direction of force on the hold. Flexing your ankle may increase the surface area of contact between sole and rock, giving you maximum holding power. Leaning away from the rock creates inward as well as downward force on the hold, increasing security.

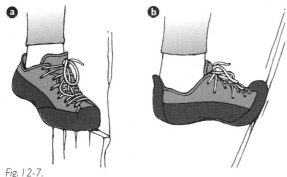

Fig. 12-7.

Footholds: a, edging; b, smearing.

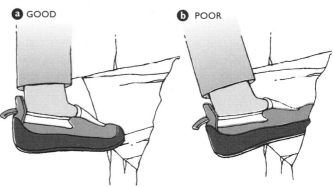

Fig. 12-8.

Bucket hold: a, use only as much of the hold as needed; b, foot too far into bucket can force lower leg outward.

When using large footholds, called buckets, place only as much of your foot as necessary on the hold (fig. 12-8a). Putting your foot too far into the bucket can sometimes force your lower leg outward, making for an out-of-balance stance (fig. 12-8b).

Avoid placing your knees on a hold, because knees are susceptible to injury and offer little stability. Nevertheless, even experienced climbers may on rare occasions use a kneehold to avoid an especially high or awkward step. The main considerations are to avoid injury from pebbles and sharp crystals and to avoid becoming trapped on your knees, unable to rise beneath a bulge or roof.

Fatigue, often aggravated by anxiety, can lead to troublesome spastic contractions of the leg muscles, jocularly known among climbers as "sewing-machine" or "Elvis" legs. The best way to stop it is to relax your mind and change leg position, either by moving on to the next hold, lowering your heel, or straightening your leg.

Friction or slab climbing requires liberal use of smearing (also called frictioning) moves. Balance and footwork are the keys to success, and the primary technique is smearing with your feet.

Remember to flex your ankle (lowering your heel) and keep weight directly over the ball of your foot for maximum friction between rock and sole (fig. 12-9a). Avoid leaning into the slope with your body, which causes your feet to slide down (fig. 12-9b). Instead, keep your weight over your feet, bending at the waist to

a GOOD

b POOR

Fig. 12-9.
Slab (friction) climbing:
a, keep weight over feet and
push hips away from rock;
b, avoid leaning into the slope,
which causes feet to slide.

allow your hands to touch the rock and pushing your hips and buttocks away.

Take short steps to maintain balance with your weight over your feet. Look for the small edges, rough spots, or changes in angle that provide the best foot placements. Sometimes you will actually have to feel with your hand or foot to find the irregularities.

Other techniques can also be useful on friction slabs. Face holds and cracks may be intermittently available for your hands or feet. On small edges or irregularities, use downpressure (see below) with your fingertips, thumb, or the heel of your hand. A lieback (see below) with one hand might be possible using tiny edges. Look for an opportunity for stemming (see below), which could mean a chance to rest.

Downpressure

For the downpressure technique, place your fingertips or the palm, side, or heel of your hand on the hold and press down (fig.12-10). Pressing down with your thumb can be useful on very small holds.

Holds are often used as cling holds from below and then as downpressure holds as you move above them. Downpressure holds may be used by themselves or in combination with other holds, such as in counterforce with a lieback hold or as part of a stemming move. With

your arm extended and elbow locked, you can balance one-handed on a downpressure hold as you move the other hand to the next hold.

Fig. 12-10.
Downpressure
using left hand.

216

Mantel

The mantel is a specific use of the downpressure technique. It lets you use hand downpressure to permit your feet to get up onto the same hold that your hands are using, when no useful handholds are available higher.

The classic mantel is easiest if the ledge is about chest-high (fig. 12-11a). Walk your feet up the rock (fig. 12-11b) until you can place both hands flat on the ledge, palms down, with the fingers of each hand pointing toward the other hand. Then raise your body up onto

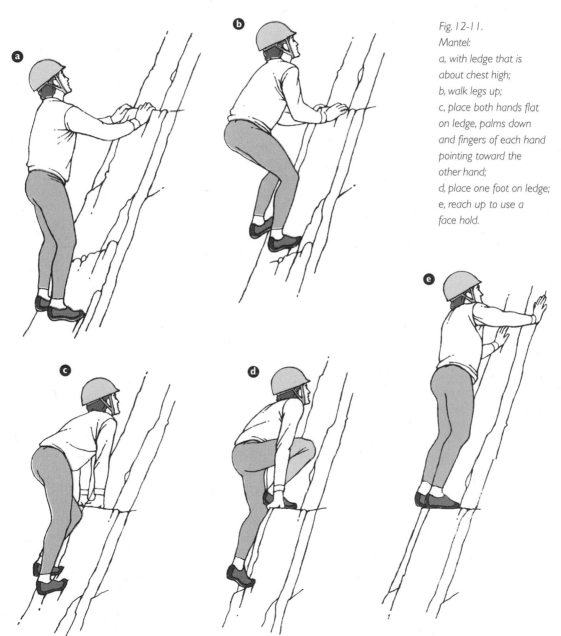

Fig. 12-11.
Mantel:
a, with ledge that is
about chest high;
b, walk legs up;
c, place both hands flat
on ledge, palms down
and fingers of each hand
pointing toward the
other hand;
d, place one foot on ledge;
e, reach up to use a
face hold.

12

stiffened arms (fig. 12-11c). Continue to walk your feet up the rock or, if you can, spring up from a good foothold, lift one foot up onto the ledge (fig. 12-11d), and stand up, reaching for the next handholds for balance (fig. 12-11e).

This basic mantel, however, is not always possible, because a ledge is often higher, smaller, or steeper than you might wish. If the ledge is narrow, you may be able to use the heel of your hand, with your fingers pointed down. If the ledge is over your head, you will use it first as a cling hold and then convert to a downpressure hold as you move upward. If the ledge is not big enough for both hands, you will mantel on just one arm while the other hand makes use of any available hold, or perhaps just balances against the rock. Do not forget to leave room for your foot.

Avoid using your knees on a mantel because it may be difficult to get off your knees and back on your feet, especially if the rock above is steep or overhanging. Sometimes in midmantel you will be able to reach up to a handhold to help as you begin standing up.

Counterforce

Counterforce plays a part in many of the climbing maneuvers described in this chapter. Counterforce is the use of pressure in opposing directions to help keep you in place. For instance, place both hands in a vertical crack and pull in opposite directions on the sides of the crack—a pulling-apart action (fig. 12-12a)—to create outward pressure. Or pull in on widely spaced holds—a pulling-together action (fig. 12-12b)—or press in on both sides of a sharp ridge (fig. 12-12c) to create inward pressure. You can also use your hands in counterforce to your feet, as in the undercling (see below).

Stemming

Stemming (also called bridging) is a valuable counterforce technique that lets you support yourself between two spots on the rock that might be of little or no use alone. It often provides a method of climbing steep rock where no holds are apparent, simply by pressing in opposing directions with your feet or with a hand and a foot.

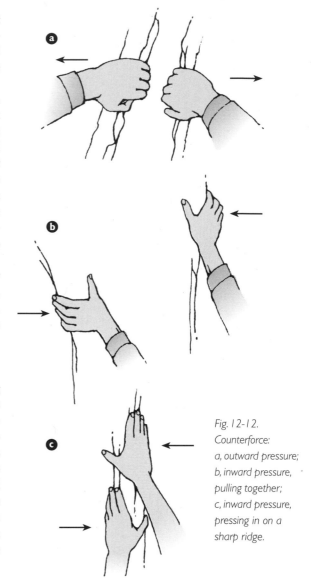

Fig. 12-12.
Counterforce:
a, outward pressure;
b, inward pressure, pulling together;
c, inward pressure, pressing in on a sharp ridge.

The classic use of stemming is in climbing a rock chimney. It also comes into play in climbing a dihedral (also called an open book), where two walls meet in an approximately right-angled inside corner. One foot presses against one wall of the chimney or dihedral, while the other foot or an opposing hand pushes against the other wall (fig. 12-13a).

Stemming may also open an avenue of ascent on a

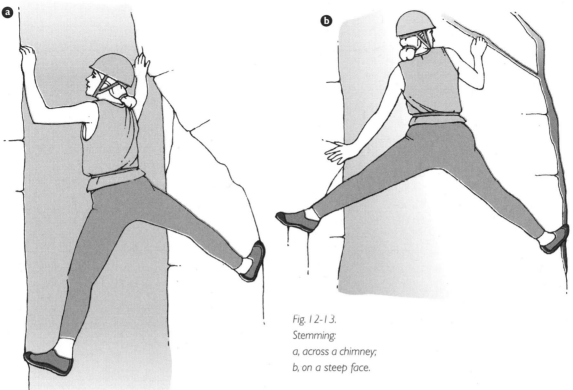

Fig. 12-13.
Stemming:
a, across a chimney;
b, on a steep face.

steep face, where you can press one foot against a slight protrusion while the other foot or a hand gives opposing pressure against another wrinkle (also known as a rugosity) in the rock (fig. 12-13b).

Undercling

In the undercling, your hands (palms up) pull outward beneath a flake or lip of rock while your body leans out and your feet push against rock (fig. 12-14). Your arms pull while your feet push, creating a counterforce. Try to keep your arms extended. Both hands can undercling at the same time, or one hand can undercling while the other uses a different type of hold.

An undercling hold may have multiple uses. For example, from below a rock flake, you can hold its bottom edge in a pinch grip and then convert to an undercling as you move up to the flake.

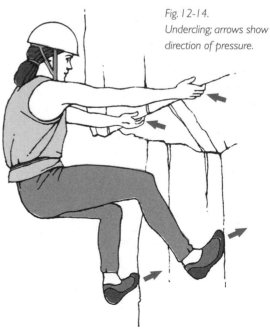

Fig. 12-14.
Undercling; arrows show
direction of pressure.

219

Liebacking

The classic lieback technique, another form of counterforce, uses hands pulling and feet pushing in opposition as you move upward in shuffling movements (fig. 12-15a). It is used to climb a crack in a corner, a crack with one edge offset beyond the other, or along the edge of a flake. Grasp one edge of the crack with both hands and lean back and to the side, away from the crack, on straightened arms. At the same time, push your feet against the opposite wall of the crack. Keep your arms extended to minimize muscle stress. Keep your feet high enough to maintain friction on the rock, but not so high that it is too strenuous. As always, feel for your body's balance and adjust accordingly. This is a strenuous technique, and it is difficult to place protection when you are liebacking.

The lieback can be used along with other holds as the rock allows. You can lieback on a single handhold in combination with other holds, or use one hand and foot in a lieback while using face holds for the opposite hand and foot (fig. 12-15b).

When you are using the lieback technique, your body will sometimes have a tendency to swing sideways out of balance toward the crack, in what is known as the "barn-door" effect, which usually results in a fall. To avoid the barn-door effect, do not apply too much pressure with the leg closest to the rock.

Counterbalance

Counterbalance, or flagging, is not a specific type of move but, rather, a principle that can be used in all kinds of climbing. It is the principle of distributing your body weight in a way that maintains your balance. This means selecting holds that do the best job of keeping your body in balance. But it also sometimes means putting a hand or foot in a particular location, even if no hold is available there, in order to provide counterbalance to the rest of your body. Your hips and shoulders also come into play as you move them to provide counterbalance. Flagging is useful because it enables you to extend your reach (fig. 12-16).

Fig. 12-15.
Lieback:
a, a classic lieback;
b, combining a
lieback (right
hand and foot)
with face holds.

Fig. 12-16.
Two examples of counterbalance: a, the left foot is flagged to the side to provide counterbalance; b, the left foot is flagged behind the right for counterbalance.

Long Reaches

There are several techniques you can use when the next available handhold is a long reach away, or even out of reach. First, make the most of available holds. Move as high as you can on your existing holds. Stand on your toes, but remember that this is strenuous and can contribute to sewing-machine leg if you continue too long. Sometimes a longer reach is possible if you stand on the outside edge of your boot, which tends to turn your body somewhat sideways to the rock. The longest reach possible is with the hand that is opposite the foot you are standing on.

Another option is to consider quick intermediate moves, using holds that are marginal but will be used just long enough to allow you to scamper up to the next good hold. This leads to using a dynamic move (or dyno)—a lunge or simply a quick move before you lose your balance. The time to grab the next-higher handhold while making a dynamic move is at the "dead point"—at the apex of your arc of movement when your body is weightless for a fraction of a second before it begins to fall. Movement is most efficient at that point.

Make a dynamic move only after calculating and accepting the consequences of failure. If a dynamic move fails, a fall is likely. Do not make a dynamic move out of desperation. You should know beforehand that the protection is secure and that a fall onto the protection will not result in hitting a ledge or the ground.

Exchanging Placements

Sometimes you need to move one foot onto a small hold already occupied by the other foot, or one hand onto a hold being used by the other hand. Either move can be made several different ways.

To exchange a foot placement, you can make an intermediate move using a poorer, even marginal, hold to get the one foot off the good hold long enough for the other one to take it over. You can also hop off the hold as you replace one foot with the other. You can also try sharing the hold by matching feet, moving one foot to the very edge of the hold to make enough room for the other. Another technique is the crossover (fig. 12-17a), in which you cross one foot in front of the other (fig. 12-17b) to occupy a small spot on the hold while

Fig. 12-17.
Foot crossing to change feet on a small hold:
a, right foot is on a hold;
b, cross left foot in front of the right;
c, left foot is on the hold and right foot moves off;
d, right foot reaches next hold.

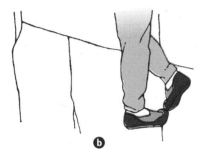

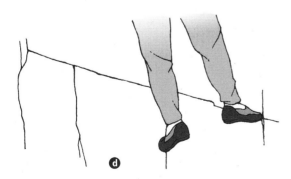

you move the first foot off that hold (fig. 12-17c) to another (fig. 12-17d).

To trade hands, you can make an intermediate move, much as you might in exchanging feet. You have the option of placing both hands on the same hold, one on top of the other. If space is limited, you can also try picking up the fingers of one hand, one finger at a time, and replacing them with the fingers of the other hand. The crossover technique also is occasionally useful.

CRACK CLIMBING

Many climbing routes follow the natural lines of cracks in the rock. Cracks have the advantage of offering handholds and footholds virtually anywhere along their length, as well as protection opportunities (see Chapter 13, Rock Protection). Some climbers seem to find crack-climbing technique more difficult to develop than face-climbing technique. Perhaps this is because even easy crack climbs demand a higher proportion of technique to strength than do face climbs. However, as with face climbing, balance and continued practice are the keys to success.

Jamming

Jamming is the basic technique of crack climbing. To jam, place a hand or foot into a crack, then turn your foot or flex your hand so that it is snugly in contact with both sides of the crack. This wedging must be secure enough that your hand or foot will not come out when weighted. Look for constrictions in the crack, and place hand and foot jams just above these constrictions. When you are learning to crack climb, it is a good idea to try weighting jams as a test—while you remain balanced on the other points of contact—before you actually try moving up on the jams.

Cracks may be climbed with a pure jamming technique, with both feet and hands using jams, or in combination with other types of holds. As you move up on a jam, you can maintain the jammed position by using downpressure. Of course, there is nothing to stop you from also using any nearby face holds (fig. 12-18).

The following technique descriptions are basic guidelines that may be adapted to the varying size and configuration of the particular crack you are on. With

Fig. 12-18.
Combining jamming
with face climbing.

The thumb-down technique may allow a more secure reach to a jam high above your head, because your hand can be twisted for better adhesion and you can lean in any direction off this jam (fig. 12-19c). Climbers use a combination of thumbs up and thumbs down, especially in diagonal cracks, where it is often useful to jam the upper hand thumb down and the lower hand thumb up (fig. 12-19d).

With hand jams, keep alert to the effect of your elbow and body position on the security of the hold. As

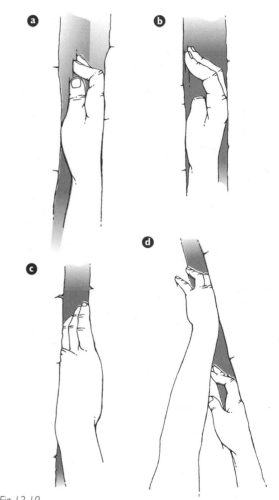

Fig. 12-19.
Hand jams: a, thumb-up jam; b, with thumb tucked across palm; c, thumb-down jam; d, combining thumb-down and thumb-up jams in a diagonal crack.

practice, you will become more adept at selecting the appropriate technique to apply in a given situation.

Hand-Size Cracks

The easiest crack to master is the hand-size crack. As the name implies, you insert your entire hand, cupping it as needed and pressing downward with your thumb to provide adequate expansion against the walls of the crack (fig. 12-19a). To increase pressure against the walls, you will sometimes tuck your thumb across your palm, especially in wider cracks (fig. 12-19b). You can often improve the hold by bending your wrist so your hand points into the crack rather than straight up and down.

The hand jam is done either thumb up or thumb down. Thumb up often is easiest and most comfortable for a vertical crack, and it works especially well when your hand is relatively low. The thumb-up configuration is most secure when your body leans to the same side as your hand that is jammed.

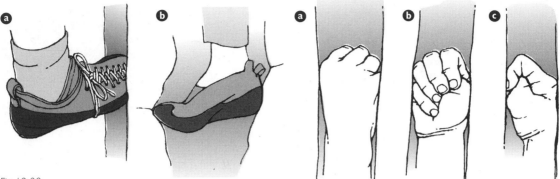

Fig. 12-20.
Foot jams: a, foot jam in a hand-sized crack; b, heel and toe jam in an off-width crack.

Fig. 12-21.
Fist jam: a, palm facing in; b, palm facing out; c, palm facing the side.

you move up, you may have to rotate your shoulder or trunk to keep sufficient torque and downward pressure to maintain the jam. Direction of force should be pulling down, not out of the crack. In general, keep your forearm parallel to the crack as you climb.

In dealing with hand jams, you will run across variants at both ends of the size scale: thinner cracks that will not admit your entire hand but are larger than finger cracks, and wider cracks that are not quite large enough for a fist jam but require extra hand-twisting to create enough expansion for a secure jam. The size of your hand is a major factor in determining the appropriate technique and the degree of difficulty of any particular crack.

Hand-size cracks are good for foot jamming, and it is generally possible to wedge a shoe in as far as the ball of your foot. Insert your foot sideways, with the sole facing the side of the crack, and then twist it up to jam (fig. 12-20a). Avoid twisting your foot so securely that it gets stuck.

Fist-Size Cracks

In a crack that is too wide for a hand jam, you can insert your fist. Your thumb may be inside or outside your fist, depending on which provides the best fit. Your palm may face the back of the crack (fig. 12-21a), the front (fig. 12-21b), or either side (fig. 12-21c). Flexing the muscles in your fist can expand it slightly to help fit the crack. Fist jams are often painful, but they can be very useful. For the most secure hold, try to find a constriction in the crack and jam your fist above it.

Fist-size cracks can generally accept your entire foot. As with hand-size cracks, insert your foot sideways, sole facing the side of the crack, and rotate your foot to jam it securely in place. In even wider cracks, you can jam your foot diagonally or heel to toe (see Figure 12-20b).

Finger-Size Cracks

Finger jams make it possible to climb some of the narrowest cracks, where you may be able to insert only one or more fingers or perhaps just your fingertips. Finger jams are commonly done with your thumb down. Slip your fingers into the crack and twist your hand to lock your fingers in place (fig. 12-22a). You get added strength by stacking fingers and also by pressing your thumb against your index finger in a ring jam (fig. 12-22b and c).

In slightly wider cracks, you can try a thumb lock, also called a thumb cam (fig. 12-22d). Place your up-pointing thumb in the crack, your thumb pad against one side of the crack and your knuckle against the other. Slide the tip of your index finger tightly down over the first joint of your thumb to create the lock.

The pinkie jam is done with your thumb up (fig. 12-22e and f). Put your little finger in a crack and stack the other fingers on top (fingertips down, nails up). In slightly larger cracks, you may be able to wedge the heel of your hand and your smaller fingers into a crack that is not quite wide enough for a full hand jam. The weight here is borne by the heel of your hand.

For another variation done with your thumb down,

12

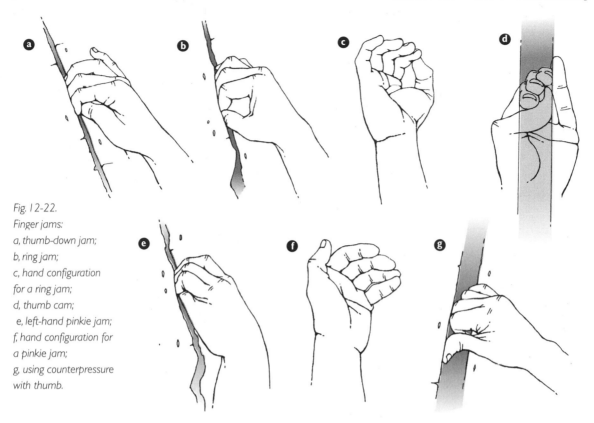

Fig. 12-22.
Finger jams:
a, thumb-down jam;
b, ring jam;
c, hand configuration
for a ring jam;
d, thumb cam;
 e, left-hand pinkie jam;
f, hand configuration for
a pinkie jam;
g, using counterpressure
with thumb.

use the counterpressure of your thumb pushing against one side of the crack and your fingers pushing against the other (fig. 12-22g).

Finger-size cracks are not big enough to accept your foot, but there is often room for your toes. You can wedge your toes into a crack by turning your foot sideways—usually with the inside of your ankle up—inserting your toes in the crack and then twisting your foot to jam it (fig. 12-23a). You can also wedge your toes into a steep inside corner with a smearing technique, keeping your heel lower than your toes and putting pressure down and in to keep your toes in place (fig. 12-23b). Using smearing and friction for your feet also works well when you are climbing a finger-size crack.

Chimneys

A chimney is any crack big enough to climb inside, ranging in size from those that will barely admit your body (squeeze chimneys) to those that your body can barely span.

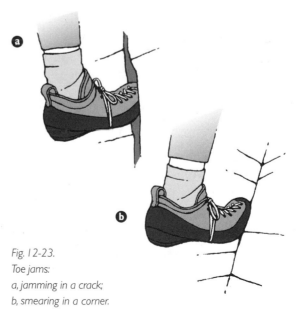

Fig. 12-23.
Toe jams:
a, jamming in a crack;
b, smearing in a corner.

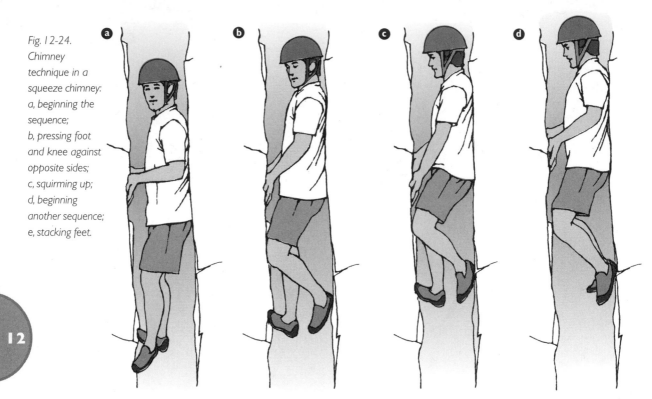

Fig. 12-24.
Chimney
technique in a
squeeze chimney:
a, beginning the
sequence;
b, pressing foot
and knee against
opposite sides;
c, squirming up;
d, beginning
another sequence;
e, stacking feet.

12

The basic principle is to span the chimney with your body, using counterforce to keep from falling. Depending on the width of the crack, you either face one side of the chimney or face directly into or out of the chimney. The best body position and technique to use depend on the situation, your size, and whether you are wearing a pack. Which direction you face may depend on what holds are available outside the chimney and on how you plan to climb out of it.

In squeeze chimneys, wedge your body in whatever way works best (fig. 12-24a and d) and squirm upward (fig. 12-24c). Look for handholds on the outside edge or inside the chimney. Arm bars and arm locks (see "Off-Width Cracks," below) may be useful. It is helpful, sometimes, to press your foot and knee of one or both legs, for example, against opposite sides of the chimney (fig. 12-24b). You might try stacking your feet in a T configuration, with one foot placed parallel to one side of the rock and the other placed perpendicular to it, jammed between the first foot and the opposite wall (fig. 12-24e). Climbing squeeze chimneys can be very strenuous.

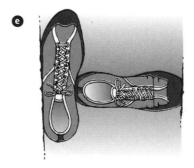

In a crack that is somewhat wider than a squeeze chimney, there is some more room to maneuver. You can press your back and feet against one side of the chimney as your knees and hands push against the other side (fig. 12-25a). You can move upward by squirming your way. Or try a sequence of wedging your upper body while raising your feet and knees and then wedging them and raising your upper body.

A wide chimney calls for stemming technique, where you face directly into or out of the chimney (fig. 12-25b). Counterforce is applied between your right

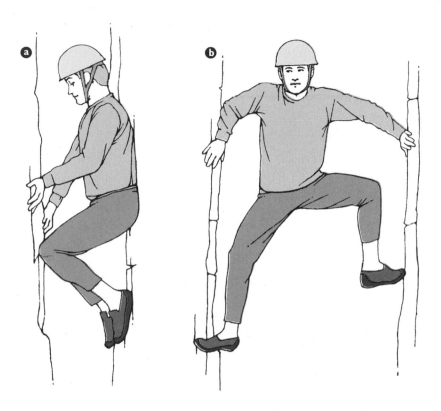

Fig. 12-25 (left).
Chimney techniques:
a, in a narrow chimney;
b, in a wide chimney.

Fig. 12-26 (below).
Chimney techniques in a
moderate-width chimney:
a, using counterforce
between hands and
between feet;
b, moving up;
c, using counterforce
between buttocks and feet;
d, beginning the sequence
again.

12

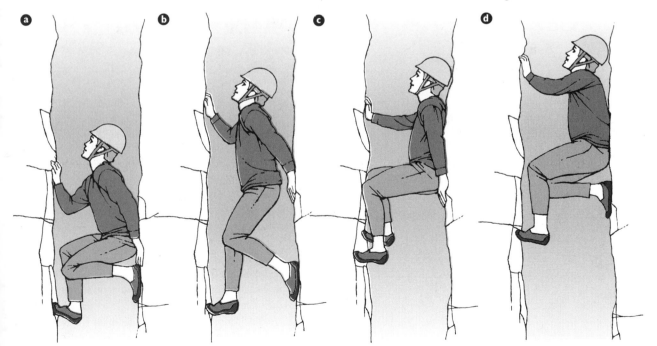

hand and foot on one side of the chimney and your left hand and foot on the other side. Press down as well as against the sides, especially if there are holds on the sides of the chimney. Ascend either by alternately moving your arms and legs or by moving each leg and then each arm.

In a standard moderate-width chimney, perhaps 3 feet (1 meter) wide, again face one wall of the chimney, your back to the other. For your upper body, your hands may push against one wall in counterforce to your back pressed against the other, or the counterforce may be between your hands on opposing walls (fig. 12-26a, b, and c). For your lower body, your feet may push against one wall in counterforce to your buttocks against the other (fig. 12-26c), or the counterforce may be between your two feet (12-26a, b, and d).

To climb a moderate-width chimney, use the following sequence: Start with your back toward one wall.

Press one foot against each wall and one hand against each wall (fig. 12-26a). Move upward by straightening your legs and then reestablishing hand positions (fig. 12-26b). Immediately bring your back leg across to the same side as the forward leg (fig. 12-26c). Then swing your forward leg across to the back position (fig. 12-26d). You are now again in position to move upward by straightening your legs.

Beware of getting too far inside a chimney. Although psychologically it may feel more secure, you can get lodged deep inside and find it difficult to move back out. You have a better chance of finding useful handholds and footholds if you stay near the outside of the chimney.

Climbing deep inside the chimney also can make it harder to exit at the top. The transition from the top of the chimney to other types of climbing is often challenging and may require extra thought and creativity.

Chimney technique may be useful in places that do not look like classic chimneys. It can be used to climb dihedrals (fig. 12-27) or short, wide sections of otherwise narrower cracks. Knee pads can be very useful when you are climbing routes with extensive chimney sections.

Off-Width Cracks

Climbers have figured out ways to jam their arms, shoulders, hips, knees, and just about anything else into the difficult and awkward features known as off-width cracks. They are "off-width" because they are too wide for hand or fist jams but too narrow to admit your entire body for chimneying.

The basic off-width technique calls for standing sideways to the crack and inserting one full side of your body into it. When you are confronted by an off-width crack, first decide which side of your body to put inside the crack. This depends on several things, such as holds in the crack or on the face, the direction in which the crack leans, and whether it flares larger in places.

After you have settled on which side to use, your inside leg goes inside the crack and forms a leg bar, usually with counterpressure between foot and knee or foot and hip. This foot is often placed in a heel-toe jam (fig. 12-28). Your outside foot also is inside the crack in a heel-toe jam. Try to keep your heel above your toe

Fig. 12-27.
Chimney techniques
in a dihedral.

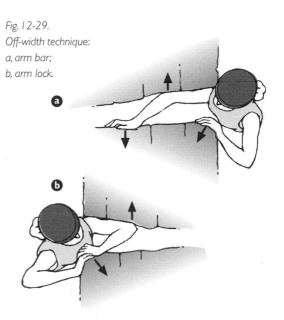

Fig. 12-29.
Off-width technique:
a, arm bar;
b, arm lock.

a

b

Fig. 12-28.
Climbing an
off-width crack.

(for better friction) and turned into the crack (to allow your knee to turn out).

A primary body-jam technique is the arm bar (fig. 12-29a). With your body sideways to the crack, insert one arm fully into the crack, with your elbow and the back of your upper arm on one side of the crack giving counterpressure to the heel of your hand on the other side. Get your shoulder in as far as possible, and have the arm bar extend diagonally down from your shoulder.

In the arm lock, a variation of the arm bar, fold your arm back at your elbow before inserting it in the crack, and press your palm against the opposite side in counterforce to your shoulder (fig. 12-29b).

In either the arm bar or the arm lock, use your outside arm to give downpressure to help hold you in the crack, or bring it across the front of your chest and push it against the opposite side of the crack, elbow out.

You are now wedged securely in the crack. To climb, move your outside leg upward to establish a higher heel-toe jam. When this jam is set, stand up on it. Then reestablish the inside leg bar and arm bar (or arm lock), and reposition your outside arm. This again wedges your body in the crack. You are now ready to move your outside leg upward again to establish a yet higher heel-toe jam. Continue repeating this procedure.

You may use your outside foot occasionally on face holds, but watch out for the tendency for these outside footholds to pull you out of the crack.

Combining Crack and Face Climbing

Cracks also may be climbed with a pure lieback technique or by liebacking with one arm in combination with face holds for the other hand (fig. 12-30). This may result in a kind of stemming action.

Dihedrals may be climbed by using various combinations, such as hands jammed in a crack splitting the dihedral, combined with feet stemming on opposite sides of the dihedral (fig. 12-31).

You may find useful edges or other holds hidden within cracks—on the sides or even at the back of wide cracks. Horizontal cracks can also be used as cling holds.

12

Fig. 12-30.
Liebacking
combined
with face holds.

Fig. 12-31.
Climbing a dihedral
using stemming
and hand jams.

Fig. 12-32.
Climbing an
overhanging route.

OTHER CLIMBING TECHNIQUES
Negotiating Overhangs and Roofs

Remember the main points for any climbing: Stay in balance and conserve strength. Identify handholds you will use to move up and over the bulge. Make the most of footholds by keeping your feet high and your hips low to help press weight against the footholds (fig. 12-32). In some situations, it means pressing your hips into the rock, with your back arched, to keep weight over your feet while poised under an overhang.

To conserve strength, weight your feet as much as possible, even when you are negotiating a roof (fig. 12-33a). Keep your arms straight while raising your feet (fig. 12-33b). Avoid hanging on bent arms, because this will quickly exhaust your arm strength. Push your body up with your legs rather than pulling with your arms (fig. 12-33c). Move quickly to minimize the time you spend in these strenuous positions. Occasionally you may need to rise up on your feet while making a dynamic reach to a handhold. Another trick is to throw one foot up onto a ledge while pushing with your other foot and pulling with your arms to swing up onto your top foot (fig. 12-33d).

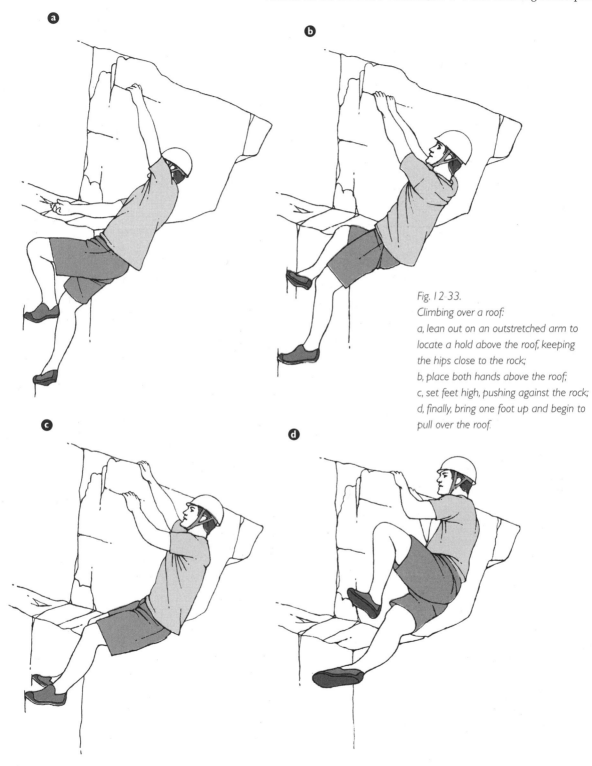

Fig. 12-33.
Climbing over a roof:
a, lean out on an outstretched arm to
locate a hold above the roof, keeping
the hips close to the rock;
b, place both hands above the roof;
c, set feet high, pushing against the rock;
d, finally, bring one foot up and begin to
pull over the roof.

Traversing

Traversing—going sideways across a section of rock—calls for a wide variety of climbing techniques. The main ones are side clings, liebacks, and stemming. Good balance and being aware of your center of gravity are especially important during traverses.

Usually you face into the rock, your feet pointed away from each other (fig. 12-34a). Commonly you shuffle your hands and feet sideways, although it can be very useful to exchange one hand for the other, or one foot for the other, on a single hold. You may occasionally cross one foot behind the other to reach the next hold, or cross one hand over the other (fig. 12-34b and c).

A hand traverse is necessary when footholds are marginal or nonexistent. Your hands grip a series of holds or shuffle along an edge, while your feet provide a counterforce by pushing against the rock, as in a lieback or undercling (fig. 12-35a). Keep your feet high and your center of gravity low so your feet are pushed into the rock. Cross one hand over the other (fig. 12-35b). Again, keep your arms straight to conserve arm strength and to let your legs do as much of the work as possible.

Exiting onto Ledges

As you approach a ledge, continue to walk your feet up the rock, and then use downpressure with your hands near the edge of the ledge. Avoid the temptation to reach forward and pull yourself onto the ledge; this may throw you off balance and also make it impossible to keep an eye on your footholds (fig. 12-36b). Often a classic mantel is an excellent exit move (fig. 12-36a).

Down-climbing

Efficient down-climbing is useful on many alpine climbs. Down-climbing is sometimes faster, safer, or easier than rappelling, and may provide another retreat option when necessary.

When you are down-climbing, the holds are harder to see than when you are climbing upward. The steeper the face, the harder the holds are to see. It is difficult to test holds without committing to them.

On low-angle rock, face outward for the best visibility

Fig. 12-34.
Traversing a steep face (an advanced technique): a, start the sequence with right foot on a hold in the direction of the traverse; b, twisting the body, reach through with the left hand; c, move the right hand to a new hold.

Fig. 12-35.
Hand traverse:
a, feet push against rock, providing counterforce;
b, one hand crosses over the other.

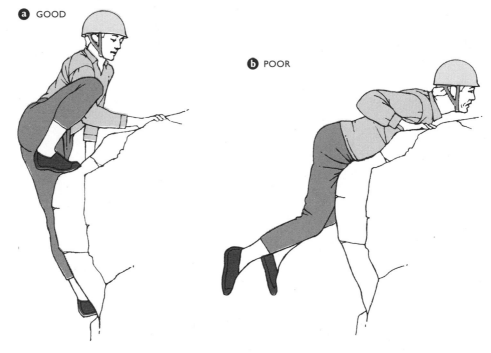

Fig. 12-36.
Exiting onto a ledge:
a, keep hands close to lip of ledge and step up;
b, trying to pull yourself up with your hands causes your feet to lose their hold.

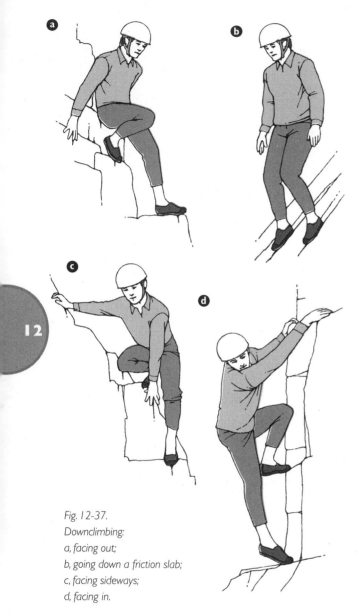

Fig. 12-37.
Downclimbing:
a, facing out;
b, going down a friction slab;
c, facing sideways;
d, facing in.

(fig. 12-37a). Keep your hands low and use down-pressure holds whenever possible. Keep your weight over your feet to maximize friction, especially when you are going down slabs. It may help to keep your center of gravity low, with your knees well bent (fig. 12-37b). As the rock steepens, turn sideways, leaning away from the rock for better visibility (fig. 12-37c). If the angle gets even steeper, face into the rock (fig. 12-37d).

234

STYLE AND ETHICS

Climbers debate endlessly over which styles are fair and which are less than sporting, over which practices are harmful to the environment and which are not. Climbers soon discover that getting to the end of the pitch or the top of the peak is not the only goal—another is getting there in a way that feels right, that respects the rock, and that tests your skill and resolve as a climber. These are matters of style and ethics.

The terms "style" and "ethics" are sometimes used interchangeably by climbers, but style is generally an individual attribute, and ethics are considered in the overall application of the pursuit. For example, style refers to your personal mode of climbing; in other words, is it fair to say you have led a first ascent if you first climbed the route on a top rope? Ethics pertain to issues concerning preservation of the rock itself.

Diversity of Styles

Styles change and attitudes evolve, but the core of the debate on climbing styles is about how to maintain the challenge of climber against rock and how to play the game in a way that fairly tests the climber.

Climbers adhering to traditional style prefer to climb each route strictly from the ground up, with no help from such aids as top ropes or preplaced protection such as bolts. New routes are explored and protected only on lead. This type of climbing characterizes rock climbing in the alpine setting, but it is also found at many popular crags.

Climbers following the European-influenced sport-climbing style are more likely to find other techniques acceptable as well. This can include inspecting the route on rappel before trying to lead it from below. It can also mean cleaning the route (removing protection placed by the lead climber or by another climber) and perhaps placing protection on rappel. Routes may be climbed with multiple falls, by resting on the rope while checking out the next move (hangdogging), or by rehearsing moves with the help of a top rope. These techniques have made it possible to climb harder and harder routes with the climber assuming less risk.

A particular climbing area may lend itself more to one style than another because of the type of rock, the difficulty of the routes, or the conventional style of the local climbers. In the world of climbing, there is room for a diversity of styles, and most climbers experience a variety of them.

Ethics and the Rock

The subject of ethics has to do with respecting the rock and every person's chance to use it. Unlike climbing style, ethics involves personal decisions that do affect others' experience and enjoyment. This includes the sticky question of the manner in which bolts are placed on a route. Are bolts that are placed on rappel different—less "ethical"—from bolts placed on the lead? Some climbers may argue that bolts placed while on rappel rob others of the chance to try the route from the ground up, and are often placed at less-convenient places than bolts would be if they were placed on a ground-up ascent. But other climbers may say that placing the bolts on rappel gives them a chance at a route that otherwise would be unclimbable at the present time.

Each area has its own tradition of what styles and ethics are acceptable. Visiting climbers should observe the local standards, which are usually described in local guidebooks, as well as any land manager regulations. Sometimes locals may disagree among themselves. This book does not try to resolve issues of style and ethics, but there is general agreement on a couple of principles.

Preservation of the rock is paramount. Chipping the rock to create new holds is unacceptable and destroys a natural feature—and who knows? It may be climbed someday as it is. Although bolt-protected routes are common in many areas, bolting should not be indiscriminate. In the mountains or other wilderness areas,

away from concentrated centers of rock climbing, it is particularly important to preserve the environment for those who follow. If possible, stick to clean climbing, using only removable gear for protection. (See Chapter 13, Rock Protection, for more on this.)

It is almost never justifiable to add a bolt to an existing route (retro-bolting). If you feel you cannot safely climb the route as it is, do not try it. Retro-bolting usually occurs when a consensus of local climbers agree that more bolts should be placed to promote safety and enjoyment. This may occur with the agreement of the first ascensionists.

There should be no objection to replacement of an old bolt with a newer, stronger one at an established belay or rappel point, provided you have the necessary skills and experience.

Courtesy

Keep other climbers in mind when you are out climbing. If your party is moving up a multipitch route at a pace that is much slower than that of the people behind you, let the following party pass you at a safe spot, such as a belay ledge.

Beware of tackling climbs that are beyond your abilities. Try climbs at your limit on the crags rather than in the mountains. If your inexperience gets you in trouble in the mountains, you may involve other climbers in a time-consuming and dangerous rescue of your party. Come prepared to handle the possibilities inherent in your climb. Aim to be self-reliant within your climbing party, and capable of self-rescue. This competence will add to your confidence and enjoyment of the alpine environment.

12

13

CHAPTER

Rock Protection

NATURAL PROTECTION ■ FIXED PROTECTION ■ REMOVABLE
PROTECTION ■ BUILDING YOUR SKILLS

The "rack and rope" are, collectively, the rock climber's protection. The rope connects two climbers—one leading a pitch while the other belays. Individual pieces of protection connect them both to the rock face. The belayer is connected to an anchor that is usually formed from several pieces of protection. The climber on lead places protection from the rack (the collection of gear used for protection) periodically while climbing.

The quality and location of the protection that the lead climber places largely determine the consequences of a potential fall. If a climber falls while leading, the

length of the fall will be about twice the distance between the climber and the last point of protection, plus rope stretch (fig. 13-1). If the last piece placed pulls out, the fall increases in length by double the distance to the next piece that holds. Skill in using and placing protection makes you a far safer climber.

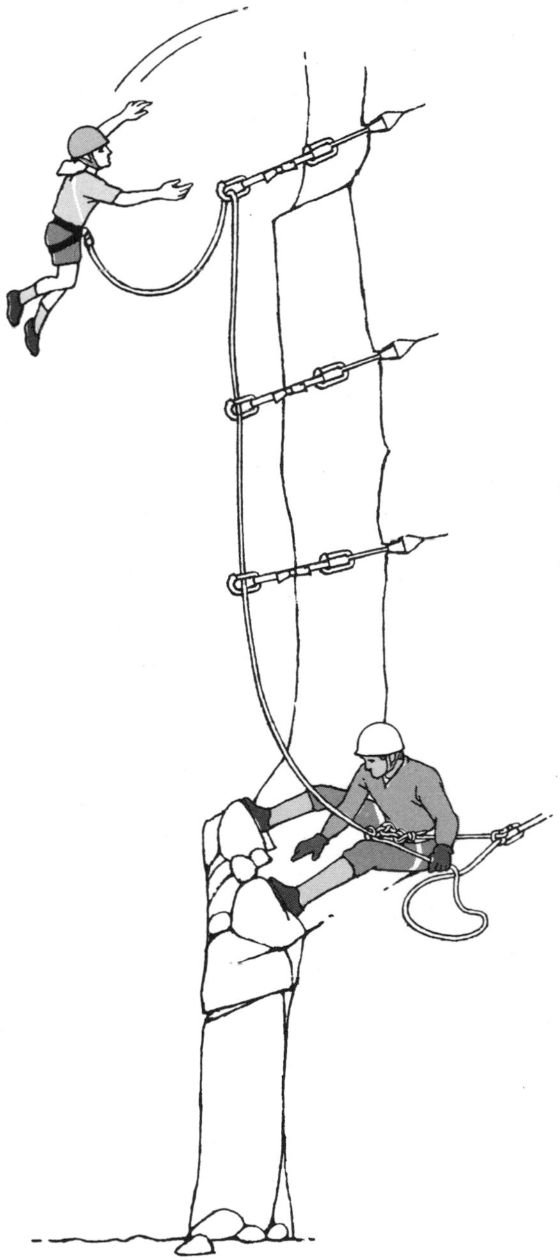

Fig. 13-1.
Leader fall with intermediate points of protection in place.

Connecting the Rope to Protection

Carabiners and runners (fig. 13-2a) are the tools you use to connect the climbing rope to protection. The carabiner should almost always be used in the down-and-out position: The gate should point down and away from the rock surface (fig. 13-2b). This position lessens the chance of accidental (and potentially disastrous) opening of the carabiner gate during a fall. The rope itself should be clipped in so that it runs freely through the carabiner in the direction of travel (fig. 13-2c): The rope should travel from the rock surface below/behind the climber upward through the carabiner and then out toward the climber. If you are not climbing straight upward, the rope exits the carabiner on one side or the other; it should exit on the side opposite from the gate. This minimizes the chance that the rope will twist across the gate and open it during a fall.

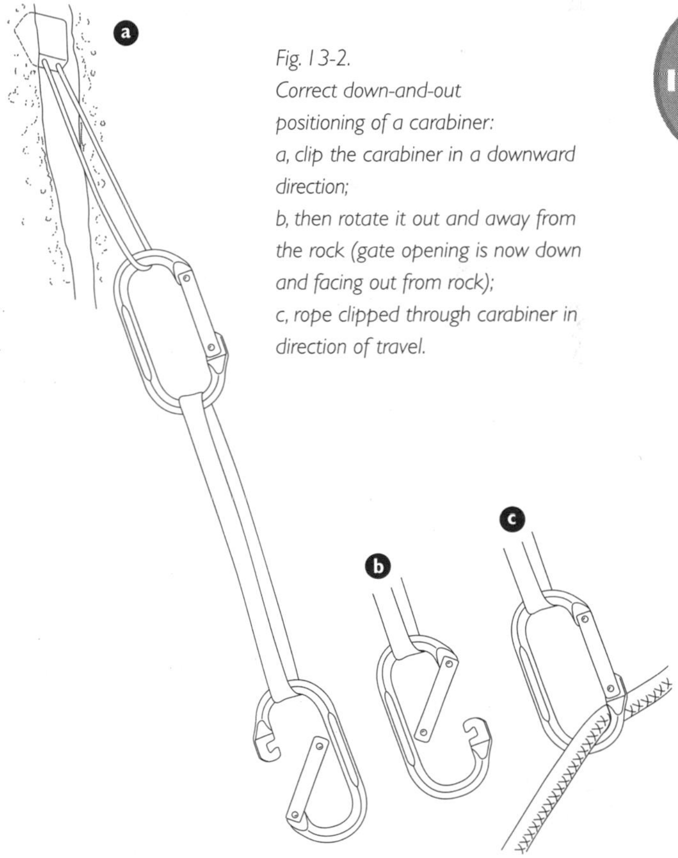

Fig. 13-2.
Correct down-and-out positioning of a carabiner:
a, clip the carabiner in a downward direction;
b, then rotate it out and away from the rock (gate opening is now down and facing out from rock);
c, rope clipped through carabiner in direction of travel.

13

237

Runners serve to lengthen the distance between the point of protection and the rope (fig. 13-3a). This helps to isolate rope movement from the protection, keeping protection from wiggling or "walking" from its intended placement, and also helps to minimize friction or rope drag on the climbing rope by allowing it to run in more of a straight line. Runners can connect directly to natural protection (fig. 13-3b, c, and d) or, rarely, to preexisting fixed protection (such as that shown in Figure 13-9, later in this chapter) without the use of an intervening carabiner.

Fig. 13-3.

Attaching the protection to the rope:
a, using two carabiners and one runner
to link a piece of artificial protection to
the rope; b, using one runner and one
carabiner to link a point of natural
protection to the rope; c, securing
a runner to a rock horn with a
clove hitch; d, slinging a horn
with a slipknot on a runner.

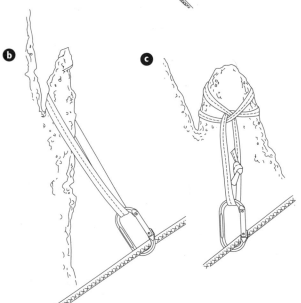

NATURAL PROTECTION

Trees and rock features can provide excellent protection, conserve gear, and frequently be a quicker alternative than a difficult gear placement, but you must carefully evaluate them for stability and strength. "Test before you trust" is a good rule. Be wary of rock that is brittle, vegetation that is poorly rooted, and other suggestions of weakness. An error in judgment could result not only in failed protection but also in a rock or tree crashing down upon you, your belayer, or other parties on the route.

Trees and large bushes provide the most obvious points of attachment. Do not trust a brittle, weak, or loose tree or shrub. Look for a healthy trunk with live branches and a solid root system. If there is any question, test smaller trees by pushing against them with one foot. A common method of attaching a runner to a tree is to loop the runner around the trunk and clip the ends together with a carabiner (fig. 13-4a). You can also untie a runner and then retie it around the trunk (fig. 13-4b). A third method is to use a girth hitch (fig. 13-4c). The runner usually should be as close to the roots as possible, although with a strong tree it may be placed higher if necessary.

Rock features—horns, columns, rock tunnels such as those formed by the contact point between two boulders, and large and flat-bottomed boulders—are common forms of natural protection. In evaluating a rock

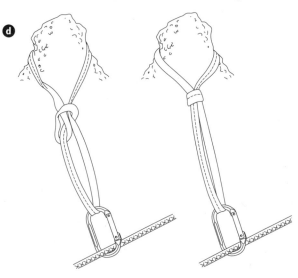

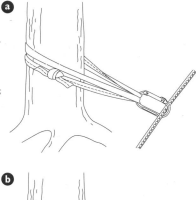

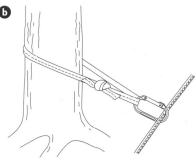

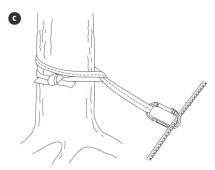

*Fig. 13-4.
Methods of
attaching a runner
to a tree trunk:
a, looped around
the trunk, the ends
clipped together
with a carabiner;
b, retied around
trunk;
c, girth-hitched
around trunk.*

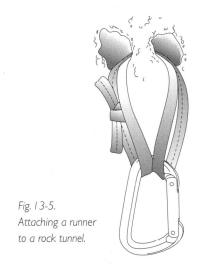

*Fig. 13-5.
Attaching a runner
to a rock tunnel.*

feature, consider its relative hardness, how friable or broken up it is, and whether it is firmly attached to the rock around it. Attempt to move the rock, being careful not to pull it loose. Whack it a few times with your hand or fist. Beware of hollow sounds or brittleness. Horns (also called spikes, knobs, or chicken heads, depending on their shape and size) are the most common type of natural rock protection. If there is any question about rock horns, test them by pushing against them with one foot.

To attach to a rock horn, a runner can be simply looped over the horn and clipped in to the rope (see Figure 13-3b, above), but it may be pulled off the horn

by rope movement. Use a clove hitch (see Figure 13-3c) or slipknot (see Figure 13-3d) to tighten the runner around the horn to help prevent it from slipping off. The slipknot requires less sling material than a girth hitch or clove hitch.

To attach to a rock column or chockstone or through a rock tunnel, first thread a runner around the feature, then connect the ends with a carabiner (fig. 13-5). Alternatively, secure the runner to the rock feature with a girth hitch or untie the runner and retie it after threading it through the point of protection.

See "Natural Anchors" in Chapter 10, Belaying, for related information about selecting natural anchors.

FIXED PROTECTION

On established routes, climbers may encounter previously placed bolts and pitons (see also "Artifical Anchors" in Chapter 10, Belaying). Climbers may also encounter other fixed pieces, usually removable protection that became fixed when someone could not remove it. On rock-climbing topo maps, bolts and fixed pitons are often shown as "x" and "fp," respectively.

Bolts

Bolts are most common in sport-climbing areas, but you may find them on traditional or aid-climbing routes. Bolt hangers allow carabiners to be attached to bolts (fig. 13-6).

13

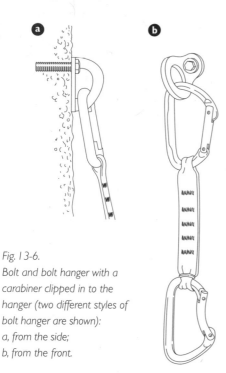

Fig. 13-6.
Bolt and bolt hanger with a carabiner clipped in to the hanger (two different styles of bolt hanger are shown):
a, from the side;
b, from the front.

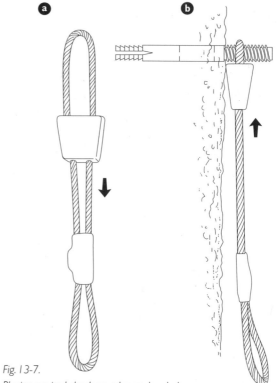

Fig. 13-7.
Placing a wired chock on a hangerless bolt:
a, create a loop by sliding the chock down the chock's wires;
b, then slip the upper wire around the hangerless bolt and slide the chock up the wires to form a noose around it.

A well-placed bolt will last for years, but age and weather can compromise it. Be especially wary of ¼-inch bolts, which were placed primarily in the 1960s and 1970s. Bolts measuring ⅜ to ½ inch in diameter have been used since the mid-1980s and are now the standard. Standard metric bolts are 10, 12, and 14 millimeters in diameter.

Visually check both the bolt and its hanger for signs of weakness, especially for cracks, excessive corrosion, or brittleness. A rust streak below the bolt indicates metal wear. Do not trust an old sheet metal–style hanger with heavy rust. Test whether the bolt is securely anchored into the rock by clipping in to the bolt hanger with a carabiner and trying to pull the bolt around or out. Any bolt that can be moved in any direction, however slightly, is probably not trustworthy. Avoid banging on the bolt, which weakens it. Back up any suspect bolt with another point of protection wherever possible. If the bolt and its placement seem solid, use a carabiner to clip a runner to the bolt hanger.

You may encounter bolts without hangers, but they are not reliable protection. If you anticipate hangerless bolts, carry extra hangers and nuts; slip an extra hanger over the bolt stud and then screw on an extra nut to secure the hanger. If a bolt has no hanger, there is a makeshift, last-resort solution: Slide a chock down its wire (fig. 13-7a), then slip the upper wire around the bolt stud and snug the chock up tight against the bolt to secure it (fig. 13-7b). Use a small chock, but not one with the smallest-diameter wire. Then use a carabiner on the lower end of the chock wire, a runner, and another carabiner to attach it to the rope. However, if the bolt stud has no nut, the wire stopper is easily levered off.

Pitons

Pitons were commonly used in mountaineering through the 1970s but are rarely used today, because placing and removing them scars the rock. However, many pitons remain as fixed placements on various routes.

Fig 13-8.
Piton driven into rock.

Pitons, even more than bolts, are vulnerable to weathering. Years of melt-freeze cycles widen cracks in the rock and loosen pitons. Examine pitons closely for signs of corrosion or weakness; examine the cracks they are in for deterioration around the pitons. Heavy use, failed attempts at removal, and falls on a piton can lead to cracks in the metal around the eye or other damage.

Ideally a piton was driven in all the way, with the eye close to the rock and the piton perpendicular to the likely direction of pull (fig. 13-8). If the piton seems to be strong, secure, and in good condition, clip a carabiner (with runner attached) through the eye of the piton. Try to place the carabiner so that under a load it will not be levered against the rock, which could cause the carabiner to break or the gate to open.

If a piton is only partially driven in but otherwise secure, use a runner to tie it off next to the rock, with a girth hitch or a clove hitch (fig. 13-9). This tie-off reduces the leverage on the piton under the impact of a

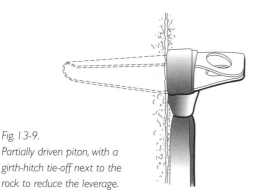

Fig. 13-9.
Partially driven piton, with a girth-hitch tie-off next to the rock to reduce the leverage.

fall. Thoroughly inspect the setup, especially noting whether the piton has sharp edges that could cut the runner. Do not rely on this setup if there is better protection available.

Other Fixed Pieces

Removable protection may be abandoned when a party is unable to remove it. When you encounter these "fixed" pieces, examine them carefully before deciding to use them as protection.

Note whether the sling attached to the chock appears to be worn or damaged. Be suspicious of possible failure of the sling, especially if it is made of accessory cord or webbing rather than wire cable. Study the condition of the rock and test whether the chock remains securely lodged. Check whether it is oriented properly to hold a fall. Because of these chocks' questionable integrity, consider them primarily as backup protection.

REMOVABLE PROTECTION

Removable protection, also known as chocks, includes the various types of artificial protection other than bolts and pitons. A chock generally consists of a metal device that can be secured into the rock, with a sling for use in linking the metal piece to the rope.

For environmental reasons, using removable protection is preferred to placing new pitons or bolts. Removable protection is relatively easy to place and remove, and leaves no scars on the rock, unlike bolts and pitons.

Removable protection generally falls into one of two categories: without moving parts (passive) or with moving parts (active). Passive removable protection pieces are made from a single piece of metal without moving parts other than a connecting sling or cable (fig. 13-10a–g). A typical placement is into a constriction in a crack. Shapes can vary from a tapered wedge, often called nuts or stoppers (fig. 13-10a), to a deformed hexagonal tube, often called hexes (fig. 13-10b–f), to the more unique-shaped piece such as the Tri-cam (fig. 13-10g) that can be used in a camming (torquing) orientation with counterforce exerted between the piece's point and its curved side when both are in contact with the rock.

13

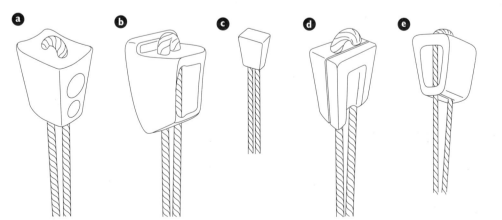

Fig. 13-10.
Protection:
a, stopper;
b, wired hex;
c, hex slung with
Spectra cord;
d, curved hex,
wired;
e, hex slung with
high-strength
webbing;
f, curved hex slung
with high-strength
webbing;
g, Tri-cam;
h, spring-loaded
camming device
(SLCD), four-cam;
i, SLCD, three-cam.

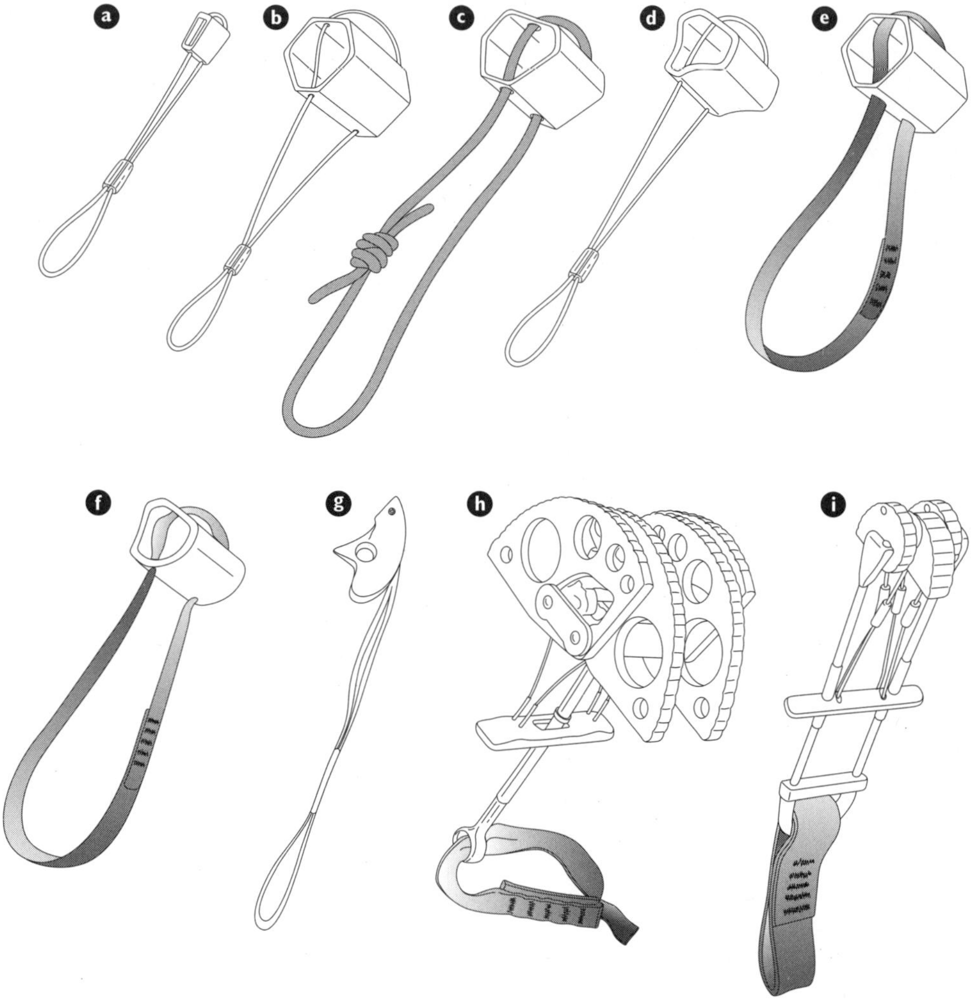

Fig. 13-11.
Passive
wedging chocks:
a, curved nut;
b, Wallnut;
c, RP (micronut);
d, Hugh Banner
(HB) offset;
e, stopper.

Spring-loaded camming devices (SLCDs) are active devices that use spring-loaded mechanisms to allow portions of the device to cam against opposite walls of a crack (fig. 13-10h and i). Loading the device increases the pressure against the rock. Triggers on the device retract the parts, allowing insertion and removal.

Tube chocks, often called Big Bros (see Figure 13-13, below) do have movable parts—they telescope out to a desired size—but they are passively placed much like a hex or a Tri-cam.

Passive Removable Protection

Passive wedging chocks come in a wide variety of shapes and sizes, but most have a generally wedge-shaped appearance (fig. 13-11). They are called by a lot of names, from brand names such as Stoppers (fig. 13-11e) to simply wired nuts or wedges.

These chocks are narrower at the base than at the top, which lets them slip down into a constriction, and toward the top they widen on all sides. Variations include chocks with flat faces, chocks with curved faces (fig. 13-11a and e), chocks with more-curved faces (fig. 13-11b), chocks with notches or grooves in the faces (fig. 13-11d), sides that may be parallel or offset, etc.

Some of the smallest wedging-type chocks, referred to as micronuts, are designed for very thin cracks and for aid climbing (fig. 13-11c). Manufacturers construct the nuts with softer metals so that the rock will bite into them better than it will into standard aluminum chocks—but this also makes micronuts less durable. In addition, micronuts frequently are manufactured so the cable does not pass through and over the top of the nut, but is soldered into the nut. The thinness of the micronut's cable makes it more prone to damage from normal use. Inspect the micronut and cable often for nicks and other signs of wear, and retire it if you see any cable damage.

Hexentrics and other similar chocks take their name from their hexagonal shape. Each pair of opposing sides on a Hexentric is a different distance apart, permitting four different placement options per piece. The chock sling can be placed off center to create the torquing action (fig. 13-12a), or the piece can be wedged in a constriction. More rounded versions of the hex work on the same principles. Some hex-shaped chocks come

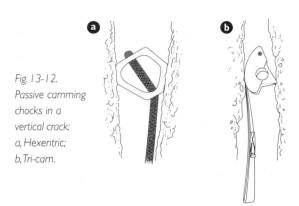

Fig. 13-12.
Passive camming chocks in a vertical crack:
a, Hexentric;
b, Tri-cam.

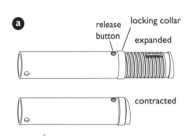

Fig. 13-13.
Spring-loaded tube chock: a, contracted and expanded;
b, correctly placed in a vertical crack, where it acts as a passive cam.

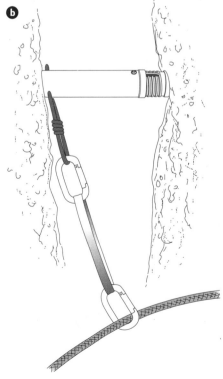

13

with wire cables and others come with holes through which cord must be threaded.

Tri-cams are curved along one side; the curved side rails oppose a point, or stinger, on the other side. Torquing action is gained by running the sling between the curved side rails and positioning the piece so that the stinger is set in a small depression or irregularity in the crack (fig. 13-12b); the load on the sling rotates the device into the rock with a camlike action. These chocks can also be used as passive devices simply set into a constriction (see Figure 13-20c, below).

Another device that acts as a passive chock (even though it is spring loaded) is the telescoping tube chock called the Big Bro. This chock has a spring-loaded inner sleeve that telescopes out to bridge a crack when a release button is pressed (fig. 13-13a). The extended sleeve is then locked into place by spinning the collar down snugly against the outer tube. The sling is attached at one side so, when it is loaded, a torquing action adds to stability (fig. 13-13b). Tube chocks are specialized for wide cracks, from about 3¼ inches (8 centimeters) to about 12 inches (30 centimeters).

Slings on Passive Removable Protection

Most wedge-shaped chocks and some hex-shaped chocks are slung with wire cable, which is much stronger than cord or webbing of the same size. The stiffness of the wire cable sometimes aids in placing the chock, but if the wire cable is very long, the chock may be awkward to carry.

Some larger chocks come with holes drilled for an accessory cord, or may be preslung with webbing by the manufacturer. If a chock is not preslung, follow the manufacturer's instructions for attaching a sling. Inspect the holes that are drilled in the chock for the cord. They should have smooth, rounded edges to avoid damaging the sling. Some manufacturers provide plastic inserts for these holes, through which the cord is threaded. Most larger chocks are designed to accept 5.5-millimeter Spectra cord or Gemini (Spectra/Kevlar) cord. A chock sling is usually 8 to 10 inches (20 to 25 centimeters) long when tied. The cord used for making a sling should be twice as long as the desired sling length, plus another 12 inches (30 centimeters) or so for the knot. Due to the greater stiffness of Spectra and

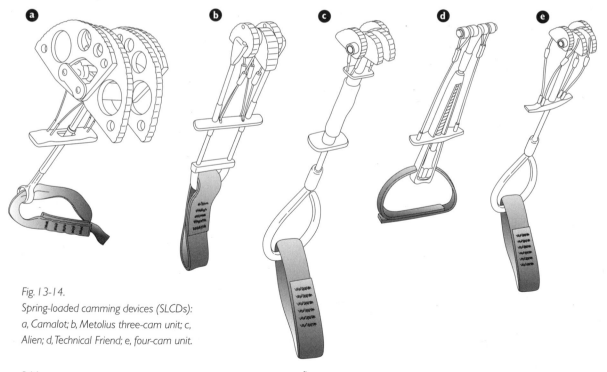

Fig. 13-14.
Spring-loaded camming devices (SLCDs):
a, Camalot; b, Metolius three-cam unit; c,
Alien; d, Technical Friend; e, four-cam unit.

Gemini cord, a triple fisherman's knot is recommended for tying the sling (see Figure 13-10c, above). Leave at least a 1-inch (2.5-centimeter) tail on each side of the fisherman's knot. Tighten the knot under body weight, and check it frequently.

Active Removable Protection

Spring-Loaded Camming Devices (SLCDs)

The first spring-loaded cams, called Friends, were introduced in the mid-1970s. They quickly expanded the limits of free climbing by providing protection that could be placed easily and quickly with one hand and that could adapt to a variety of cracks. Now many brands of spring-loaded camming devices (SLCDs) are manufactured in a wide size range (fig. 13-14).

The basic design has four blades—called a four-cam unit—that rotate from one or two axles, connected to a trigger mechanism on a stem (fig. 13-14a, c, d, and e). When the trigger is pulled, the blades retract, narrowing the profile of the device for placement in a crack or pocket (fig. 13-15a). When the trigger is released, the blades open up against the sides of the rock (fig. 13-15b).

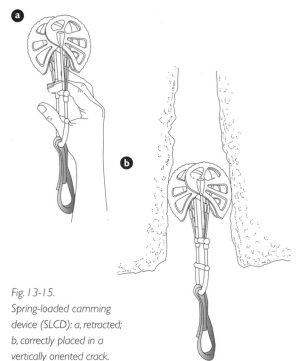

Fig. 13-15.
Spring-loaded camming device (SLCD): a, retracted; b, correctly placed in a vertically oriented crack.

The cams move independently of each other, permitting each to rotate to the point needed for maximum contact with the rock. This movement sets the device in place. If you fall, the stem is pulled downward or outward, increasing the camming action and increasing the outward pressure of the cams on the rock.

Variations of SLCDs include specialized cams that fit into narrower placements (side to side) such as Aliens (fig. 13-14c) and three-cam units (fig. 13-14b) as well as two-cam units (not shown); double-axle cams that can be used in the totally open position—called Camalots (fig. 13-14a)—and those that cannot; cams with rigid stems or flexible stems; specialized cams designed to hold better in sandstone—called Fat Cams; cams with different trigger designs; cams with different types and lengths of attached slings; specialized cams designed for flaring cracks; and cams in sizes that accommodate tiny or very large cracks.

Spring-Loaded Wedges

Spring-loaded wedges (fig. 13-16a) use a small sliding piece to expand the profile of the chock after it is placed in a crack. To operate the device, first retract the smaller piece by pulling back on the spring-loaded trigger, thereby narrowing the profile of the chock so it can be inserted into a thin crack (fig. 13-16b). Then release the trigger, permitting the smaller piece to press up between the larger piece and the rock, filling in the gap and increasing the area of the chock that is in contact with the rock (fig. 13-16c).

Spring-loaded wedges work particularly well in small, parallel-sided cracks where other devices may be difficult or impossible to place. But, like micronuts, these chocks have less holding power than larger

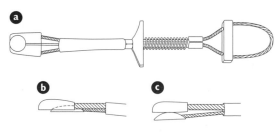

Fig. 13-16.
Spring-loaded wedging device (a); b, contracted; c, expanded.

245

TABLE 13-1. SIZE RANGE OF PASSIVE AND ACTIVE PROTECTION		
Type of Protection	**Range in Inches**	**Range in Centimeters**
PASSIVE		
Wedge-Shaped Devices		
Astro Nuts #6–#10	0.16–0.55	0.41–1.39
Curved nuts	0.36–1.20	0.91–3.05
Offsets	0.15–0.92	0.38–2.34
Peenuts	0.20–0.37	0.51–0.94
Rocks	0.17–1.22	0.43–3.09
Stoppers	0.17–1.38	0.43–3.51
Wallnuts	0.10–1.12	0.25–2.84
RPs	0.09–0.44	0.23–1.12
Hexagonal Devices		
Curved hex 2000	0.42–2.92	1.07–7.42
Hexentric	0.45–3.51	1.14–8.92
Rockcentric	0.94–2.89	2.40–7.35
Other Passive Devices		
Big Bros	3.20–12.0	8.13–30.48
Tri-cams	0.60–5.50	1.52–13.97
ACTIVE		
Spring-Type Slider		
BallNutz	0.12–0.63	0.31–1.60
Sliders	0.12–.63	0.31–1.60
Removable bolts	½–¾	1.00–1.90
Spring-Loaded Camming Devices		
Aliens	0.33–2.50	0.84–6.35
Camalots	0.34–7.0	0.86–17.78
DMM	0.50–3.90	1.27–9.91
Friends	0.50–7.50	1.02–19.05
Metolius	0.50–4.20	1.27–10.67
Splitter Gear	0.70–1.50	1.78–3.81
Trango	0.60–5.40	1.78–13.72

Note: Measurements in inches are given as decimals or fractions per manufacturers' literature.

wedges because of the smaller surface area gripping the rock and because the spring may allow some movement—or "walking"—within the crack after placement.

Other Active Removable Protection

Removable bolts (RBs) are spring-loaded devices that fit into empty drilled holes in the rock. Splitter Gear makes a new type of spring-loaded camming device that fits into narrow placements; both two-cam units and four-cam units are available.

Placing Removable Protection

Placing protection in the rock is both art and science. Developing an eye for good placement sites, and then being able to slip just the right piece into the right place safely and efficiently, is a skill that requires practice to perfect.

Look for constrictions in a crack, irregularities in crack surfaces, and prominences behind a flake. A good site for chock placements has solid rock sides—free of vegetation, dirt, or deteriorating rock. Check for loose blocks or flakes by hitting the rock with your fist or shaking it; if the rock moves or sounds hollow, look for a better spot.

The next consideration is what type of chock to use. Wedges work best when placed behind constrictions in a vertically oriented crack. Hexes or Tri-cams can work well in horizontal cracks and behind small irregularities in cracks or flakes where it may be difficult or impossible to position wedges. Tri-cams are often the only device that will work in shallow, flaring pockets.

SLCDs are easier to place, but they are heavier and more expensive, and placement integrity can be more difficult to evaluate. However, SLCDs often work in parallel-sided or slightly flaring cracks where it is difficult or impossible to get anything else to hold.

More than one type of chock may work in a given spot. Make your choice based on ease of placement and what you may need later on the pitch. Ration the chocks you expect to need higher up.

Placing Passive Wedges

The basic procedure is quite simple: Find a crack with a constriction at some point, place an appropriate-size chock above the constriction (fig. 13-17a), slide it into place (fig. 13-17b), and pull down on the sling to set the chock firmly in position (fig. 13-17c). Slot the chock completely into the crack, with as much of the chock surface as possible contacting the rock.

The best choice of chock for any given placement is whichever size and shape offers the best fit. As a general rule, greater contact between chock and rock means a stronger placement. Therefore, larger chocks generally are stronger than smaller ones, and wide-side placements (fig. 13-18a) are stronger than narrow-side placements (fig. 13-18b).

13

GENERAL CONSIDERATIONS IN PLACING REMOVABLE PROTECTION

- Learn to estimate the right chock size and shape for a particular placement. The better your estimate, the more efficient the placement.
- Choose the best chock, not necessarily the largest or the most easily placed. In the vast majority of cases, chocks fail because they pull out under load rather than break. Placement integrity is more important than chock size. Choose the piece that will provide the best fit.
- Decide whether a particular chock is likely to be adequate, based on the characteristics of the rock and the magnitude of a possible fall. Some things to consider include the relative hardness of the rock, the direction of the fall, and how well the chock is placed. Reinforce doubtful pieces with another chock, use a load-limiting runner to decrease forces on the piece, or find a better placement.
- Recheck the chock after you place it. Look to see that it is placed correctly, in good contact with the rock. Give the piece a sharp tug. This sets the piece and tests the reliability and security of the placement, especially in the likely direction of pull.
- Guard against the chock being dislodged by rope movement. Clip a runner between the chock and the rope to minimize the effect of rope movement on the piece. An adequate length of runner not only prevents pulling on the piece, but also helps prevent rope drag (see Chapter 14, Leading on Rock).
- Guard against the chock being dislodged by an outward or upward pull in a fall. Many chock placements are one-directional—they will take a load in only one direction. If a one-directional placement could come under load from different directions, make it multidirectional by placing opposing chocks (see "Opposition Placement" later in this chapter) or use a different placement.
- Remember the climber who will be following behind you and removing the protection. Make your placements secure, but also try to make them reasonably easy to remove and within reach of a short follower.

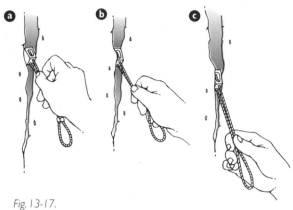

Fig. 13-17.
Placing a passive wedge: a, placing wedge into crack above constriction; b, sliding it into place; c, tugging on chock sling to set it.

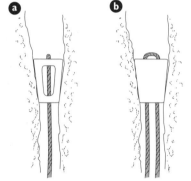

Fig. 13-18.
Placement of passive wedging chocks: a, wide sides are in contact with the rock, a stronger placement; b, ends are in contact with the rock, a weaker placement.

Carefully evaluate the potential effects of rope drag and the direction of loading in the event of a fall. In vertical cracks, gravity usually keeps the chock in place, as long as the rope is not pulling it sideways or upward. In horizontal cracks, it may be more difficult to keep the chock in position, because rope movement will pull it out of place. It helps to set the piece tightly in position. You can also place opposing chocks, with a second chock to help hold the first one in place (a technique discussed in "Opposition Placement," later in this chapter).

If a micronut must be used for climbing protection, place it especially carefully and make sure it has excellent contact with the rock.

Placing Hexes and Tri-cams

In addition to being used as a chock in a constriction, a hex or a Tri-cam is also designed to pivot on a corner under load. In parallel-sided cracks, you must use this feature for the placement to work. A good placement is tight enough to have good contact with the rock and to avoid being displaced by the rope, yet positioned to allow torquing action under load.

In vertical cracks, the piece will be more secure if it is placed just above a constriction or irregularity in the crack, and if it is oriented so that the torquing action pulls it more tightly against any irregularity (figs. 13-19a and 13-20a).

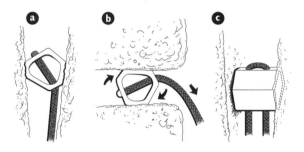

Fig. 13-19.
Placements of a Hexentric chock: a, in a vertical crack as a passive cam; b, in a horizontal crack as a passive cam—sling exits near the roof of the crack for proper camming action; c, sideways in a crack as a passive wedging chock.

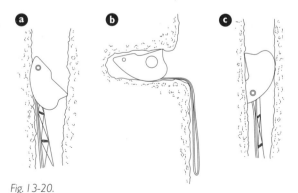

Fig. 13-20.
Placements of a Tri-cam: a, in a vertical crack as a passive cam; b, in a horizontal crack as a passive cam; c, in a vertical crack as a passive wedging chock.

In horizontal cracks, the piece must be placed so that the downward pull of a potential fall will create the maximum torquing action. Hexes should be positioned so that the sling leaves the crack closer to the roof than to the floor (fig. 13-19b). Tri-cams are more stable if the sling is on the floor of a horizontal crack, with the stinger pointing up (fig. 13-20b).

Placing Spring-Loaded Camming Devices

An SLCD can be placed very quickly. It is the device of choice for parallel-sided cracks that lack the constrictions or irregularities needed for more traditional chocks. It can also be used in slightly flaring cracks, in parallel-sided spaces behind flakes, and in cracks under roofs where other chocks may be difficult to place or questionable to use.

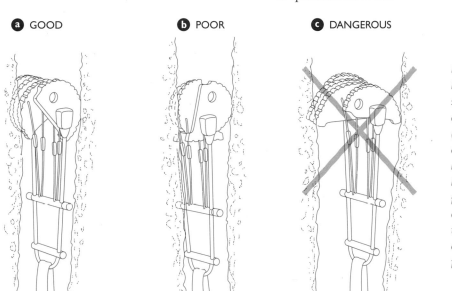

ⓐ GOOD   **ⓑ** POOR   **ⓒ** DANGEROUS

Fig. 13-21. Placement of a spring-loaded camming device (SLCD): a, correct—cams expanded to midpoint, stem in likely direction of pull; b, cams are overretracted—hard to remove; c, cams are overexpanded—failure likely.

TIPS FOR PLACING SLCDS

Despite how easy it is to place spring-loaded camming devices, here are a few things to be aware of:

■ If the cams are fully retracted in the placement, the device may become jammed in the crack and impossible to remove (see Figure 13-21b, above).

■ If the cams are overexpanded, little camming action will occur, and the device is likely to pull loose during a fall (see Figure 13-21c, above).

■ In soft rock, such as sandstone or limestone, spring-loaded camming devices can be pulled out by a hard fall even when they are placed properly.

■ For the placement to be stable, all cams must contact the rock. To permit proper camming action, the cams should be placed somewhat in balance, with each pair of cams expanded about the same amount.

■ Rope movement can cause the entire piece to "walk," moving it either deeper into or out of the crack, jeopardizing stability of the placement. Minimize this walking by making a careful placement and using a suitable runner. Devices with three cams, though not as strong, do not walk as much as those with four cams.

■ When you are using a three-cam unit in a horizontal crack, place the side with two cams on the bottom for best stability. In vertical cracks, place the two cams on whichever side provides the best fit in the crack.

Within their given range, the three or four individual cams in the device will adjust to the width and irregularities of the crack as the trigger is released. The stem of the device must be pointed in the likely direction of pull during a fall to provide maximum strength and to help keep it from being pulled out of position (fig. 13-21). Spring-loaded camming devices work best in harder rock—for instance, granite rather than sandstone—and in cracks with relatively even sides.

If the SLCD you are using has a solid stem rather than a flexible one, make sure that the stem will not be forced against the edge of the crack during a fall, which could cause the stem to bend or break. This is especially important in horizontal or near-horizontal cracks, where the stem hangs out over the edge of the crack. A flexible-stem device is more reliable in this situation (fig. 13-22a), but if a solid-stem device must be used, then place a tie-off loop through one of the holes in the stem (fig. 13-22b). The force of a fall will then be less likely to break the stem.

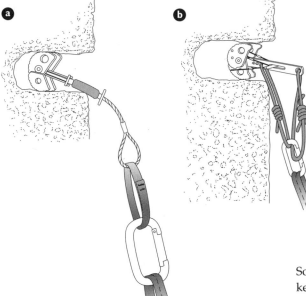

Fig. 13-22.
Spring-loaded camming device (SLCD) placement in a horizontal crack: a, flexible cable stem can bend and adjust to the direction of pull; b, a tie-off loop can reduce the danger of solid-stem breakage.

Placing Spring-Loaded Wedges

Spring-loaded wedging chocks can be used almost anywhere that a passive wedge would be used, but they really come into their own in thin cracks, including parallel-sided cracks (fig. 13-23).

In placing spring-loaded wedges, select just the right size for the crack because the placement size range for any one of these devices is quite narrow. They are susceptible to being pulled out of place by rope movement, so it is advisable to attach a runner to the piece. As with any piece of rock protection, place the device to be strongest in the direction of the force of a potential fall. A miscalculation may result in the spring-loaded wedge rotating out of its placement.

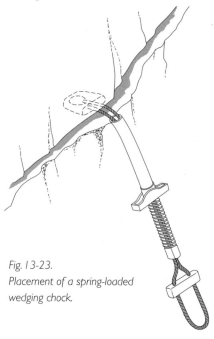

Fig. 13-23.
Placement of a spring-loaded wedging chock.

Opposition Placement

Sometimes a second chock must be placed in order to keep the first one in position. Single placements can sometimes be dislodged by sideways or upward pulls on the rope as the lead climber advances, because of changes in the direction of the route. In horizontal cracks, or when the rope changes angle, the chock must sometimes be pulled into the crack constriction by another piece to be effective in holding a fall.

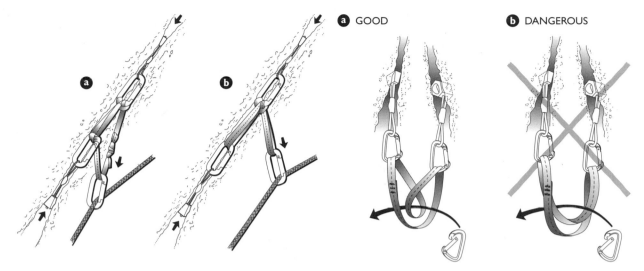

Fig. 13-24.

Opposing chocks: a, in a vertically oriented crack, connected by a runner secured with clove hitches; b, in a vertically oriented crack, using one long runner and a clove hitch to hold the tension between the chocks.

Fig. 13-25.

Constructing two-point equalizing protection: a, good—the carabiner is clipped from one loop of the twisted runner to the other; b, dangerous—the carabiner is clipped across the runner and will fail if one of the chocks pulls out.

To form an opposition placement, place two pieces that will pull toward each other when linked. Depending on how far apart the pieces are, use either carabiners or slings to link the chocks; slings are preferable because they can be tensioned. Ideally the chocks should be held together under a slight tension: Use clove hitches to tie a runner between the carabiners on the chock slings and cinch up the runner (fig. 13-24). The climbing rope may then be clipped into the slack side of the runner.

Equalizing Protection

A leader who is faced with a hard move or questionable protection may decide to place two pieces of protection close together. If one piece fails, the other remains as a backup.

Another option is to equalize the load over two protection points, subjecting each to only a portion of the total force. (For equalizing belay points to establish an anchor, see Chapter 10, Belaying.)

Equalizing the forces between two points of protection can be accomplished with one hand and requires only one runner. First clip the runner into one chock.

Twist the runner in the middle, and then clip it into the second chock. Then simply clip an extra carabiner through the twist in the runner, with the rope attached to this carabiner (fig. 13-25a). If one chock later pulls out, the twist in the runner will slide down and catch around the carabiner so that the rope remains connected to the remaining chock. Avoid clipping the carabiner across, rather than through, the twisted runner (fig. 13-25b), because the entire setup will then fail if one chock comes loose.

Stacking

If nothing on your rack will accommodate the crack in which you need to place protection, the advanced technique called stacking can sometimes do the job. You will need two passive wedges. Place the wedges in opposition to each other in the crack, with the larger one on top (fig. 13-26). A downward pull on the larger chock causes it to wedge between one side of the crack and one side of the other chock. Seat the larger chock with a firm tug before using it, and connect it to the rope in the usual way. Use a runner to tie the smaller chock into something, or use a carabiner to clip the smaller

251

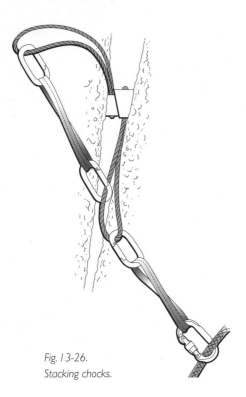

Fig. 13-26.
Stacking chocks.

chock to the wire of the larger chock. This will keep the smaller chock from becoming a flying missile when it is removed by the follower or if it comes loose in a fall. Use only chocks that seat well against one another; otherwise stacking is not effective.

BUILDING YOUR SKILLS

The way to become proficient at placing protection is very simple: practice. First, practice by placing protection while you are standing on the ground. When you are following as a second, observe closely how the leader places protection. Practice placing pieces while you are climbing on a top rope. When you believe you are ready to try leading, start on an easy pitch that you have already climbed as a second or while top-roped. Place more pieces than are needed, just for the practice. Do not be discouraged if the first time turns out to be harder than it looks. Bring along a knowledgeable, experienced climber as your second—it is a great way to get valuable feedback. Just keep at it, and soon you may be the one giving advice.

13

14

CHAPTER

Leading on Rock

LEADING ON NONTECHNICAL TERRAIN ■ **LEADING TECHNICAL CLIMBS** ■
LEADING ON ROCK, STEP BY STEP ■ **PERSONAL RESPONSIBILITY**

Rock climbing is a vertical dance between climber and belayer. The climber on lead determines the route ahead, places the protection, and sets the pace. The belayer feeds the rope in pace and anticipates the leader's need for more or less rope. The belay forms a pact between belayer and leader, binding both through the rope to the rock. The climber on lead accepts the responsibility, the risk, and the rewards of leading the pitch. The belayer agrees to hold any fall.

Imagine two climbers high on a rock face, in a scene reenacted daily in many rock-climbing areas. One is on lead, climbing up a crack, belayed by rope through numerous points of protection from a partner anchored to a ledge below.

The leader gives a sharp yank to the stopper he just placed in the crack. Grasping the rope tied to his harness, he pulls it up and clips it into the protection. His belayer yells up to him "Halfway!" indicating he has reached the midpoint on the rope. He exhales deeply,

253

switches hands in the crack, and shakes out his arm before raising his eyes to study the route ahead.

He sees that the thin splitter crack continues up steeply, with a few uneven pockets where a hand jam appears solid. From his rack, he readies a cam he feels would be ideal for placement when he reaches the most promising pocket several moves up. He mentally rehearses his moves, then resumes climbing.

Leading on rock requires a merging of climbing skill and psychological readiness. How do you decide whether you are ready? Others can help you assess your skills; only you can assess your mental preparation, so you must search deeply within yourself. Prepare by practicing and gaining confidence with placing rock protection, building anchors, belaying, rope management, and an understanding of fall forces. Work on rock technique, a methodology of gear selection and placement, and routefinding. Use every pitch you follow as an opportunity to observe and learn. Experience helps refine judgment.

LEADING ON NON-TECHNICAL TERRAIN

A climbing party may travel unroped or unbelayed over third-class and fourth-class rock, each person climbing in balance and maintaining three points of contact with the rock. If the risks of the climb escalate beyond the party's comfort level, a leader has several options for using a rope to help minimize danger, short of full belayed climbing.

Hand Line

A fixed hand line can be set up for members of an unroped party (fig. 14-1). The leader anchors a rope at the bottom of a difficult section and then scrambles up this section, bringing along the loose end of the rope. At the top, the leader anchors the rope taut, taking care not to place the rope under tension over sharp edges. The other climbers then move up, either holding on to this hand line or prepared to grab it if it is needed. If they are wearing harnesses, they can also choose to clip in to the line with a carabiner attached to a runner from their harness or to clip a carabiner directly from their harness into a sling attached to the line with a prusik knot. The last climber breaks down the hand line while ascending.

Running Belay

The running belay is another option that is sometimes useful when a team is climbing over relatively easy terrain but is still roped together (fig. 14-2). Roped climbing teams normally consist of only two people. To establish a running belay, the lead climber simply clips the rope in to some rock protection at appropriate intervals. At least two pieces of protection should be in place, clipped in to the rope between the leader and the follower at all times. The follower removes the protection while climbing. If one climber takes a fall, the

Fig. 14-1.
A hand line as limited protection for an unroped party.

rope will remain linked to the protection—and the weight of the other climber will naturally arrest the fall at some point.

The running belay is less secure than belayed climbing but considerably safer than no protection at all. The lead climber needs to be sensitive to the skill level of the climber who follows and be ready to set up an anchored belay if the follower needs that degree of security.

Hip Belay

The hip belay (see Chapter 10, Belaying) can be a fast and efficient technique for providing a secure belay for the leader of a climbing team that is moving together on relatively low-angle rock. If the difficulty or exposure becomes great enough, the leader may call for a belay for security over a worrisome section. The second climber sets up a belay anchor and clips in to it, and then can simply use the classic hip belay to protect the leader. Of course, the belayer also has the option of using a belay device, but the hip belay is a practical way to protect the leader on a lower-angle, lower-grade route. It should not be used for belaying on continuous difficulties because of the danger of rope burns—which could compromise the belay if a long, hard fall occurs.

LEADING TECHNICAL CLIMBS

Technical rock climbing begins when anchored belays are needed for the party's safety. Each pitch will be led and belayed. The leader accepts more risk than the second, who is belayed from above and does not have to worry about falling more than a very short distance. An aspiring leader should learn the mechanics of leading while climbing well below his or her actual climbing ability. It may sound obvious, but always be sure your climbing ability is consistent with the route you decide to lead. For example, you may be good at face climbing but have trouble with cracks; in that case, if a route requires crack climbing, make sure that it is rated lower than what you are accustomed to handling on a face climb.

Steep, bolt-protected sport-climbing routes can be relatively safe places to attempt leading hard moves. An overhanging 5.11 route can be safer to lead than a

5.7 climb of ledges if the only risk in a fall off the former is hitting air. Evaluate routes in terms of potential risk and your ability to manage the consequences of a fall.

On a long, remote alpine climb, the consequences of a fall can be great. In addition, your climbing will be greatly affected by your having to carry a pack and wear cumbersome mountain boots. For those reasons, be more conservative in choosing an alpine route and gear.

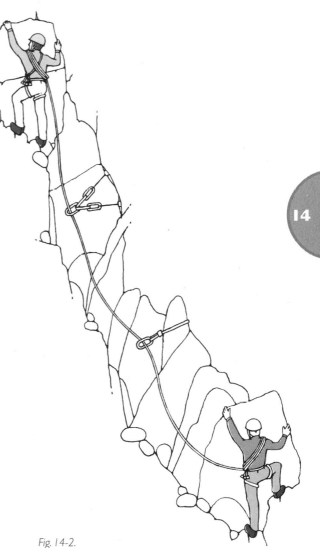

Fig. 14-2.

A running belay as limited protection for a two-member climbing team.

14

The Rack

The collection of gear used for protection is called the rack. Each climbing team prepares just one rack, which is carried by whoever is leading. During the climb, the leader places some of the individual pieces of protection from the rack; the follower removes these and carries them up while climbing, and at the top of the pitch, the rack is reorganized and the leader takes the gear needed for protecting the next pitch. The decision about what to bring is determined by the climb and each climber's comfort level. If the selected climb is in an area covered by a guidebook, check the guidebook for general information such as the type of rock and what a "standard rack" for that area contains. The climbing route topo (fig. 14-3) for the selected climb, if there is one, may show the width of cracks, the amount of fixed or natural protection, the length and direction of each

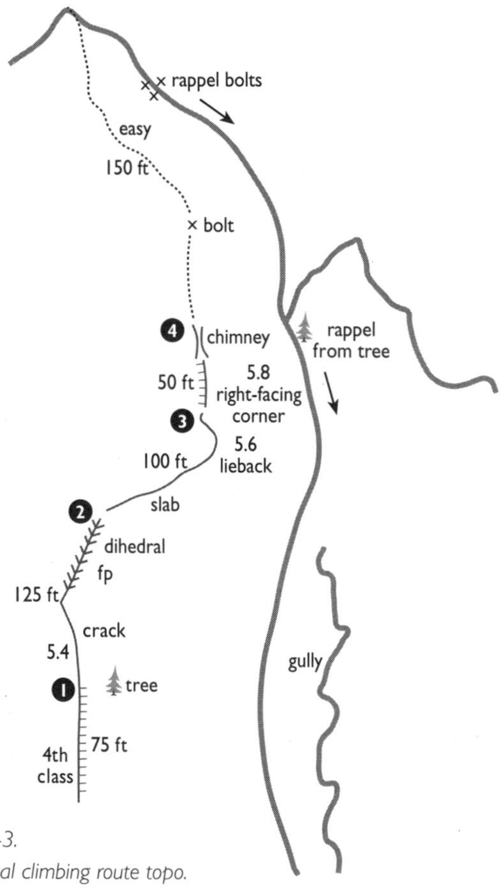

Fig. 14-3.
A typical climbing route topo.

pitch, the difficulty of each section and the overall climb, and perhaps even the precise sizes of chocks needed.

If the selected climb is in a remote area, usually not as much information is available. Take too big a rack, and the extra weight and equipment can impede your climbing. Take too little protection or the wrong pieces, and you may not have what you need to safely climb the route. Research the climb by consulting several guidebooks or talking with other climbers who have done the route.

A typical rack includes a selection of chocks, carabiners, and runners. The specific selection of protection varies with each route. A long, thin crack might dictate small wired nuts and some small cams. A wide crack may require the largest cams, hexes, or tube chocks. Other cases may be less clear-cut, and you may need a full range of sizes.

The pieces of protection typically connect to the rope though two nonlocking carabiners and a runner or quickdraw. Locking carabiners should be used in cases in which the gate might be forced open. Carry a few extra carabiners as insurance against running short of them. The ideal runner at any protection point is just long enough to help the rope stay in as straight a line as possible. A runner that is longer than necessary lengthens a fall, and one that is shorter than necessary causes rope drag. Quickdraws may work well for a straight-up climb. A zigzag line, roofs, or turns on the pitch require longer runners. Additional runners may be needed for belay anchors, unanticipated protection placements, and rappel slings.

The chock pick, a thin metal tool designed to help extract pieces of protection (fig. 14-4), is carried by each climber to use when following a pitch; if your team is swinging leads, both climbers will by turns be following. Also known as a cleaning tool, the chock pick can help you retrieve pieces of protection that do not come out easily.

In addition to carrying chocks, carabiners, runners, and a chock pick, a rock climber usually carries a belay device, a cordelette, a tie-off loop (a short loop of accessory cord for emergency prusiking, tying off a climber after a fall, or a rappel backup—see Chapters 9, Basic Safety System, 10, Belaying, and 11, Rappelling), a pocketknife for removal of old slings (or for emergencies), and

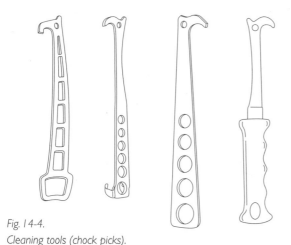

Fig. 14-4.
Cleaning tools (chock picks).

perhaps chalk for keeping hands dry. Overall equipment choices, which are influenced by the setting and the type and length of the rock climb, warrant careful consideration and planning.

How to Rack

Typically, protection is racked on a gear sling, which is slung over one shoulder and under the opposite arm (see Figure 14-6b, below). A padded gear sling from a climbing shop may be the most comfortable choice, but a single-length runner can also be used for the job. Commercial gear slings are available with partitions and without (fig. 14-5).

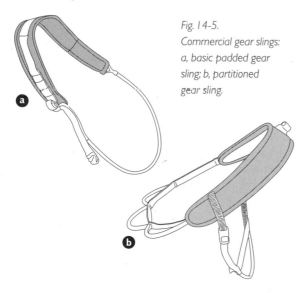

Fig. 14-5.
Commercial gear slings: a, basic padded gear sling; b, partitioned gear sling.

The ideal racking method permits the leader to place protection efficiently and to climb without awkwardness despite carrying the gear; it also allows easy transfers between climbers for swinging leads. Keeping the hardware away from the rock makes it more readily available. For instance, when you are climbing an inside corner with your left side in, it is easier to have the rack hang from your left shoulder and under your right arm. No racking method is perfect, but several are commonly used.

Put each chock on its own carabiner: This method (fig. 14-6a) can be very efficient for placing protection. The leader simply places the chock in the rock, clips the chock's carabiner to a runner, and clips the runner's carabiner to the rope. However, this method has the major disadvantages of bulkiness and poor weight distribution. This rack tends to be relatively wide and cumbersome, with few free carabiners. If you choose the wrong-size chock, you waste time and energy in returning to the rack to find the right one.

Combine several pieces of protection of a similar size on each carabiner: This method (fig. 14-6b) reduces the number of carabiners you need for carrying the chocks, and this method can make climbing easier because it results in a less-bulky rack with better weight distribution. To choose the best chock for a placement, you unclip the carabiner of chocks for that size range and hold the whole batch of chocks up to the placement, eyeing each chock for fit. Then unclip the carabiner from the chosen chock, place the chock, and return the carabiner and unused chocks to the gear sling. This method of racking gear increases the risk of dropping gear, and it also means you handle more gear every time you place a piece. With this method, you usually have two carabiners preattached to each runner or quickdraw because the placed protection lacks a carabiner (remember that one carabiner attaches to the protection and the other carabiner attaches to the rope; see Figure 13-3a in Chapter 13, Rock Protection). Many climbers feel that the extra work is worth the increased ease of climbing offered by this racking method.

Rack gear on the gear loops of your climbing harness: This method (fig. 14-6c) helps distribute the weight of the rack, and you can separate the different types of protection: Rack the chocks on one side of the

257

Fig. 14-6.
Examples of racking methods:
a, method in which almost every
piece of protection is attached to
its own carabiner;
b, climber carrying runners and a
typical rack, with similar-size pieces
of protection sharing a carabiner;
c, method in which pieces of
protection are attached to gear
loops on the seat harness.

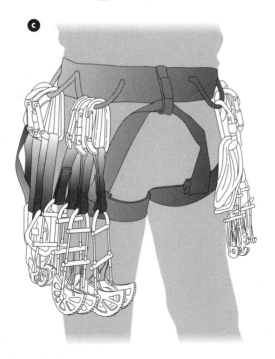

harness and rack the runners, quickdraws, and carabiners on the other side. Be sure the gear does not hang down far enough to interfere with your footwork. This method makes transfer of gear at belays more troublesome.

Of course, climbers may use a hybrid of these systems. For example, you could combine similar-sized wire stoppers on one carabiner, but reserve one carabiner for each camming device. Or you might combine some gear on a sling over your shoulder and some on the harness.

Whatever method you use, rack the protection in a systematic order so that you can find a particular piece in a hurry. The usual order is to start at the front with the smallest wired chocks and work back with larger pieces. For each carabiner clipped to the rack, use the same orientation so that each one unclips in exactly the same way. Climbing partners should agree on using one racking technique; otherwise, much precious time may be lost in reracking at each belay when climbers are swinging leads.

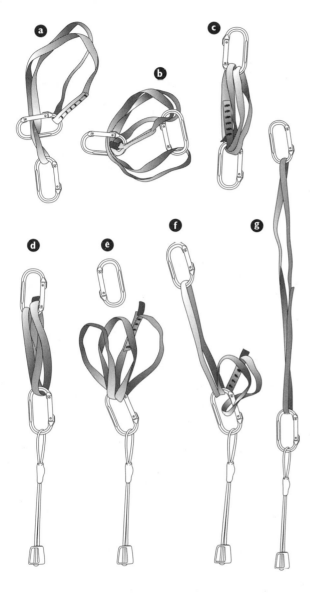

Runners need racking as well. Quickdraws can be racked on the harness or on a sling. You can carry single-length runners over one shoulder, but if you carry a number of them, it can be difficult to retrieve just one from the tangle. You can carry a single-length runner quickdraw-style by attaching two carabiners to it, putting one carabiner through the other, and clipping the resulting loop (fig. 14-7a–d). Such runners can be quickly extended by unclipping one carabiner, reclipping a single strand of the runner, and pulling it out (fig. 14-7e–g). You can carry double-length runners looped over your shoulder and connected with a carabiner (see Figure 14-6b, above); you can easily retrieve them. Alternatively, you can chain the runner (fig. 14-8) before attaching it to the harness, and when

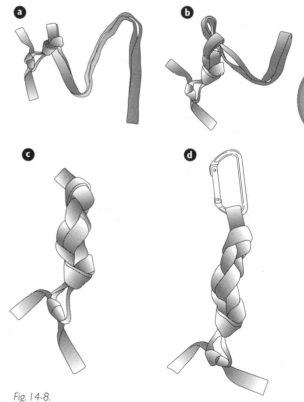

Fig. 14-7.

How to rack and extend a single-length runner quickdraw-style:
a, pass one carabiner through the other;
b, clip the first carabiner back into the newly formed loop;
c, straighten;
d, clip one carabiner in to the protection;
e, unclip the second carabiner and fan out the loops;
f, clip the carabiner back into one loop;
g, straighten and extend.

Fig. 14-8.

Chaining a long runner: a, form a slipknot; b, pull runner through the loop formed by the slipknot; c, repeat this process until the runner is chained; d, the final loop can be attached to a carabiner for carrying and to ensure it does not unravel.

you need it, pull or shake it out to remove the loops. You can also fold a double- or triple-length runner several times and tie it in an overhand knot, then clip it to your harness.

If you are climbing with a pack, put it on first, then the rack. If you are carrying double-length and single-length runners over your shoulder(s), put the single-length runners on top so that the doubles can be removed without displacing the singles.

Carry your cordelette, cleaning tool (chock pick), and belay device on the harness gear loops so that they are easily accessible. Other gear such as a pocketknife and tie-off loop can be clipped to the harness or carried around your neck so they are out of the way but accessible.

LEADING ON ROCK, STEP BY STEP

Whether you are leading the next pitch or the next climb, you need to plan the route, evaluate rope and rack requirements, and know the descent. Leading is a complex business. Beginners usually need an apprenticeship, moving behind seasoned climbers before they can safely "take the sharp end of the rope" (lead). Never take the lead if you do not feel ready, and do not pressure others into leading. Keep the art of leading exciting, challenging, satisfying, and safe, as it ought to be.

Planning the Route

Planning a route begins with determining where it goes. The skill required depends on the location and nature of the climb. Routefinding can be as easy as following a guidebook picture with a climbing route topo, or following a line of bolts on a crag. Even then, confirm the descent and if it is not obvious, perhaps check with others who have done the route. Decide whether boots are needed for the descent. For rappels, make sure the rope is long enough.

Routefinding on alpine routes or some long crag routes can be much more complex. Longer routes often are less clearly defined. The guidebook description may be sketchy: "Ascend northeast buttress for several hundred feet of moderate climbing." The descent may be complicated and vaguely described.

Study the route on the approach if possible. Look for major features that the line of ascent might follow: crack systems, dihedrals, chimneys, areas of broken rock. Note areas of small trees or bushes that could indicate belay ledges and/or rappel anchors. Identify landmarks that, when you reach them, will help you determine your position on the route. For this kind of small-detail planning, your eyes will tell you what the topographical map cannot.

Watch out for deceptively tempting lines that lead to broad roofs, blank walls, or false summits. These may

---

QUESTIONS TO ASK YOURSELF BEFORE YOU LEAD A PITCH

- How long and hard is the pitch?
- Can I see the general path of the pitch, and where the next anchor will be?
- What is the nature and location of the crux (most difficult move of the pitch)?
- What sizes, types, and amount of protection will I need?
- How much protection will I need, including carabiners and runners?
- What gear will I need to build the anchor at the end of the pitch?
- What climbing techniques will I use? Liebacking? Chimneying? Jamming? As a result, on what side should I rack?
- Do I want my partner to shout out how much rope is left as I climb (calling out "halfway," "20 feet," "10 feet")? Is the middle of the rope marked?
- Can my belayer and I hear each other throughout the climb? If not, do we have rope signals? Radios?
- How will a fall affect the belay? Could I drop past my belayer in a fall? Is my belayer well secured for any pull from a potential fall of mine?
- Where and how will the first piece of protection be placed? Will it minimize the fall factor and minimize the chance of setting off the zipper effect? (See "The Zipper Effect" later in this chapter.)

14

not be visible once you are on the climb and, if you climb them in error, they may dead-end after several pitches.

Develop a plan for the line of ascent, but keep likely alternatives in mind. Continue planning the route-finding as the actual climb begins, looking for more local features and landmarks. Seek out natural lines to follow as you lead the route. Form a tentative plan for each pitch, perhaps including a place for the first piece of protection and a spot for the next belay station. Do not hesitate to look around the corner for easier route alternatives that may not be visible from below.

If you are faced with a choice between pitches of varying difficulty, consider the rest of the climb. Two moderate pitches are better than an easy pitch followed by one beyond the party's ability.

On the way up, keep track of retreat possibilities in case the climb is aborted, and study, to the extent possible, your party's planned descent route.

Protecting the Lead

Placing protection every few feet requires a big rack and eats up time. Placing very little protection at all greatly increases the risk of a long leader fall and potential injury. Learning the appropriate balance requires practice. You certainly should protect moves you expect to be hard. Always space the protection to avoid potential falls that are excessively long or dangerous. Protection above a move provides the safety of a top rope. In deciding when to place another piece of protection, keep in mind the quality of the placements you have already made. Consider how to minimize

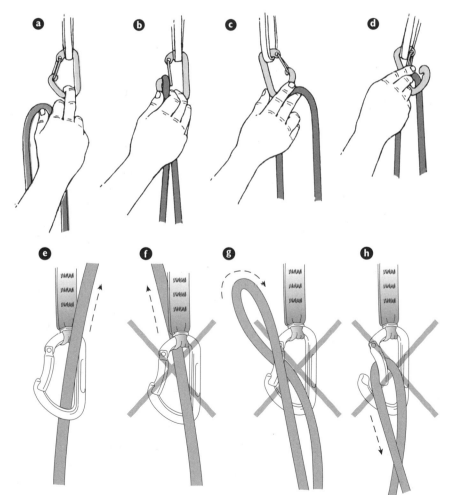

Fig. 14-9.
Clipping technique:
a–b, using the right hand to clip in to a carabiner with the gate facing left;
c–d, using the right hand to clip in to a carabiner with the gate facing right;
e, correctly clipped carabiner;
f, back-clipped carabiner (incorrect);
g–h, back-clipping causes carabiner gate to open and rope to come unclipped in a fall.

14

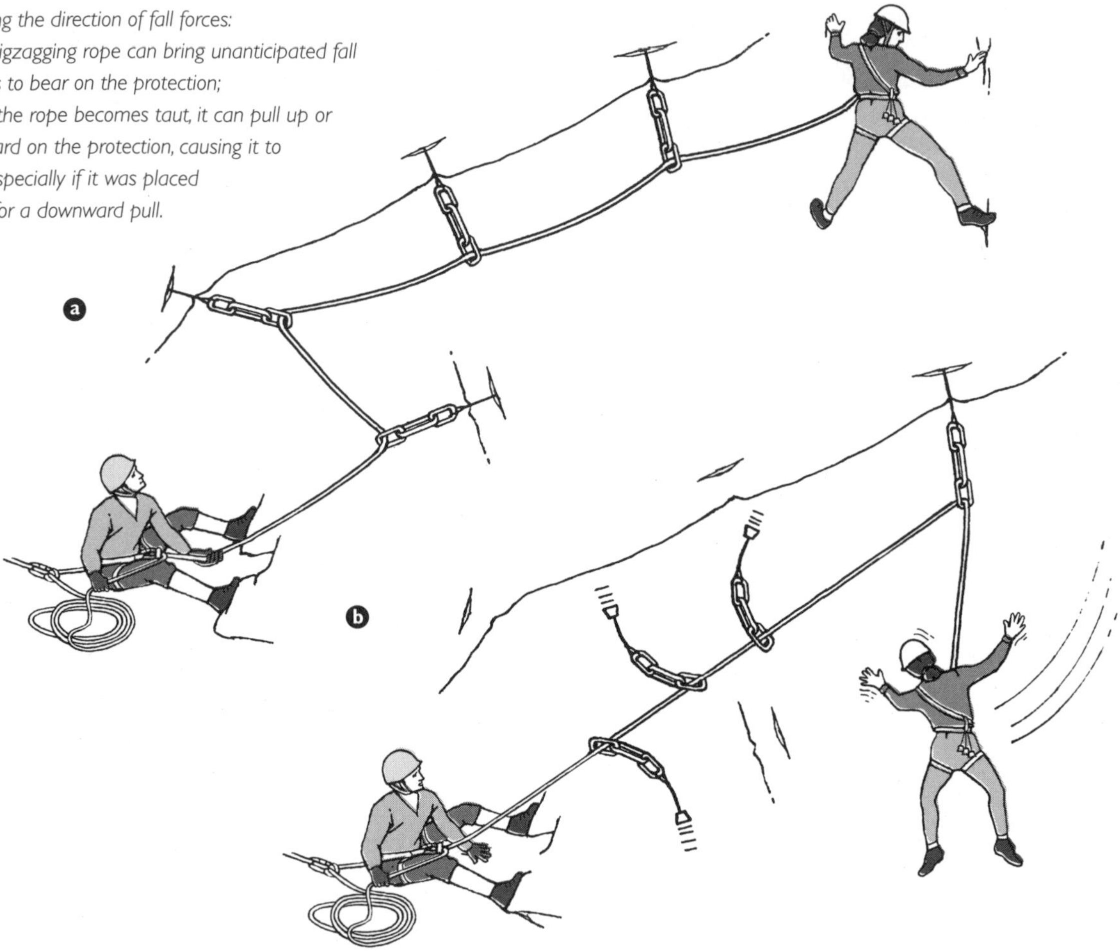

Fig. 14-10.
Judging the direction of fall forces:
a, a zigzagging rope can bring unanticipated fall forces to bear on the protection;
b, as the rope becomes taut, it can pull up or outward on the protection, causing it to fail, especially if it was placed only for a downward pull.

dangerous rope drag and how to take the fall factor into account (see Chapter 10, Belaying).

Selecting and Making a Placement

The perfect placement is a combination of a crack sized and shaped ideally for placing protection with a comfortable stance from which to place it, located right at the next hard move—but two out of three is not bad either. When you are on the sharp end of the rope, avoid making difficult moves far away from your last protection.

To place protection, find a stance that is secure enough that you can release one hand, because you must be able to make the placement and then clip in to it without falling or seriously tiring. Take advantage of natural protection—a tree, bush, rock tunnel, or horn—when possible because it can be easy to use and is often multidirectional, and doing so can save on chocks. You must be able to quickly place and clip sound protection with either hand, whether the carabiner gate faces left (fig. 14-9a and b) or right (fig. 14-9c and d), to make your lead safer. Study diagrams on clipping technique and then practice clipping with either hand until you are fluid and fast.

Suppose you are faced with a choice between two or more possible placements. Ask yourself:

■ Which placement combines the best fit with stability in the direction(s) of pull?

- Which placement will be stronger?
- What size chocks should be conserved for use higher on the pitch?
- Which placement will be easier for the second to remove?
- Will one placement interfere with a needed foothold or handhold?
- Which placement will minimize rope drag?

If your unfortunate choice is between questionable protection or none at all, by all means place something, but also plan to place additional protection as soon as possible. Placing and equalizing two pieces can also help (see Chapter 13, Rock Protection). Do not let such placement give you a sense of false security, however. Treat obviously bad protection as though it is isn't even there.

Suppose you face a hard move without apparent protection. Restudy the rock for some less-obvious way of protecting the move. Evaluate whether there is a movement sequence or rock feature you did not see at the outset. Your options are to:

- Protect the move after all, and then resume climbing.
- Go ahead and attempt the move without good protection.
- Down-climb and see if the belayer will lead the pitch.
- Find an easier line to climb.
- Consider retreating from the climb.

After studying the situation and evaluating the consequences of a fall, carefully and calmly weigh the options, and then decide on the course of action that seems best.

Judging the Direction of Fall Forces

You must anticipate the direction of forces on the protection in order to make your placements, but this judgment must take into account the entire climbing system. A protection point may seem solid for a fall when it is placed, but later could pop out when the system causes pulls in directions you did not initially anticipate.

A zigzagging climbing rope causes severe directional forces as well as rope drag that, at its worst, can immobilize the leader. Chocks that may have been placed to hold only a downward pull now are in danger of taking sharp pulls from quite different directions in case of a fall (fig. 14-10a). In catching a fall, the rope loads and straightens from the belayer up to the highest protection point and then back down to the falling climber. When the protection has been placed in a zigzag, pieces can be pulled sideways or upward by the tightening rope. If protection is placed for only a downward pull, it can be pulled out (fig. 14-10b).

During a fall, the top piece of protection is loaded with high forces: the force of the falling climber plus the force from the belay in arresting the fall (fig. 14-11). If the top piece will possibly fail, the lower pieces, which

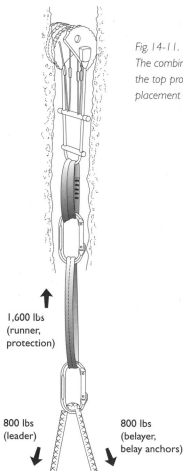

Fig. 14-11.
The combined force on the top protection placement during a fall.

1,600 lbs
(runner,
protection)

800 lbs
(leader)

800 lbs
(belayer,
belay anchors)

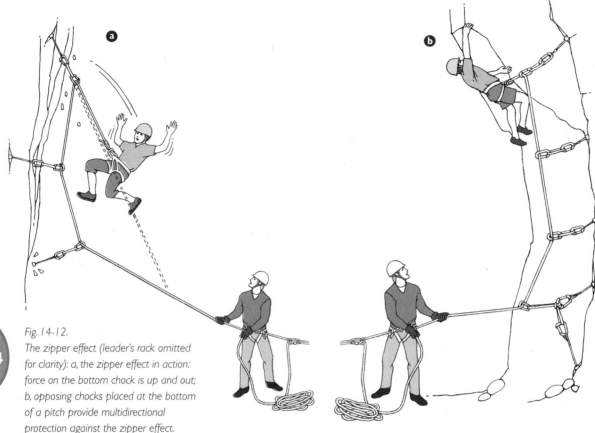

Fig. 14-12.
The zipper effect (leader's rack omitted
for clarity): a, the zipper effect in action:
force on the bottom chock is up and out;
b, opposing chocks placed at the bottom
of a pitch provide multidirectional
protection against the zipper effect.

back it up, should be placed to avoid being compromised.

Protection that allows the rope to follow in a straight line helps preserve the integrity of the system and minimizes rope drag. Extend protection with runners where needed. Rope drag not only can immobilize the climber, but it also decreases the rope's ability to absorb forces in case of a fall. Make placements multidirectional when a bend in the climbing line must be made—use natural protection, opposing chocks, or cams that can safely rotate with minimal walking (see "Opposition Placement" in Chapter 13, Rock Protection). Or consider placing the belay on the other side of the bend.

The Zipper Effect

The full-scale zipper effect is a dramatic demonstration of the importance of anticipating force directions. The zipper effect occurs most readily where the belay is established away from the base of the pitch (fig. 14-12) or, as in Figure 14-10, where the rope runs in a zigzag up the route. Again, as the rope loads during a leader fall, the bottom chock can have a tremendous outward pull placed on it. If it pulls out, the next piece becomes subject to the outward pull. Each in turn could fail, causing the line of chocks to be yanked out one by one as the "zipper" opens from the bottom up (fig. 14-12a). Overhangs and sharp traverses also have the potential to zipper.

The zipper effect can be prevented by making the suspect placements multidirectional through the use of opposing chocks, SLCDs, and/or natural protection, and by eliminating the potential for outward pull by extending pieces with runners. The belayer in Figure 14-12b could also reduce outward pull by belaying closer to the base of the route.

Protecting Special Situations

Overhangs

Keep the rope running as free of an overhang as possible. Extend the rope with runners in order to reduce rope drag, prevent dangerous fall forces such as the zipper effect, and keep the rope from being cut by the edge of the overhang (fig. 14-13). On small overhangs, leaning out and placing protection above it may be the most effective strategy.

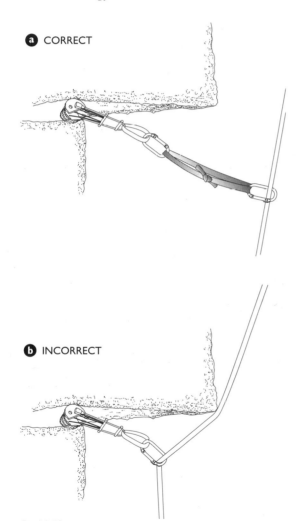

ⓐ CORRECT

ⓑ INCORRECT

Fig. 14-13.
Placements under overhangs: a, good—rope runs free of the overhang; b, poor—bends cause rope drag and rope could be cut by rock edge during a fall.

Traverses

When you are leading a traverse, place protection both before and after a hard move (fig. 14-14a). This guards not only you but also the follower from the possibility of a long pendulum fall (fig. 14-14b). In addition to the danger of injury, that kind of fall could leave the second in a tough spot, off route and with no easy way back.

ⓐ GOOD

ⓑ POOR

Fig. 14-14.
Protecting a traverse:
a, good—placing protection both before and after a hard move on a traverse can reduce potential for a long pendulum fall;
b, poor—if the climber falls on a traverse with inadequate protection, the climber faces a long pendulum fall.

As you lead a diagonal or traversing section, keep in mind the effect each placement could have on the second climber. Put yourself in the second's shoes and ask yourself, "Would I like some protection here?" If so, place it.

Consider belaying the second with an extra rope, which may help protect against a long pendulum fall and provide better protection than using the leader's rope. If you are using double-rope technique (described later in this chapter), do not clip in both ropes during the traverse, so that the follower can receive a belay from above on the free rope.

Clipping Bolts

The carabiner clipped in to a bolt hanger should normally have its gate facing away from the subsequent direction of travel of the leader (fig. 14-15). Otherwise it may lift up and open itself against the bolt hanger and potentially come unclipped. However, not all carabiners and bolt hangers are alike, so the leader should evaluate each circumstance with that in mind.

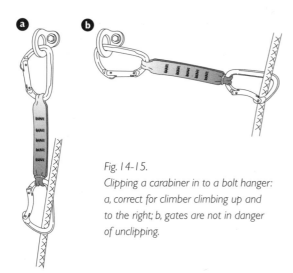

Fig. 14-15.
Clipping a carabiner in to a bolt hanger: a, correct for climber climbing up and to the right; b, gates are not in danger of unclipping.

Arriving at the Next Belay

At the top of the pitch, clip in to a solid anchor before signalling "off belay." Add additional pieces as needed to form a multidirectional belay anchor. (See Chapter 10, Belaying.) Make sure the anchor secures you against being pulled from the stance by the second.

Think through the belay sequence before you settle in so you know which hand to use for the braking hand and where you will flake the rope as you belay up the second. Keep the belay system simple. Strive for straight, easily traceable lines from the anchors to you.

Never lay belay devices, gloves, carabiners, or other items on the ground. If you are not using an item, keep it attached to yourself or to an anchor. Have only one item, such as the rope, a chock, or a carabiner, in your hand at a time. The moment you no longer need this item for whatever you are doing, reattach it to yourself or an anchor. Unattached objects are easily knocked or blown off the belay ledge.

Take off your pack and your rack and attach them to an anchor, but keep them within easy reach. That way, you will be more comfortable as you belay your second.

When you are settled in, haul up the slack rope until it is taut. The second should yell, "That's me." After you place the second on belay, yell, "On belay."

Cleaning a Pitch

The climber who follows the leader should climb as quickly and efficiently as possible after being put on belay. While ascending, this second climber cleans the pitch: removes the protection from the rock in an orderly way, organizes it, and efficiently transfers it to the belayer at the end of the pitch.

The second can minimize the risk of dropping gear by using a careful cleaning procedure, which may depend on the method used to rack the hardware. Consider a typical placement consisting of chock-carabiner-runner-carabiner-rope. If your rack features one carabiner on each chock and on each runner, the following cleaning procedure is very efficient:

1. First remove the chock from the rock.
2. Holding the carabiner that is clipped to the chock, clip the carabiner-chock combination directly to your gear sling.
3. Then unclip the carabiner-chock combination from the runner.
4. Next, loop the runner over your head, unclip the runner-carabiner combination from the rope, and rotate the carabiner-runner combination so that it is under one arm.

14

TIPS TO SAVE TIME AND ENERGY AS THE SECOND

- Start preparing to climb as soon as the leader is off belay. Begin breaking down the belay station (but always stay clipped in to at least one anchor until the leader has you on belay).

- Put your pack on before anything else. If you are already carrying climbing hardware on a gear sling, put it on next. Plan where you will put the gear that you clean, whether on the gear sling, your harness, or another sling.

- Give the area a last look to make sure you are not leaving anything behind. Then, once you are on belay, yell, "Climbing!" and start out.

- Remove each chock in the opposite way of how it was placed. A stopper slotted down and behind a constriction should be removed by pushing it back and up.

- Be persistent but sly. Use the chock pick to tap on a stubborn wedge or hex-shaped chock to loosen it, then lift the chock out gently. Prying and tugging often only tightens or wedges the chock more and can damage the wires. You can use a loose rock or other object, if available, to tap on the end of the chock pick.

- Spring-loaded camming devices can sometimes "walk" back into a crack, so that you cannot retract the trigger with your fingers. Sometimes you can use chock picks to retract the triggers. Or, use the wires of two stoppers to snare the trigger device to retract the cams.

- If a chock refuses to budge, consider asking your belayer for tension so you can put your weight on the rope, freeing your hands to work on removing the piece.

- As a final option, simply abandon the chock. Too much time and effort can be wasted on a chock that is not going to come out.

5. Continue climbing to the next piece of protection, and repeat.

If the placement uses a quickdraw instead of a runner:
1. First remove the chock from the rock.
2. Next clip the carabiner that connects the chock and quickdraw in to your racking sling.
3. Last, unclip the quickdraw's other carabiner from the rope.

In general, cleaning from rock to the rope is best. This keeps the pieces clipped to something at all times, and there is little possibility of dropping any gear. In any racking procedure, minimizing the handling of unattached gear also lessens the risk of dropping it.

Transferring Equipment at the Top of a Pitch

The first thing the second climber needs to do when arriving at a belay station—before being taken off belay—is to clip in to the belay anchors. If the climbers are swinging leads, then the belayer need not remove the rope from the belay device, but can back it up with an overhand or figure-eight knot on a bight. If they are not swinging leads, the climbers have to trade places. In either case, if the second was neat, organized, and efficient in cleaning the pitch, the transfer of gear at the belay station should go quickly, whether the original leader transfers the rest of the rack to the second, who will now lead, or the second transfers the cleaned pieces back to the leader's rack.

Follow this sequence:
1. Both climbers always stay anchored to the rock. First, reconstruct the rack. Clip the cleaned pieces to the rack, whether the original leader has it or the new leader. Be careful not to drop any gear.
2. Then hand the removed runners and/or quickdraws over to whoever will lead.
3. If either climber is wearing a pack, it can be removed and clipped in to the anchor.
4. If the original leader plans to lead the next pitch, reflake the rope and then the second should settle into the belay position.

Swinging leads is more efficient, but requires both climbers to be competent at leading. The new leader shoulders the reconstructed rack, and then racks the runners according to the climbers' chosen system. The

14

new leader rechecks and adjusts the rack to ensure that everything is ready for the next pitch. A look at the route description may be in order. The leader is placed on belay and then unclips from the anchor, and the climbing resumes.

Climbing with a Party of Three

Most rock climbing is done in pairs, but occasionally a party has three climbers. A three-person team generally is more awkward and less efficient than a two-person team. However, it has the advantages of having an extra person for hauling, rescue, etc. A team of three is faster than two teams of two. Two ropes are required unless the pitches are extremely short.

Using two ropes sequentially: In a team of three, the leader climbs with one rope while the second belays and the third remains anchored at the belay station. At the top of the pitch, the leader sets up a belay and brings up the second, who is belayed by the first rope and has the second rope either clipped with a locking carabiner to the harness's back haul loop or tied in at the front of the harness; the second rope will be used by the third climber. If the pitch follows a straight line up, the second can clean the pitch; remember, a top belay is very safe, and if a fall occurs, the climber falls only a very short distance. If the pitch includes some traversing, the protection should stay in for the third climber, to help prevent a pendulum fall. In this situation, the second climber unclips each piece of protection from the first rope and clips it to the second rope. Once the second is at the top of the pitch, the first rope is now completely at the top belay and the second rope is put on belay to bring up the third climber. When the third climber reaches the top of the pitch, the climbers then may decide to swing leads, with the third climber leading the next pitch using the second rope. For the second to lead, you will need to retie the ropes and perhaps restack them.

Using two ropes simultaneously: Another way to climb with three is this. The leader ties in to both ropes while the second and third climbers each tie in to one of the other ends. The leader then climbs the pitch, belayed on both ropes. The belay can be provided by one belayer with two ropes in one device, or by two belayers with one rope per belayer. At the top of the pitch, the leader sets up a belay station. Then the leader can either belay one follower at a time or bring both up together, one slightly ahead of the other. A specialized belay device called a GiGi (manufactured by Kong and not to be confused with a Petzl Grigri) works well for belaying two climbers at a time. Double ropes (half ropes) can be used for this method instead of two larger-diameter single ropes (see the next section).

This technique takes more rope management—but this way, three climbers can ascend nearly as fast as two. The original leader remains on lead throughout the climb. With the additional rope and climber involved in a three-person team, belay stations can be more confusing and messy. Each of the three climbers must remain securely anchored when not climbing.

Double- and Twin-Rope Techniques

Most of this book describes climbing situations in which a single rope is usually used. However, climbers can opt for one of the methods that use two smaller-diameter ropes: double-rope technique or twin-rope technique.

Double-Rope Technique

The double-rope technique uses two ropes that serve as independent belay lines. Each rope is referred to as a "half rope," is approved by the UIAA/CEN for such use, and is marked by a "½" on the end of the rope. It is usually 8.1 to 9.1 millimeters in diameter. The leader clips each rope in to its own protection on the way up, and the belayer manages the ropes separately. Most belay devices with two slots can be used, but some are designed specially for use with double ropes.

Although this technique is more complicated than using a single rope, it does offer some advantages. Rope friction can be greatly reduced, falls can be shorter, two ropes are less likely than one to be severed by rockfall or sharp edges, and two ropes are available for rappel. The technique is widely used by British climbers, in waterfall climbing, and by an increasing number of climbers everywhere to increase protection on highly technical routes. The ropes should be different colors to allow for clear communication about which rope needs slack or tension.

14

The double-rope technique offers great advantages when the route meanders. With a series of zigzag placements, one rope can be clipped in to the left pieces and one rope into the right, allowing the ropes to remain relatively straight, in roughly parallel lines that do not cross (fig. 14-16a), thereby preventing rope drag. When both ropes are clipped to the same protection placement, each rope is attached using a separate carabiner.

Traverses can be better protected with the double-rope technique, especially when the route traverses at the start of a pitch and then heads straight up. The leader can use one rope for protection on the traverse and leave the other free to belay the second climber from above. If the climbers were using only a single rope, the second climber could risk a long pendulum fall (fig. 14-17a). But with double ropes, the belay on the free rope can minimize or prevent a long pendulum (fig. 14-17b and c).

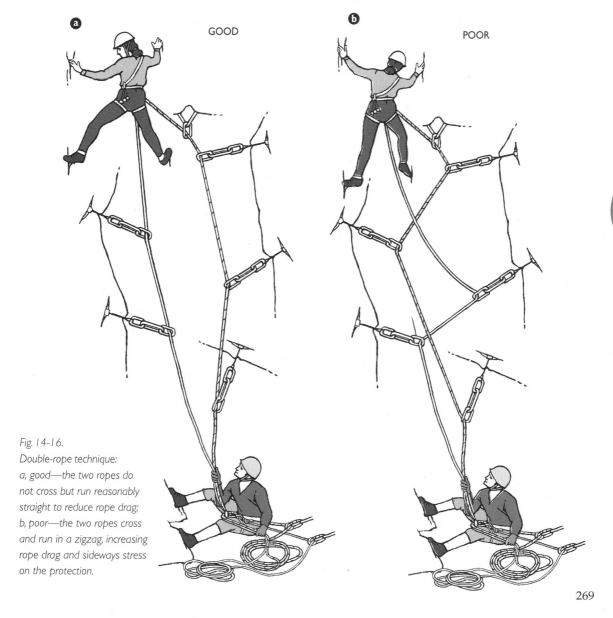

a GOOD

b POOR

Fig. 14-16.
Double-rope technique:
a, good—the two ropes do not cross but run reasonably straight to reduce rope drag;
b, poor—the two ropes cross and run in a zigzag, increasing rope drag and sideways stress on the protection.

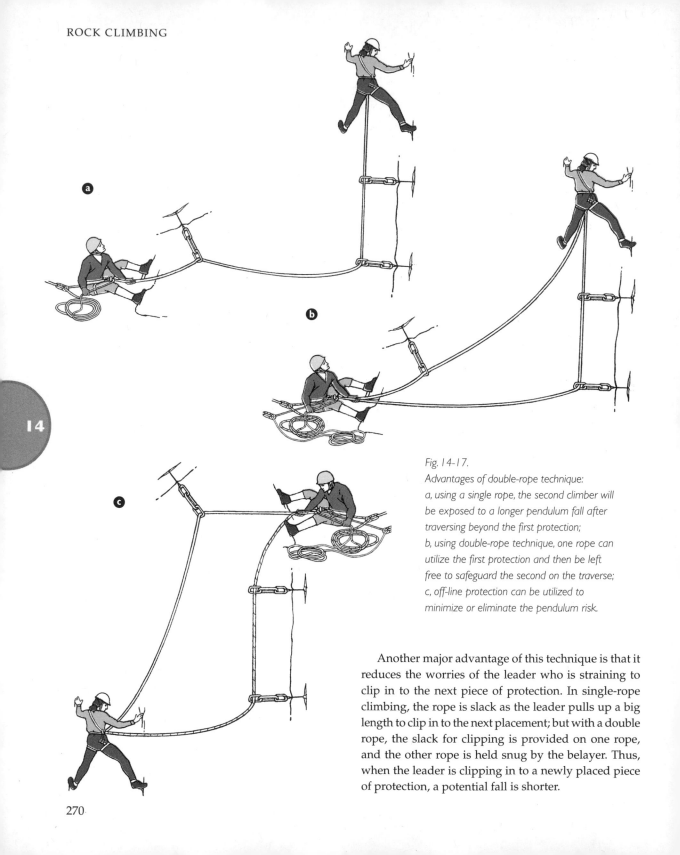

Fig. 14-17.
Advantages of double-rope technique:
a, using a single rope, the second climber will
be exposed to a longer pendulum fall after
traversing beyond the first protection;
b, using double-rope technique, one rope can
utilize the first protection and then be left
free to safeguard the second on the traverse;
c, off-line protection can be utilized to
minimize or eliminate the pendulum risk.

Another major advantage of this technique is that it reduces the worries of the leader who is straining to clip in to the next piece of protection. In single-rope climbing, the rope is slack as the leader pulls up a big length to clip in to the next placement; but with a double rope, the slack for clipping is provided on one rope, and the other rope is held snug by the belayer. Thus, when the leader is clipping in to a newly placed piece of protection, a potential fall is shorter.

One disadvantage is that the belayer's job is more complex, handling the movements of two ropes at the same time—often letting out slack on one rope while taking it in on the other. Also, the two ropes weigh and cost more than a single rope or twin ropes. Another drawback is that the technique requires more practice for both leader and belayer than does single-rope technique.

However, many climbers find that on long, challenging, and complex rock pitches, the advantages greatly outweigh the disadvantages.

Twin-Rope Technique

UIAA/CEN-approved twin ropes are generally 7.4 to 8.1 millimeters in diameter, and are not rated for use as single ropes. The ends of the rope are marked with a symbol of two overlapping circles.

The twin-rope technique shares some characteristics with the single-rope technique and some with the double-rope technique. Two ropes are used, but they are each clipped in to the same piece of protection, as a single larger-diameter rope would be (fig. 14-18).

The twin ropes together absorb more energy and can withstand more falls than a single rope. Though twin ropes are smaller-diameter, severing both at one time is less likely than severing one larger-diameter rope. Plus, two ropes are available for double-rope rappels.

A disadvantage is that the thinner the rope, the more likely it is to tangle. Also, together, twin ropes weigh and cost more than a single rope. Another disadvantage is that the technique lacks the specific advantages of the double-rope system on meandering routes, traverses, and shorter falls. As with double-rope technique, the belayer has to deal with two ropes, but separate management of each rope is greatly lessened.

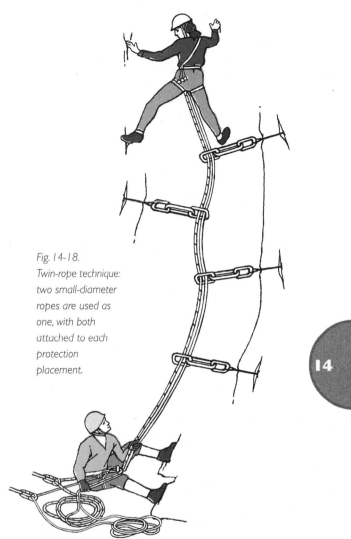

Fig. 14-18. Twin-rope technique: two small-diameter ropes are used as one, with both attached to each protection placement.

Inclement Weather and Other Emergencies

Rain, lightning, unexpected wind or cold, injury, or illness may make it prudent to retreat from the route. As the climb progresses, evaluate it for changing conditions of route, weather, or party. Know your alternative responses to those changes, weighing all of your resources. Know descent or escape routes in case they are needed. See the chapters in Part 5, Emergency Prevention and Response.

PERSONAL RESPONSIBILITY

Leading on rock is serious business. You face decisions in which a poor choice may be fatal. It is impossible to have a complete set of rules that cover every situation. Memorized dogma will not ensure your safety. Accurately evaluating the risks of climbing requires instead a fundamental understanding of the risks of the environment and the consequences of your own actions. Act not from superficial rules but from the knowledge gained through study and experience.

15 CHAPTER

Aid Climbing

CLEAN AID CLIMBING ■ **TYPES OF AID CLIMBING** ■ **AID-CLIMBING EQUIPMENT** ■
AID PLACEMENTS ■ **BASIC AID TECHNIQUES** ■ **SECONDING** ■ **BIG-WALL**
MULTIDAY TECHNIQUES ■ **THE FUTURE OF AID CLIMBING**

Aid climbing **is the technique of using gear to support your weight as you climb. It can be as simple as pulling on a quickdraw or as complex as climbing an entire multiday route with your weight suspended from gear you have placed. Aid climbing is an intricate and personal art, and everyone who participates does it somewhat differently.**

Aid climbing is clearly a sharp departure from free climbing, wherein weighting the rope or the protective hardware is generally considered poor style. Cutting-edge first ascents are often accomplished using the skills of the aid climber. Although free ascents are one of the goals of the sport of climbing, aid climbing remains a valuable skill for ascending currently unfreeable routes, to move through unappealing terrain, and to push the horizons of modern alpinism.

As free-climbing skills continue to rise, climbers are

freeing (free climbing) many routes originally climbed with aid. But despite the rise in free-climbing standards, there will always be tempting routes that are more difficult still—and so devoid of natural features—that a climber will need some of the aid-climbing skills described in this chapter.

Skills in aid climbing can also help overcome unexpected difficulties during normal free climbing. They can provide a way to move safely up or down when bad weather or an accident puts a climbing party in jeopardy. Many routes have short sections of very difficult climbing or poor rock that may be negotiated by aid climbing to gain access to excellent free climbing and/or an objective summit. Aside from their practical applications, aid-climbing techniques give experienced and technically advanced climbers access to the vertical world of the big-wall routes that so many climbers dream of tackling.

Aid climbing requires skill, judgment, and a lot of practice. To learn both the basics and the many tricks of aid climbing, work with an experienced partner, and climb often.

CLEAN AID CLIMBING

Aid climbing takes a lot of gear, but it does not need to damage the rock. With all the chocks and camming devices available, climbers now have a better chance of climbing routes clean (without putting in a single piton or bolt). A clean placement is one that is not a bolt, piton, copperhead, or any other placement that mars the rock. Chocks and other clean devices can be removed without defacing the rock, leaving no trace that you were there.

When climbers make the first ascent of a major wall, they often carry bolts and pitons to make the ascent possible. Once this gear is placed, the best approach is to leave it intact so that future parties can use it without marring the rock further by placing other fixed gear.

A clean ascent of an aid route usually entails using the existing fixed gear, and may include carrying a hammer in case some of that gear has been removed or is no longer serviceable. Climbing hammerless (without a hammer) means not relying on previously fixed gear. Hammerless climbing of a route that has essential fixed gear may be naive and possibly dangerous if you do not understand the consequences of expecting that the fixed gear will all be in place, or if you are not up to the challenge of broken or missing fixed gear, such as thin pitons or copperheads. Some climbers enjoy the challenge of hammerless climbing of established aid routes with known fixed gear, or even new routes. The clean and hammerless styles of climbing present an additional level of commitment.

Aid climbing may require placement of bolts and pitons, but keep them to a minimum. Pitons chip the rock, especially when they are removed. On popular routes, tiny cracks sometimes evolve into finger or hand cracks after generations of climbers force them to accept pitons. In general, make clean climbing your goal.

TYPES OF AID CLIMBING

Aid climbing can be roughly categorized based on the extent of its use on a particular climb. See Appendix A, Rating Systems, for information on the various grades of difficulty in aid climbing.

Mountaineering alpine aid climbing: This uses a minimum of aid techniques and equipment to overcome short, blank (or extremely difficult) sections of a route that otherwise can be free climbed. This type of climbing often requires little or no specialized aid equipment; usually climbers just use the free-climbing gear they have along. Sometimes pulling on gear is intentionally done to speed progress and/or minimize exposure to objective hazards or other risks in the mountains.

General aid climbing: Aid is often used for extended distances, although aid- and free-climbing techniques may be interspersed. Long one day climbs may involve fixing the initial pitches on a preceding day: putting up ropes and leaving them in place so they can be climbed quickly with mechanical ascenders the following morning to reach the previous day's high point and complete the route on the second day.

Big-wall aid climbing: Ascents of big walls typically take longer than one day to complete, even if the initial pitches are fixed. These climbs usually involve either a hanging bivouac or ledge bivouac, and require sack-hauling techniques. However, with the proliferation of speed-climbing techniques, many big walls that originally took many days to ascend are now being climbed in a day.

AID-CLIMBING EQUIPMENT

This section details the range of equipment used in aid climbing, building on all the gear and techniques described in Chapter 13, Rock Protection, and Chapter 14, Leading on Rock. The true "nuts and bolts" of the sport, from beginning to big wall, are described here.

Basic Equipment for Clean Aid Climbing

Clean aid relies heavily on standard free-climbing equipment. Aid climbers may simply need more of it.

Chocks and Camming Devices

Because climbers set placements every several feet, a long pitch can require more than fifty assorted chocks and camming devices. If the slings attached to placements are used as the clip-in points for the etriers (ladderlike slings), they should be as short as possible to help you get the maximum elevation gain out of each placement.

Carabiners

Although you need a minimum of 40 free carabiners on an aid rack, it is not unusual to use 80 on a long pitch and more than 100 on a particularly difficult pitch. Many aid climbers prefer oval carabiners rather than D-shaped carabiners because ovals minimize the unnerving shifting that occurs when a D carabiner takes your weight. Regardless of the carabiner's shape, you need to be able to open the carabiner gate whenever you wish, even while it is holding your weight.

Small Nuts

Aid racks include small nuts that are even more specialized than those for free-climbing racks. These tapered nuts are often used instead of thin pitons, but they are not as strong. They are designed to support only your body weight, and may fail if a fall occurs.

Three general styles of nuts are available. The first is the common contoured nut used for free climbing. The second type is a smaller version of the classic tapered stopper. The third style has both horizontal and vertical taper and is more secure in flaring cracks and old piton scars.

The heads of small nuts are made from aluminum, brass, or stainless steel. The rock bites into aluminum or brass and so these tend to hold better in marginal placements, but steel nuts are less likely to deform and fail if you take a fall on one of them.

Ropes

The tough duty of aid climbing usually requires a 10- to 11-millimeter kernmantle lead rope, 60 meters (approximately 200 feet) long. The haul line is typically a second lead rope or a 9-millimeter static line that doubles as a second rope for long rappels. If the route entails long pendulums or other unusual problems, a third rope may be needed—either another kernmantle rope or another static line. When you are selecting a rope, keep in mind its resistance to abrasion and edge cutting, because of the typically rough terrain and demands associated with aid climbing. See "Ropes" in Chapter 9, Basic Safety System.

Hero Loops

These tie-off loops—4 to 6 inches (10 to 15 centimeters) long—are threaded through fixed placements in lieu of a carabiner. Climbers usually tie their own out of ½-inch or ⁵⁄₁₆-inch webbing. Hero loops are also used to prevent the loss of stacked pieces (described in "Piton Placement" later in this chapter) and to tie off partially driven pins (see "Knots" in Chapter 9, Basic Safety System). Hero loops are often carried on big walls to replace old, worn slings on fixed gear.

Slings

Carry at least twelve single-length slings for establishing anchors, extending placements to reduce rope drag, and other normal rock-climbing uses. Single-length slings are the most useful because you can carry them easily; they can also be carried like quickdraws and easily extended to full length after the first half is clipped to the placement (see Figure 14-7 in Chapter 14, Leading on Rock).

Quickdraws are very useful for clipping in to a placement that will be a key point of protection. The proper

15

use of the quickdraw (i.e., no back-clipping; see Figure 14-9 in Chapter 14, Leading on Rock) assures that the rope will lie properly on the wide, rope-bearing portion of the carabiner in the event of a fall.

Slings that attach protection to the climbing rope in aid climbing are typically shorter than those used in free climbing. This is because aid pitches tend to be vertical, overhanging, and more direct and thus do not need extension to allow the rope to run freely. The use of shorter slings, when appropriate, reduces the distance that you could fall.

Chock Picks

Picks used for aid climbing should be sturdy, because you often hammer on your pick to tap out lodged nuts. There are myriad styles with features such as integral wrenches, bottle openers, and integral "light" hammers (see Figure 14-4 in Chapter 14, Leading on Rock).

Gloves

Over and above their value for belaying and rappelling, leather gloves protect your hands while you are jugging (ascending the climbing rope with mechanical ascenders) and removing protection placements.

Shoes

If the route involves only a small amount of aid, normal free-climbing rock shoes perform best. If you anticipate sustained aid climbing, boots with greater sole rigidity provide a better working platform and more comfort. Some boots that are available provide a rigid arch support and good torsional rigidity for aid climbing, yet have a flexible toe and a sole of soft friction rubber for good free-climbing capabilities.

Eye Protection

This is important both for leaders and followers, to protect climbers' eyes from falling debris, equipment that comes loose, flying pieces of ice, and other hazards. Protection should be industrial quality, fitting snugly around the eye area, with no gaps.

Load-Limiting Runners

These slings are sometimes used to climb above placements of questionable strength. In a fall, the slings limit the shock delivered to the protection. (See Figure 10-13 in Chapter 10, Belaying.)

Universal Aid-Climbing Equipment

In addition to equipment normally used in free climbing, aid climbers need a selection of gear that is used both for clean aid climbing and for aid that may involve placing pins.

Helmets

A helmet is absolutely essential for aid climbing. See Chapter 9, Basic Safety System. Steep terrain, daisy chains (sewn slings with sewn loops), large racks (which make the climber top-heavy), and the dynamics of a popped placement tend to send aid climbers into head-first falls. A chest harness will keep you upright if the rope draws taut prior to contacting the rock, but this in no way replaces your need for head protection.

Etriers (Aiders)

These ladderlike slings (fig. 15-1), also called aiders, allow you to step up from one placement to the next when the etriers are clipped to a chock, piton, or other aid piece. When you are making or buying etriers, consider their intended use. For alpine climbs, minimize weight by using a single lightweight pair of etriers (fig. 15-1a). For most aid climbing, four-step (fig. 15-1b), five-step (fig. 15-1c), or six-step etriers sewn from 1-inch webbing are standard. They are used in pairs, in leap-frog fashion as you ascend. Etriers should be long enough to let you step smoothly from the top step of one to the bottom step of the other that has been clipped into a piece at arm's reach above.

Some aid climbers use two pairs of etriers and others use a single pair; it depends on the nature of the route and on how much and at what angle(s) you want to weight your placement. Two pairs of etriers—of equal length but different colors—allow you to use one set to ascend "quietly" (more smooth and in balance) and stand more securely while placing the next piece of protection to which the second set is then attached. (See "The Basic Sequence" later in this chapter.) Other styles of aiders have been developed and have become quite popular. The adjustable type (fig. 15-1d) tends to

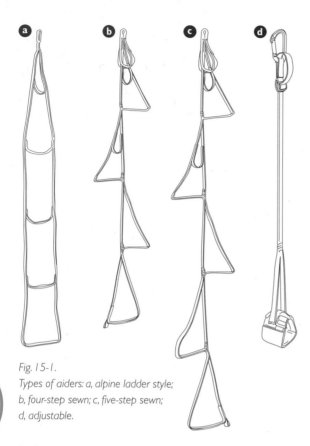

Fig. 15-1.
Types of aiders: a, alpine ladder style;
b, four-step sewn; c, five-step sewn;
d, adjustable.

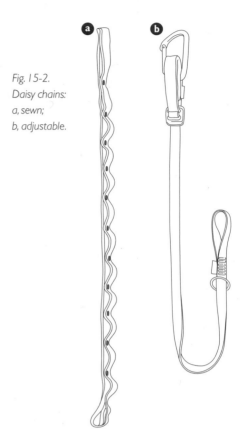

Fig. 15-2.
Daisy chains:
a, sewn;
b, adjustable.

be lighter, is especially well suited for quick adjustment for optimal jugging, and permits seamless transition to free-climbing movements with the aiders still strapped onto your feet.

Daisy Chains

Daisy chains are sewn slings with multiple loops (fig. 15-2a)—formed by stitching—every 3 to 6 inches (8 to 15 centimeters). These are used to keep new placements and aiders attached to the lead climber, and are an integral part of the jugging setup. A daisy chain should, when attached to your harness, reach at least as far as your raised hand. Typical daisy chains are 45 to 55 inches (115 to 140 centimeters) long. The loops are used to shorten the daisy chain when it is used in the jugging mode, or to clip in short when you are passing under roofs or very steep sections, which relieves your arms from the chore of holding up your weight. See "The Basic Sequence," later in this chapter.

Usually two daisy chains are carried, one for the left-side etrier and one for the right-side etrier (or pair of etriers). One end of each daisy chain is usually girth hitched into the climbing harness while the other end is attached to the appropriate etrier with a carabiner. This prevents the loss of an etrier if a hook placement fails or if you drop the etrier, and allows you a convenient method for resting on a placement if the daisy is shortened up by clipping another one of the loops in to the etrier. The daisy chains and etriers are adjusted when jumaring (ascending the climbing rope with mechanical ascenders) so that your body weight can be left on the rope at the end of each arm extension. The upper daisy should be adjusted so that it draws tight prior to a full arm extension, preventing the ascender (see "Mechanical Ascenders" later in this section) from ever getting out of reach. Adjustable daisies (fig. 15-2b), a new option for the modern aid climber, provide a viable option to the classic daisy chain.

Fig. 15-3.
Fifi hook.

Fifi Hooks

Fifi hooks (fig. 15-3) function somewhat like daisy chains but are attached to your harness with a sling or adjustable daisy. You can quickly hook in to an aid piece, allowing you to rest on your harness. Be careful: If you release the tension or change the angle, it could come unhooked.

Double Gear Sling

A double gear sling distributes the weight of the hardware with equipment slings on both sides of your body (fig. 15-4). It improves balance and comfort, and reduces the neck strain caused by the single bearing point of a traditional free-climbing gear sling. If it is designed as such, a double gear sling can also serve as a chest

harness as you jug up a rope with mechanical ascenders, or to keep you upright during a fall. Some climbers carry a single gear sling in addition, for their free carabiners or to provide the means to quickly put together a supplemental free-climbing rack.

Belay Seat

A belay seat with a two- or three-point attachment (fig. 15-5) is a great creature-comfort during hanging belays. One urgent warning: Never let the belay seat be your sole means of attaching to an anchor. Clip in from your harness to the anchor with the climbing rope as usual and attach the belay seat to the anchor point with its own nonlocking carabiner.

Fig. 15-5.
Belay seat attached
directly to the anchor,
not to the climbing rope.

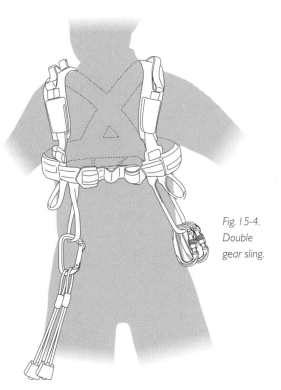

Fig. 15-4.
Double
gear sling.

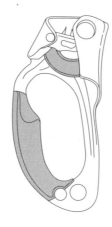

Fig. 15-6. Ascender for the left hand (right-hand ascender is a mirror image).

Mechanical Ascenders

Serving the same function as prusik knots, mechanical ascenders (fig. 15-6) are stronger, safer, faster, and less tiring. The devices are very helpful for sack hauling on big walls.

All ascenders employ a cam, allowing them to slide freely in one direction on a rope but to grip tightly when pulled in the opposite direction. Ascenders also have a trigger or locking mechanism to keep them from accidentally coming off the rope. Some triggers are difficult to release, decreasing the chance of accidental removal but making it harder to get them off when you want to.

For cold-weather climbing, look for a pair of ascenders with openings large enough to accommodate heavily gloved hands. Carabiner holes at the top and the bottom of the ascender come in handy for a number of purposes, such as sack hauling and locking the ascender to a fixed rope during jumaring.

Piton Hammers

These tools have a flat striking surface for cleaning and driving pitons and a blunt pick for prying out protection, cleaning dirty cracks, and placing malleable pieces. A hammer shaft should be long enough so you can forcefully drive pins and short enough to fit comfortably in a belt holster. The shaft should also be sturdy and taped for protection. A carabiner hole in the head is useful for cleaning pins and malleable pieces (see "Cleaning" later in this chapter).

Attach a sling to the hammer that allows full arm extension when you use the hammer (fig. 15-7). If you

Fig. 15-7. Chouinard-style hammer with sling.

drop the hammer, it will just hang on the sling somewhere below your feet. Be sure to check the sling regularly for wear.

Skyhooks

Skyhooks, which come in many shapes, are commonly used to grip ledges or small holes (fig. 15-8). Skyhooks should be made of chromium molybdenum steel (for strength) and curved (for stability), and the nonhook end should be wider than the hook end. Attach a sling to the bottom of a hook by feeding a separate loop through from the back until the knot jams (see Figure 15-8). The sling should hang from the rock side of the hook, with the knot on the other side. This puts the line of force next to the rock and eliminates rotation of the tip of the hook off the rock feature.

The standard skyhook (fig. 15-8a) is useful for small flakes and ledges. You can achieve greater stability on some placements if the tip of the hook is filed to a point that can be set into small holes drilled at the back of tiny ledges. Fishhooks (fig. 15-8b) are large skyhooks used to grip larger flakes and ledges. Logan hooks (fig. 15-8c) are L-shaped: The wide style is stable on tiny ledges and flakes, and the narrow style can be used in shallow pockets. Bat hooks (fig. 15-8d) are basically a narrow-style Logan hook with a pointed blade, used in shallow, ¼-inch (6-millimeter) holes drilled for their use.

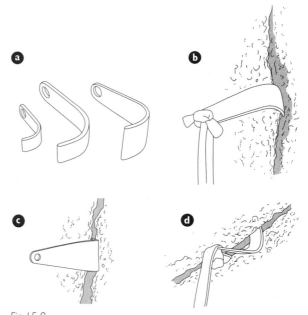

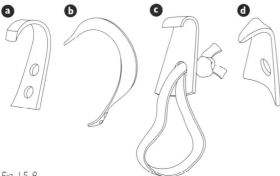

Fig. 15-8.
Skyhook types: a, standard; b, fishhook; c, wide Logan hook; d, bat hook.

Fig. 15-9.
Camming hooks: a, typical camming hook sizes; b, camming hook in shallow flaring crack; c, solid camming hook placement; d, camming hook upside down under a roof.

Camming Hooks

Camming hooks can be used in any crack that is at least as wide as the thickness of the metal and no wider than the width of the hook's tip. Camming hooks have different tip widths and "arm" lengths (fig. 15-9), which produce different leverages on the rock features. Too much leverage may bite into the rock or expand a flake, whereas too little leverage may make the placement insecure. Narrow camming hooks tend to have higher leverage; wider camming hooks tend to have lower leverage. Camming hooks can be used in leapfrog style to advance quickly on relatively easy terrain where placements are made only to protect in case of a fall rather than to hold your weight as you climb, much the way one protects a free-climbing pitch.

Wire Hangers

Wire hangers (fig. 15-10a and b) are loops of wire ⅛ inch or 3/32 inch in diameter, with a slider to cinch the wire tight over bolt studs and rivets (which are, basically, bolts with a wide head). Small nuts with wire

Fig. 15-10.
Hangers: a, wire; b, self-cinching wire hanger on a bolt; c, keyhole.

slings can also be used for this purpose, with the chock itself acting as the slider to tighten the wire against the bolt stud. However, because chocks have a longer wire loop than do wire hangers, you do not get as much elevation gain from them.

Regular Hangers and Keyhole Hangers

Serving a similar function to wire hangers, regular and keyhole hangers are shaped pieces of metal rather than wire loops (fig. 15-10c). They are useful especially at belay anchors and for fixed bolts that have no hangers. On keyhole hangers, the metal between the bolt hole and carabiner hole is filed out to allow placement over rivets and buttonhead bolts.

Ironmongery for Full Aid Climbing

To master the full range of aid-climbing techniques, you must have a knowledge of pitons, bashies (see "Malleable Hardware," below), and bolts.

Pitons

Modern pitons—also called pins—are made of hardened chromium-molybdenum steel or other suitable alloys such as titanium alloys. Rather than molding to cracks the way the malleable pitons of old did, they mold the crack to their form. With the proliferation of contoured nuts, spring-loaded camming devices (especially smaller units and asymmetric SLCDs), and camming hooks, larger pins are seldom used. They are still important, however, on sections of poor-quality rock and very thin cracks. Even then, their use should be limited to crucial points of protection. For winter mountaineering, when cracks are filled with ice, they may offer the only viable means of protection. To fit the diverse cracks encountered on rock walls, pitons vary tremendously in size and shape (fig. 15-11).

Realized Ultimate Reality Piton (RURP): This is the smallest piton, a postage-stamp-size, hatchet-shaped pin (fig. 15-11a) used in incipient cracks. It will usually support only body weight and derives what little strength it has by minimizing the leverage between the piton and carabiner supporting your etriers. Some styles come with offset sides for use in corners.

Birdbeaks: Also called seam hooks, these are similar to RURPs but have a longer arm for attaching a carabiner or sling (fig. 15-11b). They are generally easier to place and remove.

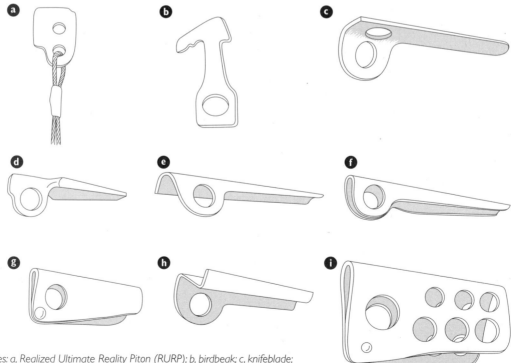

Fig. 15-11.
Piton (pin) types: a, Realized Ultimate Reality Piton (RURP); b, birdbeak; c, knifeblade; d, Lost Arrow; e, shallow angle; f, angle; g, large angle, sawed off; h, Leeper Z type; i, bong.

Knifeblades: Blade-type pitons are long and thin and have two eyes—one at the end of the blade and a second in the offset portion of the pin (fig. 15-11c). They come in different lengths and in thicknesses ranging from $\frac{1}{16}$ to $\frac{3}{16}$ inch. They are commonly used to fit many cracks that are too thin for tiny nuts.

Lost Arrows: These pitons are similar to knifeblades but have a single eye that is centered and set perpendicular to the end of the blade (fig. 15-11d). These too are still commonly used and come in several lengths and thicknesses—$\frac{5}{32}$ to $\frac{3}{8}$ inch. They are very good in horizontal cracks.

Angles: These are pitons formed into a V shape (fig. 15-11e, f, and g). The V varies in height from $\frac{1}{4}$ to $1\frac{1}{2}$ inches (6 millimeters to 4 centimeters)—smaller ones are most popular. Their strength is derived from the metal's resistance to bending and spreading. Angles and other large pitons have largely been replaced by modern free-climbing hardware.

Leeper Zs: This type of piton obtains its thickness through its Z-shape profile (fig. 15-11h), as opposed to the V profile of an angle. These pitons often make very solid placements and work well for stacking because of their short length, which makes them useful in bottoming cracks.

Bongs: These are large angle pitons that vary from 2 to 6 inches wide (fig. 15-11i). Spring-loaded camming devices have largely replaced the need for bongs.

Sawed-off pitons: These are handy for protection on routes that have been heavily climbed using pitons, leaving shallow pin scars. Several $\frac{3}{4}$-inch and 1-inch angles with a few inches cut off the end are useful for shallow placements (see Figure 15-11g above). Camming hooks work well in shallow pin scars to hold body weight and aid in advancement; however, the hooks will not hold in a fall and so cannot replace sawed-off pitons for protection.

Malleable Hardware

Also called bashies or heads, malleable hardware is designed to hold weight by melding the soft head of the piece to the irregularities of the rock. The security of bashies varies greatly and it is difficult to gauge their strength, making them last-resort equipment, generally capable of holding only body weight.

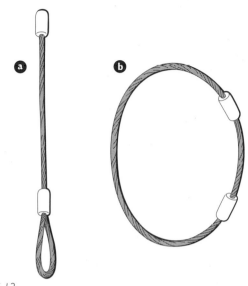

Fig. 15-12.
Malleable head types: a, copper or aluminum head; b, circlehead.

Copper or aluminum heads: These have a swage of copper or aluminum attached to one end of a short cable that has a loop at the other end (fig. 15-12a). They are placed by pounding the relatively soft metal end into an irregularity in the rock. Copper forms well and is more durable than similar pieces with aluminum heads. Aluminum heads are not as strong as copper heads but are more malleable, so they tend to be used in larger sizes, whereas the smaller heads are usually copper.

Circleheads: These consist of a wire loop with an extra copper or aluminum swage on the loop (fig. 15-12b), which is pounded into the rock the same as a regular head. They are used in horizontal cracks, overhead placements, and other applications where the symmetry of the wire loop's attachment point balances rotational forces and effectively reduces twisting of the attachment point.

Bolts

Chapter 13, Rock Protection, includes a section on the use of existing bolts found on climbing routes. Proper bolt placement is a special skill, beyond the scope of this book. Bolt placement is best left to the skill and judgment of very experienced climbers.

Big-Wall Equipment

Climbers undertaking a big wall have other specialized equipment needs to consider. Safeguard important equipment taken on a big-wall climb by using tie-in loops or lanyards to attach anything that might be dropped. Bring gear that will get you through the worst possible weather, because there is not likely to be any easy way to retreat.

Be sure your equipment is durable, and beef up any item that could fail. Select only the most durable water bottles.

Pulleys

Pulleys are necessary to ease the chore of sack hauling. They receive much abuse, so they must be durable. Pulleys with bearings and larger wheels operate more smoothly. Pulleys with self-locking cams are especially useful for extensive hauling.

Haul Bags

These carry clothing, water, food, sleeping bag, and other nonclimbing paraphernalia. A good haul bag has adequate cargo capacity, a solid haul suspension, durable fabric, no snag points, and a removable backpacking harness system. It is a good idea for the haul bag to have a top cap to protect the knot connecting the sack to the haul line and to help reduce snagging problems while it is being hauled. An effective top cap can be readily fashioned from an empty 2-liter plastic bottle.

Cheater Sticks

These allow you to clip a carabiner into a piece of hardware beyond your reach. They are often used to avoid top stepping (see "The Basic Sequence," later in this chapter) in etriers or to speed progress. Cheater sticks should have a means of holding a carabiner solidly while you clip it in with your arm fully extended. Because the clipped placement will be out of range for close inspection, give additional consideration to bounce testing. Cheater sticks may be mandatory for shorter climbers, especially when the gear is fixed and intermediate placements are not available. If a fixed placement is missing, broken, or otherwise not serviceable, using a cheater stick to reach another placement provides a viable option to placing new pitons, bashies, or bolts.

Knee Pads

These protect your knees, which are regularly in contact with the rock during low-angle, big-wall aid climbing. Knee pads should be comfortable and allow good circulation.

Portaledges

A portaledge is a lightweight cot (fig. 15-13) that offers greater comfort from a single point of suspension than the classic hammock. Unfortunately, portaledges are much heavier and bulkier. As with belay seats, when using portaledges, climbers must always be anchored to the rock.

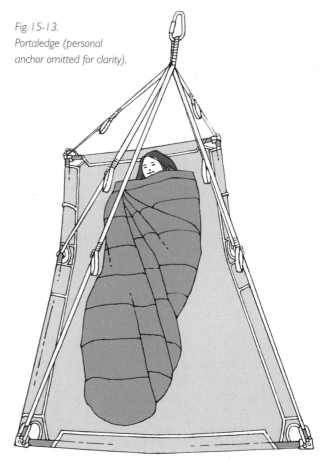

Fig. 15-13. Portaledge (personal anchor omitted for clarity).

Poop Tubes

On big-wall ascents, poop tubes must be carried to haul human waste. They may be simple units handmade from materials purchased at a hardware store or elaborate, commercially available containers. (See Chapter 7, Leave No Trace.)

AID PLACEMENTS

The general rule for aid climbing is to place each aid piece as high as possible. Making placements at 5-foot (1.5-meter) rather than 4-foot (1.2-meter) intervals, over the course of a 160-foot (50-meter) pitch, saves eight placements, many more carabiners, and much time.

Most of the techniques for placing free-climbing protection apply to aid climbing. For aid climbing, shorten the slings to your pieces, if possible, to reduce the potential fall distances. You will make many placements that are generally suitable to hold only body weight, not fall forces. It is important to keep in mind good basic protection skills and free-climbing concepts.

Using a solid camming-hook placement rather than placing a nut or piton can save considerable time for both leader (placement is much simpler) and follower (because there is little to clean), but this provides no protection against the consequences of a fall.

Placing small nuts during an aid climb is similar to placing larger ones on a free climb, but because aid nuts take the weight of the lead climber, and because they may be smaller than the chock pick, they can be difficult to remove. Place small nuts near the outside of a crack; they are easier to remove and there is less danger of damaging them in the process. Test small nuts gently before committing your weight to them.

Evaluate fixed pins, bolts, and other fixed gear before using them (see Chapter 13, Rock Protection). If you decide to use a fixed piece, you can save a carabiner by threading a hero loop through its eye and clipping a single carabiner in to the two ends of the loop. **Note:** Use a direct carabiner clip-in, not the hero-loop method, for all critical points of protection and, as a minimum, for every third or fourth placement. The hero-looped pieces are not as reliable for stopping a fall because of the danger that the loop could be cut by the edge of the metal eye. It is also wise to carry a few bolt hangers and nuts, in both ¼- and ⅜-inch (6- and 10-millimeter) sizes, for bolts with missing or damaged hangers.

Piton Placement

A properly sized pin can be placed one-half to two-thirds of the way by hand; the remainder of the pin is hammered in place. Select the correct pin to fit the crack. Do not try to make the crack fit the pin; this practice causes needless destruction of the rock. A sound piton rings with a higher-pitched *ping* with each strike of the hammer. After the pin is driven, tap it to test for rotation; if it rotates, the pin is not biting the rock. Replace such a pin with a larger one. Knowing just how much to hammer a piton is a matter of touch and experience. Excessive hammering wastes energy, makes it harder for the second to remove the piton, and needlessly damages the rock. Underdriving a piton, however, increases the risk of it pulling out. If several pins are underdriven, the failure of one could result in a long fall as the series of pins zippers out.

Below are some additional guidelines for the sound placement of pitons.

- Consider hand placement of pitons to eliminate further damage to the rock.
- Horizontal placement of pins is generally more secure than vertical placement because rotation is reduced or eliminated.
- Ideally, the eye should point downward.
- As with chocks, place pins in locally wider portions of a crack. If the crack is thinner below and above the pin, the pin will be supported when it has to take your weight (fig. 15-14a).
- When possible, avoid placing a pin in a three-way corner. Such placements are often impossible to clean because the pin cannot be tapped back and forth for removal. Just leave it as a fixed pin.
- If the position of the piton causes the connecting carabiner to extend over an edge, add a hero loop to the piece (fig. 15-14b). This prevents loading the carabiner across its sides.
- Place knifeblades in vertical cracks with the offset eye down (fig. 15-14a).
- When you are placing angles, keep the three points of the V in contact with the rock (fig. 15-14c). The back (the point of the V) must always be in contact

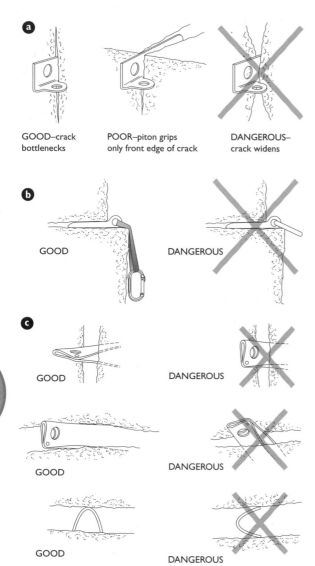

GOOD–crack
bottlenecks

POOR–piton grips
only front edge of crack

DANGEROUS–
crack widens

GOOD

DANGEROUS

GOOD

DANGEROUS

GOOD

DANGEROUS

GOOD

DANGEROUS

Fig. 15-14.
*Piton placements: a, blade placements; b, safely extending a piton
to avoid side-loading the carabiner; c, angle piton placements.*

with one wall, while the edges (the two tips of the V) are in contact with the opposing wall. In a horizontal crack, put the back of the angle up and the edges down.

■ Bongs, typically made of aluminum, are quite fragile, so pound them as little as possible.

Expanding flakes and/or cracks present problems for pins because as subsequent pins are placed, lower pins loosen. When possible, use chocks in such situations, because they minimize flake expansion. If you must use pins, try to work with long, minimum-taper pins placed lightly in natural slots, to minimize expansion of the rock flake. Placements in expanding features are generally good for holding only body weight. Wide camming hooks may be more useful for such placements. Pre-expanding an expanding crack with a weighted SLCD (weighted with your body weight) may improve the potential for reliable placement of a nut or other chock by taking the initial spring out of the feature—if the feature does not detach in the process.

■ In shallow cracks and flutings, a piton may be driven over a chock or hand-placed in conjunction with a chock (fig. 15-15). The chock creates a second "wall" against which the pin wedges, or vice versa. Because the chock or pin would fall and be lost if either failed, attach a keeper sling (which acts as a lanyard) to the secondary piece and clip it in to the sling or carabiner of the load-bearing piece. The keeper sling must not bear any weight.

■ When a pin bottoms out in a crack (that is, cannot be driven in all the way), stop hammering, to avoid loosening it. The piton must be tied off around the shaft at the point where it emerges from the rock. A hero loop tied to the piton with a girth hitch or clove hitch supports your weight and reduces the levering action on the pin (fig. 15-16). Loop a longer keeper sling (or a second carabiner) through the eye of the pin and clip it in to the hero loop or hero-loop carabiner. The keeper sling does not bear weight, but will catch the pin if it pops out.

Stacking and Nesting

When no single pin, chock, or camming device fits the crack at hand, aid climbing gets very creative. Whether you have run out of the proper-size pieces or are facing a shallow, flaring crack and need a placement to provide protection against a fall, it is time to improvise by stacking or nesting the hardware in whatever combination works. Blades are nested back to back and are usually driven together. If a third blade is necessary,

Fig. 15-15.
Sawed-off piton driven over a stopper. Note the non-load-bearing keeper sling on the stopper.

Fig. 15-16.
Tied-off piton. Note the use of a keeper sling through the piton eye.

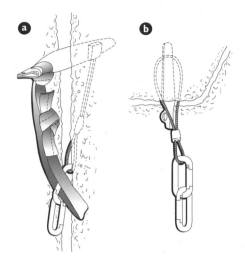

Fig. 15-17.
Camming combinations: a, piton and chock; b, piton and wire hanger (keeper sling omitted for clarity).

the first two are inserted by hand, and then the third is driven in between them.

There is some disagreement about the best way to stack angles. Some climbers stack them by keeping the spines of both angles against each other and the edges of each piton into the rock, but any combination will work. Try to avoid stacking angles by simply placing one over the other, because these may be very hard to separate once they are removed. The Leeper Z-style pitons are especially useful for stacking.

It may be possible to use a camming combination of a pin and a chock (fig. 15-17a)—or a pin and a wire hanger (fig. 15-17b)—in very difficult situations. The concept relies on the camming force exerted by the chock or wire on the back of the pin. The chock or wire loop is partially inserted into the crack. Then the pin is inserted to anchor the chock or wire and to create an artificial wall against which the chock or wire can cam. A solid aid placement can often be achieved this way with minimal use of the hammer. Note, however, that wires used this way wear quickly.

These special combinations present another

situation that requires non-load-bearing keeper slings to catch any pitons should the placement fail.

Many of the above time-consuming and complicated placements can be avoided by using camming hooks. These placements should be contemplated only if the placement must be made to protect against the consequences of a fall.

Skyhook and Camming Hook Placement and Use

Before placing a hook, clip an etrier to it and make sure to connect a sling (or daisy chain) between the etrier's carabiner and your harness. This connection, and the carabiner connecting the etriers and daisy chains, will prevent the loss of gear if the hook pops off its purchase. Test all hook types gently before applying your full body weight (or gently "ooze" your weight onto the hook). Avoid standing with your face directly in front of the hook because it could pop out with a good deal of force. When you are choosing the kind of hook to use, always consider the type of rock you are climbing. For example, sandstone (especially when it is wet)

285

may fail if it is loaded by a camming hook, which may create too much bearing stress on the rock.

To place a skyhook, set the hook on the ledge, flake, or hole where it will be used. If the hook is used in a shallow bolt hole, it is sometimes useful to give a very slight tap to set the hook's point. However, this practice increases the possibility that the hook will pop out. It also erodes the existing hole or feature, which means that eventually it will be enlarged to the point where a bolt will need to be placed. A skyhook can sometimes be placed on a fixed bashie that has lost its wire.

Camming hooks should be placed in the crack or pocket in a fashion that will cause the hook to bind up and cause the rotation of the device to create a bearing force on the rock. These camming-hook placements rely on the large friction force created by the torque of the hook into the rock. With practice, you can place camming hooks in many unlikely positions and orientations. Many camming-hook designs are available, with various bearing stresses. Some camming hooks are designed specifically for delicate expanding flakes and features. The tighter the camming hook fits into the crack (the closer the width of the metal sheet is to the width of the crack), the more secure the placement and the less potential there is to do any damage to the rock.

Malleable Placements

Because you often cannot tell how secure placements of malleable heads are, do not use them except in a pocket or flare where other protection just will not work.

Copper heads, aluminum heads, and circleheads take more practice to place than other types of aid, and placing them requires some specialized tools. The hammer pick works for setting large heads, but small heads require a striking tool such as a blunt chisel or, in a pinch, a Lost Arrow. Using a striking tool reduces the likelihood of a missed hit, which causes undue damage to the rock. Figure 15-18 illustrates the following procedure for placing a head.

1. **Place it:** Insert a head as you would a chock—in a narrowing portion of a flare or seam (fig. 15-18a).
2. **"X" it:** Pound it in using angled strokes that form an X pattern on the head (fig. 15-18b).
3. **Paste it:** Now pound the right and left sides to "pin" the head (fig. 15-18c).
4. **Rotate it:** Hit the bottom and top to see whether the head rotates (fig. 15-18d). If so, X it and paste it again.
5. **Use it:** Heads are used like any other aid piece—but remember their inescapable weakness. Inspection cannot guarantee that the head has been molded to the rock. Some heads may hold a short fall, others will support just your body weight, and others might fail. All malleable head placements are suspect, and acceptance of this fact is inherent to their use.

BASIC AID TECHNIQUES

Before you start to lead any aid pitch, study the terrain and make a plan. Determine the best rest spots. Figure out how to minimize rope drag. Plan what gear you will need and what you can leave for the second to carry. Spot any obstructions that might plague sack hauling. Decide whether to save aid pieces of certain sizes for the end of the pitch.

Then gear up for the pitch. Place chocks and other

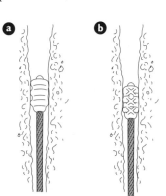

Fig. 15-18.
Placing a malleable piece:
a, place it;
b, "X" it;
c, paste it;
d, test it for rotation.

gear for clean aid climbing on one side of the rack, with the larger pieces to the rear. Place pitons (between three and six to a carabiner) and hooks on the other side of the rack, again with the larger pieces to the rear. Some climbers clip camming hooks or other commonly used pieces directly into their etrier/daisy chain carabiner to allow them to leapfrog where a point of protection is not available or not needed. Balance the rack's weight by racking free carabiners in groups of four (two pairs). Single slings are best racked over your shoulder or shortened like quickdraws. Quickdraws and/or short slings should be clipped to an easily accessible part of your harness. Often it is useful for the leader to have a chock pick to coax difficult gear into acceptable placements or to remove unsettled placements. Finally, check that your hammer, if you are carrying one, is accessible, with its sling untangled.

The Basic Sequence

The basic aid sequence (fig. 15-19) is the same whether you are starting from the ground, from a comfortable free stance, or from the top step of your etriers.

1. Look at and feel the terrain above you, and select an aid piece to place at the highest spot within reach (fig. 15-19a).
2. Place the piece (fig. 15-19b).
3. Clip in a free carabiner. Some climbers prefer to clip in a two-carabiner chain (fig. 15-19c); the second carabiner will later take the climbing rope. Other climbers feel that two carabiners get in the way at this point. Still others climbers prefer to first clip a single sling with two carabiners, or a quickdraw, in to the placement.
4. If the aid piece on which you are currently placing your body weight (weighting) is questionable and if you are positive the higher placement is solid, you may want to immediately clip the rope to the second carabiner of the higher piece. Otherwise do not clip the rope into the higher piece yet. Note that this "quick clipping" adds considerable distance to a potential fall.
5. With a single oval carabiner, clip your free etrier(s) and the end of the daisy chain into the carabiner on the higher piece—the higher of the two carabiners if two were used (fig. 15-19c).

6. Test the new piece with a gentle, one-footed hop (keep your other foot in an etrier on the lower piece). If the new piece is questionable, not intended for more than body weight, or behind an expanding feature, you may decide to avoid the body-weight test, hand-set the placement (if appropriate) with a firm tug, and simply "ooze" onto the new placement, applying your weight as gradually and smoothly as possible. Some climbers rely on their experience and knowledge of the specific rock type to set good placements and forgo anything more than hand-setting the placement. Others believe that the only method for maintaining good health is vigorous full-body-weight-bounce testing. The only certainty is that vigorous testing requires vigorous cleaning of most clean placements and may accelerate wear or damage to the gear, particularly stems and trigger wires of SLCDs. Warn your belayer when you are about to test or move onto a dubious placement.
7. Move onto the higher etrier(s) (fig. 15-19d). Clip the daisy chain in short to the new piece while you are still in the lower step, if you wish.
8. Remove the lower etrier(s) (fig. 15-19d). For extended aid climbing, some climbers carry two pairs of step-type etriers. In that case, remove the lower pair and clip it to your harness. (If you are climbing with just a single pair of etriers or the adjustable type of etriers, remove the lower etrier and clip it to the highest aid piece or to the lower carabiner on the higher piece.) Climb up the etriers until the daisy chain (or fifi hook) can be clipped in close to the new piece, if you wish. This can reduce fatigue by allowing you to rest on your harness while you assess the next move.
9. Add a second carabiner (in chain fashion) to the new piece and clip in the rope. If you initially clipped two carabiners to the piece, clip the rope in to the lower carabiner (fig. 15-19e).
10. Study the area immediately above you to determine likely spots for the next placement. Then climb as high as possible, reclip the daisy if desired, and begin the process anew. How high you climb in your etriers depends on the terrain but, ideally, place the new piece from the top step.

15

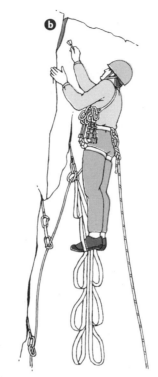

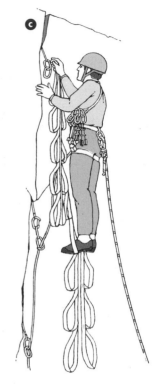

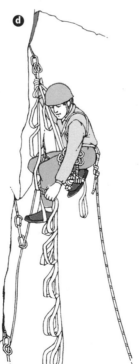

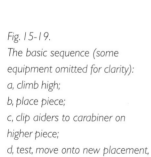

Fig. 15-19.
The basic sequence (some
equipment omitted for clarity):
a, climb high;
b, place piece;
c, clip aiders to carabiner on
higher piece;
d, test, move onto new placement,
remove lower aiders;
e, clip rope into lower carabiner
on new piece and clip in daisy
chain if desired.

SPECIAL CONSIDERATIONS

Problems you encounter while aid climbing may cause you to add variations to the basic sequence.

■ As in free climbing, rope drag can become a problem. Use long slings and/or quickdraws to keep the rope running straight. Still, always clip at least one etrier in to the highest carabiner of the next higher piece so that you get the maximum elevation gain from each placement.

■ You may also realize that you are short on aid pieces of a certain size and will need to reuse these sizes. As you move onto a higher placement, pull the piece you were just using and save it for future use. If this can be foreseen, using a good camming-hook placement is much more efficient.

■ As a general rule, leave at least every other piece in as protection against a fall. Always leave all critical protection placements to protect against an injurious fall onto slabs, ledges, and/or pendulums into corners or other features. Remember, falls while leading aid climbing tend to be head first.

Top Stepping

Moving onto the top step of your etriers can be unnerving, but being able to do so greatly improves the efficiency of aid climbing. The process is simple on low-angle rock, where the top steps are used like any other foothold and your hands provide balance. Sometimes it is faster and less fatiguing to make multiple placements from lower than the top step. However, the ideal is to top-step in a timely fashion.

Vertical and overhanging rock make top stepping difficult because your center of gravity moves away from the rock and above the point where the etriers are clipped to the aid placement. If the rock offers any features, your hands or a handheld intermediate placement may provide the balance. If the rock is blank and the placement suitable, keep your weight on your feet while you lean back and apply tension to the daisy chain between your harness and your aid placement. That tension provides the means of balancing yourself (fig. 15-20).

Resting

Do not wear yourself out. Climb in a relaxed fashion and take rests as often as necessary to conserve your strength or plot the next series of moves. Here is a quick and easy rest position:

With each foot in separate etriers and one foot one step below the other, bend the knee of your higher leg and bring that foot under you. Most of your weight now rests over your bent leg. Your outstretched leg takes minimal weight but maintains balance (fig. 15-21).

You can also clip your daisy chain or fifi hook into the piece supporting you and rest in your harness.

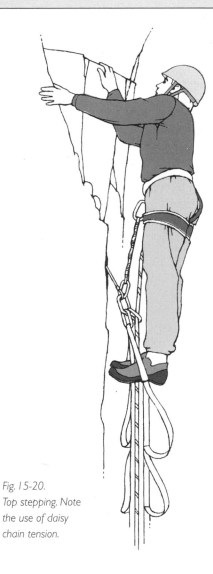

Fig. 15-20.
Top stepping. Note
the use of daisy
chain tension.

15

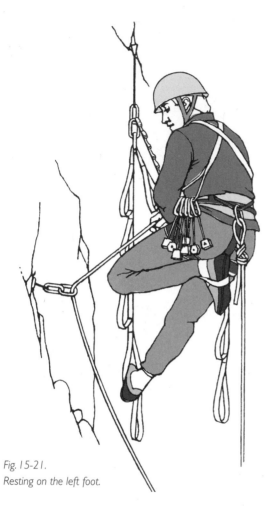

Fig. 15-21.
Resting on the left foot.

15

From Free to Aid

Free climbers must remember that the switch to aid requires some preparation. Begin the aid sequence before stretching yourself to the limit of your ability. This is easy if you know you will be changing to aid, but if you are not expecting to use aid and suddenly need it, problems arise. Finding yourself in this bind, you can improvise etriers by interconnecting several slings and then aid-cimb your way over the blank area. Such creativity is particularly important when you are climbing in a remote alpine environment. It may damage the climb's style, but it will spare time and your body.

From Aid to Free

It is best to continue climbing on aid until you can comfortably switch to free techniques. If you make the change too early, retrieving your etriers from the last aid placement may be difficult. To free-climb a few moves during an aid pitch, simply clip the etriers to the back of your harness and then make the moves.

When you are beginning a longer section of free climbing, clip etriers and daisy chains to your harness gear loops and be sure they will not hinder your movement. This may entail removing most of your aid implements and hanging them on the back of your harness.

Tension Traverses and Pendulums

Tension traverses and pendulums allow you to move horizontally across blank sections of a wall that would normally require placement of bolts.

Tension Traverses

This is the simpler technique, useful for short traverses. The leader takes tension from the belayer and then leans to the side and uses friction on small holds to work sideways.

Pendulums

Pendulums let you cross wider blank sections without bolts, but often they require more ropes and pose special problems for the second climber. Start by placing a bombproof anchor at the top of the planned pendulum. The equipment used for this anchor cannot be retrieved unless it is possible to come back to it from above.

Next, have the belayer lower you (or you can rappel

Once you have clipped the climbing rope in to the supporting piece, you can ask the belayer for tension and rest on the climbing rope. This is not an efficient method, however, due to stretch in the rope and the need for verbal communication. It also places unnecessary strain on the belay system.

Finally, you can often find relaxing stances in your etriers. Generally, you get the greatest stability by standing with your heels together and toes spread apart against the rock.

Switching Between Aid and Free Climbing

Timing is the key problem in switching between the techniques of aid and free climbing.

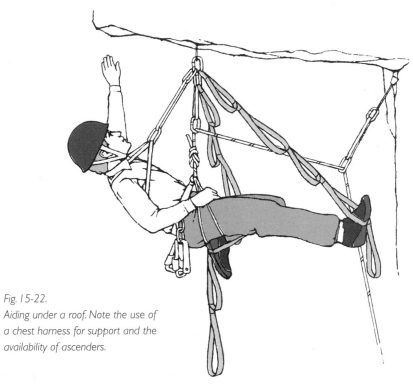

Fig. 15-22.
Aiding under a roof. Note the use of
a chest harness for support and the
availability of ascenders.

while on belay) until you have enough rope to run back and forth across the rock and swing into a new crack system. If you use a rappel for the pendulum, an extra rope is required. When you are being lowered by the belayer, it is better to be lowered too little than too much, because if you are too low, it may be very difficult to correct the error.

Once you are in the new crack system, climb as high as safety allows before clipping your belayed climbing rope into aid pieces for protection. The higher you get, the easier and safer it is for your belayer, who will second the pendulum.

For more details on pendulum technique, see "Seconding Pendulums" later in this chapter.

Overhangs

Before you lead an overhang, check that you have enough equipment for the job. It may be impossible to obtain more gear later from the second climber. Keep your ascenders handy, because if a piece pulls out and you end up hanging, you will need ascenders to climb back up to your last secure piece. Also, check that your belayer is securely anchored (as always!), or

in the event of a fall you could both end up hanging free in space.

It is difficult to balance while you are scaling an overhang because you cannot effectively place your feet against the rock. You can use a daisy chain or fifi hook, however, which allows you to hang from the harness and achieve a stable position. As an overhang becomes horizontal, achieve even greater balance by clipping a sling from your chest harness to the supporting aid piece (fig. 15-22).

Despite the difference in balance, for aiding over a roof you use the same basic sequence as described in "The Basic Sequence," above. Expect to experience some swinging. Because your belayer will probably aid-climb over the overhang rather than use ascenders, consider the length of your partner's reach when you make your placements. Consider back-cleaning the roof to allow the second to simply jumar up the fixed line, although this may cause the second climber to experience a pendulum into space.

Rope drag is a common side effect of overhangs, but liberal use of longer slings helps. You may also want to pull along a second belay rope and start climbing on it

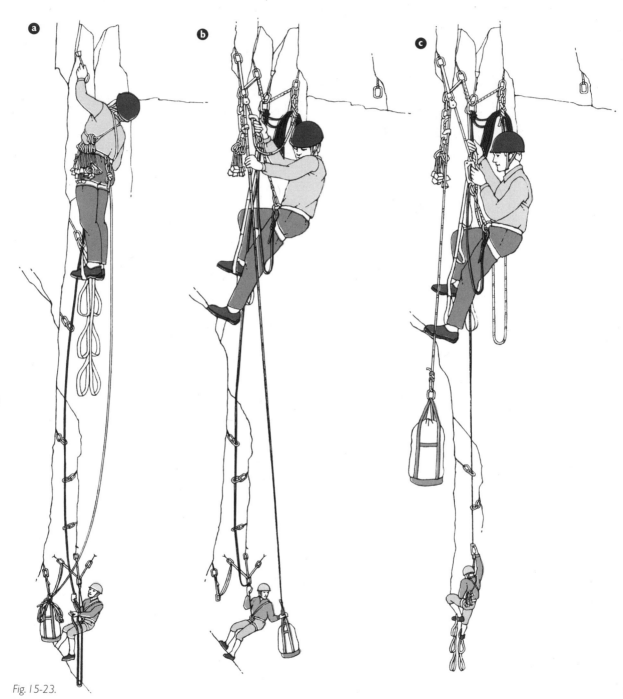

Fig. 15-23.

Hanging belay sequence: a, leader establishes anchor; b, with climbing rope anchored and the haul system set, the second frees the haul sack (note that the first piece of the next pitch is set); c, while the second jugs, the leader hauls the sack; d, the haul sack is anchored, and the second moves onto the first piece of the next pitch; e, after reracking, the new leader begins to lead.

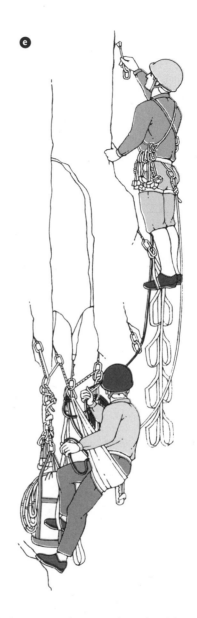

after you clear the lip of the overhang. Finally, try to relax when you are working out over a big roof. Have confidence in your pieces. Clutching at them will not keep them in place, but will drain your strength.

Hanging Belays

Upon reaching the end of a pitch, the leader establishes an anchor as a new belay station (fig. 15-23a). Place this anchor, when possible, to the side of the route (especially if you are sack hauling) so that your second can easily climb through (climb past it). Also try to place at least one aid piece at the start of the next pitch (fig. 15-23b) to give the second a stance while you are changing leads (fig. 15-23e).

When you are establishing your anchor, make sure all anchor points (including the haul anchor) are connected to all other anchor points. If an existing anchor system is in place, do not simply place a sling over the system. This is an easy mistake to make, and experienced climbers have paid for this error with their lives.

Instead, clip in in such a way that, should any portion of the anchor fail, your attachment will not slide off the failed end.

Similarly, complete anchor systems have failed when a separate haul anchor, which was not interconnected with the main anchor, failed. In these cases, the force generated by the falling haul sack overloaded the main anchor.

Once you are clipped in to the anchor system, you can anchor the climbing rope with a figure-eight loop knot so that the second can ascend it as a fixed line. Consider first pulling up the slack in the rope to be fixed. Inform the second that the rope is fixed. Now prepare the hauling system, if one is needed (see "Hauling," later in this chapter). Inform the second to free the haul sack so that you can hoist it while the second ascends the fixed climbing rope (fig. 15-23c).

After the hauling is completed (or after the climbing rope is fixed, if you are not hauling), establish your belay seat, get comfortable, and prepare for the exchange of leads. Sort the rack, organize the ropes, prepare your belay system, and so forth (fig. 15-23d).

Tyrolean Traverses

Tyrolean traverses are most often used to return to a main wall after you ascend a detached pillar. Ropes are strung between the main wall and the top of the pillar, allowing you to traverse through the air, attached to the rope. A Tyrolean traverse can be established this way:

1. After you set up a bombproof anchor on the main wall—one that can take both a horizontal and a vertical pull—rappel on two ropes to the saddle between the main wall and the pinnacle. (Use just one rope for the rappel if the traverse is short enough.) Do not pull down the rappel ropes. If it takes more than one rappel to reach the saddle, tie a light line to the two ends of the main rappel rope to make it possible to retrieve the ends once you are atop the pinnacle.

2. Climb the pinnacle using an additional climbing rope. The second climber brings up the free ends of the rappel ropes.

3. Once both climbers are atop the pinnacle, stretch the free ends of the rappel ropes (now the traverse ropes) tight and anchor them to the pinnacle. After the traverse, you will not be able to recover the equipment used for the pinnacle anchor.

4. While you are belayed, you now jug across the open area on one of the ropes, using the Texas prusik (see "Rescue Methods" in Chapter 17, Glacier Travel and Crevasse Rescue). The forward ascender is attached to your harness with a daisy chain, an etrier is attached to the rear ascender, and a daisy chain is attached to your harness. Finally, connect an additional safety sling between the traverse rope and the harness. This sling rides on a carabiner between the two ascenders. What would normally be the lower ends of the ascenders must be clipped to the rope with a safety carabiner (as recommended by the ascender manufacturer).

5. After you have jugged across, the second climber unties the ropes at the pinnacle anchor, threads the end of one rope through the anchor, and ties the ropes together as if preparing a rappel. The second notes which rope will be pulled when it comes time to retrieve the ropes. (If it is a short traverse and just a single rope is being used, the climbers on each side of the traverse need to pull the rope around so that its center moves to the pinnacle anchor and the two ends are back on the main wall; otherwise, you will have problems retrieving the rope later.)

6. You then tighten and anchor the rope ends on the main wall and belay the second, who traverses in the same manner as you.

7. Once both climbers are reunited, untie the ropes at the main wall and retrieve them by pulling on the appropriate rope.

SECONDING

On short sections of aid, the second climber usually follows the same sequence as the leader, except that the second is belayed from above. However, the second unclips the rope from a placement before clipping on the etriers, and cleans the placement below after stepping up higher. If the second cannot reach a lower piece after moving up, lengthen the etriers with another sling and then step down to clean the piece.

Long sections of aid call for a different strategy. Use mechanical ascenders to jug the fixed climbing rope and clean the route as you go. Before you head up, free the haul bag so the leader can start hauling it up the route. If it hangs up along the way, you will be the one to free it.

Using Ascenders

Although the second could ascend fixed climbing ropes on slings attached with prusik knots, mechanical

Fig. 15-24.
*Use of ascenders. Note
daisy chains from each
ascender to harness,
and climber tied in short.*

you are ascending. Remaining tied in serves as a backup in case both ascenders fail. To further decrease the likelihood of a long fall, periodically "tie in short."

Tying in short is an easy precaution that has saved lives. As the second ascends, an ever-lengthening loop of climbing rope forms below the climber, making for a long fall if the ascenders fail. To avoid this danger, stop periodically and, using the climbing rope just below the ascenders, tie a figure-eight loop and clip the loop into your harness with a locking carabiner. This guarantees a much shorter fall. Repeat this procedure about every 20 feet (6 meters). Each time, unclip and untie the last figure-eight loop after the new figure-eight loop is clipped in to your harness. If there are rock features that may snag the rope loop as you ascend, consider transferring the figure-eight loop to a harness gear sling. Even when you are tied in short, do not untie from the end of the rope.

Often while you are jugging, particularly on diagonal sections, you must remove the upper ascender from the rope and place it above a piece from which the rope cannot be unclipped while it is weighted from below. This same situation arises when the rope runs over an edge. It is convenient to tie in short before you remove the ascender.

After you reattach the upper ascender above the piece, check that the ascender's cam trigger is fully locked so that the ascender cannot pop off the rope. This is especially crucial when you are jugging on a diagonal rope, because the ascender has a tendency to twist to a vertical position once weighted. Minimize twisting by clipping a carabiner between the ascender and the rope. Once the upper ascender is reattached and your weight is on it, unclip the rope from the problem piece of aid. Take care to assure that the lower ascender is far enough below the piece of aid so that when the ascender above is weighted, the rope does not jam the lower ascender into the piece of aid.

There are other precautions to take while you are ascending. First, carry a spare prusik sling just in case an ascender fails. And, as in all climbing, beware of sharp edges. Jugging places the rope under tension, and sharp edges can cut it. Ascend as smoothly as possible to minimize the sawing motion of the rope running over an edge.

ascenders are more efficient (fig. 15-24). Attach an etrier and a daisy chain to each ascender. The etriers give you a platform to stand on, and the daisy chains positively connect the ascenders to your harness. Use a carabiner—not a fifi hook—to clip each daisy chain and etrier to an ascender. To expedite the process of preparing your ascenders, mark the loops on both the daisies and etriers where the gear is adjusted for the proper length while you are jugging.

Do not untie from the end of the climbing rope while

TIPS FOR CLEANING PINS

1. Attach a cleaner biner (a carabiner no longer used for climbing) and a sling to the pin. Pull out on the sling while tapping the pin back and forth until the pin pops out (fig. 15-25a).
2. Place the pick of the hammer in the pin's eye and pry out on the loose pin, taking care not to break the hammer (fig. 15-25b).
3. Attach a cleaner biner and sling to the loose pin, and then attach the sling to the hammer's eye with another carabiner. Starting with slack in the sling, swing the hammer in the direction the pin should come out (fig. 15-25c).
4. Because you can reuse the heads of malleable placements only a limited number of times, it is often best to leave them fixed. This is especially true if it seems likely that the wire will pull off the head as you remove the piece. If you decide to remove a malleable piece, attach a cleaner biner and sling between the head and your hammer. Then, as with pins, give the hammer a quick swing outward. It may take several swings before the head pops out. Inspect the head closely before you reuse it, because they deteriorate quickly. If your attempt to remove the head merely strips the wire away, take the time to clean the head out of the rock. It is easier for you to do so on a fixed rope than for another climber on lead.

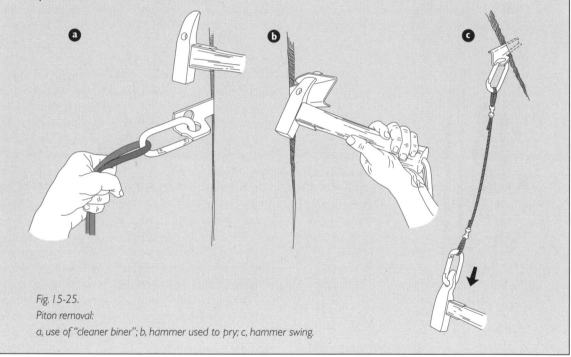

Fig. 15-25.
Piton removal:
a, use of "cleaner biner"; b, hammer used to pry; c, hammer swing.

Cleaning

Efficiency in aid climbing is very much related to organization. While you are ascending and cleaning a pitch, rack the equipment as it will be placed on the lead rack. This greatly facilitates the lead changes.

Clean protection and aid placements that are lightly set often pop out if you jug right through them. Lift up on the placement as you slide your ascender up the rope. If clean aid has been used, you can often ascend from one tying-off-short spot to the next without stopping. After tying in short again, rack the pieces that have accumulated on the rope above your ascender.

This general system works even if a placement does not pop out as you move the ascenders up. Keep the piece clipped in to the climbing rope and use a chock pick and hammer to dislodge it. Once it pops free, continue ascending without reracking until you tie in short again. If, however, you must remove the upper ascender frequently, rack the pieces as they are removed.

Fixed pins found on the route should be left in place unless they are obviously unsafe or interfere with a chock placement. Take care not to break the eyes off these old pins, which leaves them useless.

When you are cleaning one of your own pins, pound it upward, along the axis of the crack, as far as it will go and then back down to its original position. This technique, rather than pounding it back and forth as far as it will go in each direction, tends to create a future nut placement. Once the pin is loose enough to move easily back and forth, remove it by any of several means shown in Figure 15-25 (see sidebar).

Seconding Traverses and Overhangs

When you are traversing a long distance, it is generally more efficient to aid across the traverse as if you were leading. Aiding in this fashion, you can receive a belay from above. You can also self-belay by attaching ascenders to your harness with slings and sliding the ascenders along the climbing rope as you aid. When using the latter method, tie in short from time to time.

You can cross short traverses and those that are more diagonal than horizontal by using normal jugging (mechanical ascender) techniques. The closer to horizontal the traverse is, the less efficient this technique becomes, because at each piece, you are faced with a small pendulum.

When you are jugging, remove the upper ascender at each placement and move it as far as possible above the currently weighted piece. This practice minimizes the pendulum that results when you transfer your weight onto the upper ascender. Before you do this, however, allow some distance between the lower ascender and the placement so that the lower ascender does not jam into the piece as you transfer your weight to the upper ascender. Also, be sure to still tie in short at regular intervals.

The same basic methods just described for traverses also apply to seconding overhangs.

Seconding Pendulums

The best method for seconding a pendulum depends on the length of the pendulum and the ropes that are available. The placements, slinging, and carabiner for the pendulum anchor usually all must be left behind, unless they can be reached from above after the pendulum is completed.

Seconding Long Pendulums

All long pendulums require at least one rope in addition to the climbing and haul ropes. There are a number of ways to second a long pendulum, but the following method (fig. 15-26) will handle all such cases.

1. All pendulums begin with a leader, of course, who rappels off a bombproof pendulum point using either one rope or two ropes tied together, depending on the width of the pendulum; clip the rappel rope in to the anchor so there is no danger of losing it. While on the pendulum, the leader is belayed on the climbing rope, which is not clipped in to the pendulum anchor (fig. 15-26a). At the bottom of the rappel, the leader runs back and forth across the rock to gain enough momentum to swing into the new crack system. On a very long pendulum, the leader may haul along an extra belay rope. The belayer keeps one end of this rope as the leader drags the other end.

2. The leader ascends the new crack system (fig. 15-26b) and sets up an anchor. The leader attaches the climbing rope and the extra belay rope to the new anchor, the latter to serve as a belay rope for the second climber.

3. With the leader now set to belay, the second climber frees the haul bag or lowers it. The follower also unclips the rappel rope tie-in from the pendulum anchor so the rope can be retrieved later. (The follower can clip one end of the rappel rope to an out-of-the-way place on the seat harness to again ensure that the rope cannot be dropped.)

4. The follower rappels the pendulum, with the leader belaying and helping to pull the follower toward the new crack system at the end of the pendulum (fig. 15-26c). (If the leader did not drag an extra pendulum rope across, there is an alternative: The

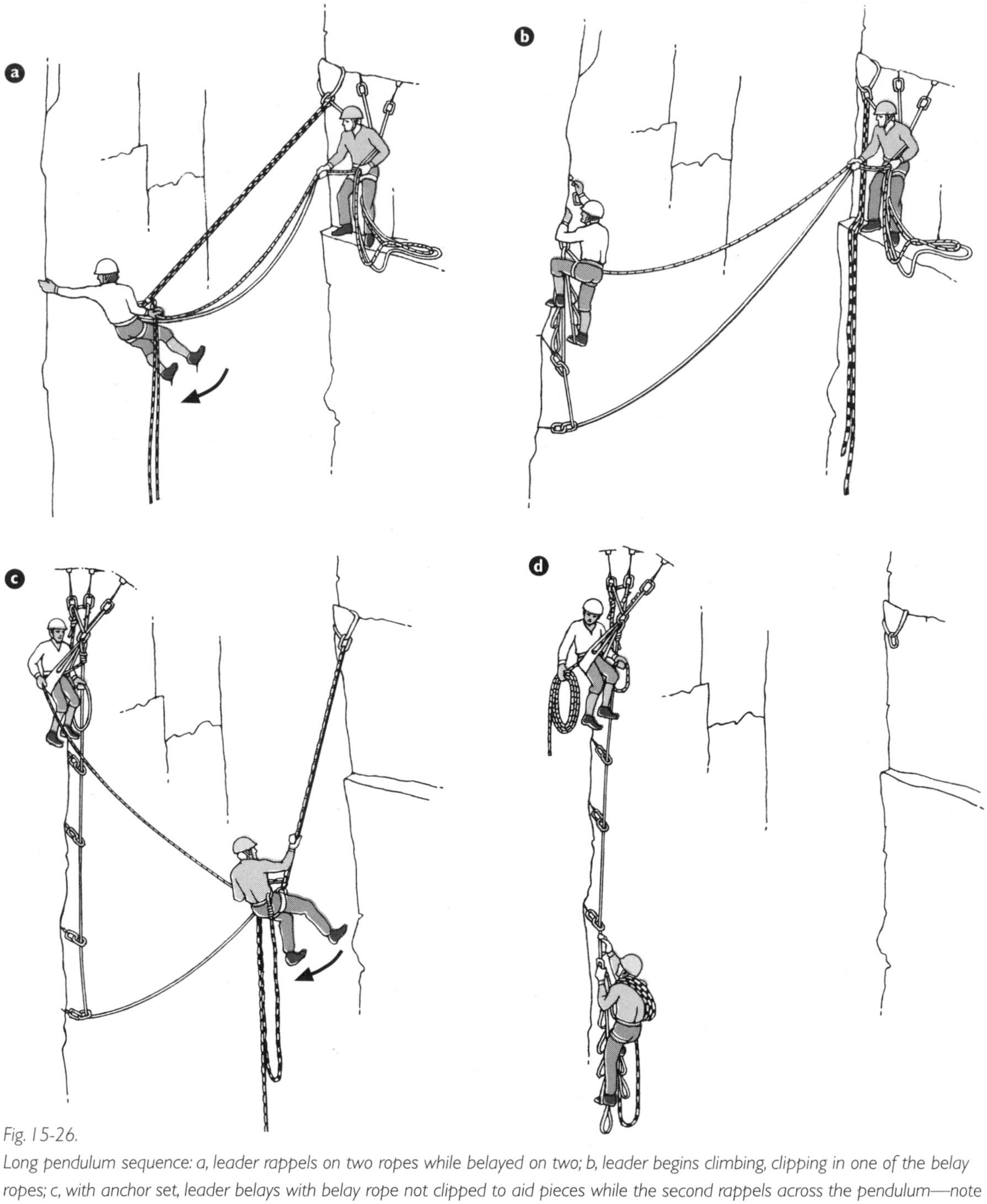

Fig. 15-26.
Long pendulum sequence: a, leader rappels on two ropes while belayed on two; b, leader begins climbing, clipping in one of the belay ropes; c, with anchor set, leader belays with belay rope not clipped to aid pieces while the second rappels across the pendulum—note that the end of one rappel rope is attached to the second climber to prevent its loss; d, the second pulls the rappel ropes, ties in short, and jugs the anchored climbing rope.

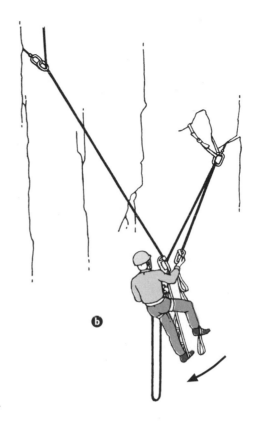

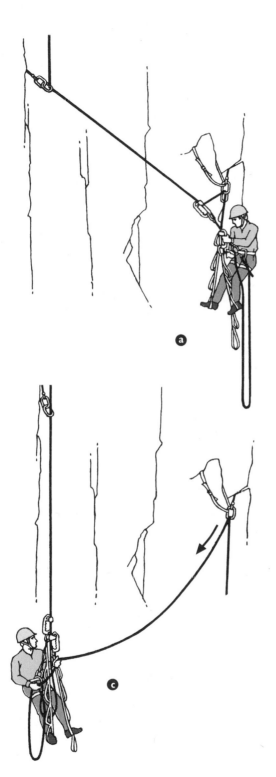

Fig. 15-27.
Seconding a short pendulum: a, after climbing to the pendulum anchor, the second prepares ascenders; b, the second lowers himself across the pendulum with a rappel device and lower ascender held open; c, the second ties in short, unties from the end of the rope, pulls the rope through the anchor, and reties the end of the rope.

15

TIPS FOR CHANGING LEADS

Following are several methods to improve organization of the belay station:

- All ropes should be different colors so you can easily separate and keep track of them.
- After hauling the sack, the leader stacks the haul line and organizes the other ropes and hardware at the anchor.
- Once the second arrives at the anchor and begins consolidating the lead rack, the original leader (now the belayer) makes butterfly coils in the climbing rope and stacks these coils at the anchor with a sling. This prevents the climbing rope from getting snagged and tangled and helps it pay out smoothly.
- If the second is carrying a rucksack, pack it with gear that will not be used on the next pitch and clip the rucksack in to the anchor.
- The original second (now the leader) clips the free end of the haul rope to the harness, is placed on belay, and starts climbing.

---

second can pull across the pendulum on the lead climbing rope by hand or with the help of mechanical ascenders.) Safely across, the second attaches ascenders to the climbing rope, ties off short, retrieves the rappel rope, and is ready to climb up the new crack system (fig. 15-26d).

Seconding Short Pendulums

Climbers also have a variety of ways to handle the challenge of seconding a short pendulum. One clever and useful method is shown in Figure 15-27. For this method to work, the slack rope from the pendulum anchor to the follower's harness must be at least double the arc of the pendulum. The follower stays tied in to the climbing rope during the sequence. The follower can second a short pendulum in this manner:

1. Facing across the pendulum, connect the upper ascender with its attached etrier to the climbing rope beyond the pendulum anchor (fig. 15-27a). Clip a daisy chain from your harness to the ascender. Connect the lower ascender and etrier to the section of rope between the pendulum anchor and yourself. Clip it in with another daisy chain. Place your weight on the upper ascender.
2. Next, attach a rappel device to the rope, below the lower ascender, and grasp the rope where it exits the device. Then, while keeping the safety trigger locked, release the cam of the lower ascender by pulling on the rope below it (this takes some effort). You are now ready to move.
3. With one hand grasping the climbing rope as it leaves the rappel device and the other hand

sliding the lower ascender, lower yourself across the pendulum (fig. 15-27b). To put the brakes on at any time, simply let go of the lower ascender and the cam will again lock. (If you do not use a rappel device, this ascender will often lock onto the rope by itself, requiring you to repeat the previous tactic of pulling hard on the rope below it.)

4. Once you are across the pendulum, tie in short and move the lower ascender above that point (fig. 15-27c). Now untie yourself from the end of the rope so you can pull it through the pendulum anchor. Once you have retied into the end of the climbing rope, you are set to ascend the climbing rope again.

When seconding a short pendulum, the rappel device makes it easier to hold the rope while lowering yourself across the pendulum; however, you can also second a short pendulum as described above without the device.

Changing Leads

Unorganized belay stations can become a rat's nest of tangled ropes, twisted slings, and assorted hardware. Basic organization (see "Tips for Changing Leads" sidebar) keeps the belay station manageable and the team functioning efficiently.

BIG-WALL MULTIDAY TECHNIQUES

"Big walls," the saying goes, "are 90 percent work and 10 percent fun." Not everyone agrees with those percentages, but few climbers will say big walls are easy. There is no question that proper conditioning is essential for hauling the heavy loads and scaling multiple aid pitches.

Big walls also call for a high degree of mental composure. Inexperienced wall climbers easily find themselves the victim of heightened fears brought on by prolonged and severe exposure. If you are new to the game, perhaps you can soothe your fears by realizing that techniques for dealing with major walls are much the same as those needed for smaller climbs. Concentrate on the problem at hand and work away at the objective one move at a time.

Guidebooks and other climbers are helpful sources of information in preparing for a big wall. Beware, however, of overdependence on climbing route topos and equipment lists. Routes do change over time, especially if pins are used regularly.

Solid, efficient aid technique is a prerequisite if you are to complete a major wall within the time constraints dictated by reasonable food and water supplies. For success on the big walls, develop competence in hoisting heavy sacks up a route and the ability to live comfortably in a vertical world for days at a time.

Hauling

After anchoring yourself and fixing the climbing rope for the second, the leader begins hauling (fig. 15-28):

1. Attach a pulley, through which the haul line passes, to the haul anchor.
2. Attach an upside-down ascender to the haul line on the haul-sack side of the pulley. Clip the end of the ascender closest to the pulley (normally the bottom) in to the anchor, while counterweighting the end pointing toward the haul sack with the remains of the rack (or another weight). Alternately, you can use a pulley with an integral locking cam to simplify the system.
3. Attach a second ascender, in the normal direction, to the haul line on the opposite side of the pulley (between yourself and the pulley). Use a daisy chain to connect this ascender to your harness.
4. Push back from the wall using your legs and palms; your body weight will raise the haul sack. When you stop pushing, the upside-down ascender acts

right-side up ascender

pulley

upside-
down
ascender

15

Fig. 15-28.
Sack-hauling system: hauler is preparing to move ascender up haul line and ascend aiders for the next power haul.

as a brake to prevent the haul bag from slipping backward. You need a little slack in the climbing rope between yourself and the anchor to allow your hauling movement.

You can also haul by allowing slack of 6 to 8 feet (2 to 3 meters) between you and the anchor. Then, with the daisy chain connected between your harness and the haul-line ascender, walk down the wall 6 to 8 feet until the anchor rope tightens. Climb back to your original position by jugging or stepping up in etriers attached to the anchor, pulling the ascender with you. Repeat the process.

This method is also used if you need two people to lift a very heavy bag. Both climbers clip to the ascender on the haul rope, allow 6 to 8 feet of slack, and walk down the wall together.

Regardless of which method you use, always connect yourself to the anchor with the climbing rope.

Fixing Pitches

On long climbs, often climbers fix pitches—put up ropes and leave them in place so they can be climbed quickly with mechanical ascenders the following morning to reach the previous day's high point. Climbers fix two, three, or more pitches above the ground or beyond the bivouac site, and at the high point they leave gear that is not needed for the bivouac. The lower end of each fixed rope is attached to the anchor of the previous pitch. Take care to protect the rope from sharp edges or abrupt contours by using duct tape or other material to cover the rope or the offending feature. Intermediate anchor points, if available, reduce the bouncing that can arise from jugging multiple ropes connected in a series. Intermediate anchor points can also be used to redirect the rope around abrasion points.

The next morning the fixed pitches are jugged—one climber on a rope at a time. This gives a head start on the day and lets you warm up before new climbing begins.

Retreating

Before a major climb, plan retreat lines in case of bad weather, an accident, or another emergency. Locate other easily reached routes with speedier ascents or fixed retreat lines.

If there is no retreat route, consider carrying a bolt kit for emergencies, allowing you to place rappel anchors. Also, as you climb each pitch, consider how you would descend it. On major walls, rescues may be slow and difficult, if they are possible at all. It may be up to you to get back down in an emergency.

Living in the Vertical World

Living for days on a vertical wall of rock brings some intriguing problems. Once you drop gear, for instance, it is gone for good. All vital items must have clip-in loops. Learn about your gear so that you can use it confidently. Get acquainted with unfamiliar items, such as portaledges or hammocks, beforehand.

Climbers usually must carry all their water with them. Each climber generally needs a minimum of 2 quarts (liters) per day. For hot weather, especially if the route gets a lot of sun, carry even more, usually 1 gallon per person per day.

Waste disposal poses another challenge. Do not toss garbage down the wall. Haul it up and off the climb. Keep all bivouac sites clean and sanitary, with no sign of your passing. Chapter 7, Leave No Trace, covers disposal of human waste during big-wall climbs.

After you complete a major wall, you need to get your gear back down. Do not toss the haul bag loaded with gear off the wall. Sack tossing is illegal at popular climbing areas such as Yosemite; it endangers climbers below. Furthermore, many climbers have discovered that their gear has been stolen by the time they got back down. Carry down what you hauled up.

THE FUTURE OF AID CLIMBING

Free climbers may feel that aid climbing isolates the climber from the rock. However, anyone who has struggled to place a piece of aid while standing above a series of marginal placements understands that aid climbing is not only climbing, but a test of your technical abilities and nerves. To ensure that these routes continue to be a test of skill and nerves, aid climbers are asked to respect certain ethics.

If you are climbing an established route, adhere to the ethics of the first-ascent climbers and the current local ethics. If the first-ascent party did not need a piton or bolt, do not place one. Use creativity and boldness to overcome the difficulty. Camming hooks and other similar body-weight-only placements, including hand-placed pitons, can greatly speed a party's ascent without adding unreasonable risk. A party following you on a route should find it in the condition you found it.

Many long routes that originally required "thin nailing" (placement of very small pitons due to the very small width of the natural crack) tend to be "beaten out" until they can accept camming-hook placements and chock placements. Find out the current status of routes to check whether you need to use a hammer, and resist the temptation if possible. Nonetheless, some seldom-climbed pitches on less-than-solid rock may always require the use of a hammer.

If you are putting up a new route, you are establishing the style for those who follow. Remember that routes once considered to be difficult aid climbs have now been free climbed. Although the majority of future ascents of current aid lines will continue to be climbed with at least some aid, consider future free ascents before you reach for the hammer.

Similarly, free-ascent attempts of aid lines should not introduce new bolts to protect hard free moves. This may detract from the original challenge of the aid route. Make it your goal to climb cleanly and in a style that climbers can respect. As time goes on, more sections of today's aid routes will be free-climbed by a higher percentage of those who climb them. Many more will be climbed hammerless as the next wave of aid climbers push their limits on ever thinner and more remote climbs.

15

Next page: *Ice climber in Ouray, Colorado* (Photo by James Martin)

4

SNOW, ICE, AND ALPINE CLIMBING

Snow Travel and Climbing

EQUIPMENT ■ TECHNIQUES OF SNOW CLIMBING ■ ROPED SNOW-CLIMBING
TECHNIQUES ■ ROUTEFINDING ON SNOW ■ AVALANCHE SAFETY ■
AVALANCHE RESCUE ■ SAFE SNOW TRAVEL

**Climbing in snow is fundamental to mountaineering. Snow is magical stuff, cloaking the
landscape in a sparkling mantle. Gently falling snowflakes can be a balm to the human
spirit, an aesthetic delight. But technically, snow is rather dryly defined as
"a consolidated mass of water crystals." It is the degree of
consolidation that is significant to the climber.**

Snow falls in a variety of forms ranging from tiny
crystals to coarse pellets. Initially the snowpack can
consist of up to 90 percent air by volume. Once the
snow is on the ground, a cyclic process of melting and

freezing begins. Even though a snow climber might
be literally walking on air, climbing in snow is not to be
taken lightly. The snow becomes increasingly dense as
the air is displaced. Ultimately, the density of glacial ice

can be the same as that of ice formed directly from water. See Chapter 26, The Cycle of Snow, for more about snow.

Snow displays a broad spectrum of physical characteristics, and the distinction between hard snow and ice is rather arbitrary. Snow climbing is described in this chapter, whereas ice-climbing techniques are discussed in Chapter 18, Alpine Ice Climbing, and Chapter 19, Waterfall Ice and Mixed Climbing, but note that the techniques overlap with no distinct separation.

Climbers travel in a world that is affected by snow on two very different scales. On a rather grand scale, snow—in the form of glaciers—sculpts the terrain. On a more human scale, snow often is the climbers' landscape, largely determining how and where they can travel.

Snow travel is trickier than trail hiking or rock climbing. A rock face is essentially unchanging, whereas the snowpack undergoes rapid changes. Depending on the degree of consolidation, snow can present a widely variable surface: seemingly insubstantial and bottomless unconsolidated powder, a consistently firm and resilient surface, or rock-hard alpine ice. A snowpack that appears to be firm can under certain conditions suddenly collapse and flow (avalanche) and then quickly set as hard as concrete. Safe snow travel requires judgment based on experience.

During a single season, a snowfield may start as a dusting of snow over a brushy slope, progress to a bowlful of powder ready to avalanche, then change to a solid surface offering firm footing, and finally revert back to scattered snow patches. In the course of a day, snow can change from a firm surface in the morning to slush in the afternoon.

Snow can facilitate travel, making climbs easier by providing a pathway over brush and other obstacles on the approach hike and reducing the danger of loose rock on the ascent. But snow conditions also affect decisions on routefinding and climbing technique. Should the climbing party hike up the comfortable, snow-covered valley bottom or on the ridge crest away from avalanche hazard? Should you go for easy step-kicking up the sunny slope or the more labor-intensive climb on the firmer, more stable snow of the shaded hillside? Is it safer to travel roped or unroped? The changeable nature of snow requires you to be flexible in choosing your mode of travel, ready to use snowshoes, skis, or crampons.

EQUIPMENT

Ice axes and crampons are at the top of the basic snow-climbing equipment list. Snowshoes, skis, and ski poles are other important snow-travel aids, as are wands and shovels. Snow climbers must also construct anchors in snow (snow protection equipment is discussed under "Snow Anchors" later in this chapter).

Ice Ax

The ice ax or *piolet* (fig. 16-1) and skill in its use allow you to venture onto all forms of snow and ice, enjoying a greater variety of mountain terrain during all seasons of the year. The ice ax, an inherently simple tool, has many uses. Below the snow line, it can serve as a walking cane or be used to help you brake when you are going downhill. But its main role is in snow and ice travel, where it is a balance aid, a tool to prevent a fall, and a tool to stop a fall.

Selecting an ice ax means choosing between features designed for specific uses. A long ax is suitable for cross-country travel and scrambling, in which it is used as a cane and to provide security in low-angle climbing. However, on steeper slopes, a shorter ax is better. Axes designed for ice climbing have even shorter shafts and specialized features including the shape of pick and adze and the placement of teeth. (Ice tools are discussed in Chapter 18, Alpine Ice Climbing.)

Weight is another consideration. The adage says "Light is right"—but this should not be taken too far. Be sure to select an ax that is designed for general mountaineering. Some very light axes are meant for only light

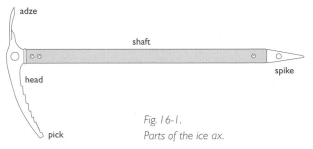

Fig. 16-1.
Parts of the ice ax.

use—that is, ski mountaineering or trekking. Ice axes that meet the CEN standards for general mountaineering (see Chapter 9, Basic Safety System) are designated by a "B." At the other extreme, technical ice axes tend to be heavier (and more expensive) than general mountaineering axes. Tools that meet the CEN standards for technical mountaineering are designated by a "T."

Parts of the Ice Ax

Head: The head of an ice ax—the pick and the adze—is typically made of steel alloy. The hole in the ax head, the carabiner hole, is used by most climbers to attach the ice-ax leash.

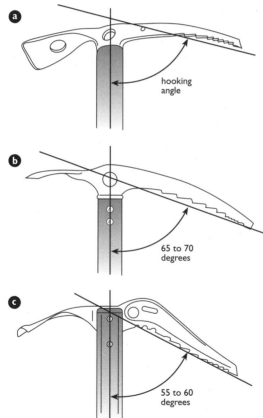

Fig. 16-2.

Ice-ax picks: a, the hooking angle is the angle of the pick relative to the shaft; b, a general mountaineering ice ax has a hooking angle of 65 to 70 degrees; c, an ice ax for technical ice climbing has a hooking angle of 55 to 60 degrees and teeth along the entire length of the pick.

Pick: The pick is curved or drooped (fig. 16-2), a design that provides better hooking action in snow or ice, enabling the ax to dig in when you are trying to stop yourself (self-arrest) after a fall. A moderate hooking angle of 65 to 70 degrees relative to the shaft is typical of general mountaineering axes (fig. 16-2b). A sharper angle of 55 to 60 degrees is better for technical ice climbing (fig. 16-2c); the more acutely angled pick holds better in ice and snow, and coincides with the arc of the tool head as you swing it. The pick teeth provide grip in ice and hard snow. Ice axes designed for general mountaineering typically have aggressive teeth only at the end of the pick, as shown in Figure 16-2b. Picks of ice axes and tools designed for technical climbing typically have teeth along the entire length, as shown in Figure 16-2c.

The pick may have positive, neutral, or negative clearance (fig. 16-3). The clearance is determined by comparing the angle of the pick tip relative to the axis of the shaft. In theory, the degree of clearance affects how the ax performs in self-arrest. A pick with positive clearance should penetrate more readily; a pick with negative clearance would tend to skate on ice or hard snow. However, the clearance actually makes little difference: Self-arrest is almost impossible on ice, and in softer snow the pick will dig in regardless of clearance. In any case, clearance can always be modified by using a hand file.

Adze: The adze is used mainly to cut steps in hard snow or ice. The flat top of the adze also provides a firm, comfortable platform for your hand when you are

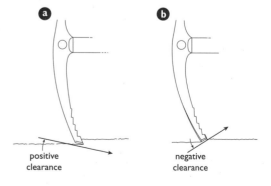

Fig. 16-3.

Ice-ax clearance: a, positive; b, negative.

using the self-belay grasp (see "Techniques of Snow Climbing" later in this chapter). Most adzes for general mountaineering are relatively flat and straight-edged and have sharp corners (see Figure 16-2a above). This is the best all-around design for cutting steps.

Shaft: Ice-ax shafts are made of aluminum or a composite material (fiberglass, Kevlar, or carbon filament), or a combination of these. Such materials are much stronger and more durable than wood, which they have replaced.

Some shafts are covered at least partly by a rubber material, which gives you a better grip and, hence, better control of the ax, and also dampens vibrations and increases your control in planting the pick. If the ax shaft lacks a rubber grip, you can wrap the shaft with athletic grip tape (for example, bicycle handlebar tape) or you can wear gloves with leather or rubberized palms. However, the friction of any shaft covering may impede the ax from readily penetrating the snow when you are using it for a boot-ax belay, for probing, or for self-belay.

Spike: The spike—the metal tip of the ax—should be sharp enough to readily penetrate snow and ice. Using the ice ax for balance on rocky trails and talus slopes dulls the spike. (See "Ice-Ax Maintenance and Safety," later in this section.)

Ice-Ax Length

Ice axes (which are described only in metric units) range in length from 40 centimeters to 90 centimeters—still much shorter than the 5-foot (1.5-meter) alpenstocks used by the alpine pioneers. The shortest axes are for technical ice climbing; the longest ones are for tall mountaineers using the ax as a cane on easy terrain.

The optimal length for an ice ax depends more on your intended use than on your height. For general mountaineering, a 70-centimeter ax is the best choice for the majority of climbers. This length offers the best compromise of balance and appropriate length for use on steep snow slopes.

Axes less than 60 centimeters long are technical ice-climbing tools, excellent for placements on very steep slopes. However, these ice tools are not as good for self-arrest; the shorter shafts offer less leverage, and many of the technical pick designs do not lend themselves to

the self-arrest technique. A 70-centimeter ax is the longest that is generally useful for technical ice climbing. Thus, a length of 60 to 70 centimeters works well in most alpine situations, where climbing is on moderately steep snow slopes and you are using the ax for self-belay and self-arrest. Longer axes are better for cross-country travel and scrambling, for snow anchors, and for probing for cornices and crevasses.

Ice-Ax Leash

The ice-ax leash provides a sure way to attach the ice ax to your wrist or harness. A leash is valuable insurance on crevassed glaciers or long, steep slopes where losing an ax would leave you without a principal safety tool and put climbers below you in danger from the runaway ax. A leash also allows you to let the ice ax hang free while you make a move or two on the occasional rock you encounter during a snow climb.

There are two schools of thought regarding the use of an ice ax leash during snow travel that requires using self-belay technique. Most climbers use a leash so that the ice ax is secure against loss. However, some climbers believe that a flailing ice ax, hanging by the leash from your wrist after you have lost your grip on the shaft, is a potential threat during a fall. Ultimately, it is a judgment call.

The leash typically consists of a piece of accessory cord or webbing attached to the carabiner hole in the ice ax head (fig. 16-4). A vast array of commercially manufactured leashes are also available. You can make a leash using either 5- or 6-millimeter perlon accessory cord or ½- to 1-inch tubular webbing. Tie the ends of the material together with a suitable knot to create a sling, girth-hitch the sling through the carabiner hole, then tie an overhand knot to form a wrist loop.

The length of a leash can vary. Short leashes (fig. 16-4a) are favored by those using ice axes for basic snow and glacier travel. The short leash is easy to use and allows you to regain control of the ice ax quickly during a fall. During an uncontrolled fall in which you lose your grip on the ax, an ax on a short leash will not flail around as much as one on a longer leash.

However, most climbers prefer a longer leash (fig. 16-4b). When you are shifting the ax from one hand to the other while you are changing direction up a snow

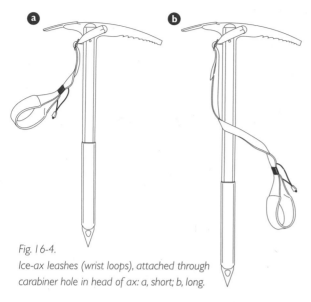

Fig. 16-4.
Ice-ax leashes (wrist loops), attached through carabiner hole in head of ax: a, short; b, long.

slope, a long leash does not need to be switched from wrist to wrist. A long leash can also be chained to a runner clipped to your seat harness, so that the ax can be used as a personal anchor. The long leash also makes the ax more versatile for climbing steep snow or ice. A long leash is usually about as long as the ax shaft, and if it is adjusted correctly, it will reduce arm fatigue during step-cutting and ice climbing. With your hand through the wrist loop, you should be able to grasp the end of the shaft near the spike.

Ice-Ax Maintenance and Safety

Ice axes require very little special care. Before each use, inspect the shaft for deep dents that might weaken it to the point of failure under load (but do not worry about minor nicks and scratches). After each climb, clean mud and dirt off the ax. Use a combination of solvents (such as a lubricating and penetrating oil) and abrasives (scouring pads or a soft ski hone—a soft synthetic block with embedded abrasive) to remove any rust.

Check the pick, adze, and spike regularly for sharpness. To sharpen, use a hand file, not a power-driven grinding wheel. High-speed grinding can overheat the metal and change the temper, diminishing the strength of the metal.

Guards are available to cover the sharp edges and points of the pick, adze, and spike.

Crampons

Crampons are a set of metal spikes you strap on over your boots to penetrate hard snow and ice where boot soles cannot gain sufficient traction. When should you wear crampons? There is no steadfast rule. Make this decision based on your skill and experience, and on your assessment of conditions. If you feel that you need to wear crampons, put them on.

Choosing among the different crampon designs involves making a trade-off between features that are essential for general alpine use and those designed for technical ice climbing.

Crampon Points

The early-model ten-point crampon was eclipsed in the 1930s by the addition of two forward-slanting or front points, which created the twelve-point crampon (see the "History of Crampons" sidebar). The front points

---

HISTORY OF CRAMPONS

Crampons are an ancient tool, invented more than 2,000 years ago. Early inhabitants of the Caucasus region wore leather sandals soled with spiked iron plates to travel on snow and ice. Celtic miners were using iron foot spikes as early as 2,700 years ago. Medieval alpine shepherds wore three-point crampons—horseshoe-shaped frames bearing three sharp spikes.

At the end of the nineteenth century, the four-point crampon was state of the art. Then in 1908, Oscar Eckenstein created the ten-point crampon. Many alpinists thought the gadgets were an unsporting advantage. However, these crampons served to relieve climbers of the tremendous tedium of cutting steps and opened up a vast array of unclimbed snow and ice faces. In 1932 Laurent Grivel added two front points, creating the twelve-point crampon, which was specifically designed for climbing steep, hard snow and ice. They have evolved into today's crampons that are essential for mountaineering.

reduced the need for step-cutting and permitted front-pointing up steep snow and ice (see Chapter 18, Alpine Ice Climbing). Currently crampons designed for general mountaineering include both twelve-point and lighter ten-point models, but all have front points.

Most crampons are made from chromium molybdenum steel, an extremely strong and lightweight alloy. However, some models are fabricated from aircraft-grade aluminum alloys, which are lighter than steel but also much softer, and these may not stand up to the rigors of rock underfoot. Snow and ice routes often include short sections of rock that are climbed wearing

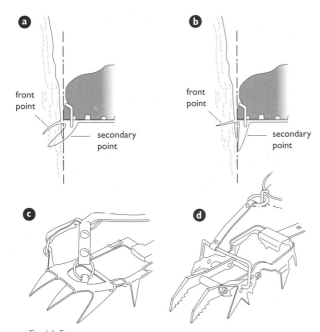

Fig. 16-5.

Angle of first two rows of points: a, best suited for front-pointing; b, for general mountaineering; c, horizontal front points; d, vertical front points.

crampons. The crampons should be able to take the punishment, but very much of this will dull the points.

The relative angles and orientation of the first two rows of points determine the best use for a set of crampons. When the first row (front points) is drooped and the second row (secondary points) is angled toward the toe of the boot (fig. 16-5a), the crampons are better suited for ice climbing (front-pointing) than for general mountaineering. This configuration allows easier engagement of the secondary points when front-pointing, which greatly reduces calf strain (see Chapter 18, Alpine Ice Climbing). In contrast, downward-angled secondary points (fig. 16-5b) facilitate a more ergonomic walking motion on moderate terrain.

Front points can also be either horizontally (fig. 16-5c) or vertically oriented (fig. 16-5d). Vertically oriented front points are designed for technical ice climbing. Their shape mimics that of an ice-ax pick. They are well suited for penetration into hard water ice, but in softer alpine ice and snow, they are prone to shearing through unless they are deeply set. In contrast, horizontally oriented front points are designed for the alpine ice and snow conditions encountered in most general mountaineering situations. They provide a larger surface area and therefore are more stable in softer snow conditions.

Hinged, Semi-rigid, and Rigid Crampons

Mountaineering crampons can be categorized into three types: hinged, semi-rigid, and rigid.

Hinged: These crampons are designed for general mountaineering (fig. 16-6a). They fit a wide variety of mountaineering boots, are light, and flex with the natural rocking action of walking. Attached to a stiff boot, hinged crampons perform nearly as well for ice climbing as rigid crampons because the boot provides the stable platform, although there may be more vibration than with a stiffer crampon.

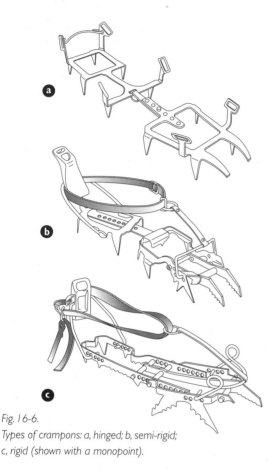

Fig. 16-6.
Types of crampons: a, hinged; b, semi-rigid; c, rigid (shown with a monopoint).

16

Semi-rigid: These crampons are designed for both general mountaineering and technical ice climbing (fig. 16-6b). They have some flex, which creates some give with a fairly stiff-soled boot. Semi-rigid crampons are designed with either horizontally or vertically oriented front points. Some semi-rigid crampons are designed so that with a reconfiguration of the linking bar, the crampon can be converted to a more ergonomic flexible walking mode, compatible with a flexible boot. They can then be readjusted for any technical front-pointing that may lie ahead.

Rigid: These crampons are designed for technical ice climbing (fig. 16-6c). They vibrate less than hinged crampons when they are kicked into the ice, and their stiffness provides more support, which helps you to conserve energy. Most rigid crampons require a very stiff boot, because a flexible boot is likely to flex out of

the attachment system, causing the crampon to pop off. Rigid crampons are generally more awkward when you are traveling on flat or rocky terrain, where some flexibility is desired, and they are typically the heaviest of all crampon types.

Crampon Attachment

There are three main crampon attachment systems available today: strap-on, step-in, and hybrid systems (fig. 16-7). In general, hinged crampons work best with strap-on systems and flexible boots. Rigid crampons work best with step-in systems and very stiff boots. And hybrid attachment systems, those with a combination of straps over the front of the boot and a rear clip, work best with semi-rigid crampons and fairly stiff boots. Ultimately the choice of an attachment system is largely dictated by the attachment platform that the boot provides.

Straps: Buckled straps do a good job of attaching crampons to nearly any boot. Neoprene-coated nylon is an excellent strap material because it is strong, does not absorb water, will not stretch, and can be easily transferred from one pair of crampons to another. Nylon webbing is strong but it absorbs water, which may cause the webbing to freeze, making it harder to manipulate. Leather straps are less expensive but stretch when wet and will eventually rot or break. Three strap-on designs are in general use:

- **The "Scottish" system:** A strap with a ring in the middle is permanently attached to the two front attachment posts. A second strap then runs from one side post through this ring to the other side post. The rear (third) and longer strap wraps around the ankle, buckling to a (fourth) short strap and connecting the two rear posts. This strap system (fig. 16-7a) is quick and convenient to use.
- **Two independent straps per crampon:** One strap wraps over the instep, connecting the front four attachment posts, and the other wraps around the ankle, connecting the two rear posts (fig. 16-7b).
- **Four independent straps per crampon:** Two short straps, with buckles, are attached to one side of the crampon and two longer straps are attached to the other side. One of the long straps wraps over the instep, buckling to the front short strap and

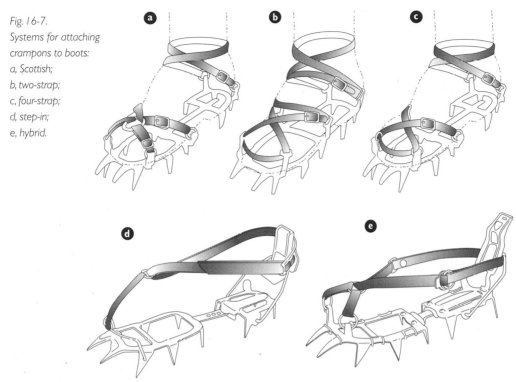

Fig. 16-7.
Systems for attaching
crampons to boots:
a, Scottish;
b, two-strap;
c, four-strap;
d, step-in;
e, hybrid.

connecting the front four attachment posts. The second long strap wraps around the ankle, buckling to the other short strap and connecting the two rear posts (fig. 16-7c).

When you are attaching straps to crampons, place the buckles on the outer side of each crampon to minimize your chances of catching an inside crampon point on a buckle. With the two-strap and four-strap systems, reduce the danger of the front straps loosening by making sure that the strap that goes through the hole at each front attachment post is threaded from the outside in, and then give it an extra twist.

Step-in bindings: The crampons attach to the boot with a wire toe bail and a heel clip or lever (fig. 16-7d). These systems are fast and easy to use. With step-in bindings, the fit of the crampon to the boot is much more critical than with crampons that are strapped on. In order to fit securely, the boot must have pronounced grooves at both the heel and toe. When the crampon is sized correctly, the heel clip should decisively "snap" into place, forcing the wire toe bail firmly into the boot

toe groove. Step-in bindings typically include a safety strap that is wrapped around your ankle to secure the crampon if it pops off your boot. Some step-in bindings also include a metal strap attached to the toe bail. The safety strap is threaded through the metal strap to prevent the crampon from popping off the boot.

Hybrid bindings: These feature toe straps combined with a heel clip (fig. 16-7e). These bindings are popular because they work well on boots that have a pronounced heel groove but lack a toe groove. As with step-in bindings, the heel clip should decisively "snap" into place, forcing the boot into the front attachment posts. These are excellent bindings for use with a mountaineering boot covered by an insulating overboot.

Crampon Fit

It is critical that crampons fit boots perfectly. When you are purchasing crampons, bring your boots to the shop for a proper crampon fitting. If the crampons will be used on more than one pair of boots, check the fit on all pairs. Be sure to purchase crampons that match the intended usage.

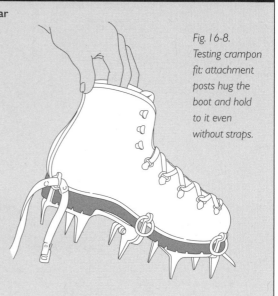

TIPS FOR FITTING CRAMPONS

- The crampon strap attachment posts at the front and rear should hug the boot snugly. Test the fit by lifting the boot with the crampon. The posts should hold to the boot without the use of the straps (fig. 16-8).
- The welt on a boot is especially important with step-in bindings, which grip the boot at toe and heel. Step-in bindings require well-defined grooves at the toe and heel on plastic and very stiff leather boots.
- The front crampon points should protrude ¾ to 1 inch (2 to 2.5 centimeters) beyond the toe of the boot.
- If you will be wearing supergaiters with a rubber rand that fits around the rand and instep of the boot, be sure to wear the gaiters when fitting the crampons.
- In very cold conditions, most climbers wear overboots to help insulate their feet from the cold and snow. As with supergaiters, crampons must be fitted with the overboots on. Make sure any attachment straps are long enough.

Fig. 16-8. Testing crampon fit: attachment posts hug the boot and hold to it even without straps.

Practice putting on the crampons while in the comfort of home. There will be plenty of opportunity to put them on under less-ideal conditions: by feel in dim light or in the limited illumination of a headlamp, fumbling with cold, numbed fingers.

Crampon Maintenance and Safety

Regular simple maintenance is required to keep your crampons safe and dependable. After every climb, clean and dry the crampons and inspect them for wear. Repair or replace worn straps, nuts, bolts, and screws. Check the points: They should be clean and reasonably sharp, though very sharp points are needed only for technical ice climbing. As with ice axes, use a hand file to sharpen overly dull crampon points (fig. 16-9). Also

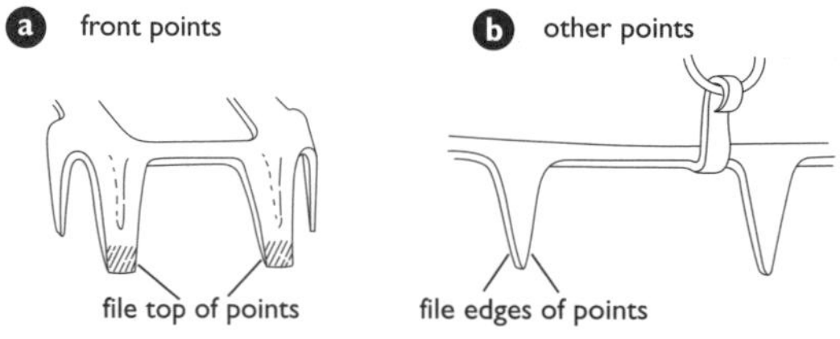

ⓐ front points   **ⓑ** other points

file top of points   file edges of points

Fig. 16-9.
How to sharpen crampons: a, front points; b, other points.

check alignment of the points—splayed points make the crampons less efficient at penetrating snow and ice and more likely to slash pants, gaiters, and legs. It is probably best to retire a pair of crampons whose points have been badly bent or overly filed.

In soft, sticky snow, crampons can accumulate a growing buildup of snow. This ball of snow can interfere with the crampon points' penetration and be dangerous, particularly where sticky snow overlays an icy base. To minimize this hazard, you can use manufactured "anti-balling plates," plastic, rubber, or vinyl sheets that fit the bottom of the crampon. Alternatively, you can wrap the bottom of the crampon with duct tape. When you encounter soft, sticky snow, consider whether crampons are really needed. It may be possible to proceed more safely without them.

Instep and Approach Crampons

Small instep crampons with four or six points are designed for crossing an occasional short snowfield. Because there are no points at the heel or toe, these crampons are not suitable for mountaineering and can be dangerous on steep snow or ice.

Approach crampons are flexible, full-length plates

CRAMPON SAFETY RULES

In the mountains, follow a few rules to protect yourself, your gear, and your climbing companions from sharp crampon points.

■ Use a crampon pouch or a set of rubber point protectors when you are carrying crampons.

■ Always bring the tools needed to adjust the crampons, as well as any necessary spare parts.

■ While climbing, step deliberately to avoid snagging pants or gaiters, gashing a leg, or stepping on the rope.

■ Be careful not to snag gear hanging low from gear loops on your harness; avoid having slings hang below your thigh.

---

that typically have eight points. Approach crampons are designed for use on moderate terrain, and also are not suitable for mountaineering.

Instep and approach crampons are not a substitute for ten- or twelve-point mountaineering crampons.

Wands

Mountaineers often use wands to mark their route to be able to retrace their path during inclement weather. Wands may also be used to indicate potential danger. Two wands forming an X indicate a known danger, such as a weak snow bridge. Wands can also be used to mark the boundaries of safe areas for unroped walking at camp and the location of buried supplies (caches).

Wands are available commercially, but climbers usually make their own, using green-stained bamboo garden stakes, topped with a colored duct-tape flag (fig. 16-10). Wands vary in length from 30 to 48 inches (0.7 to 1.2 meters). If the wand is less than 30 inches, the flag may not be seen easily; if longer than 48 inches, the wands are awkward to carry in pack compression straps.

Mark your wands with your initials and the date to be certain that you are retracing your own party's path,

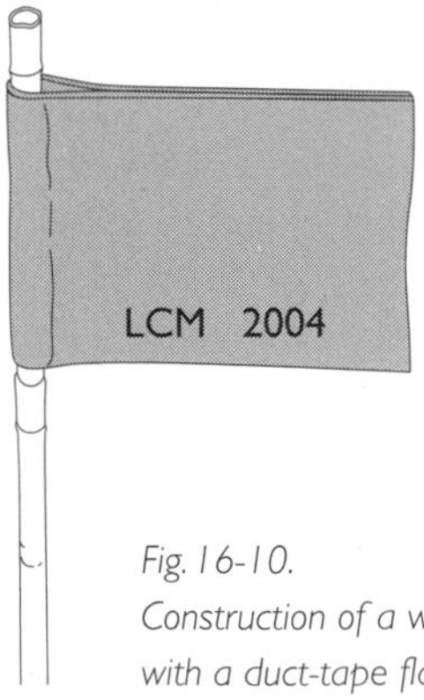

Fig. 16-10.
Construction of a wand
with a duct-tape flag.

not someone else's. Insert the wands firmly into the snow, planting them deeply enough to compensate for melting or high winds. Place them so that they indicate the direction of travel. Use long wands in winter, when they have to be inserted deeper in soft snow and when heavy snowfall can bury them. Retrieve wands on the descent.

Ski Poles

Ski poles are not only used for skiing. Ski or trekking poles can be used whether you are traveling by foot, snowshoes, or skis. Poles are better than an ice ax for balance when you are carrying a heavy pack over level or low-angle snow, slippery ground, or scree or when you are crossing a stream or boulder field. Poles also can take some of the weight off your lower body. And the basket at the bottom keeps the poles from penetrating too deeply into soft snow, which ice axes do unless they are fitted with a special snow basket.

Some ski and trekking poles have features helpful to the mountaineer. Adjustable poles enable you to set the length to suit the conditions or the terrain; on a traverse, the uphill pole can be set to a length shorter than the downhill pole. These poles can be fully compressed for easy packing. Adjustable poles require more maintenance; after each trip, disassemble, clean, and dry them.

Poles with removable baskets can serve as probes for crevasses. Some poles are made so that a pair can be fastened together to form a serviceable avalanche probe. However, this is only a poor substitute for a commercial avalanche probe.

Some ski poles can be fitted with a special self-arrest grip that has a plastic or metal-tipped pick, but on technical terrain this definitely is not a substitute for an ice ax.

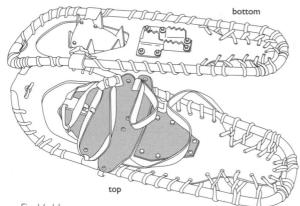

Fig. 16-11.

Modern snowshoes for winter mountaineering, with a tubular aluminum frame, a polyurethane deck, aluminum cleats, and nylon straps.

Snowshoes

Snowshoes are a traditional snow travel aid, and their design has been updated into smaller, lighter models (fig. 16-11). Modern designs include models consisting of tubular metal frames with lightweight, durable decking materials, as well as plastic composite models. Modern bindings are easy to use, are more stable than older models, and include cramponlike toothed metal plates designed to improve traction on hard snow. Many models also include serrated heel and/or side plates that decrease side-to-side slippage.

Snowshoes permit efficient travel in soft snow, where hikers laboriously posthole (sink deeply with each step). Snowshoes can be used to kick steps uphill. Although travel on snowshoes may be slower than travel on skis, snowshoes can be used in brushy or rocky terrain where skis would be awkward, and they are often more practical than skis when you are carrying a heavy pack. If the climbing party includes some people who are not very good on skis, it is much less frustrating and more efficient for the group to travel on snowshoes. Snowshoe bindings can be used with almost any footwear, whereas most ski bindings require specialized boots.

Skis

Nordic and mountaineering skis fitted with climbing skins provide a convenient mode of travel in the

mountains. The Nordic ski binding leaves the heel free and is worn with a special boot (fig. 16-12a). Depending on the design and purpose of the skis and boots, they may be used for cross-country, touring, or telemark skiing. The free heel allows the Nordic skier to use the telemark turn for downhill travel.

Ski mountaineering employs a wider, heavier ski (sometimes called a randonée ski) that is closer to a traditional alpine (downhill) ski (fig. 16-12b). The randonée binding also leaves the heel free for uphill travel, but the heel can be locked down for standard alpine downhill technique. Special randonée or alpine touring boots are designed for use with mountaineering skis. Some bindings can accommodate plastic mountaineering boots, but with significant loss of skiing performance.

Both Nordic and randonée skis permit climbers to travel the backcountry. Climbing skins (strips of rough-textured material) that can be attached temporarily to the bottom of the skis provide traction for uphill travel (fig. 16-12c).

Climbers who are not accomplished skiers may find certain disadvantages to using skis in the backcountry. When the skis must be carried, they are awkward and heavy. Wearing skis complicates self-arrest. Skis can be awkward on rocky or forested slopes, and skiing can be difficult when you are carrying a heavy pack. Every party member must have similar skiing ability for the group to keep a steady pace. This is especially true for roped glacier travel.

Skis can be faster for basic snow travel, and they can provide a way to reach areas that are otherwise not accessible. Skis offer a bonus for glacier travel: They distribute your weight over a larger area and may decrease the chance of breaking through snow bridges. Skis can also come in handy for rescue work, because they can be converted into a makeshift stretcher or sled.

Backcountry skiing is a complex activity, with special techniques and equipment. For detailed information, see Appendix C, Supplementary Reading, at the back of this book.

Shovel

A broad-bladed shovel is both a tool and a safety device for the snow traveler. A shovel is a necessity for

*Fig. 16-12.
Ski equipment for
mountaineering:
a, Nordic ski boot and
three-pin binding;
b, randonée boot and
randonée binding;
c, climbing skins for skis.*

uncovering an avalanche victim. Shovels are also used for constructing snow shelters and tent platforms, and have even been used as climbing tools to ascend particularly snowy routes. Keep your shovel readily available.

A good shovel (see Figure 3-9a and b in Chapter 3, Camping and Food) has a blade large enough to move snow efficiently and a handle long enough for good leverage but short enough for use in a confined area (2 to 3 feet/60 to 90 centimeters long). Some shovels feature extendable and/or detachable handles. Another desirable feature is a blade that can be rotated perpendicular to the handle and locked so that the shovel can be used as a trenching tool. A D-shaped grip on the handle can make shoveling more comfortable. Some models have a hollow handle, where you can carry a snow saw or avalanche probe.

In dry, powdery snow, a plastic-bladed shovel provides a good compromise of weight to strength. However, metal-bladed shovels are much stiffer and therefore better for chopping through hard snow or avalanche debris. The edge of a shovel blade (whether metal or plastic) can be sharpened with a file.

TECHNIQUES OF SNOW CLIMBING

The first priority of snow travel is to prevent a slip or fall, but if you do slip on snow, you must know how to regain control as quickly as possible. Without an ice ax and the skill to use it, it is dangerous to travel up steep alpine snow slopes.

Using the Ice Ax

How to Carry an Ice Ax

Always carry an ice ax carefully. Be aware of what its sharp points and edges can do to you and others in your climbing party.

When you do not need your ax, carry it on your pack. Slip it down through the pack ice-ax loop, flip the shaft up, and strap it to the pack (fig. 16-13a). Keep guards on the pick, adze, and spike. To carry the ax in one hand, grasp the shaft with the spike forward and pick down to avoid jabbing the person behind you (fig. 16-13b).

Fig. 16-13.

Carrying an ice ax: a, attached to a pack by an ice-ax loop, with guards on the pick, adze, and spike; b, in the hand while walking; c, temporarily between back and pack.

When travel on snow alternates briefly with areas of rocks or steep brush, where both of your hands need to be free, slide the ax diagonally between your back and the pack (fig. 16-13c). Place the spike down and the pick between the two shoulder straps, clear of your neck and pointing in the same general direction as the angle of the shaft. The ax can be stowed and retrieved quickly in this position.

How to Grasp an Ice Ax

There are two ways to grasp an ice ax (fig. 16-14). Conditions determine which grasp is best at any moment.

Self-arrest grasp: Place your thumb under the adze and your palm and fingers over the pick, near the top of the shaft (fig. 16-14a). While you are climbing, the adze points forward. The self-arrest grasp puts you in position to go directly into arrest in case of a fall.

Self-belay grasp: Rest your palm on top of the adze and wrap your thumb and index finger under the pick (fig. 16-14b). While you are climbing, the pick points forward. The self-belay grasp provides a firmer anchor and may keep you from slipping in the first place.

When you are using the self-belay grasp, you must be able to instantly change to a self-arrest grasp in case you slip. Grab the shaft of the ax, momentarily loosen your grip on the head, and rotate the head 180 degrees into the self-arrest grasp. This takes practice. If you lack

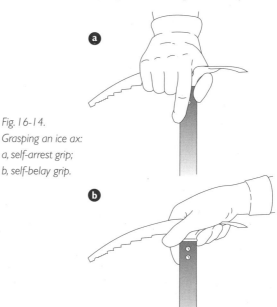

Fig. 16-14.
Grasping an ice ax:
a, self-arrest grip;
b, self-belay grip.

the skill to do it, it is safer to do self-belays while holding the ax head in the self-arrest grasp.

Some climbers simply choose to use the self-arrest grasp at all times. Others prefer the comfort of the self-belay but shift to the self-arrest grasp whenever they feel there is a significant danger of slipping.

Self-Belay

Self-belay can keep a simple slip or misstep on a snow slope from turning into a serious fall. Wear gloves; hard snow is quite abrasive, and sliding unprotected over its surface can cause your hand to lose its grip.

To self-belay, be sure both your feet are secure, then jam the spike and shaft of the ice ax straight down into the snow (fig. 16-15a). Continue to grip the head of the ax with your uphill hand while moving forward. (Use either the self-belay grasp or the self-arrest grasp to perform self-belay.) Take a step or two, pull out the ax, and replant it. For self-belay to work, you must place the shaft deep enough in firm snow to hold your full weight.

If you slip, keep one hand on the head of the ax and grab hold of the shaft at the surface of the snow with your other hand (fig. 16-15b). The key to successful self-belay is to grab the shaft right next to the surface, so that you pull against the buried shaft. Your hand on the head of the ax minimizes the risk of levering the ax out (fig. 16-15c).

If self-belay fails and you begin an uncontrolled slide down the slope, you must immediately self-arrest.

Self-Arrest

Preventing a fall is a primary goal while climbing, but if you do fall, your life can hinge on self-arrest skills. Self-arrest technique holds your fall or the fall of a rope mate. During glacier travel, self-arrest stops the rest of the team from sliding into a crevasse (discussed in Chapter 17, Glacier Travel and Crevasse Rescue). For climbers who practice and master self-arrest, steep alpine snow slopes become highways to the summit.

The goal of self-arrest is to stop safely in a secure and stable position. The last panel of Figures 16-16, 16-18, and 16-19, below, illustrate the completion of a successful self-arrest: lying face down in the snow with the ice ax beneath you.

Fig. 16-15.
The self-belay:
a, climbing;
b, falling;
c, recovering.

16

- **Your hands** hold the ax in a solid grip, one hand in the self-arrest grasp with your thumb under the adze and fingers over the pick (see Figure 16-14a, above), and your other hand on the shaft just above the spike.

- **The pick** presses into the snow just above your shoulder so that the adze is near the angle formed by your neck and shoulder. This is crucial. You cannot exert sufficient force on the pick if the adze is not in the proper position.

- **The shaft** crosses your chest diagonally and you hold the spike end close to the hip that is opposite the ax head. Grip the shaft near the spike end to prevent that hand from acting as a pivot point around which the spike can swing to jab your thigh. (A short ax is held the same way, although the spike will not reach the opposite hip.)

- **Your chest and shoulder** press down on the ice-ax shaft. Successful self-arrest relies on your body weight falling and pressing on the ax, rather than just arm strength driving the ax into the snow.

- **Your head** is face down, the brim of your helmet in contact with the slope. This position prevents your shoulders and chest from lifting up and keeps your weight over the adze.

- **Your face** is in the snow. Your nose should be touching the snow.

- **Your spine** arches slightly away from the snow. This places the bulk of your weight on the ax head and on your toes or knees, which are the points that dig into the snow to force a stop. Pull up on the spike end of the shaft, which starts the arch and rolls your weight toward your shoulder by the ax head.

- **Your knees** are slightly bent and against the surface to slow the fall in soft snow. On harder surfaces, where your knees have little stopping power, they help stabilize your body position.

- **Your legs** are stiff and spread apart, toes digging in. If you are wearing crampons, dig in with your knees and keep your toes off the snow. Crampon points can catch on hard snow or ice and flip you over backward, out of control.

Your self-arrest technique depends on the position you are in after a fall. You will be sliding in one of four positions: head uphill or head downhill and, in either case, face down or on your back.

If you are falling, your immediate goal is to get your body into the only effective self-arrest position: head uphill, feet downhill, and face pressed into the snow. The first move toward that goal is to grasp the ax with both hands, one hand on the ax head in the self-arrest grasp and the other hand at the base of the shaft. The next moves depend on your position while falling.

Head uphill, face down: You are already in self-arrest position. All you have to do is get the pick pressed into the snow and your body over the ax shaft, ending in a secure self-arrest.

Head uphill, on your back: This position (fig. 16-16a and fig. 16-17a) is not much more difficult to self-arrest than the face-down position. Roll toward the head of the ax and aggressively plant the pick into the snow at your side while rolling over onto your stomach (fig. 16-16b). Roll in the direction of the ax head (fig. 16-16c). Beware of rolling toward the spike, which can jam the spike in the snow before the pick (fig. 16-17b) and wrench the ax from your hands (fig. 16-17c).

Head downhill, face down: Self-arrest from a headfirst fall is more difficult because your feet have to first be swung downhill. In this face-down predicament, reach downhill and off to the ax-head side (fig. 16-18a) and get the pick into the snow to serve as a pivot to swing your body around (fig. 16-18b). Work to help swing your legs around so they are pointing downhill (fig. 16-18c and d). Never jab the spike into the snow and pivot on that end of the ax. That will bring the pick and adze of the ax across your slide path and on a collision course with your chest and face.

Head downhill, on your back: Hold the ax across your torso and aggressively jab the pick into the snow (fig. 16-19a); then twist and roll toward it (fig. 16-19b). Once again, the pick placed to the side serves as a pivot point. Planting the pick will not bring you around to the final self-arrest position. You need to work at rolling your chest toward the ax head while you work your legs to swing around and point downhill (fig. 16-19c). A sitting-up motion helps the roll.

Practice self-arrest in all positions on increasingly steeper slopes and hard snow above a safe runout. Practice with a full pack. The key to success is to get quickly

Fig. 16-16.
Correct self-arrest technique when you fall on your back with your head uphill: a, falling; b, rolling toward the pick onto your stomach; c, the completed self-arrest.

into the arrest position and dig in. During practice, leave the ice-ax leash off your wrist so there is less chance of the ax striking you if you lose control of it. Cover or pad the adze and spike to minimize chances of injury.

The effectiveness of the self-arrest depends on your reaction time, the steepness and length of the slope, and snow conditions.

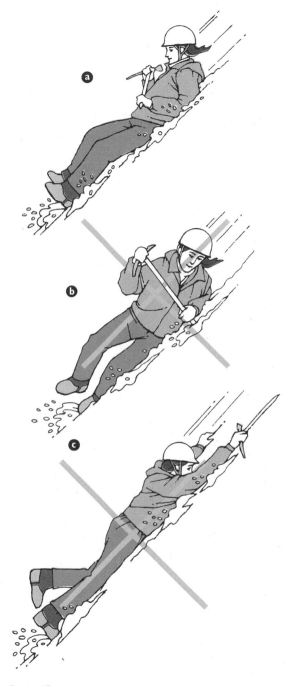

Fig. 16-17.
Incorrect self-arrest technique when you fall on your back with your head uphill, a, falling; b, rolling toward spike; c, ax is wrenched out of your hands.

321

Fig. 16-18.
Self-arrest
technique when you
fall with your head
downhill, face down:
a, reach downhill
and off to the
ax-head side;
b, get the pick
into the snow;
c, pivot body
on pick;
d, swing legs
downhill;
e, the completed
self arrest.

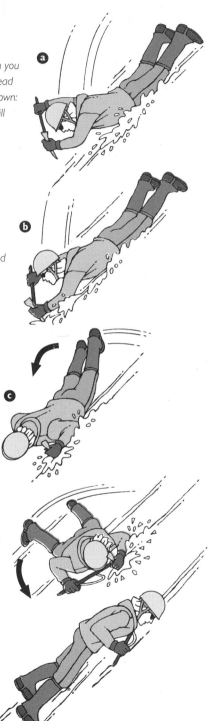

Fig. 16-19.
Self-arrest
technique, when
you fall on your
back with your
head downhill:
a, plant the pick;
b, twist and roll
toward pick;
c, swing legs
downhill and roll
chest toward pick;
d, the completed
self-arrest.

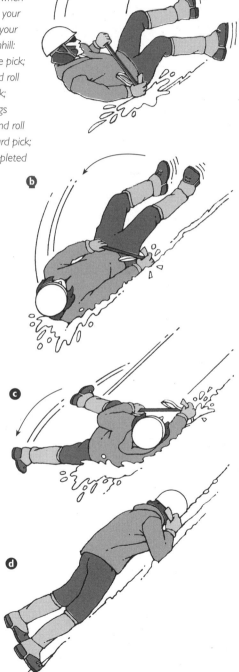

16

On steep or slippery slopes: When the slope is too steep or slippery, even the best technique will not stop your slide. Acceleration on hard snow, on even a modest snow slope, can be so rapid that the first instant of the fall is the whole story: You rocket into the air and crash back to the unyielding surface with stunning impact, losing uphill-downhill orientation.

On hard or loose snow: Arrest on hard snow is difficult, if not impossible, but always give it a try, even if you are on belay. In loose snow, the pick may not be able to reach compact snow, making the usual self-arrest useless. The best brakes in this case are your feet and knees and elbows, widely spaced and deeply pressed into the snow.

If your initial efforts at self-arrest are unsuccessful, do not give up. Keep fighting. If you do not stop, the attempt itself may slow you down and help prevent rolling, tumbling, and bouncing. It may also help keep you sliding feet first, the best position if you end up hitting rocks or trees. If you are roped to other climbers, anything you can do to slow your fall increases the chance that their self-arrests or belays will hold.

Without an ax: If you lose your ax in a fall, use your hands, elbows, knees, and boots to dig into the snow slope, using positioning similar to what you would use if you still had the ax. Try to clasp your hands together

against the slope so that snow is accumulated in them and creates more friction.

There are times when self-arrest should not be trusted, such as when a slope seems too fast or the runout too dangerous, or when members of the climbing party doubt their strength or skill. If this is the case, back off, look for another route, or rope up and put in protection. (See "Roped Snow-Climbing Techniques" later in this chapter.)

Ascending Snow

Climbing up snow slopes takes a set of special skills. Different techniques come into play, depending on the slope's hardness or steepness. The direction of ascent can be either direct or diagonal.

Climbing in Balance

Although you need to be proficient at ice-ax self-arrest, it is important to make every effort not to have to use it. You climb in balance to avoid falling. Climbing in balance means moving from one position of balance to another, avoiding any prolonged stance in an out-of-balance position.

Fig. 16-20.
Ascending a snow slope, diagonally, in balance: a, placing the ice ax from a position of balance; b, advancing a step into an out-of-balance position; c, advancing another step back into a position of balance.

323

On a diagonal uphill route, you are in a position of balance when your inside (uphill side) foot is in front of and above your outside (downhill side) foot, because your body weight is evenly distributed between both feet (fig. 16-20a). When your outside foot is forward, you are out of balance because your trailing inside leg, which is not fully extended and therefore cannot make use of the skeletal structure to minimize muscular effort, is nonetheless bearing most of your body weight (fig. 16-20b).

The diagonal ascent is a two-step sequence: from a position of balance through an out-of-balance position and back to a position of balance. From the position of balance, place the ax above and ahead of you into the snow in the self-belay position (fig. 16-20a). Move up one step, bringing your outside (downhill) foot in front of your inside (uphill) foot, which puts you out of balance (fig. 16-20b). Then move up another step, putting your inside foot in front of your outside foot, which puts you back in the position of balance (fig. 16-20c). Then reposition the ice ax. Keep your weight over your feet and avoid leaning into the slope. Keep the ax on your uphill side.

If you are heading straight up the fall line, there is no longer an uphill or downhill reference for arms and legs. Just carry the ax in whichever hand feels comfortable and climb in a steady, controlled manner. Regardless of the direction of travel, place the ax firmly before each move to provide self-belay protection.

The Rest Step

Climbing a long, featureless snow slope can give you the frustrating sensation of getting nowhere. Few landmarks help measure progress. Novice climbers try a dash-and-gasp pace in an attempt to rush the objective. But the only way to the top of the slope is to find a pace that you can maintain—and then maintain it. The solution is the rest step, a technique that conserves energy as it moves you methodically forward. Use the rest step whenever your legs or lungs need a bit of recuperation between steps. At lower elevations, it is usually your leg muscles that require a break; at higher elevations, your lungs need the pause. See Chapter 6, Wilderness Travel, for a description of the rest step.

Step-kicking

Step-kicking creates a path of upward steps with the best possible footing and the least expenditure of energy. Climbers move in single file up the steps, improving them as they go. The head of the line has the hardest job: kicking fresh steps and looking for the safest route up the slope.

The most efficient kick to use for creating snow steps is to swing your leg and allow its own weight and momentum to provide the impact, with little muscular effort. This works well in soft snow. Harder snow requires more effort, and the steps may be smaller and less secure.

An average climber needs steps deep enough to place the ball of the foot when going straight up and at least half of the boot on a diagonal ascent. Steps that are kicked level or tilted slightly into the slope are more secure. The less space there is on a step, the more important it is that the step be angled into the slope.

When you are kicking steps, keep other climbers in your party in mind. They can follow up your staircase if the steps are spaced evenly and somewhat close together. Make allowance for climbers whose legs are shorter than yours.

Followers improve the steps as they climb. The follower must kick into the step, because simply walking onto the existing platform is not secure. In compact snow, drive your toe in and deepen the step. In soft snow, bring your boot down onto the step, compacting the snow and making the step stronger.

Switch leads occasionally to share the heavy work. The leader can step aside and fall in at the end of the line. (The related skills of step-cutting and cramponing are discussed in Chapter 18, Alpine Ice Climbing.)

Direct Ascent

Speed is a consideration on a long snow climb, and a direct ascent is a good choice if you face bad weather, avalanche or rockfall danger, poor bivouac conditions, or a difficult descent. Ice-ax technique varies according to snow conditions and steepness.

Cane position: On a slope that is at a low or moderate angle, climb with the ax in the cane position, holding it in one hand by the head (by whatever grasp you prefer) and using it for balance (fig. 16-21). You can continue in the cane position as the snow gets steeper, as long as it feels secure. Setting the ax firmly before each move provides a self-belay.

Stake position: As the snow gets steeper, you may choose to switch to the two-handed stake position (fig. 16-22). Before moving upward, use both hands to plant the ax as far as it will go into the snow. Then continue

Fig. 16-23.
Direct ascent with ice ax in horizontal position.

Fig. 16-21.
Direct ascent with ice ax in cane position.

Fig. 16-22.
Direct ascent with ice ax in stake position.

to grasp it with both hands on the head or with one hand on the head and one on the shaft. This position is useful on steeper soft snow.

Horizontal position: This is an effective technique on steep, hard snow that is covered with a soft layer. Hold the ax with both hands, one in the self-arrest grasp on the head and the other near the spike end of the shaft. Jab the ax horizontally into the snow above you, the pick down and the shaft at right angles to your body (fig. 16-23). This jabs the pick into the harder base while the shaft gets some purchase in the softer surface snow.

Diagonal Ascent

When time and weather conditions permit, you may prefer a longer, diagonal ascent, switchbacking up moderately angled slopes. In marginal conditions, a diagonal route may be more difficult because of the work of kicking numerous edged, traversed steps in hard snow. Again, ice-ax technique varies according to snow conditions and steepness.

Cane position: The ax works fine in this position on moderate slopes (see Figure 16-21). As the slope gets steeper, the cane position becomes awkward.

Cross-body position: Hold the ax perpendicular to the angle of the slope, one hand grasping the head and the other holding the spike end of the shaft, which you jab into the snow (fig. 16-24). The ax crosses diagonally in front of you, the pick pointing away from your body.

16

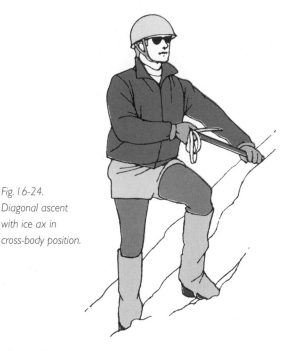

Fig. 16-24. Diagonal ascent with ice ax in cross-body position.

1. Start from a position of balance, with your inside (uphill) foot in front of and above your outside (downhill) foot. Jab the ax shaft straight down into the snow at a spot as directly above your location as possible.
2. Move your outside foot forward, bringing you into the out-of-balance position (fig. 16-25a). Grasp the head of the ax with both hands. Continue holding onto the head with both hands while moving into a stance facing uphill, turning your inside foot toward the new direction of travel and ending with splayed feet (fig. 16-25b).
3. Kick steps into the slope if your splayed feet feel unstable.
4. Turn your body toward the new direction of travel, returning to a position of balance. Your new uphill foot is now in front and above (fig. 16-25c).

With the cane position, your new uphill hand now grasps the ax head (fig. 16-25c). With the cross-body position, the hands holding the head and the shaft are now reversed.

The shaft should bear your weight, while your hand on the head of the ax stabilizes the ax.

Changing directions: Diagonal ascents often mean changes in direction, or switchbacks. There is a sequence of steps for a safe change in direction on a diagonal route, whether the ax is in the cane position or the cross-body position.

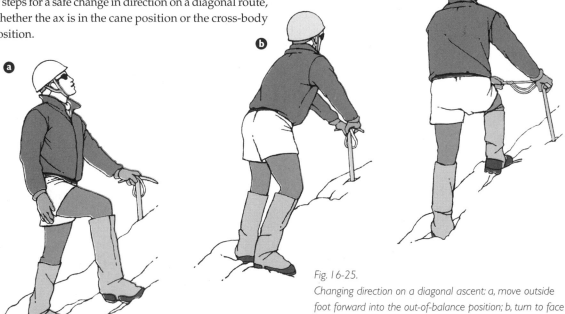

*Fig. 16-25.
Changing direction on a diagonal ascent: a, move outside foot forward into the out-of-balance position; b, turn to face uphill with feet splayed; c, turn in new direction of travel.*

Traversing

Long horizontal traverses that neither gain nor lose elevation are best avoided. This "sidehill gouging" is fine on soft snow at low and moderate angles, although it is not as comfortable or as efficient as a diagonal route. If you must traverse over hard or steep snow, face directly into the slope and kick straight into it for the most secure steps.

Descending Snow

One mark of a skillful snow climber is the ability to go downhill efficiently and confidently. Many otherwise competent and aggressive climbers blanch at the prospect of going forward down a steep, exposed snow gully. To be able to move down, you must place the ax low down, which provides a less-comfortable stance and handhold than on the way up. Master the following descent techniques to help you conquer any uneasiness about downhill travel.

Plunge-stepping

When you are going down, technique is determined mainly by the same factors as when you are going up: the hardness and angle of the snow. In soft snow on a moderate slope, simply face outward and walk down. With harder snow or a steeper angle, use the plunge step.

The plunge step is a confident, aggressive move. Face outward, step assertively away from the slope, and land solidly on your heel with your leg vertical, transferring weight solidly to the new position (fig. 16-26a). Avoid leaning back into the slope, which can result in less-secure steps or perhaps an unplanned glissade. Keep your knees slightly bent, not locked, and lean forward to maintain balance. How much you bend your knees depends on the angle of the slope (the steeper the slope, the greater the bend) and the firmness of the surface (the harder the snow, the greater the bend). Plunge-stepping can be secure with steps that hold only the heel of the boot, but most climbers do not trust steps shallower than that.

When you plunge-step, maintain a steady rhythm, almost like marching. This helps maintain balance. Once you find a comfortable rhythm, do not stop. Plunge-stepping in a stop-and-start fashion can cause you to lose your balance.

When you are plunge-stepping, hold the ice ax in one hand in either the self-arrest or self-belay grasp, with the spike close to the surface, well forward and

Fig. 16-26.
Descending on snow:
a, plunge-stepping on moderate slope;
b, using a self-belay on steeper slope.

16

ready to plant in the snow (fig. 16-26a). Spread out your other arm and move it for balance. Some climbers hold the ax in both hands in the full self-arrest position— one hand on the head, the other near the end of the shaft—but this allows less arm movement for maintaining balance.

An aggressive stride creates a deep step. Take care in deep, soft snow not to plunge so deeply that your legs get stuck and you fall forward, injuring yourself. When the snow is too hard or steep to plunge-step, begin to descend in a crouched position, planting the ax as low as possible in a self-belay with each step (fig. 16-26b).

Glissading

Glissading is the fastest, easiest, and most exhilarating way down many snow slopes if you are on foot. On slopes where you can control your speed, it is an efficient alternative to walking or plunge-stepping.

Glissading can be hazardous. Do not glissade in crevassed terrain. Glissade only when a safe runout is close enough that if you slide out of control, you will not be injured before reaching it. Unless you can see the entire descent route, the first person down must use extreme caution and stop frequently to look ahead. The biggest risk is losing control at such a high speed that self-arrest is not possible. This is most likely to happen on the best glissading slope—one with firm snow.

Before you glissade, remove your crampons and stow them and other hardware in your pack. Crampon points can catch in the snow and send you tumbling. Wear rain pants to keep dry. Wear gloves to protect your hands from the abrasive snow.

Always maintain control of the ice ax. If you wear an ice-ax leash, you risk injury from a flailing ax if it is knocked loose from your grip. If you do not use a leash, you risk losing your ax.

Effective glissading requires a smooth blend of several techniques. Climbers who lack finesse in the standing glissade (see below) often use a combination: breaking into a plunge step to control speed, stepping off in a new direction rather than making a ski-style turn, and skating to maintain momentum as the slope angle lessens.

Sometimes in soft snow, a glissader accidentally sets off a mass of surface snow, which slides down the slope with the glissader aboard. These are small avalanches, known as avalanche cushions. The trick is to decide whether the avalanche cushion is safe to ride or is about to become a serious avalanche. If the moving snow is more than a few inches deep, self-arrest will not work because the ice-ax pick cannot penetrate to the stable layer below. Sometimes you can drive the spike deep enough to slow the glissade, although probably not deep enough to stop you. Unless you are sure the cushion is safe and your speed is under control, get off. Roll sideways out of the path of the moving snow and then self-arrest.

There are three methods of glissading—the sitting glissade, the standing glissade, and the crouching glissade. The one to use depends on snow and slope conditions, the appearance of the runout, and your mastery of the technique.

Sitting glissade: This works on soft snow on which you would bog down if you tried a standing glissade. Sit erect in the snow, bend your knees, and plant your boot soles flat along the surface (fig. 16-27a). Hold the ice ax in self-arrest position while you are going downhill. To maintain control, run the spike of the ax like a rudder along the snow on one side of you. Keep both hands on the ax. Put pressure on the spike to reduce your speed and to thwart any tendency to pivot the ice-ax head downward.

The standard posture, with your knees bent and feet flat, also reduces speed. This posture is good when the snow is crusted or firmly consolidated, pitted with icy ruts or small "sun cups" (hollows melted by the sun), or dotted with rocks or shrubs. It provides more stability and control than having your legs straight out in front and helps minimize wear and tear on your bottom.

To stop, use the spike to slow down, then dig in your heels—but not at high speed, or a somersault may be the result. For an emergency stop, roll over and self-arrest.

Turns are almost impossible in a sitting glissade. The best way to get around an obstruction is to stop, walk sideways to a point that is not directly above the obstacle, and glissade again.

Standing glissade: This is the most maneuverable

Fig. 16-27.
Glissades:
a, sitting;
b, standing;
c, crouching.

technique, and saves clothes from getting wet and abraded. This glissade is similar to downhill skiing. Crouch slightly over your feet, bend your knees, and spread out your arms (fig. 16-27b). Your feet provide stability and can be spread out or placed together, with one foot slightly forward to improve stability and prevent nosedives. Bring your feet closer together and lean forward over them to increase speed.

To slow down and stop, stand up and dig in your heels, turn your feet sideways and dig their edges into the slope, or crouch and drag the ice-ax spike as in the crouching glissade (see below).

You can also perform a turn similar to skiing in which you rotate your shoulders, upper body, and knees in the direction of the turn and roll your knees and ankles in the same direction to rock your feet onto boot edges.

The standing glissade is most effective on a firm base with a softer layer on top. The softer the snow, the steeper the slope needed to maintain speed. It is possible to do a standing glissade down slopes of harder snow, but these are usually slopes of lower angles with a safe runout. You can skate slopes of very low angles if the snow is firm.

Changes in the snow texture are tricky. If you hit softer, slower snow, your head and torso will suddenly outpace your legs, so move one boot forward for stability. If you hit harder, faster snow or ice below the surface, lean well forward to prevent a slip. Keep your speed under control by regular braking and traversing.

Crouching glissade: This is slower than a standing glissade and easier to learn. From the standing glissade position, simply lean back, hold the ice ax in the self-arrest position to one side of your body, and drag the spike in the snow (fig. 16-27c). Because it uses three points of contact, it is also more stable. However, it is more difficult to turn and to control your speed.

Down-climbing

On steep snow where you do not feel secure glissading or plunge-stepping, face into the slope and climb down backward, kicking steps straight into the slope. Use the ice ax in the stake position (see Figure 16-22, above) as a self-belay.

ROPED SNOW-CLIMBING TECHNIQUES

On a glacier, teams always rope up for protection from hidden crevasses. On a nonglaciated snow slope, the decision is not so clear-cut, and climbers have to weigh several options.

The party can climb unroped, relying on each individual to stop a personal fall. They may decide to travel roped together but unbelayed, which offers some security for a weaker climber and gets the rope set up in case no convenient rope-up place exists later. The party may also decide to travel roped together and to use belays, because route conditions or the climbers' abilities dictate this level of protection.

16

The risks of roping up are not trivial. One climber can fall and pull the entire rope team off the mountain. There is also a higher risk of avalanche and rockfall exposure. The party also will move more slowly.

Options for Roped Team Protection

If the climbing party decides it is safer overall to rope up, there are several different ways to match the type of rope protection to climbing conditions and climbers' strengths.

Team Arrest (Roped but Unbelayed)

Team arrest depends on individual climbers to stop their own falls and to provide backup in case someone else falls. Relying on team arrest as the ultimate team security makes sense only in certain situations, such as on a low- or moderate-angle glacier or snow slope. The proficient members of the rope team can save a less-skilled climber from a dangerous slide.

On steeper, harder slopes, the party has to decide which option is safest—continuing to rely on team arrest, using anchors for protection, or unroping and letting each climber go it alone.

To increase the odds that team arrest will work on a snow slope, use the following procedures:

- **If there are any climbers below you, carry a few feet of slack rope coiled in your hand.** If a climber falls, drop the loose rope, which gains you an extra instant before the rope is loaded; this gives you a moment to get the ice ax into self-belay position and to brace yourself before the falling climber's weight impacts the rope. However, if you carry too much slack, you will increase the distance that your rope mates will slide before you stop them.
- **Put the weakest climber on the downhill end of the rope.** As a rule, the least-skilled climber should be last on the rope while ascending and first on the rope while descending. This puts the climber most likely to fall in a position where a fall will be less serious: below the other climbers, where the impact will be quickly felt along the rope.
- **Climb on a shortened rope.** This technique is best for a two-person rope team. A climbing pair that uses only a portion of the rope reduces the sliding distance

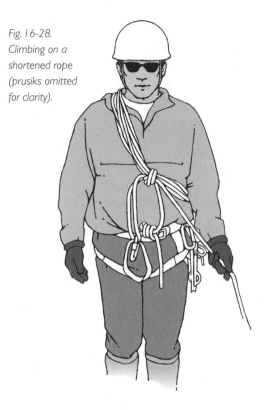

Fig. 16-28. Climbing on a shortened rope (prusiks omitted for clarity).

and the tug from the fall if one partner falls. To shorten the rope, wind as many coils as necessary until the desired length remains. Then use a loop of the climbing rope to tie an overhand knot through the coils, and clip the loop into your harness with a locking carabiner. Carry the coils over one shoulder and under the opposite arm (fig. 16-28). If more than two climbers are on the rope, the middle climber or climbers should take coils in the direction of the leader. See "Special Rescue Situations" in Chapter 17, Glacier Travel and Crevasse Rescue, for a description and illustration (fig. 17-23) of a similar technique, called the adapted Kiwi coil.

- **Climb in separate parallel tracks.** This is also best for a two-person rope team. The climbers are abreast of each other, separated by the rope. A falling climber will pendulum down, putting force on the rope to the side of and below the partner. The tug on the rope will be less than if the climber fell from high above. Also, the friction of the rope as it pendulums across the snow will absorb some of the force. On ascents where kicking two sets of steps would be a waste of time and energy, this style may be impractical, but on ascents of harder snow and on descents, it can be good.

- **Handle the rope properly.** Keep the rope on the downhill side of the team so that there is less chance of stepping on it. Hold the rope in your downhill hand, in a short loop. You can then take in or let out the rope, adjusting to the pace of the person ahead of you or the person behind you, rather than getting into a tug-of-war.
- **Observe your rope mates' pace and position and adjust and prepare accordingly.** When the rope goes taut, it may be hung up on the snow, or your rope mates may be in a delicate situation in which any additional tug on the rope could yank them off their feet.

- **Yell "Falling!" whenever any climber falls.** All rope partners can self-arrest and avoid getting pulled off their feet.

Running Belays

Roped climbers can move together on snow with the help of running belays. This technique saves time over regular belayed climbing but still allows for protection. Running belays, which are also useful in rock climbing, ice climbing, and alpine climbing, are discussed in Chapter 14, Leading on Rock, and Chapter 18, Alpine Ice Climbing.

The running belay offers an intermediate level of protection, somewhere between team arrest and fixed belays. It helps when a successful team arrest is improbable but fixed belays are impractical. For example, running protection may do the job on long snow faces and couloirs.

To place running belays, the leader puts in pieces of snow protection when necessary and uses a carabiner to clip the rope in to each one. (For more information on snow anchors, see the next section.) All members of the rope team continue to climb at the same time, just as in unbelayed travel, except that now there is protection in the snow that will be likely to stop a fall (fig. 16-29). To pass each running belay point, when the middle climbers reach an anchor, they unclip the rope that is in front of them from the carabiner attached to the protection, then clip the rope that is behind them to the

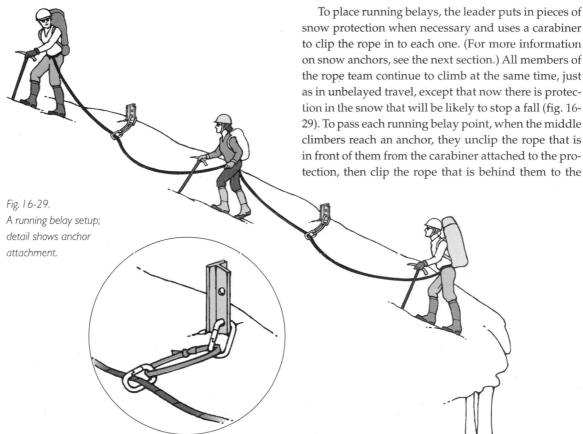

Fig. 16-29. A running belay setup; detail shows anchor attachment.

16

331

carabiner. The last climber on the rope removes each piece of protection.

Combination Protection Techniques

Long snow routes usually demand fast travel to reach the summit. Climbers often use a combination of roped and unroped travel, mostly unbelayed. They rely primarily on team arrest or running protection, and some sections of the climb will warrant unroped travel. Belays are typically used on steeper, harder snow or when climbers are tired or hurt. The option of turning around is always worth considering. The party can select a new route, choose another destination, or just head home.

Snow Anchors

Snow anchors provide protection and secure rappels and belays. The strength of a snow anchor placement depends on the strength of the snow. The greater the area of snow the anchor pulls against and the firmer the snow, the stronger the anchor. Ultimately, the strength of snow anchors depends greatly on proper placement and snow conditions. Common snow anchors are pickets, deadman anchors, flukes, and bollards.

Picket

A picket is a stake driven into the snow as an anchor. Aluminum pickets are available in lengths ranging from 18 to 36 inches and in different styles, including round or oval tubes and angled or T-section stakes.

The angle for placing a picket depends on the angle of the slope. The picket should be placed so that it can withstand the direction of pull while having the greatest

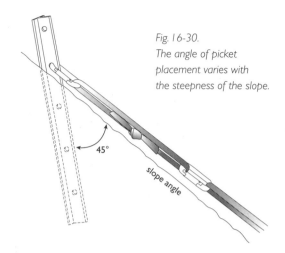

Fig. 16-30.
The angle of picket placement varies with the steepness of the slope.

45°

slope angle

possible area of snow to pull against (fig. 16-30). On a gentler slope, the placement should be vertical or at an angle of a few degrees toward the top of the slope. On a steeper slope, the placement should be at an angle of about 45 degrees from the direction of pull. Attach a carabiner or runner to the picket at the level of the snow surface—not higher on the picket, or a pull may lever it out of the snow. Drive a picket into the snow with a rock, the side of an ice ax, or an ice hammer. An ice ax or ice tool can also serve as a makeshift picket.

A picket works best in firm, hard snow. If the snow is too soft, use the picket as a deadman (see below). Make sure the picket is not pulling out of the snow and that there are no visible cracks in the snow in the area against which the picket exerts force.

Inspect a picket after every use. If you are on a rope team using a running belay, check the picket when you pass it.

DECISION-MAKING FOR ROPED SNOW TRAVEL

A team always ropes up on glaciers, but on snow or mixed terrain, the climbing team has a few considerations:

1. Is each member of the party able to use self-belay or self-arrest? If the answer is yes, the party can continue unroped. If the answer is no, go on to question 2.
2. Can the team stop all falls by roping up and relying on team arrest? If so, rope up and continue climbing, unbelayed. If not, then go on to question 3.
3. Can the team use some form of belay (running or fixed) that will provide adequate protection? If so, begin belaying. If something hinders a belay—for example, poor terrain or a lack of time—then go on to question 4.
4. Should the party turn around, or should the team proceed unroped and assume the risks?

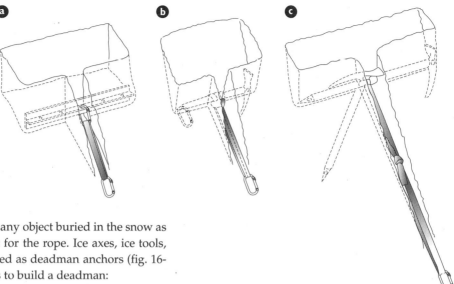

*Fig. 16-31.
Deadman anchors:
a, picket;
b, one ice ax, buried
horizontally;
c, two ice axes, one
horizontal and one
vertical (the T-ax
anchor).*

Deadman

A deadman anchor is any object buried in the snow as a point of attachment for the rope. Ice axes, ice tools, and pickets can be used as deadman anchors (fig. 16-31). Here are the steps to build a deadman:

1. Dig a trench as long as the item being used and perpendicular to the load.
2. Girth-hitch a runner to the item at its midpoint and place the item in the trench. To prevent the runner from sliding off the ends, use a carabiner: For a picket, clip a carabiner to the picket's midpoint and to the runner (fig. 16-31a). For an ice ax or ice tool, clip a carabiner to the hole at the spike end (fig. 16-31b).
3. Cut a slot in the snow that is as deep as the trench, to let the runner lie in the direction of pull. If this slot is shallower than the trench, there will be an upward pull on the anchor.
4. Cover everything with snow except the tail of the runner. Stamp down on everything to compact and strengthen the snow.
5. Clip in to the end of the runner.

If the snow is soft, increase the strength of the deadman placement by increasing the area of snow it pulls against; do this by using a larger object. Try using a pack, a pair of skis, or a long, large stuff sack tightly filled with snow. Do not use ski or trekking poles—they are not strong enough.

In a variation of the buried-ax deadman anchor, place a second ax vertically behind the horizontal ax (fig. 16-31c). In this variation, called the T-ax anchor, girth-hitch a runner to the vertical ax and run the shaft of the horizontal ax through the runner.

As with all snow anchors, inspect a deadman after every use. Look for cracks and bulges in the snow above the buried item.

Snow Fluke

The snow fluke is a specially shaped aluminum plate with a metal cable attached (fig. 16-32a). A buried fluke should be angled back about 40 degrees from the direction of pull (fig. 16-32b). Dig a slot in the snow to permit the cable to be pulled in as direct a line as possible.

In theory the snow fluke serves as a dynamic anchor, planing deeper into the snow when it takes a load. In practice, a fluke may behave in more complicated ways, even coming out if its top is tipped too far forward (fig. 16-32c) or backward or if the load is not in a direct line (fig. 16-32d), such as to the side rather than straight out.

Flukes work best in snow that is moist and heavy. They are less reliable with snow layers of varying density: If the fluke or its cable travels down into the snow and hits a harder layer, the fluke could be deflected and pull out. Neither do flukes do well in dry, unconsolidated snow.

Snow Bollard

A snow bollard is a mound carved out of snow. When rigged with rope or webbing, bollards can provide

16

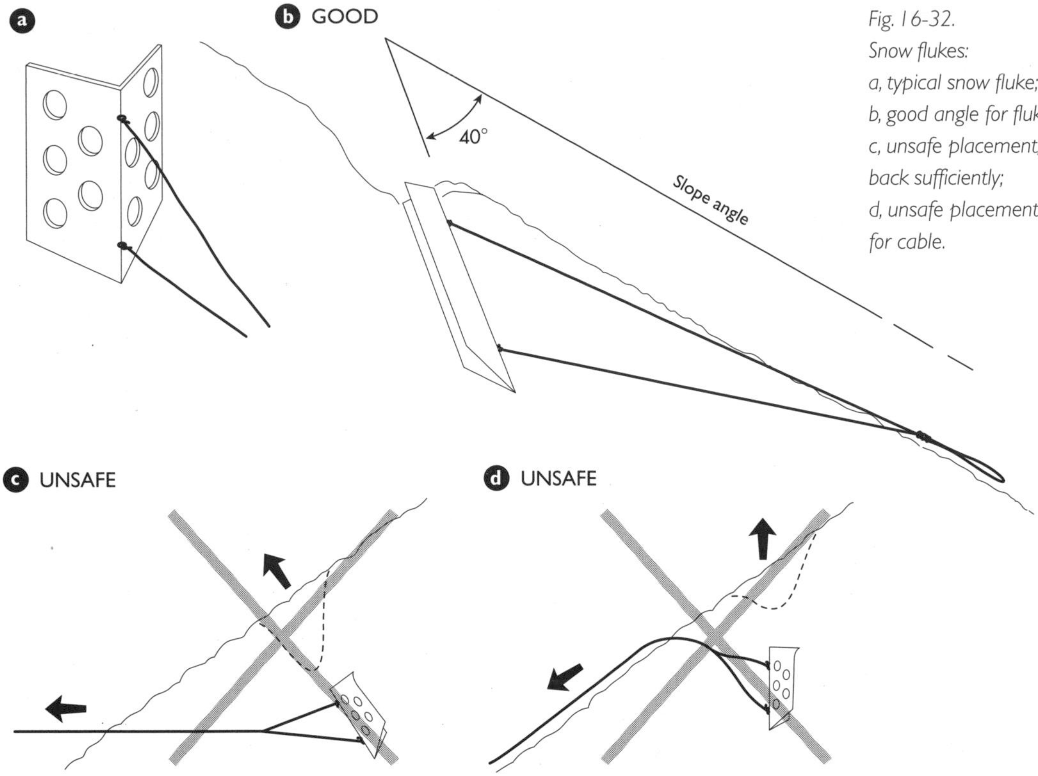

a

b GOOD

40°

Slope angle

Fig. 16-32.
Snow flukes:
a, typical snow fluke;
b, good angle for fluke placement;
c, unsafe placement, not angled
back sufficiently;
d, unsafe placement, no slot
for cable.

c UNSAFE

d UNSAFE

16

strong, reliable snow anchors (fig. 16-33a). However, building bollards can be time consuming.

Create the mound by making a horseshoe-shaped trench in the snow, with the open end of the horseshoe pointing downhill (fig. 16-33b). In hard snow, chop out the trench using the adze of an ice ax; in soft snow,

stamp out a trench or dig one. The trench should be 6 to 8 inches (15 to 20 centimeters) wide and 1 to 1½ feet (30 to 45 centimeters) deep (fig. 16-33c). In hard snow, the mound should be at least 3 feet (1 meter) in diameter, and in soft snow it should be up to 10 feet (3 meters).

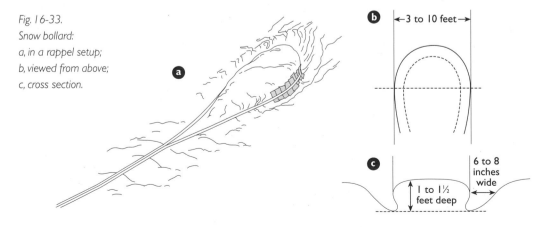

Fig. 16-33.
Snow bollard:
a, in a rappel setup;
b, viewed from above;
c, cross section.

a

b ←3 to 10 feet→

c 6 to 8 inches wide

1 to 1½ feet deep

The bollard should not be in an oval teardrop shape in which the legs of the trench come together. This configuration results in a weaker anchor by not taking advantage of the entire snow slope in front of the mound.

During construction, assess the snow in the trench for changes in consistency or weak layers that will allow the rope or webbing to cut through the mound. Webbing is less likely than rope to saw into the mound. Avoid pulling on the rope or webbing after you have placed it. Ice axes planted vertically at the shoulders of the trench prevent rope or webbing from cutting in. Pad the rear and sides of the mound with packs, clothing, or foam pads. Inspect the bollard for damage after each use.

Multiple Anchors

Multiple anchors are safest. They can be placed one behind the other to provide backup and absorb any remaining force (fig. 16-34a), or placed independently and

connected to share the load (fig. 16-34b). (More details and illustrations on joining multiple anchors are found in "Equalizing Multiple Anchors" in Chapter 10, Belaying, and in "Equalizing Protection" in Chapter 13, Rock Protection.) Keep the anchors several feet apart so they do not share any localized weaknesses in the snow. Inspect every anchor after each use.

Belaying on Snow

Snow climbers set up belays using established snow anchors, or they give quicker and less-formal belays using an ice ax. No matter what the belaying technique, every snow belay should be as dynamic as possible to help limit the force on the anchor. The standard hip belay provides a more gradual, dynamic belay than do mechanical belay devices. Plan your stance so your body takes the force, which is dissipated as much as possible by the belay. The dynamic, shock-absorbing quality of climbing rope also helps to minimize chances of an abrupt stop to a fall.

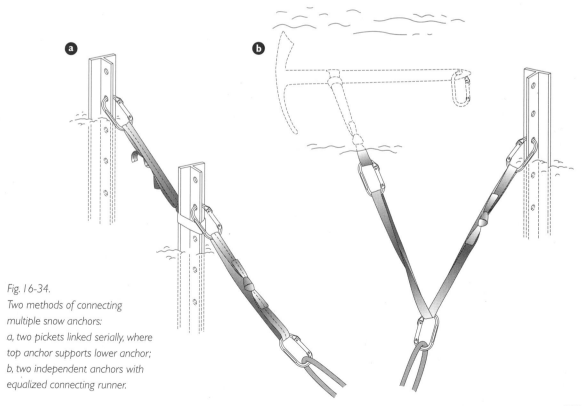

Fig. 16-34.
Two methods of connecting multiple snow anchors:
a, two pickets linked serially, where top anchor supports lower anchor;
b, two independent anchors with equalized connecting runner.

Set up a belay close to the climbing difficulties. To belay the lead climber, get out of the line of fire by setting up the belay stance to one side of the fall line. If the leader is heading up on a diagonal, get outside any point where that climber's route can cross directly above you. On a ridge crest, it is not always possible to predict a fall line and plan a belay in advance. If a rope mate slips off one side of the ridge, the best tactic may actually be to jump off the opposite side, with the rope running over the ridge and thus saving both climbers.

Quick Belays

Boot-ax belay: This is a fast and easy way to provide protection as a rope team moves up together. The boot-ax belay is primarily a form of dynamic belay, and cannot hold the force of a high fall from above the belay. Use this when protecting a rope mate who is probing a cornice or crevasse edge, or when providing a top belay. With practice, this belay can be set up in a matter of seconds with a jab of the ice ax and a quick sweep of the rope. Follow these steps:

1. Stamp a firm platform in the snow, big enough for the head of an ice ax and your uphill boot.
2. Jam the ice-ax shaft as deeply as possible into the snow at the rear of the platform, the shaft tilted slightly uphill against the force of a possible fall. Place the pick perpendicular to the fall line, thus applying the broadest side of the shaft against the fall force.
3. Stand below the ax, at a right angle to the fall line, facing the climber's route.
4. Plant your uphill boot into the snow against the downhill side of the shaft, so that your foot braces the ice ax against a downward pull.
5. Plant your downhill boot in a firmly compacted step far enough below the uphill boot so that your downhill leg is straight, providing a stiff brace (fig. 16-35a).
6. Flip the rope around the ax. The final configuration has the rope running from the direction of potential load across the toe of your uphill boot, around the uphill side of the ax, and then back across your boot above the instep (fig. 16-35b).
7. Hold the rope with the downhill (braking) hand, applying extra friction by bringing the rope uphill

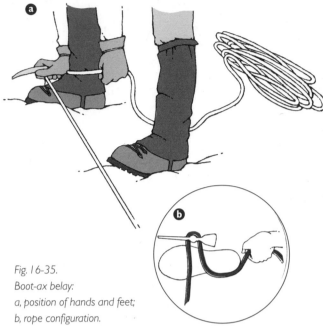

Fig. 16-35.
Boot-ax belay:
a, position of hands and feet;
b, rope configuration.

behind your heel, forming an S-bend (see Figure 16-35b, above). The braking hand must never leave the rope.
8. Use the uphill hand for two jobs: to grasp the head of the ax to further brace the shaft (see Figure 16-35a, above) and then, as the belayed climber moves upward, to take in rope.

Carabiner–ice ax belay: Also called the stomper belay, this provides the same level of security as a boot-ax belay, with easier rope handling. One good thing about the carabiner–ice ax belay is that the force of a fall pulls the belayer more firmly into the stance.

To set it up, plant the ax as deeply as possible, the pick perpendicular to the fall line. Girth-hitch a very short sling to the ax shaft at the surface of the snow, and clip a carabiner to the sling. Stand at a right angle to the fall line, facing the same side as the climber's route. Brace the ax with your uphill boot, standing atop the sling but leaving the carabiner exposed (fig. 16-36). Keep crampons off the sling. The rope runs from the potential direction of pull up through the carabiner and then around the back of your waist and into your uphill (braking) hand.

TIP FOR A QUICKER BOOT-AX BELAY

Some climbers find the following alternate method for setting up the boot-ax belay to be quicker and easier:
1. Stamp out the platform in the snow and position your feet as described above.
2. Holding your ice ax by its head, sweep up a short length of the climbing rope with the shaft, and jam the ax into position in the snow, with the rope now in place.

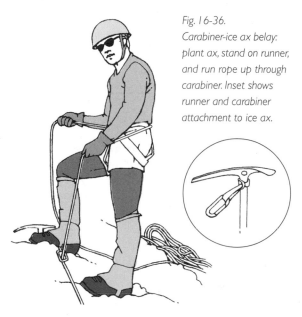

Fig. 16-36.
Carabiner-ice ax belay: plant ax, stand on runner, and run rope up through carabiner. Inset shows runner and carabiner attachment to ice ax.

Anchored Belays

Other snow belays are used with anchors such as pickets or bollards.

Sitting hip belay: Used with an anchor, this belay is inherently dynamic and very secure on hard snow or deep, heavy, wet snow. It does have its drawbacks. The sitting belayer may face the prospect of a cold, wet assignment, and the belay can be difficult to work if the rope is frozen.

To set up the belay, stamp or chop a seat in the snow as well as a platform to brace each boot against. Put down a pack, foam pad, or other material as insulation from the snow, and then settle into a standard hip belay, with your legs outstretched and stiffened (fig. 16-37).

Standing hip belay: This is easier to set up than a sitting hip belay, but it is far less secure because the belayer tends to topple under the force of a fall. Standing hip belays must be backed up with an anchor.

The belayer faces into the slope, out away from the slope, or sideways. Facing into the slope is the poorest choice because the belayer will be completely wrapped by the rope if the climber falls below the belay stance, and it is difficult to pay out rope for a smooth belay. Facing out is an improvement because it gives a less-complete wrap around the belayer and also permits a view of a fall below, important in timing a dynamic belay. But it shares a major weakness with the face-in stance: There is no way to brace your legs against toppling downhill. In both stances, the belayer can lean into the slope against a downhill pull.

For the most reliable standing hip belay, stand sideways, facing the same side as the climber's route. Your downhill leg is straight at the knee and braced in a snow slot. Your uphill leg is in a line with the downhill leg and the direction of a potential fall. Your downhill hand is the braking hand to allow for best control of a gradual dynamic belay.

Mechanical belay devices: These can be used in snow belaying. However, they provide a less-dynamic belay than a hip belay, increasing the force on the anchor.

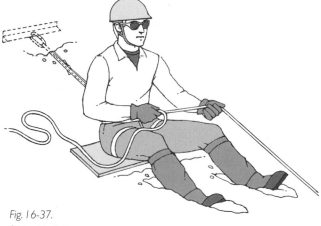

Fig. 16-37.
Sitting hip belay.

16

Consider using mechanical belay devices only when multiple anchors are being used. Belaying directly from the anchor with a device, rather than belaying from your seat harness, permits you to get into a drier, more comfortable position. They are easy to set up and operate even with wet or icy ropes.

ROUTEFINDING ON SNOW

Snow can provide passage over some frustrating obstacles, such as tundra, talus, brush, streams, and logging debris. At its best it provides a smooth, uniform surface and a straight shot up the mountain.

At its worst, snow can be too soft to support your weight, or it can be hard and dangerously slick. It can obscure trails, cairns, ridge crests, and other guideposts to the route, especially above tree line. Dangers often lie beneath the surface: moats, creeks, or glacier crevasses hidden by a thin snow cover. Unstable snow slopes may avalanche.

Minimize the frustrations and dangers of snow travel by studying the medium. See Chapter 26, The Cycle of Snow, for information on snow formation, types of snow, and the creation of glaciers. Learn how seasonal weather patterns affect snow accumulation and avalanche conditions. Hone your navigation skills. Let the snow work for you by reading the snow surface and terrain features to determine a safe, efficient route.

Routefinding Aids

A good routefinder uses a variety of tools, including map, compass, altimeter (see Chapter 5, Navigation, for details on use of these as well as GPS receivers), wands, the sun, and other visual landmarks. Wands are used to mark the return route, but they can also mark points of danger (such as moats and crevasses) and changes in direction.

Surface Considerations

The best snow to travel on is snow that will support your weight and provide easy step-kicking, as well as being stable enough not to avalanche. The location of the best snow varies from day to day, even from hour to hour. If the snow in one spot is slushy or too hard or too crusty, look around: There may be better snow a few feet away. Here are some tips for making the best use of the snow surface:

- To find patches of firmer snow on a slushy slope, walk in shade or use sun cups as stairs.
- On a slope that is too firm for good step-kicking, try to find patches of softer snow.
- When the going is difficult, detour toward any surface that has a different appearance.
- To find the best snow on a descent, use a different route if necessary.
- To find a firmer surface, look for dirty snow. It absorbs more heat and therefore consolidates more quickly than does clean snow.
- Remember that in the northern hemisphere, south and west slopes catch the heat of afternoon sun and consolidate earlier in the season and quicker after storms. They offer hard surfaces when east and north slopes are still soft and unstable.
- After a clear, cold night that follows a hot day, get an early start in order to take advantage of strong crusts on open slopes before they melt.
- Beware of hidden holes next to logs, trees, and rocks, where the snow has melted away from these warmer surfaces.
- If you do not like the conditions on one side of a ridge, gully, clump of trees, or large boulder, try the other side. The difference may be considerable.

Visibility Considerations

The creative use of several routefinding methods becomes especially important when visibility is poor. In a whiteout, it is possible to lose all orientation. Distinguishing between uphill and downhill is difficult, as is distinguishing between solid snow and dense clouds. A whiteout can be caused by a temporary cloud cover or blowing snow that limits visibility and makes navigation difficult and hazardous. Care must be taken to avoid going off route. If a whiteout seems to be approaching, place wands so you can find the way out. This is the time to get out map, compass, and altimeter to navigate. Other options include waiting it out a while before proceeding, or turning back. If possible, retrace the wanded route.

16

Terrain Considerations and Features

Major terrain features present obstacles as well as opportunities (fig. 16-38). Know which ones to use and which ones to avoid.

Ridges

A ridge (fig. 16-38b) may be the route of choice if it is not too steep or craggy. Ridges are generally free of rockfall and avalanche hazard. However, ridge routes take the full brunt of wind and bad weather, and you must be alert to the hazard of cornices, which form on ridge crests (see below).

Cornices

Cornices form when windblown snow accumulates horizontally on ridge crests and the sides of gullies, and hangs suspended out past the supporting rock. The shape of a ridge determines the extent of the cornice that can develop (fig. 16-38d). A ridge that slopes on one side and breaks into an abrupt cliff on the other is a good candidate for a gigantic cornice. A knife-edge ridge (where snow cannot accumulate) or a ridge that is gentle on both sides (where snow can disperse) typically has only a small cornice, if any at all—although exceptions do exist.

When the physical features are right for building cornices, wind direction decides the exact location of the cornice. Because storm winds have definite patterns in each mountain range, most cornices in the same area face the same way. In the Pacific Northwest region of the United States, for example, most snowstorms come from the west or southwest, so the majority of cornices form on the north and east sides. These same northern and eastern exposures were made steep by past glaciation, making the ridges ideally shaped for cornice formation.

There are exceptions. Temporary or local wind deflection can contradict the general pattern. In rare instances, cornices are even built one atop the other, facing opposite directions, the lower one partially destroyed and hidden by later formations.

Cornices are a hazard. If a climbing party is climbing on a cornice, it could collapse spontaneously or under the added load of their weight, or climbers could break through the cornice. Collapsing cornices can trigger avalanches. Cornices can fracture, falling into gullies or along the slopes below, or can separate slightly from their host ridge, forming a crack or cornice crevasse. (See Figure 26-3 in Chapter 26, The Cycle of Snow.)

The safest course along a corniced crest is well behind the probable fracture line. Do not be misled by appearances. On a mature cornice, the probable line of fracture could be 30 feet (9 meters) or more back from the lip—farther back than you might expect upon examination. Usually the fracture line is not visible. Look for any crack or indentation in the snow, which indicates a cornice that has partially collapsed and recently been covered with new snow.

The colder the weather, the more secure the cornice. A late-season cornice that is almost completely broken down also is not a problem. The safest strategy with cornices is to avoid them. Do not travel on them, under them, or through them.

Approaching from windward: The back side of a cornice appears to be a smooth snow slope that runs out to meet the sky.

Look at nearby ridges for an idea of the frequency, size, and location of cornices in the area. Try to view the lee side of the ridge from a safe vantage point, such as a rock or tree jutting through the crest.

Although rocks and trees projecting from the snow are safe, they do not indicate a stable route across the entire ridge. These can easily be on the tops of buttresses that randomly jut out perpendicularly to the ridge. The area directly in front of and behind these outcroppings may be all cornice. Many climbers have had the enlightening experience of looking back along a ridge and discovering that their tracks pass above a chasm.

When you are approaching from windward, if you suspect there is a cornice, stay well back from the crest. If the crest must be approached, consider belaying the lead climber, who should probe carefully while advancing. The belayer also assumes a risk. If the cornice collapses, the belayer may have to bear the weight of the falling snow in addition to that of the climber.

Approaching from leeward: A cornice cannot be missed from the leeward side. Resembling a wave frozen as it is breaking, a large cornice close above a climber is an awesome sight. If cornice's stability is doubtful, stay

Fig. 16-38.
Alpine terrain
features.

a. Horn or aiguille
b. Ridge
c. Rock arête
d. Cornice
e. Glacier basin
f. Seracs
g. Fallen seracs
h. Icefall
i. Glacier
j. Crevasses
k. Lateral moraine
l. Snout
m. Moraine lake
n. Terminal moraine
o. Glacial runoff
p. Erratic blocks
q. Rock band
r. Shoulder
s. Col
t. Couloir or gully
u. Hanging glacier
v. Bergschrund
w. Buttress
x. Cirque or bowl
y. Headwall
z. Flutings
aa. Ice wall
bb. Summit
cc. Ice arête
dd. Towers or gendarmes
ee. Avalanche chute
ff. Avalanche debris
gg. Snowfield

16

among trees or on the crest of a spur ridge while traveling below it.

Occasionally it may be necessary to climb directly through a cornice to force your way to a ridge crest or pass. Penetrate at an overhang or rock spur or where the cornice has partially collapsed. The lead climber cuts straight uphill at the point of least overhang, carefully tunneling and upsetting as little of the mass as possible.

Couloirs

Couloirs—steeply angled gullies (fig. 16-38t)—can provide a main avenue to the summit. Their overall angle is often less than that of the cliffs they breach, offering technically easier climbing. Couloirs are also the deadly debris chutes of mountains: Snow, rocks, and ice blocks that are loosened by the sun often pour down couloirs. Here are some tips for using couloirs:

- Try to be out of couloirs before the sun hits them. They can be safer in early morning when the snow is solid and rocks and ice are frozen in place.
- Keep to the sides, because most of the debris comes down the center.
- Always listen for suspicious sounds from above and keep an eye out for quiet slides and silently falling rock.
- Examine a gully carefully before ascending it. Couloirs can become increasingly nasty higher up, with extreme steepness, moats (see below), rubble strewn loosely over smooth rock slabs, thin layers of ice over rock, and cornices.
- Bring crampons. Deeply shaded couloirs may retain a layer of ice year-round. Early in the season, they are covered by hard snow and ice caused by freezing or avalanche scouring. Later in the season, you encounter the remaining hard snow and ice, sometimes with steep moats lining its edges.
- Observe snow and avalanche conditions above steep gullies and on their floors. Avalanches scour deep ruts in the floors of many steep couloirs. Cornices can hang above. Early in the year, the floors of the ruts offer the soundest snow available, and in cold weather they may be quite safe, particularly for a fast descent. If these conditions do not exist, cross the ruts rapidly or avoid them altogether.
- During the ascent, look for alternative descent

routes, just in case time or changing snow conditions prevent descending the couloir on your return.
- Research the area beforehand. Finding the correct couloir on a particular route can be challenging. They often look alike, and there may be several in the area. Rely on route information and knowledge of the terrain in order to choose the couloir that gives access to the summit rather than leading to a dead end.
- Beware of meltwater streams running above or underneath the snow. Listen for water. Look for sagging or holes in the snow where the stream may be. Walk on the sides of the gully and avoid any water; it may be slick with ice.

Bergschrunds

A bergschrund is the giant crevasse found at the upper limit of glacier movement, formed where the moving glacier breaks away from the permanent snow or ice cap above (fig. 16-38v). The downhill lip of the bergschrund can be considerably lower than the uphill edge, which may be overhanging. Sometimes the bergschrund is the final problem of the ascent. (See Chapter 17, Glacier Travel and Crevasse Rescue, for more information.)

Moats

Moats occur when snow partially melts and settles away from warmer rocks or trees. Moats are encountered on snowfields, around rock outcroppings and trees on ridges and along slopes, and in couloirs. Crossing a moat at the top of a snowfield where it separates from its rocky border can be as tough as getting past a bergschrund, with the main difference being that the uphill wall of a moat is rock, whereas the uphill wall of a bergschrund is ice.

Moats around trees and rocks may not be visible, appearing as merely an unstable layer of snow but actually covering an unseen large hole underneath. Stay away from treetops poking through the snow, and probe uncertain areas with an ice ax before stepping onto them. If a wide moat borders both sides of a slope along a steep couloir, it may indicate an equally wide moat at the head of the gully. You may have to cross it or, worse yet, retreat and find an alternate ascent.

16

Rockfall

Snowfields and glaciers are subject to rockfall from bordering walls and ridges. Wear helmets in hazardous areas. Try to schedule climbs for less-dangerous periods. Early-season outings face less rockfall than summer climbs because snow still cements loose rock in place. In the northern hemisphere, southern and eastern slopes get the sun first, so climb these slopes early. The shaded northern exposures offer less rockfall danger.

AVALANCHE SAFETY

Mountaineers seek the freedom of the hills, and no freedom is harder to earn than the freedom of the *snowy* hills. In North America, according to the International Commission on Alpine Rescue, avalanches kill more winter recreationists than any other natural hazard: forty-eight fatalities in 1998–99, thirty-two fatalities in 1999–00, and forty-five fatalities in 2000–01. Nearly all avalanches that involve people are triggered either by the victims themselves or by a member of their party; according to avalanche expert Bruce Tremper, about 85 percent of avalanche victims trigger their own slide.

Climbers, backcountry skiers, and snowshoers are prime victims of avalanches. Better mountain gear and changing trends in backcountry recreation are leading more and more people to have fun where there are avalanche-prone slopes. The high level of risk to climbers and backcountry skiers can be explained by two factors:

1. Climbers and backcountry skiers' destination may be avalanche terrain; therefore they spend time in avalanche terrain, exposed to the potential of random events—in a way "in the line of fire." Increased time in avalanche terrain equals more risk of involvement in an avalanche.
2. Climbers and backcountry skiers' route to their destination may be avalanche prone, so they travel in avalanche-prone areas where human triggering is possible or even likely.

Reaching a climbing objective often involves traveling on steep and exposed avalanche start zones (see below). In choosing among route options, climbers must contend with the challenges of evaluating avalanche hazard. Early start times, moving really fast, and brute ambition are not enough to evade all avalanches. Avalanche hazard, unlike high-mountain exposure and severe weather, is not always obvious.

However, avalanches are not a mysterious phenomenon. Avalanche education can help backcountry travelers make better decisions about safe snow travel. This section introduces the subject of avalanches and reviews some of the ways that snow travelers can evaluate hazards and minimize risk; the next section explains methods of searching for avalanche victims. This material is not intended to be comprehensive. For a more complete understanding of the subject, consult specialized publications (see Appendix C, Supplementary Reading) and take advantage of courses in avalanche awareness. For an explanation of the formation of avalanches and an assessment of dangers associated with various forms of snow, see Chapter 26, The Cycle of Snow.

Understanding Avalanches

Snow, which is part of the allure of a climbing, snowshoeing, or skiing trip, is the source of avalanche hazard. Natural avalanches occur when snow deposited by storm systems places too great a load on the snowpack. The imposed stress exceeds the strength of the snowpack, and an avalanche is the result. A skier or climber may add sufficient stress to set off a slide.

Most avalanche victims are involved in small to medium-sized slides. Imagine a snowfield of an area that is the size of a couple of tennis courts; it is poised on a slope, with weak layers hidden beneath the surface. A climber or skier enters the scene, and the additional load causes a failure: *crack!* The slab is off and away. The snow breaks and shears along the bed surface (the ground, ice, or hard snow layer that forms the sliding surface), between the weak layers, and across the top a fracture line marks the point where the tension holding the snow to the slope failed. Below the avalanche start zone (typically a 25- to 50-degree slope), the slab breaks up, and the churning snow accelerates down the avalanche track and into the runout zone, where the dense deposit accumulates and buries victims, on average, nearly 3 feet (a meter) deep. Because the motion is sudden, it has an unbalancing effect; the suddenness, speed, and power of the avalanche typically

16

sweep victims off their feet or skis, sometimes hurtling them into bad terrain or forcing them through confined tracks and burying them deeply in a cementlike medium tightly packed in a terrain trap.

Many avalanches create a destructive force capable of breaking trees, crushing a car, or wiping out a small cluster of buildings. Avalanche movement is varied; imagine slow lava, flowing white water, or 220-mile-per-hour (350-kilometer-per-hour) airborne turbulent masses.

Evaluating Avalanche Hazard

The interaction of three crucial variables—terrain, snowpack, and weather—determines whether or not an avalanche is possible (fig. 16-39). Is the terrain capable of producing an avalanche? Could the snowpack slide? Is the weather contributing to instability? However, to determine whether an avalanche hazard exists, another variable must be added: the backcountry traveler.

All of the information needed to evaluate avalanche hazards is generally available through observations and tests. Your decisions will be based on the results of these observations and tests. The results, if interpreted correctly, can reduce your risk of being caught in an avalanche. It is critical to learn the observations and

tests, and then go to the backcountry to practice them in a safe area.

Terrain

Avalanches can occur only on slopes steeper than about 25 degrees, and they occur most often on slopes of between 35 and 45 degrees. Learning to recognize avalanche terrain is the first step in the process of evaluating avalanche hazard. The steepness of a slope, its aspect (which direction it faces), and the slope's shape and natural features (its configuration) are all important factors in determining whether a slide can occur on a particular slope.

Slope angle: Of all of these factors, the steepness, or slope angle, is the most important (fig. 16-40). Slab avalanches commonly occur on slopes with starting-zone angles between about 30 and 45 degrees, but slab avalanches occasionally occur on slopes of less than 30 and greater than 45 to 55 degrees. Slopes steeper than about 50 to 60 degrees tend to slough snow constantly, and slopes of about 25 degrees or less are generally not steep enough. It is difficult to estimate the angle of a slope just by looking at it. Use a clinometer. Simple plastic models are available, and many compasses have clinometers built into them (see Chapter 5, Navigation, for a discussion of clinometers).

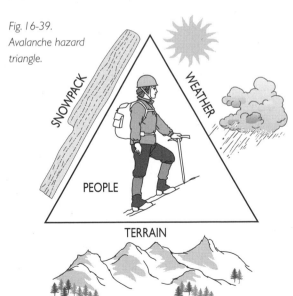

Fig. 16-39.
Avalanche hazard
triangle.

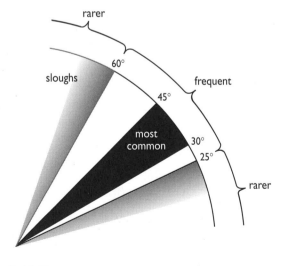

Fig. 16-40.
The frequency of avalanches on slopes of various angles.

The slope you are on is not the only concern, because an avalanche could start from an adjacent slope. You do not have to be climbing or skiing on a slope for it to avalanche. This is a very important concept: All of the snow is connected. You can be traveling on a gentle slope or snow-covered road, and if the snowpack is unstable enough, you can trigger a slide on the steeper slope above you, even though you are not *on* a steep slope. All of the snow is connected, remember? It is critical for you to know what is above you as you travel.

Slope aspect: The direction a slope faces—its slope aspect—determines how much sun and wind the slope gets, and this indicates a great deal about its avalanche potential. Here is how it works in the northern hemisphere; it is just the opposite on mountains south of the equator.

South-facing slopes receive more sun; therefore, snow settles and stabilizes faster than on north-facing slopes. In general (with plenty of local exceptions), this may make south-facing slopes somewhat safer in winter. They tend to release avalanches sooner after a storm, so if they *are* avalanching, it is an indication that slopes facing in other directions may soon follow their lead. As warmer spring and summer days arrive, south slopes become prone to wet-snow avalanches, and north-facing slopes may be safer.

North-facing slopes receive little or no sun in the winter, so consolidation of the snowpack takes longer. Colder temperatures within the snowpack create weak layers. Therefore, in general (again, with local exceptions), north slopes are more likely to slide in midwinter. In spring and summer, as south slopes become dangerously wet, look to the north side for firmer, safer snow.

Windward slopes—those that face into the wind—tend to be safer than leeward slopes. Windward slopes may be blown clear of snow, or the remaining snow may be compacted by the force of the wind.

Leeward slopes—those that face away from the wind—are particularly dangerous because of wind-loading. These slopes collect snow rapidly when high winds move snow from windward slopes onto the leeward side. The result is cornices on the lee side of ridges, snow that is deeper and less consolidated, and the formation of wind slabs ready to avalanche.

Slope configuration: Smooth slopes—those that, beneath the snow, are covered with grass or smooth rock slabs—generally have a poor bond with the snow and provide a slick surface for a slide. Trees and rocks may serve as anchors that tend to stabilize the snow—at least until the snow covers them. But, in general, to act as effective anchors the trees and rocks need to be so close together that it can be difficult or impossible for a climbing party to move through them. After these trees and rocks are buried by snowfall, they can actually become a source of weakness in the snowpack; as foreign bodies, the trees and rocks can inhibit or interfere with the bonding of the snow layers. Slides are not

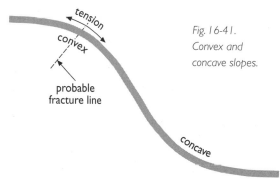

Fig. 16-41.
Convex and
concave slopes.

TIPS FOR EVALUATING SLOPE CONFIGURATION

Look around while you are traveling:
- Are there shattered trees in avalanche fans and wide swaths cut through old timber? This is evidence of large avalanches penetrating thick forest.
- Does a slope grow only brush and small trees? Do they all slant downward? This is probably a slope that avalanches so often that timber has no chance to grow.
- Are tree limbs missing from the uphill side in open timber? It might be the result of avalanches. Open timber that can be easily skied through offers little or no avalanche protection.

likely to originate in a dense forest, but they can run through dense forest from above.

The shape of a slope affects the hazard level. Snow on a slope that is straight, open, and moderately steep presents the most obvious danger. Snow on a convex slope, under tension as it stretches tightly over the curve of the hill, is more prone to avalanche than snow on a concave slope (fig. 16-41). Fracture lines frequently occur just below a convex area.

Snowpack

Slab configuration: What is the composition of the snowpack? The typical snowpack comprises a series of discrete layers. The layers are characterized by relative strength, hardness, and thickness. The depth and distribution of weak layers within the snowpack are significant factors in determining the stability of the snowpack.

Bonding ability: Throughout the winter, the snowpack accumulates layer by layer with each new precipitation, temperature, and wind event. There are both strong and weak layers within a snowpack. Strong layers tend to be denser layers composed of small, round snow grains that are packed closely together and are well bonded to each other, or cohesive. Weak layers tend to be less-dense layers that are composed of poorly bonded or cohesionless grains. These layers often appear loose or "sugary." Because weak layers prevent strong layers from bonding with one another, it is important for the backcountry traveler to know the relationship of these layers.

Sensitivity to stress: The snowpack exists in a balance between its strength and the stresses placed upon it. When the snow's strength is greater than the stresses, the snow is stable. Fortunately, this is most often the case; otherwise, snow would never stay on a hillside. But sometimes the balance between strength and stress is almost equal and then the snowpack is unstable. Avalanches occur only when and if the snowpack is unstable. For an avalanche to occur, something must disturb the balance so that the stress on or within the snowpack exceeds its strength. The snowpack can adjust to only a limited amount of stress and only at a certain rate of speed. Add another stress such as a rapid load of precipitation, a sudden increase in temperature,

windblown snow, or the weight of a climber or skier, and an avalanche could be triggered.

Weather

Before and during any backcountry trip, study the weather closely. Heavy precipitation, high winds, or extreme temperatures mean changes in the snowpack. Be prepared to look critically at the snow to see how the snowpack has been affected by recent weather. The snowpack adapts poorly to sudden changes, so rapid turns in the weather contribute to instability of the snowpack. The snowpack can bend and adapt when forces are applied slowly, but sudden stress can cause it to break. (See "The Formation of Snow Avalanches" in Chapter 26, The Cycle of Snow.)

Precipitation: Precipitation is either solid (snow and hail) or liquid (rain). Both forms add to stress on the snowpack. Avalanche danger increases rapidly with snowfall of 1 inch (2.5 centimeters) or more per hour. The threshold of 12 inches (30 centimeters) or more in a day is critical. If a heavy load of new snow accumulates too quickly for the strength of the existing snowpack, an avalanche may result.

Rain can percolate into the snow, weakening bonds between layers. Rain tends to lubricate the layers, making it easier for a slide to start. Rain adds significant weight, and it may also rapidly warm the snowpack. Avalanches can be triggered very quickly after rainfall begins.

With either rain or new snow, the questions to consider are: How well does it bond with the snowpack? How big a load does it represent? The weight of the water in the new snow is the primary contributor of stress on the snowpack.

Wind: The high winds that transport snow from windward slopes and deposit it on leeward slopes break the interlocking bonds between snow crystals. These particles, once they are made smaller, pack closely together, forming cohesive slabs that fracture efficiently, resulting in avalanches. High winds also shape the cornices that overhang lee slopes. Cornices can break and fall, sometimes triggering an avalanche.

Temperature: Significant differences in temperature between the ground and the snow surface promote growth of highly faceted snow crystals (depth hoar, or "sugar snow") that cannot support much load. This temperature differential and the resulting sugar snow especially appear early in the season, notably in interior, snowy climates such as that in the Rocky Mountains. Less-severe temperature gradients and a deeper snowpack act as insulation that may allow this snow to stabilize. But highly faceted snow can persist as a dangerous underlying layer well into the snow season or until avalanches release it.

Another type of weak crystal growth, similar to dew, is surface hoar. It is common in all areas. The conditions that encourage its growth are cool, cloudless nights that are calm or nearly calm at the snow surface. When the thin, feathered crystals of surface hoar are covered by subsequent snowfall, they can form weak layers that—like sugar snow—increase avalanche hazard.

Temperature affects snow stability, especially that of new snow, in complicated ways. Warm temperatures accelerate settling, causing the snowpack to become denser and stronger, and thus, over the long term, more stable. But rapid, prolonged warming, particularly after a cold spell, initially weakens the snow cover, making it less stable and more susceptible to human-triggered failure. The snowpack remains unstable until temperatures cool down. Cold temperatures make dense snow layers stronger but are unlikely to strengthen weak layers of new, low-density snow.

Know Before You Go

It is up to you to gather important data before you head into avalanche terrain. There are many ways to minimize the risk of avalanches and to increase your chances of survival if one hits. In addition to evaluating avalanche hazard during a trip, you can also reduce avalanche risk by the things you do before you head into the mountains.

Take a class. Avalanche awareness and education are critical to making good decisions. Reading this chapter gives you an introduction to decision making in avalanche terrain. However, after you take an avalanche course, you should be able to identify avalanche terrain; to identify basic snow grain types, weak layers, and strong layers; to perform field tests to determine snowpack stability/instability; to recognize weather and terrain factors contributing to instability; to perform rescue through fast and efficient transceiver use; and to apply safe travel techniques. There is no such thing as too much avalanche education.

You can also improve your safety margin by taking some of the normal precautions of any climbing trip or ski tour, such as studying maps and photos of the area, researching alternative routes, preparing for an emergency bivouac, and identifying possible retreat routes. Determine the route—including its slope aspects, elevations, slope sizes/shapes, and exposure—and identify the probable locations of hazards.

TIPS FOR SELECTING A SAFE ROUTE

Travel safely in the backcountry by seeking routes that limit your exposure to danger. The following guidelines are based on some of the important considerations discussed in this chapter:

- Favor windward slopes, which tend to be more stable.
- Avoid leeward slopes where winds have deposited snow slabs.
- Choose the least-steep slopes that will get you to your objective.
- Favor the edges of slopes; avalanches are less likely, and safer terrain is closer in case one occurs.
- Be suspicious of the convex rollover at the top of a slope—a point of stress that can trigger an avalanche.
- Be careful of shaded slopes in winter and the very warm, sunny slopes of spring.
- Be particularly cautious of slopes of 35 to 45 degrees; use a clinometer to identify them. The majority of avalanches occur on slopes of 38 degrees.
- Avoid gullies, which can be chutes for large quantities of snow that can deeply bury you or sweep you away.
- Keep aware of the runout zone below snow slopes and gullies, especially avoiding areas with cliffs below.
- Avoid camping in valleys that can be exposed to avalanche danger from above.
- Develop "avalanche eyeballs" by continually evaluating avalanche danger and its potential consequences.

16

Finally, be sure the people in your climbing party have adequate training and equipment for heading into areas of possible avalanche risk. Be prepared to recognize, evaluate, avoid, and mitigate avalanche risk.

Check Weather and Avalanche Forecasts

It is obvious advice, but check the weather and avalanche forecasts before your trip. In many mountain areas, detailed avalanche reports are available by telephone and through the Internet from local avalanche forecast centers. Most local avalanche centers issue avalanche warnings (see Table 16-1) throughout the winter. Before you head out, check the avalanche hazard rating for the area you plan to visit and use this forecast to make your decisions. If possible, follow the weather trends and snowfall history of the area. This will provide information about the snowpack. Talk to people with local knowledge of your intended route, including any ranger who may be responsible for that area. Do not be afraid to rethink well-laid plans if you uncover crucial pretrip information.

Consider Human Factors

In evaluating avalanche hazard, a prime component is the human factor. The judgments that mountaineers make affect the level of risk they face. The Avalanche Hazard Evaluation Checklist in Table 16-2 asks all members of a mountaineering party to ask questions of themselves and to reach a judgment on several points.

Attitude: What is the general attitude of the party

What	Why	Where	What to Do
TABLE 16-1. U.S. AVALANCHE DANGER SCALE			
Danger Level (and Color)	*Avalanche Probability and Avalanche Trigger*	*Degree and Distribution of Avalanche Danger*	*Recommended Action in the Backcountry*
Low (green)	Natural avalanches *very unlikely*. Human-triggered avalanches *unlikely*.	Generally stable snow. Isolated areas of instability.	Travel is generally safe. Normal caution advised.
Moderate (yellow)	Natural avalanches *unlikely*. Human-triggered avalanches *possible*.	Unstable slabs *possible* on steep terrain.	Use caution in steeper terrain on certain aspects.
Considerable (orange)	Natural avalanches *possible*. Human-triggered avalanches *probable*.	Unstable slabs *probable* on steep terrain.	Be increasingly cautious in steeper terrain.
High (red)	Natural and human-triggered avalanches *likely*.	Unstable slabs *likely* on a variety of aspects and slope angles.	Travel in avalanche terrain is not recommended. Safest travel is on windward ridges of lower-angle slopes without steeper terrain above.
Extreme (red with black border)	Widespread natural or human triggered avalanches *certain*.	Extremely unstable slabs *certain* on most aspects and slope angles. Large destructive avalanches *possible*.	Travel in avalanche terrain should be avoided and travel confined to low-angle terrain well away from avalanche path runouts.

Note: Italics in table for emphasis.

TABLE 16-2. AVALANCHE HAZARD EVALUATION CHECKLIST

Critical Data		Hazard Rating		
Parameters:	**Key Information**	**Green Light** (go/OK)	**Yellow Light** (caution/potentially dangerous)	**Red Light** (stop/ dangerous)
Terrain: Is the terrain capable of producing an avalanche?				
■ Slope Angle (steep enough to slide? prime time?)		☐	☐	☐
■ Slope Aspect (leeward, shadowed, or extremely sunny?)		☐	☐	☐
■ Slope Configuration (anchoring? shape?)		☐	☐	☐
Overall Terrain Rating:		☐	☐	☐
Snowpack: Could the snow fail?				
■ Slab Configuration (slab? depth and distribution?)		☐	☐	☐
■ Bonding Ability (weak layer? tender spots?)		☐	☐	☐
■ Sensitivity (how much force to fail? shear tests? clues?)		☐	☐	☐
Overall Snowpack Rating:		☐	☐	☐
Weather: Is the weather contributing to instability?				
■ Precipitation (type, amount, intensity? added weight?)		☐	☐	☐
■ Wind (snow transport? amount and rate of deposition?)		☐	☐	☐
■ Temperature (storm trends? effects on snowpack?)		☐	☐	☐
Overall Weather Rating		☐	☐	☐
Human factors: What are the alternatives and their possible consequences?				
■ Attitude (toward life? risk? goals? assumptions?)		☐	☐	☐
■ Technical Skill Level (traveling? evaluating avalanche hazard?)		☐	☐	☐
■ Strength/Equipment (strength? prepared for the worst?)		☐	☐	☐
Overall Human Factors Rating:		☐	☐	☐
Decision/Action:				
Overall Hazard Rating/Go or No Go?		GO ☐ or NO GO ☐		

Source: © Fredston and Fesler, Alaska Mountain Safety Center, Inc. *(reproduced by permission)*

toward its goals, toward risk, and toward the hazard data each member has been collecting? Consider the party's tolerance for risk and its degree of commitment to a climbing objective even in the face of hazard. Decide how willing the group is to look objectively at information on terrain, the snowpack, and weather. Many parties allow their desires to cloud the hard facts. Most avalanche victims were aware of the hazard but chose to interpret the information in such a way that an accident occurred. An unsafe attitude can be fatal.

Technical skill level: How skilled are members of the party at snow travel and at evaluating avalanche hazard? Are the party's overall mountaineering skills high? Just average? Low? A balanced party of able, experienced mountaineers can be expected to do well at avoiding avalanches and at responding efficiently if one strikes. A relatively untested party, or one whose members have a great difference in experience and skill levels, may need to be more conservative in its decisions.

Strength and equipment: What shape is the party in? Decide whether members of the group are strong and healthy enough to go on a demanding and possibly

349

hazardous trip. How well equipped is the party to deal with an avalanche? Determine whether the party is actually prepared for the worst, with shovels, rescue transceivers, first-aid supplies, and other gear that would be needed.

Deciding "Go" or "No Go": Before Leaving Home

After all the avalanche hazard information has been collected and evaluated, the climbing party must make the go/no go decision.

Every member of the party needs to give their opinion freely. Groups that take each person's thinking into account usually make better decisions than individuals. All climbers have an obligation to express their concerns clearly, even in the face of differing opinions. When the party faces the risk of fatalities, prudent reservations, based on sound information, are essential.

Each person must understand the possible consequences of the decision and any alternatives to it. Everyone should understand any assumptions underlying the go/no go decision, including the thinking that resulted in assessments of the party's risk tolerance or its ability to deal with an avalanche. The party's decision-making process should proceed in this manner:

1. Identify potential hazards.
2. Continuously collect, evaluate, and integrate information.
3. Consciously explore assumptions, the consequences of a particular decision, and alternatives to that decision.
4. Make a decision—but be willing to reevaluate based on new information.

The information in this chapter can help simplify the decision-making process. Using the Avalanche Hazard Evaluation Checklist in Table 16-2, the party will assign each step of the evaluation with a green go-ahead light, a yellow caution light, or a red stop signal. The completed checklist then points the way to a sound decision.

Use Your Skills in the Field

Once you have learned (and practiced) the fundamentals of avalanche safety, you must use these skills in the backcountry. Identifying avalanche terrain or suspect weather patterns is not enough; you must know how to put it all together. This section helps prepare you for making decisions and taking action in the backcountry. As with other aspects of avalanche safety, practice the techniques before finding yourself in hazardous terrain or involved in an avalanche rescue.

Observing Snow Conditions

Climbers need to know where they are going and, before they get there, what actions they are going to take. Look at conditions on similar terrain as soon and as often as possible. Observe the big picture first: on the road, up the trail, at camp, out on the terrain. Then fit your party's plans and situation into that picture. Use this perspective to decide where the party will test the snow for its stability and what tests will be used, and also use this perspective to aid the party in avoiding avalanche hazard.

To travel safely in the backcountry, you must be able to recognize unstable conditions. Generally, when unstable snow conditions exist, the majority of results from observations and tests will confirm that conditions are unstable on certain slope aspects, at certain elevations, and within a certain range of slope angles. Because there will be some uncertainty, particularly when the weather is changing, an extra margin of safety is required. Always make observations, looking for obvious signs of instability. Use the major clues shown in Table 16-3.

Testing Snow Stability

You can get a lot of information on possible avalanche danger simply by paying close attention to the obvious signs of instability outlined in this section. You can also test for snow stability. The Rutschblock test has shown a high degree of reliability, though several other methods can also secure information on snow stability. These other methods are briefly introduced below, but you must refer to specialized publications and expert instruction to learn how to carry them out and evaluate them correctly.

Rutschblock (glide block) test: This reliable test is considered a particularly good indicator of how likely a slope is to slide. The Rutschblock test puts stress on a

TABLE 16-3. CLUES TO SNOWPACK STABILITY

Clue	Message
Recent avalanche activity	Best clue to instability. *Slopes of similar elevation and aspect should be considered suspect.*
***Whumphing* noises**	Sounds caused by a sudden collapse of a weak subsurface layer; indicates extreme instability in the area. *Pick routes across gentle slopes (slopes with angles of less than 25 degrees) and avoid runout zones of steeper slopes.*
Shooting cracks	A form of brittle failure caused by the sudden release of stored elastic energy (i.e., extreme instability is present). As a rule, the longer or deeper the crack, the more serious the instability. *Avoid avalanche terrain, including the runout zones of steeper slopes above.*
Pluming and wind transport	Wind pluming (wind-generated snow clouds), which results from snow being eroded from the windward slopes and new snow being rapidly deposited on leeward slopes, is a major clue that conditions have changed for the worse on leeward slopes. If wind loading persists, the period of instability is usually followed by repeated cycles of avalanche activity and reloading. *Avoid these leeward slopes and terrain below them.*
Storm activity	Tends to make conditions more unstable. These periods of instability are generally of shorter duration in warmer snow climates, but persist for long periods of time in colder climates. *Avoid travel in the backcountry.*

Note: Italics in table for emphasis.
Source: © Fredston and Fesler, Alaska Mountain Safety Center, Inc. *(reproduced by permission)*

TABLE 16-4. INTERPRETING THE RUTSCHBLOCK TEST RESULTS

Results	Stability
Fails while excavating the site	Extremely Unstable
Fails while approaching the test site after excavation	Extremely Unstable
Fails while standing on the block	Extremely Unstable
Fails while flexing for a jump	Unstable
Fails (to a questionable degree) with a jump	Unstable
Fails after repeated hard jumps	Relatively Stable
Does not fail with repeated jumps; try jumping without skis on	Stable

large block, or column, of snow (fig. 16-42), which provides better results than other tests, such as the shovel shear test (see below). In the Rutschblock test, a person on skis stands atop the block. Follow these steps to conduct the Rutschblock test:

1. Find a spot that is representative of the slope aspect and incline that the party expects to encounter. The best information is usually garnered from an area that is not near trees or a ridge.

2. Using a shovel, a snow saw, or a ski, excavate to create three sides of a rectangular snow block: front (downslope) and two sides. Dig down at least 3 feet (a meter), or deeper if necessary, to reach suspected weak layers. The length of the block in the cross-slope direction should be about the same as the length of a ski; the width of the block in the downslope direction should be about the same as the length of a ski pole. Make clean, vertical sides

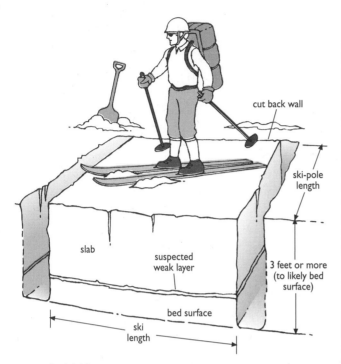

cut back wall

ski-pole length

slab

suspected weak layer

3 feet or more (to likely bed surface)

bed surface

ski length

Fig. 16-42.
In the Rutschblock test for snow stability, a person on skis puts stress on top of a block of snow.

on the snow block; do not disturb the snow on top.

3. Cut the fourth side of the rectangle—the back wall of the block—free of the slope, using a saw, ski, or rope. It may be difficult to cut through hard or icy layers without a snow saw.

4. Have a person on skis step onto the center of the block from the slope above. If the block supports the skier, that person then stresses the block with a series of jumps, leaping up with both skis. The amount of stress required to cause the block to shear (fail) at a weak layer indicates the relative stability of the slope.

5. Use the criteria in Table 16-4 to interpret the Rutschblock test results. Keep in mind that the result of the Rutschblock test is just one piece of information among many that must be collected to assess avalanche danger. After conducting the test, fill in the hole so that it is not a hazard for other travelers.

Shovel shear test: This test can detect the presence of snow layers that are likely to slide. The procedure involves excavating a column of snow that is freestanding on the front and sides and has a cut at the back that is deep enough to allow you to insert a shovel. The column should be approximately as wide as the shovel. The tester stands in front of the column, inserts the shovel in the cut at the back, and pulls forward on the shovel handle with both hands. If the snow has a pronounced sliding layer, the column will shear off evenly at that point. This test has been criticized for not providing reliable information on the amount of force needed to cause shearing. Although the shovel shear test may provide information about layering and stability, multiple test sites may be required. The Rutschblock test has proven to be a much more reliable indicator of snow stability.

Snow-pit observation: Observe the pattern of layering in a snow pit (perhaps the one dug for the Rutschblock test). The snow pit should be in a safe location that has an angle, aspect, and elevation similar to the nearby slopes that the party plans to cross. It should be in a spot away from trees. It is not difficult to identify the various snow layers and determine their relative hardness and strength by pushing against each one with a fist or jabbing them with a finger, pencil, or knife. Very hard layers or very soft layers may not bond well with other layers. Snow pits may not yield as much useful information as the Rutschblock test.

Ski-pole probe: Use a ski pole to puncture the snow surface and get an indication of what is below. If the snow is very soft, push the basket end of the pole smoothly into the snow; then pull it slowly out, trying to feel any hard or soft layers. It may be possible to reach down into the ski-pole hole and feel the snow layers with your fingers. In most other snow, use the handle end of the ski pole or remove the basket to penetrate the snow. Regularly making these observations and discussing them with party members reinforces an awareness of avalanche hazard and preparedness. This informal test will not give information on the bonding of snow layers and it will miss thin shear planes, but it can reveal gross discontinuities in the snowpack structure that suggest instability.

16

Deciding "Go" or "No Go": During the Approach

Snow travelers facing possible avalanche hazard want the answer to one basic question: Is it a "go" or a "no go"? That is, can the party proceed, or must they turn back or find another route? Table 16-2 above provides a checklist of critical data that snow travelers can use both at home in preparation and in the field en route to evaluate avalanche hazard and reach a go/no go decision. The checklist can guide the party in responding to four principal questions:

1. Is the terrain capable of producing an avalanche?
2. Could the snow fail?
3. Is the weather contributing to instability?
4. What are the alternatives and their possible consequences?

To respond effectively to these overall questions, the party needs to come up with answers to a series of secondary queries about the terrain, snowpack, weather, and the climbing party. Using the checklist in Table 16-2 above, answer each one with an assessment of relative hazard, expressed as a green light (OK), a yellow light (caution), or a red light (danger). Keep in mind that most avalanche incidents occur on days when yellow signals are noted. A review of the completed checklist should give the party enough input to reach a go/no go decision at each encounter with possible avalanche hazard.

Crossing a Questionable Slope Safely

Nobody likes it, but sometimes there is no way to avoid questionable avalanche terrain. The task then is to make the passage with the least danger of disturbing the slope and to minimize the consequences of a possible avalanche.

Before you head out onto the slope, put on your hat, mittens, and warm clothing, and zip up your clothing. Undo ski-pole straps. If you are on skis or snowshoes, use releasable bindings and remove the safety straps that connect the boots to the bindings. (Skis and snowshoes spread a person's weight over a relatively large area, putting less strain on the slope than boots do.)

When the route lies up a slope (and the party is walking, not skiing), head straight up the fall line instead of switchbacking, which can undercut the snow.

On a traverse, only one person moves at a time, and everyone else watches from safe places, ready to shout if a slide starts. Cross with long, smooth strides, being careful not to cut a trench across the slope. Each climber follows in turn, stepping in the leader's footprints. Everyone listens and watches for an avalanche. The route should follow a line as high on the slope as practical. It may be possible to hug cliff bands at the top of the slope.

Move from one position of safety to another, minimizing the exposure period. Do not fall; falling puts a sudden load on the snowpack. On an avalanche-ready slope, the impact of a falling body is like the detonation of a little bomb.

Think twice before roping up on questionable slopes. Decide whether the risk of the slope avalanching is greater than the risk of a climber falling. If you choose to use a rope, belay directly off the anchor. The belayer should not tie in to the rope, because this would risk the belayer being pulled into an avalanche. If there are no solid anchors from which to belay, go unroped.

Surviving an Avalanche

You must think ahead about what you would do in the event of an avalanche, because after one starts, there is no time.

While you are traveling, keep an eye out for escape paths. If you are caught in an avalanche, do not give up. Fight to survive. Try to get off the moving snow. Yell to your climbing partners. Jettison any gear you want to get rid of, including skis and ski poles. You might want to keep your pack: Larger objects tend to be transported to the surface of avalanche debris; your pack may help keep you near the surface, and it may help protect you from trauma. If you survive the traumatic forces of the avalanche, you will certainly need the clothing and equipment in your pack.

At the start of an avalanche, try to stop before being swept away. Grab a rock or tree, or dig your ice ax or a ski pole into the snow, and hold on. If that does not work, try to stay on the surface by using swimming motions, flailing your arms and legs, or by rolling. Try to move to the side of the slide.

16

If your head goes below the surface, close your mouth to avoid being suffocated by snow. As the avalanche slows, thrust upward. If you are buried, try to make a breathing space by putting an elbow or hand in front of your face. Inhale deeply before the snow stops, in order to expand your ribs; as the snow closes around you, it will become impossible to move. Do not shout or struggle. Relax. Try to conserve oxygen and energy. Your climbing partners should know what to do, and they will begin immediate rescue efforts.

AVALANCHE RESCUE
The Well-Prepared Party

A climbing party's level of preparedness is an important factor in minimizing avalanche hazard. A well-prepared party has the training and practice, conditioning, equipment, and critical judgment to evaluate hazard and to respond effectively to an avalanche. Members of the party must have electronic avalanche rescue transceivers, shovels, and probe tools to perform a rescue, and they must have developed the skills to use them. They know that seconds do count in the safety of their party.

The well-equipped party may carry other tools to evaluate the snowpack and aid in avoiding an avalanche. A snow-study kit with a snow crystal card, a clinometer, and a snow saw help in analysis of slopes and the snowpack. New products to help avalanche victims survive include the Black Diamond Avalung II, avalanche air bags, and avalanche balls. Research and try out any avalanche safety item before you rely on it in the backcountry.

The mountaineer's primary emphasis should be on avalanche evaluation and safe travel. Every party needs rescue skills and equipment, but they are no substitute for the ability to make sound judgments that promote safe travel in avalanche terrain.

Using Avalanche
Rescue Transceivers

The electronic avalanche rescue transceiver is the principal tool for finding buried victims. A rescue transceiver can be switched to either transmit or receive signals.

The international standard frequency for avalanche transceivers is 457 kilohertz. Transceivers that work at 2,275 hertz are obsolete and should not be used. Some rescue groups may use dual-frequency transceivers, but the recommended transceivers for backcountry travelers and climbers operate exclusively at 457 kilohertz. The new standard transceivers have a greater range.

Further progress in the avalanche safety field has produced transceivers with digital processors. Analog and digital transceivers are compatible and both utilize the 457 kilohertz standard. The two types of transceivers have different features, so before investing money and time in one, read product reviews, talk to experienced users, and try out different units.

Digital tranceivers convert the analog signal to a digital readout. Digital units typically provide both audible and visible signals in the search (receive) mode. Digital units do offer some advantages; the primary one is that almost all users will experience a shorter learning curve with a digital transceiver than that experienced with an analog transceiver.

Rescue depends on each member of the party carrying a transceiver. All members of a party must know how to use the transceivers correctly. This is a skill that requires regular practice, so practice before and during every season.

At the trailhead and at the beginning of each day, the group should verify that all transceivers can transmit and receive signals properly. Fresh batteries usually last for about 300 hours, but carry extras in case the signal from any transceiver weakens.

Strap the transceiver around your neck and torso. Carry it under a shirt or jacket to keep it from being lost in an avalanche. Do not carry it in your pack. During the climb, transceivers are left on, set to the transmit mode. If you are staying overnight in a snow cave or in an avalanche-prone area, consider leaving the transceiver on, set to transmit, even at night.

Once a search begins, unstrap the device and bring it out for rescue work; all rescuers switch their transceivers to the receive mode to locate the transmission from a victim. It is critically important that every searcher switch to receive; if a searcher's transceiver is left in the transmit mode, searchers will waste valuable

16

time receiving this signal rather than the signal from the victim.

Each searcher listens for beeps and/or watches an optical display to detect the buried victim. A rescuer should be able to locate the buried victim in less than 5 minutes. It is essential to practice using rescue transceivers to ensure that searchers have the best chance of locating victims before they suffocate.

First Steps in a Rescue

The rescue effort starts even before the avalanche has stopped. In the shock of the moment, the first step in a successful rescue is a tough one: Someone must pay attention to the point where a victim is last seen. Identify the area to be searched based on the Last Seen Area.

Do *not* go for help. This is a critical principle of avalanche rescue. Do not send anyone for help. *Stay and search.* Survival depends almost certainly on locating the victim quickly. A person located in the first 15 minutes has an approximately 90 percent chance of survival. The probability of survival drops off rapidly after that time. After 90 minutes, the probability of survival is approximately 25 percent. After the victim is unburied or after search efforts turn out to be futile, then send someone for help.

Select a search leader to direct a thorough and methodical rescue effort. Before you enter the search area, consider the safety of the search party. Evaluate the potential for other slides in the area, choose a safe approach to the search area, and designate an escape path in case of another avalanche.

The Three Phases of a Transceiver Search

A transceiver search for an avalanche victim proceeds through three phases: coarse, fine, and pinpoint. The coarse phase and the pinpoint phase rely on a traditional technique called the bracket or grid method. But for the fine search phase, a newer method—the tangential or induction method—is up to 50 percent quicker when used by trained individuals. It is essential that you master the bracket method. However, you should also learn the tangential method because of the critical time it can save during the fine-search phase.

Coarse Search

The coarse search starts with an initial rapid "scuff search" of the snow surface. Rescuers look for someone partially buried, any castoff equipment, or any logical spot where the victim might have come to a stop against a tree or rock. Use anything to mark the location of any clues as an aid to further search, and probe the likely catchment areas. The missing climber could turn up in this fast and immediate search.

Then move quickly into the transceiver search. Put the volume control or signal level all the way up on every transceiver. Searchers, spaced no more than 50 or 60 feet (15 to 18 meters) apart, should move in a clearly defined pattern over the search area. It is usually easier to move downhill while searching. Work rapidly but efficiently. You may need to consciously control your feelings of shock and anxiety in order to be effective at trying to find the missing person.

Because a transceiver's wire wrap antenna has directional characteristics, signals may be stronger or weaker depending on the position in which you hold your search transceiver, relative to the victim's transmitting transceiver. For this reason, it is important to rotate the transceiver left and right, forward and back, trying to find the strongest signal position.

When a signal is picked up, one or two persons start to track down the signal with a fine transceiver search while other rescuers get ready to dig out the victim. If there is more than one victim, the rest of the rescuers continue the coarse search. As each victim is found, turn off that person's transceiver so that searchers will not continue to pick up those signals.

Fine Search

Bracket method: Using a single rescue transceiver, searchers employing the bracket method follow a series of steps to find their way to a spot very near the buried victim (fig. 16-43).

1. Orient the transceiver for maximum signal strength, moving the unit vertically and horizontally to find the best signal position. The transceiver is now oriented toward the strongest sound. (Some transceivers provide a visual display to show the strongest

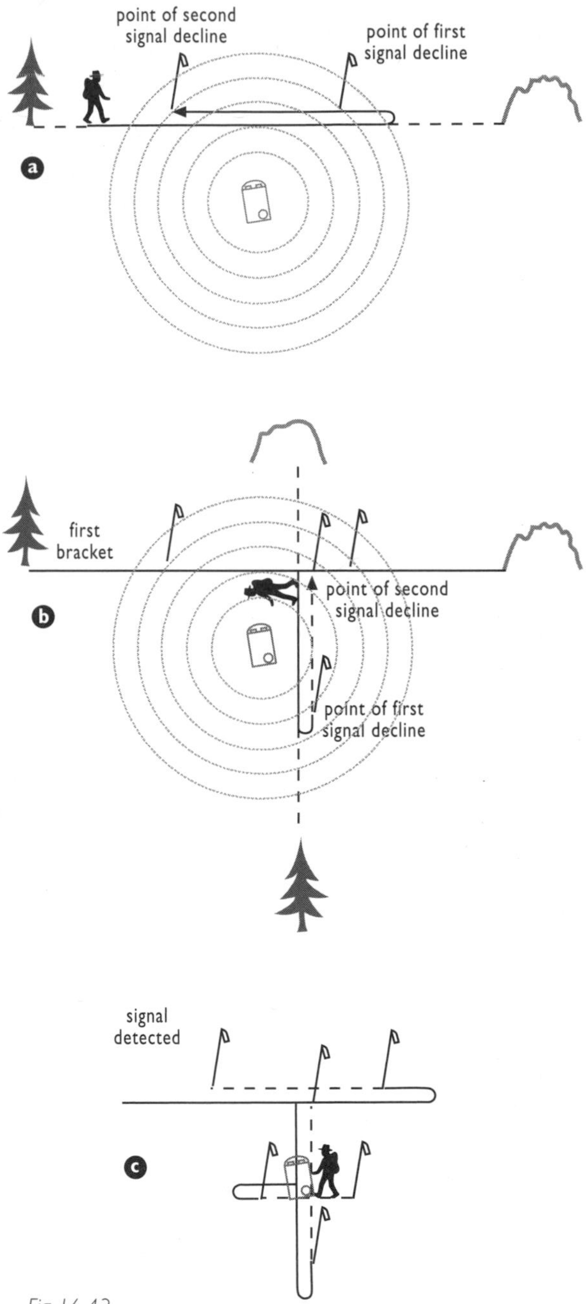

Fig. 16-43.
Fine search, using the bracket method: a, first bracket; b, second bracket; c, summary of beacon search bracketing. (Adapted from illustrations by Ray Smutek, used by permission.)

signal.) This orientation must be maintained throughout the search.

2. Reduce the volume to be as low as possible while still allowing you to hear the signal. (Your ear is better able to distinguish changes in volume for low-volume sounds.)

3. Keep the transceiver in the same orientation while you walk in any straight line. As soon as the signal reaches a peak and begins to drop, again reduce the volume to be as low as possible.

4. Still holding the transceiver in the same orientation, continue on the same path. When the signal fades out, mark the spot.

5. Without changing orientation of the transceiver, turn around 180 degrees and retrace the same pathway. When the signal fades out again, mark that spot. There is now a straight line bracketed at the end by points where the signal disappears (fig. 16-43a).

6. Return to the center of this bracketed line and make a 90-degree turn. Now repeat the process: Reduce the volume to a minimum and walk in a straight line until the signal fades out. Mark the spot, turn around 180 degrees without disturbing the orientation of the transceiver, and retrace your steps until the signal again fades; mark that spot. There is now another straight line bracketed by two fade-out points (fig. 16-43b).

7. Return to the center of this new line and again make a 90-degree turn in the direction of the signal. Work fast and efficiently, without worrying too much about precision. Continue this process of making bracketed lines until the distance between fade-out points on a line is less than 6 feet (1.8 meters). You can usually reach this stage within the first three brackets. You are now very close to the victim (fig. 16-43c) and ready to move into a pinpoint search.

Tangential method: The tangential method is an alternative to the bracket method for the fine search. The tangential method is faster when performed by a trained rescuer, but it takes more effort to learn and is not always successful. Be prepared to switch back to the bracket method if the tangential method does not give the needed results. Following are the steps to

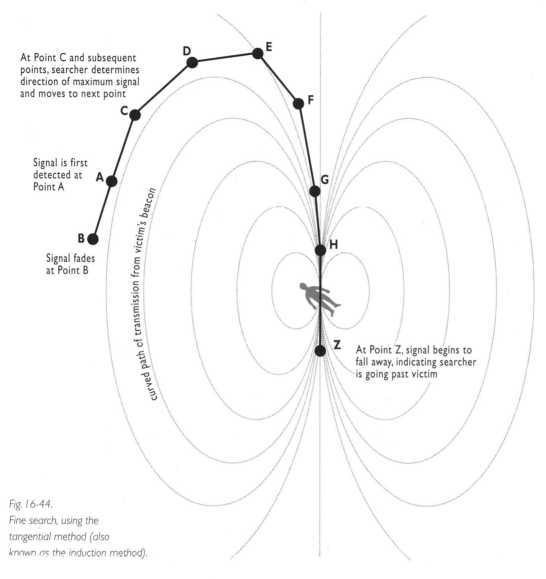

At Point C and subsequent points, searcher determines direction of maximum signal and moves to next point

Signal is first detected at Point A

Signal fades at Point B

curved path of transmission from victim's beacon

At Point Z, signal begins to fall away, indicating searcher is going past victim

Fig. 16-44.
Fine search, using the tangential method (also known as the induction method).

follow for the tangential method (fig. 16-44). The first two steps are identical to the bracket method.

1. Orient the transceiver for maximum signal strength, moving the unit vertically and horizontally to find the best position. The transceiver is now oriented toward the strongest sound. (Some transceivers provide a visual display to show the strongest signal.) This orientation must be maintained throughout the search.

2. Reduce the volume to be as low as possible while still allowing you to hear the signal. (Your ear is better able to distinguish changes in volume for low-volume sounds.)

3. Head off in the direction of the strongest sound. If the volume drops before you have traveled about 15 feet (about 4.5 meters) on this first leg of the fine search, turn and walk in the opposite direction.

4. After walking about 15 feet, again adjust the

orientation of the transceiver for maximum signal, reduce signal volume to the minimum, and start off in the direction of the strongest signal.

5. After walking another 15 feet, again adjust orientation and signal volume. Continue with a series of these 15-foot walks and signal adjustments, each time setting off again toward the strongest signal. On each leg, signal volume should increase as you walk.

These repeated procedures are designed to lead the searcher progressively closer to an area very near the victim. Because transmissions from the victim's transceiver follow a curved path, searchers will be following a curved arc to the buried person. Searchers know they are near the person when signal volume fades rather than increasing as they walk—the signal will fade as searchers pass the victim's location. They are now very close to the victim and ready to move into a pinpoint search.

Pinpoint Search

With your transceiver close to the snow surface, begin to pinpoint the victim by moving the transceiver from side to side and front to back in a small crisscross. When the volume is set very low, a loud signal means you are very close to the victim. If the transceiver can identify only a fairly large space—perhaps several feet across—mark the four corners of this area of maximum signal.

Using an avalanche probe, very carefully probe to determine the exact location of the person. Probe gently to avoid injuring the victim. As soon as the person is located, begin digging. Leave the pole in place to guide the digging.

Take care to avoid injuring the victim with shovels or probes or otherwise endangering the person you are trying to save. Some people report that the most terrifying part of their avalanche experience was having their air space trampled on as they were being rescued.

Probing

Formal probe searches for avalanche victims are not very effective because they take so much time, even for small areas. However, spot-probing is necessary for checking likely burial spots, especially the area identified by the pinpoint search with the rescue transceiver.

Probing is a slow and uncertain mechanical process, but it may be the only alternative if rescue transceivers fail to locate a victim or if the party is traveling without transceivers. Probe first at likely areas: near pieces of the victim's equipment, at the points of disappearance, and around trees and rocks. Probing in a group is a skill that must be practiced before it is needed. It is hard work involving discipline and concentration. In the backcountry, there may not be enough people to carry out formal probe procedures.

Commercial avalanche probes work far better than any other alternative. However, to find one buried victim, use whatever you have as a probe, including commercial avalanche probes, ski poles, ice axes, or wands.

If you have ski poles that can be joined together to create an avalanche probe, test them to verify whether they really work. You may conclude they do not. You may find you have difficulty removing the baskets, screwing in the adapter piece, or assembling the parts. Furthermore, the poles may not be strong enough to penetrate hard avalanche debris. Remember, these poles are only a poor substitute for a commercial avalanche probe.

Recovery

As the victim is uncovered, check to see that the person's mouth is not filled with snow and that there are no other obvious obstructions to breathing. Clear snow away from the victim's chest to allow room for it to expand and take in air. Be prepared to start cardiopulmonary resuscitation (CPR); the person need not be fully extracted from the snow before you begin CPR. Be aware that suddenly moving a burial victim may cause cardiac failure as cold blood from the extremeties moves to the heart. Make the person as warm and comfortable as possible, and be prepared to treat for hypothermia and injuries. (See Chapter 23, First Aid.)

If the avalanche buried more than one person, remember to switch off the transceiver carried by the rescued individual so that its transmissions will not interfere with the ongoing search for other victims. Once you have determined that the rescued individual does not need urgent care, continue to search for the other buried victims.

SAFE SNOW TRAVEL

Snow is a constantly changing medium. Safe snow travel requires alertness, preparation, and a constant reassessment of conditions. Here is a checklist of points to remember:

- Continually assess the stability of the snow. What is the relative level of avalanche hazard?
- When you are traveling in avalanche terrain, carry the necessary rescue gear: avalanche transceivers, probes, shovels, and first-aid kit.
- Use proper snow travel techniques. Practice and be proficient at self-belay and self-arrest.
- Keep your ice ax secure at all times, either leashed to you or strapped to your pack.
- Wear gloves whenever you are on snow, even when the weather is warm and you would prefer to take them off. You can fall at any time.
- Yell "Falling!" whenever someone, including you, falls. This notifies the rest of the party that someone is falling and, if the party is roped up, they themselves may need to arrest.
- Follow up with "Arrest! Arrest!" until the fallen climber has safely come to a stop—even if that fallen climber is you. This can be life saving for unroped climbers who fall and have no backup. It helps remind disoriented, falling climbers about what they have to do.
- Do not rely on self-arrest if there is dangerous runout. While you are ascending, if you are uncomfortable using the self-belay, arrange for an anchored belay or turn back and find another route.
- If you are on an exposed slope and have to adjust equipment such as crampons, anchor yourself. Plant your ice ax firmly in the snow and clip in to your leash.
- Carry and use appropriate gear for protection on snow climbs.
- Inspect a snow anchor after every use, and consider using multiple anchors whenever it is prudent.
- Bring crampons on snow climbs, even in warm weather. They are not just for glacier travel. You may encounter a shady couloir or slope with ice or hard snow.
- Observe the party's overall condition and climbing ability. Late in the day, exhaustion may diminish your reaction time in the event of a fall.

16

Glacier Travel and Crevasse Rescue

GLACIERS AND CREVASSES ■ EQUIPMENT FOR GLACIER TRAVEL ■
FUNDAMENTALS OF GLACIER TRAVEL ■ CREVASSE RESCUE RESPONSE ■
INSIDE THE CREVASSE ■ RESCUE METHODS ■ SPECIAL
RESCUE SITUATIONS ■ PATHS TO THE SUMMIT

Glaciers can offer a convenient route to alpine summits. However, glaciers hold many hazards. Glacier travelers should learn about crevasses, the chasms that split a glacier as its great mass of consolidated snow flows slowly downhill, and other glacier hazards. Although glacier travel is a very specialized skill, it is very necessary to mountaineering, for one principal reason: As a mountaineer, you must contend with crevasses.

To travel safely on a glacier, you first need all the basic snow travel skills outlined in Chapter 16, Snow Travel and Climbing. To that you must add the ability to detect and avoid crevasses and other glacier hazards. If you regard crevasses with a healthy respect, you may never fall into one. If a fall does occur, it is imperative that you know the techniques that provide the best chance of safe recovery and escape from a crevasse. Before stepping onto a glacier, you must have a clear appreciation of the dangers as well as confidence in dealing with them.

GLACIERS AND CREVASSES

Glaciers constantly change as snow supply and temperature influence their advance and retreat. In classic form, glaciers look like a frozen river creeping down a mountain (fig. 17-1), yet they differ from a river in many ways. Some glaciers are small, relatively stagnant pockets of frozen snow. Others are ice fields of immense proportions, full of teetering forms and dramatic releases of ice. (See Chapter 26, The Cycle of Snow, for information on the formation of glaciers.)

Glacial flow patterns can be very complex, but a typical mountain glacier may flow between 150 and 1,300 feet (roughly 45 to 400 meters) per year. Most glaciers flow faster in the warmth of summer than in winter because they are lubricated by increased meltwater. Glacial flow breaks the surface of the ice into those elemental obstacles of mountaineering known as crevasses.

Crevasses often form where the angle of the slope increases significantly, putting tension on the snow and ice, which then split open (fig. 17-2). Crevasses also commonly form where a glacier makes a turn, with the outside edge usually crevassing more; where the distance between valley walls either narrows or expands; or where two glaciers meet. Crevasses may also develop around a bedrock feature that obstructs the glacial flow, such as a rock formation protruding through the ice (a *nunatak*, as shown in Figure 17-1d, above). At the point where a moving glacier breaks away from the permanent snow or ice cap above, the large crevasse called a bergschrund is formed (as shown in Figure 17-1b, above). The middle of a glacier tends to have fewer crevasses than the sides, and a gently sloping glacier

usually has fewer crevasses than a steep, fast-moving one.

Crevasses are most dangerous in the accumulation zone (as shown in Figure 17-1h, above), that portion of a glacier that receives more snow every year than it loses to melting. Here, crevasses are frequently covered with snow bridges that may be too weak to support a climber. Below the accumulation zone is the area of the glacier where annual melting matches or exceeds the yearly snowfall. Between the two zones is the firn line, also known as the névé line (as shown in Figure 17-1c, above), words for "old snow."

The deeper layers of a glacier, denser and more plastic than the upper section, can move and deform without cracking (fig. 17-2c). If this deeper, older ice becomes exposed, the glacier takes on a folded, seamless appearance, often without any true open crevasses. Travel on such a glacier can be relatively simple and safe. They are usually fairly flat, with narrow, shallow crevasses that are not difficult to cross.

Other Common Glacier Hazards

Ice avalanches: These can pour from the steep, jumbled glacial sections known as icefalls (see Figure 16-38h in Chapter 16, Snow Travel and Climbing) when seracs (towers of ice) come crashing down (see Figure 16-38f and g). The inexorable movement of a glacier means that ice avalanches can occur anytime; their activity is only partly related to season, temperature, or snowfall. Serac collapse does seem to happen frequently when the temperature rises above freezing, and at night when it drops below freezing. Travel through these areas should be prudently swift if it cannot be avoided.

Moats: These big gaps that appear when winter snows melt back from a rock face (as shown in Figure 17-1a, above) can present major barriers to glacier travelers who need to regain the rock in order to stay on route. Belayed mountaineers may be able to cross a snow bridge over a moat or climb into the moat and back up onto the rock on the other side.

Glacial moraines: These mounds of rocky debris that were carried and then deposited by the glacier (as shown in Figure 17-1i, j, and k, above) make rugged venues indeed for mountain travel, impeding efficient movement by a climbing party. The moraines are typically steep-sided, narrow ridges with partly

17

ICE FEATURES

a. Moat
b. Bergschrund
c. Firn line
d. Nunatak
e. Crevasses
f. Marginal crevasses
g. Terminus (snout)
h. Accumulation zone

MORAINE FEATURES

i. Medial moraine
j. Lateral moraine

k. Terminal moraine
l. Moraine lake
m. Braided outwash stream
n. Old terminal moraine

o. Old lateral moraine
p. Outwash plain and ground moraine
q. Erratic (boulder)

Fig. 17-1.
Aerial view of a glacier showing some principal features.

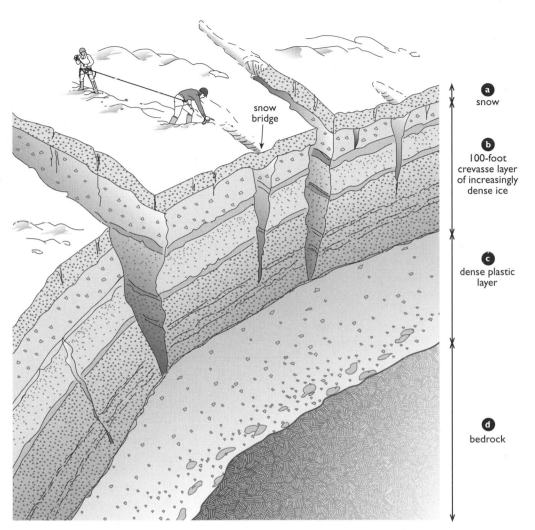

Fig. 17-2. Crevasses open up in the upper snow and ice layers (a and b) as glacier angle increases. The denser lower area (c) moves without splitting.

a snow

b 100-foot crevasse layer of increasingly dense ice

c dense plastic layer

d bedrock

snow bridge

17

buried boulders ready to dislodge at the slightest touch. The moraine surface is often as hard as cement. As you approach the fringe where the glacier begins, there may be a soupy mix of ice and moraine gravel, or rocks skating around like ball bearings on hard ice.

Meltwaters: The runoff flowing from a glacier (as shown in Figure 17-1m, above) can be a chilling challenge to cross. During warm weather, consider waiting to cross until the cooler hours of the next morning, when flow should be at its lowest. (See Chapter 6, Wilderness Travel, for more advice on crossing rivers.)

Whiteouts: In a whiteout on a glacier, sky and snow merge into a seamless blend of white—with no appar-

ent up or down, east or west—taxing routefinding skills to the utmost. Climbers can defend against a whiteout by taking such precautions as placing route-marking wands and noting compass bearings and altimeter readings during the ascent—even when it looks as though clear weather will prevail. If snow or clouds close in and leave the climbing party in a whiteout, these simple precautions will pay off on the descent.

Rockfall: Glaciers are subject to rockfall from bordering walls and ridges. For glacier climbs, whatever the season, the general rule is: early on and early off. The nighttime cold freezes rock in place and prevents most rockfall, whereas direct sun melts the bonds. The greatest hazard comes in the late morning, when sun melts the ice, and in the evening, when meltwater expands as it refreezes, breaking rocks loose.

EQUIPMENT FOR GLACIER TRAVEL

Take a look at your gear with glaciers and crevasses in mind. Here are some considerations in getting ready for glacier travel.

The Rope

Ropes with "dry" treatment, although more expensive, absorb much less water from melting snow and pick up less grit from a glacier. This makes them lighter and easier to work with following an overnight freeze. The type of rope you need depends on the glacier.

For general glacier use, a single 8.5- to 9-millimeter rope will handle crevasse falls and save some weight in your pack. A 9-millimeter rope that is 50 meters (165 feet) long weighs only two-thirds as much as a standard 11-millimeter rope—about 6 pounds (2.7 kilograms) compared to about 9 pounds (4 kilograms). The lighter, thinner rope is more than adequate for general glacier use, because crevasse falls put a relatively gradual impact on the rope due to rope friction on the snow and over the lip of the crevasse.

Steep technical climbing, however, which has the possibility of severe leader falls, requires a standard 10- to 11-millimeter climbing rope or two smaller ropes used in the double-rope or twin-rope technique (see Chapter 14, Leading on Rock).

A rope team traveling alone should also carry a lightweight 100-foot (30-meter) accessory line as a precaution for rescue situations.

Harnesses

For glacier travel, be sure the waist belt and leg loops of your seat harness can adjust to fit over several layers of cold-weather clothing. Glacier travelers also wear a chest harness, which can be made from a piece of 1-inch webbing. Commercial full-body harnesses are more expensive, heavy, and cumbersome, and are not commonly used. See "Harnesses" in Chapter 9, Basic Safety System.

Ice Ax and Crampons

An ice ax and crampons are as important for safe glacier travel as they are for travel on any firm, sloped surface of snow or ice. The ice ax aids with balance and provides a means for self-belay and self-arrest. If a rope mate drops into a crevasse, other climbers on the rope use their ice axes to go into self-arrest, controlling and stopping the fall. The ax needs a uniform taper from the spike to the shaft, because a blunt spike or jutting ferrule (metal cap or ring on the shaft) makes it hard to feel the snow when you are probing for crevasses.

Crampons give you secure footing and enable efficient travel on refrozen snow, which is typically very hard in the early morning. A word of warning about using crampons for descending steep glacial terrain: A number of accidents and falls have resulted from crampon points getting caught on climbers' clothing, gaiters, or gear hanging low from gear loops. It is important to develop good habits of foot placement, and avoid having slings hang below your thigh (see the "Crampon Safety Rules" sidebar in Chapter 16, Snow Travel and Climbing).

Ascenders

Prusik Slings

For personal safety, one of the most important pieces of gear a glacier traveler can carry is a set of prusik slings for ascending the rope after a crevasse fall. The slings are two loops of 5- to 7-millimeter perlon accessory cord attached to the climbing rope with friction knots. When you put your weight on a prusik sling, the knot grips the rope firmly; when you remove your weight, the knot can be loosened and moved up or down the rope.

Figure 17-3 gives details on how to make the Texas prusik slings, using 6-millimeter accessory cord. As with all prusik systems, sizing the slings correctly for your height is critical (see Table 17-1, below). Figure 17-4 shows a way to approximately gauge the correct sizing. When you are standing in the sling (as shown in Figure 17-20c in "The Texas Prusik" later in this chapter), the top of the foot sling should be at about waist level and the top of the seat-harness sling should be at about eye level. The distance between the two knots is the distance that you will move up for each movement

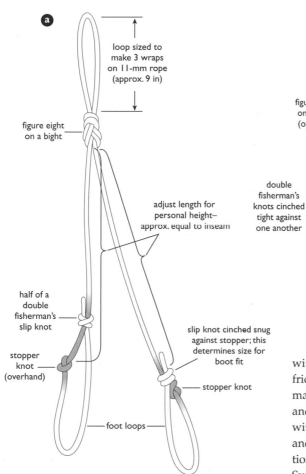

a

loop sized to make 3 wraps on 11-mm rope (approx. 9 in)

figure eight on a bight

adjust length for personal height– approx. equal to inseam

half of a double fisherman's slip knot

stopper knot (overhand)

slip knot cinched snug against stopper; this determines size for boot fit

stopper knot

foot loops

b

approx. 9-in loop

figure eight on a bight (optional)

double fisherman's knots cinched tight against one another

loop length approx. equal to distance from belly button to eyebrows

Fig. 17-3. How to make Texas prusik slings using 6-millimeter accessory cord: a, the foot sling, with two foot loops; b, the seat-harness sling.

The two slings are commonly attached to the rope with prusik knots. Some climbers prefer the Bachmann friction knot because it incorporates a carabiner, which makes a good handle to use while you are loosening and sliding the slings because it can be gripped easily with a gloved hand. If you do not have accessory cord and must use webbing, the Klemheist is the best friction knot to use. (See "Knots" in Chapter 9, Basic Safety System.)

cycle you make using the Texas prusik.

Before you take your slings out onto a glacier, check their sizing at home. Dangle yourself in the slings from a rope thrown over a garage rafter or a tree limb to find out what adjustments you need to make in the sling lengths.

Etriers (Aiders)

Some climbers attach etriers (also called aiders) rather than conventional slings. The steps in these ladderlike slings can help you climb up and over a crevasse lip if the rope is entrenched in the snow. (See "Etriers" in Chapter 15, Aid Climbing.)

TABLE 17-1. SIZING PRUSIK SLINGS		
Climber's Height	**Foot Prusik Length**	**Harness Prusik Length**
5 feet (1.5 meters)	11 feet (3.4 meters)	5 feet (1.5 meters)
5 feet 6 inches (1.7 meters)	11 feet 6 inches (3.5 meters)	5 feet 6 inches (1.7 meters)
6 feet (1.8 meters)	12 feet (3.6 meters)	6 feet (1.8 meters)
6 feet 6 inches (2 meters)	13 feet (3.9 meters)	6 feet 6 inches (2 meters)

17

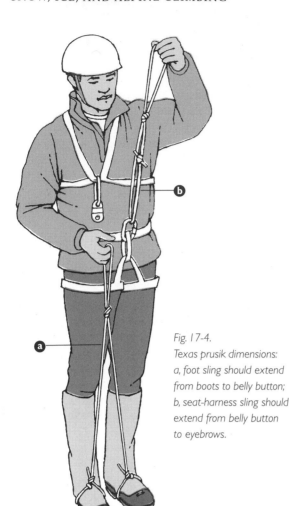

Fig. 17-4.
Texas prusik dimensions:
a, foot sling should extend
from boots to belly button;
b, seat-harness sling should
extend from belly button
to eyebrows.

Mechanical Ascenders

Some glacier travelers carry mechanical ascenders, which attach to the rope more easily than friction knots. On icy ropes, the ascenders work better and can be operated more readily with gloved hands. A disadvantage is that ascenders traditionally have been heavy and expensive, though a number of cheaper, lightweight devices are now available. Titanium models (made by Ushba) have smooth, rather than toothed, cams. These ascenders grip the rope by pure camming action, and so they may be safer to use in situations when high fall forces may occur, such as in a crevasse fall. (See "Mechanical Ascenders" in Chapter 15, Aid Climbing.)

Other Standard Glacier Gear

Often each climbing party carries a shovel, which is useful for flattening camping places and in rescue situations. Each party member should also carry the following gear:

Rescue pulley: Many models of pulley have been designed for use in climbing. Pulleys for use in rescue hauling systems should be compatible with a friction knot (that is, the pulley should not get jammed when used with a prusik or Bachmann knot). If no pulley is available, a carabiner can be used in the rescue hauling system, but it adds considerable friction.

Anchor: If conditions warrant, carry a snow or ice anchor such as a snow picket, a snow fluke, or an ice screw. (See "Snow Anchors" in Chapter 16, Snow Travel and Climbing, and "Ice Screws" in Chapter 18, Alpine Ice Climbing.)

Runners: Bring at least two single-length and one double-length runner for attaching to anchors. Tied runners, rather than sewn runners, work better for crevasse rescue, because you can more easily adjust their length.

Belay device.

Carabiners: Carry one locking carabiner and at least four regular carabiners.

Clothing

To be ready for a fall into a crevasse, you need to dress for the frigid interior of the glacier even when it is a hot day on top. Priorities collide here, because you are preparing for the cold but at the same time are trying to minimize sweating and keep well hydrated.

Select outer garments that can be ventilated easily, such as pants with side zippers and a wind parka with armpit zippers. Zip these closed if you end up in a crevasse. Consider strapping a jacket to the outside of your pack, where you can reach it easily. Stash a hat and gloves in the pockets.

On a warm day, the insulating layer will be your outer layer. For this layer next to your skin, use reflective colors, such as white; light-colored garments reflect the heat of the sun but still provide warmth if you end up inside a crevasse. To thwart the cold dampness in a crevasse, wear a synthetic-fiber shirt and long-underwear bottoms for optimal comfort over a wide range of temperatures.

Skis and Snowshoes

Skis or snowshoes are essential for winter or arctic mountaineering because they distribute your weight over a larger area, thus keeping you from sinking too deeply into the snow. Skis or snowshoes also reduce your chance of breaking through snow bridges over hidden crevasses, which is helpful on some glacier climbs. Snowshoes are usually more practical than skis for roped glacier travel unless all members of the rope team are highly skilled skiers (for further information on ski mountaineering see Appendix C, Supplementary Reading, at the back of this book).

Wands

Wands mark the location of crevasses, identify turning points, and show the climbing route in case a whiteout occurs on the return. (See "Wands" in Chapter 16, Snow Travel and Climbing.) Space between wands should be a distance equal to the total length of the climbing party when roped and moving in single file. A party of nine (three rope teams) will use ten to twelve wands for each mile (1.6 kilometers) of glacier walking; smaller teams will need more.

FUNDAMENTALS OF GLACIER TRAVEL

Climbers need to be moving well before the sun rises and begins weakening snow bridges and loosening avalanche slopes. For glacier climbs, climbers grow to appreciate alpine starts: the brilliance of stars at higher altitudes, perhaps the glow of moonlight on snow, the distinctive sounds of crampons on ice, the tinkling of carabiners in the still night. Sometimes the climbing party is alone on the glacier; other times, distant trains of lights show that other parties are also on the route. The magic of watching a sunrise from high on a mountain above a sea of clouds remains with you long after your memories of the trip's exertion have faded.

Using the Rope

The first rule of safe glacier travel is very simple: Rope up. This rule holds whether or not you are familiar with the glacier and whether or not you believe you can see and avoid all of its crevasses. Roping up is especially important in areas above the firn line, where every year the glacier gets more snow than it loses to melting, making it likely that snow covers some crevasses.

It is tempting to walk unroped onto a glacier that looks like a benign snowfield, especially if you have gone up similar routes time after time without mishap. Avoid the temptation. Like wearing a seat belt in a car, taking the extra time and trouble to deal with the rope greatly increases your chances of surviving the most likely accident on a glacier: falling into a crevasse. Some climbers travel unroped on certain glaciers in the area below the firn line if crevasses are stable and easily seen, but this kind of unroped travel is best left to people with a great deal of glacier travel experience.

On bare ice, as in the late season, it is dangerous to rope up, because crevasse falls are almost impossible to arrest on hard ice, and likely consequences are broken ankles and more climbers in crevasses. However, consider the conditions and determine if using a running belay would be prudent (see "Running Belays" in Chapter 16, Snow Travel and Climbing).

Rope Teams

Rope teams of three climbers each are ideal for travel on glaciers where no technical climbing will be encountered. With a rope team of three, two people are available to arrest a rope mate's fall into a crevasse. A minimum party size of two rope teams is recommended so that a team involved in an accident will have backup help. In some instances a party of four may climb on a single rope; for example, if one of the climbers may not be able to arrest a crevasse fall, or if just one of the party is experienced in crevasse rescue.

Glacier travelers usually put three people on a 37-meter (120-foot) rope, and three or four people on a 50- or 60-meter (165- to 200-foot) rope. These configurations space the climbers far enough apart so that as the rope team crosses a typical crevasse, only one person at a time is at risk. Where there are truly humongous crevasses—in the Himalaya or the Alaska Range, for example—greater spacing may be necessary.

On technical glacier terrain—with slopes steeper than 40 degrees or with severe crevassing—belaying may be necessary, making it more efficient to travel in two-person rope teams. In this situation, having a second

17

rope team as rescue backup becomes even more important. While the person who is on the same rope as the fallen climber holds the rope fast, the second team can set up a snow anchor and initiate the rescue (see "Crevasse Rescue Response" later in this chapter).

Tying In

It is best to tie the rope directly into the tie-in loops on your seat harness—rather than tying a figure-eight loop in the rope and clipping that loop in to a locking carabiner at the harness—because the carabiner adds an unnecessary link between climber and rope. Of course, a clip-in connection makes it easy to disconnect and reconnect to the rope, but this is not normally done repeatedly over the course of a day on a glacier. Following are some general glacier tie-in procedures, depending on the size of the rope team.

Three-person rope: This is the standard size for a

rope team on a nontechnical glacier. Two of the climbers tie in at the very ends of the rope, usually with a rewoven figure eight through the tie-in loops of their seat harnesses (fig. 17-5). The middle climber ties in to the very center of the rope, most commonly with a double bowline knot (fig. 17-6a). The small loop that remains at the end of the bowline should be clipped to the harness with a carabiner to ensure that the knot cannot come untied. The butterfly knot is also good for the middle-person tie-in (fig. 17-6b); it has the advantage of being easier to untie after having been weighted. Use a locking carabiner to clip it in to the harness's tie-in loop.

Four-person rope: Divide the rope into thirds. Two climbers tie in at the ends; the other two tie in at the one-third points.

Two-person rope: Although a three-person rope is the standard for glacier travel, sometimes it is more

Fig. 17-5.
Rigged and ready end climber on a three-person rope; note prusik slings attached to the rope— the other ends of the foot prusiks can be clipped to the harness or stuffed in a pocket.

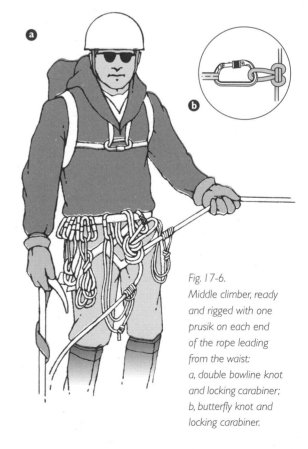

Fig. 17-6.
Middle climber, ready and rigged with one prusik on each end of the rope leading from the waist: a, double bowline knot and locking carabiner; b, butterfly knot and locking carabiner.

efficient to have rope teams of only two climbers; for instance, on technical glacier terrain where belaying may be necessary. The most convenient procedure is to have only a portion of the rope stretched between the climbers, because a full rope length can have too much slack as the climbers weave through a maze of crevasses. Using only part of the rope also leaves some rope free for rescue use. The adapted Kiwi coil system is the preferred method for tying in to a shortened rope. This is illustrated and explained in "Special Rescue Situations" later in this chapter.

Chest Harness

Put the chest harness on over the layer of clothing next to your skin before you head out onto the glacier. Whether you clip the rope through the chest harness at this point depends on the situation. In expedition travel when you are carrying a heavy pack, clipping the chest harness will help you stay upright in case of a fall; not clipping the chest harness may make it very difficult for you to regain an upright stance inside a crevasse. Traveling with the chest harness clipped to the rope hampers your ability to perform self-arrest in cases of a teammate's fall, though, because the tension on the rope comes high on your body.

There is a good compromise: Clip the climbing rope in to your chest harness anytime you cross a snow bridge or otherwise face obvious immediate danger of a crevasse fall; otherwise, travel with the chest harness unclipped (as shown in Figures 17-5 and 17-6).

Prusik Slings

Attach prusik slings to the climbing rope just as soon as you rope up to begin glacier travel, so that the slings are ready for immediate use in an emergency (see Figure 17-5). If you are a middle person on the rope, you do not know which end of the rope you might have to climb after a fall; therefore, attach one prusik to the section of rope that goes to the climber in front of you and the other prusik to the section that goes to the climber behind you (see Figure 17-6). After any fall, you will have to move only one of the prusik slings to the side of the rope that you must climb. Regardless of how you attach the prusik slings, stuff both foot loops into your pockets, so they are ready to be pulled out and slipped onto your feet when you need them, or clip them to the seat harness.

If you are using mechanical ascenders, do not attach them to the rope until after a crevasse fall; if an ascender receives a shock load, it can cut the rope.

Some climbers girth-hitch a sling and carabiner to their pack haul loop and clip them to a shoulder strap, so that if they fall into a crevasse, the pack is easier to secure and take off. This also makes it easier to anchor a pack on steep sections of the glacier.

Rope Management

No slack: The first rule of rope management on a glacier is to keep the rope extended—not taut, but without undue slack. A rope that is fully extended between climbers is insurance against a long plunge into a hidden crevasse. Increasing slack in the climbing rope puts additional force on the next climber (because the first climber is falling deeper in the crevasse), making it more and more difficult to arrest promptly. The falling climber therefore drops farther, increasing the chance of hitting something or becoming wedged if the crevasse narrows. For the climbers holding the fall, a slack rope can also pose the danger of being dragged into the hole themselves.

To keep slack out of the rope, a rope leader needs to set a pace the others can follow for a long time. For their part, the second and third climbers must try to closely match the pace of the leader so the rope stays extended. Be alert going downhill, when it becomes easy to walk too fast.

At sharp turns, the rope tends to go slack when the climber in front of you heads in a new direction and then tightens when you near the turn yourself. Throughout the turn, adjust your pace to keep the slack out of the rope. At sharp turns, it is usually necessary to make new tracks, outside the leader's footsteps, in order to keep the rope fully extended (although at other times you normally follow the leader's path for safety and ease of travel).

To keep the right amount of tension in the rope, travel with a small loop of the climbing rope 6 to 12 inches (15 to 30 centimeters) long, held in your downhill hand. Gripping this makes it easier to feel the progress of your rope mates so you can adjust your pace

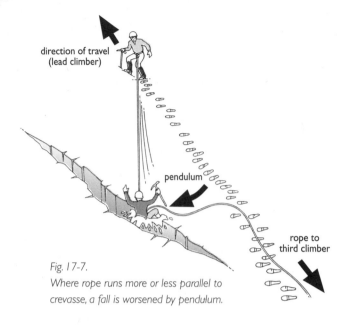

Fig. 17-7.
Where rope runs more or less parallel to crevasse, a fall is worsened by pendulum.

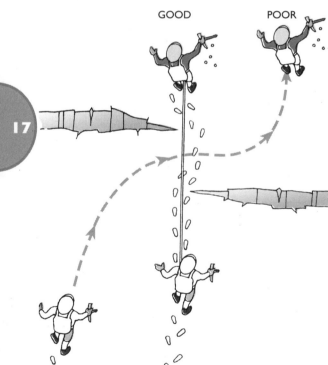

GOOD   POOR

Fig. 17-8.
Be aware of your rope partner's position in order to keep the rope as perpendicular to the crevasse as possible.

as needed. Keeping the rope on the downhill side of a glacier lets you keep the rope out from under your feet and helps avoid entangling the rope in your crampons.

Do not forget safety when you reach a rest stop or campsite. Always belay climbers into and out of all rest and camp areas. The rope must stay extended and slack-free until the area has been thoroughly probed for crevasses. If you must camp on the glacier, probe and then mark the boundaries of the safe area with wands.

Right angle to crevasses: The second important rule of rope management on a glacier is to run the rope at right angles to a crevasse whenever possible. A rope team that travels more or less parallel to a crevasse is risking a lengthy pendulum fall for a climber who falls in (fig. 17-7). Although it is not always possible to keep the rope at right angles to a crevasse, keeping this in mind helps you choose the best possible route (fig. 17-8).

Detecting Crevasses

The first step in safe glacier travel is figuring out where the crevasses are and picking a route through them. On many glaciers, routefinding is part planning, part experience, and part luck.

Sometimes you can get a head start on the planning by studying photographs of the glacier before the trip, because some crevasse patterns remain fairly constant from year to year. Seek out recent reports from parties who have visited the area, though in summer reports older than a week are not generally too helpful, due to melting.

On the approach hike, try to get a good up-valley or cross-valley look at the glacier before you reach it. You may see an obvious route that would be impossible to discover once you are there. Make notes or sketches to help you remember major crevasses, landmarks, and routes.

Though looking at guidebook photographs and getting distant views of a glacier are useful, prepare to be surprised when you actually get there. What appeared to be small cracks may be gaping chasms, and major crevasses may not have been visible from your angle of view. Plan alternative routes from a distance if possible.

Once the climbing party is on the glacier, you play a continuous game of "Find the Crevasse." Just because

TIPS FOR DETECTING CREVASSES

- Keep an eye out for sagging trenches in the snow that mark where gravity has pulled down on snow over a crevasse. This is a prime characteristic of a hidden crevasse. The sags are visible by their slight difference in sheen, texture, or color. The low-angle light of early morning and late afternoon tends to accentuate this feature. (The sags may be impossible to detect in the flat light of a fog or in the glare of the midafternoon sun, and it takes additional information to distinguish them from certain wind-created forms.)
- Be wary after storms. New snow can fill a sagging trench and make it blend into the surrounding surface. (At other times, however, the new snow can actually make the sagging trench more apparent by creating a hollow of new snow that contrasts with surrounding areas of old snow.)
- Be especially alert in areas where crevasses are known to form; for example, where a glacier makes an outside turn or where slope angle increases.
- Regularly sweep your eyes to the sides of the route to check for open cracks to the left or right. Cracks could hint at crevasses that extend beneath your path.
- Remember that where there is one crevasse, there are often many.

you cannot see a crevasse does not mean it is not there. After you set up base camp, have an advance party spend a little time scouting out the first portion of the route in daylight; this can sometimes save you many hours of predawn routefinding.

Snow Probing

Snow probing is the technique to use if you have found a suspicious-looking area and want to search it for crevasses. If a probe locates a crevasse, continue probing in all directions around this area to find the crevasse's true lip.

Probe with the ice ax, thrusting the shaft into the snow a couple of feet (a half meter or so) ahead. Keep the ax perpendicular to the slope and thrust it in with a smooth motion. If resistance to the thrust is uniform, the snow is consistent to at least the depth of the ax. If resistance lessens abruptly, you have probably found a hole. If the route must continue in the direction of this hole, use further ax thrusts to establish the extent of the hole. The leader should open up the hole and mark it with wands.

The value of probing depends on your skill and experience at interpreting the changes you feel in the snow layers. An inexperienced prober may think the shaft has broken through into a hole when all it has done is hit a softer layer of snow. The ice ax is a limited probe because it is relatively short. The lead climber can also use a ski pole (with the basket removed), which is

lighter, longer, and thinner than an ax, for easier, deeper probes.

Crossing a Crevasse Field

Climbers have a number of ways to get safely across a field of crevasses. The techniques described here are typical, but you will have to adapt them as needed in the field. Routefinding on a glacier involves finding a path around or over all the visible crevasses, guarding all the time against hidden crevasses. The crossing is seldom without its detours as you carefully pick your way over the glacier.

The End Run

Crossing directly over a crevasse is rarely a preferred choice. Where a crevasse narrows in width, often near its end, the safest and most dependable technique is to go around it, in an end run. A 0.25-mile (600-meter) walk may gain the rope team only 20 or 30 feet (7 to 10 meters) of forward progress, but it is often better than a direct confrontation with the crevasse. In late summer when the winter snow has melted down to the ice, you may be able to see the true end of the crevasse, but if seasonal snows still blanket the glacier, the visible end of the crack may not be its true end. Make a wide swing around the corner, probing carefully (fig. 17-9). Look closely at adjacent crevasses to judge whether one of them could be an extension of your crevasse; you might actually be crossing a snow bridge.

Fig. 17-9.
*End run around a crevasse,
keeping the rope fully extended
by not following in the
leader's footsteps.*

Snow Bridges

If an end run is impractical, the next choice is to cross a snow bridge. Deep winter snow hardened by wind can create a crevasse bridge that lasts into the summer climbing season. Other, sturdier bridges are actually thin isthmuses between two crevasses, with foundations that extend deep into the body of the glacier.

Study a bridge carefully—try for a side view—before you put any faith in it. If in doubt, the leader can go in to probe and get a close-up look while the second climber stays braced against the taut rope to help guard against possibly breaking through, being prepared to drop into self-arrest if needed (fig. 17-10). After the leader gets across, the rest of the party follows exactly in the leader's steps, also receiving a degree of protection from a taut rope held by a braced climber.

A snow bridge's strength varies tremendously with temperature. A bridge that might support a truck in the cold of winter or early morning may collapse under its own weight during an afternoon thaw. Use caution every time you cross a snow bridge. Do not assume that a bridge that held in the morning during the ascent will still be safe during the descent in the afternoon. In cases of dubious snow bridges, setting up a belay may save having to execute a time-consuming crevasse rescue.

Jumping

Jumping is one of the least-common tactics for crossing a crevasse (fig. 17-11). Most jumps across crevasses are short, simple leaps. If you are planning a desperate

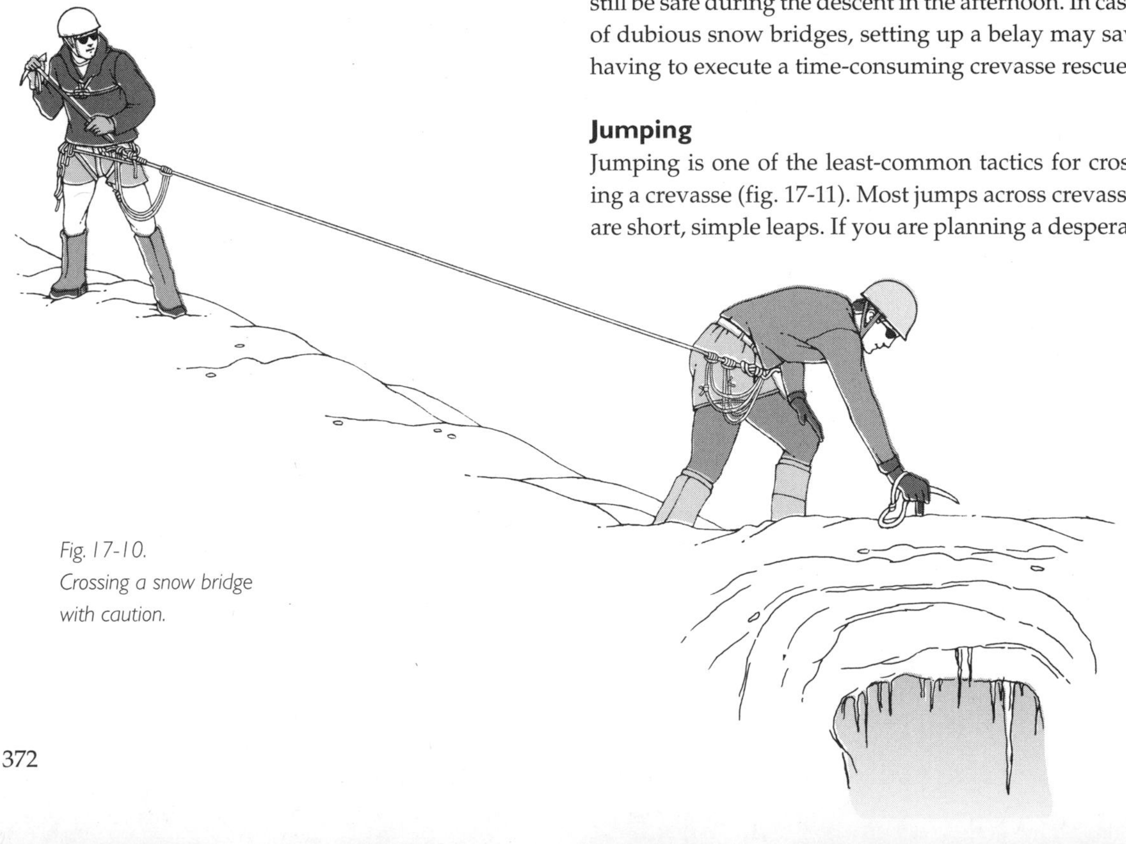

Fig. 17-10.
*Crossing a snow bridge
with caution.*

lunge, be sure you have ruled out all the alternatives and see that you are well belayed.

While you are well supported by a taut rope or by a belay, probe to find the true edge of the crevasse. If you need a running start for the jump, tramp down the snow for better footing. Put on your parka, mittens, and hat; check your prusiks and harness; and spool out the amount of rope slack needed from the belayer. Then jump—with your ice ax in the self-arrest position, ready to help you claw over the edge if you fall shy of a clean landing on the other side.

Once you are safely on the other side, the rope is now linked to the landing side, so the other climbers have a less-dangerous jump ahead: The belay rope can help pull up any jumper who falls just short of the target.

Use caution and common sense if the leap is from the high lip of a crevasse over to a lower side. (Bergschrunds, for example, often have a high overhanging wall on the uphill side.) Injuries are possible in a long, hard leap. If you must make such a leap, keep your feet slightly apart for balance, your knees bent to absorb shock, and your ice ax held ready for a quick self-arrest. Beware of getting your crampons caught on your gaiters.

Fig. 17-11.
Jumping a crevasse (belay not shown).

Into the Crevasse

On rare occasions, it may be practical to get to the other side of a shallow crevasse by climbing down into the crevasse, crossing it at the bottom, and climbing up on the other side. This tactic should be attempted only by a strong, highly trained, well-equipped party that is ready to provide a good belay. One further caution: Often what appears to be a solid bottom is not; if the crevasse bottom collapses and leaves you hanging, the party must be able to provide assistance.

Echelon Formation

Certain crevasse patterns preclude the rule of keeping the rope at right angles to the crevasses. If the route demands travel that is parallel to crevasses, it sometimes helps to use the echelon formation: climbers somewhat to the side of and behind the leader, as in a series of stair steps (fig. 17-12). This formation is safest on stable, heavily crevassed glaciers on which the location of crevasses is known and the risk of hidden holes

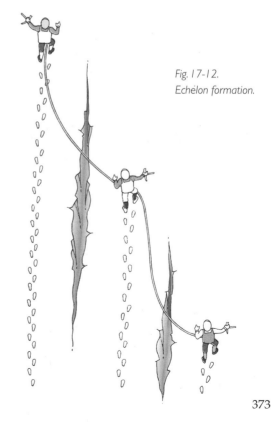

Fig. 17-12.
Echelon formation.

17

*Fig. 17-13.
Stop and hold the fall. Here the
leader has fallen into a crevasse.*

is small. The formation offers an alternative to following in the leader's footsteps through a maze of crevasses where single-file travel is impractical. Avoid moving in echelon formation where hidden crevasses are likely.

CREVASSE RESCUE RESPONSE

The depths of a great crevasse exhibit an awful beauty, both enticing and repellent. On a fine day, the walls are a sheen of soft blue ice in the filtered light from high above, and the cavern is cool and still as a church, or a tomb. It is a place every climber should visit occasionally—for crevasse rescue practice. But if there are other times you end up in a crevasse, hopefully it will be in the company of climbers who know the rescue techniques described in this section.

It is typically the first person on the rope who falls in when a rope team crosses a hidden crevasse. Here is the scene: You are the middle person on a three-person rope team traveling up a moderately angled glacier. The rope mate walking 50 feet (15 meters) in front of you suddenly disappears beneath the snow. What do you do? (A middle-climber fall is discussed in "Special Rescue Situations" later in this chapter.)

Stop the fall immediately! Drop into self-arrest (facing away from the direction of pull) and hold the fall. The other rope partner (the end climber) will do the same thing. (Chapter 16, Snow Travel and Climbing, has details on ice ax self-arrest.)

Once the fall is stopped (fig. 17-13), the critical steps in crevasse rescue begin. Learning these procedures well requires training in the field, augmented with annual practice. The principal steps in a successful crevasse rescue, beginning the instant the fall is stopped, are listed briefly here, and discussed in detail in the sections that follow.

Step 1. Set up a secure anchor system.
Step 2. Communicate with the fallen climber.
Step 3. Devise a rescue plan. There are two basic choices:
    Option 1. Self-rescue—the fallen climber ascends the rope with prusik slings.
    Option 2. Team rescue—team members use a hauling system to pull the climber out.
Step 4. Carry out the plan:
    Option 1. For a self-rescue, assist the fallen climber as needed.
    Option 2. For a team rescue, set up the chosen hauling system, then haul the climber out.

Step 1: Set Up a Secure Anchor System

The goal is to anchor the climber who is in the crevasse and allow the rescuers safe access to communicate with the climber who has fallen.

17

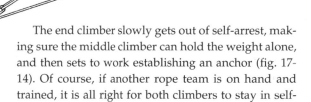

Fig. 17-14.
End climber sets up the initial anchor; meanwhile, fallen climber gets into prusik slings (pack attachment simplified for clarity).

The end climber slowly gets out of self-arrest, making sure the middle climber can hold the weight alone, and then sets to work establishing an anchor (fig. 17-14). Of course, if another rope team is on hand and trained, it is all right for both climbers to stay in self-arrest while the other team sets up the initial anchor.

In snow, a picket is often a good choice for the initial anchor because it can be placed quickly; failing that, an ice ax may also be used. (See "Snow Anchors" in Chapter 16, Snow Travel and Climbing.) Place the anchor 5 to 10 feet (1.5 to 3 meters) down-rope from the middle climber, toward the lip of the crevasse, and angled back 20 degrees from vertical, away from the victim. (If the anchor is placed instead up-rope from the middle climber, tension on the rope that eventually builds up could make it impossible for that person to untie.)

Attaching the Rope to the Anchor

The person who has set up the anchor now attaches a short sling to the climbing rope with a prusik knot; a Bachmann friction knot may also be used (see "Knots" in Chapter 9, Basic Safety System). This person then attaches a runner to the sling with a carabiner, and clips the other end of the runner to the anchor with a locking carabiner (see Figure 17-14, above).

The next move is to slide the friction knot down the rope, toward the crevasse, until the sling assembly is tight, ready to take a load. Now anyone who is still in self-arrest can ease the load onto the anchor (but still remains in self-arrest, to back up the initial anchor).

The Initial Anchor

The end climber has responsibility for setting up the initial secure anchor. To free up the end climber, the middle climber on the three-person rope stays in self-arrest to support the weight of the fallen climber, usually an easy task because rope friction across the snow does much of the work.

375

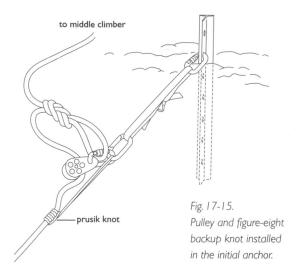

Fig. 17-15.
Pulley and figure-eight
backup knot installed
in the initial anchor.

Confirm that the anchor is solid and that the knot is gripping the climbing rope tightly. (Keep in mind that, if a prusik knot is used, one rescuer will have to tend the knot later, whenever the fallen climber is being pulled up. The Bachmann friction knot, on the other hand, usually requires less tending.)

Just as soon as the load is transferred to the initial anchor, back up the friction knot. Tie a figure-eight loop in the climbing rope a foot or so (about 30 centimeters) up-rope from the friction knot (fig. 17-15). At the same time, use a locking carabiner to clip a rescue pulley to the carabiner already on the sling, running the climbing rope through the pulley. Clip the figure-eight loop in to this new carabiner. With the pulley in place, the beginnings of a 3:1 (**Z**) pulley hauling system are now created (see "Step 3" below), saving time later if such a system needs to be set up to haul the climber from the crevasse.

The Second Anchor
Never trust a single anchor that you know will be fully weighted. Back it up. With a single anchor now in place, set up a second anchor. Meanwhile, the middle climber remains in self-arrest position as a temporary backup to the existing anchor.

The second anchor makes the anchor system as fail-safe as possible. This anchor needs to be good, so take the time to do it right. As with the initial anchor, use a picket or a deadman for snow or an ice screw for ice. In

snow, a good combination is a picket for the first anchor and a deadman (such as a buried picket) for the second anchor (fig. 17-16).

Link the second anchor to the sling that is tied to the climbing rope with a prusik knot in the same way that you linked the initial anchor to the sling: Attach a runner to the sling with a carabiner (also clipping through the pulley carabiner at the same time), and then clip the other end of the runner to the second anchor with a carabiner. Try to make a taut connection from anchor to sling, and remember the principles of equalization: Keep the angle between the two anchor slings small (see "Equalizing Multiple Anchors" in Chapter 10, Belaying).

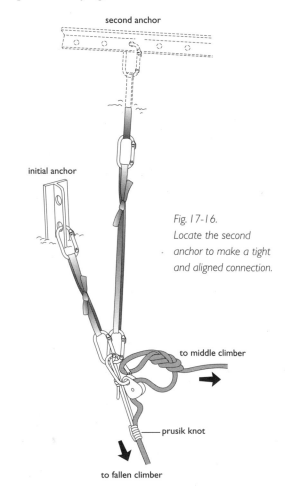

Fig. 17-16.
Locate the second
anchor to make a tight
and aligned connection.

Step 2: Communicate with the Fallen Climber

To develop a complete understanding of the fallen climber's situation so you can devise the rescue plan, someone now needs to check the fallen climber's situation closely.

A rescuer can be belayed from the anchor by a teammate or, better yet, a rescuer can move to the lip of the crevasse with a self-belay. Use a prusik knot to connect a sling to a rope that is attached to the anchor (this can be the climbing rope or a separate rope that is anchored), then clip the sling to your harness with a locking carabiner. By sliding this prusik knot along the rope, you can move toward the crevasse edge on an anchored self-belay (fig. 17-17).

Probe with the ice ax when you are approaching the crevasse lip to discover where the snow surface may be undercut by the crevasse. Approach the lip somewhat to the side of where the fall occurred so you do not knock snow down onto the fallen climber.

Try to talk with the fallen climber. If you hear no answer, the fallen climber may simply be out of earshot, or a noisy wind on the glacier may be masking the response. If further attempts still bring no response, you can rappel or be lowered on belay into the crevasse to help the climber. (See the information on an unconscious fallen climber in "Special Rescue Situations" later in this chapter.)

If the fallen climber responds to your voice, ask questions to find out the full situation. Is the climber wedged in? Injured? In need of more clothing? Is the climber now standing in prusik slings? Most importantly, assure the climber that things are progressing topside but that the rescuers need help in deciding the best way to carry out the rescue.

The fallen climber should be able to tell you whether self-rescue—by climbing up the side of the crevasse or by prusiking out—is a good possibility or whether a hoist from above will be needed. There may even be the option of lowering the climber farther down, to a ramp or ledge where self-rescue or hauling might be easier. The rescuer perched at the lip of the crevasse will gain the most complete picture of the situation above and below, so will have the most important input in the decision on a rescue method.

Fig. 17-17.
Anchor system complete; communicate with fallen climber (pack attachment simplified for clarity). Note anchored ice ax protecting rope from entrenchment.

Minimize Entrenching of the Rope

Regardless of the rescue method that will be chosen, you must pad the lip of the crevasse to minimize further entrenching of the rope. An entrenched rope will sabotage the rescuers' efforts to hoist the climber up over the lip and will confound a fallen climber's own attempts to prusik over it. It may take some excavation to properly prepare the lip. In fact, the extent to which the rope has been entrenched by the climber's fall may force rescuers to consider setting up a different rescue rope from the one the climber is on.

For padding, slide the shaft of an ice ax, a ski (watch the sharp edges), a foam pad, or even a pack under the rescue rope as close to the edge of the crevasse as can safely be reached. Anchor the padding so it cannot fall into the crevasse (see Figure 17-17, above).

Step 3: Devise a Rescue Plan

Choose a method for getting the fallen climber safely out of the crevasse. Will the climber attempt self-rescue? Or will the team members topside set up a hauling system to pull the climber out? After choosing between self-rescue or team rescue, the party must choose among the various methods of either self-rescue or team rescue. Factors that affect these decisions include: the condition of the climber, the number of rescuers, the equipment available (ice-climbing tools, additional ropes, pulleys, and so forth), weather conditions, topography of the crevasse area, and any other variables that will affect the safety of victim and rescuers.

Option 1: Self-Rescue

Self-rescue is often the easiest and fastest form of crevasse rescue, regardless of party size. It has the added advantage of keeping the fallen climber active and warm. Of course, it requires that the fallen climber be basically uninjured and able to maneuver in the crevasse.

For small parties that lack the muscle power to hoist the fallen climber or that are pinned down holding the rope, self-rescue may be the only practical option. This is especially true for a two-person party traveling alone.

A good self-rescue method for ascending the rope is the Texas prusik (see "Rescue Methods" later in this chapter).

Option 2: Team Rescue

Climbers have several choices among team-rescue methods, each with its own particular advantages. These methods are described and illustrated in "Rescue Methods" later in this chapter; here, they are summarized as part of the decision-making process.

Brute force: For a large party with an unentrenched rope, direct pull using brute force works excellently. It is fast and uncomplicated, uses minimal equipment, and requires little or no help from the fallen climber. It works best when perhaps a half dozen strong rescuers can haul on the rope and when the pullers are on flat ground or downhill from the fallen climber.

2:1 (single) pulley method: For a badly entrenched rope or when there are few haulers, the single-pulley method may be best. An entrenched rope will not matter because this method requires a separate length of rope—either the unused end of the accident rope or another rope entirely. The length of available rope must be at least twice as long as the distance from the initial anchor to the fallen climber. The mechanical advantage of the pulley makes hoisting this way a lot easier than by using brute force alone, though it still usually takes a minimum of three or four people to do the pulling. The fallen climber must be able to contribute to the rescue, with at least one good hand for clipping in to the rescue pulley and for maintaining balance.

3:1 (Z) pulley method: For a fallen climber who is unable to help in the rescue or when few haulers are available, the 3:1 pulley is likely the best method. The pull force is on the accident rope, which may be partially entrenched in the snow, but the high mechanical advantage of the system gives haulers the power to overcome some entrenchment.

Piggyback pulleys: Even more power can be gained by piggybacking two systems together, such as a single-pulley setup hauling on a 3:1 pulley system.

Alternatives

A climber who falls into a crevasse does not necessarily have to come back out at the same spot. Check the possibility of lowering or swinging the fallen climber to a ledge. It might be a good spot for the victim to rest, as well as perhaps a gateway to a different part of the crevasse where rescue will be easier. Consider whether the bottom of the crevasse looks solid. This could offer another resting spot and a possible path to a climbing route or a snow ramp back to the surface.

Step 4: Carry out the Plan

Now you must get the fallen climber safely out of the crevasse. If self-rescue is the chosen plan, climbers topside assist as needed. If it will be a team rescue, the climbers topside set up the selected hauling system and pull the fallen climber out. See "Rescue Methods" later in this chapter.

A party with enough people should assign one climber as the communicator at the lip of the crevasse throughout the rescue. Good communication is especially important as the fallen climber approaches the lip.

In cases where the fallen climber has trouble climbing out over the crevasse lip due to an entrenched rope, consider lowering gear (ideally linked to a different anchor) such as slings tied together, carabiner chains, etc., to provide additional support points away from the embedded rope.

INSIDE THE CREVASSE

While the climbers on top are taking the steps for rescue, the fallen climber has work to do down below, beginning with the moment of recovery from the fall. Below are the immediate actions the fallen climber should take.

Get Pack and Ice Ax Out of the Way

If possible, send your pack and ice ax up on a rope lowered by the rescuers. If this is not possible, clip the ax to your seat harness, letting it hang so it does not interfere with your movement. If at the beginning of the climb you did not rig a runner to the pack's haul loop (see "Using the Rope," earlier in this chapter), do this now: Girth-hitch a short sling through the pack's haul loop, and then clip the sling with a carabiner in to the climbing rope between your seat harness and prusik attachments. The pack will then hang below you; as you prusik up the rope, the hanging pack will slide freely along the bottom of the loop of climbing rope and weight the rope, making it easier for you to climb (fig. 17-18).

Attain an Upright Position

If you did not do so instinctively, work yourself into an upright position. Normally you do this by clipping the climbing rope through the carabiner at your chest harness. (This may be difficult or impossible to do until you have hung your pack, as described above.)

Get into Prusik Slings

Remove the prusik slings' foot loops from your pocket and slip one of the two adjustable loops over each boot

Fig. 17-18.
Preparing for self-rescue: clip ice ax to seat harness, girth-hitch a short sling to the pack's haul loop, and then clip it to the climbing rope between the seat harness and prusik attachments.

(see "Using the Rope" earlier in this chapter). If you are wearing crampons, it will not be easy. Cinch the slipknot to tighten them around your boots. Getting into your prusik slings that are attached to the climbing rope permits you to alternate between standing in the foot sling and sitting from the seat-harness sling as you dangle (fig. 17-19). You will be a lot more comfortable and will be ready to climb up the rope using the slings.

As soon as you have gotten yourself upright, clipped in to your chest harness, moved your pack and ice ax out of the way, and caught your breath, it is usually okay to begin prusiking partway to the top if you are

17

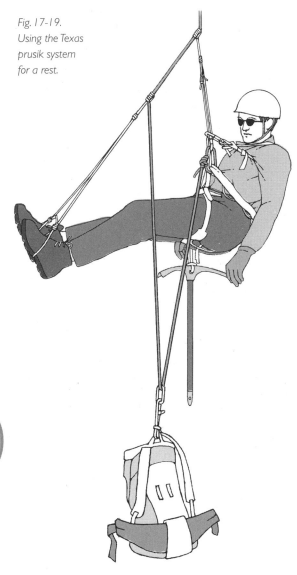

Fig. 17-19.
Using the Texas
prusik system
for a rest.

This preliminary prusiking gets you closer to the glacier surface, where it is easier to communicate with rescuers. You and the other climbers can then decide together on the best rescue plan. If the final plan is to use a hauling system, your initial prusiking will have helped by making the haul shorter. Even if the final plan is self-rescue by prusiking, you will probably need their help in getting over the crevasse lip.

If the fall did not leave you dangling free but, instead, dropped you onto a ledge, where most of your weight is off the rope, a different approach to prusiking is required. In this case, go ahead and get into the prusik slings, but wait to begin prusiking until you have talked it over with your rescuers. If you were to start prusiking without an OK from topside, your full weight coming suddenly onto the rope could unbalance and endanger the whole team.

Keep Warm

Close your parka, put on the hat and gloves you stuffed in its pockets earlier, and try to put on additional layers of clothing.

RESCUE METHODS

This section describes the principal prusiking method for self-rescue and hauling methods for team rescue.

Option 1: Self-Rescue

The Texas prusik is a simple system that permits more progress per cycle and more comfortable rests than other methods such as the stair-step prusik. A climber with an injured leg can still ascend the rope with the Texas prusik by using just one of the foot loops. Unlike the stair-step prusik, the Texas prusik is easy to learn and execute. It will keep you upright without having to be connected to a chest harness. In fact, you may find it easier to move the upper prusik when you are unclipped from the chest harness.

The Texas Prusik

This method of ascending the rope, developed by spelunkers (cavers), uses one sling for the feet and a separate sling for the seat (which is clipped with a locking carabiner to your seat harness). The foot sling has two

just dangling free in the crevasse (see "Rescue Methods" below for a description of the Texas prusik). If possible, let your rope mates know what you are doing. Move carefully and deliberately so that you do not put sharp or sudden tugs on the rope that could interfere with their work in holding your weight and setting up an anchor. Normally, though, the snow provides enough friction to help to hold the rope, especially at the lip of the crevasse, that your prusiking will not hamper your rescuers.

Fig. 17-20.
Ascending a rope using
the Texas prusik system
(pack and ice ax omitted
for clarity): a, sitting/
resting position; b, sitting
on heels, ready to stand;
c, standing position.

loops, one for each foot, tied so that they will adjust and cinch down on your boots. This is how to use the Texas prusik after you have recovered from a fall into a crevasse (fig. 17-20):

1. Stand up in the foot loops. You are now ready to move upward.
2. Unclip from the chest harness.
3. Loosen the friction knot attached to the seat-harness sling and slide it up the rope until it is taut.
4. Sit down in the seat harness, putting all your weight on the seat-harness sling, which releases your weight from the foot sling (fig. 17-20a).
5. Loosen the friction knot attached to the foot sling and slide it up the rope—18 to 24 inches (50 to 75 centimeters), if the sling is properly adjusted. Raise your feet with it (fig. 17-20b).
6. Stand up again in the foot loops (fig. 17-20c).
7. Keep repeating Steps 3 through 6.

Option 2: Team Rescue

All rescues are team rescues to some degree, because even in a self-rescue the fallen climber usually needs some help getting over the crevasse lip. A full team rescue usually involves hauling the fallen climber to safety. The principal hauling methods—brute force, 2:1 (single)

pulley, 3:1 (Z) pulley, and piggyback systems—are described in the sections that follow. In any rescue system calling for pulleys, carabiners can be substituted if necessary. However, carabiners create far more friction and make the rope harder to pull, and the load on the anchor system is correspondingly increased.

Brute Force

A half dozen or so strong haulers line up along the accident rope and grasp it. They position themselves up-rope beyond the point where the initial anchor is attached to the climbing rope with a prusik knot or Bachmann friction knot. The knot is then in the right place to hold the rope if the haulers slip or need a rest. Before the hauling begins, unclip the backup figure-eight loop from the anchor system (as shown in Figures 17-15, 17-16, and 17-17, above). Then the haulers can go to work, pulling hand over hand on the rope or moving step by step away from the crevasse.

17

One rescuer tends the knot, making sure the rope moves smoothly through it, and also keeps an eye on the anchor system. If there are enough people, another person can be stationed at the lip of the crevasse to stay in communication with the fallen climber.

The haulers should pull the rope at a slow, steady pace, especially when the fallen climber reaches the crevasse lip. If the rope has cut into the lip, the fallen climber could be hurt by being pulled into the crevasse wall. At this point, rescuers may ask the fallen climber to scramble over the lip (with the help of an ice ax) while they hoist.

2:1 (Single) Pulley System

The 2:1 pulley system theoretically doubles the amount of weight that each hauler could raise without a pulley,

though friction lowers this ratio somewhat. Because this method uses a length of rope that is separate from the rope going to the fallen climber, this is the method of choice if the accident rope is entrenched into the edge of the crevasse. However, it also requires the assistance of the fallen climber, and so cannot be performed when the fallen climber is unconscious. To carry out a rescue using the 2:1 pulley system, follow these steps:

1. Find a rescue rope (the unused end of the accident rope or a separate rope altogether) that is at least twice as long as the distance from the initial anchor down to the fallen climber. Attach the rope to either the existing anchor system or a new rescue anchor (fig. 17-21a).

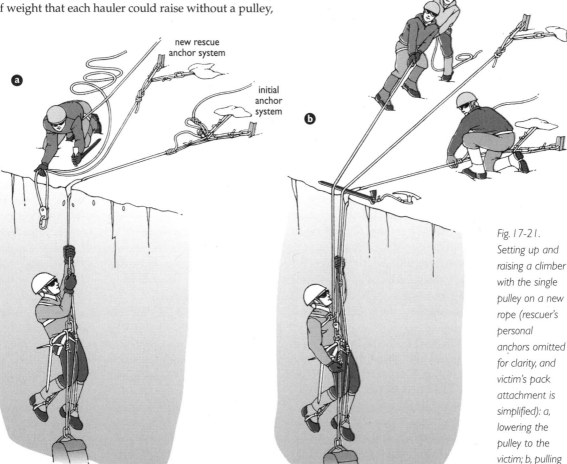

new rescue anchor system

initial anchor system

Fig. 17-21. Setting up and raising a climber with the single pulley on a new rope (rescuer's personal anchors omitted for clarity, and victim's pack attachment is simplified): a, lowering the pulley to the victim; b, pulling the victim up.

2. At the point where the rescue rope will go over the lip of the crevasse, prepare the lip with padding, such as an ice ax or pack, to keep the rescue rope from entrenching itself in the snow (fig. 17-21b).

3. Double the rescue rope into a big loop. Affix a pulley to the loop and attach a locking carabiner to the pulley. Leave the carabiner unlocked.

4. Lower the pulley and carabiner dangling from the loop down to the fallen climber. Have the climber clip and lock the carabiner in to the seat harness. Confirm that this has been done. Check that all the climber's equipment is secure and ready for hauling to begin. Have the climber clip the rescue rope—the portion that is between the pulley and the pulling rescuers above (not the portion that is between the pulley and the anchors above)—in to the chest harness, to help stay upright.

5. Assign a rescuer to attend to the slack that will develop in the original accident rope as the fallen climber is raised. It is critically important that this person pull slack through the friction knot so that the rope is always ready to accept the fallen climber's weight, in case the pullers slip or need a rest. If the fallen climber's pack is clipped to the accident rope, there will be considerable weight on the rope, and it may require two people to take in the slack. Keep the existing figure-eight backup knot to the initial anchor in the system while the slack is taken in; do not remove the knot.

6. With everything ready, the haulers start pulling on the unanchored end of the rescue rope. To ease their task somewhat, the fallen climber can pull up on the anchored side of the rescue rope while the hauling proceeds; this unweights the unanchored end of the rescue rope somewhat.

3:1 (Z) Pulley System

The 3:1 pulley magnifies the muscle power of small climbing parties by offering a three-to-one theoretical mechanical advantage through the use of two pulleys. It can be set up and operated with no help from the fallen climber, making it valuable for rescuing an unconscious person. The 3:1 pulley system normally uses the accident rope. It requires more equipment and is more complicated than the other hauling methods.

First confirm the solidity of the initial anchor system, because the 3:1 pulley system puts considerable stress on it. With the initial climbing rope (the rope attached to the fallen climber), take the loose end—the end that extends unweighted beyond the anchor—and lay out a long loop on the snow. This loop and the rest of the rope going from the anchor to the fallen climber should form a giant flat S in the snow, somewhat like a Z or a backward Z with the sharp edges worn off (fig. 17-22).

At the first bend in the Z (by the initial anchor system), the first pulley for hauling is already in place; this is the pulley attached to the initial anchor system with a locking carabiner when the system was first set up. Also clipped into the locking carabiner are the prusik sling (also called the ratchet or keeper sling or prusik) and the backup figure-eight loop (see Figures 17-15 and 17-16, above).

At the second bend in the Z (the slack bend, closer to the crevasse lip), install a second pulley on the rope. Use a friction knot to attach a short sling to the taut section of rope going from the anchor's first pulley to the fallen climber, and clip this sling with a carabiner in to the second pulley (this is called the traveling sling or prusik). Drag the friction knot (traveling prusik) and traveling pulley as far down the taut rope as possible toward the crevasse. It may have to be seen to be believed, but this is now a 3:1 pulley system, ready for use. Here's how to haul using the 3:1 pulley system:

1. Unclip the backup figure-eight loop from the initial anchor system and untie the knot as soon as the haulers and fallen climber are ready for pulling.

2. If the ratchet or keeper sling used a prusik knot to attach the accident rope to the initial anchor system, assign a rescuer to tend the knot so that the rope slips freely through it as the rope is pulled in. If a Bachmann friction knot was used instead (fig. 17-22b), the attachment should tend itself, and the front hauler can simply keep an eye on it to see that all is well.

3. Start pulling at a steady rate, either hand over hand or by holding tight and walking backward (fig. 17-22a).

4. The hauling will soon bring the second (traveling) pulley in close to the first (stationary or ratchet) pulley at the initial anchor. Stop hauling when the

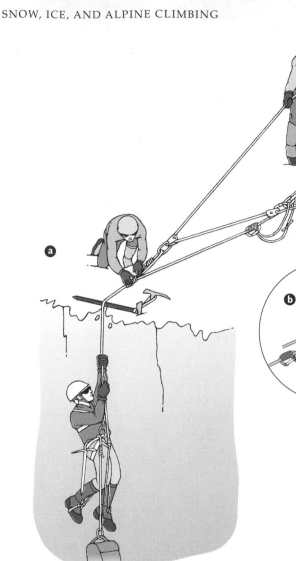

Fig. 17-22.
Raising a climber with
the 3:1 (Z) pulley (pack
attachment simplified for
clarity): a, setting up the
second pulley; b, detail
showing Bachmann
friction knot.

As the fallen climber nears the lip of the crevasse, beware of the pulling power of the 3:1 (**Z**) pulley system. If care is not used, the climber can be injured by being pulled sharply up into the lip.

Piggyback Pulleys

To get even more mechanical advantage out of a rescue hauling setup, you can combine, or "piggyback," two systems. For example, establish a separate 2:1 pulley setup to haul on the rope coming from a 3:1 pulley system. This now gives a 6-to-1 theoretical mechanical advantage. Or set up a 2:1 single-pulley system to haul on another 2:1 pulley system for a 4-to-1 advantage. (See Chapter 24, Alpine Rescue.)

One note of caution: Beware of using piggyback systems to overcome the resistance of pulling the victim over the crevasse lip; serious injuries have resulted.

pulleys are still a couple of feet (about a half meter) apart. If they are pulled too close, the figure **Z** is collapsed and the mechanical advantage is lost.

5. Now that you have stopped hauling, relax your pull on the rope enough to transfer the fallen climber's weight back onto the ratchet or keeper sling at the initial anchor.

6. Reset the traveling pulley by loosening the traveling sling that is linked to the traveling pulley and sliding it back down the taut accident line toward the crevasse lip once again.

7. Keep repeating Steps 3 through 6.

SPECIAL RESCUE SITUATIONS

A crevasse rescue can be complicated by any number of unusual twists. This section describes some special situations that you could encounter, and ideas on how to deal with them. The situations can become complicated, and you will have to adapt your response to the conditions of the moment. Anything that works safely is fine. (See Chapter 24, Alpine Rescue, for more details on accident response and additional rescue techniques.)

When the Middle Person Falls In

It is awkward at best when the middle person on a three-person rope team falls into a crevasse, especially if no other climbers are around to set up the rescue anchor. With no second team, the only two people who can help are separated by a crevasse, each in self-arrest. Here is a general procedure for getting out of this fix.

The climbers begin by deciding which side of the crevasse will be the rescue side—that is, which side the fallen climber should come out on. Usually, one of the two rescuers in self-arrest is holding more weight than the other. The one holding the least weight usually has the best chance to get up and establish an anchor while the rescuer on the other side stays in self-arrest to hold the fall.

After the climber on the rescue side sets up the rescue anchor (see "Step 1: Set Up a Secure Anchor System," above), the climber in self-arrest on the other side of the crevasse can slowly release tension on the climbing rope and ease the fallen climber's weight onto the anchor.

If the climber who was in self-arrest is needed to help in the rescue operation, the climber on the rescue side now tries to belay the climber on the self-arrest side over to the rescue side. The rope on the rescue side can be used for belaying, if it is long enough, or a lightweight 100-foot (30-meter) accessory line—a precaution for a rope team traveling alone—can provide the belay. If no belay or safe route across the crevasse is available, however, the climber on the self-arrest side could be stuck there. This climber would then set up an anchor and stay put.

The most advantageous rescue plan now is for the fallen climber to self-rescue by ascending the rope on prusik slings, coming out on the rescue side, where the anchor has been placed. If a self-rescue by prusiking is not possible, then a 3:1 pulley or a piggyback system could be tried. This all takes plenty of time, competence,

equipment, and resourcefulness. Learn to use the Bachmann friction knot for times when you might have to haul alone, because the knot requires less tending than a standard prusik knot in a hauling system.

In the case of a four-person rope team, the situation is a little simpler in the event that one of the two middle members falls into a crevasse. Conduct the rescue in a routine manner from the side that has two climbers topside.

A Two-Person Team Alone

For a party of two people with no other rope team nearby, glacier travel is risky indeed. Both climbers absolutely need to know their rescue techniques, period. The climber who stops a fall must set up an anchor alone while in self-arrest and then create a hauling system if one is needed. Therefore each climber needs to carry at least two pieces of snow or ice protection for an anchor appropriate to the conditions, plus the equipment (pulleys, carabiners, slings) to set up a hauling system. And all of this must be readily at hand, clanking from seat harness or pack straps.

Rope teams of two should use the tie-in method known as the adapted Kiwi coil (see below), which automatically makes available an extra length of rope for rescue use. Packing along a 100-foot (30-meter) accessory line is also good precaution. The climbers should not have the rope clipped in to their chest harnesses, because this makes rescue very difficult. And with only two people, it is even more important than usual to travel with your personal prusiking system ready for use.

If you end up as the sole rescuer in a two-person rope team, holding your partner's fall with your self-arrest, begin your rescue efforts by augmenting the security of your arrest position by digging in your feet and pressing the ice ax more firmly into the snow. Imagine that you are establishing a belay stance while lying down.

Try to free one hand by rotating the upper half of your body—but keep leaning on the ax and bracing yourself with at least one stiff leg. If the rope is clipped in to your chest harness, unclip it now.

When you get one hand free, place a fluke, picket, ice screw, second ice tool—anything secure enough to hold and allow you to get up and create a main anchor. At this point, you will see the value of keeping the appropriate anchors easily accessible.

Now follow the steps described in "Crevasse Rescue Response" earlier in this chapter, though you will probably experience more duress than would a larger rope team or group of teams: Set up a secure main anchor, communicate with your fallen partner, settle on a rescue plan, and carry it out. Ideally, your partner will be able to handle self-rescue, prusiking out. If not, try a 3:1 pulley or piggyback hauling system. Of course, if you are unable to set up an anchor in the first place, the climber in the crevasse has no choice but to try self-rescue while you remain in self-arrest.

The Adapted Kiwi Coil

The Kiwi coil was developed by alpine glacier guides in New Zealand, and an adaptation of it is the preferred tie-in method for two-person glacier travel teams. The technique results in closer spacing between rope partners for more efficient, comfortable travel, and provides some free rope for a hauling system or other rescue use.

The adapted Kiwi coil also is valuable in providing a means of quick transition between the closer spacing of roped glacier travel and the full rope-length requirements of belayed climbing. This transition is important on an alpine climb where a glacier approach is followed by belayed rock or ice climbing. To create an adapted Kiwi coil (fig. 17-23):

1. Tie in to the rope at your seat harness, as you would normally.
2. Take a series of coils of rope into your hand (usually five, but no more than nine) until you have the desired spacing between you and your rope partner. Secure the coils together by tying an overhand knot around them, using a loop of the rope (fig. 17-23a).
3. Get the coils out of the way for travel, stowing them securely anywhere, such as in the top of your pack or over one shoulder, where they are easily accessible (fig. 17-23b).
4. Tie the shortened length of climbing rope to your seat harness with a double bowline. The rope is now tied twice to the seat harness, and any force coming onto the rope will be taken by this second knot.

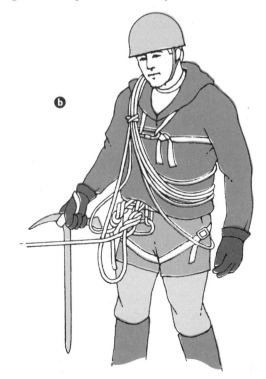

Fig. 17-23.
Adapted Kiwi coil:
a, looping and
tying the coil;
b, draping the coil
out of the way.

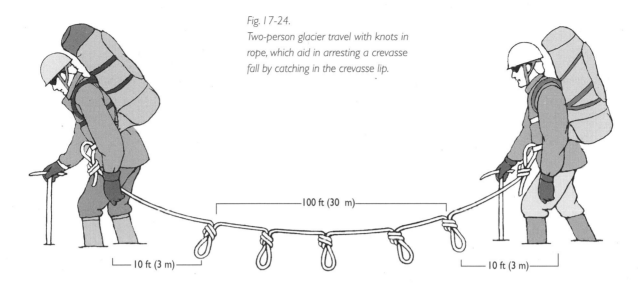

Fig. 17-24.
Two-person glacier travel with knots in rope, which aid in arresting a crevasse fall by catching in the crevasse lip.

100 ft (30 m)

10 ft (3 m) 10 ft (3 m)

Variation

A variation of the adapted Kiwi coil is often used in Europe; climbers put overhand knots on a bight in the rope (leaving a small loop) at 5-foot (1.5-meter) intervals between the two climbers, beginning with an initial 10-foot (3-meter) space between the climber and the first knot (fig. 17-24). This method works on the principle that in the event of a fall into a crevasse, the rope will entrench and the knots will catch in the crevasse lip. This takes most of the weight off the arresting climber, which makes it considerably easier to set up the initial rescue anchor.

To use this rope to extract the fallen climber from the crevasse, you must untie the knots in the rope before hauling. This may be possible because most of the load should be taken by the knot wedged in the lip of the crevasse. If you cannot do this, then rescue must be performed using either a 2:1 pulley system using the loose end of the rope, or using another rope.

An Unconscious Fallen Climber

To help an unconscious climber, a rescuer should descend by rappelling or being lowered on belay. This rescuer can administer first aid and also get the fallen climber right-side up if necessary. You can then consider using any of the standard hauling methods. To help get the fallen climber over the lip of the crevasse, a rescuer may have to work right at the edge of or from inside the crevasse. Monitor the condition of the unconscious person, taking care to cause no further injury.

More Than One Victim

In a case where more than one person has fallen into a crevasse, assess each person's condition and the best method for getting each one out, and then decide the order of rescue. Practicality usually determines the order of rescue, unless there is ample backup for rescuers and equipment. Be sure that each fallen climber is given warm clothing, if needed, and keep them informed of rescue plans as they develop.

Cramped Working Space

The climber who drops into self-arrest position to stop a rope mate's fall could be lying so close to the lip of the crevasse that there is very little room to place an anchor or pulley system. A solution to this situation is to set up the main anchor where there is enough room—on the up-rope side of the climber in self-arrest (instead of the usual place between the rescuer and the crevasse). Leave a couple of feet (60 centimeters) of slack between the main anchor and this rescuer, so that this person is not trapped in the system by tension on the rope.

Then set up a temporary anchor, between the rescuer and the crevasse, that will take the weight of the

17

Fig. 17-25.
Adding another pulley to
the 3:1 (Z) pulley system
in a tight space, such as
between two crevasses.
(Victim's pack attachment
simplified for clarity.)

fallen climber long enough to enable the rescuer to get up from self-arrest position and untie from the rope. Once hauling begins, untie the prusik sling attached to the temporary anchor.

Between Two Crevasses

Rescuers trying to work in a very narrow area between two crevasses can consider moving the operation. The

rescue might proceed better if it is run from the opposite side of the crevasse that holds the fallen climber.

Another option is to change the direction of pull on a 3:1 pulley system. Hook a third pulley to the anchor and run the hauling end of the rope through it (fig. 17-25). Now the rescuers can pull in a direction more parallel to the crevasses.

Entrenched Ropes

The upward progress of a person climbing out or being pulled out of a crevasse can be stopped cold by a rope that has dug itself into the lip. This situation calls for some improvisation. For instance, a rescuer can attach prusik slings or etriers (aiders) above the entrenched portion of the rope and drop them down for the climber to step into.

Another option is to switch to a new rescue rope. A rescuer can lower a new rope to the fallen climber (as shown in Figure 17-21a, above). Or the fallen climber can, in effect, provide a new rope by tossing the loose end of the climbing rope up to the rescuers. This is done by prusiking up to the lip, tying in higher up on the climbing rope, untying from the loose end of the climbing rope, and throwing the loose end up to the rescuers.

A new rescue rope, carefully padded at the lip of the crevasse so it does not also get entrenched, opens up several rescue possibilities. The fallen climber can switch prusik slings from the original climbing rope to the new free rope. Or the rescuers can haul the fallen climber up and out on the new rope. Or the fallen climber can merely transfer all weight to the new rope to give rescuers a much better chance of freeing the entrenched line.

Roofed Crevasses

Wide, roofed crevasses present special problems. The fallen climber may be hanging free, without a stabilizing wall for support, and the accident rope typically entrenches itself deeply into the snow of the crevasse roof. The fallen climber may be bombarded by snow and ice dislodged by the rescuers, who will be working in an area of proven instability.

It may be necessary to have a well-belayed rescuer take a shovel or ice ax and enlarge the hole the climber fell through. Do your best to keep snow and ice from hitting the fallen climber.

Knowledge and preparation will minimize the hazards of roofed crevasses and the other problems of traveling near crevasses.

PATHS TO THE SUMMIT

Glaciers move slowly but inexorably downward under the influence of gravity. Like rivers flowing to the sea, they follow the path of least resistance. Glaciers can appear to be obvious, rather convenient routes to alpine summits, but in reality they are massive, dynamic systems that hold many hazards. Climbers who seek the freedom of the glaciated peaks must learn how to safely negotiate crevasses and other dangers. Clearly the best strategy for travel on a glacier is to minimize your exposure to such hazards; take precautions to avoid falling into crevasses. Even when precautions are taken, however, falls and other accidents can occur. Anyone planning to travel on a glacier must master the techniques for dealing with the hazards and effecting a successful recovery if necessary. With these skills, you can safely take advantage of these paths up the glaciated summits.

17

18

Alpine Ice Climbing

EQUIPMENT ■ TECHNIQUES OF ALPINE ICE CLIMBING ■ ROPED CLIMBING
TECHNIQUES ■ PRACTICE FOR THE FREEDOM OF THE HILLS

**Ice is found on or around the summits of many alpine peaks, and developing
ice-climbing skills increases your opportunities for safe exploration
of those summits. With proper skills you will be able to use
ice as yet another avenue to the alpine realm.**

To climb ice, mountaineers use a lot of what they
have learned about rock and snow climbing, adding
the special tools and techniques needed for climbing
ice. Ice climbers experience the same joys as do snow
climbers, along with the perils: avalanches, hazardous
couloirs and unstable cornices, ice blocks, and icefalls.

You can find ice-climbing opportunities year-round, from
climbing waterfall ice on the short, dark days of winter
to ascending alpine ice on long, warm summer days.

Ice can appear in a variety of forms. Under the combined effects of pressure, heat, and time, snow and other
forms of frozen precipitation metamorphose into the

alpine ice of glaciers, ice fields, and couloirs. There is no clear distinction between alpine ice and hard snow. Alpine ice sometimes appears as blue ice; this hue means that the ice is relatively pure. Black alpine ice—old, hard ice mixed with dirt, pebbles, or other debris—is another common variation. Liquid water freezes to form water ice. Water-ice formations can be as dramatic as a frozen waterfall or as common as *verglas,* the thin, clear coating of ice that forms when rainfall or melting snow freezes on a surface, such as rock. Verglas is difficult to climb because the thin, weak layer provides scant purchase for crampons and ice tools. Water ice is usually harder, steeper, and more brittle than alpine ice, but under some conditions—for example, high altitudes and low temperatures—the two may be indistinguishable.

Ice is as changeable and ephemeral as snow. A rock route is likely to be there for years or decades, but what was an ice route in the morning may by that afternoon be nothing but a jumbled pile of ice blocks or a wet spot on the rock. You must learn to anticipate the changeability of ice. Ice can exhibit a wide range of characteristics. At one extreme, it can seem as hard as steel; ice tools bounce off it, barely scratching the surface. Hard ice can also be as brittle as glass, requiring you to expend time and energy chopping away at the surface until you can plant an ice tool without the placement shattering. At other times, ice can be soft and plastic, allowing you to make secure placements effortlessly with a single swing—an ice climber's dream. However, ice can be too soft and weak to provide good protection placements or to support your weight. It takes experience to assess the relative condition of ice.

As is true of all types of climbing, the steepness of the slope greatly affects which ice-climbing technique is appropriate. On flat ice, such as level areas on a glacier or a frozen stream, it is usually possible to walk without crampons, especially if rocks and dirt are embedded in the surface. On short slopes, you can use an ice ax to chop steps, but longer sections call for crampons. As the slope angle increases, climbers can use French technique—"flat-footing"—but only up to a point. The very steepest routes require front-pointing, also called German technique.

This chapter uses the descriptive terms in Table 18-1 in referring to the approximate steepness of slopes.

TABLE 18-1. STEEPNESS OF SLOPES

Descriptive Term	Angle of Steepness
Gentle	0° to 30°
Moderate	30° to 45°
Steep	45° to 60°
Extremely steep	60° to 80°
Vertical	80 to 90°
Overhanging	Greater than 90°

EQUIPMENT

Continuing refinements in equipment have helped ice climbers improve and expand their techniques and use them to undertake greater climbing challenges. Manufacturers are producing a steady stream of specialized and innovative clothing, boots, crampons, ice tools, and ice protection. (See Chapter 16, Snow Travel and Climbing, for a general description of gear such as crampons and ice axes.) This section describes the equipment that is specific to alpine ice climbing.

Clothing

Clothes for ice climbing should offer a combination of comfort and function. Employ a layered system, with layers appropriate to the conditions. Some climbers wear bibs or a one-piece suit as an alternative to the conventional outfit of jacket (or anorak) and pants. A one-piece suit of windproof, waterproof synthetic material retains warmth and repels debris. The suit should provide a convenient means of ventilation—for example, an armpit zipper that opens from elbow to midriff and a second zipper that opens from front to back via the crotch. The one-piece suit should not be confused with the expedition suit (a heavily insulated one-piece suit designed for the extreme conditions of high-altitude or arctic environments.)

Waterproof: Ice climbing is a wet activity, so the clothing system must be designed to keep you dry.

Unrestrictive: Freedom of movement is essential, so in choosing a jacket or anorak, make sure you can reach your arms high overhead without having the garment hem rise above your waist level. Otherwise, your torso will be exposed to the elements when you reach high to make a tool placement.

Windproof: The chilling effect of wind means that

18

391

you should always pack a complete layer of windproof clothing. The windproof layer must fit over all the insulating layers that you are likely to wear, and should overlap or tuck together to provide a solid shield. Fabrics vary in their relative level of wind resistance, so get recommendations from other climbers and from staff at outdoor stores. Laminated fabrics such as Gore-Tex are among the most windproof.

Gloves and Mittens

Ice climbers' hands need protection from cold and abrasion. Climbing alpine ice on a summer day may require nothing more than a pair of lightweight gloves, but other conditions usually require much more elaborate layered systems. Many glove and mitten systems are available. Features to look for include waterproof shells (sealed Gore-Tex shells are good), articulated designs, removable liners, and retainer loops. Mittens are warmer than gloves but more cumbersome; as a compromise, several manufacturers offer mittens with a separate index finger compartment, which can be used in opposition with the thumb.

Ease of use: It should be possible to adjust straps using your teeth. Check to see whether any straps or buckles interfere with the leashes of your ice-climbing tools. The components of the layered system protecting your hands must be compatible and should be easy to remove and replace, because you may have to remove a glove or mitten to manipulate climbing gear.

Materials: Gloves or mittens should have high-friction material on the palms to help you grip ice tools; some fabrics, especially nylons, tend to be rather slippery. Leather is the best material for standing up to the rigors of rope handling. High-density, boiled-wool mittens or gloves have one rather esoteric advantage: You can temporarily freeze a mittened or gloved hand to the ice, which can help you work through a move.

Boots

When selecting boots, it is essential to get a precise fit: room for the toes to wiggle but snug in the instep and heel, with minimal lift at the heel while walking. Be sure to fit boots to accommodate the stocking system you will wear. Most modern mountaineering boots

have molded toe and heel grooves, so they are compatible with step-in crampons.

Leather: For alpine ice climbing in moderate conditions, modern leather mountaineering boots are a good choice. However, if leather boots will be used for extensive front-pointing, they must be stiff-soled. Insulated leather boots are available that are specifically designed for technical ice climbing. In French technique (flat-footing), ankle rotation is very important, so boots must permit good range of motion; leather boots are usually better in this regard.

Plastic: In extreme cold, ice climbers use plastic boots more commonly than leather boots. Plastic boots are warm and dry, and they also provide a rigid platform for crampons, which is especially important for front-pointing.

Gaiters

Ice climbers need full-length gaiters that come up to just below the knee. Make sure the gaiters fit your boots and can accommodate any layers of insulation you wear on your legs. If you will wear insulated supergaiters for added warmth, check to see that they are compatible with your boot-crampon system.

Crampons

Crampon points must be sharp, and the harder the ice, the sharper the points should be. Check the points before each climb and sharpen them if necessary. (See "Crampons" in Chapter 16, Snow Travel and Climbing.)

Hinged

Properly fitted, hinged, twelve-point crampons are suitable for most alpine ice climbing. They work well with most types of climbing boots and are lighter and less expensive than rigid-frame designs.

Rigid and Semi-Rigid

Climbers who do a lot of front-pointing prefer rigid or semi-rigid crampons, which vibrate less than hinged crampons when they are kicked into water ice, which is denser. Rigid crampons should be worn with stiff leather or plastic boots to prevent overstressing the crampon frame. Although some rigid crampons are

*Fig. 18-1.
Angle of crampon
points for alpine ice.*

heavy head penetrates most readily, but it may be difficult to extract.

Ice tools, unlike ice axes, can have a hammerhead opposite the pick rather than an adze (fig. 18-2). Ice climbers either can use matched ice tools—both having a hammerhead—or can use one with a hammerhead and one with an adze. Many tools feature modular designs. Some models are semimodular; that is, only the pick is interchangeable (fig. 18-2b). Fully modular tools provide the option of interchangeable picks and adze/hammerheads (fig. 18-2c). Being able to replace picks, adzes, and hammerheads as the need arises makes the tool more complex, and the additional parts can fail or become lost, but it also provides added flexibility because the tool can be assembled to accommodate prevailing conditions. Also, a broken pick can be replaced in the field—even in midpitch, theoretically, if the fastening system is not too complex.

There is no standard fastening system for interchangeable parts on modular ice tools. Components of one manufacturer's system are not compatible with those from another company, and some systems are easier to use than others. The trend has been to design fastening systems that require a minimum of tools. The components of some ice tools are designed to be changed using the pick or spike of another ice tool made by the same manufacturer.

What is the "perfect" ice tool? Most of the ice tools that are now available work quite well. The number of different designs and models is rapidly growing. Try out a variety of ice tools to determine which ones work best for you.

On alpine ice, some climbers use a full-length general mountaineering ice ax and a shorter, straight-shafted ice tool such as a classic north wall hammer (as shown in Figure 18-2a). On more technical routes, many

strong enough to be worn with softer boots, a soft boot could twist out of a step-in crampon binding.

Front and Secondary Points

The angles of the front points and the secondary points are critical in determining the best penetration. For alpine ice, the front points are straight-shaped but bent slightly downward, and the secondary points are angled slightly forward (fig. 18-1). Chapter 19, Waterfall Ice and Mixed Climbing, discusses front-point angles preferred for waterfall ice climbing, including mono and dual front points. Table 18-2 compares advantanges of various front-point angles.

Ice Tools

Ice tools have shorter shafts than the standard ice ax used for general mountaineering. The short shaft, commonly 50 centimeters (ice tool lengths are described only in metric units), is easier to control, increasing the accuracy of pick placement and reducing the shaft vibration that can fatigue arm muscles. Ice tools generally weigh 680 to 907 grams (24 to 32 ounces), and some feature removable head weights that allow you to fine-tune the tool's "swing weight." An ice tool with a relatively

TABLE 18-2. COMPARISON OF CRAMPON FRONT-POINT ANGLES	
Orientation of Front Points	**Advantages**
Horizontal front points	Work well in warm ice, bad ice, alpine ice, and mixed climbing. If you own only one pair of crampons, then these are the ones to get.
Vertical mono front points	Work best on specific features, cold water-ice climbs, and mixed climbs.
Vertical dual front points	Work well for water ice that is in less than perfect condition.

18

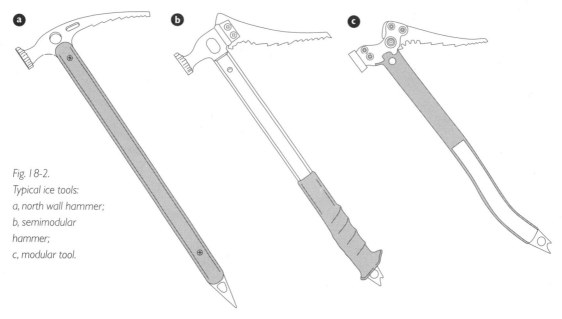

Fig. 18-2.
Typical ice tools:
a, north wall hammer;
b, semimodular
hammer;
c, modular tool.

climbers use two short ice tools. A versatile combination is a pair of ice tools, one with an adze and one with a hammer. The adze is used to chop and scrape ice for steps, belay positions, ice protection, and ice bollards; the hammer is used to drive in pieces of protection. Some climbers prefer to hold the hammer in their dominant hand, making it easier to start ice screws or place pitons.

Some climbers carry a third tool, which can be used as a temporary personal anchor at belay points, placed as a piece of protection, or used to replace a lost or broken tool. The third tool can be a full-size ice tool, or it can be a shorter (35- to 40-centimeter) and lighter (454-gram/16-ounce) "third tool" model (as shown in Figure 18-2b). The spike of a holstered tool is a potential hazard, so you may decide to carry a third tool that does not have a spike.

The styles of ice tools vary greatly. The following sections describe the principal design variations of the parts of the ice tool: shaft, pick, adze/hammerhead, spike, and leash.

Shafts

Ice tool shafts are manufactured from aluminum alloy, carbon fiber composites, and titanium alloy. A number of shaft designs are available, including a straight shaft (fig. 18-3a). Bent-grip models (fig. 18-3b) decrease strain in the wrist. Check to see that the curve of the bend and the swing weight complement your natural swing. A bent-grip design will not keep you from bashing knuckles; this is usually the result of poor technique. Bent-grip designs have some disadvantages: The bend may impede plunging the shaft into snow, the bend makes hammering or chopping somewhat awkward, and a bent-grip tool may be difficult to remove from a holster. A bend high on the shaft near the head (fig. 18-3c) increases clearance around bulges or cauliflower ice (see Chapter 19, Waterfall Ice and Mixed Climbing).

QUESTIONS TO CONSIDER WHEN SELECTING ICE TOOLS

When you are selecting ice tools, ask yourself the following questions:
1. Do the tools fit me?
2. Can I comfortably grip the tools?
3. Are they designed for the kind of climbing I intend to do?

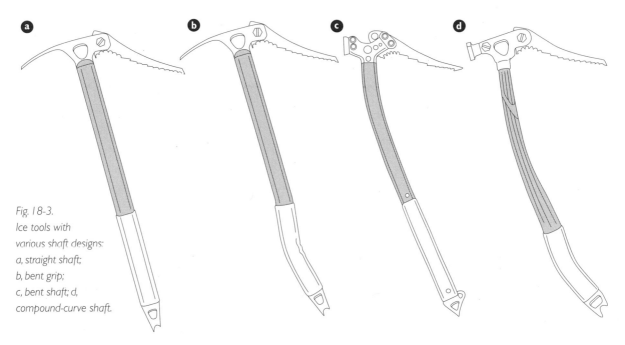

Fig. 18-3.
Ice tools with
various shaft designs:
a, straight shaft;
b, bent grip;
c, bent shaft; d,
compound-curve shaft.

Some tools have both kinds of bends (fig. 18-3d)—that is, a bend at both top and bottom. Other tools feature shafts that have a continuous, long-radius curve. If the slope of the ice is less than 60 degrees, a bent-shaft tool is awkward to place.

The circumference and cross-sectional shape of the shaft affect your grip. A particular shaft might be too large or too small for your hand. A shaft that is too large in circumference is fatiguing to grip. A shaft that is too small in circumference is hard to control.

The array of grip styles—bumps, knobs, pommels, etc.—and shaft covering materials can be bewildering. Most ice tools have a shaft covering of high-friction material that facilitates grip. To further help you grip the ice tools, wear gloves or mittens with leather or rubberized palms. A tool should be comfortable to grip when you are wearing the various glove and mitten combinations you use while climbing.

Picks

The pick must penetrate the ice, hold against a downward pull, and release easily when its grip is no longer needed. The holding and releasing characteristics of a pick are determined by its geometry, thickness, and tooth configuration. Modular ice tools typically include a variety of pick designs, but not all manufacturers offer all types.

The steeper the droop of a pick and the sharper, deeper, and more numerous the teeth, the better the pick will hold; the smoother the pick, the easier it is to remove. The teeth should be shaped to bite into the ice as you pull on the end of the shaft. In most cases, only the first few teeth provide any useful bite into the ice. Although thin picks penetrate and hold best, they are more vulnerable to damage. A thick-bladed pick, on the other hand, requires more force to place and is more likely to shatter the ice, but it is less prone to breaking.

Modular tools give you the option of choosing one of several types of interchangeable picks, so you can choose the right one for a particular climb or replace a broken pick instead of having to discard the tool.

Technically curved: The pick of a general mountaineering ice ax curves slightly downward, whereas the technically curved pick of an ice tool (fig. 18-4a) curves down more sharply and thus holds better in ice. It is most often used on alpine ice and glacial ice climbs. It is the most effective technical pick for self-arrest.

Reverse curved: The reverse-curved pick (fig. 18-4b) is both secure and easy to remove, making it the overwhelmingly most popular choice for extremely

18

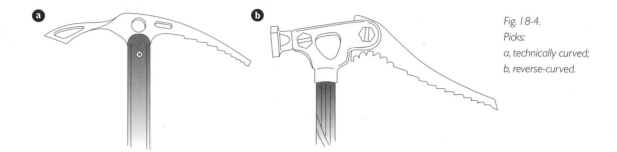

Fig. 18-4.
Picks:
a, technically curved;
b, reverse-curved.

steep ice routes. During self-arrest, this pick grabs so well that you may not be able to hold on to the tool.

The shape of any pick can be easily changed with a hand file, but be judicious in removing metal. Consider beveling the top of the pick to aid in removing the tool from the ice (fig. 18-5). Be careful not to weaken the pick by overheating it or by removing too much material. You can also change the tooth pattern of a pick that either sticks too well or does not stick well enough. Modifying the pick clearance will affect its hooking ability; a more pronounced positive clearance should make the pick better for hooking with the tip. (See Figure 16-3 in Chapter 16, Snow Travel and Climbing, for positive and negative clearance.) Some picks are designed with a pounding surface or anvil. This permits you to use a second tool to drive in a placement. This feature is useful if a tool will be used as a temporary personal anchor.

Adzes and Hammerheads

The adze of an ice tool can be used to chop steps, clear ice to make a good surface for a screw placement, or cut footholds at belay stances. Hammerheads are used to drive pickets or pitons or to pound in screws and ice hooks.

Fig. 18-5.
Close-up view of a reverse-curved pick. Note that the tip and top edge are sharp, and the sides of the teeth are beveled.

As with picks, adzes come in an array of shapes and sizes. Modular ice tools give you the option of replacing a broken adze or changing adzes depending on ice conditions. An adze can even be exchanged for a hammerhead. Some climbers dislike having a sharp adze edge near their face so they use two hammers. However, an adze is more convenient if it is necessary to chop a stance or clear rotten ice.

The most common adze is straight, extending more or less perpendicular to the shaft or drooping slightly downward (see Figure 18-4a). The straight adze's sharp corners are excellent for cutting steps. Some adzes curve downward like a technically curved pick (see Figures 18-3a and b, above). On some adzes, the very end of the working edge curves slightly inward, although this may impede cutting steps because it diffuses the full force of a swing. Drooped adzes can be used for climbing snow or rotten ice. The majority of adzes and hammerheads are now designed to be used for hooking or camming placements in rock.

Spikes

To penetrate ice, the spike on the bottom of an ice tool's shaft must be sharp, and the joint between spike and shaft must be smooth. Most spikes have carabiner holes (see Figures 18-2 and 18-3, above), to which you can clip when you are using the tool as a temporary personal anchor. This setup should not be used as part of a belay anchor.

Leashes

A wrist leash mounted on each ice tool serves several purposes. The leash secures a dropped tool, helps in the work of swinging the tool, and lets you rest your grip by hanging your weight from it. The wrist leash is an energy-saving necessity on steep or vertical ice.

A variety of leash features are available, designed to increase comfort and security. The leash can be attached through a hole or slot in the head of the tool or in the tool shaft, and it should be adjusted so that it is just long enough to let you grasp the shaft above the spike. The wrist loop should be adjusted to snugly, but comfortably, fit your gloved hand.

An increasing number of quick-release leashes are available to allow you to quickly free your hand from the tool. They are time- and energy-saving devices. If you choose a quick-release leash, be sure to take the time to practice releasing and securing yourself to the tool. Do not wait until you are at midpitch to discover that you cannot release the leash or, worse yet, resecure it. Quick-release leashes are not recommended for use in general mountaineering.

The leash should be adjusted to help hold your hand in the desired spot and to direct a downward pull straight along the shaft (fig. 18-6). Used in this manner, the leash shares the work of holding and swinging the ax. The leash also makes it possible for you to hang from an ice tool without maintaining a forearm-killing grip.

Maintenance

Inspect ice tools before each outing, checking for cracks and other signs of wear or damage. Be sure that adzes, picks, and spikes are sharp. Keep these sharp edges covered with guards when they are not in use. If the tools are a modular design, also check to see that all fastening systems are secure. Consider using an industrial thread lock (such as Loctite) to ensure that parts will not work loose during a climb.

Ice Screws

Modern tubular ice screws (fig. 18-7a) are made from steel, aluminum, or titanium alloy. Ice screws come in a variety of lengths ranging from 10 to 22 centimeters (ice screws are commonly measured in metric units). The length and diameter of an ice screw have a great bearing on its strength; a large-diameter screw supports more weight than a smaller-diameter screw of the same length. A longer screw is stronger, but only if the length isn't greater than the depth of the ice. The latest screw designs include integral spinning knobs, which make placement and removal almost effortless. The tubular design minimizes fracturing of the ice by allowing the displaced ice to work itself out through the hollow core of the screw.

18

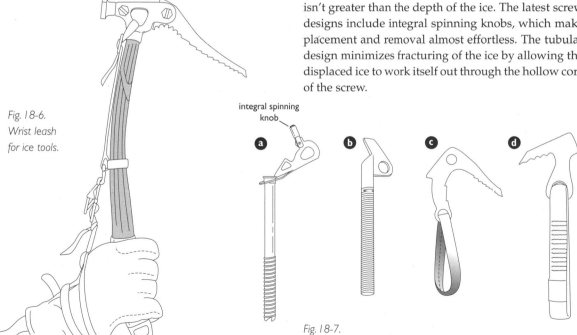

Fig. 18-6.
Wrist leash
for ice tools.

integral spinning
knob

a **b** **c** **d**

Fig. 18-7.
Ice protection: a, tubular ice screw with knob; b, tubular pound-in/
screw-out design; c–d, ice hooks.

HISTORY OF ICE SCREWS

Until the mid-twentieth century, ice pitons were extra-long, blade-type rock pitons with holes, notches, or bulges to increase their grip in ice. After World War II, climbers experimented with new designs that featured a greater surface area (to decrease the load per square inch on the ice) and more holes (to help the shaft freeze into the slope). In the early 1960s, when ice pitons evolved into ice screws, enthusiasts claimed that they would revolutionize ice climbing, bringing security to the slopes. Critics theorized that the screws were not much better than the older ice pitons. This was true of the lightweight, relatively weak "coat-hanger" ice screws, which are no longer in use. Ice screws have continued to improve and now provide reliable protection when placed in good ice.

Another type of tubular ice screw is hammered into place but screwed back out (fig. 18-7b). This type was developed in an attempt to make an easy-to-place screw. However, the "knobbed" screw with an integral spinning knob as shown above in Figure 18-7a is easier and faster to place, and has eclipsed many of the advantages of the pound-in design.

The ice hook, another type of pound-in protection, is designed for thin ice (fig. 18-7c and d). The ice hook may be used to hook features in either ice or rock; driven into the ice as a piton using ice-tool or monopoint placements as starter holes; or pounded into ice-filled cracks. Typically, use ice hooks in conjunction with a load-limiting runner. This type of protection usually needs to be chopped out by the second, an arduous task.

Other Gear

Holsters

Use a holster or harness gear loop to temporarily hold an ice tool. You can add two holsters or a double-size holster to your seat harness or pack hip belt. Try out the tools in the holster before using it. The tools may be hard to remove if the holster was designed for rock-climbing hammers, which have thinner and smoother shafts.

Racking Devices

A variety of devices are designed to facilitate the racking of ice screws and ice tools (fig. 18-8). Base your selection on how well the device works for you and on its compatibility with your harness or gear sling. Some of these devices attach directly to the harness waist belt (fig. 18-8a); others rigidly hold a carabiner attached to the harness gear loops or gear sling (fig. 18-8b and c). These devices allow ice screws to be racked securely, yet provide easy, one-handed unclipping when you need the gear. The larger devices can also be used for temporarily securing ice tools.

Ropes

Standard single ropes (10 to 11 millimeters in diameter) are most commonly used for ice climbing, though this

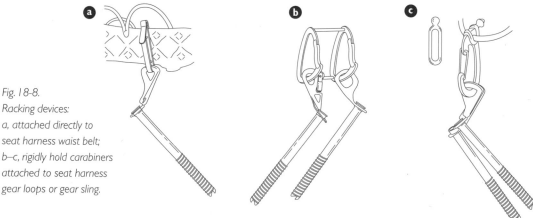

Fig. 18-8.
Racking devices:
a, attached directly to
seat harness waist belt;
b–c, rigidly hold carabiners
attached to seat harness
gear loops or gear sling.

depends on the type of climb and the climbers' preference. Using a rope longer than the standard 50 meters (165 feet) permits longer pitches. Double-rope and twin-rope techniques (see Chapter 14, Leading on Rock) are an option for ice climbing. Some climbers feel more comfortable using a two-rope system for ice climbing—which uses ropes along with sharp implements amid sharp falling debris—because it provides redundancy.

Because ice climbing can be wet, water-repellent ("dry") ropes are probably worth the extra cost. In comparison with untreated ropes, dry ropes retain more strength and are less likely to freeze—though a dry rope can still become ice-coated, and the water repellency may not last the lifetime of the rope.

Head and Eye Protection

Prudent ice climbers wear helmets. The helmet should be fitted to accommodate a hat or balaclava. Ice climbers should also protect their eyes from flying debris and ultraviolet light by wearing either goggles or sunglasses. Goggles must fit when you are wearing a helmet and have adequate ventilation to minimize fogging, which is a constant problem.

Load-Limiting Runners

Consider using load-limiting runners, also known as energy-absorbing runners or slings (see Figure 10-13 in Chapter 10, Belaying). It is advisable to use a load-limiting runner on the first piece of protection or when the protection placement is in ice of questionable quality. These runners can provide an extra margin of safety. Load-limiting runners can be placed in series, to increase the total energy absorption, or ganged, to increase the force required to activate the runner.

V-Thread Tools

The V-thread tool is a hooking device used to pull cord or webbing through the drilled tunnel of V-thread anchors (see "Setting Up Ice Anchors" later in this chapter). Two styles of V-thread tools are available commercially. One consists of a piece of wire cable with a hook swaged to one end (fig. 18-9a). The second type is a piece of stamped metal with a hook on one end (fig. 18-9b). Both types have advantages and disadvantages. The cable type is less likely to impale you, but is less

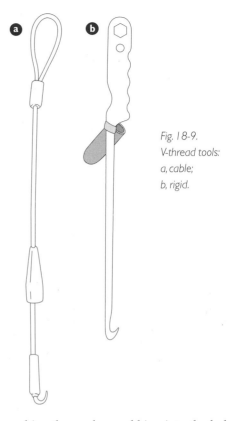

Fig. 18-9.
V-thread tools:
a, cable;
b, rigid.

suited to pushing the cord or webbing into the hole. The rigid type is a better tool for pushing the cord or webbing down into the hole, but is also more likely to stab you. A V-thread tool can also be made from a piece of wire hanger. Remember to keep the hook sharp.

TECHNIQUES OF ALPINE ICE CLIMBING

Climbing the perennially shaded side of a mountain can be an exhilarating passage over an ever-changing medium in a steep and cold environment, all of which challenges both mind and body. An alpine ice climber must move quickly and efficiently up long and sometimes sparsely protected faces to reach the summit, and then safely descend within the allotted time. On alpine ice, climbers use surface features, seeking out depressions, pockets, and ledges for tool placements, crampon purchase, and belay points. Unlike rock climbers, ice climbers are not in direct contact with the surface of the mountain. The ice climber must rely on ice tools, axes, and crampons. They make do with anchors and protection placements that can be uncertain.

Climbing without Crampons

Alpine climbers often encounter short sections of ice or frozen snow. Negotiating these sections without crampons requires balance-climbing, moving up from one position of balance to the next. At each position of balance, your inside (uphill) foot is in front of and above your trailing outside (downhill) foot. The ax, in your uphill hand, moves only after your body and feet are in balance, and your feet move only after you have moved the ax forward. You shift weight from one foot to the other smoothly as though friction-climbing on rock. While you are climbing, look for irregularities in the surface of the ice such as sun cups (small hollows that have been melted by the sun) or imbedded rocks to use as footholds.

If the slope is too steep for secure balance-climbing and you plan to proceed without crampons, consider taking another route or try cutting steps. Step-cutting is a good method if the steps can be cut quickly and efficiently.

Step-Cutting

For the earliest alpinists, chopping or cutting steps was the only technique available for climbing steep ice and hard snow. The invention of crampons reduced the need for step-cutting but never eliminated it. There are several good reasons for developing a good working knowledge of the technique of cutting steps with the ice ax. Sometimes you are not carrying crampons but still encounter areas of ice, or you may face short ice problems that do not merit taking the time to put on crampons. A broken crampon, or an injured or inexperienced climber, may be reason enough to cut steps. Even if you are wearing crampons, you might welcome a slight step for added security or to serve as a small platform on which to rest. And you should be able to chop out a comfortable belay platform.

The adze of the ice ax can be used for cutting steps two ways. The adze can be used to slash the ice by swinging the tool in a motion nearly parallel to the surface of the ice to create a slash step (fig. 18-10), or it can

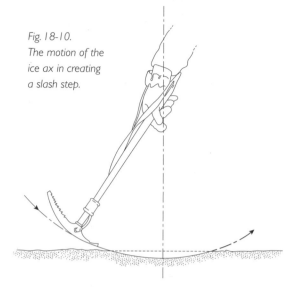

Fig. 18-10. The motion of the ice ax in creating a slash step.

be swung perpendicular to the ice to chop out a pigeonhole step (see below). For all step-cutting, use a wrist leash to help support the hard-working hand holding the ax and to keep from losing the ax if you drop it.

Slash steps: The most frequently used step-cutting technique is for slash steps, for traversing up or down gentle to moderate slopes. To cut ascending slash steps, stand in a position of balance, holding the ax in your inside (uphill) hand (fig. 18-11). Cut two steps. Swing the adze parallel to your uphill foot and away from your body. Swing the ax from your shoulder, cutting with the adze and letting the weight of the ax do most of the work. With successive swings, slice ice out of the step, starting at the heel end of the new step and working toward the toe. Scoop out chunks of ice with the adze, and use the adze and pick to finish the step.

Pigeonhole steps: These are used on steeper slopes. Each diagonal step should slope slightly into the slope to help keep your boots from slipping downward and out of the step. On gentler slopes, it is acceptable if the step holds only a small part of your boot, but the steps on steeper slopes should be large enough for the front half of your boot. Space the steps so they are convenient for all members of the party to use. Pigeonhole steps for the direct ascent of steep ice are placed about shoulder-width apart and within easy stepping distance of each other. Each step functions as both a handhold and foothold, so each should have a small lip to serve as a handhold.

18

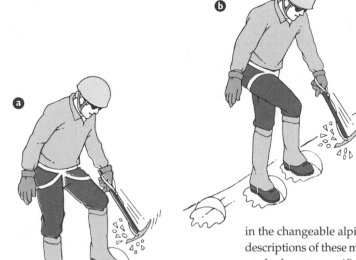

Fig. 18-11.
Cutting slash steps
on a diagonal ascent:
a, work from a position
of balance, with the ax in
the inside (uphill) hand;
b, then step uphill to an
out-of-balance position.

Ladder steps: To chop steps down an ice slope, the easiest method is to cut a "ladder" of pigeonhole steps that descend almost straight down the hill. To cut two steps in sequence, start in a position of balance, facing down the slope. Chop two pigeonhole steps directly below the ones you are standing in. When the new steps are ready, step down with your outside (downhill) foot and then your inside (uphill) foot. To cut just one step at a time, again start in a position of balance. Cut the step for your outside (downhill) foot and move that foot down into the step. Then cut the step for your inside (uphill) foot and move that foot down into it. Some climbers may opt to rappel rather than cut steps down an icy incline.

Climbing with Crampons

Ice climbers usually employ features of two basic techniques, depending on steepness of the slope, conditions of the ice, and their ability and confidence level. These are termed French technique and German technique. Although each technique has its own distinct benefits, modern ice climbing melds the two. Mastery of both French and German technique is essential for climbing

in the changeable alpine environment. Below are brief descriptions of these methods, followed by sections that apply them to specific types of terrain.

French Technique (Flat-Footing)
French technique, also called flat-footing, is the easiest and most efficient method of climbing on gentle to steep ice and hard snow. Good French technique demands balance, rhythm, joint flexibility, and the confident use of crampons and ice ax. Specifics of this technique are described in the sections that follow.

German Technique (Front-Pointing)
Developed by Germans and Austrians for climbing the harder snow and ice of the eastern Alps, German technique, better known as front-pointing, allows an experienced ice climber to go up the steepest and most difficult ice slopes. With this technique, even average climbers can quickly overcome sections that would be difficult or impossible with French technique. The German technique is much like kicking steps straight up a snow slope, but instead of kicking a boot into the snow, you kick that boot's front crampon points into the ice; you step up with the other foot, directly supported by the placed boot's front points. Just as in French technique, good front-pointing is rhythmic and balanced, with the weight of your body balanced over the crampons. It is essential to move efficiently, whether you are planting front points, placing ice tools, or moving on the ice.

18

American Technique
(Combination Technique)

Modern crampon technique evolved from the French and German styles. As on rock, climbing on ice involves the efficient and confident use of footwork to maintain balance and minimize fatigue. Flat-footing is generally used on lower-angle slopes and where crampon point penetration is easy. Front-pointing is most commonly used on slopes steeper than 45 degrees and on very hard ice. In practice, most climbers blend them into a combination approach, sometimes called American technique.

In any technique, the most important element is confident use of the crampons. Practicing on gentle and moderate slopes helps develop skill, confidence, and the aggressive approach needed at steeper angles. A skilled ice climber, whether flat-footing or front-pointing, displays the same deliberate movement as a skilled rock climber. The crampon points must be carefully and deliberately placed into the ice, your weight transferred from one foot to the other smoothly and decisively.

Boldness is essential to skillful cramponing. Exposure must be disregarded and concentration focused solely on the climbing. But boldness is not blind bravado. It is confidence and skill born of experience and enthusiasm, nurtured in many practice sessions on glacial seracs and on ice bulges in frozen gullies, and matured by ascents of increasing length and difficulty.

Ice-Climbing Terms

Table 18-3 below lists ice-climbing techniques for crampons and ice ax, along with the approximate steepness of the slope on which each technique is used. French terms are sometimes used, given in parentheses. The French word *pied* (pronounced pee-EY) means "foot"; the French word *piolet* (pronounced pee-oh-LAY) means "ice ax." Terms including the word *pied* refer to footwork; terms including the word *piolet* refer to ice-ax positions.

None of these techniques are restricted to any particular set of conditions, and all can be useful in a wide range of snow and ice situations. When you

TABLE 18-3. TECHNIQUES FOR CRAMPONS, ICE AXES, AND ICE TOOLS	
Technique	**Approximate Steepness of Slope**
Crampons	
Walking (French technique; *pied marche*)	Gentle, 0 to 15 degrees
Duckwalk (French technique; *pied en canard*)	Gentle, 15 to 30 degrees
Flat-footing (French technique; *pied à plat*)	Moderate to steep, 30 to 60 degrees and higher
Rest position (French technique; *pied assis*)	Steep, 60 degrees and higher
Three-o'clock position (combination technique; *pied troisième*)	Steep, 60 degrees and higher
Front-pointing (German technique)	Steep through vertical and overhanging, 45 degrees and higher
Ice Axes and Ice Tools (French and German Technique)	
Cane position (*piolet canne*)	Gentle to moderate, 0 to 45 degrees
Cross-body position (*piolet ramasse*)	Moderate, 30 to 45 degrees
Anchor position (*piolet ancre*)	Steep to extremely steep, 45 degrees and higher
Low-dagger position (*piolet panne*)	Steep, 45 to 55 degrees
High-dagger position (*piolet poignard*)	Steep, 50 to 60 degrees
Traction position (*piolet traction*)	Extremely steep, 60 degrees through vertical and overhanging

are practicing these techniques, keep in mind that a sharp crampon is a happy crampon, requiring only body weight to set it securely in place.

Climbing on Gentle to Moderate Slopes

Using French Technique

French technique, or flat-footing, is an essential alpine ice-climbing technique. Keep your boot soles parallel to the ice surface and your feet slightly farther apart than normal to avoid snagging a crampon point on clothing or on a crampon strap on the other foot. Firmly set all bottom points into the ice. Use the ice ax in the cane position (see Figures 18-12 and 18-13), holding the ax in the self-belay grasp (for ice ax positions and grasps, see Chapter 16, Snow Travel and Climbing). On gentle slopes, you begin by simply walking. Flexible ankles are sometimes necessary in order to keep your soles parallel to the surface. Boots that are flexible at the ankle facilitate flat-footing. Climbers with plastic boots can loosen their boot laces at the cuff for more comfortable flat-footing. Ease ankle strain by

rotating your boots more and more downhill as the slope steepens.

As the gentle slope steepens slightly, splay your feet outward in duckwalk fashion (fig. 18-12). Keep your knees bent and your weight balanced over your feet. Continue to use the ax as a cane.

As the slope gets steeper still, no longer gentle but moderate, duckwalking straight upward causes severe ankle strain. Then it is time to turn sideways to the slope and ascend diagonally for a more relaxed, comfortable step. Be sure that you are flat-footing, with all crampon points weighted into the ice (fig. 18-13). In using this technique for the first time, people have a strong tendency to edge with their crampons. The crampon points can skate off the ice, throwing you off balance. Fight this tendency, and keep the crampon points flat against the ice at all times. Start with your feet pointed in the direction of travel. As the slope steepens, you must rotate your feet more and more downward in order to keep them flat. As the slope angle increases, ease ankle strain by pointing your boots downhill more and more, so that the flex needed to keep your feet flat

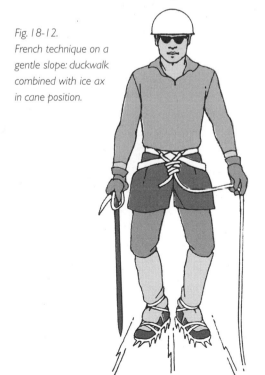

Fig. 18-12.
French technique on a
gentle slope: duckwalk
combined with ice ax
in cane position.

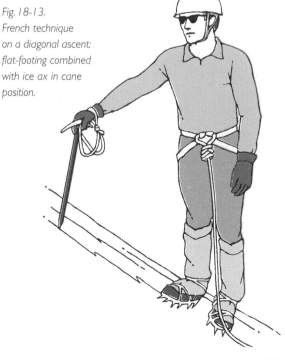

Fig. 18-13.
French technique
on a diagonal ascent:
flat-footing combined
with ice ax in cane
position.

18

comes from the more normal forward flex of the ankle and from your knees, which you bend away from the slope and spread well apart (see Figure 18-14). On the steepest slopes, your knees may be pointing straight downhill.

As the slope angle changes from gentle to moderate, using the ax in the cane position becomes awkward. You can now achieve greater security by holding the ax in the cross-body position (fig. 18-14). Grip the shaft just above the spike with your inside hand and hold the head of the ax in the self-belay grasp, pick pointing forward, with your outside hand. Drive the spike into the ice, the shaft perpendicular to the slope. In the cross-body position, most of the force on the ax should be at the hand on the shaft. The hand on the head stabilizes the ax and is a reminder not to lean into the slope. To keep your body from leaning into the ice, you need a full-length ice ax, rather than a shorter ice tool. Even experienced ice climbers have difficulty maintaining proper French technique with a short ax.

Move diagonally upward in a two-step sequence, much the same as ascending a snow slope without crampons. Remember to keep your feet flat at all times.

Start from a position of balance, your inside (uphill) foot in front of and above your trailing outside (downhill) leg (fig. 18-14a). From this in-balance position, bring your outside foot in front of and above your inside foot, into the out-of-balance position (fig. 18-14b). Cross your outside leg over the knee of your inside leg; if the cross is made at the ankle, you compromise stability and the next step is difficult to make. To return to a position of balance, bring your inside foot up from behind and place it again in front of your outside foot (fig. 18-14c). Keep your body weight over the crampons. Avoid leaning into the slope and creating the danger of crampon points twisting out of the ice. Step on lower-angled spots and natural irregularities in the ice to ease ankle strain and conserve energy.

During this diagonal ascent, plant the ax about an arm's length ahead of you (as shown in Figure 18-14a) each time before you move another two steps. Whether you are using the ax in the cane or the cross-body position, plant it far enough forward so that it will be near your hip after you move up to the next in-balance position (as shown in Figure 18-14c).

To change direction (switchback) on a diagonal ascent

Fig. 18-14.
French technique on a diagonal ascent—flat-footing combined with ice ax in cross-body position (pick forward): a, in-balance position; b, out-of-balance position; c, in-balance position.

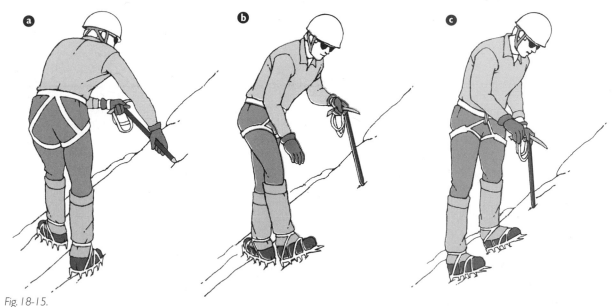

Fig. 18-15.
French technique for changing direction on a diagonal ascent—flat-footing combined with ice ax in cross-body position:
a, out-of-balance position; b, the turn; c, in-balance position.

of a moderate ice slope, use the same technique as on a snow slope where crampons would not be used, but keep your feet flat. From a position of balance, place the ax directly above your location. Move your outside (downhill) foot forward, into the out-of-balance position, to about the same elevation as your other foot and pointing slightly uphill (fig. 18-15a). Grasping the ax with both hands, turn into the slope, moving your inside (uphill) foot to point in the new direction and slightly uphill. You are now facing into the slope, standing with feet splayed outward in opposite directions (fig. 18-15b). If the splayed-foot position feels unstable, front-point. Return to the in-balance position by moving your foot that is still pointing in the original direction to above and in front of your other foot. Reposition your grasp on the ice ax, for either the cane or cross-body position. You are now back in balance and facing the new direction of travel (fig. 18-15c).

Climbing on Moderate to Steep Slopes

With steeper ice, other variations of French technique are called for. At some point, the German technique of front-pointing comes into play.

Using French Technique

On moderate to steep slopes, for more security switch the ice ax from the cross-body position to what is known as the anchor position. Your feet remain flat, with all bottom crampon points weighted into the ice at each step.

To place the ax in the anchor position, begin in a position of balance. Grip the ice ax shaft just above the spike with your outside (downhill) hand (fig. 18-16a). Swing the ax so that the pick sticks into the ice in front of and above your head, with the shaft parallel to the slope (fig. 18-16b). With the other hand, take hold of the ax head in the self-arrest grasp. Now pull on the ax while you move two steps forward to a new position of balance (fig. 18-16c). Use a gentle and constant outward pull on the ice ax to set its teeth and keep it locked into the ice. When it is time to release it, push the bottom of the shaft toward the ice and lift the pick up and out.

To keep your feet flat at these angles, your body must lean farther away from the slope, with your knees and ankles flexed, and the toes of your boots increasingly pointing downhill. Try to continue advancing upward in the standard sequence, moving two steps at a time.

18

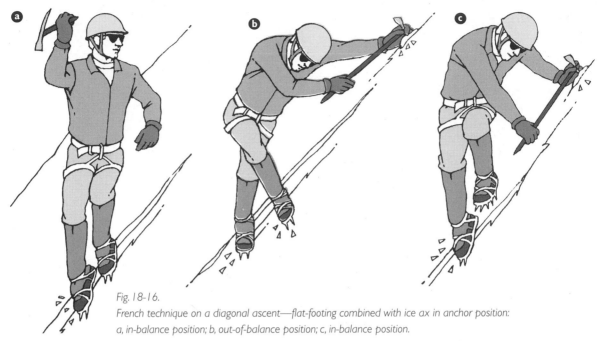

Fig. 18-16.

French technique on a diagonal ascent—flat-footing combined with ice ax in anchor position: a, in-balance position; b, out-of-balance position; c, in-balance position.

At the steepest angles, however, your feet point downhill and you must take increasingly smaller steps, essentially moving backward up the slope. But continue to plant and remove the pick from a position of balance. Your foot that is on the same side as the direction of travel should be at least slightly higher than your other foot, allowing your upper body to rotate for a smooth, strong swing of the ax.

To change diagonal direction when the ice ax is in the anchor position, use the same sequence as with the cane or cross-body position. However, on the steepest slopes, where you are stepping backward, change direction simply by switching hands on the ax and planting it on the other side. There is not much diagonal movement at this point, because you are mainly moving backward straight up the slope.

The French also devised a rest position—called *pied assis*—that gives your leg muscles a rest and provides more security for replanting the ax (fig. 18-17). From a position of balance, bring your outside (downhill) foot up and beneath your buttocks, with the boot—flat, as always—pointing straight downhill. Then sit down on the heel of that foot. This is a balanced position, a relatively comfortable one.

Fig. 18-17.
French technique of pied assis *for rest and balance.*

The invaluable technique of flat-footing, used with the ice ax in the cane or cross-body position, will serve an experienced climber for many alpine routes. For short stretches of steeper ice, flat-footing combined with the ice ax in anchor position will often work, but this marks the upper limit of French technique.

Using German Technique

On steep ice slopes, use of French technique and German technique begins to overlap. They both have a place on these slopes.

Most people pick up front-pointing quickly because it feels natural and secure. Unfortunately, this encourages you to use it on moderate slopes where flat-footing would be more efficient and just as secure. In flat-footing, most of the strain is on the large, powerful thigh muscles. Front-pointing, however, depends almost solely on the calf muscles, which burn out much faster. Even climbers who strongly prefer front-pointing would benefit from alternating the techniques to give their calf muscles a rest.

Plastic boots provide a firm base for crampons and make front-pointing easiest. Very stiff-soled leather boots are also good. Less stiff-soled boots can be used in some cases, but require more muscular effort. However, flexible-soled boots (fig. 18-18) just do not provide the necessary support for front-pointing. Pioneer ice climber Yvon Chouinard said it well: "You can't dance on hard ice with soft-soled shoes" (Chouinard, *Climbing Ice*, p. 87).

Front-pointing uses not only the primary points of the crampons, but also the secondary points immediately behind them. These points, attached to a rigid boot and properly placed in the ice, provide a platform you can stand on. The most stable placement of your boot is straight into the ice, avoiding splayed feet, which tend to rotate the outside front points out of the ice. Your boot soles should be perpendicular to the ice surface, with your heels slightly down in order to engage the secondary points into the ice and complete the four-point platform for standing (fig. 18-19). Slightly bend at the knee to reduce the strain on your calf muscles.

Resist the temptation to raise your heels. This pulls the secondary points from the ice, endangering placement of the front points, and accelerates calf muscle fatigue. Your heels will normally feel lower than they really are, so if it feels as though your heels are too low, the odds are that they are in the correct horizontal position. This is especially important when you are coming over the top of steep ice onto a gentler slope, where the natural tendency is to raise your heels, relax your level of concentration, and hurry. This is a formula for trouble because it could cause the crampon points to shear from the ice. A good way to become comfortable with the essential skills of crampon placement and foot positioning is to practice on a top rope with an experienced ice climber who can critique your style.

In the initial crampon placements on a route, concentrate on determining the amount of force required

18

Fig. 18-18.
Problems of trying to front-point with soft-soled boots.

Fig. 18-19.
Correct position for front-pointing.

to secure a foothold. After that, a single confident swing should be all that is needed. Watch out for two common mistakes: kicking too hard (which is prematurely fatiguing) and kicking too often in one place (which fractures the ice and makes it harder to get a good foothold). After you make a crampon placement, avoid foot movement because it can make the points rotate out of the ice.

Front-pointing uses a variety of ice ax positions. Dagger positions are useful in hard snow and relatively soft ice. They do not work well in hard ice. The jabbing and stabbing motions of placing the pick are not very powerful, and poor pick penetration into the hard ice could mean an insecure placement. Attempts to force a deeper placement may result in nothing more than a bruised hand. For harder ice or a steeper slope, abandon the dagger positions for the anchor and traction positions, which are also used in flat-footing.

Low-dagger position: Hold the ax by the adze in the self-belay grasp and push the pick into the ice near

Fig. 18-21. Front-pointing with ax in high-dagger position.

Fig. 18-20. Front-pointing with ax in low-dagger position.

waist level, to aid balance (fig. 18-20). This position is helpful in tackling a short, relatively steep section that requires only a few quick front-pointing moves. It tends to hold you away from the slope and out over your feet, the correct stance for front-pointing.

High-dagger position: Hold the ax head in the self-arrest grasp and jab the pick into the ice above shoulder height (fig. 18-21). Use this position if the slope is a bit too steep to insert the pick effectively into the ice at waist level in the low-dagger position.

Anchor position: While you are standing on front points, hold the ax shaft near the spike and swing the pick in as high as possible without overreaching (fig. 18-22a). Front-point upward, holding onto the shaft higher and higher while you are progressing, adding a self-arrest grasp on the adze with your other hand when you are high enough (fig. 18-22b). Finally, switch hands on the adze, converting to the low-dagger position (fig. 18-22c); when the adze is at waist level, remove it from the ice and replant it higher. Use the anchor position on harder ice or a steeper slope.

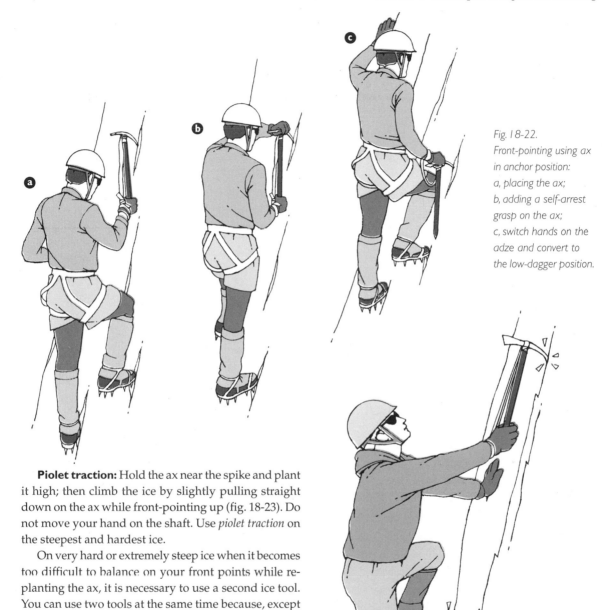

Fig. 18-22.
Front-pointing using ax
in anchor position:
a, placing the ax;
b, adding a self-arrest
grasp on the ax;
c, switch hands on the
adze and convert to
the low-dagger position.

Piolet traction: Hold the ax near the spike and plant it high; then climb the ice by slightly pulling straight down on the ax while front-pointing up (fig. 18-23). Do not move your hand on the shaft. Use *piolet traction* on the steepest and hardest ice.

On very hard or extremely steep ice when it becomes too difficult to balance on your front points while re-planting the ax, it is necessary to use a second ice tool. You can use two tools at the same time because, except for the anchor position, all ice-ax techniques used with front-pointing require only one hand.

Using two tools provides three points of support—two crampons and one ice tool—while you replant the other tool. The placements must be secure enough so that if one point of support fails, the other two will hold you until you replace the third point. Your legs carry most of the weight, but your arms help with both weight-bearing and balance.

Fig. 18-23.
Front-pointing with
ax overhead in
traction position.

18

409

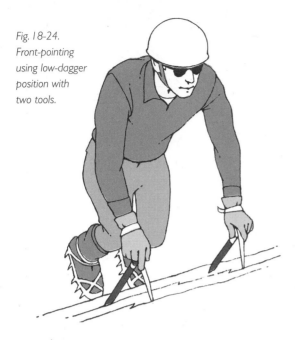

Fig. 18-24.
Front-pointing
using low-dagger
position with
two tools.

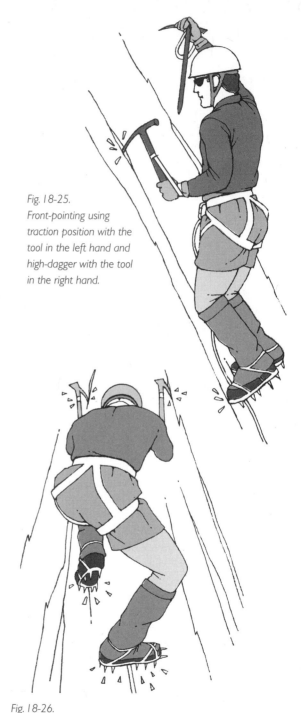

Fig. 18-25.
Front-pointing using
traction position with the
tool in the left hand and
high-dagger with the tool
in the right hand.

In double-tool technique, you can use the same ice ax method for both hands or a different method for each. For instance, climb with both tools in low-dagger position (fig. 18-24). Or place one tool in high-dagger position and the other in piolet traction (fig. 18-25). See "Climbing on Vertical Ice" later in this chapter for details of double-tool technique using piolet traction with both tools.

Using American Technique

One fast and powerful technique combines flat-footing and front-pointing. This is called the three o'clock position, *pied troisième* (fig. 18-26), because as one foot is front-pointing, the other is flat and points to the side (to three o'clock if it is the right foot or nine o'clock if it is the left). This combination technique is an example of American technique.

The three o'clock position is a potent resource for a direct line of ascent, much less tiring than front-pointing alone. The position lets you distribute the work over more muscle groups by alternating techniques with each leg. When you are climbing, seek out irregular flatter spots and any pockets or ledges for flat-footing, allowing your calf muscles to rest. Use whatever ice-tool positions are appropriate to the situation.

Fig. 18-26.
Three o'clock position for the feet, combining flat-footing (the right foot) and front-pointing (the left foot).

Climbers alternate crampon techniques depending on ice conditions. Flat-footing is usually more secure on frozen snow, ice crust over snow, and soft or rotten ice, because more crampon points dig into the surface. When soft snow covers ice or hard snow, using front-pointing technique or the three o'clock position lets you blast through the surface to get points into the firmer layer beneath. Front-pointing is often the most secure technique for the average climber to use on very hard ice on all but gentle slopes. If you are having serious problems on a climb with flat-footing—perhaps due to fatigue, winds, high altitude, or fear—switch to front-pointing or the three o'clock position.

Ice-Tool Placements

The objective of placing any ice tool is to establish a solid placement with one swing. Each swing saved during a pitch means that much less fatigue at the top. It takes a lot of practice to learn pinpoint placement, especially when you are swinging the tool with your nondominant arm. But with a combination of proper technique and equipment, you should be able to place a tool easily and precisely so that it is both secure and easy to remove.

At the base of the route, try a few tool placements to get a feel for the plasticity of the ice. Plasticity—which determines the ability of the ice to hold and release a tool—varies tremendously with temperature and age of the ice.

Study the ice for good placements. Ice holds the pick better in depressions than in bulges, which shatter or break off under the impact of an ice tool due to radiating fracture lines. Try to make placements in opaque ice, which is less brittle than clear ice because it has more air trapped inside. Minimize the number of placements needed by planting the pick as high as possible and by moving upward as far as possible with each placement. Placement techniques vary, depending on the type of pick.

Technically curved: These picks, also known as al-pine picks, are most like the pick of a standard ice ax (see Figure 18-4a, above). However, the picks are more acutely curved than that of a regular ax, to hold better in ice. A tool with a technically curved pick is placed with a natural swing from your shoulder. This pick is used in conditions ranging from soft serac ice to hard water ice, though you need to swing harder for good penetration in hard ice.

Reverse curved: The more acute angles of reverse-curved picks (see Figure 18-4b, above) require a some-what different swing, with a definite wrist snap just prior to connecting. To plant the pick, bring your arm back, with your elbow bent about 90 degrees, then swing at the desired spot. At the end of the swing, snap your wrist toward the ice. The steeper the droop of the pick, the more wrist action is needed to set the pick. The reverse-curved pick also works well for hooking holes in the ice. Large icicles often form in clusters on vertical sections, creating slots or gaps that are ideal for secure hooking placements.

Removing the Tool

In addition to learning the proper force to use in plac-ing a tool, you must also learn the best way to remove it. Unless you do it correctly, removing a tool can be more tiring than placing it. Try to remove the tool in reverse of the motion you used to set it. First, loosen the placement by rocking the tool back and forth in the same plane as the pick (fig. 18-27a and b). Then try to remove the tool by pulling up and out (fig. 18-27c and

Fig. 18-27.

How to remove an ice tool: a and b, rock it back and forth; c and d, pull up and out; e, strike up on the adze (or hammerhead).

411

d). If this fails, release your grip on the tool and try to knock it loose by hitting up against the adze with the palm of your hand (fig. 18-27e). Then grab the head and pull up and out. Never remove a tool by torquing it from side to side because the pick may break.

Climbing on Vertical Ice

The basic method of climbing vertical ice is front-pointing combined with use of two ice tools in piolet traction (fig. 18-28). The standard position for your feet is about shoulder width apart and level with each other, a stable and relatively comfortable stance. At this point

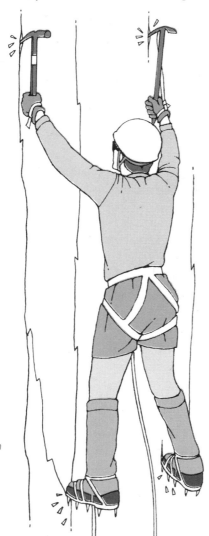

Fig. 18-28. Front-pointing on vertical ice, in an X body position with two tools overhead.

your body resembles an X against the ice. Your feet are level with each other, heels slightly down, and your arms are straight. Pull down and slightly outward on the tools to keep the picks' teeth set in the ice, and apply inward pressure on the crampon points. This is like a mild lieback position. To conserve energy, hang from the wrist leashes rather than gripping the tools tightly.

To ascend, grasp the tools and pull yourself higher while stepping upward on the front points to a new level position. Let your legs do most of the work. Do not burn out your arms by doing pull-ups while you are climbing the pitch. You are now ready to replant the ice tools. Reach up and plant the pick of one ice tool as high as possible—but off to the side a bit so you are not hit by dislodged ice or by a tool that comes loose. Then plant the other tool, in the same manner. Be careful not to overreach for a tool placement because that motion may cause your boot soles to rise from their position perpendicular to the ice.

This sequence returns you to the X body position. Repeat this sequence. Concentrate on efficient, methodical placement of crampon points and ice tools. Rhythm is as important as balance.

Climbers sometimes find themselves "barndooring"—swinging out of balance—as they remove one tool in order to place it higher. Avoid this by shifting your center of balance toward the tool that will remain in the ice (fig. 18-29a). Once that new, higher placement is made, shift your center of balance to the higher tool and then remove the lower tool (fig. 18-29b).

The monkey hang is a good technique to use for ascending ice bulges, small overhangs, and longer vertical sections. (See Chapter 19, Waterfall Ice and Mixed Climbing.)

From Vertical to a Horizontal Stretch

Oddly enough, one of the most challenging sequences involves climbing from a vertical face up onto a horizontal step or ledge. With a secure horizontal section of ice ahead, you may relax concentration and forget about good foot placement. At the same time, you face the problem that it is virtually impossible to obtain a confident tool placement by blindly swinging over a ledge. You must move high enough to see onto the ledge.

*Fig. 18-29.
Staying in balance
on vertical ice:
a, center body weight
on the right-hand tool
and remove the left-
hand tool for higher
placement;
b, then center body
weight on the
replanted left-hand
tool and remove
the right-hand tool.*

To do this, make shorter tool and foot placements for a slightly exaggerated X body position when you are approaching the lip of the ledge; then step up to a high-dagger position so you can see onto the ledge and look for a good spot to place an ice tool. You may need to remove snow or rotten ice, which often accumulates on ledges and moderate ice slopes. Place an ice tool securely into the ledge, well back from the lip, and then place the second ice tool; move your feet up until they are safely over the lip. Remember that it is especially important to keep the heels low.

Traversing Steep to Vertical Ice

The principles for traversing are much the same as for front-pointing up steep ice. However, because you are moving to the side instead of straight up, it is more difficult to keep one foot perpendicular to the ice while replacing the front points of the other foot. If your heel rotates, the front points will also rotate and come out

of the ice. Ice tools also tend to rotate out during sideways travel.

Start from a secure position with both your feet at the same level. Lean in the direction of travel and plant the leading tool in the ice (fig. 18-30a). This places the leading tool lower than it would be if you were ascending, but not so far to the side that it causes your body to rotate out from the wall when you remove the trailing tool. This also puts the trailing tool in a position so that you can pull on it in a modified lieback while you are traversing, without twisting the tool out of the ice.

Now shuffle sideways on front points (fig. 18-30b). You can also make a two-step move, crossing your trailing foot over your leading foot, and then bringing the other foot back into the lead. Most climbers prefer the shuffle, which is less awkward and feels more secure. After moving your feet, replant the trailing tool closer to your body at a 45-degree angle, replant the leading tool vertically, and repeat the process.

18

413

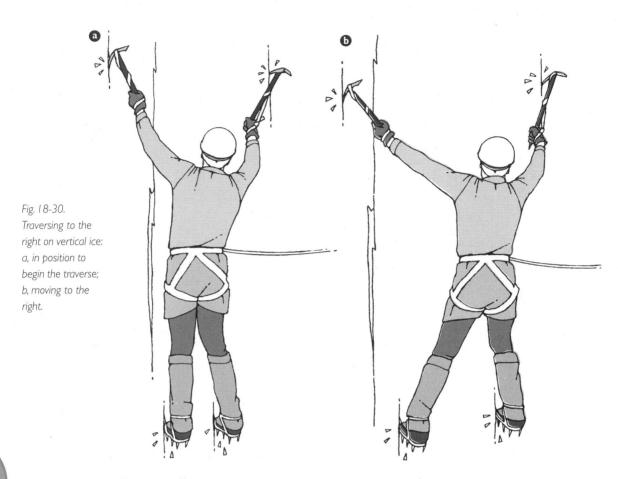

Fig. 18-30.
Traversing to the
right on vertical ice:
a, in position to
begin the traverse;
b, moving to the
right.

Descending

Using French Technique

Cane position: To descend gently sloping ice, simply face directly downhill, bend your knees slightly, and walk firmly downward. Plant all bottom crampon points into the ice with each step. Hold the ax in the cane position. As the descent angle steepens, bend your knees more and spread them apart, with your body weight over your feet so that all crampon points bite securely (fig. 18-31). Thigh muscles do the bulk of the work.

Cross-body position: For greater security, plant the ax perpendicular to the slope in the cross-body position (fig. 18-32).

Support position: For the next level of security, use the ax in the support position (fig. 18-33). Grasp the ax near the middle of the shaft and hold it beside you while

descending; the ax head points uphill, with the pick down, and the spike points downhill.

Banister position: As the slope steepens, use the banister position. Grasp the ax near the spike. Plant the pick as far below you as possible (fig. 18-34a). Walk downward, sliding your hand along the shaft toward the head of the ax (fig. 18-34b and c). Maintain a slight outward pull (away from the ice) on the shaft to keep the pick locked in the ice. With a reverse-curved pick, this is less secure; pull parallel to the ice. Keep moving down until you are below the ax head (fig. 18-34d). Then release the pick (fig. 18-34e), and replant the ax farther down.

Anchor position: On a slope too steep to safely descend facing outward, turn sideways and descend diagonally. Your footwork changes to the same flat-footing technique used to ascend diagonally. Use the ax in the

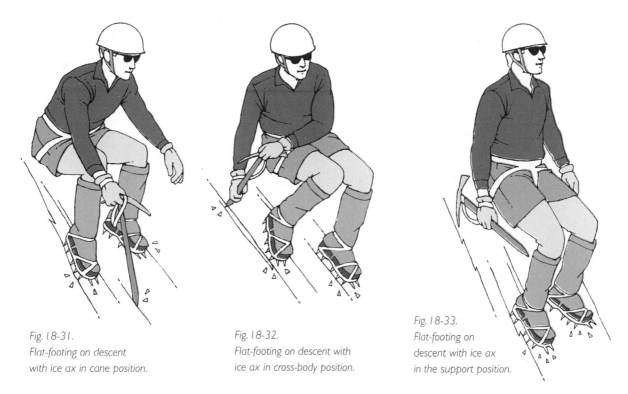

Fig. 18-31.
Flat-footing on descent
with ice ax in cane position.

Fig. 18-32.
Flat-footing on descent with
ice ax in cross-body position.

Fig. 18-33.
Flat-footing on
descent with ice ax
in the support position.

anchor position (fig. 18-35). With your outside arm, swing the ax out in front and plant the pick in the ice; take hold of the head with the other hand in the self-arrest grasp; and then flat-foot diagonally down below the ax. The shaft rotates as you pass below it.

Using German Technique

On steeper slopes, front-point and tool techniques are generally the same for going down as they are for going up. But, just as on rock, down-climbing is more difficult. There is a tendency to step too low, which keeps your heel too high, so front points may fail to penetrate in the first place or may shear out. A good view of the route is not possible on a descent (although descending on a slight diagonal helps). It is awkward to plant the ice tools because they must be placed closer to your body, so the power of a good full swing is lost. On a descent, the only feasible way to get secure placements may be to plant the tools back in the holes that you made on the ascent.

Climbers do not often front-point to descend, but it is still a valuable skill for some occasions, such as retreating from a route. Down-climbing ability also builds confidence in ascending. Ice climbers usually rappel down steeper routes (see "Rappelling" later in this chapter).

ROPED CLIMBING TECHNIQUES

Climbers usually rope up on ice. Ice pitches can be climbed using a standard single rope or by using two ropes (see "Double- and Twin-Rope Techniques" in Chapter 14, Leading on Rock). The principal exception comes when you decide that overall team safety is served best by climbing unroped. Late on a stormy day or while you are ascending a couloir threatened by rock-fall, unroped travel might offer relatively more safety with its greater speed than would continuing on the rope. It may be sensible to travel unroped through a section so difficult to protect that a fall by one roped climber would sweep away the whole team. However, make no mistake: Unroped ice climbing is serious business.

Fig. 18-34.
Flat-footing on descent with ice ax in the banister position: a, planting the ax; b–c, slide hand along the shaft like a banister; d, ready to replant the ax; e, remove and replant the ax.

Fig. 18-35.
Flat-footing on descent with
ice ax in the anchor position.

Placing Protection on Ice

Modern ice screws offer reliable protection in good ice. However, you sacrifice some safety because of the time and energy it takes to place them. Therefore leaders commonly place fewer points of protection on an ice pitch than they typically would on a rock pitch of the same length. Ice climbers also make some use of natural protection. Practice using either hand to place protection.

Natural Protection

Natural protection is oftentimes hard to come by on an alpine ice route. Good natural protection may be available not on the ice itself but in rock bordering the route or protruding through the ice. Shrubs and trees may be protection opportunities.

Ice Screws

For any given screw placement, there are dozens of variations. And you must ask some very serious questions: What is the quality of the ice? What is the depth of the ice? What is the projected amount of force on the piece? What is the projected direction of force? Which screws are left on the rack? Which will be needed later? Observations, calculations, estimates, and experience

will help you answer these questions and place gear accordingly.

Each screw placement is different—which is one of the great things about climbing ice. It is an ever-changing medium. In solid ice and under ideal conditions, ice screw placements are actually stronger if the screw is placed in the projected direction of force. In other cases, placements are stronger if the screws are oriented away from the direction of force. But you must make the decision at the time you make the placement. Practice. Take your screws and set them at various angles in different types of ice, and test them hard. Prove to yourself that they will hold you if you fall. Talk to people who have fallen on screws and had them hold. Talk to people who have ripped out every screw on a leader fall, and find out what went wrong.

A favorable location for an ice-screw placement is the same as that for an ice tool. A good choice is a natural depression, where fracture lines caused by the screw are not as likely to reach the surface (fig. 18-36). A screw placed in a bulge in the ice, on the other hand, can cause serious fracturing that weakens the placement or makes it useless. In general, keep screw placements at least 2 feet (60 centimeters) apart to reduce danger that fracture lines from one placement will reach the other, weakening both.

Fig. 18-36.
Ice-screw placement in alpine ice with the screw head angled uphill 10 degrees against the anticipated direction of pull and the screw eye facing the direction of pull.

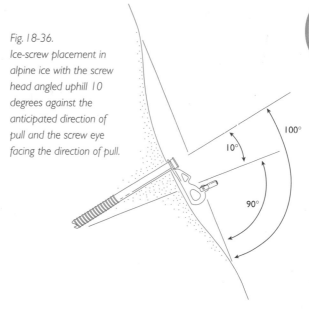

18

The procedures for placing a screw vary somewhat with ice conditions, but the basic routine is much the same in any case:

1. For maximum leverage during placement, keep the screw placement between your hip and shoulder level. Punch out a small starting hole with the pick or spike of the ice tool, to give the starting threads or teeth of the screw a good grip. Make the hole gently, with light taps, to avoid fracturing the ice. The starting hole can also be an old pick hole.

2. Start the screw in the hole set at your selected angle, press the screw firmly, and twist it into the ice at the same time. Drive the screw home. The screw hanger should be flush with the ice surface and pointed in the direction of anticipated force. Attach a carabiner, quickdraw, or load-limiting runner to the screw hanger; clip the rope.

3. Continue climbing.

A screw with sharp teeth can usually be screwed in all the way by hand. If not, drive it with the help of a lever through the screw eye; another ice screw or the pick of an ice tool works well (fig. 18-37). The knobbed screws are easier and faster to screw in and out. Clip a carabiner in to the eye, with the carabiner gate down and out. To slow the melt-out in soft summer ice or in ice exposed to direct sunlight, pack ice over the screw.

On ice topped with a layer of soft snow or rotten ice, use the adze or pick to scrape down to a hard, trustworthy surface before you make the starting hole (fig. 18-38a). In extremely rotten ice, make a large horizontal

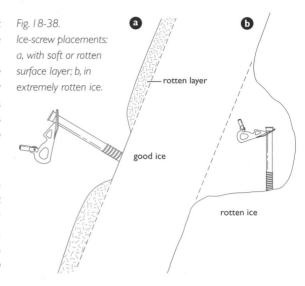

Fig. 18-38.
Ice-screw placements:
a, with soft or rotten
surface layer; b, in
extremely rotten ice.

rotten layer

good ice

rotten ice

step with an ice tool and place the screw vertically at the back of the step (fig. 18-38b). If the ice fractures and shatters at the surface, you may still get a secure placement by continuing to drive the screw and gently chopping out the shattered ice with sideways strokes of the pick.

Climbing extremely steep ice is fatiguing, both physically and mentally, so minimize the number of screw placements. If the ice is hard and solid or the slope not extremely steep, only one or two protection points may need to be placed on an entire pitch. Unless the ice is rotten, only one screw is placed at each protection point. Climbing by relying mainly on your tool and crampon placements and skills for safety (a concept known as "self-belayed" climbing) also determines the number of ice screws that you need to place.

With practice, you should be able to place an ice screw with one hand. On extremely steep ice, placing ice screws is exacting business. Try to place screws from natural resting spots on the route. Be sure to hang from your leashes; do not wear yourself out by gripping the shaft of the tool while you are placing screws. For extra support or when you need to use both hands, slip one arm through the wrist loop of a solidly planted ice tool (fig. 18-39).

On a moderate to steep slope, it may help to chop a step to stand in while you place the screw. On extremely steep ice, however, chopping steps is too difficult, so

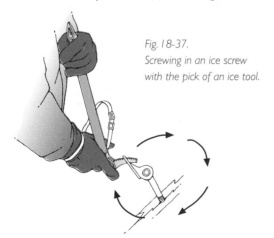

Fig. 18-37.
Screwing in an ice screw
with the pick of an ice tool.

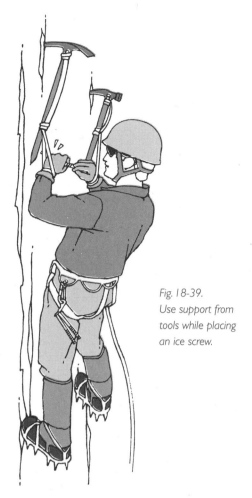

Fig. 18-39.
Use support from
tools while placing
an ice screw.

save your energy. When it is time to place an ice screw, do it efficiently and confidently from your front points, and then continue climbing.

After you remove a screw, ice inside its core must be cleaned out immediately or it may freeze in place, rendering the screw useless until it is cleared. Before climbs, squirt a lubricating and penetrating oil (such as WD-40) inside your screws. The interiors of some screws are slightly tapered, facilitating ice removal. Shake the screw to remove the ice core; if this does not work, then tap the screw against the rubber shaft of the ice tool or the side of your boot. Do not bang the screw against anything hard, such as the head of a tool or crampon rails. This will only pit the teeth and screw threads and make the screw harder to place, especially in cold conditions. If ice does freeze to the inside of the

screw, push it out with your pick or a length of stiff wire. Or try to melt the ice with your breath, with the warmth of your hand, or inside a jacket pocket.

Setting Up Ice Anchors

For belaying or rappelling, ice climbers have several options for anchors, including the V-thread, ice bollards, and multiple ice screws. This section discusses the V-thread and bollards, which are used mainly in rappelling. The next section, "Belaying on Ice," explains the standard anchor setup using two ice screws.

The V-Thread

The V-thread anchor (fig. 18-40) is popular because it is simple and easy to construct. Devised by Vitaly Abalakov, a premier Soviet alpinist in the 1930s, the V-thread anchor (also known as the ice hourglass or Abalakov sandwich) is nothing more than a V-shaped tunnel bored into the ice, with a cord or webbing threaded through the tunnel and tied to form a sling. The V-thread anchor has held up well in testing and in use, but remember that it is only as strong as the ice in which it is constructed. You can construct multiple V-thread placements and rig them together to create an equalized anchor point. Here are the steps to construct a V-thread anchor:

1. Screw a 22-centimeter ice screw into the slope. Angle the screw uphill 10 degrees against the anticipated direction of pull; also tilt it about 60 degrees to one side (fig. 18-40a).
2. Back this screw out about halfway, but keep it there as a guide. Insert a second screw into the slope 6 to 8 inches (about 20 centimeters) from the first, angling it to intersect the first hole at its bottom (fig. 18-40b). Remove both screws.
3. Thread a length of 7-millimeter perlon accessory cord or ½-inch tubular webbing into one side of the V-shaped tunnel. You need a V-thread tool to fish the end of the cord out through the other side of the tunnel (fig. 18-40c).
4. Holding both ends of the cord, saw it back and forth in the tunnel in order to smooth the sharp edge where the two screw holes intersect. Otherwise, the edge might cut the cord in a fall. Tie the cord or webbing so that it forms a sling (fig. 18-40d).

18

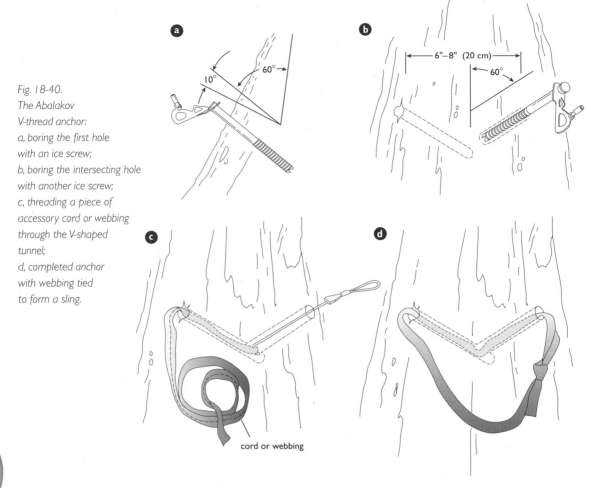

Fig. 18-40.
The Abalakov
V-thread anchor:
a, boring the first hole
with an ice screw;
b, boring the intersecting hole
with another ice screw;
c, threading a piece of
accessory cord or webbing
through the V-shaped
tunnel;
d, completed anchor
with webbing tied
to form a sling.

5. Place an ice screw 2 to 3 feet (0.6 to 1 meter) away. Clip this screw to the V-thread sling as a backup. The anchor is now complete.

For a rappel, the rope is threaded directly through the loop of webbing and then pulled free when the rappel is completed.

Many abandoned V-threads are found on popular ice climbs at rappel/belay stations. As with any other fixed anchor, check it carefully before committing your life to it. Inspect the sling material for burn or wear marks, or other damage, and check that the knot is secure. Sometimes the free tails of the knot may be frozen in place, resembling a secure portion of the sling. Be sure that the rope is rigged through the sling and not through these frozen tails. Do not make that fatal

error. Inspect the integrity of the V-shaped tunnel. See if it has melted out to an extent that it is too shallow for comfort and safety. If you have any doubt about the anchor, back it up or replace it.

Ice Bollards

A bollard can be among an ice climber's most useful anchors. Two bollards linked together, one cut for an upward pull and the other for a downward pull, form a multidirectional anchor. The strength of a bollard is proportional to its size and the quality of the ice. Made in hard, solid ice, a bollard can be stronger than the rope. The single largest disadvantage to a bollard is the long time it takes to construct one.

A completed ice bollard is teardrop-shaped when viewed from above (fig. 18-41a and c) and mushroom-

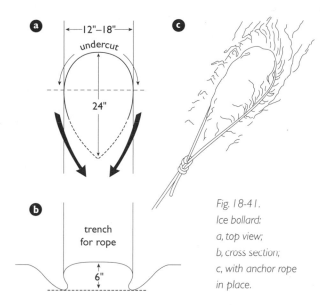

Fig. 18-41.
Ice bollard:
a, top view;
b, cross section;
c, with anchor rope
in place.

shaped when viewed from the side. All that is needed for a bollard is an ice ax and good ice, uniform and without cracks or holes. Cut the outline of the bollard with the ax pick. In hard ice, give it a diameter of 12 to 18 inches (30 to 45 centimeters) across the wide end of the teardrop (fig. 18-41a). Cut a trench around the bollard at least 6 inches (15 centimeters) deep (fig. 18-41b), working outward from the outline with both the pick and the adze. Undercut the sides and top half of the bollard to form a horn that prevents the rope from popping off over the top. This is the most sensitive part of the construction because the bollard is easily fractured or broken if you do not take care.

Belaying on Ice

Ice climbers have the options of using running belays or fixed belays, as in other types of roped climbing. They also have the use of boot/ice-screw belay techniques.

Running Belays

Ice climbers can get a measure of protection that is somewhere between climbing on belay and climbing unroped by setting up a running belay. It is another way for a team to move faster when storms or avalanches threaten—circumstances under which, more than ever, speed means safety. It can also be useful on gentle to moderate terrain where danger of falling is minimal and fixed belays would be too time-consuming.

A running belay on ice is created in very much the same way as a running belay on rock (see Chapter 14, Leading on Rock) or snow (see Chapter 16, Snow Travel and Climbing). The team members, usually just two climbers, move simultaneously. The leader places protection as they climb and clips the rope through it; the follower removes the protection. The idea is to keep at least two points of protection between them at all times to hold the rope in case of a fall. The protection is usually spaced so that as the leader makes each new placement, the follower is removing the bottom one.

Because the technique of running belays sacrifices much of the safety of true belaying, the decision to use it takes fine judgment, based on extensive experience.

Fixed Belays

Fixed belaying on ice requires a belayer, a belay anchor, and intermediate points of protection, just as it does on snow or rock. A belay anchor is set up and the leader climbs the pitch on belay, sets up another anchor, and then belays the follower up the route. The climbers can either swing leads, or one climber can continue as the leader.

The leader should, when near the end of a pitch, keep an eye out for a good belay spot, perhaps at a slight depression, where the ice is not so steep, or in an area where a platform can be chopped out quickly. Plant an ice tool off to one side and clip in for temporary protection while you chop a step large enough so you can stand facing the ice with both feet flat and splayed. On steep ice it may be possible to chop only a simple ledge the width of your foot.

Belay Anchor

A standard anchor setup for an ice belay (fig. 18-42) takes two ice screws. (Ice bollards and V-threads also can serve as belay anchors, but they are more time-consuming to set up and are used primarily for rappelling.) Place the first screw in the ice in front of you, a bit to one side, at about waist to chest level. Clip in a carabiner and tie yourself into it with the climbing rope. Use a clove hitch or figure-eight knot. Then tell your belayer that you are off belay.

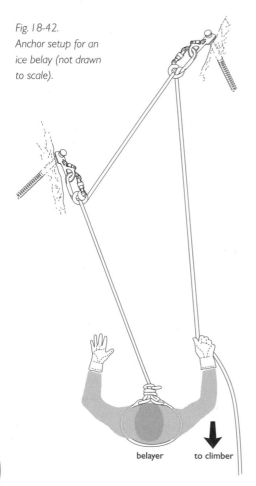

Fig. 18-42.
Anchor setup for an
ice belay (not drawn
to scale).

belayer   to climber

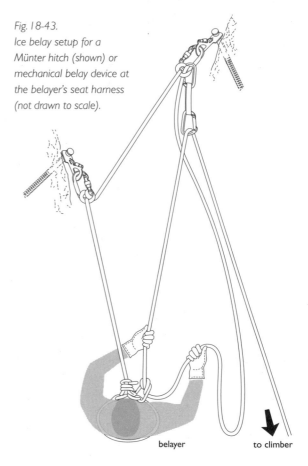

Fig. 18-43.
Ice belay setup for a
Münter hitch (shown) or
mechanical belay device at
the belayer's seat harness
(not drawn to scale).

belayer   to climber

Now place the second ice screw, above you and about 2 or 3 feet (0.6 to 1 meter) higher than the first one and off to one side. Ideally, place this screw on the side to which the route will continue. Extend the climbing rope from the first screw to the second screw and tie in with a clove hitch. There should be little or no slack between the two screws. Alternatively, use a runner. Clip the runner to both screws, then set up an equalized system. (See "Equalizing Multiple Anchors" in Chapter 10, Belaying.)

Clip a quickdraw or load-limiting runner to the carabiner on the second screw (or to the screw hanger eye, if it is large enough to accept two carabiners); clip the rope trailing down to the follower through the carabiner clipped to the quickdraw or load-limiting runner. This completes the anchor setup.

Belay Methods

Choose between using a mechanical belay device, a Münter hitch, or a hip belay. The anchor setup is the same in any case. The choice will probably depend on what you are accustomed to and on the degree of your confidence in the anchor. The hip belay tends to be somewhat dynamic, with a bit of movement at the belay—resulting in a slower stop to a fall but less force on the anchor and intermediate protection points. Belay devices and the Münter hitch, on the other hand, tend to be less dynamic, stopping a fall faster but putting more force on the anchor and intermediate protection points. (See "Choosing a Method" in Chapter 10, Belaying.)

Mechanical devices: A belay device or a Münter hitch is easy to set up and efficient to use (fig. 18-43). Many ice climbers use such a method as standard procedure.

18

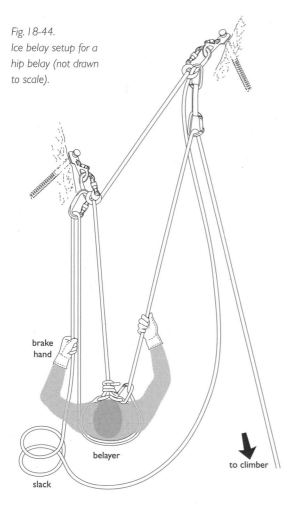

Fig. 18-44.
Ice belay setup for a
hip belay (not drawn
to scale).

brake
hand

belayer

slack

to climber

If you face outward to belay the follower, the belay rope runs directly to the device at your harness, and you tie in to the anchor much as you would in a fixed belay in rock climbing.

Hip belay: Establish a hip belay as you stand facing the ice by running the belay rope through a control carabiner at your waist, around your back, through an extra carabiner on the first screw, and then into your braking hand (fig. 18-44). You can also face outward to belay a follower with a hip belay. The hip belay is especially favored when the rope is stiff and frozen and could jam in belay devices.

Boot/ice-screw belay: This can be useful on gentle ice slopes. Place an ice screw, and then clip in a carabiner and run the belay rope through the carabiner (fig. 18-45a). Plant your uphill boot over the screw, perpendicular to the direction of pull. Place your boot so that the inside point of the midboot row of crampons goes through the carabiner (fig. 18-45b). Do not jab the rope with your crampons. Bring the belay end of the rope over your instep, around the back of your boot ankle, and into your uphill hand.

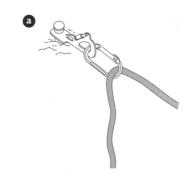

Fig. 18-45.
Boot/ice-screw belay:
a, place an ice screw;
b, plant a boot over
the screw.

18

The device is usually clipped to the seat harness, though you can also belay directly from the anchor. To belay a leader, the belayer usually faces into the ice; for belaying a follower, either face into the ice or face out.

If you face the ice to belay the follower (as shown in Figure 18-43), the belay rope runs up through the top screw in the anchor setup, directing the pull from the second climber through this screw. After the follower ascends to the belay station and starts upward to take the lead, that screw becomes the first piece of protection on the new pitch. Remember that when the rope is clipped in to the belay anchor in this fashion, forces at the anchor can be multiplied. A fall from your follower will generate two times the force at the anchor because of the pulley effect.

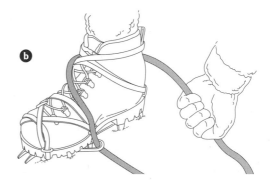

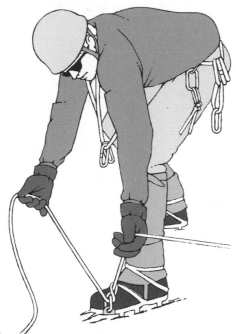

Fig. 18-46.
Boot/ice-screw belay using a Münter hitch.

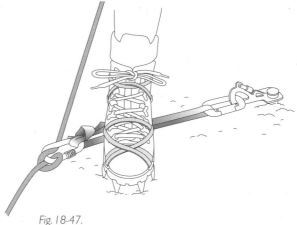

Fig. 18-47.
Boot/ice-screw belay using a Münter hitch while standing.

Control friction on the rope by the amount of wrap on your ankle, much as in a boot-ax belay (see Chapter 16, Snow Travel and Climbing). You can also adjust the space between the edge of your boot and the outside edge of the carabiner. If the climber you are belaying falls, slowly tighten the rope low against your ankle with your uphill hand.

Helpful variations of the boot/ice-screw belay include two that use the Münter hitch. Use a large pear-shaped carabiner, which has the correct radius for the Münter hitch, instead of a standard carabiner. In one method, simply use a Münter hitch at the carabiner instead of running the belay rope around your ankle (fig. 18-46). Another method permits you to operate the belay while you are standing. Use a Münter hitch at a carabiner clipped to a runner that is clipped to the carabiner at the ice screw; stand on the runner (fig. 18-47).

Rappelling

For descending steep ice, rappelling is usually the method of choice. The principal considerations for rappelling on ice are the same as for rappelling on rock (see Chapter 11, Rappelling), but there is a big difference in anchor options. On rock, you can often use a natural anchor, such as a rock horn or a tree. On ice, you frequently have to make your own anchors. The two most popular rappel anchors for ice are the V-thread and the bollard (see "Setting Up Ice Anchors," above). Ice screws are commonly used to back up an ice anchor until the last member of the party descends. The last person removes the screws and rappels on the anchor with no backup.

PRACTICE FOR THE FREEDOM OF THE HILLS

Skill and confidence in ice climbing come with long practice. The ability to assess or read the ice comes with years of experience. Link up with a steady ice-climbing partner if possible. Practice together often. Work on pinpoint ice-tool and crampon placement, which conserves energy so you can meet the rigors of serious routes. Also work to increase the speed and efficiency of your climbing, gearing it to the conditions of the ice and your body's current strength. It is up to each climber to decide when to rope up for protection—and when it is safer not to. An experienced ice climber learns these skills, continues to hone them, and applies them with confidence and good judgment.

19

Waterfall Ice and Mixed Climbing

EQUIPMENT ■ WATERFALL ICE CLIMBING ■
MIXED CLIMBING ■ CLIMBING IN THE WINTER ENVIRONMENT

As the temperature falls below freezing, liquid water freezes to a solid. Even raging torrents can become spectacular, massive, hanging waterfall ice formations. Water ice is formed by gradual buildup. The usual formation is not a single, monolithic, crystalline structure. Typically, ice formations are the result of a series of freezes, and they have a laminated or layered structure. Water ice formations can display a broad spectrum of forms: smooth, broad slabs; flat runnels; cauliflower-textured walls; latticed sheets; chandeliered curtains; massive ice pillars; fantastic, free-hanging icicles.

Compared to the life cycle of glacial ice, the life spans of winter waterfall ice formations are all too brief. During a single winter season's freeze/thaw cycles, a waterfall ice formation can form, collapse, then re-form, only to collapse again when the spring thaw arrives. When you visit the sites of winter ice climbs in warmer seasons, you may not be able to picture what is there in winter. Summer tourists traveling along the Icefields Parkway in Jasper National Park in Alberta, Canada, can easily miss the wet spot that marks the location that attracts waterfall ice climbers from around the world in winter: the Weeping Wall's spectacular ice curtain, a vertical football field of ice.

The technical difficulty of waterfall ice climbing continues to rise. The sport has transcended the traditional style—simple ascension of ice formations—and now includes dry tooling (climbing on technical rock with ice tools and crampons to link separate formations of ice). Climbing on mixed terrain (rock, thin ice, and ice) is not a new concept and has long been part of ascending Scottish gullies in winter. In the classic sense, mixed climbing meant having one foot on rock and the other on ice—usually thin ice. However, the focus of the sport has shifted. On a modern mixed route, you may spend as much or more time on rock as on ice. Often the crux of a route consists of making an athletic transition from rock to an overhanging curtain or spear of ice.

Waterfall ice and mixed-route climbers must exercise caution on terrain that changes abruptly from ice to rock and back, but they must also act with concern for the environment. The hard steel of ice tools and crampons does scratch and can break the rock surface. When you are dry tooling, exercise care to minimize damage. When you are establishing mixed routes, give major consideration to the local ethics. Avoid climbing in culturally sensitive areas (for example, cliffs with pictographs) and popular rock-climbing areas.

EQUIPMENT

This section includes a few considerations specific to waterfall ice and mixed climbing. For discussions of snow- and alpine ice–climbing equipment, see Chapter 16, Snow Travel and Climbing, and Chapter 18, Alpine Ice Climbing.

Crampons: For waterfall ice, the front points are curved or angled downward, and the secondary points are angled more forward. On extremely steep to overhanging waterfall ice or mixed terrain, the crampons of choice are rigid or semi-rigid with vertically oriented dual (fig. 19-1a) or mono (fig. 19-1b) front points. Monopoints are better for dry tooling. (See Table 18-2 in Chapter 18, Alpine Ice Climbing, for the advantages of various front-point angles.)

Ice tools: The reverse-curved pick (see Figure 18-4b in Chapter 18, Alpine Ice Climbing) is overwhelmingly the most-popular choice for water ice. Ice tools are increasingly used for dry tooling.

Ice hooks: The ice hook, a type of pound-in protection, is designed for thin ice and mixed climbing (see Figure 18-7c and d in Chapter 18, Alpine Ice Climbing). The ice hook may be used to hook features in either ice or rock.

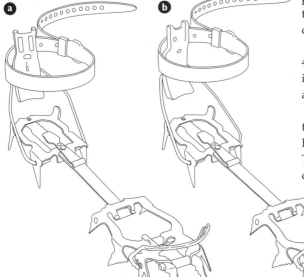

Fig. 19-1. Semi-rigid crampons with interchangeable front points: a, dual; b, mono.

WATERFALL ICE CLIMBING
Crampon Techniques

Footwork is *the* foundation of climbing techniques for steep waterfall ice. Good footwork allows you to keep most of your weight on your feet and the strong musculature of your legs, rather than on your arms, saving precious arm strength. Good footwork gives you smooth weight changes and greater efficiency. Poor footwork causes you to flail, burn out rapidly, and fall.

Front-pointing is the mainstay of footwork on vertical ice (see Chapter 18, Alpine Ice Climbing, for details on front-pointing). A good ice climber not only looks up for good tool placement opportunities, but also continually looks down for front-point placements that ease the strain on the calves. As is true for tool placements, slight depressions make for ideal front-point placements. Similarly, a spot just above a small bulge can also be a nice placement.

After you find a likely spot, use a firm kick to set the front points in place. Except in rotten, chandelier, or extremely brittle ice (see "Unusual Conditions" later in this chapter), no more than one or two kicks should be necessary. Make sure that your feet are perpendicular to the ice surface in both planes: Keep your heels low so that the secondary points engage the surface, making for a much more stable placement, and make sure the toe of your boot is squarely facing the surface at that particular spot. A pigeon-toed stance (or its opposite, a duck-footed stance) may be necessary for you to plant the front points squarely (fig. 19-2). Monopoints can be slotted in old pick placements. Once your feet are placed, try to keep them steady until you are ready to move again. Nervous feet actually weaken the placement.

Keep your feet shoulder-width apart, or slightly less, to reduce the tendency to "barn-door" to one side. Use several short steps, rather than high-stepping, to reduce the stress on your quadriceps—although high-stepping can be necessary occasionally to get past bulges.

Beyond straight-in front-pointing, footwork that is much more akin to rock-climbing techniques is very useful for the variety of features found on many waterfall ice climbs. Stemming and flagging (counterbalance)—see Chapter 12, Alpine Rock-Climbing Technique—are also very useful on waterfall ice.

Fig. 19-2.
A pigeon-toed stance may be necessary to plant front points squarely.

Ice-Tool Techniques

Just as the mainstay of footwork on waterfall ice is front-pointing, the most frequent tool placement, by far, is piolet traction (see Chapter 18, Alpine Ice Climbing). Because it becomes very tiring to swing tools above your head, do everything possible to reduce the number of swings and placements you make.

When you are ice climbing using piolet traction placements, think of it as climbing on self-belay. Before you trust the integrity of each placement, test it by loading it with partial body weight. Do this test from the relative safety of a stable stance on the ice. This is a key concept: Your goal is to create a position of strength and then to climb from that position. If each position is stable, you will climb with comfort and confidence. Do not fall into the trap of relying on a shaky placement, because this robs you of confidence and can lead to increasingly weak and unstable stances.

19

Selecting a placement and accuracy in making the placement are the keys to placing ice tools securely and quickly; strive to gain a secure placement with just one swing. One technique for hitting a precise spot is to tap the desired spot with the pick, then swing at that spot with force. The swing is more akin to a racquetball swing, with its wrist-snap just prior to connecting with the ball, than to a straight-wristed tennis swing. The steeper the droop of the pick, the more wrist action is needed to set the pick at the proper angle. (See "Ice-Tool Placements" in Chapter 18, Alpine Ice Climbing.)

Many beginning waterfall-ice climbers tend to drive their tools in too hard; take care to avoid this because it makes it much more difficult to remove the tool. (See "Removing the Tool" in Chapter 18, Alpine Ice Climbing.)

While you are climbing, look for secure placements that do not require you to swing the ice tool. Some old tool or monopoint placements may be deep enough that you can simply slot the pick in. Hooking opportunities abound on waterfall ice (fig. 19-3). Large icicles often form in clusters on vertical sections, creating slots or gaps that are ideal for secure hooking placements; tools can be slotted into gaps between icicles. Larger columns can be hooked horizontally. Reverse-curved picks are best for hooking placements, a common technique in

waterfall ice climbing. Many ice-tool picks have teeth where the pick attaches to the shaft; this provides more secure hooking.

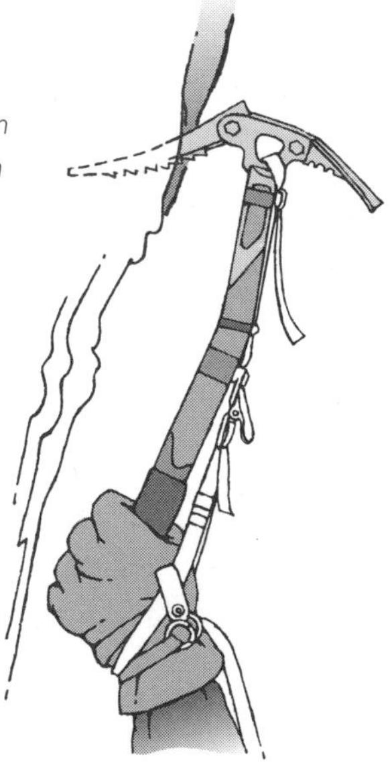

In good ice, try to vertically stagger your tool placements. By staggering the tools (rather than planting them side by side) and by relying on a single tool at a time, you reduce the number of tool placements, thus decreasing the workload on the swinging and gripping muscles of your arm and hand. If the ice, and thus the placements, are suspect, plant both tools side by side, about 2 feet (0.6 meter) apart, before moving your feet up. This decreases the load on each placement and reduces the chance that a tool will shear out under the load.

Vertical Progression

Just as in climbing on rock, climbing on waterfall ice involves a coordinated combination of climbing techniques used by a leader and a belayer, who are connected by the rope, anchors, and protection points.

The Monkey Hang

The basic technique for ascending vertical and overhanging ice is the monkey hang. Rather than a single movement, the monkey hang is a series of movements for upward progress on steep ice that allows maximum rest for the gripping muscles of your hand and forearm (fig. 19-4). Follow these steps to perform the monkey hang:

1. While you are standing on front points and with one ice tool in piolet traction, place the other ice tool at full arm's length; immediately sag down, weighting that tool's leash and loosening your grip on the tool (fig. 19-4a).
2. With the tool still weighted (your arm fully extended), move your feet up until you are in a crouching position on your front points (Fig. 19-4b).
3. Loosen, but do not yet remove, the lower of the two tools, and look above for the next placement for it.
4. In one motion, stand upright by pushing with your feet and pulling on the tools, remove the lower tool, and place it in the chosen spot, again preferably at full arm's length (fig. 19-4c).
5. Sag down, weight that tool's leash, and loosen your grip on the tool just placed (fig. 19-4d).
6. Repeat steps 2 through 5.

Fig. 19-3. Hooking a gap in waterfall ice with an ice tool.

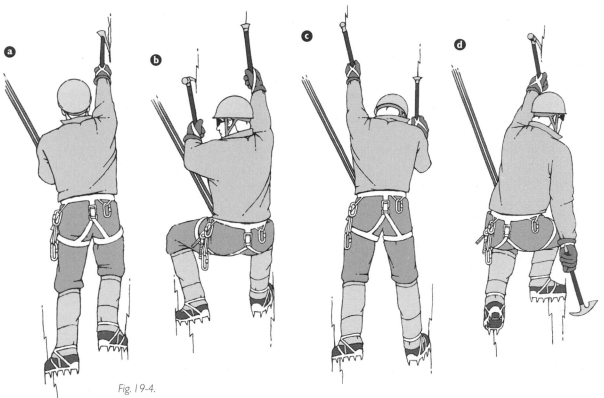

Fig. 19-4.

The monkey hang: a, place one tool at arm's length and weight its leash; b, move feet up to a crouching position; c, stand up and place the other tool at arm's length; d, weight the leash and move feet up to a crouch.

Belaying

Setting up belay anchors and belaying on waterfall ice use the same procedures as those discussed in "Belaying on Ice" in Chapter 18, Alpine Ice Climbing. Take extra care in locating belays away from the fall line to avoid being showered with debris from the leader. In gullies, site the belay to one side of the route, seeking protection from the side wall. On pillars or curtains, try placing the belay behind or to the side of the formation, but be aware that although this position provides greater protection from falling ice, it will make communication more difficult and rope drag a possibility. Look for a compromise between protection and convenience in belay stances.

Leading

Most waterfall ice climbs are led and followed in pitches, though many long climbs offer sections suitable for running belays. Ice pitches may be climbed with either a single rope or with two ropes, using either twin-rope or double-rope technique. (See Chapter 14, Leading on Rock.)

Protection

Rock Gear

On some waterfall ice climbs, there are options for using rock gear. On gully climbs, the rock side walls can provide protection opportunities. On freestanding columns or curtains, look behind the ice for placements in the back wall; these most likely will need to be extended by slings to prevent rope drag. In the winter, cracks tend to be filled by ice; as a result, pitons are used more frequently than on summer climbs, though the full variety of clean protection can be used as well.

Natural Protection

Waterfall ice offers more opportunities for natural protection than do the flows and steps of alpine ice, and

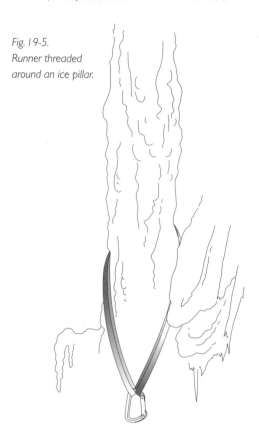

*Fig. 19-5.
Runner threaded
around an ice pillar.*

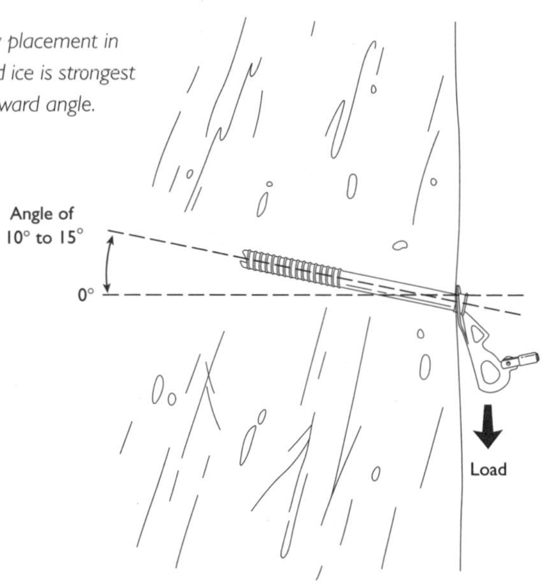

*Fig. 19-6.
Ice-screw placement in
cold, solid ice is strongest
at an upward angle.*

Angle of
10° to 15°

0°

Load

many natural placements are quicker to set up than ice screws. Runners can be placed around small ice columns (fig. 19-5). A long ice screw tied off with webbing can be inserted between two columns or through a slot in an ice curtain, then rotated sideways and used as a deadman. In thin curtains, two holes can be punched in the curtain and then threaded with webbing or perlon as for a V-thread anchor (see Chapter 18, Alpine Ice Climbing). With all these placements, it is wise to use a load-limiting runner.

Ice Screws and Pitons

Ice screws remain the most common type of protection used on waterfall ice. Although the methods for placing ice screws are the same as those discussed in Chapter 18, Alpine Ice Climbing, some considerations are specific to waterfall ice.

Over the last several years, significant testing has been done to determine the strength of ice-screw placements in solid water ice at cold temperatures. (This

testing involved ice screws with high-relief threads.) Surprisingly, under those conditions the strongest screw placements are those with the long axis of the screw placed at a 10- to 15-degree upward angle, pointing toward the direction of anticipated force (fig. 19-6). This configuration can reduce fracturing of the ice when loaded by a leader fall.

It is best to use a screw of a length that can be sunk to the hilt. If the ice is too shallow for a screw to be placed all the way in to its hanger, remove that screw and use a shorter one. Carry a variety of screw lengths to decrease your chances of needing to tie off a screw. Tie off a screw only as a last resort. When screws fail under loading, they do so by fracturing the ice below them and bending toward the direction of force. In the case of a tied-off screw, the webbing then slides to the hanger and is cut by its sharp edges.

If the screw protrudes no more than 2 inches (5 centimeters) from the surface of the ice, clip the hanger as you normally would (fig. 19-7a). If the screw protrudes more than 2 inches from the surface, the placement is highly suspect. Either clip the hanger or tie off the screw with a runner or a load-limiting runner (fig. 19-7b). In this situation, back up and equalize such a placement, climb confidently, and make better placements as soon as possible.

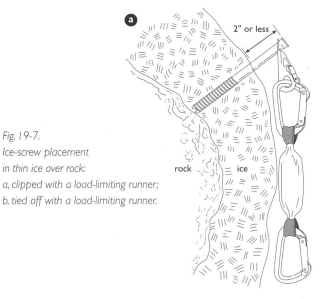
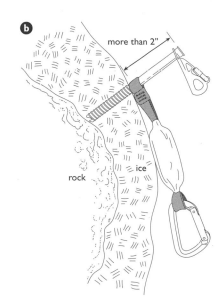

Fig. 19-7.
Ice-screw placement
in thin ice over rock:
a, clipped with a load-limiting runner;
b, tied off with a load-limiting runner.

Another type of protection is the current crop of ice pitons, also called ice hooks (see Figure 18-7c and d in Chapter 18, Alpine Ice Climbing). An ice hook can be slotted into holes in ice curtains or between the laced-together icicles in chandelier ice, and then set with a light tap. Ice hooks can also be driven into iced-up cracks.

Protecting the Leader

There are many more options for protecting the leader on waterfall ice than on alpine ice. On alpine ice, you are limited to ice screws, with occasional rock protection to the side or in rock "islands." On waterfall ice, frequently you can place rock gear to the side of or even behind an ice column, or creatively use natural protection in the ice itself, in addition to placing ice screws and ice hooks.

Racking

Although some ice climbers use gear slings to carry ice screws and other gear, many more are using harness-mounted gear racking devices. (See Chapter 18, Alpine Ice Climbing.) It can be uncomfortable and inconvenient to carry long, sharp screws on a gear sling. Here is one suggested arrangement for racking gear on the harness:

■ Rack the gear needed on lead on the same side as your dominant hand. Place ice screws in front,

arranged front to back by length, short to long, with teeth pointed to the rear. Next, rack quickdraws and load-limiting runners.

■ Use the rear gear loop of your dominant side as well as your weak-side gear loops to rack gear that you will not need immediately. This includes longer screws for belay anchors, a belay device, free carabiners, a pulley, a V-thread tool, and cordelette.

Placing Gear on the Lead

Placing ice screws while you are leading on steep ice can be very physically demanding. To conserve energy, minimize the number of screw placements; typically, on a waterfall ice pitch you make far fewer protection placements than would be placed on a rock pitch of similar length. Similarly, climbers develop techniques for placing screws that minimize the effort expended.

For example, avoid the temptation to place a screw high (above shoulder height) to gain that momentary top-rope protection (having the rope above you). In this position it is very difficult to put enough pressure on the screw so that its threads will bite into the ice. The most efficient placement is right at hip level. You have better leverage and can use your whole body weight to push the screw into the ice. Also, your arm remains below the level of your heart, and so blood flow remains constant.

431

Fig. 19-8.
Placing gear
on lead.

Fig. 19-9.
Combination footwork: front-
pointing and heel-hooking.

Here is one technique for placing screws on lead (fig. 19-8):

1. Get a good stance for both feet and (if you are right-handed) plant the left tool high (at arm's length); weight the tool leash, hang straight-armed, and loosen the grip of your left hand.
2. At hip level, use the right tool to chip away any rotten or soft ice at the desired placement and make a starter hole for the screw. Get out of that tool leash and secure the tool—holster it, clip it to your harness, or place it solidly in the ice.
3. Place the screw with your right hand; attach a carabiner, quickdraw, or load-limiting runner to the screw hanger; clip in the rope.

4. Get back into the right tool leash; place the tool high and weight it; remove the left tool and shake your arm out as needed.
5. Continue climbing.

Unusual Conditions

Unlike the more homogeneous ice of most alpine ice climbs, waterfall ice comes in an amazing and beautiful (and, many times, terrifying) array of formations, shapes, textures, features, and quality. These characteristics can make for difficult climbing with little opportunity for protection.

Pillars: These are formed when meltwater drips off a free-hanging icicle until the resulting ice stalactite and stalagmite join. Climbable pillars can range in size from less than a body's width to many feet across. Although big pillars are climbed using the monkey hang, small pillars require much more varied technique. The tools must be vertically staggered so as not to weaken the pillar by having the two tools too close together. If placing screws in the pillar might weaken it, place protection in the adjacent rock. Both the tools and the front points might need to be placed in a pigeon-toed angle to keep the points and picks going straight into the ice, perpendicular to the ice in both planes. On really narrow pillars, you may need to use a combination of front-pointing with one foot and heel-hooking with the other (fig. 19-9).

Free-hanging ice: This is formed when a pillar or curtain has not touched down onto ice or the ground or has broken off. Most of the climbing techniques are the same as for pillars. Use delicate tool and crampon placements. Place protection in the adjacent rock walls. Place screws in the ice only above its point of attachment to the rock. If screws are placed low in the formation and the formation fails, the climber, connected to the falling block, will be dragged down.

Chandelier ice: This is formed by thousands of small icicles melting and becoming laced together into a dense latticework. Chandelier ice is fairly common, beautiful to see, hard to climb, and difficult to protect. Belays must be located to avoid the constant rain of debris from the leader. Most of the time, there is little delicacy to climbing a chandelier. Kick your feet deep into the ice structure in hopes of finding secure purchase. Place the tools similarly, although you can be very creative with the tools. You might hook the slots between two larger icicles; stab the entire head of the tool directly into the ice and then rotate the tool 90 degrees so the hammer/adze and pick straddle the newly created slot; or thrust the entire tool (and your arm) through the lattice and grasp the tool midshaft, using it as a deadman. You may not be able to place a solid screw, but natural protection may exist.

Cauliflower ice: In *How to Ice Climb!*, Craig Luebben describes this as "looking like the out-turned scales of a pine cone," which forms at the "drip zone" of ice climbs. Ice domes at the bottom of pillars often sport cauliflower ice; it also forms above large ledges. The cauliflowers range in size from small—several inches—to very large—several feet wide and deep. Cauliflower ice offers many opportunities for hooking tools and often sports large footholds that can be flat-footed (see Chapter 18, Alpine Ice Climbing). Resist the temptation to place your entire foot into and onto a cauliflower. You can get your foot in so far that you are out of balance. Better to front-point it, or just set the front half of your boot on top of it. Protection can include screws in larger bulges as well as natural protection.

Brittle ice: The result of very cold temperatures, brittle ice usually appears only on the surface layers of ice formations. You have to work through the hard, brittle layers to get to the more plastic ice below, and in the process a cascade of falling ice results, ranging in size from small chips to very large dinner plates. Be sure to place the tools far enough apart that the fracturing caused by one tool does not reach the other, causing both placements to fail. Also, beware of falling dinner plates, which can dislodge front points. Place ice screws in better ice found beneath the brittle layers.

Rotten ice: Often the result of being baked by the sun or weakened by percolating water, rotten ice can run much deeper than brittle ice, even through an entire formation. Rotten ice is difficult to climb and harder to protect; a lengthy section of rotten ice may be all but unclimbable.

Thin ice: This ranges from just a glaze of ice over the rock to ice a few inches thick. Thin ice can be very exciting and fun to climb. The thinnest ice is *verglas*, thick enough to obscure the underlying rock but not thick enough to gain purchase with picks or points. Thicker ice is easier to climb, as long as temperatures are cold enough for cohesion to be maintained between the ice and the underlying rock. Make both tool and crampon placements with the gentlest of taps, swinging tools just from the wrist; sometimes you can scratch placements into place by chipping and hooking. Protection is usually found in the rock surrounding the ice. Extremely short screws may offer only psychological protection at best.

Descending

Some waterfall ice climbs, especially gully routes, allow walk-off descents to one side or the other. Most, however, are descended by a combination of down-climbing

19

and rappelling. The techniques of down-climbing ice are discussed fully in Chapter 18, Alpine Ice Climbing.

Rappelling

The principal techniques for rappelling on ice are the same as for rappelling on rock. Many rappels on popular waterfall ice climbs are done from fixed anchors, usually a combination of bolts/chains, slings on trees, or abandoned V-thread anchors. As with any fixed anchor, inspect these thoroughly before trusting them. Make sure the bolts are secure. Check the slings or perlon on the tree or the V-thread anchor for damage, wear, or burn marks, and check all knots. When in doubt, replace the material. Check found V-threads to ensure that they are still solid. If any found anchor is suspect in any way, or if there are none, place your own. The technique for building a V-thread is fully discussed in Chapter 18, Alpine Ice Climbing. Any V-thread should be backed up with a screw until the last climber removes the backup screw, then rappels.

MIXED CLIMBING

Mixed climbing combines climbing on rock, snow, and ice—and sometimes on frozen mud and moss as well. Usually you are wearing crampons. Perhaps mixed climbing is climbing a rock route in the winter, with ice-filled cracks and snow-covered ledges. Or maybe it is making an alpine ascent that requires climbing an icy face broken by a rock band. Recently, mixed climbing has come to mean climbing sections of rock between discontinuous sections of ice. In its purest form, mixed climbing has you with one crampon on rock and the other on ice, one hand inserted into a crack and one ice tool placed in a frozen smear.

Equipment and Techniques

The equipment used for mixed climbing most likely is whatever you were using right before the ice ran out. On a glacier climb, this means mountaineering crampons and a mountaineering ice ax. On a harder alpine ice climb, it most likely means a mountaineering ice ax used in combination with a shorter ice tool,

likely a hammer, and rigid crampons. On a frozen waterfall with a mixed section, it is likely to be technical ice climbing tools and rigid crampons.

Crampons

When you are climbing a mixed route, you are most likely wearing crampons. Although considerable rock may be showing, it may be impractical to remove your crampons only to put them back on when you return to the ice. Whichever crampons you choose, be sure that they are absolutely compatible with your boots. Their fit must be tight to withstand the tremendous stress of your dancing on rock while wearing crampons.

Vertically oriented front points: Many mixed climbers prefer technical, rigid crampons with vertically oriented front points (see Figure 19-1, above). Monopoint crampons (see Figure 19-1b, above) are particularly handy for precision accuracy on dime edges, vertical seams, and pick holes. Vertically oriented monopoints are also advantageous because the point mimics the pick of an ice tool. A monopoint can be delicately placed in the pick hole you made just a few moves previously.

Horizontally oriented front points: Some mixed climbers prefer crampons with horizontally oriented front points (see Figure 16-5 in Chapter 16, Snow Travel and Climbing). Such crampons have greater stability because their horizontal alignment matches the features found in the sedimentary strata of many mountain ranges. They also are less prone to shearing because of their greater surface area.

Crampon Technique

Ultimately, crampon choice is secondary to proper technique. A good mixed climber selects a foothold and delicately places a crampon point or points in the spot. Smooth weight transfer is critical as you gradually test the foothold until it is completely weighted. Once your foot is weighted, it is important to keep it still, to prevent the points from rotating out of a crack or off a ledge. Careful footwork is the key to mixed climbing. With proper technique, you will not scratch the rock and your crampon points will remain sharp for any difficult ice climbing that may lie ahead.

Hands on Rock

Although it may be impractical to remove your crampons for a rock section, it often makes sense to secure your ice tools and grasp the rock directly with your hands. Likewise, it may be next to impossible to find a pick placement on a downsloping rock ledge or fist-sized crack, but that same ledge or crack may easily yield a workable handhold.

Securing an ice tool may be as simple as releasing your grip on the shaft, as long as the leash is designed to remain snug around your wrist. This technique is particularly handy if you will need the tool again after a few moves. Then it is readily available with a flick of the wrist.

For extensive climbing using your hands on rock, it may be more practical to holster the tool. Ice tool holsters can be mounted on your harness or pack hip belt. Or slide the shaft of the ice tool into a spare carabiner. But beware: An ice tool with high-friction material on the shaft to facilitate grip may not easily slide into a holster or carabiner, and the leash may get in the way. Be absolutely sure that there is no possibility of the ice tool coming out accidentally. Dropping a tool on a one-pitch sport-style mixed route may be merely annoying and embarrassing, but dropping a tool on a committing alpine route may have devastating consequences.

The surest method of securing an ice tool is to clip the ax-head hole into a spare carabiner. To remove the tool, grasp the head of the tool and open the carabiner gate with your thumb.

Once your hand(s) are free from the tools and leashes, use them as on any rock climb. Fist jams, cling and crimp holds, liebacks, and downpressure can all be used to give your body the proper balance and positioning to support delicate footwork.

Keep in mind that while you are climbing with your hands on rock, you most likely will be wearing gloves. Technical mixed climbing, like technical rock climbing, requires dexterity. Handholds, carabiners, protection, and tool leashes must all be manipulated efficiently. It is therefore impractical to climb mixed terrain with a bulky glove system. Most mixed climbers wear one pair of midweight fleece gloves while climbing, keep a second pair warming in a clothing pocket, and have a third pair in the top lid of their pack.

Ice Tools on Rock

When the holds become too small for your hands and the cracks are filled with too much ice, it is time to use ice tools. When you are using an ice ax or ice tools on rock, use every part of the tool and engage the different parts well. Be aggressive while being creative.

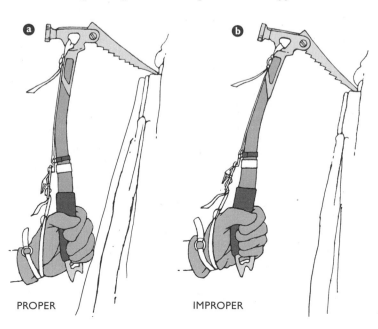

Fig. 19-10. Standard hooking technique: a, with proper downward force; b, improper technique with outward force.

PROPER

IMPROPER

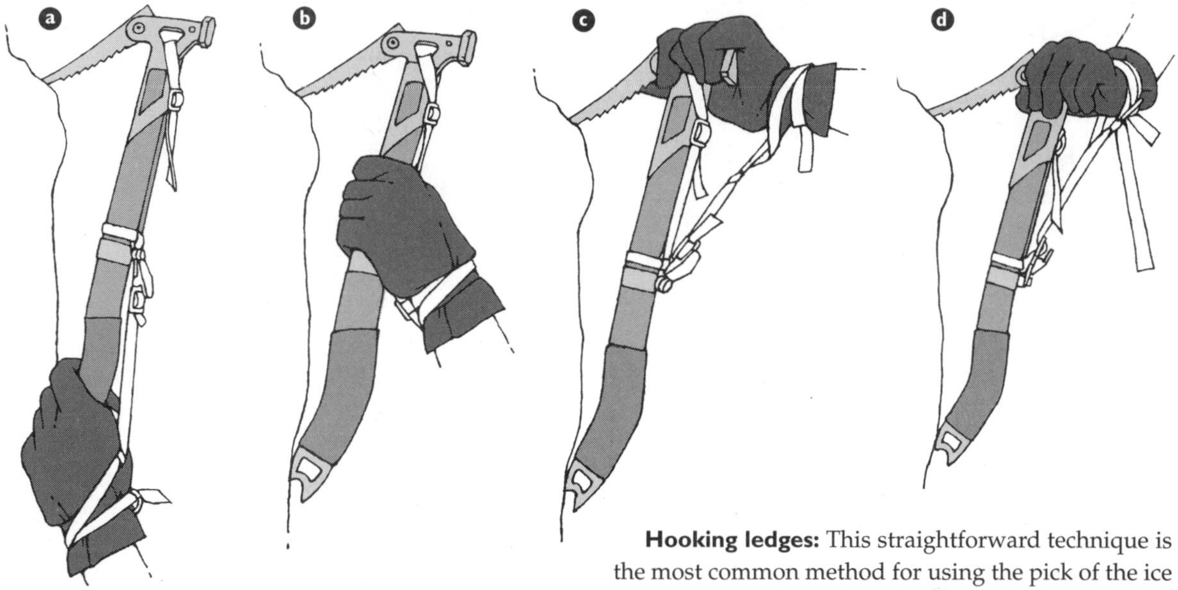

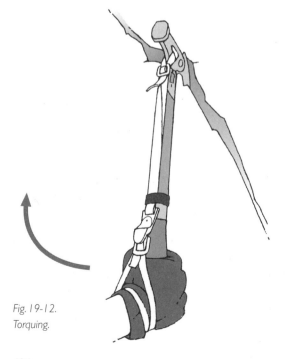

Fig. 19-11.

Turning a hook into a mantel: a, hook the ledge; b, work your hand up the shaft; c, climb up, grasping the head of the tool; d, work your feet higher and mantel.

Fig. 19-12.
Torquing.

Hooking ledges: This straightforward technique is the most common method for using the pick of the ice tool to climb rock. However, it is critical that, while you are pulling through the move, you hold the shaft of the tool steady against the rock (fig. 19-10a). If you pull outward on the shaft, the pick will skate off the hold (fig. 19-10b). You can also use the hammer or adze of the ice tool to hook rock holds, although you must exercise caution because the pick will be pointing toward you.

While you are moving up, it is sometimes advantageous to turn a hook placement into a mantel by grasping the head of the tool (fig. 19-11). This technique is especially handy if the next tool placement is far above you.

Torquing: Slide the pick into a crack that is a little too wide to be secure, and twist the shaft of the tool until the pick wedges itself securely (fig. 19-12). As long as you maintain adequate pressure, the placement will be secure. Or torque by using the hammer, adze, or even the shaft of the tool.

The "stein puller": A very stable technique, the stein puller is most often performed by inserting the pick upside-down into a downward-facing seam or flake (fig. 19-13). Then, just as a bartender would pull down on a bar tap, pull down on the shaft of the tool, engaging the pick into the hold and forcing the head of the tool against the rock, creating opposing force. The harder you pull down, the stronger the tool placement becomes.

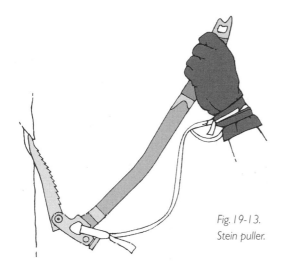

Fig. 19-13.
Stein puller.

A great advantage of the stein puller is that a hold above your head can be hooked (fig. 14a); then you can climb up (fig. 14b), turning the stein puller into a mantel without removing the tool from the rock (fig. 19-14c and d).

Matching: This is another technique that is particularly useful while you are dry tooling. Just as on a rock climb when you place both hands on one hold, one hand on top of the other, one hold is used for both ice tools. One of the great things about the pick of the ice tool is that it is so narrow. Both tool picks can easily fit side by side on the same hold, as long as the hold is wider than about ¼ inch (6 to 7 millimeters). When you

are matching, be sure that the hold is strong enough to withstand the tremendous force that can be generated by the two ice tools.

Stacking: This technique is also used frequently in dry tooling. If there is one very good tool placement surrounded by bad ones, try hooking the pick of the good tool placement with the other tool (fig. 19-15). When you are stacking, once again make sure that the hold is strong enough to withstand the tremendous force that can be generated by the two ice tools.

Body Positioning

In order to climb mixed terrain well, you must combine precision crampon and tool placements with calculated body positioning. Rarely do you simply pull down on hooked placements and walk your feet up the wall.

For instance, picture a ledge that slopes down to the right. In order to hook this ledge and keep the tool placement stable through a series of foot placements, pull down and to the left (fig. 19-16). Conversely, a right-leaning lieback is futile unless your crampons are in a position to allow you to push sideways to the right (fig. 19-17).

With lots of practice on mixed terrain, you will gain confidence in your crampon and tool technique. Climb as many mixed routes on top-rope as possible, no

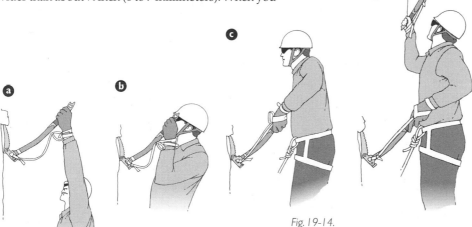

Fig. 19-14.
Stein puller to mantel: a, place the stein puller; b, work your feet higher; c, mantel on tool; d, reach up and place the other tool.

matter how hard the routes may look. If a certain move is elusive, examine your body positioning. A slight change in the way you are leaning may be the difference between frustration and exuberance.

Protection

Previous chapters contain detailed discussions of the various types of protection used on rock (Chapter 13, Rock Protection), snow (Chapter 16, Snow Travel and Climbing), and ice (Chapter 18, Alpine Ice Climbing). Also see "Protection" in the "Waterfall Ice Climbing" section earlier in this chapter. When you are combining the various types of protection for mixed climbing, here is an additional consideration.

If you have a choice between a rock anchor and a snow or ice anchor, use the rock anchor. It is relatively easy to evaluate the soundness of rock anchors, but this is not so with most snow or ice anchors. It might be necessary to do some digging and grooming to clear away snow, ice, and debris in order to place a piece of

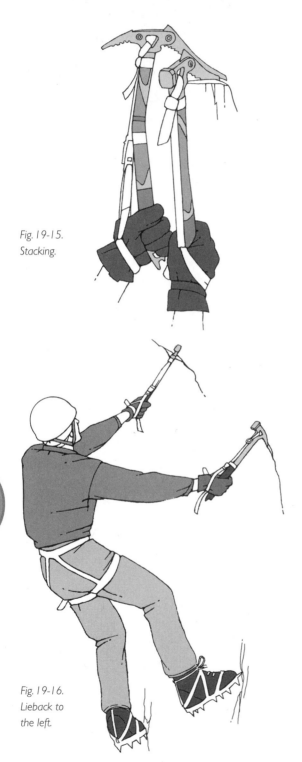

Fig. 19-15.
Stacking.

Fig. 19-16.
Lieback to
the left.

Fig. 19-17.
Lieback to
the right,
pushing
with feet.

THE RACK FOR MIXED CLIMBING

A mixed climbing rack contains gear that is appropriate for the climb: Some modern mixed climbs are fully bolted, requiring only a set of quickdraws for protection. Longer classic mixed climbs require a full rock rack combined with a full ice rack. A typical mixed climbing rack might contain some or all of the following gear:

- Six to twelve screws of varying lengths appropriate for the thickness of the ice
- An assortment of nuts, Hexentrics, and Tri-cams that can be slotted or pounded into cracks
- Spring-loaded camming devices (SLCDs), both three- and four-cam units
- An assortment of pitons for ice-filled cracks
- Several runners or quickdraws
- A few long runners or cordelettes for threading gaps between the rock and the ice or ice columns
- Several load-limiting runners
- An ice hook (as shown in Figure 18-7c and d in Chapter 18, Alpine Ice Climbing) for quick protection, frozen seams, and moss
- A V-thread tool (as shown in Figure 18-9 in Chapter 18, Alpine Ice Climbing)
- A few pieces of $^{11}/_{16}$-inch tubular webbing or 6- to 8-millimeter perlon cord for constructing rappel anchors
- A knife to cut webbing and perlon

protection in the rock. You can knock off powdery snow with your hands, but you will probably need an ice tool to clear hard snow or ice. If a crack is filled with ice, a piton or ice hook may be useful. Wired nuts can be pounded into cracks with the pick of the ice tool to create solid placements.

Belaying and Reducing Forces on the Climbing System

Because of the possibly dubious nature of mixed protection, a dynamic belay is required. As always, use a strong, multipoint, multidirectional belay anchor with well-placed screws or pitons. (See Chapter 10, Belaying.)

A dynamic belay may be partially obtained by using a rope that has a relatively low impact force (4 to 7 kilonewtons). Several half-rope systems offer low impact forces. Keep in mind that low-impact-force ropes are stretchier than the "fat" rock-climbing rope with which you are probably more familiar. Therefore, if a fall occurs, you would fall a greater distance, so watch out for any ledges.

It is also a good idea to use load-limiting runners on lead gear as well as incorporating them into the belay anchor. This further reduces forces on the climbing system.

Minimizing rope drag is also important when you are leading on shaky protection. If the rope zigzags up

the route between points of protection and a fall occurs, the friction generated at the bends in the rope would prevent the rope from elongating as it should by design. If this occurs, a disproportionate amount of force is applied to the protection nearest to the fallen climber. Keep the rope running as straight as possible, use double-rope technique, and use long runners.

Leading

Leading on mixed terrain can be an exhilarating experience, but it is not for everyone. By its very nature, mixed leads tend to be bold and committing. Taking a leader fall while you are wearing crampons and holding ice tools is serious business. Before you decide to lead a mixed pitch on ice gear, be honest about your ability to climb it responsibly. If you have decided that you can indeed climb and protect the pitch safely, here are a few tips to keep in mind:

- Examine the crux or cruxes carefully. Figure out the moves before you get there. Devise a plan and a back-up plan for protecting and climbing through the crux.
- Once you are on route, place gear at rests, before the hard parts, instead of halfway through a crux sequence of moves.
- Calculate your moves and climb with confidence.
- Relax and breathe deeply; this will calm stressed nerves.

- If you are stumped by a sequence of moves, down-climb to the last rest spot, reevaluate, and try again, perhaps using a slightly different technique. If the sequence remains elusive, down-climb or lower off.
- Be prepared to leave some gear behind.
- If a fall is imminent, check the landing zone. Be sure that you will fall away from the trailing rope, which can be damaged by crampons or tools. Disengage your tools, then your crampons, and push away from the wall. Aim picks away from you and to the sides. Direct crampons toward the wall and keep your knees slightly bent to absorb the impact.

CLIMBING IN THE WINTER ENVIRONMENT

The extreme conditions of winter can create fantastic, almost surreal landscapes. On clear winter days, the bright blue sky is a perfect backdrop for the vivid blues of water-ice formations. The water ice glistens in the sunlight and leads skyward.

Waterfall ice and mixed climbing build on the skills of alpine mountaineering and can involve severe conditions that require specialized equipment, a high level of skill, and a tremendous will to succeed. Exposed to the harsh wind and cold, the climber stands armed and armored cap-à-pie, like a medieval knight. However, the climber's weapons are ice tools and crampons, and the armor is fleece, Gore-Tex, and plastic.

Equipped for the winter environment, the mixed climber combines the disciplines of rock climbing and ice climbing. The mixed climber is well schooled in leading on rock and ice and is well versed in avalanche assessment skills. But more importantly, mixed climbers have an excellent understanding of their own abilities; they have nothing to prove and climb without egotism. The mixed climber tests the smallest holds, the thinnest ice, and the steepest routes not for glory or recognition, but to fully experience the freedom the hills.

19

20

Expedition Climbing

PLANNING AND PREPARATION ■ EXPEDITIONARY CLIMBING TECHNIQUES ■ EXPEDITION WEATHER ■ HIGH-ALTITUDE HEALTH HAZARDS ■ AN EXPEDITION PHILOSOPHY

Climbing the high and remote peaks of the world requires significant commitment of both time and effort. Expedition mountain travel allows us the opportunity to explore faraway lands, immerse ourselves in local mountain cultures, challenge our minds and bodies against huge mountaineering objectives, and build strong, lifelong relationships with climbing partners.

Many of the considerations for expeditions are similar to those for shorter climbs. However, there are some significant differences in planning, techniques, and health issues. Moreover, the required level of commitment is much higher.

Expedition climbing does not entail a different type or standard of climbing as much as an expansion of the time scale for a trip. A weekend trip may involve several hours to approach a peak, a day to climb it, and several hours to return home. An expedition may

441

> We've come this far. Let's make the last step together.
>
> — *Jim Wickwire to Lou Reichardt, putting their arms around one another and together becoming the first Americans to reach the summit of K2 in 1978*

involve two or three days of air travel, followed by a day or two of land travel, and then a ten-day trek just to get to base camp. On an expedition, a rest break may be an entire day spent lounging and hydrating rather than a 15-minute sit-down.

The actual climbing is much the same as what is discussed in earlier chapters. The main differences between expedition climbing and other types of mountaineering are the logistics of tackling a remote peak, the more severe weather likely to be encountered, and the difficulties of climbing at high altitude—and often the challenge of dealing with local customs and the daunting red tape of climbing regulations in a foreign country. In addition, expeditions require special skills such as performing crevasse rescues while tied in to a sled, ascending and descending fixed lines, and functioning in extreme cold.

PLANNING AND PREPARATION

Planning an expedition involves selecting a destination, choosing the climbing party, determining a climbing schedule, preparing supplies, and making sure the team members are in condition. You might also decide whether to hire guides. Travel necessities such as passports, immunizations, and insurance also cannot be overlooked.

Choosing an Objective

In deciding what peak to try and which route to climb, you must consider a number of factors: the difficulty of the route, whether the expedition will tackle alpine- or expedition-style climbing, how long the expedition will last, what time of year it will take place, its costs, and the location.

Difficulty of the Route

It is generally best to choose a route well within the climbing ability of the party because the challenges of remoteness, altitude, changeable weather, and routefinding will add to the route's difficulties. Until you have gone on a few expeditions, you should think of the trip as an opportunity to apply well-practiced climbing skills in a new environment, rather than to push the limits of your technical ability.

Choosing a Climbing Style

The route, the size and strength of the party, and the preference of the climbers will help them choose a style of climbing—alpine-style, expedition-style, or somewhere in between. The choice will affect the length of the trip, the amount of risk involved, and the kinds of equipment and technical gear necessary, so it is an important decision and must be made early in the planning process.

Alpine-style: This means moving camps up the mountain in a continuous push, so that you climb the route only once. All equipment and supplies are carried with the team at all times. There is less margin of safety on alpine-style trips because you cannot bring as much equipment and supplies as a team on an expedition-style trip can. However, because the team moves faster, there is also less exposure to objective hazards such as storms and avalanches.

Expedition-style: This involves multiple trips between camps, during which food, fuel, and supplies are carried to higher camps. Total group sizes are larger because more supplies and equipment must be carried. Technically difficult sections of the route are often protected with fixed lines—ropes anchored in place to minimize danger during repeated trips up and down the route. For these reasons, expedition-style climbing takes longer. This can be an advantage because you have more time to acclimatize when you are ascending slowly in stages.

Duration of the Climb

Again, be realistic. Do not try to cram a twenty-five-day route into two weeks of annual leave. Remember that the time it takes to get to the mountain and then to return home can be a significant part of the expedition's schedule. Each individual climber's schedule should include extra time.

Time of Year

Study information on seasonal temperatures, winds, storms, precipitation, and amount of daylight in the area you are considering for the expedition to take place.

Costs

Expeditions are costly because of the large amounts of time, equipment, and food that are required. Major costs include equipment for the climb, transportation and other expenses on the way to the peak, and hiring porters or pack animals to haul gear to base camp. In many cases, expenses incurred within a country are minor compared to the cost of getting there. Estimate costs based on your research about the peak and the area.

Some climbers try to save a few dollars by not using porters or pack animals to haul their gear to base camp. Do not scrimp in this regard only to waste extra days and exhaust the party just getting to the mountain. Be sure to budget adequate compensation for porters and other support staff, as well as supplies they will need for their own safety and comfort. The climbing party should be prepared to provide essential equipment, such as sunglasses and extra stove fuel, which many porters may not have. Know the going rates for support staff services and be sure to pay them accordingly; it is always best to set rates for their services before you head out on the expedition.

Location

There are so many choices for an expedition. Alaska, Mexico, South America, New Zealand, China, Nepal, Pakistan, India, Europe, Russia, Kazakhstan, and Africa all boast difficult, remote peaks. The experience of traveling in a new country is often one of the most enjoyable and rewarding aspects of an expedition.

After you choose a peak, research the mountain and its routes. Talk to climbers who have been there; look for descriptions in the journals of the American Alpine Club, the Alpine Club of Canada, and other climbing organizations. Seek out guidebooks, videos, and articles in climbing magazines, and research online sources. Note that in some countries, maps are considered restricted military information. Consider whether anyone in the party speaks the local language. Get all possible details on logistics, potential problems, where to buy fuel, what foods are available, objective hazards on the mountain, and so forth.

Research a backup route in case the original objective must be scratched because of avalanche hazard, bad weather, inability of some party members to continue, or any other reasons. If you have chosen a highly technical route up the mountain, consider acclimatizing by climbing the standard route first and then taking on the tougher challenge.

Find out what climbing and communication-device permits and approvals are necessary and how long in advance you must make application. It helps to have typewritten itineraries, climbing résumés of party members, equipment lists, and medical information in hand ahead of time and while you are traveling to the peak. Evidence of good organization impresses bureaucrats around the world.

Choosing the Team

Choosing a compatible team is the first and most essential step toward an enjoyable experience. Expedition climbing is full of stress, and climbers can be taxed to their physical and mental limits. Climbing literature abounds with "climb and tell" accounts of expeditions in which, it seems, team members despised their fellow climbers. Do not let your expedition end up being another such example. Make it your goal to head out as friends and return as friends.

The skill of the team must, of course, be equal to the demands of the climb. Climbing with people of similar technical ability may improve compatibility. Personalities also need to be compatible, and team members must be able to live harmoniously with others in close quarters under stressful conditions. The climbers should agree on the philosophy of the trip in terms of climbing style, climbing goals, environmental impact, and degree of acceptable risk.

It is important to agree on leadership before the trip gets under way. If all climbers are of roughly equal experience, democratic decision-making usually works well. If one climber is clearly more experienced, that person can be given the leadership role. Even if

20

democratic decision-making works for the majority of situations on the climb, you need to have a designated leader who will step in when necessary, especially in urgent situations. Even if a single leader is designated, areas such as finances, food, medicine, and equipment should be delegated to others to lessen the leader's load and to keep everyone involved and informed. This also helps build expedition leaders for the future.

The number of climbers in the expedition depends on the route and on the climbing style that you have chosen. A party of two or four climbers may be best on technically difficult routes because of the efficiency of two-person rope teams and the limited space at bivouac sites. However, climbing with a very small team means that if even one person becomes ill or cannot continue, the entire team may have to abandon the climb.

When the route itself does not determine the optimum party size, logistics become the deciding factor. As the number of climbers increases, issues of transportation, food, lodging, and equipment become more complicated. Climbing parties of six or eight have the advantage of strength and reserve capacity: If one climber is unable to continue, the rest of the party still has a chance to go on with the expedition. Larger parties are also better able to carry out self-rescue than smaller teams. However, an expedition with more than eight members can become logistically burdensome.

The Climbing Itinerary

Once you have researched your mountain and picked your team, set up an itinerary that includes a good estimate of the number of days needed for the journey. Allow for the approach to the peak, carrying loads up the mountain, climbing, sitting out storms, and resting. An average elevation gain of 1,000 feet (300 meters) per day allows for acclimatization, and this figure should be correlated, where possible, with good campsites. Rest days built into the schedule provide time for mental and physical recuperation, equipment sorting, and a time buffer for unplanned delays caused by storms, illness, or other problems. If a storm hits, try to adjust the itinerary to allow a rest period for the same time, making the best of a bad day.

Guided Expeditions

Guided climbs are available to just about any expedition destination. Consider hiring a guide if this is your first expedition, if you lack capable partners, or if the prospect of organizing such a major adventure is overwhelming. Using a guide on an expedition allows you to spend more time enjoying the experience and less time organizing it. You will be able to concentrate on mental and physical preparation.

Conversely, a guided climb costs more than a privately organized venture. You lose control over the selection of party members and other decisions that may affect your safety or prospects for the summit. Also, there may not be the same unity of purpose and team spirit that characterize the best expedition experiences.

Supplies

On expeditions to the remote mountains of the world, climbers either take it with them or they do without it. Having the necessary equipment—and having it in working order—is much more critical than on a weekend climb where home is a short drive away. An expedition needs a complete equipment list, including both group and personal gear, agreed upon by all team members. (See Table 20-2, Sample Expedition Equipment List, later in this section.)

Food

Food is the heaviest supply carried on an expedition. You will, however, be grateful for every ounce of it. Food provides the necessary fuel for your body to carry

> If there is a deeper and more lasting message behind our venture than the mere ephemeral sensation of a physical feat, I believe this to be the value of comradeship and the many virtues which combine to create it. Comradeship, regardless of race or creed, is forged among high mountains, through the difficulties and dangers to which they expose those who aspire to climb them, the need to combine their efforts to attain their goal, the thrills of a great adventure shared together.
> —*Sir John Hunt, leader of the 1953 British Everest Expedition*

20

loads and climb the route. It can also serve as one of the great pleasures of the trip.

Every climber has preferences in food, so conduct a team survey of strong food likes and dislikes before you plan menus. Try out all the food ahead of time, preferably on training climbs with the team. Combat the danger of carrying unpopular foods by providing a lot of variety. This ensures that if some team members do not like one item, there should be several others they will find tasty, or at least palatable. A condiment and seasoning kit with Tabasco sauce, spices, soy sauce, margarine, and mustard adds interest to bland packaged foods, and perhaps will salvage the unpopular foods.

Although fats have the highest caloric density—at 9 calories per gram (calories are uniformly measured in metric units)—carbohydrates (4 calories per gram) are easiest to digest, providing the quickest energy. Proteins have about the same caloric density as carbohydrates, but are not as easy to digest and are usually accompanied by substantially more fat. For a reasonable expeditionary diet, try to consume total calories in roughly the proportions shown in Table 20-1 (compare with Table 3-3 in Chapter 3, Camping and Food).

TABLE 20-1. CALORIC PROPORTIONS FOR EXPEDITIONS

Food Source	Percentage of Daily Calories
Carbohydrates	50 to 70 percent
Fats	20 to 30 percent
Proteins	15 to 20 percent

Plan to provide about 35 ounces—roughly 2¼ pounds (1 kilogram)—of food per person per day. With no waste, 35 ounces would provide more than 5,000 calories. In reality—because of packaging, nonnutritive fiber, and the food's irreducible water content—the food will provide only about 3,900 calories per day. Experi-

ence will tell you whether this is just right, too much, or not enough. Too much food means carrying extra-heavy loads between camps and possibly a slower trip. Too little means you will begin losing weight or have to abandon the climb; on a trip of three or four weeks, weight loss should not cause a problem, but on longer expeditions, too much weight loss may affect the team's strength and endurance.

It is tempting to take plenty of extra food. Keep in mind, however, that someone has to carry it up the mountain. Do you want that extra weight in *your* pack? Plan carefully. Take enough to remain adequately nourished and comfortable, but do not take unneeded supplies.

Packaging and organizing food is an important element of planning. Repackage food in appropriately sized portions (either individual portions or meal-size portions for the entire group), perhaps adding spices or other ingredients, to get rid of unnecessary packaging. Keep the preparation instructions with the repackaged food. Measure the food into the correct portions (so much per person per day) and label it. Clear plastic sacks help organize the food while keeping the contents visible.

Adequate hydration is the first line of defense against altitude sickness. Bring plenty of soups, hot drinks, and cold-drink mixes to keep climbers motivated to drink the necessary fluids. Contaminated water plagues nearly every part of the world. The expedition kitchen must be able to furnish adequate potable water for everyone through chemical decontamination, filtering, or boiling.

For early in the trip, plan foods that differ from those for later on when you are up on the mountain. Foods for lower elevations and warmer climates include those that are more time-consuming to prepare, such as pancakes; items that cannot withstand freezing (e.g., cheese and peanut butter); and canned foods. Foods carried to higher altitudes should be very light and require minimum preparation, such as freeze-dried items, instant noodles, instant rice, and instant potatoes. Try to eat local food on the approach and at base camp. Not only will this help prevent you from getting tired of expedition food, but it will also give you an opportunity to sample the local fare.

Vitamins are another important item to take on an expedition. Take along vitamin C, vitamin E, and multivitamins to bolster overall health. These vitamins may also decrease susceptibility to upper-respiratory illness, which is common on expeditions.

Fuel

Regulations for transporting fuel vary from airline to airline and destination to destination. Research the regulations for the party's specific airline and destination well ahead of time. It is likely that you will not be permitted to take fuel on the flight, so make sure the fuel you need is available at the destination.

Fuel containers are usually available in Alaska or Canada, but elsewhere you must provide your own. Aluminum containers (plastic bottles have a reputation for leaking) as small as 1 liter (1 quart) are fine if you do not need to carry much fuel. For larger quantities, bring empty 1-gallon gas cans or sturdy, approved plastic fuel containers. They must be new, because some airlines object to containers with residual vapors. All fuel containers should be kept separate from other gear, especially food.

Multifuel stoves are good insurance in countries where white gas is not readily available. Even with a multifuel stove, check the fuel's compatibility with the stove before you head into the mountains. If you will use kerosene or a similar low-volatility fuel, be sure to buy alcohol or white gas for priming the stove. It is preferable to prime with and burn the same fuel whenever possible. The cleanliness of fuel in some areas is questionable. Bring a fuel filter, and filter all fuel before you use it. Clean the stove often.

Plan on using between ½ and 1 cup (0.1 to 0.2 liter) of fuel per person per day, depending on how much water must be boiled for purification or melted from snow or ice. Bring sufficient stoves and fuel for any

porters or other local individuals who will be part of the expedition, so that no fires will be needed for cooking. Adequate cooking equipment will help reduce the entire team's impact on the environment.

Group Gear

Kitchen: For communal cooking, take pots large enough for group meals and for melting large amounts of snow. Water bottles will need to be filled daily, so pots must be easy to pour from; a 2-quart (2-liter) coffeepot works well. Bring at least one cook pot per stove. Bring a metal gripper to use on pots that lack handles or bails, or use wool gloves as potholders. Be careful using synthetic gloves, which will melt if they get too hot.

Shelter: Tents are another item the expedition will share. Decide beforehand how many and what kind of tents are best. If necessary, also decide ahead of time who will stay in what tent, keeping in mind the importance of making everyone comfortable for a good night's rest.

Other group gear: To save a bit of weight, the party can carry an altimeter and a compass as pieces of group equipment, rather than having each climber carry their own. Note that if the climb objective is in the southern hemisphere, the compass must be balanced for the southern hemisphere (see "Dip" in Chapter 5, Navigation).

Wands, which are used to mark routes, camp perimeters, gear caches, and snow shelters, are another group gear item. The number of wands needed varies according to the specifics of the climb, such as length, terrain, and route. (See "Wands" in Chapter 16, Snow Travel and Climbing.)

The party may carry communication devices to get weather information, call for emergency help, or allow communication between climbers at different locations. The main choices are citizens-band radios, marine band FM radios, and cellular or satellite telephones. Investigate these options to determine both the technical feasibility and the legality of their use.

Repair kit: Be prepared for critical equipment failure under the prolonged and rugged demands of an expedition. Put together a comprehensive repair kit, keeping in mind the relative importance of each piece

20

of equipment to the progress of the group. (See Table 20-2 later in this chapter.)

First-aid kit: An expedition should include a comprehensive first-aid kit, which is assembled after everyone in the party has had input on the contents. Keep in mind how isolated the peak is, and consider the specific medical conditions of team members and their medical knowledge. Discuss the group's medical needs with a doctor who is familiar with mountaineering.

The first-aid kit may include such specialized or prescription items as a strong painkiller, antibiotics, a dental repair kit, and a suture kit. Be sure to carry a first-aid manual. (See "First-Aid Supplies" in Chapter 2, Clothing and Equipment, as well as Chapter 23, First Aid.)

Check on any restrictions or cautions regarding transporting drugs and medical equipment to a particular destination. Find out whether different climates or altitudes adversely affect medications that you will take on the expedition. Also, bear in mind that just because certain drugs are legal in your country of origin does not mean they will be legal everywhere in the world.

Climbing Gear: Communal or Personal?

The route and the chosen climbing style determine what climbing gear you need. A route that involves only glacier travel may require just the basics—rope, ice ax, crampons, and crevasse rescue gear. Technical routes can take the whole gamut of equipment, from ice screws, snow flukes, and pickets to camming devices, nuts, and pitons.

Depending on the climbing style and organization of the trip, climbing gear can be personal or common. On a technical route, where climbers operate in self-sufficient pairs, climbing gear should be personal or left to each rope team to work out. In other cases, virtually all climbing gear—carabiners, runners, screws, and so forth—can be treated as group equipment. The choice is up to the team. Certain pieces of climbing gear, such as crampons and ice axes, are indispensable, and a large party may want to carry spares.

Ropes: Deciding what rope to take depends on the route and its difficulty. Keep in mind, however, that an expedition can put extraordinary wear and tear on

ropes with daily use in bright sunlight. The team needs to decide how much rope to bring for fixed lines along the route. Fixed lines usually use nylon kernmantle rope due to its strength and abrasion resistance.

Backpacks: Every person on an expedition team needs a backpack, with a capacity between 5,500 and 7,000 cubic inches (90 and 115 liters), because at times climbers will be called on to carry extremely large and heavy loads. The pack must be comfortable while worn with a climbing harness.

Ascenders: The cam of a mechanical ascender permits one-way movement, gripping or squeezing the rope when the ascender is pulled downward, but freely sliding upward. Ascenders make it easier to haul heavy, bulky expedition loads and handle crevasse rescues. Expedition climbers prefer ascenders over prusik slings, both for crevasse rescue and for self-belay while climbing with a fixed line—climbers accept the extra weight because of the greater utility. A pair of handled ascenders is the norm, although one ascender plus a prusik sling or a mini-ascender can work if you need to cut down on equipment weight. Regardless of the choice, make sure you can operate the system while you are wearing bulky gloves or mittens.

Personal Gear

Clothing: Expedition climbers need clothing that can stand up to prolonged use under severe conditions. The suggestions on clothing and equipment in the preceding chapters of this book (Chapter 2, Clothing and Equipment; Chapter 16, Snow Travel and Climbing; and Chapter 18, Alpine Ice Climbing) are generally applicable to expeditions.

Sleeping bag: Your sleeping system's comfort rating should be based on the anticipated climate, season, and altitude of the area you will be visiting.

Other personal gear: Consider including the following:

- Prescription sunglasses—If you require prescription glasses, carry an extra set of prescription sunglasses as well.
- Journal—An expedition can make you introspective. A journal made of waterproof paper (look under surveyor supplies at a bookstore or stationery supply store) and some pencils can help pass the time.

20

TABLE 20-2. SAMPLE EXPEDITION EQUIPMENT LIST
GROUP GEAR

Shelter

Expedition-quality tent(s)

Ground cloths

Snow stakes and/or tent flukes

Sponge and whisk broom

Snow shelter construction tools: large snow shovel (for moving a lot of snow), small snow shovel (for delicate trimming), snow saw (for cutting blocks)

Group Climbing Gear

Ropes

Hardware: snow and ice gear (pickets, flukes, ice screws), rock gear (pitons, spring-loaded camming devices, chocks), carabiners, runners, daisy chains, fixed line, extra climbing equipment (spare ice ax or tool, spare crampons, spare rescue pulleys)

Kitchen

Stove gear: stove, windscreen and stove platform, fuel containers and fuel filter, matches and/or butane lighters, firestarter

Cooking gear: pots, pot cozy, pot gripper, sponge/scrubber, dip cup, cooking spoon, snow sack (for collecting clean snow to melt for water)

Food

Water treatment: filter, chemicals

Repair Kit

Tent repair kit: pole splices, spare pole

Stove repair kit

Crampon repair kit: extra screws, connecting bars, straps

Tape (duct, filament, fabric repair)

Adhesive-backed repair cloth

Seam repair compound

Tools: slotted and Phillips screwdrivers; Allen wrenches; small pliers; small wire cutter/shears; file

Sewing kit: assorted needles and thread; awl; assorted buttons, snaps, buckles, and D-rings; Velcro (hook and pile), fabric (Cordura, ripstop nylon), flat webbing

Other: wire, accessory cord, pack buckle, extra ski-pole basket, patch kit for inflatable foam pads

---

First-Aid Kit

Most expeditions carry a comprehensive group first-aid kit. In addition to normal first-aid items, the kit should include the following drugs, plus others recommended by a physician.

Prescription drugs vary with the destination, but should include: antibiotics, strong analgesics, anti-diarrhetics, laxatives, and altitude medications (acetazolamide, dexamethasone).

Nonprescription drugs vary with the destination, but should include: cough suppressants, decongestants, mild analgesics (aspirin, ibuprofen).

Other Group Gear

Wands

Altimeter, map, compass

Radio transceiver and extra batteries

Two-way radios

Weather radio

Satellite phone

GPS receiver

Latrine equipment

TABLE 20-2. *Continued*

PERSONAL GEAR

Clothing

Synthetic-fabric underwear	Plastic boots
Insulating layers	Supergaiters and/or overboots
Down clothing	

Wind-protection and rain-protection garments (top and bottom)

Extremities: hands (liner gloves, insulating gloves, mittens), feet (liner socks, insulating socks, vapor-barrier socks), head (balaclava, sun hat, face mask, wool hat)

Other: bandannas, sun shirt, synthetic fill/down booties

Sleep System

Sleeping bag	Vapor-barrier liner
Bivouac sack	Inflatable foam pad or closed-cell foam pad

Climbing Gear

Ice ax	Rescue pulley
Second ice tool	Ascenders/prusiks
Seat harness with ice-tool holster	Helmet
Chest harness	Large-volume pack
Crampons	Pack cover
Personal carabiners and slings	Snowshoes or skis
Chock pick	Sled with associated hardware for pulling
Belay device	Duffel bag

Other Gear

Ski poles	Headlamp and extra batteries and bulbs
Avalanche transceiver	Watch with alarm
Avalanche probe	Wide-mouth water bottles
Sunglasses and goggles	Insulated mug, bowl, spoon
Spare prescription glasses	Passport
Pocketknife	Sit pad

Personal hygiene: toilet paper, pee bottle, toothbrush, comb, chemical wash/wipes, sunscreen, lip balm, foot powder, earplugs

Personal recreation: camera and film, books, journal, pen or pencil, personal stereo, playing cards

20

■ Books—Catch up on reading while you are waiting for flights or during rest days and storm days in the field. Coordinate your selection of books with other team members to avoid repetition and provide variety.

■ Personal hygiene items—On cold-weather trips where water is at a premium, chemical wash/wipes can provide a refreshing sponge bath, and talcum powder can take the edge off the often strong odors that develop over the course of an expedition.

■ Pee bottle—The pee bottle eliminates those unpleasant trips to the latrine during storms and cold nights. Be sure the bottle has a secure top and is clearly labeled. The pee bottle should be a unique shape or have some obvious tactile difference from your water bottles so you do not mistake one for the other in the middle of the night.

Physical and Mental Conditioning

Training for an expedition involves both physical and mental preparation. For your body, emphasize both cardiovascular and strength training (see Chapter 4, Physical Conditioning). Cardiovascular conditioning is important for physical activity at high altitudes. Strong muscles are essential for carrying heavy loads up mountains, not to mention hoisting and climbing with a large expeditionary pack.

Climbing itself is the best training. Climb often and in all weather conditions, carrying a heavy pack. If you are able to go on a typical two- to three-day climb while carrying gear for camping and climbing, gaining 3,000 to 5,000 feet (900 to 1,500 meters) per day, and feel you still have plenty of physical reserves, you are probably sufficiently fit for an expedition. You need the endurance to carry 40 to 60 pounds (18 to 27 kilograms)—sometimes in addition to pulling a sled—for an elevation gain of 2,000 to 3,000 feet (600 to 900 meters) every day, day after day.

Your mind and spirit also need to get in shape for the rigors of an expedition. Learn about the special challenges of expedition travel and prepare to accept them. Otherwise, you may be overwhelmed by the size and remoteness of the climbing area, or you may lose your good spirits during a long storm or a bout with the flu.

Expedition success often goes to the climbers who have the desire or will to succeed, even though they may be physically weaker than other climbers. It takes more than physical strength to deal with extreme cold, sickness, cramped quarters, poor food, conflict with teammates, the stress of technical climbing, and the lethargy brought on by high altitude.

Work on both physical and mental conditioning by seeking out experiences that come as close as possible to what you can expect on the expedition. Prepare for the expedition by going on winter climbs and on longer trips. Once you are on the expedition, you may not be able to alter such objective factors as extreme cold or illness, but with preparation, you can learn to exercise a great deal of mental control over your attitude toward and actions about them.

Before Leaving Home

Food and gear must be packed and repacked to accommodate the various transportation modes used to get to the mountain. Become familiar with the requirements that face the expedition, such as airline regulations on bag sizes and weights, or muleteer requirements on load balancing. Develop, and carry along on the expedition, detailed equipment lists, including what items are in what containers so that any item can be retrieved readily. Research what documentation is required for importing equipment to the destination (for example, a packing list or bill of lading).

Before leaving home, plan travel arrangements for each leg of the journey, making reservations where possible. Try to work with a travel agent who has booked trips to the region before.

Well before the departure, secure the following: passport, visa, medical insurance coverage, and required or suggested immunizations.

You should be as healthy as possible when you leave home, because, in all likelihood, you will not get better while traveling. Have a dental exam, and have any dental care done before you leave. To stay healthy once you

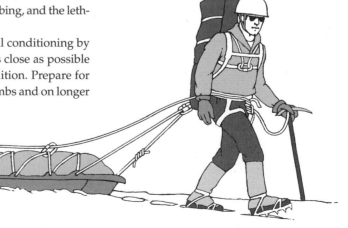

Fig. 20-1.
Sled and climber
rigged for glacier travel.

reach the destination, purify all water and be cautious about eating fresh vegetables or fruit, dairy products, and uncooked food (for proper precautions, see *The Pocket Doctor* by Stephen Bezruchka).

Finally, through all the complicated hurry and scurry of getting ready for a big expedition, remember that the goal is to get away from it all and climb a mountain.

EXPEDITIONARY CLIMBING TECHNIQUES

Expedition mountaineering calls for the rock-, snow-, ice-, alpine-, and winter-climbing techniques that are covered throughout this book. An expedition also adds some new techniques to your climbing repertoire: hauling sleds and using fixed lines.

Sled Hauling

To move loads of gear and supplies on long glacier approaches, expedition members often pull sleds or haul bags behind them (fig. 20-1). You may carry a normal load in a backpack and pull a sled with another pack's worth of gear. Before the expedition, practice on various types of terrain.

A commercial haul sled features zippered covers to hold the load, a waist harness, and rigid aluminum poles connecting the sled and harness. The poles help you control the sled when you are traversing or going downhill. You can add an optional brake made out of a flat piece of lightweight material, such as aluminum, to the rear of the sled, which prevents backsliding on steeper terrain.

A cheaper but usable alternative is a plastic children's sled with holes punched in the sides as rope attachment points. Load your gear into a duffel bag and tie it to the sled. You can use 5- to 7-millimeter perlon accessory cord to pull such a sled. Most climbers prefer to attach the cord to their pack rather than their climbing harness.

Another alternative is to drag a haul bag, constructed of durable slick material to help it slide over the snow. A swivel connector that attaches the haul line to the haul bag keeps the bag's rolling from putting twists in the line.

As the route steepens, the amount of weight you can pull in a sled decreases. Sleds cannot be used at all on steep technical climbing terrain. Haul bags may then be what is needed (see "Hauling" in Chapter 15, Aid Climbing).

Hauling a sled can get complicated during roped travel on glaciers. A fall into a crevasse is more treacherous with a sled plunging down behind the fallen climber. Even if the fallen climber is not injured by the plummeting sled, the sled's presence and added weight make rescue more difficult. A brake added to the rear of the sled can prevent backsliding on steeper terrain. Minimize the danger of getting hit by the sled during a crevasse fall by using this simple preventive technique:

Where the climbing rope runs past the sled, tie it snugly with a clove hitch or prusik knot to a carabiner attached to the rear of the sled. Be sure to clip the duffel bag on the sled to the rope as well. In a crevasse fall, first you will drop into the crevasse, followed by the sled. The sled, however, will be stopped above you by the tie-in to the climbing rope (fig. 20-2). If you are using a hauling tether to the sled instead of rigid aluminum poles, be sure the tether is long enough so that you are well below the sled as it hangs from the climbing rope.

This technique does depend on having a team member on the rope behind the fallen climber, to arrest the fall of both the climber and the sled. Therefore, it will not work for the last climber on a rope. The last person either assumes the extra risk, or the team can decide to haul only two sleds for every three climbers on a three-person rope team.

Crevasse Rescue

There are special procedures for crevasse rescue involving a sled, beyond those discussed in Chapter 16, Snow Travel and Climbing. As you dangle in the crevasse, your weight may be on the sled haul line (or towing poles, if you are using a commercial sled). First of all, transfer your weight to the climbing rope by standing in slings attached to your ascending system—whether that is mechanical ascenders, prusik slings, or a combination (see Chapter 17, Glacier Travel and Crevasse Rescue). Next, disconnect the attachment between you and the sled. If a haul line is attached to your pack, simply take off the pack and let it hang from the line.

20

Once you are free of the sled, try to rescue yourself or wait for your climbing mates to get you out. If you start up the climbing rope on your own, the sled probably will complicate matters. You may need to ascend around the knot in the rope holding the sled. In this case, remove your ascenders, one at a time, and reattach them above the knot.

A fallen climber may also need to untie from the climbing rope in order to move past the sled and reach the lip of the crevasse. To make it easier to disconnect from the climbing rope, many sled-pullers travel with the rope clipped to a locking carabiner on their harness, rather than tying the rope directly to the harness itself. If you need to unclip from the climbing rope, use extreme caution to ensure that your ascenders are secure.

A fall into a crevasse with a sled can also mean extra effort for topside teammates if they must pull out the fallen climber and the sled. If the fallen climber cannot disconnect from the sled, or if no extra rescue rope is available, topside teammates must haul both climber and sled at the same time. Using a 3:1 pulley system will give the most mechanical advantage pulling on the climbing rope (see Chapter 17, Glacier Travel and Crevasse Rescue). It is far preferable to use a spare rope to pull out a fallen climber, and then use the climbing rope to haul out the sled.

Fixed Lines

A fixed line is a rope that is anchored and left in place on the route. It allows safe, quick travel up and down a difficult stretch. You protect yourself by tying in to a mechanical ascender on the fixed line, eliminating the need for time-consuming belays. If you fall while climbing next to the fixed line, the ascender cam locks onto the fixed line to hold you (see "Using Ascenders" and "Fixing Pitches" in Chapter 15, Aid Climbing).

The fixed line simplifies the movement of people and equipment, especially when numerous trips are required, and permits less-experienced climbers to follow a route. Fixed lines have been common on large expeditions to major peaks to provide protection on long stretches of exposed climbing or to protect porters while they make carries from camp to camp in the face of such obstacles as icefalls, glaciers, and steep rock or ice. The lines make it possible for climbers and porters

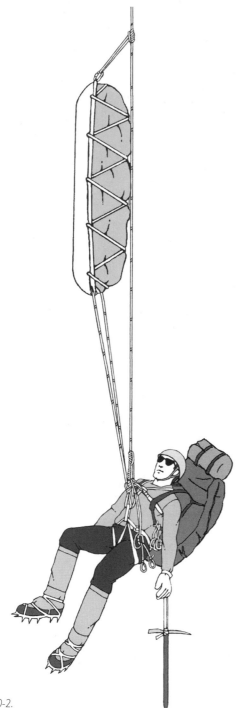

Fig. 20-2.
After a fall into a crevasse, the prusik knot (or clove hitch) takes the weight of the sled.

to carry heavier loads than they could safely carry without them.

Fixed lines are sometimes used as a siege tactic on difficult rock and ice faces, with climbers retreating down the lines each night to a base camp and then ascending again the next day to push the route a little farther.

Exercise extreme caution in deciding whether to make use of a fixed line already in place on a route. It is hard to determine the integrity of an existing line and its anchors. Age, exposure to weather, or the ice tools or crampons of climbers who used the line before you may have damaged the rope.

Some climbers argue that fixing ropes is an outdated technique, no longer required to climb any established route. This is not the majority view, but the technique should not be abused. Fixed lines should not be used to supplement the climbing ability of an expedition team. Fixed lines should not be added on popular routes or in violation of the local climbing ethic.

Equipment for Fixed Lines

To set up and use fixed lines, the party needs rope, anchors, and ascenders. Climbing ropes do not make good fixed lines because they are designed to stretch when weighted, which is undesirable for a fixed line. A more static rope—that is, one with low elongation under load—is best. Nylon rope is the most common type for fixed lines. Kernmantle construction is best, though braided ropes can be used.

The diameter of fixed lines usually varies between 7 and 10 millimeters. The ideal size depends on the terrain and the amount of use the line is expected to get. Try to carry long sections of fixed line. They are usually manufactured in lengths ranging from 90 to 300 meters (300 to 1,000 feet), depending on diameter.

Anchoring Fixed Lines

Every fixed line needs an anchor at the bottom and a bombproof (secure) anchor at the top. To anchor the fixed line to the mountain, employ attachment points that are normally used in belaying and climbing on rock, snow, or ice—pitons, chocks, natural outcrops, ice screws, pickets, and snow flukes or other deadman anchors. Mark the location of the bottom and top anchors with wands, making it easier to find them during or after a snowstorm.

Place a series of intermediate anchors between the bottom and top of the fixed line. Tie off the fixed line at each anchor (intermediate as well as top and bottom) so that every section of line is independent of the others. This permits more than one climber at a time on the line. Be sure that a fall by any climber would not cause rope movement, rockfall, or anything else that could endanger a team member. Passing should be done at an anchor.

Follow several rules of thumb when you decide where to place anchors: Place them at points where the direction of the line needs to change or to prevent pendulum falls. An anchor at the top of a difficult section of the route is helpful. If possible, place the intermediate anchors at natural resting spots, making it easier for climbers to stand and move their ascenders past them.

Always bury or cover snow and ice anchors, and inspect them regularly for possible failure from creep or melting. Keep a close eye on any rock anchors capable of creeping or loosening. Place anchors at locations that will keep the line from rubbing on rough or sharp surfaces, or pad the line at points of abrasion. Even small amounts of wear can multiply into dangerous weak spots on fixed lines, which are typically lighter-weight rope. Falls will also damage the line. After any fall on the line, inspect it for damage and check the anchors for indications of possible failure.

Setting Up Fixed Lines

You can use a variety of methods to set a fixed line, each appropriate for certain conditions, climber preferences, and types of line. The key is to think through your chosen system prior to starting out and, if you can, test and refine it before it is actually needed. It is a big job. Here are three possible methods:

■ The most common way is for two or three climbers to ascend the route, using a standard climbing rope to belay one another or to establish a running belay, and to set a fixed line as they climb. The climbers carry the whole spool of fixed line with them, letting it out as they ascend and tying off at each intermediate anchor along the way. Carrying a spool of rope is difficult.

20

453

Another option is for the climbers to pull the end of the fixed line up as they ascend, clipping the fixed line in to each anchor with carabiners. After anchoring the top of the fixed line, the climbers go back down, tying off the line at each anchor along the way. It is difficult to pull up on the end of the line and overcome the tremendous friction that develops as the line travels through the carabiners and over the route.

Another option is to set the fixed line on the descent. This means, of course, that the material for the fixed line first must be carried to the top of the route. Tie the line in to a bombproof anchor at the top, then rappel or down-climb to tie the line off at intermediate anchors. These can be anchors that were placed on the earlier ascent of the route, although new ones may be added just for the fixed line.

To tie off the fixed line at each intermediate anchor, use a figure-eight knot (the preferred method) or a clove

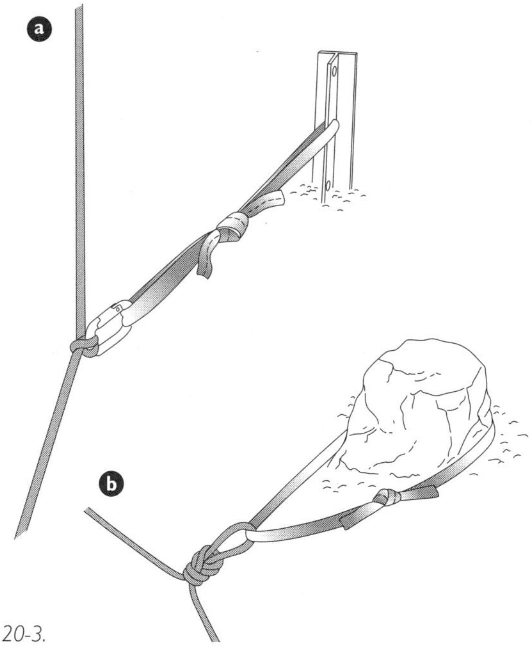

Fig. 20-3.

Intermediate anchors on a fixed line: a, anchor with carabiner clove-hitched to fixed line; b, anchor without carabiner, using a figure-eight knot to attach to fixed line.

hitch in the line. Tie a sling directly to the anchor and clip the figure-eight loop or clove hitch in to a carabiner attached to that sling (fig. 20-3a). Or better yet, minimize use of carabiners and have one less link in the system by tying the sling directly through the figure-eight loop (fig. 20-3b).

Ascending Fixed Lines

Ascending with a fixed line is just like regular climbing, except your harness is attached by a sling to a mechanical ascender, which you place on the fixed line and use as a self-belay in case of a fall (fig. 20-4).

Tie the sling to your seat harness where you normally tie in with the climbing rope, or clip the sling into a locking carabiner attached to the harness. Make the sling short so the ascender is not out of reach if you fall. If you are climbing a near-vertical section or climbing with a heavy pack, pass the sling through your chest harness as well to prevent tipping upside down in a fall.

Attach the ascender to the fixed line, following the specific directions for that brand of ascender. The ascender should be oriented so that a fall will cause it to clamp the rope. It should slide easily up the line, but lock tight when pulled down the line. Test it, and check the fittings on your seat harness, before starting upward.

Attach a carabiner clipped to the ascender sling, or clipped to a separate sling attached to your seat harness (fig. 20-4a), to the fixed line to serve as a backup safety link. If you fall and the ascender fails, the safety carabiner will slide down the fixed line, stopping at the next anchor below to arrest the fall.

At each intermediate anchor, you must pass the knot in the fixed line. This is the most dangerous moment in fixed-line travel, particularly if conditions are severe and you are exhausted. It is best to move the safety carabiner first (fig. 20-4b). Unclip the carabiner, then reclip it above the anchor. Then move the ascender (fig. 20-4c). This sequence offers more security than moving the ascender first. Another option is to briefly clip in to the anchor while you relocate the ascender. Be sure that the safety carabiner stays on the line when the ascender is detached. Think the procedure through in

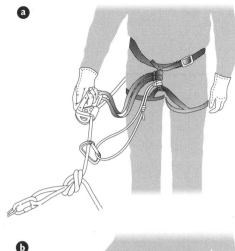

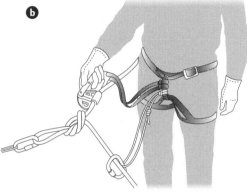

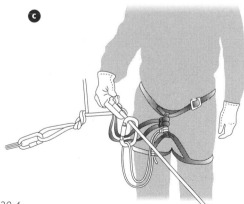

Fig. 20-4.
Mechanical ascender attachment to fixed line: a, set up for normal movement; b, passing an anchor, move the safety carabiner first; c, moving the ascender past the knot.

advance and practice it often so you can perform it reliably under the worst possible conditions.

Descending Fixed Lines

Climbing down with a fixed line is similar to climbing up. Attach the ascender sling to your seat harness. Attach the ascender to the fixed line in the same way as on the ascent. Double-check that the ascender locks onto the rope when you pull down on it and that it will be within reach if you end up hanging from it after a fall. Attach the safety carabiner.

Begin the descent. As you climb downward, move the ascender down the rope, keeping it with you. Use a light grip on the ascender release, which allows you to let go of it instantly in a fall so the ascender will grab the rope. It is natural to try to hang onto something if you lose your balance, but the last thing you should grab is the ascender release!

Be very careful in removing and reattaching the ascender while you are descending past anchors. Move the ascender, then move the safety carabiner (the opposite order from ascending a fixed line). Remember: Never detach the ascender and the safety carabiner at the same time. Keep in mind that you can temporarily clip in to the anchor while you are relocating the ascender. On steep sections of fixed line, rappelling the fixed line may be a good alternative to down-climbing.

Removing Fixed Lines

Climbing rope of any type is not a natural or biodegradable material. It must be packed out. Teams have the responsibility of removing any fixed lines that they have placed and hauling them out. When you are setting them up, always bear in mind that you will need to remove them. In some cases you may be able to use a "moving" fixed line, removing it and moving it higher as the party ascends the mountain, then descending via a safer route. If the party is leaving the mountain and thus going down a fixed route for the last time, plan a strategy (down-climbing or rappelling, or a combination) that will permit the party to remove the fixed line. Practice Leave No Trace guidelines (see Chapter 7), and respect the importance of taking everything with you when you leave.

20

EXPEDITION WEATHER

On an expedition, climbers need to become amateur weather forecasters because their safety and success are so closely bound to nature's moods. When you reach the climbing area, talk to other climbers and to people who live there about local weather patterns. Find out the direction of the prevailing winds. Ask about rain and storms. On the mountain, make note of weather patterns. The altimeter can serve as a barometer to signal weather changes.

Take clues from the clouds. Cirrus clouds (such as mares tails) warn of a front bringing precipitation within the next 24 hours. Lenticular clouds (cloud caps) mean high winds. A rapidly descending cloud cap is a sign that bad weather is coming. If you climb into a cloud cap, expect high winds and poor visibility. (See Chapter 27, Mountain Weather.) Be prepared for the fact that big mountains typically have big storms, strong winds, and rapidly changing weather. Wait out a storm if possible because of the risk inherent in descending under bad conditions. If the party expects to be stuck for some time, start rationing food and conserve on fuel.

Fair weather poses problems too. If it is hot and sunny, glaciers intensify solar radiation. The result can be collapsing snow bridges, crevasse movement, and increased icefall. In such conditions, it is best to climb at night, when temperatures are lowest and snow and ice are most stable.

HIGH-ALTITUDE HEALTH HAZARDS

Expedition climbing is physically taxing. Inadequate levels of oxygen, extreme cold, and dehydration, among other things, are all potential health hazards. Learn to recognize, prevent, and treat potential health hazards when they occur (see Chapter 23, First Aid). Consult a first-aid manual, specialized texts, or physicians familiar with mountaineering for detailed information.

On high peaks, temperatures drop well below zero. Although this is good for keeping snow stable, it can have a detrimental effect on your body. Everyone in the expedition party must be aware of the dangers of frostbite, as well as wind- and sunburn.

Expedition climbing, like any mountaineering, takes you to altitudes where the human body no longer feels at home. Every climber is affected to one degree or other by reduced oxygen at higher elevations, often leading to acute mountain sickness (altitude sickness). This can lead to the life-threatening conditions of high-altitude pulmonary edema (HAPE) and high-altitude cerebral edema (HACE). These illnesses are generally avoidable, however, through proper acclimatization and hydration.

Acclimatization

The best way to combat altitude illness is to prevent it in the first place. The best way to do this is to ascend slowly. Your body needs time to acclimatize to higher altitude, though how much time it takes varies from person to person.

Ascend at a moderate rate, averaging 1,000 feet (300 meters) a day in net elevation gain. If suitable campsites are 3,000 feet (900 meters) apart, carry one day to the next camp (3,000-foot gain), move camp the next day, and rest the third day at the new camp, for a net gain of 3,000 feet every three days. Try not to push your limits until you have become well acclimatized. Schedule rest days after big pushes.

Above 18,000 feet (5,400 meters), most people begin to deteriorate physically regardless of acclimatization. Minimize your stays at high altitudes, and periodically return to lower altitudes to recover. The old advice is good: Climb high, sleep low. Your body acclimatizes much faster during exertion than during rest, and recovers more quickly at a lower altitude. Expedition-style climbing takes advantage of these concepts by carrying loads to a high camp, returning to lower altitude to recover, and then ascending again.

Hydration

Hydration is critical in avoiding altitude illness. Everyone should be drinking 5 to 7 quarts (5 to 7 liters) of water a day, and avoiding alcohol and caffeine, which have a dehydrating effect. To supply that much water for everyone, several hours each day must be dedicated to melting snow. This is time well spent, however, because adequate hydration is an important key to the success of an expedition.

20

In addition to using these figures for daily liquid intake, monitor your urine output and color. Urine should be copious and clear. Dark urine indicates that you are not drinking enough water.

Climbers usually lose their appetites at high altitudes. Everyone tends to eat and drink less than they should. This is why a varied menu—one that includes food and drink that is appealing to each member of the party—is so important.

AN EXPEDITION PHILOSOPHY

Members of an expedition need a common code to live by during their weeks of traveling and climbing together. One good code is summed up in three promises that you and your teammates can make to one another: to respect the land, to take care of yourselves, and to come home again.

Respect the land: Every day, an expedition party has the chance to put the health and beauty of the land ahead of its own immediate comfort. The easy way out might be to burn wood fires, set up camp in a virgin meadow, or leave garbage and human waste on the ground. But if all the climbers have promised to respect the land, they will be aware of their impact and be responsible. Leave no trace.

Those who follow your trail will not want to see the wrappers from your snacks or other signs that your group passed through the area. If you pack it in, pack it out. Be sensitive to local customs. Local land managers may have specific wishes about the treatment of their areas. Learn what their expectations are ahead of time and be respectful.

Take care of yourselves: If you and your climbing partners have promised to take care of yourselves, you have made a commitment to group self-reliance. You may have no choice in the matter, because you will likely be a long way from rescuers, helicopters, hospitals, or even other climbers. Prepare by thinking through the possible emergencies that the party could face and by making plans for responding to those. You will feel reassured that plans are ready if you have to use them, and grateful if you do not.

In addition, foster team spirit by checking on one another throughout the day regarding adequate fluid intake, use of sunscreen, and other necessities that will keep team members healthy and in good spirits. After all, as the late, renowned climber Alex Lowe said, "The best climber in the world is the one having the most fun!"

Come home again: The third promise might be the hardest to keep, because it can conflict with that burning desire for the summit. It is really a promise to climb safely and to be willing to sacrifice dreams of the summit in favor of survival. Expedition climbing is, after all, about pushing limits and testing yourself in a very tough arena.

Each person and each team must decide what level of risk they are willing to accept. Keep the third promise by being sure before ever setting out that the team agrees upon what is safe and what is unsafe. Out of that discussion, decisions flow daily regarding how fast to ascend, what gear to carry, when to change routes, and when to back off.

Most climbers would rather return home safely than push for the summit under unsafe conditions. Having the freedom of the hills does not only mean reaching the summit; you can measure your expedition's success in many ways.

20

Next page: *On Ross Island near the base of Mount Erebus, south Antarctica* (Photo by Scott Darsney)

21 CHAPTER

Leadership

THE CLIMB LEADER ■ ORGANIZING THE CLIMB ■ BECOMING A LEADER

Just as every climbing party needs a map and compass, every climb needs good leadership—but the style and form of that guidance varies with the venture. It is one thing to head out with some longtime climbing companions for a sunny weekend of peak bagging, and another to mount an extended technical climb with mountaineers who do not know one another to a peak none of them has ever seen.

Climbers who know one another well achieve good leadership very informally, probably without even knowing it. An expedition of climbers less familiar with one another requires a more formal, structured organization. But in both cases, leadership provides the same things: a way to put a climb together and make it a safe and enjoyable success.

THE CLIMB LEADER

A climb leader is someone who has special responsibility for organizing the climb and for making decisions en route. Depending on the nature of the party, the degree of formal organization may vary from highly structured to virtually nonexistent. Nevertheless, certain necessary functions of the group are performed one way or another. The position of leader may be conferred by a sponsoring organization or may develop informally and spontaneously, but the fact is that most climbs have a leader.

Small, informal parties often do not select a leader. Everyone feels responsible for organizing, sharing work, and team building. It is easy for each member to know what the others are doing, so coordination is not much of an issue. The climb organizer or most experienced party member may be tacitly recognized as leader of such a group, but should try not to be too directive.

Large groups, on the other hand, do not lead themselves and usually do better with a designated leader. Members of the climbing party cannot know what every other person is doing, so someone needs to be chief organizer if only to make sure no critical details are overlooked. Large groups may also need more focus on team building, because it is likely that the members will not all know one another.

The leadership structure of most climbing parties tends to fit into one of the following categories.

Peers: This is a group of acquaintances that decide to go climbing. Usually there is no designated leader, but members informally allocate key functions. One climber may take responsibility for organizing equipment, another for transportation and food, and so forth. Most decisions are made by consensus. Even in this least-formal type of organization, one member will usually emerge as "first among equals" and be regarded as leader. It will be the person who displays initiative, good judgment, and concern for the group and who generally inspires the most confidence.

Climb organizer: This is the person who organizes the climb—the one who has the original idea for the venture and then recruits others. The organizer is usually recognized as de facto leader, even if the position is never formalized.

Most experienced: A group tends to bestow leadership upon, and to defer to the judgment of, a climber who is clearly the most experienced in the party.

Climbing clubs and schools: Leadership is formally conferred by the sponsoring group when a climb is part of an organized program. Often leaders must go through an accreditation process to ensure a certain level of experience and competence. There may even be a hierarchy among the leadership, with an overall leader and assistant instructors to help. There is no doubt who is leader, and it is not up to the party to select one. The leader is expected to research the climb and to take charge of equipment, transportation, and other logistical matters. Such climbs are often teaching situations; students are expected to follow the leader's guidance, but they are also supposed to be learning and gaining self-sufficiency.

Guided climbs: Climbers pay guide services to provide competent leadership. Professional guides are often outstanding climbers and are completely in charge of their groups. Guides make the decisions for their clients and assume responsibility for their safety.

> Fail to honor people,
> They fail to honor you;
> But of a good leader, who talks little,
> When his work is done, his aim fulfilled,
> They will say, "We did this ourselves."
>
> —*Lao-tzu*

Roles of the Leader

The leader's role is to help the party achieve the team's objectives in a safe, enjoyable manner, with minimum impact on the alpine environment. A leader must be experienced, with technical skills appropriate for the climb, but is not necessarily the most experienced in the group or the best climber. A leader should be in good enough shape to keep up, but need not be the strongest in the party. A leader does need an abundance of good judgment, common sense, and a sincere interest in the welfare of the entire party. Along the way, a leader simultaneously adopts many roles, such as the following.

Guardian of safety: The paramount concern of any party is safety, starting in the planning stage. A leader should ensure that everyone has appropriate equipment, experience, and stamina and that the route chosen is reasonable for the party and in safe condition. En route, when climbers become tired, impatient, or excited, they get careless. This can also happen if they are inexperienced. A leader learns to see these conditions as warnings and become more alert, watching, gently reminding, and even nagging when necessary. When tough

21

decisions have to be made, such as turning back due to weather or time, it is often up to the leader to initiate the unpleasant discussion before the situation becomes critical. (See Chapter 22, Safety.)

Planner: Many details need attention if a group of people is to be at the right place at the right time with the right equipment to mount a successful attempt. A leader does not have to do all the planning personally, but does bear responsibility for seeing that all necessary preparations are being attended to by someone in the group.

Expert: Giving advice when asked or when needed is an important leadership role. Training, experience, and judgment are the prerequisites for this job. A person does not have to be the party's best climber to be an effective leader, but certainly needs enough experience to have developed "mountain sense." A range of skills is needed in addition to technical climbing knowledge. Leaders should know something about equipment, navigation, first aid, rescue techniques, weather—in fact, all the topics addressed in the various chapters of this book.

Teacher: When less-experienced climbers are along, teaching becomes part of the leadership role. Usually this involves nothing more than occasional advice and demonstrations. However, if some members lack techniques required for safe progress, it may be wise to halt and conduct a little hands-on learning right then and there. Many seasoned mountaineers find that passing along their hard-won knowledge is a fulfilling experience—but it should be done with a careful touch. Novices may be embarrassed by their relative lack of skill or intimidated by the physical danger. This is no time for bullying. Instead of using the approach that says someone else is wrong, try saying, "Let me show you what works for me." The exception is when a student is doing something dangerous; then a more direct approach is needed.

Coach: This is a little different from the role of teacher. The coach helps people get past difficulties by adding encouragement and support to a base of knowledge. Often the real obstacle is lack of self-confidence. Assisting a companion through some difficulty helps that person and also keeps the entire party moving forward. Coaching effectively, helping people do their best and emerge smiling, can be one of the particular delights of leadership.

Initiator: A climb progresses by the party making a series of decisions: Where shall we make camp? Which route should we take? What time should we get up? When should we rope up? Often the decisions themselves are not hard to make, but they need to be made in a timely fashion. The function of leadership is not necessarily to dictate answers but to get the right issues on the table at the appropriate time.

Arbiter: Once a discussion is under way, differences of opinion will arise. It is good to collect opinions and get all viewpoints out into the open, but this can lead to indecision ("Which course do we select?") or argument ("You are wrong!"). Anyone in a position of leadership, whether or not formally conferred, has some leverage that can be used to advantage in these instances. If the party seems to be making a technically incorrect or dangerous decision, if tempers are rising, or if the discussion is aimlessly wandering, the weight of the leader's opinion will often settle matters and get the climb moving again.

Guardian of the environment: Climbers must do their best to leave the alpine environment undisturbed so that future generations may sample the same pleasures. Leaders should set the example by always practicing minimum-impact techniques (see Chapter 3, Camping and Food, and Chapter 7, Leave No Trace). If others fail to follow this example, they should be reminded, gently at first, insistently if necessary.

Styles of Leadership

Two broad categories characterize what leaders do.

Goal-oriented style: This has to do with process and structure—what to do, who will do it, and how. Goal-oriented leaders concentrate on making decisions and directing others.

Relationship-oriented style: This has to do with showing consideration and helping a group of people become a supportive, cooperative team. Relationship-oriented leaders take a personal interest in people and their views, consulting with them on decisions and thereby building group cohesion and morale.

Most people lean toward one style or the other, but

it is not an either/or choice. Neither style should be neglected, and effective leaders balance both styles. The proper balance depends on the nature of the party and the needs of the moment.

Each leader must develop a personal style through the process of learning the craft of mountaineering and discovering effective ways of relating to climbing companions to help them become a happy, effective team.

Beyond that, leaders should be themselves. Some people are jolly and talkative; some are more reserved. Successful leaders are found among all types of people. It is more important to be genuine than to try copying some idealized style.

Leading in a Crisis

Everyone hopes it will never happen, but sometimes things go wrong. Perhaps conditions turn dangerous or someone is injured. Then the group focus shifts from recreation to safety and survival. The leader's role also changes. If you are the designated leader, this is the time for you to switch to a decisive style. The small, informal group may find that a leader emerges. There is a clear need for coordination, and people will tend to look to the most-experienced person or the one who, for whatever reason, inspires the most confidence.

When an accident occurs, there is no time for lengthy debate. Prompt, effective action is needed, and it should be directed by someone with training and experience. Nevertheless, the leader should stay "hands off" as much as possible, directing others, maintaining an overview, and thinking ahead to the next steps.

The party should be guided by the three rules of rescue (see Chapter 24, Alpine Rescue) in managing a crisis:
- The safety of the rescuers comes first—even before that of the victim.

- Act promptly, but deliberately and calmly.
- Use procedures that have been learned and practiced; this is no time to experiment.

It is easy to think of all climbing mishaps as life-and-death situations in which the outcome depends solely on what the rescuers do. In fact, neither is usually the case.

First, most accidents result in cuts and bruises, sprains, sometimes broken bones, but only occasionally anything worse.

Second, the outcome is usually determined by factors beyond the rescuers' control. All that can reasonably be expected is that the climb leader will draw upon training and experience to devise an appropriate plan and then carry it out as safely and effectively as conditions permit.

The best way to avoid trouble is to anticipate it. Leaders should always be thinking ahead, asking "What if?" In camp, they think of the climb; on the ascent, of the descent; in success, of retreat. They look for early signs of fatigue in companions, mentally record bivouac sites, keep track of the time, and note any changes in the weather. Everywhere on trips, leaders mentally cross bridges before reaching them; they borrow trouble. By staying a step ahead, they hope to avoid problems or to catch burgeoning ones before they become crises.

Accidents are unexpected, but you can prepare for them by taking courses, reading on the subject, and mentally rehearsing accident scenarios. First-aid training is a must. Chapter 23, First Aid, describes the prevention and treatment of medical conditions commonly experienced by mountaineers, but it is not a substitute for hands-on training. Public and private agencies

---

TIPS FOR BECOMING A LEADER

There is no simple formula for becoming a leader, but there are guidelines:
- A leader cannot be self-centered; decisions are made for the good of the party, not the leader.
- A leader's genuine interest in every party member will influence the degree to which they care about each other and will strengthen the group.
- A leader cannot pretend and cannot show off; the leader should be honest about personal limitations. Leaders should admit it when there is something they do not know—and get the group to help them figure it out.
- A sense of humor helps.

offer first-aid courses, and some climbing clubs give mountain rescue training.

Also, climbers can benefit from studying the experiences of other climbers. The American Alpine Club and the Alpine Club of Canada jointly publish *Accidents in North American Mountaineering*. This instructive annual publication contains detailed descriptions and analysis of mountaineering accidents.

ORGANIZING THE CLIMB

Even a simple climb is a complex undertaking. Once an objective is chosen, the leader needs to gather information on the approach and the climbing route itself. The party must be selected, and decisions must be made regarding what equipment is needed and who will bring it. A schedule should be made to assure that there is enough time to complete the climb with a margin for contingencies. Everyone needs transportation to the trailhead. And in the days leading up to the climb, snow conditions and weather trends should be monitored. The checklist in Table 21-1 is a useful guide to this process.

Researching the Climb

Typically, climbers research the trip so they will know what to expect and can prepare accordingly. Guidebooks are available covering most popular climbing areas. They usually have written descriptions of approaches and routes, maps, drawings, and sometimes photos. Topographic maps are invaluable—be sure to know how to read them (see Chapter 5, Navigation).

Some climbing clubs keep files of trip reports from their outings; these can be valuable both in themselves and because they often give the names of those who went on the climb. Firsthand information from someone who has recently done the route can add significantly to information you find in guidebooks. For peaks on public land, government agencies such as those in charge of national parks or forests can be good sources of information. Be sure to check for permit requirements, access restrictions, and fees (see "Permits and Fees," below).

For a full discussion of researching a route, see "Gather Route Information" in Chapter 6, Wilderness Travel.

Checking Conditions and Weather

The understanding of current and anticipated route conditions and weather remains as much an art as it is a science. However, mountaineers have ever-increasing access to weather and current route conditions, primarily via the Internet. The amount of information available for a given area, mountain, or specific route will vary greatly, and for many ranges and mountains, little or no current information is readily available.

Useful Internet sites include those of local and regional governments, national or regional parks, and private recreation areas, and those that detail weather and road conditions. Some of these sites include real-time weather and web cams for an up-to-the-minute view of conditions. Local climbing sites can also be useful for current route conditions, or you may be able to post a question. However, the best source of information concerning current route conditions will be from a reliable individual who has recently been on the mountain and route you are considering; a phone call to a park office, climbing shop, bush pilot, or friend in the area is a good idea. This is especially true if the climb involves a long drive or approach.

The "art" portion of understanding conditions and weather forecasting involves knowing how a change in weather will affect the route and your climbing objectives. In many areas the only certainty about the weather is that it will change. How will specific changes in temperature, wind, humidity, and precipitation affect your climb? Having alternate objectives in mind is a good idea and will help you to avoid "forcing" a climb—nearly always a bad decision.

Permits and Fees

Permit, registration, and recreational fee requirements vary greatly from region to region. Many publicly owned parks, forests, and wilderness areas have some form of governmental regulation. Typically, regulations are designed to preserve the ecology of an area or to increase the value of the wilderness experience. Some are in place for the safety of visitors; others are in place to gather fees for rescue or for maintaining an area's infrastructure; others still may limit where you can camp, which can affect the logistics of a climb.

For popular climbing areas or specific climbing

TABLE 21-1. CHECKLIST FOR ORGANIZING AND LEADING A CLIMB

BEFORE THE CLIMB

Research the route

Review guidebooks and maps.

Talk with others who have done the route.

Determine the technical level and any special problems of the route.

Estimate the levels of climbing skill and physical condition required.

Determine whether wilderness permits or reservations are required, and obtain if necessary.

Determine optimum party size.

Determine equipment needs

Personal equipment: clothing, boots, food, camping equipment, crampons, ice ax, helmet, other technical gear.

Shared equipment: tents, stoves, ropes, hardware.

Make arrangements for sharing tents, cooking equipment, and climbing gear

Research the approach

Driving route: check to be sure backcountry roads are open.

Hiking route: check trail conditions.

Develop a trip itinerary

Estimate: Check weather forecast and avalanche conditions.

    Miles/hours of driving   Leave trip itinerary with a responsible person.

    Miles/hours of hiking to high camp or start of climb

    Hours to summit

    Hours back to cars

ON THE WAY

Make a final check of weather forecast and avalanche conditions.

Register with park or forest agencies if required.

AT THE TRAILHEAD

Check equipment and discuss plan

Personal equipment: make sure everyone has enough food, clothing, and essential equipment; inadequately equipped climbers should not continue.

Shared equipment: make an inventory of tents, stoves, ropes, and hardware.

Redistribute group equipment, if necessary, to equalize loads.

Discuss the plan: route, campsites, time schedule, expected hazards.

ON THE APPROACH

Keep the party together. Agree to regroup at specified times or places—especially at trail junctions.

Decide on formation of rope teams.

ON THE CLIMB

Establish a turnaround time. Continuously evaluate, and adjust that time based on actual conditions encountered if appropriate.

Keep rope teams close enough to be in communication with each other.

ON THE WAY OUT

Assign a "trail sweep."   Regroup periodically.

Be sure that no one leaves the trailhead until everyone is out and all cars have been started.

21

routes, it may be necessary to obtain a reservation a year or more in advance. Some areas, on the other hand, have a first-come-first-served approach to permitting. In either case, the time required to get a permit, and the hours in which the permit will be issued, should be calculated as part of the overall climb logistics. If there is any question about regulations, it is best to call ahead to get the latest information. As with the case of changeable weather and route conditions, the lack of permit availability may require a change in plans.

Forming the Party

Party Strength

A climbing party must have adequate strength in order to have a safe, enjoyable, and successful trip. Strength refers to the group's ability to accomplish the climb and to cope with situations that may arise. The party's strength is determined by the mountaineering proficiency of the members, their physical condition, the size of the party, and their equipment. Intangibles such as morale, the members' degree of commitment to the climb, and the quality of leadership also affect party strength.

A strong party consists of several experienced, proficient climbers, well equipped and in good condition. What constitutes weakness is not as easy to define because a party is strong or weak only in relation to its goals. On a very challenging climb, the addition of a single ineffective member would make a party too weak. On easier trips, a party may be strong enough if it has only two strong climbers and several weaker ones; in fact, this is common on guided climbs. A party with no experienced members is weak in any situation.

Researching the route helps determine what party strength is needed for a particular climb. Is the route or the approach physically arduous? What level of technical challenge does it pose? Is the place so remote that the party will be completely on its own, or are there likely to be many other people in the vicinity?

Who Should Go?

Experience: Every member of a climbing party must be up to the challenge, both physically and technically. Some climbers will go with only proven companions when they are attempting routes near the limit of their abilities. When a leader is considering inclusion of a climber whom the leader does not know, some questions should be asked. Experience is the surest indicator of ability; someone who has climbed several times at a given level is probably capable of doing so again. Climbing skills should match the chosen route's requirements. For instance, experience gained from an indoor climbing gym will not necessarily translate to an alpine environment. Expedition leaders sometimes even request written résumés, but for a weekend climb, a bit of probing conversation is probably enough to ascertain a person's fitness. However, leaders should be aware that inexperienced people may not realize they are unprepared for the planned climb.

A party that includes novices, or even experienced people who have never before climbed at the route's required level of skill, will need veteran climbers who are willing and able to coach. The climb almost surely will take longer, and the chance of success will be reduced. Be sure everyone in the party understands this situation and accepts it.

Often the group is formed before the objective is selected. Several climbers may decide to "get together and do something." Then the selection process is reversed and it becomes a matter of picking a climb to fit the group. It is important to gauge everyone's skill and stamina and to choose a peak that the party can realistically attempt safely. Usually the weakest member is the limiting factor.

Compatibility: Fortunately, most people seem to be on their best behavior while they are on climbs. The unspoken knowledge that climbing companions will soon be literally holding one another's lives in their hands does much to promote accommodation. Nevertheless, consider compatibility when you are forming a climbing party, especially for a long or arduous trip. Expedition literature is filled with engaging tales of squabbling parties. To say the least, dissension in a climbing party is no fun. It may reduce the party's chance of success; it is guaranteed to eliminate much of the enjoyment and can even compromise safety.

People who are known to dislike each other should not be on the same climb. The tensions and close proximity of the climb situation will only exacerbate their animosity. If two people are not getting along during the climb, other party members should do their best to keep the situation from erupting into open conflict.

How Many Should Go?

The size of the party must be appropriate to the objective. Both strength and speed should be considered—and sometimes these two factors are at odds.

Minimum: The Climbing Code given in Chapter 1, First Steps, recommends three climbers as the minimum for safety: If one climber is hurt, the second can go for help while the third stays with the injured person. Another good conservative rule recommends at least two rope teams for safe travel on a glacier: If one team is pinned down holding a colleague who has fallen into a crevasse, the second team is there to effect the rescue.

These rules are general guidelines for minimum party size, but the specifics of the proposed trip may introduce other considerations. A prolonged wilderness venture may require a larger group to carry equipment and supplies, as well as to provide better backup in case of emergency. Some rock climbs require double-rope rappels on the descent. This dictates a minimum of two rope teams unless a single team wants to carry two ropes. Technical rock and ice climbs are best done with just two climbers on each rope; for these climbs, whatever the size of the party, there should always be an even number of climbers.

Sometimes speed is safety, and experienced alpinists know that a larger group always moves more slowly. On certain routes, for example, climbers must move quickly to ensure finishing before dark, and fewer climbers are less likely to start dangerous rockfall. As a general rule, the more difficult the route, the smaller the group should be. In the extreme case, some long technical climbs are done by parties of just two fast, experienced people, despite the general rule that three is the minimum safe party size.

Maximum: Maximum party size is determined by considerations of speed and efficiency, by concerns about environmental impact, or by land-use regulations. A large group can carry more gear and offer more helpers in case of emergency, but a bigger party is not necessarily a safer one. A larger party tends to get more spread out, can start bigger avalanches, and may kick down more loose rock.

Large groups have the potential to damage the fragile alpine environment. They also erode the wilderness experience. Park and wilderness areas typically have party size limits (often twelve people maximum) to reduce impact and preserve aesthetic values. At the very least, these limits must be respected. Responsible mountaineers may even choose to impose tighter restrictions on themselves in particularly fragile places.

Equipment

The party needs to make decisions about equipment, both personal and group.

Personal equipment is what each climber must bring—ice ax, pack, and clothing, for example. Some personal items, such as crampons or avalanche transceivers, are useful only if everybody brings them, so coordination is essential. In a large party, someone should take the lead in coordinating equipment.

Group equipment is shared: tents, stoves and pots, food, ropes, racks, and snow shovels are examples. Someone needs to determine what is needed, survey the climbers to see who owns what, and then decide who will bring which items.

The party can give itself a margin of safety by planning to arrive at the trailhead with a little extra equipment. Surplus gear can be left out of view in vehicles, but if conditions are more severe than anticipated, or if someone forgets an item or fails to show up, then the party may still be adequately equipped.

Leaders should double-check their own gear before they leave home. It is embarrassing for the leader to forget some critical piece of equipment.

Time Management

Mountaineers can never be more than visitors to the alpine world. On every trip there comes a time when climbers run out of daylight, supplies, or good weather; then it is time to return to lowland homes. Time has to be carefully rationed on a climb, and the important thing is not how fast to go but how wisely and well to use your time.

Establish a schedule before the climb. Estimate the length of each segment and allow some extra time for the unexpected. A typical estimate might be what is shown in Table 21-2.

TABLE 21-2. ESTIMATING TRIP TIME	
Trip Segment	**Estimated Time**
Hike up the trail	2.0 hours
Cross-country approach	1.0 hour
The climb itself	4.0 hours
Time on the summit	1.0 hour
Descent time	2.0 hours
Return to the trail	1.0 hour
Hike out	1.5 hours
Total time estimate	12.5 hours
Contingencies	2.0 hours
Total time allowance	14.5 hours

In the estimate shown in Table 21-2, if it gets dark at 9:00 P.M. and the climbers want to be back at the trailhead by 8:00 P.M., they must start at 5:30 A.M.

Setting a turnaround time is a good practice. In the example just given, the party estimates 4.5 hours from summit to trailhead for the descent, with no margin for the unexpected. They might decide it is reasonable to allow 5.5 hours. This means they must be descending by 3:30 P.M. or risk walking out in the dark.

Most guidebooks give times for popular climbs and sometimes for the approaches as well. Keep in mind, though, that times vary greatly from party to party. Experience with a particular guidebook will indicate whether its estimates tend to be faster or slower than your personal times; adjust accordingly. Another good source for time estimates is someone who has done the climb.

If no information is available, use rules of thumb based on experience. For example, many climbers have found that they can average 2 miles (3+ kilometers) per hour on an easy trail and 1,000 vertical feet (300 vertical meters) per hour on a nontechnical approach with light packs.

Avoid scheduling important business meetings, airplane flights, or social events for several hours after the scheduled end of a trip. Climbs frequently take significantly longer than expected. Climbing companions will not be happy if they have to turn back short of the summit or stumble out in the dark because someone in the party has a plane to catch.

Planning for Self-Reliance

When should the climb organizers allow themselves to feel that their preparation is adequate? When is it enough? A good way to gauge is to ask whether the party has the people, proficiency, and equipment it needs to be self-reliant under normal circumstances. In the event of a serious accident, the party should call upon nearby climbers, and when needed, the party should request assistance from mountain rescue groups (see Chapter 24, Alpine Rescue).

Having "a little extra": Any climbing party should be prepared to take care of itself in case of a minor mishap or downturn in the weather. In practice, this means having "a little extra" to provide a margin of safety: extra time, extra clothing, extra food, extra flashlight batteries, extra climbing hardware, and, above all, extra reserves of strength. As a general rule, climbers should plan to be self-sufficient for 24 hours in excess of the planned trip and understand that if help is needed, it may be delayed by weather and/or terrain. Balancing the benefit of extra supplies against the drag of their weight is an art every climber must develop.

Leaving an itinerary with a responsible person: Leave a copy of the climb itinerary with a responsible person at home, specifying when the party expects to return and how long the person should wait before notifying authorities if the party is overdue. Be realistic when estimating how long the climb will take. Specify which authorities are to be notified if the party is overdue. For example, in the United States, the National Park Service has responsibility for mountain rescue in national parks; in most other areas of the United States, it is the county sheriff.

Carrying wireless (cell) phones: Wireless telephones are becoming more popular among mountaineers as the technology improves while their weight and cost decline. They can dramatically shorten the time it takes to summon rescuers. The devices are also useful for telling people back home that the party will be late but is not in trouble and, thus, can be used to avoid unnecessary rescue efforts.

Understanding the limits of cell phones is as important as understanding their usefulness: The batteries can be depleted, and they are unable to transmit or receive in many mountain locations. Cell phones should be viewed as an adjunct to, not a substitute for, self-reliance. No party should set out ill prepared or inadequately equipped, or attempt a route beyond the ability of its members, with the notion that they will just call for help if needed. This attitude will imperil both the climbing party and the rescuers who may have to help them out.

On the Climb

Before the party leaves the trailhead, take a few minutes to check that all necessary equipment and supplies are in the climbers' packs. Anyone who has been climbing very long has had a weekend ruined by a missing but critical item. Some climbers even use a written inventory checklist as a memory aid while they are packing.

On the approach and on the climb, set a steady pace, not necessarily a fast one. In the long run, the party cannot move faster than its slowest member; progress may even be slowed if that person is reduced to exhaustion. The important thing is to keep moving steadily. Periodic rest stops for the whole party are more efficient than random halts whenever someone decides to stop.

A climbing party should stay together—not necessarily in a tight knot, but at least close enough to be in communication with one another. After all, mountaineers climb in groups partly because there is some safety in numbers. That safety is compromised when the party splits. Typically, the stronger members forge ahead, leaving those most likely to need help isolated from those best able to give it. The danger of getting separated is greatest on the technical portions of a climb, where the more-skilled climbers move much faster, or on the descent, where some want to sprint while others may be dragging due to fatigue.

A small party of friends will naturally tend to stick together. Problems are more likely with larger groups. A large party usually benefits from having a designated leader, and one reason is that the leader can coordinate its movement. Climbers should be free to hike up the trail at their own pace, but ought to regroup at designated rendezvous points, especially at:

■ Trail junctions—to make sure everyone goes the right way

■ Danger spots (such as hazardous stream crossings)—in case anyone needs help
■ The bottom of glissades—because they naturally tend to split the party

It may be wise to appoint a strong member as trail sweep, especially on the descent, to ensure there are no stragglers.

A leader need not be at the front of the party. In fact, many prefer to lead from the middle, to better keep an eye on the whole group. However, the leader should be ready to swing into the forefront when a difficulty arises, such as a routefinding puzzle or a patch of demanding technical terrain.

A leader's responsibility is to get things done, but not necessarily to do them. Delegating tasks has a host of benefits. It allows you to maintain an overview of the entire trip, rather than being tied down by every little problem and decision. It builds team spirit by giving people a chance to get involved and be useful. Also, delegation fosters individual responsibility by clearly demonstrating that doing and deciding are not the tasks of the leader alone. If someone is having difficulty and needs special help, a strong, experienced climber might be delegated the role of personal coach. In a larger group, especially in a teaching situation, the leader should appoint an assistant who can help keep things moving and who can take over if the leader is incapacitated.

BECOMING A LEADER

The responsibility of leadership is a burden, but the job can have great rewards. It gives the experienced alpinist an opportunity to pass along knowledge gained over the years: how to set a measured pace, how to read terrain and pick a route, how to deal with difficulties of many sorts. Mountaineers do not climb because they must; they climb because they love mountains. Climb leaders help others enjoy the sport, and that can be deeply satisfying.

Some climbers may never want to take on the role of leader, but they will find that possessing a certain degree of leadership is almost inevitable as they gain experience. A party naturally tends to look to its more

21

seasoned members for guidance, especially in a crisis. Therefore, all climbers should give some forethought to what they would do if they were suddenly called upon to take charge.

Climbers who do aspire to leadership should make it their business to climb with people they regard as capable leaders. Study them; observe how they organize the trip, make decisions, and work with people. Offer to help in order to participate in some of these activities. Veteran leaders report that they think ahead, anticipating problems that might arise and concocting solutions. This type of mental rehearsal is excellent training for future leaders. Climbers should develop the habit of thinking about the entire climb and the whole party, not just their part of it.

Studying respected leaders is always worthwhile, but it may be a mistake to copy anyone too closely. A group must believe that its leader is genuine, and therefore all leaders must develop their own style. Exercising leadership is not always easy, but it should be natural. For example, a reserved type should not strain to act outgoing. Anyone who has technical skill, confidence, and a sincere interest in the party's welfare can succeed as a leader.

On your first time out as a leader, choose a climb comfortably within your abilities. Perhaps invite a proficient friend, someone to rely on. Spend some extra time organizing, and seek input from the more experienced members of the party. Be sure to delegate in order to take advantage of their skills. Do not make an issue of the fact that this is your debut as a leader; that will only undermine the group's confidence.

The Climbing Code in Chapter 1, First Steps, is a sound set of guidelines for making leadership decisions. It is deliberately conservative. Following the code may cost you some summits, but it is unlikely to cost a life. Seasoned leaders may draw on experience to safely modify some of the rules, but they are not likely to depart from it radically because the code embodies a commonsense approach to safe mountaineering.

Everyone a Leader

Everyone on a climb needs to be a full partner in the twin tasks of moving the group safely toward its goal and of building group cohesion. In other words, each individual must share leadership responsibility. Individual leadership means, for example, being aware of the group and its progress: Is someone lagging behind? Ask whether there is a problem, offer encouragement, and look for ways to help. A group of climbers is weakened whenever the climbers become separated from each other. Work at being aware of where climbing companions are at all times, and help to keep the party together. When you are out front and moving fast, remember to look behind you from time to time. When you are too far ahead, stop and let the group catch up—then let them have a breather before you start off again.

Take part in routefinding. Study guidebooks and maps to become familiar with the approach and the climbing route. The climbing party is much less likely to get lost if everyone is actively involved in navigation. Use the map, compass, and route description frequently to always be oriented and know where the party is.

Everyone should participate in the group decision-making. Each person's experience is a resource for the party, but that resource goes untapped if that person fails to speak up.

Establishing a supportive atmosphere is one very important role of leadership. People need to know that their companions care about them and will help them. Be part of this effort: Help set up a tent, fetch water, carry the rope, share a cookie. Morale is intangible, but it makes a party stronger. Morale is often the deciding factor in party success, and it is always the deciding factor in making the climb enjoyable. Morale is everybody's job.

Assume responsibility also for your own knowledge, skill, and preparedness. Research the climb before committing yourself to it; make sure it is within your abilities. Be properly supplied and equipped. If you have questions about whether the climb is appropriate for you, or about what gear to take, ask your companions in advance. If you ever think that you are getting in over your head, speak up. Better to get some help over a rough spot or even quit the climb than to create an emergency. Thinking about the party, its welfare, and how you can contribute is in itself preparation—perhaps the very best preparation—for leadership.

21

22
CHAPTER

Safety

LEARNING FROM EXPERIENCE ■ OBJECTIVE HAZARDS ■
SPHERE OF ACCEPTABLE RISK ■ JUDGMENT

No mountaineer begins a climb with plans of getting hurt. Yet every year,
climbing accidents affect both novice and experienced climbers. This entire book
imparts knowledge and techniques that can prevent injuries from climbing
accidents. This chapter introduces principles that support safe climbing:
understanding the causes of mountaineering accidents, dealing with
the objective hazards posed by a climb, determining the party's
tolerance of risk, and learning how to exercise good judgment
regarding the party's skill level and strength,
especially as conditions change.

> As an alpinist who carries a long list of dead friends and partners, I approach the mountains differently than most. I go to them intending to survive, which I define as a success. A new route or the summit is a bonus.
> —*Mark Twight*, Extreme Alpinism *(1999)*

LEARNING FROM EXPERIENCE

There is no question that learning from your mistakes in the mountains helps you develop better judgment. However, your mistakes had best be small ones, because the mountains can be unforgiving of errors. It is best to learn from the experience of others. For the beginning mountaineer, this means seeking qualified instruction and skilled climbing partners. For mountaineers at all levels, this means studying reports of climbing accidents to learn what can go wrong and to apply the lessons others have learned to their own climbing.

Causes of Mountaineering Accidents

One of the best sources of mountaineering accident information is *Accidents in North American Mountaineering,* published annually by the American Alpine Club and the Alpine Club of Canada. By studying each year's issue, you can learn from the misfortunes of others and continue your personal education in the proper use of equipment, technique, and judgment. These reports also influence climbers' attitudes toward climbing safety, because few people can read them without gaining a better appreciation of the consequences of accidents in the mountains.

According to *Accidents in North American Mountaineering,* the following are the most frequent causes of mountaineering accidents.

Most Frequent Immediate Causes
1. Fall or slip on rock
2. Slip on snow or ice
3. Falling rock, ice, or object

Most Frequent Contributing Causes
1. Climbing unroped
2. Exceeding one's abilities
3. Having inadequate equipment/clothing
4. Placing no/inadequate protection
5. Weather

OBJECTIVE HAZARDS

When climbers speak of objective hazards, they are talking about the physical hazards associated with a climbing route. Common objective hazards are:
- Rockfall
- Loose rocks (rockfall induced by the climbing party)
- Unstable snow
- Cornices and icefalls
- Crevasses and moats
- Exposure (the distance a climber could fall)
- High altitude (its effects on the human body)
- Weather

Most of these hazards are present regardless of human activity; you should consider them not only when you are choosing a route but also as the climb progresses. Strategies for preventing accidents due to these hazards are presented throughout this book.

Some objective hazards are predictable, such as loose rock in a gully or visible crevasses in a glacier. Other objective hazards, however, may be unpredictable, such as glacier crevasses hidden by a fresh snow cover. Judgment regarding how, when, and where to cross such a hazard—or whether to cross it at all—determines the amount of risk a party takes. This is especially true for difficult climbs at high altitude, where the margin of safety is slim. Despite using the best judgment they can, parties on such climbs have the odds stacked against them and must sometimes trust their luck if they are to survive. Most climbers will not be comfortable with this level of risk.

It is important that climbers match their skill level to the hazards they will face. Good questions to ask yourself when you are considering the objective hazards on a route are:
- What are the objective hazards?

22

- How can I avoid them or protect myself from them?
- How should I adjust my plans to respond to the objective hazards?
- Does everyone in my party have the skills needed to deal with the hazards safely?

Once you are on the route, continue to ask these questions and make decisions accordingly. Consider how the climbing party is performing—both mentally and physically—and how changes in the weather may impact the risks posed by the objective hazards. Be ready to adjust your plans if necessary.

SPHERE OF ACCEPTABLE RISK

Climbing involves risk, and the level of risk an individual climber is willing to accept is a personal decision. Some climbers are happy in limiting their mountaineering adventures to an occasional snowfield traverse or rock scramble. Others seek out the most challenging peaks that require commitment, the best gear, and advanced technique.

A useful model for visualizing risk is a sphere or bubble, with the climber at the center (fig. 22-1). Anything within the sphere is what that person considers

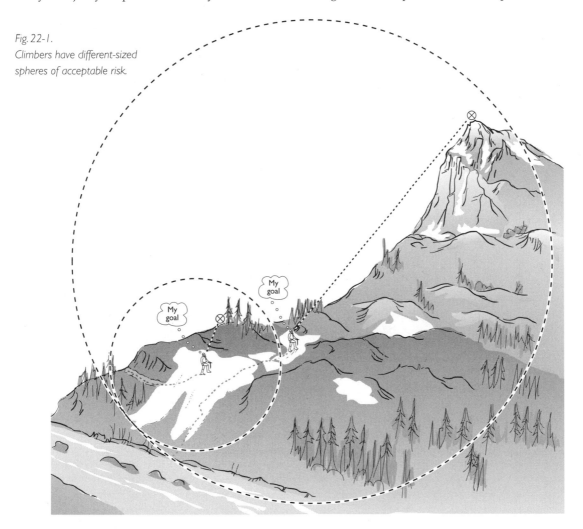

Fig. 22-1.
Climbers have different-sized spheres of acceptable risk.

22

an acceptable risk. Outside the sphere are risks the climber chooses not to accept. Most climbers probably have a good idea what mountaineering risks are acceptable to them. The diameter of each climber's sphere depends on skill level, equipment available, individual goals, and, most importantly, personal comfort level with the objective hazards encountered while climbing.

As you gain experience, your sphere tends to grow as you become more confident in all kinds of mountain terrain. Yet most climbers will reach a point when they are satisfied with the level of risk they are taking and wish to take no more. The spheres of some climbers may also get smaller if they scale back their climbing goals based on family responsibilities or in response to an accident involving themselves or friends. It is important to understand what risks are acceptable to everyone in a climbing party.

Choose routes that are within the party's sphere of acceptable risk. This may be done from the comfort of home by consulting guidebooks and talking to people who have tried the route that the party is studying. Find out what the hazards are, what preventive measures are necessary, and whether the resulting plans are within the party's sphere of acceptable risk. If not, plan a different route. On some trips, it may be appropriate to turn back or pick a new route if the selected route becomes harder than what the party members are comfortable with or if it requires more equipment than the climbers have brought with them. Often there are many ways up a mountain, and it may be possible to reach a sought-after summit without subjecting the party to risk outside of its bubble.

JUDGMENT

It is often easy to see in hindsight what went wrong on a climb. In the middle of the climb, however, exercising good judgment is rarely that easy. Many factors can influence a climber's judgment, and understanding them may help each climber make better decisions.

Desire to reach the summit is probably the most common factor affecting your judgment while you are climbing. This is especially true on expeditions and even on climbing vacations, in which considerable time and effort have been invested toward the goal. It may

help if the party agrees in advance that the first goal of the trip is for everyone to return safely. If conditions take a turn for the worse, reflecting on that goal may help the party find alternatives for safe travel or make it easier to decide to retreat.

Lack of knowledge may also influence judgment, especially for newer climbers. A party may not realize the seriousness of the objective hazards. Or they may misuse a new piece of equipment. Over time they may forget some of the things they learned as novice climbers and develop some dangerous habits.

Be aware that practicing a dangerous habit or making a poor judgment can have positive consequences that hide the real risk being faced. For example, you may cross an avalanche slope without releasing the snowpack or you may set up a weak belay anchor that is never tested by a fall. However, the difference between safe travel and an accident may be just a few degrees in temperature or one leader fall. Do not rely on luck to avoid injury. Continually update your knowledge of climbing safety and evaluate your decisions and technique to make sure you are not setting yourself up for an accident.

While you are learning to climb, other more-experienced members of the climbing party may make many of the decisions about climbing safety. It is important for you to learn how they evaluate hazards and make decisions so that you can do the same analysis later when you are climbing without them. When you are doing this, you need to evaluate what you hear and be alert for climbing advice that may not provide the level of safety you desire—it may be offered by climbers who have not yet had to pay for their errors. Keep in mind that climbers may not have all of the information they would like to have: Guidebooks cannot be expected to mention all hazards, for instance. Be alert for situations that may require different safeguards from what you expected for the climb.

Overconfidence is another human factor to consider. In the lists given earlier in this chapter, climbing beyond one's personal abilities was cited as the second most-frequent contributing cause of mountaineering accidents. It takes years to develop the judgment needed for safe climbing, but many new climbers have difficulty containing their enthusiasm for the sport. As a result, they may get into situations that are beyond their capabilities and be hurt in the process. Images of experts leading or soloing sheer rock and ice couloirs are inspiring, but you may not appreciate the years of training and experience that prepared the pictured climbers for the route. Nor do the pictures reveal the detailed process of risk evaluation that the climbers undoubtedly undertook.

Many factors contribute to a successful climb: good routefinding, technical skills suited to the task, favorable weather, stamina, and efficient use of time. Problems with any one of these factors can put party members at risk. When problems arise, party members need to evaluate the difficulties they encounter, discuss alternatives for overcoming them, and assess how they fit within their collective sphere of risk. Often they will find a solution that will allow them to attain their climbing goal, but at times the best solution may be to descend and try again another day.

Breaking the Chain of Poor Judgment

Often climbing accidents result from a series of problems or errors that combine to put the climbers in perilous situations. A good example may begin with a simple routefinding error: The party enters the wrong gully on the descent. Not realizing this, the climbers continue, trying to make sense out of the route description. Ultimately, they have descended so far that, even though they now realize they made a mistake, it makes more sense to fight their way down than to ascend and find the right gully. This routefinding error has of course taken extra time, and now darkness and fatigue become issues. Good decision-making becomes harder. About this time, the climbers reach the hardest part of the descent, and the party members are at greater risk of injury as they operate outside their normal sphere of acceptable risk.

This chain of poor judgment tends to happen without anyone realizing it. There are several reasons why:

- One poor judgment increases the probability that another will follow. For example, climbing beyond the party's turnaround time increases the chances that they will rush their climbing, just when they are most tired.
- Each error in judgment provides false information

that can lead to additional errors. For example, after making a routefinding error, climbers will be looking for any features that match the route description. If they find something that appears to be right, they may continue the wrong way.

- As the poor-judgment chain grows, the alternatives for a safe outcome decrease. Climbers may find themselves in a desperate situation.

> It was diabolic machinery, into the cogwheels of which all of us were imperceptibly but irretrievably being sucked—the mechanism being so complicated that it was not recognizable to the individual: every way that might have led us out eventually became blocked by the taking of single decisions, which by themselves would never have been so critical, but in their conjunction opened the death trap for seven people up at 8,000 meters.
> —*Kurt Diemberger,* The Endless Knot *(1991)*

Learn to recognize the complicated machinery of the poor-judgment chain. For safety's sake, keep alert to the clues that the party may no longer be fully aware of its situation. Watch for these signs:

Failure to meet planned targets: Consider why targets are not being met; should party strength, routefinding, or other factors be addressed?

Preoccupation with one aspect of a climb: Are other factors changing, such as weather or party strength, while climbers focus on a hard section of the climb?

Violating the sphere of acceptable risk: Is the party climbing a route that is beyond the capabilities of its members?

Unresolved discrepancies: Are the features being climbed inconsistent with the route description?

Gut feeling that something is wrong: Could your body be conveying something that your mind has not yet processed?

These steps can help break the poor-judgment chain:

1. Be willing to recognize your own poor judgment. Seek feedback on personal decisions—from your own senses and from the climbers around you. For this process to work, there must be open communication among climbing partners and teams.

22

2. Check for stress. A moderate level of stress sharpens your ability to make good decisions while you are climbing. A very low level of stress breeds complacency and inattention; too much stress brings panic.
3. Be alert for groups of poor judgments. If you recognize one poor judgment, look for others before you decide that only the first one is affecting the situation.
4. Review an original poor judgment as soon as the poor-judgment chain has been broken. This review provides the feedback you need to avoid beginning a similar poor-judgment chain in the future.

The Master Warning Panel

Here is a mental technique for improving your decision-making. Imagine a master warning panel in your mind, with green lights indicating informed awareness, yellow caution lights, and red warning lights (fig. 22-2). The panel is connected to your senses, to your brain, and to someplace deep down in your stomach.

What turns on the caution and warning lights? That is up to each climber. What is your personal level of strength? Are you out of shape or fatigued? The yellow warning lights should go on. Deteriorating weather conditions should turn on at least one red light, as will continuation of the climb beyond the planned turn-around time or an extremely long, difficult approach hike. Are some members of the party inexperienced or has a climbing partner seemed inattentive while belaying? Expect yellow lights, which could easily turn to red. The caution lights should go on whenever a party is short on equipment, water, or food. When a route's difficulty is at the limits of any of the climbers' ability, caution lights should go on. High-altitude climbs have inherent risks that might cause a yellow warning light to go on. Plus each climber can add other considerations as the situation warrants, such as "avalanche danger" or "exposure." And as for those connections to the stomach—pay closest attention anytime a gut feeling sets off a caution or warning light.

When you are visualizing a personal master warning panel, think back to your last climb. At any point in that climb, would your panel have shown yellow or red lights? Would enough of them have lit up to indicate that you were moving outside your sphere of acceptable risk? A warning panel bright with yellow or red lights is a signal to end the climb before an accident happens. Yet most climbers have read accounts of climbs on which their personal warning panels would have been lit up like a Christmas tree.

Give the warning panel a try on your next climb. First decide just how your panel will look, and what lights and gauges it will display. Then think about which yellow or red lights could light up without making it mandatory that you discontinue the climb. A personal warning panel, activated by an understanding of the many factors contributing to mountaineering safety, will help you make good decisions as you climb.

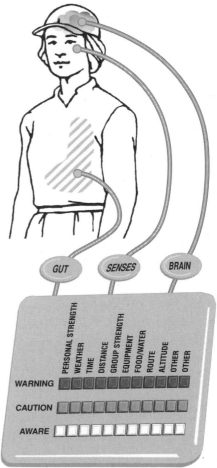

Fig. 22-2.
Master warning panel.

23
CHAPTER

First Aid

PLANNING AND PREPARATION ■ **THE SEVEN STEPS IN ACCIDENT RESPONSE** ■ **MOUNTAIN MALADIES** ■ **INJURIES** ■ **FIRST-AID KIT**

Accidents and illness can strike mountaineers, just as they can hit urban dwellers at home. However, mountaineers are far away from expert help and must be able to manage the situation, providing first aid to the patient. The mountain environment and the physical demands of wilderness travel can entail not only everyday injuries and ailments, but may also introduce new hazards to your well-being.

The most artful mountaineers grow adept at minimizing the hazards of life in the mountains, preventing exposure to risk whenever possible. It is vastly preferable for the members of a mountaineering party to be skillful in preventing injuries to themselves than to being experts at treating injuries after they occur.

Even if you are aware of accident prevention, you could become the individual who requires first-aid help:

The first-aid expert of the group could become the patient. Therefore, all members of the party should be trained in first aid through the mountaineering-oriented first-aid courses offered by many organizations.

The fun part of learning to climb certainly is not the first-aid training. It is tempting to assume that reading first-aid texts carefully is sufficient training. Unfortunately, first aid is very much like any other skill. You can read, even memorize, all of the greatest texts on skiing, and yet if you do not practice, you simply will not be a good skier. The same is true with first aid; to be truly competent in first aid, you must practice it. This is because of two elements of serious first-aid situations: uncertainty and alarm.

In most serious first-aid situations, there is a large element of uncertainty: uncertainty about what happened; uncertainty about the nature, extent, or seriousness of injuries; uncertainty about what should be done and what the outcome will be. No one who is injured wears a big sign that says precisely what is injured and how to care for it. Sometimes it is obvious, but more often it is not.

A second fundamental element of first-aid situations is that people react to them with alarm. Serious accidents are frightening and tend to flood people's minds with a spectrum of emotions, which can interfere with a calm, thoughtful, rational response. Although alarm is perhaps the most difficult challenge to overcome, practicing first-aid scenarios such as those included in many outdoor first-aid classes can help you respond well even when the situation is enormously stressful.

It is strongly recommended that all mountaineers take one of the many outdoor first-aid classes offered around the country, and that they refresh their skills over time, because only with practice will they develop solid first-aid skills.

There are essentially two categories of first-aid skills: the framework for responding to an accident, and the techniques for treating specific conditions. This chapter first presents the framework, in the form of seven simple steps that are appropriate responses to most backcountry accidents. Following that is a brief discussion of medical conditions that are more frequently encountered in the backcountry. However, many of the essential first-aid skills, such as cardiopulmonary resuscitation (CPR), splinting, and wound care are omitted because this book is not intended to be a comprehensive first-aid text. As noted above, these skills are best learned if practiced through outdoor first-aid classes.

PLANNING AND PREPARATION

Before leaving the trailhead, a mountaineering party should have a designated first-aid leader, as well as a clearly identified climb leader. The climb leader is responsible for the welfare of the entire party; the first-aid leader assumes leadership of any first-aid scenario in the field. If evacuation of a patient becomes necessary, the climb leader—not the first-aid leader—orchestrates the evacuation.

The climb leader and first-aid leader should check with party members to learn of any relevant medical conditions (such as an allergy to bee stings) or use of medications (such as insulin for diabetes). Opinions differ on the best format for gathering this information. Some climb leaders like to ask for medical information individually from each party member in advance of the trip. The information is then shared with any assistant leader and with the first-aid leader. This approach protects individual privacy, but it has the disadvantage of not giving other party members the information they might need to be most helpful to a stricken person. Thus another approach is to ask for this information from the group as a whole, at the trailhead.

Before departing, the leaders should confirm that the party has sufficient first-aid supplies. See "First-Aid Kit" at the end of this chapter.

THE SEVEN STEPS IN ACCIDENT RESPONSE

An orderly reaction to an emergency can make all the difference in how party members translate their first-aid knowledge into effective action. The effective response to an accident in the mountains can be simplified into seven steps, as shown in Table 23-1. The rest of this section covers these seven steps in detail.

TABLE 23-1. THE SEVEN STEPS IN ACCIDENT RESPONSE	
Step	**Action to Take**
1. Take charge of the situation.	The climb leader is in charge of the entire group's welfare and any evacuation efforts; the first-aid leader is in charge of the first-aid effort.
2. Approach the patient safely.	Protect the patient from further injury, and protect the party by choosing a safe approach to the patient.
3. Perform emergency rescue and urgent first aid.	The first-aid leader directs moving the injured person to a safer location if necessary and conducts a primary examination to identify and treat potentially fatal conditions. The first-aid leader checks ABCD—Airway + Breathing + Circulation + Deadly bleeding—and administers CPR if needed.
4. Protect the patient.	The first-aid leader is alert for the signs and symptoms of shock and provides insulation, dry clothing, pain management, and psychological support, including reassurance and sensitive care.
5. Check for other injuries.	The first-aid leader conducts a thorough secondary examination and records findings on an accident report form (see Figure 23-1).
6. Make a plan.	The climb leader decides how best to evacuate the injured person.
7. Carry out the plan.	Keep the needs of the patient in mind and constantly monitor the patient's condition and the progress of the plan.

Step 1: Take Charge of the Situation

Establish the leadership roles that were planned at the trailhead. The climb leader is responsible for decisions that involve the welfare of the entire party, such as surveying the accident scene to determine objective hazards, and the first-aid leader directs all first-aid-related actions.

Survey the accident scene, noting all victims, current objective hazards, and the likely cause of the accident. See whether anyone can provide an account of what happened and when.

If there are several patients, triage decisions are needed to direct the party's limited resources toward actions likely to have the most benefit and away from actions that are either trivial or hopeless. Triage decisions are modified as each patient's condition and triage status change. In a serious accident with numerous patients, triage consists of sorting patients into groups, based on priority in receiving assistance.

First priority goes to seriously injured people who have a good chance of survival if they are given immediate help; second priority is seriously injured people whose conditions are stable and who can wait perhaps an hour or two for first aid; third priority is people with minor injuries who can wait for simple first aid or can administer it themselves with a little help; the final group consists of critically injured people with very little chance of survival no matter what treatment is attempted.

Making decisions about who receives care first is a wrenching task, but it is essential to using the party's efforts to best effect. A triage viewpoint also helps in evaluating which patients are most in need of evacuation to outside medical help.

Step 2: Approach the Patient Safely

In the effort to reach an injured person, do not endanger uninjured party members, which might increase the severity of the disaster. If avalanche or rockfall is a danger, the climb leader can designate a lookout to keep watch while the first-aid effort proceeds, but everyone needs to be alert to physical limits and dangers, both present and potential. Discuss before acting.

Step 3: Perform Emergency Rescue and Urgent First Aid

At this point, the first-aid leader should move a patient *only* if one of two conditions is present:

1. The rescuer is in imminent danger in the present location.
2. The patient is in danger of further harm in the present location.

23

Absent one of these two conditions, *do not move the patient*. Patients do not have to be lying on their backs to be treated, and the risk of harm from prematurely moving the patient can be significant.

If the patient must be moved out of a danger zone, do so swiftly, safely, and without causing further injury. Note the patient's body position, and decide whether it is likely that a back or neck injury has occurred. If so, support and immobilize the injured area as you carry out further measures.

Conduct a primary examination to recognize and treat any potentially fatal conditions. Quickly note the patient's level of consciousness. The four levels of consciousness, in decreasing order of responsiveness, are:

1. Alert
2. Responsive to vocal stimuli
3. Responsive to painful stimuli
4. Unresponsive

Now check the patient's ABCD indicators:
Airway is clear of obstruction.
Breathing is spontaneous and adequate.
Circulation of blood is adequate, indicated by a beating heart and enough blood pressure to supply a pulse.
Deadly bleeding is absent.

If any of the patient's ABCD indicators do not check out, take the following actions:

Airway: If the airway is blocked, clear it.

Breathing: If not breathing, start rescue breathing.

Circulation of blood: If circulation is absent (no pulse), start CPR.

Deadly bleeding: If there is deadly bleeding, control dangerous blood loss with direct pressure over the site of hemorrhage. Do not substitute direct pressure with the use of pressure dressings, although you should use pressure dressings in conjunction with direct pressure. Direct pressure is almost always effective. If it is not, a second-level effort to stop serious bleeding is to compress the artery supplying blood to the injury site. Limb tourniquets should be used only after neither direct pressure nor compression of the relevant arterial pressure point have stemmed a life-threatening hemorrhage and only when the party is prepared for the likelihood that the affected limb will be lost.

Step 4: Protect the Patient

The first-aid leader should protect the patient from the environment (heat, cold, rain, etc.) and make every effort to maintain the patient's body temperature. Also provide the patient with as much reassurance and psychological support as possible. Initial protection from the elements can be done quickly and usually without moving the patient. As in Step 3, the patient should not be moved unless it is absolutely necessary to prevent further injury, particularly of the spine.

One of the key goals of Step 4—along with maintaining adequate breathing and blood circulation and controlling blood loss—is to prevent or limit shock. Shock is the simultaneous depression of vital body processes, including blood pressure. Ultimately, blood circulation collapses. Shock is progressive and potentially fatal. Be aware of the symptoms and signs of shock (see sidebar).

You can limit shock by insulating the patient and replacing wet garments with dry ones, to prevent body-heat loss; by providing pain management; and by offering reassurance and orientation to the patient's circumstances and surroundings. Provide fluids if the patient is able to swallow. Remain vigilant because shock may emerge later in the course of care; a patient who becomes more withdrawn and less responsive could well be drifting into shock.

At this stage, psychological support becomes important for the patient, anyone involved in helping the patient (accident responders), and any bystanders. Responders should keep an eye out for anyone behaving irrationally or in an agitated or dazed fashion. Often such individuals can be assigned a simple task that will refocus them on the work of the group. Members of the accident response party should learn the names of each patient, use their names when talking to them, and tell them the names of the accident response party members. Give the patients reasonable updates about how each person is doing and about the overall plan in progress. It is not reassuring to keep a patient "in the dark," and empty statements that "everything's going to be fine" tend to be alienating and unsettling. Keep in mind the vantage point of each patient: While you are maneuvering around the first-aid scene, avoid stepping over injured persons as if they were pieces of wood.

SYMPTOMS AND SIGNS OF SHOCK

Symptoms that may be experienced by the patient:
- Nausea
- Thirst
- Weakness
- Fear/restlessness
- Sweating
- Shortness of breath

Signs that may be noted by observers:
- Pulse rapid but weak
- Breathing rapid and shallow
- Skin cool and clammy
- Lips and nail beds blue
- Restlessness
- Face pale
- Eyes dull
- Pupils dilated
- Unresponsiveness (a late sign)

Step 5: Check for Other Injuries

Once the patient has been stabilized and treated initially for life-threatening conditions, the first-aid leader checks for other injuries. Conduct a systematic head-to-toe secondary examination, so that no injury goes undiscovered. The secondary examination can bring into view less-severe injuries and problems that could turn critical if left untreated. Only one person should perform the examination, because more than one set of hands on a patient may result in misleading findings, as well as anxiety for the injured person. (When two people attempt to do an examination, it is not uncommon for a portion of the patient to be left unexamined when each examiner assumes that the other checked it. A discussion between the examiners right there, over the patient, often ensues, leaving the patient unsure if the examiners know what they are doing.) It is important to examine bare skin while making thorough observations for possible injuries. Protect the patient from exposure to the elements, and replace clothing after examining any area of the body. Specific clues of injury that may be noted during this examination include the following:

- Deformity compared with another body part (e.g., one arm is different from the other)
- Discoloration or bruising
- Bleeding or loss of other fluids
- Swelling
- Pain or tenderness
- Limited range of motion
- Guarding of a particular body part

The person conducting the examination should use an accident report form, such as the one shown in Figure 23-1, to guide the exam. All findings must be recorded in detail on the form. The report provides essential information in the event of a change in the patient's condition or in case evacuation becomes necessary and the injured person is turned over to others for treatment.

Step 6: Make a Plan

Essentially three plans need to be made:
1. The first-aid leader makes a plan for further first aid for the patient.
2. The climb leader makes a plan for the evacuation of the patient.
3. The climb leader makes a plan for the rest of the party.

Up until now, the steps primarily have included urgent first aid and thorough assessment. Additional first aid may be required, such as splinting an injured limb. The first-aid leader makes this first part of the plan.

Next, the climb leader must make a decision about whether the patient can self-evacuate, or whether an outside evacuation is needed. A patient who is not ambulatory nearly always requires an outside evacuation. Carrying a patient requires proper equipment and a large number of people to assist and is generally beyond the capabilities of most climbing parties. Self-evacuation should *not* be attempted if there are any indications of serious head, neck, or back injuries (see "Injuries" later in this chapter). Factors to consider in deciding whether to attempt a self-evacuation (in addition to the patient's condition) include the terrain, the weather, the strength

23

© The Mountaineers

Fig. 23-1.
Accident report form.

RESCUE REQUEST
Fill Out One Form Per Victim

TIME OF INCIDENT

A.M. _____ P.M. _____ DATE _____

NATURE OF INCIDENT

FALL ON ☐ ROCK ☐ SNOW ☐ FALLING ROCK
☐ CREVASSE ☐ AVALANCHE
☐ ILLNESS ☐ EXCESSIVE ☐ HEAT ☐ COLD

BRIEF DESCRIPTION OF INCIDENT

FIRST AID GIVEN

INJURIES
(List Most Severe First)

SKIN TEMP./COLOR:

STATE OF CONSCIOUSNESS:

PAIN (Location):

RECORD:

	Initial	When leave scene
Time		
Pulse		
Respiration		

VICTIM'S NAME _____ AGE _____

ADDRESS _____

NOTIFY (Name) _____

RELATIONSHIP _____ PHONE _____

OTHER COMMENTS:

DETACH HERE—SEND OUT WITH REQUEST FOR AID
- -
TEAR HERE—KEEP THIS SECTION WITH THE VICTIM

FIRST AID/ACCIDENT REPORT FORM

START HERE	FINDINGS	FIRST AID GIVEN

Airway, Breathing, Circulation
Deadly Bleeding

ASK WHAT HAPPENED:

ASK WHERE IT HURTS:

TAKE PULSE AND RESPIRATIONS | PULSE | RESPIRATIONS

HEAD-TO-TOE EXAMINATION

HEAD: Scalp—Wounds
Ears, Nose—Fluids
Eyes—Pupils
Jaw—Stability
Mouth—Wounds

NECK: Wounds, Deformity

CHEST: Movement, Symmetry

ABDOMEN: Wounds, Rigidity

PELVIS: Stability

EXTREMITIES: Wounds, Deformity
Sensations & Movement
Pulses Below Injury

BACK: Wounds, Deformity

SKIN: Color
Temperature
Moistness

STATE OF CONSCIOUSNESS

PAIN (Location)

LOOK FOR MEDICAL ID TAG

ALLERGIES

VICTIM'S NAME _____ AGE _____

COMPLETED BY _____ DATE _____ TIME _____

23

SIDE 2 RESCUE REQUEST

EXACT LOCATION (Include Marked Map If Possible)
QUADRANGLE: _____ SECTION: _____
GPS INFO: _____
AREA DESCRIPTION: _____

TERRAIN:
- ❑ GLACIER
- ❑ BRUSH
- ❑ FLAT
- ❑ OTHER: (Describe) _____
- ❑ SNOW
- ❑ TIMBER
- ❑ MODERATE
- ❑ ROCK
- ❑ TRAIL
- ❑ STEEP

ON-SITE PLANS:
- ❑ Will Stay Put
- ❑ Will Evacuate To _____

Can Stay Overnight Safely ❑ Yes ❑ No
On-Site Equipment:
- ❑ Tent
- ❑ Flares
- ❑ Ropes
- ❑ Sleeping Bags
- ❑ Saw
- ❑ Stoves
- ❑ Ground Insulation
- ❑ Hardware
- ❑ Fuel

Other: _____

LOCAL WEATHER: _____

SUGGESTED EVACUATION:
- ❑ Carry-Out
- ❑ Lowering
- ❑ Helicopter
- ❑ Raising

EQUIPMENT NEEDED:
- ❑ Rigid Litter
- ❑ Water
- ❑ Other _____
- ❑ Food

PARTY MEMBERS REMAINING (Indicate Numbers):
_____ Scrambling Students   _____ Basic Students   _____ Basic Grads
_____ Intermediate Students   _____ Intermediate Grads

ATTACH THE PRE-TRIP LIST OF PARTY MEMBERS, including names, addresses, and phone numbers. Update the list to accurately reflect party membership and persons to notify in case of delays.
PARTY LEADERS: _____

NAMES OF MESSENGERS SENT FOR HELP: _____
WHOM TO NOTIFY TO INITIATE THE RESCUE:
IN NATIONAL PARK: Notify the Park Ranger
OUTSIDE NATIONAL PARK: Sheriff/County Police (Call 911)
IN CANADA: RCMP

VITAL SIGNS RECORD

Record TIME	BREATHS		PULSE		PULSES BELOW INJURY	PUPILS	SKIN	STATE OF CON-SCIOUS-NESS	OTHER
	Rate	Character	Rate	Character					
		Deep, Shallow, Noisy, Labored		Strong, Weak, Regular, Irregular	Strong, Weak, Absent	Equal size, React to Light, Round	Color, Temp, Moist-ness	Alert, Confused, Unrespon-sive	Pain, Anxiety, Thirst, Etc.

Other Observations:

23

and skills of other party members, and the practicality of stopping en route if an outside evacuation clearly becomes the preferred option.

Finally, the climb leader makes a plan for the rest of the climbing party. If self-evacuation is the plan, party members will have to organize and plan that. On the other hand, if the climb leader decides to seek outside help, the party will need a plan for getting that done and taking care of all members remaining in the field. See Chapter 24, Alpine Rescue, for more details.

Step 7: Carry Out the Plan

The climb leader is in charge of carrying out the plan. Party members may need to prepare to spend time where they are: setting up a shelter, heating water, and perhaps getting ready for a night in the wilderness. In all the preparations, keep the needs of the patient in mind. When you are dispatching people to find help, try to send at least two of the party's stronger and more competent members, along with the completed accident report form with information on the patient's condition, the condition of the rest of the party, and their specific location. (See Chapter 24, Alpine Rescue, for details on rescue and evacuation methods.) The most essential elements of Step 7 are for the first-aid leader to constantly monitor the condition of the patient and for the climb leader to monitor the progress of the plan.

MOUNTAIN MALADIES

The mountain environment presents hazards that are, for the most part, predictable. One study of the National Outdoor Leadership School courses over a five-year period showed that 80 percent of the injuries were sprains, strains, and soft-tissue injuries. Sixty percent of the illnesses were nonspecific viral illnesses or diarrhea; hygiene appeared to have a significant impact on these illnesses (see "Intestinal Disorders" later in this chapter). Table 23-2 lists some of the conditions that can arise from the stress these hazards apply to the human body.

Dehydration

Maintaining good hydration reduces the risk of heat-related illness, cold-related illness (including frostbite), and altitude illness. Your overall physical performance is improved dramatically as well.

Individuals vary in the rate at which their bodies lose water. Water loss occurs through sweating, respiratory loss, urination, and diarrhea. You may not be aware how much water your body is losing; for instance, in winter you can experience substantial fluid loss from sweating and other causes while feeling that you are not sweating much at all. Conditioning can play a minor role in the body's efficient maintenance of water balance by aiding the body in maintaining water balance more effectively. Various medications can influence your

TABLE 23-2. ENVIRONMENTALLY RELATED CONDITIONS AND INJURIES		
Environmental Stressor	**Generalized Conditions** (Potentially Affecting Entire Body)	**Localized Conditions** (Affecting Only Portion of Body)
Heat	Heat exhaustion, heat stroke ○	Heat cramps
Cold	Hypothermia ○	Frostbite, immersion foot
Ultraviolet radiation		Sunburn, snow blindness
High altitude	Acute mountain sickness, high-altitude pulmonary edema ○, high-altitude cerebral edema ○	
Lightning	Cardiopulmonary arrest ○, shock ○, coma ○	Burns, eye or ear injuries, nerve damage
Insect bites or stings	Sting-induced allergic response ○, tick-introduced illness	Localized pain and swelling
Snake bites	Generalized envenomization reaction ○	Localized tissue damage
○ Indicates urgent or life-threatening condition		

body's ability to maintain water balance, by changing how much you sweat or feel thirst, or by increasing or decreasing your urine output.

Always begin mountaineering outings well hydrated. Drink a cup of water or its equivalent 15 minutes before you start out. Once you are under way, continue drinking fluids at a rate of 1 to 1½ cups (0.2 to 0.3 liter) every 20 to 30 minutes. This rate of drinking helps you maintain hydration without making your stomach distended from the volume taken in. Do not rely on your sense of thirst as a gauge of when to drink; drink more before you feel thirsty. If you do not need to urinate periodically during the day, or if your urine color becomes unusually dark, you are not drinking enough fluids.

Commercial sports drinks are not usually necessary in a mountaineering setting, although they can help to make fluid replacement more palatable. Juices, if used, should be diluted by at least 50 percent in order to prevent diarrhea. Electrolytes—body salts—lost through sweating can be replaced by eating snacks that have some salt content to them.

Heat-Related Conditions

If you build up more heat than your body can lose, heat-related illness can result. Heat builds up by extreme exertion or by exposure to a hot environment.

Heat Cramps

Muscle cramps can develop if you become dehydrated or electrolyte-imbalanced during sustained exertion. Rest, massage, and gentle, slow stretching of the affected muscles usually help. Replacing water and electrolytes is the most important treatment. Heat cramps are avoidable if you replenish fluids and electrolytes throughout the climb.

Heat Exhaustion

Of the two major kinds of heat illness, heat exhaustion is the milder kind (the more serious kind is heat stroke, discussed below). In the effort to reduce body temperature, blood vessels in the skin become so dilated (and sweating-related moisture loss is so pronounced) that circulation to the brain and other vital organs is reduced to inadequate levels. The result is an effect similar to fainting. All or some of the following symptoms may be present: cool and clammy skin, faintness, weakness, nausea, and perhaps a rapid pulse.

Treatment consists of resting (feet up, head down a bit), preferably in the shade, and drinking plenty of liquids and electrolytes.

The following people appear particularly susceptible to heat exhaustion: the elderly, individuals on medications that interfere with sweating, people inadequately acclimatized to a hot climate, and individuals who are dehydrated or salt-depleted.

Heat Stroke

Heat stroke, which is sometimes called sunstroke, is an emergency. In heat stroke, the body's heat gain is so substantial that body core temperature rises to dangerous levels—105 degrees Fahrenheit (41 degrees Celsius) or more. Symptoms of heat stroke include the following:

■ Altered mental state (confusion or uncooperativeness, advancing toward unconsciousness)
■ Rapid, full pulse
■ Headache
■ Weakness
■ Flushed, hot skin (sometimes, but not always, dry)

The most reliable symptom is altered mental state.

Treatment must be immediate, despite the patient's potential inability to cooperate. Get the patient into the shade. Cool the head and body by packing them in snow or through evaporative cooling by splashing on water and vigorously fanning them. Once body temperature has dropped to 102 degrees Fahrenheit (39 degrees Celsius), you can stop the cooling efforts. However, continue to monitor the patient's temperature and general condition, because temperature instability may continue for some time and body temperature could climb again, necessitating recooling. If the patient's gag reflex and swallowing ability are intact, you may provide cold drinks.

A heatstroke patient must be evaluated by competent medical personnel and should not resume activity until after such an evaluation.

Cold-Related Conditions

Cold-related illness can strike if a person loses more body heat than the body can restore. Body heat is lost

23

to the environment through evaporation, radiation, convection, and conduction. (See Appendix B, Wind Chill Temperature Index, for the effects of wind on temperature and body-heat loss).

A cold-related illness that affects the entire body is hypothermia. Like heat stroke, hypothermia is an emergency condition that must be treated immediately to prevent the patient's death. In contrast, the other cold-related illnesses—frostbite and immersion foot—are localized in their effects. In triage (deciding which condition to treat first) of a patient with hypothermia and frostbite, you must treat and adequately stabilize the potentially deadly generalized condition of hypothermia before you devote energy to treating the localized injury of frostbite.

Hypothermia

Hypothermia results when the body's core temperature drops to 95 degrees Fahrenheit (35 degrees Celsius) or less. Hypothermia occurs as blood is diverted away from the skin surface and from extremities in an attempt to preserve the core temperature.

Wet clothing and exposure to wind greatly increase the risk of excessive heat loss. Dehydration also can be a risk factor. (In cold conditions, your body may jettison some of its fluids by sending more water out through urination, resulting in dehydration.) Usually hypothermia occurs after prolonged exposure to chilly environs rather than being the result of extreme cold. A drizzly day with the temperature around 50 degrees Fahrenheit (10 degrees Celsius) and a strong breeze is a more typical setting for hypothermia than a minus-30-degree-Fahrenheit (minus-34-degree-Celsius) cold snap at the ice cliffs.

Hypothermia symptoms vary dynamically depending on the severity of the loss in body core temperature. For example, shivering appears in mild hypothermia—body temperatures of 90 to 95 degrees Fahrenheit (32 to 35 degrees Celsius)—as the body attempts to heat back up through the muscular work involved in shivering. In mild hypothermia, symptoms include intense shivering, fumbling hand movements, stumbling, dulling of mental functions, and uncooperative or isolative behavior. Typically, the hypothermia patient will not notice these early signs. If you are in doubt

about the presence of mild hypothermia, have the person walk an imaginary tightrope for 15 feet (5 meters), heel to toe. Loss of coordination tends to become apparent during this test.

As hypothermia progresses to a more severe level, shivering ceases. In severe hypothermia—body temperatures below 90 degrees Fahrenheit (32 degrees Celsius)—shivering stops, but muscle and nervous system functioning obviously decline. The patient may not be able to walk but may still be able to maintain posture. Muscles are stiff and movements uncoordinated. Behavior is confused or irrational; stupor or actual unconsciousness may occurr. As hypothermia progresses, you may find it extremely difficult to observe a pulse or respiration. The patient's pupils may dilate.

Hypothermia is an emergency condition that unless treated immediately will lead to the patient's death. Treatment of hypothermia begins with ending further heat loss by stopping the patient's exposure to the elements. Get the patient out of the wind and wet, and remove wet clothing. In mild hypothermia cases, supplying dry clothing and shelter may suffice. If the patient's gag reflex and swallowing ability are intact, offer liquids and, later, sugar-based foods. Contrary to mountain lore, supplying warm drinks is not as important in mild hypothermia as is simply replenishing fluids. (Consider this: Pouring a teaspoonful of warm water into a cupful of ice water would not be an effective way to warm up the cup.) Dehydration should be treated until urine output is restored. In some cases, these measures alone may not be enough to warm the patient back up, and direct body contact with a (warm) party member may be needed.

In severe hypothermia, gentle rewarming is necessary. If possible, evacuate the patient promptly for rewarming at a hospital. The hypothermia patient must be handled very gently, to avoid inadvertently sending a spurt of cold blood from the surface circulation back to the heart; this could cause heart rhythm abnormalities. Rewarming shock also is a danger.

If field rewarming is necessary, hot water bottles wrapped in mittens or socks can be placed at the patient's neck, armpits, and groin, where large blood vessels are located near the body surface. Body-to-body contact inside a sleeping bag (or other dry insulation)

TIPS FOR PREVENTING HYPOTHERMIA

Follow these bits of common sense:

- ■ Avoid being wet; if you do get wet, get out of the weather and into dry clothes.
- ■ Avoid being exposed to the wind; if you cannot do this, at least get out of the wind as soon as possible.
- ■ Avoid dehydration; if you do become dehydrated, replenish fluids.
- ■ Have adequate insulation.

with a warm party member may be necessary. Do not offer oral liquids to a semiconscious patient. As in heat stroke, once the severe hypothermia patient is back to normal core temperature, you must still monitor the patient because temperature-regulating mechanisms may not be stable for a considerable period.

Because a severely hypothermic person may appear dead, it is essential to not give up on resuscitation efforts until the patient is warm, has had apparently adequate CPR, and still shows no signs of life. Keep in mind the saying that "no one is dead until warm and dead." Accompany or follow careful rewarming by CPR or rescue breathing, as circumstances dictate.

The party members must know when to call off the summit quest. Shivering must never be ignored. Because hypothermia interferes with a mountaineer's judgment and perception, typically climbing partners must be annoyingly persistent to get a shivering party member to don warmer gear. Forestall exhaustion by keeping tabs on the condition of one another. When a party member becomes exhausted, that person is often "too tired" to bother adding clothing or to eat or to drink, making hypothermia more likely.

Frostbite

Frostbite is the actual freezing of the blood vessels and surrounding tissues of a body part. Blood vessels can be severely and even permanently damaged. In the small vessels that nourish the skin, early in the freezing process, blood cells clump in a reversible fashion, but after prolonged freezing these clumps may become permanent plugs. Skin injury is common, with the epidermis separating from deeper dermis. Frostbitten tissue is cold, hard, and pale or darkly discolored. Blisters may appear on the skin. Frostbitten tissue is fragile and never should be massaged or mashed.

Intervention in frostbite starts with treatment of any

hypothermia. Following that, the party must assess whether field rewarming is appropriate or desirable. Usually it is not. If there is any chance that a frostbitten body part, once thawed, might refreeze during the trip, the patient should be evacuated instead so that rewarming can be done in a medical setting. If the body part is thawed and then refreezes, the line of tissue death will probably extend to the refreeze line.

If a person has a frostbitten foot, the foot must be kept frozen. Once the foot has thawed, it will be impossible to walk on, and the patient will have to be carried out.

In the rare instance that field rewarming is considered advisable, the frostbitten part should be rewarmed in a water bath that is 104 to 108 degrees Fahrenheit (40 to 42 degrees Celsius), never warmer. Do not use hot water; the frostbitten part is extremely susceptible to thermal injury. The frostbite patient should lie down with the injured part elevated.

Blisters often emerge during rewarming. Management of blisters in frostbite is controversial. Black or blue blisters definitely should be left alone. Some advocate the sterile drainage of pink or white blisters due to the presence of thromboxane (a tissue-damaging substance) in such blisters; others insist that the safer course is to leave these blisters alone as well, in order to reduce the risk of infection. Any open wounds or blisters should be washed gently with a skin antiseptic and covered with sterile dressings. Aspirin or ibuprofen may be administered, if the patient is not allergic to these, to relieve pain and counteract the production of thromboxane.

More definitive treatment of frostbite should be reserved for competent medical care.

Immersion Foot

Immersion foot occurs when a person's feet have been wet and cool—but not freezing cold—for long periods.

23

Climbers on Mount McKinley (Denali) who wear vapor-barrier socks but neglect to dry and warm their feet each night are prime targets for this condition. Similarly, tundra hikers who clamber through the muskeg day after day but never dry their feet at night can be affected. The injury appears to be a kind of trauma to nerves and muscles caused by diminished oxygen distribution (hypoxia), rather than an injury to blood vessels and skin as in frostbite.

Immersion foot reveals its presence in pale, pulseless, tingling feet. Typically, the unhappy mountaineer discovers these symptoms in the tent at night. Very careful rewarming is needed—in a water bath just slightly warmer than body temperature—or gangrene can occur. During rewarming, the affected feet shift to a painful hyperemic phase (congested with blood): They become reddened and swollen with a bounding pulse. It may be necessary to slightly cool the feet in order to tone down the intensity of this phase. During the subsequent days of the recovery period, the patient may be at risk for recurrence of immersion foot.

UV Radiation–Related Conditions

Sunburn

Intense ultraviolet (UV) radiation from the sun, particularly when it is reflected off snow and ice, can burn an unprepared mountaineer at high altitudes. Burn injuries from overexposure to UV radiation are potentially serious but preventable. Certain medications (such as tetracycline and oral medicines for diabetes) can increase the skin's sensitivity to sun and thus to the danger of burning.

To prevent sunburn, you must be aware of the risk of getting burned. UV radiation is not filtered out effectively by cloud cover, so you must maintain skin protection even on an overcast day.

The most effective prevention is to cover exposed skin with clothing. Clothing's ability to screen UV radiation depends on its weave and fiber. A tighter weave works better, though it is hotter to wear. Lightweight garments have been specifically developed for their sunscreening capability (an example is the material sold under the name Frogwear). Hats should include a wide brim to protect the back of your neck as well as your face and ears.

When your skin must be exposed, sunscreen products extend the time that you can spend in the sun without getting burned. Properly applied, sunscreens can work remarkably well. Chapter 2, Clothing and Equipment, discusses sunscreens. Be sure to use sunscreen with an SPF rating that is appropriate for the conditions. Some sunscreens can be difficult to extract from their containers in cold weather, so assess this potential problem with your favorite sunscreen before your next chilly glacier morning.

Sunburn should be treated like any other burn: Cool the burned area, cover it, and treat for pain. Blistered areas in particular should be covered with sterile dressings to minimize the risk of infection. Drink plenty of fluids.

Snow Blindness

Snow blindness is a potentially serious problem that results when the outer layers of the eyes are burned by UV radiation. The cornea (the clear layer at the front of the eye) is most easily burned. Its surface can become roughened and blistered. With further radiation, the lenses of the eyes can become burned as well. Snow blindness sets in 6 to 12 hours after the radiation exposure. The first symptoms, therefore, do not appear until after the damage is done. Dry, sandy-feeling eyes become light-sensitive, then reddened and teary, and then extremely painful. Recovery takes from one to several days.

Treatment of snow blindness includes providing pain relief and preventing further injury. Remove contact lenses, and protect the eyes from bright light. Advise the snow-blindness patient to avoid rubbing the eyes and to try to rest. To prevent irritation from eyelid movement, cover the eyes with sterile dressings and padding. Recheck for light sensitivity at half-day intervals. When the eyes are no longer extremely light-sensitive, you can remove dressings, but the patient should wear protective sunglasses.

Prevention of snow blindness is straightforward. In high-UV environs, you must wear either goggles or sunglasses with side shields. This eyewear needs to filter out 90 percent of the UV wavelength that burns. Glare can be filtered out with a darkly tinted lens, but the tint itself will not filter out the burning UV light. Polarizing layers on the lenses can help in settings where reflection is especially intense. If you lose your eye protection, emergency goggles can be fashioned out of duct tape or cardboard by cutting narrow horizontal slits for each eye. (See "Sun Protection" in Chapter 2, Clothing and Equipment.)

High-Altitude Conditions

As you climb to higher elevations, the altitude begins to change the way your body functions. As the air gets thinner, the amount of available oxygen in each breath decreases. Just as important, the mechanism that is instrumental in permitting your body to absorb oxygen from your lungs also decreases. Your body's tissues have a harder time getting the oxygen they need for metabolism, and you enter the state of reduced oxygen called hypoxia.

Your body attempts to adapt to this drastic environmental change, but adaptation (acclimatization) takes time (see sidebar). There is great variation in how rapidly and how completely each individual acclimatizes.

Physiological Adaptations to Altitude

Increased breathing rate: One adaptation to high-altitude hypoxia is an increase in the rate of breathing. After you have ascended to high altitude, your breathing rate continues to increase for several days. As this occurs, dissolved carbon dioxide in your bloodstream decreases (as carbon dioxide is exhaled).

Diuresis: Another normal adaptation to high-altitude hypoxia is that the kidneys send more water on to the bladder as urine, ridding the body of more fluid. This diuresis makes the blood slightly thicker. This change begins promptly upon ascent and continues for several weeks. Eventually your body produces a greater number of red blood cells in an effort to increase oxygen-carrying capacity. This change, called polycythemia (many cells in the blood), makes the blood considerably thicker and can even interfere with circulation to some tissues.

Insomnia: Your ability to sleep soundly deteriorates at high altitude. Most mountaineers have insomnia at altitude, waking up more often during the night and getting less deep sleep. Commonly, an irregular breathing rhythm appears during sleep and sometimes during wakefulness, too: machinelike cycles alternating between very slow breathing rates and hyperventilation. (This alternating rhythm is known as Cheyne-Stokes respiration.) The low carbon dioxide content of the blood appears to drive this odd change in breathing rate. Experts do not recommend using sleeping pills to relieve climbers' insomnia, because they may depress respiration. A small dose of acetazolamide (¼ tablet) at bedtime acts as a respiratory stimulant and may aid your sleep.

It is difficult to work as efficiently or powerfully at high altitude as at lower elevations, due to the effect of hypoxia and the related changes in how your body functions. For good acclimatization, it is critical to maintain adequate fluid intake amid these physiologic changes. Three high-altitude-related conditions—acute mountain sickness (AMS), high-altitude pulmonary edema (HAPE), and high-altitude cerebral edema (HACE)—all seem to involve abnormal shifts in body fluids caused by the stress of high altitude. It is important to differentiate AMS from the more ominous, related conditions of HAPE and HACE.

Acute Mountain Sickness

At least half of the sea-level residents who travel rapidly to moderate altitude—8,000 to 14,000 feet (2,400 to 4,300 meters)—experience some degree of acute mountain sickness (AMS). This is a collection of nonspecific symptoms that can resemble a case of flu, carbon monoxide poisoning from stove use inside an inadequately ventilated shelter, or a hangover. AMS can vary widely in severity. Signs of acute mountain sickness are:

- Headache
- Insomnia

23

TIPS FOR ACCLIMATIZATION

These are rough guidelines for controlling your rate of ascent to allow your body to acclimatize:
- Above 10,000 feet (about 3,000 meters), limit increases in sleeping elevation to about 1,000 feet (300 meters) per day.
- Two or three times a week, allow an additional night at the same elevation as the night before.

- Listlessness
- Loss of coordination
- Puffiness around eyes and face
- Cough
- Shortness of breath
- Fullness or tightness in chest
- Irregular breathing
- Loss of appetite
- Nausea
- Vomiting
- Reduced urine output
- Weakness
- "Heavy" feeling in legs

AMS settles in within a day of the initial ascent, and if it is mild, it lasts only a day or so; however, it can progress in severity. In cases where symptoms (such as headache and nausea) progress, a descent of 2,000 to 3,000 feet (600 to 900 meters) in elevation is the best treatment. The diagnosis of AMS is confirmed if the condition improves upon descent.

Some medicines can be used to deal with altitude-related health problems; ask your physician about the appropriateness of such drugs for your situation. For example, some mountaineers use acetazolamide (Diamox) for several days prior to ascent and through the first 48 hours at high altitude in order to prevent AMS or block its recurrence. Potential problems caused by this medication are tingling of the extremities, ringing in the ears, nausea, frequent urination, and a change in the sense of taste; individuals with sulfa allergies must not take it at all. Acetazolamide does appear to be effective in preventing and treating AMS as well as the irregular breathing brought on by high altitude.

High-Altitude Pulmonary Edema

In high-altitude pulmonary edema (HAPE), body fluids leak into the lungs to a degree that interferes with respiratory function. HAPE is a potentially fatal condition, and survival depends on a rapid response.

Early signs may overlap with more benign problems, such as a persistent cough caused by simple bronchial irritation from dry, high-mountain air. Decreasing ability to exercise, accompanied by breathlessness and a

hacking cough, appears as HAPE develops. Rates of breathing and pulse increase.

If HAPE is allowed to advance, breathing will require effort and will include bubbling noises. Lips and nail beds may appear dusky or tinged with blue, reflecting the body's inability to transfer oxygen into arterial blood due to the water barrier in the lungs. Some affected people also develop a fever, making it difficult to distinguish HAPE from pneumonia; one indicator of HAPE is how rapidly it worsens with continued ascent.

The key to treating HAPE is to descend. A descent of 3,000 feet (900 meters) will resolve nearly all HAPE cases that are caught early. On some expeditions, portable hyperbaric chambers (such as the Gamow bag) are used to create a temporary artificial "descent" environment in the effort to stabilize the patient for a few hours. Supplemental oxygen can also be helpful in temporary stabilization. Ultimately, however, real descent must occur. Some mountaineers use the drug nifedipine to help prevent or treat HAPE.

High-Altitude Cerebral Edema

High-altitude cerebral edema (HACE) usually develops in unacclimatized climbers above 10,000 feet (about 3,000 meters), although it can occur as low as 8,500 feet (2,600 meters). Generally, it takes from one to three days at altitude for HACE to develop. Vessels in the brain respond to the stress of high altitude by becoming leaky, resulting in the brain swelling with increased fluid. Ultimately the brain swells inside its rigid container of cranial bones.

Early signs of this deadly condition include deteriorating coordination (ataxia), headache, and loss of energy. Use the coordination test in which you ask a person to walk an imaginary tightrope for 15 feet (5 meters), heel to toe, to check for ataxia. Nausea and forceful vomiting may be present.

As HACE advances (which can occur rapidly), the patient's thinking becomes clouded and there may be an onset of various neurologic problems, such as loss of muscular control of one side of the body, stupor, and coma. Descent is critical to survival. Drugs such as dexamethasone are used by some expeditions as an additional part of the treatment.

Lightning-Caused Injuries

The high-mountain environment receives many more thunderstorms each year than coastal areas do, as the weather systems mass against the mountains before rising over them. Summer afternoons are the most likely time for thunderstorms, and therefore lightning, to endanger the mountaineer. Lightning strikes can emanate from several miles away toward high points ahead of (or, less frequently, behind) the main thunderhead cloud formation—"out of a clear blue sky." Therefore, mountaineers can be in danger of a lightning strike at times even when the storm is not directly overhead.

Lightning can strike you in various ways:

■ *Direct strike* of a mountaineer in the open who could not find shelter
■ *Splash strike,* in which the lightning current jumps from an object it initially hit onto a mountaineer who sought shelter nearby
■ *Contact injury,* from holding an object that lightning hits
■ *Step voltage,* transmitted along the ground or through an object near a mountaineer
■ *Blunt trauma,* created by the shock wave from a nearby strike

Lightning-caused injuries include cardiac arrest, burns, and internal injuries.

Cardiac arrest: This is the most immediate danger from being struck by lightning.

Burns: Lightning burns often take several hours to develop after the strike. These burns are usually superficial (similar to first-degree burns) and do not usually require treatment, although serious internal injuries can also occur.

Internal injuries: The eyes, a vulnerable port of entry for electrical current, can be damaged in a lightning strike. Ear damage also may occur; a patient might not respond to your questions because of a loss of hearing caused by the strike.

After the lightning strike, the patient does not present an electrical hazard to rescuers. Proceed promptly with first aid, assessing the airway, breathing, circulation, and deadly bleeding (ABCD) indicators. It is important to get the lightning patient to a medical facility, because vital body functions may remain unstable for a considerable time after resuscitation.

For information on how to avoid being struck by lightning see "Thunder and Lightning" in Chapter 27, Mountain Weather.

Intestinal Disorders

On mountaineering trips, the most common cause of gastrointestinal infections that entail diarrhea and abdominal cramping is fecal-oral contamination. Most often, the source of the feces is mountaineers themselves. Your hands can be contaminated without your realizing it. When soap and wash water are not available, you can use hand cleansers and towelettes to prevent contaminating your hands. Inadequate handwashing after a toilet break is the typical problem. Some rock-climbing routes may be contaminated with feces from previous parties. On glacier routes, handling ropes that have dragged through soiled snow and ice can lead to contamination. Clean your hands before eating. Water bottles as well as food can become contaminated from your hands. Climbers often are gregarious at rest stops—but think twice before offering your snack bag for each person to plunge a hand into; pouring some contents into each person's hands is less risky.

Animal wastes also present a risk. Many small rodents live in the same crags that mountaineers climb, and your hands may rest on mouse scat on the way up a cliff. Avoid camping near rodent burrows. Cover food and water so that they are secure from rodent invasion during the night.

Giardiasis, caused by a waterborne protozoan (*Giardia lamblia*) traveling in cyst form from an infected animal host's feces, is prevalent in the United States, particularly in the West. *Giardia* infection has a long incubation period, ranging from one to three weeks (averaging a week and a half) after you swallow the organism. Usually symptoms do not develop until after you have returned from the wilderness outing. Watery, explosive diarrhea may erupt, accompanied by abdominal cramps, flatus, bloating, nausea, and vomiting. After three or four days, the condition simmers down into an unpleasant subacute phase marked by greasy, mushy stools; mild abdominal cramping; belching; etc.

Before this ailment can be treated it must be diagnosed by laboratory tests. Tinidazole is the treatment of choice in countries other than the United States, where it has not yet received government approval. Various other drugs, such as quinacrine (not always available) or metronidazole, are used for giardiasis treatment in the United States.

To protect against giardiasis and other waterborne diarrheas, always sanitize your water. All ingested water, including that used in dishwashing and toothbrushing, must be purified. (See "Water Purification" in Chapter 3, Camping and Food.)

If you are heading into regions with questionable hygiene and water disinfection practices, seek medical advice about antibiotics that you can take to help ward off infection and about antimotility ("antidiarrheal") drugs. However, taking drugs is not a substitute for dietary discretion. Avoid eating raw fruits or vegetables, raw meat, raw seafood, tap water, and ice. Instead, stick to boiled water, properly cooked meat and vegetables, bottled beverages, and reputable eating establishments.

For most intestinal infections associated with diarrhea, treatment during a trip consists of adequately replacing fluids and electrolytes. This can be challenging if you are also nauseated. Mix packets of replacement electrolytes into a quart (liter) of drinking water. If these are not available, simply replace fluids. Eat palatable foods and broths with a substantial salt content.

Blisters

Blisters are dreaded by all wilderness travelers. These bubbles under the skin, filled with clear or blood-tinged fluid, probably represent the most common health-related reason for ending outings. Small blisters generally are a source of minor irritation and discomfort. Larger blisters can cause significant pain and, if ruptured, can lead to serious infection and ulceration.

Often blisters are caused by new or poorly fitted boots. Blisters result from the skin rubbing against socks and the inner lining of the boot. This happens when your boots are too large or too loosely laced, or when your socks are lumpy or wrinkled. Moisture tends to soften your skin, so wet boots or socks promote blister formation.

To prevent blisters, fit your boots properly. Break them in slowly and thoroughly before you launch into any extended hikes. The areas most prone to blistering are over the heel or Achilles tendon at the back of the

ankle and on the toes. If you tend to blister easily, pad the blister-prone areas with Moleskin or other adhesive foam, but do not pad them so much that you create a new pressure point around the edge of the Moleskin. Keep your feet dry and wear adequate and well-fitting socks.

A blister usually becomes noticeable first as a hot spot, a localized sensation of heat that increases in size and intensity over time. Inspect such spots immediately, and take preventive measures. Place a generous strip of waterproof, plastic adhesive tape or Moleskin over the spot (fig. 23-2b). Other suitable products include Second Skin and Dr. Scholl's Molefoam, and some sufferers are successful with duct tape or waterproof first-aid tape. Avoid using adhesive bandage strips (such as Band-Aids) for covering hot spots; these strips seem to promote blister formation because the nonadhesive dressing pad balls up and rubs against the already sensitive skin.

Once a blister has formed, avoid opening it unless absolutely necessary; opening a blister may introduce infection to the area. Your body will reabsorb the blister fluid after several days, and it will heal. If you must continue the hike or whatever activity caused the blister, pad the blister and protect it from rupture (fig. 23-2c). Layer a "doughnut" of padding until it reaches the proper depth so that the blister itself does not receive pressure. The padding doughnut must be deeper and wider than the blister. Tape the padding well to prevent it from becoming displaced.

If a blister breaks open on its own, wash and dress it with sterile dressings, as with any open wound. Infection is a concern, and further tissue damage should be avoided if at all possible.

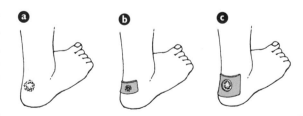

Fig. 23-2.
Ways to treat a blister (a): b, tape a hot spot; c, doughnut-cushion around a blister.

23

Panic/Anxiety

Mountaineering outings can be refreshing and rejuvenating experiences. They also can induce stress in climbers. In extreme situations, such as a serious accident, nearly everyone has to deal with their own and each other's anxiety or even panic. A challenging situation or a difficult climbing move may evoke a more intense anxiety response than you anticipate. This is unpleasant, especially if it occurs when you are halfway up a cliff. It is important to be able to manage these responses without becoming disabled by them.

Some people have a tendency toward intense anxiety in response to certain physical situations in climbing, such as exposure to heights or to enclosed spaces. This tendency can erupt in a panic response during a step-across move on a cliff face or while you are squeezing up a rock chimney. If affected, you may freeze and refuse to go on. You may hyperventilate (breathe rapidly) or be unable to recognize that there are safe movements available. Your ability to fully assess the situation will be blocked temporarily; physical movements will be clumsy and fearful, raising the risk of a mishap.

Self-calming techniques are helpful in such situations. One approach involves a five-step process:
1. Identify the panic response for what it is (simply a physical adrenaline reaction to perceived risk).
2. Decide to deal with the panic response effectively.
3. Refocus on slow, steady, deep breathing (perhaps enhanced with a mental image of exhaling the worry out with each breath).
4. Identify, systematically, the options for safe movement.
5. Carry out one of these options.

If hyperventilation is a problem, try the old trick of breathing into a paper bag to increase the concentration of carbon dioxide in the inhaled air, which can slow down the hyperventilation trend. Redirecting your focus onto a useful physical task can be an excellent strategy for interrupting the snowballing effect of panic. Fellow climbers can be most helpful by calmly and matter-of-factly prompting you to use the self-calming techniques, by maintaining an atmosphere of confident acceptance and support, and by pointing out an option for retreat if appropriate.

INJURIES

To minimize injuries from a mountaineering accident, it is critical to immediately apply skillful and caring first aid. Specific treatments for serious injuries are beyond the scope of this book. Hands-on instruction in mountaineering first aid is essential. (See Appendix C, Supplementary Reading, for the titles of detailed first-aid texts.)

Head, Neck, and Back Injuries

Head and spine injuries are common causes of death in alpine wilderness accidents. Any injury to the head or spine is potentially life-threatening. Such injuries often are caused by falling objects, such as rock or ice, or by a fall in which your head or back strikes a hard object. The spine can also be injured by deceleration, even if you do not actually strike anything during a fall, such as coming to an abrupt stop at the end of a rope while still suspended in air.

For all head injuries, you must assume that there is a cervical spine (neck) injury until a thorough examination proves otherwise. For all cervical spine injuries, the patient must be monitored for potential head and brain injury. Indicators of possible head injuries include the following:
- Unconsciousness
- Drainage of blood or clear fluid from the ears, nose, or eyes
- Unequal eye pupil size or unequal constricting response of the pupils to light
- A very slow pulse or noticeable fluctuations in respiratory (breathing) rate
- A headache generalized over the entire head
- Disorientation and confusion

The head and spine are so delicate that the slightest mistake in first-aid response may cause further injury or death, yet symptoms of injury are often so nonspecific that it can be difficult to choose a course of action. It is usually a question of whether the patient can be moved safely or whether treatment on the spot is essential. As noted above, specific treatment for serious injuries such as head injuries requires skills that are beyond the scope of this book. Hands-on practice is essential.

Avoid head injuries . . . *wear a helmet!*

23

FIRST-AID KIT

In a mountaineering party, each member must carry a basic personal first-aid kit. Suggested contents of a basic personal first-aid kit are given in Table 23-3. On trips where dampness is a possibility, it is wise to put the kit in a plastic bag to keep the bandaging materials dry.

In addition, the party often brings group first-aid supplies, depending on the nature and duration of the outing. Many parties carry a compact splint (such as a SAM splint), an oral antihistamine, and a pair of bandage scissors. Note that pharmaceuticals should

be used only by the person to whom they were prescribed, and then only as directed. Giving medications to others runs the risk of serious drug reactions or drug interactions.

Be aware that the longer and more remote the adventure, the more supplies are appropriate, yet typically the more weight-conscious the party needs to be. Avoid the temptation to strip a first-aid kit below the bare minimum simply to reduce weight. On most trips, you will not need your first-aid kit, but that does not make it less essential.

TABLE 23-3. BASIC PERSONAL FIRST-AID KIT

Item	Quantity/Size	Use
Adhesive bandages	Six 1-inch	To cover small minor wounds
Butterfly bandages or Steristrips	Three, in various sizes	To close minor lacerations
Sterile gauze pads	Four 4-inch by 4-inch	To cover larger wounds
Carlisle dressing or sanitary napkin	One 4-inch	To absorb and control severe bleeding
Nonadherent dressings	Two 4-inch by 4-inch	To cover abrasions and burns
Self-adhering roller bandages	Two rolls, 2-inch width by 5 yards	To hold dressings in place
SAM splint	One	To splint
Athletic tape	One roll, 2-inch width	Multiple uses
Triangular bandages	Two 36-inch by 36-inch by 52-inch	To use as a sling or cravat (for splinting)
Moleskin or Molefoam	4-inch to 6-inch square	To cushion blister areas
Tincture of benzoin	One 0.5-ounce bottle	To aid in adherence of adhesive tape; to protect skin
Providine iodine swabs	Two packages	Antiseptic for surface wounds
Alcohol or soap pads	Three packages	To cleanse skin
Thermometer	Range of 90 to 105 degrees Fahrenheit (30 to 41 degrees Celsius)	To measure body temperature
Sugar packets	Four packets	To treat diabetes; for hypoglycemia intervention
Aspirin	Six tablets	To treat headache, pain; if the party includes children, bring acetaminophen tablets instead of aspirin.
Anaphylaxis (epinephrine) kit (EpiPen)	One	To treat severe allergic reaction. Climbers should carry if known to have severe allergy.
Elastic bandage	One 2-inch width	To wrap sprains; for compression of injured area
Latex gloves	Two pairs	To serve as an infection barrier
Safety pins	Two	Multiple uses
Tweezers	One pair	To remove splinters, ticks, wound debris
Plastic bag	One 12-inch by 18-inch	To hold contaminated materials
Breathing barrier	Disposable	To administer CPR, rescue breathing

23

Alpine Rescue

RESCUE TRAINING ■ ACCIDENT RESPONSE ■ RESCUE FROM
TECHNICAL TERRAIN ■ EVACUATION ■ SEARCHES ■ OUTSIDE
RESCUE ASSISTANCE ■ USING ALL THESE SKILLS

**Climbing instruction emphasizes techniques for staying safe and uninjured.
However, even the best-prepared climbers may eventually encounter a situation
requiring first-aid and rescue skills. With outside assistance hours or days away, a
climbing party needs to be able to perform immediate first aid and begin rescue efforts.
It is possible for a small party of climbers to carry out a difficult rescue quickly
and efficiently, using only normal climbing gear. Additional assistance
from nearby climbing parties is sometimes available.**

This chapter focuses on rescue training, accident response, small-party rescues from technical terrain, evacuations, search techniques, and interaction with outside rescue agencies. Each climbing party needs to be prepared to perform a self-rescue and go to the aid of other parties. Each climber should add to personal knowledge of rescue systems and techniques, and practice setting up and running these systems. Consider taking courses from the many organizations that offer classes in alpine rescue.

RESCUE TRAINING

Every serious climber's education should include training for rescue. First aid, rescue systems, and leadership training should be a part of the curriculum.

First aid: The urgent first-aid skills taught in most urban and workplace classes are designed to help a severely injured patient survive the first hour. Wilderness or mountain-oriented first aid helps a patient survive the first day in an often hostile outdoor environment. Chapter 23, First Aid, is a good place to learn more.

Rescue systems: Rescue skills build on climbing skills. You should know accepted rescue safety standards, and practice with systems for raising and lowering an injured climber. Information on the strength of available materials helps you build anchors and systems that are strong enough for the task, but not overengineered and complex.

Knowledge about rescue systems is continually growing. A system considered safe today may be re-evaluated in light of new information and deemed unsafe tomorrow. It is the climber's responsibility to monitor advances in this area.

Leadership training: This training prepares you to organize and direct teams of climbers effectively. Leading a climbing team is a challenge. Leading a climbing team in an emergency can be overwhelming. Most leaders lose control when they get too involved in a particular task. Knowing how to delegate tasks and keep a wide focus of attention makes a leader's job easier. See Chapter 21, Leadership, for more information.

ACCIDENT RESPONSE

Accidents occur unexpectedly. Stress rapidly increases. Decisions made in the first few minutes can decide the outcome. The following checklist—a modified version of "The Seven Steps in Accident Response" in Chapter

23, First Aid—may help reduce the pressure on the climbing team as it converts to a rescue team. Note that the seven steps in first aid are different from the seven steps of alpine rescue. The main focus of first aid is on treating a patient who is safe and secure, whereas alpine rescue's main focus is on safely securing the situation and, when needed, transporting an injured individual.

Step 1. Take Charge of the Situation

Take a few slow, deliberate breaths to overcome the initial adrenaline rush and give your mind a chance to work again. A recognized leader (either the designated climb leader or one who steps forward) needs to evaluate the situation, plan the response, and delegate tasks. If no first-aid leader was designated at the beginning of the trip, one needs to be selected now. Table 23-1 in Chapter 23, First Aid, shows how the climb leader and the first-aid leader share decision-making throughout the seven steps of first aid.

Step 2. Proceed Safely

The climb leader needs to keep in mind that:

- Rescuer safety comes first—do not allow any member of the rescue team to become part of the problem.
- Response must be deliberate—anticipate rather than simply reacting.
- Follow your training—you usually cannot improvise successfully under stress.

Step 3. Perform Immediate and Urgent First Aid

The first-aid leader evaluates the patient's condition. This may require scrambling, rappelling, or being lowered to the patient.

Get the injured person out of harm's way (rockfall or icefall) if necessary. Perform urgent first aid if needed. If the injured climber is hanging in the seat harness, lower the patient to a safe spot. Studies indicate that 30 minutes is about the longest amount of time a healthy person can be suspended from a seat harness without serious physiological stress. Injured climbers have a much lower tolerance. Begin treating for shock.

Step 4. Assess the Situation

The climb leader needs good knowledge of the current situation before being able to formulate a plan. The climb leader should evaluate the following:

- Patient's condition—The severity of the injury is likely the most important factor affecting the plan. The first-aid leader performs the secondary examination and fills out an accident report form (see Figure 23-1 in Chapter 23, First Aid).
- Accident terrain—What kind of rescue system is needed? Is there helicopter access?
- Weather conditions—Temperature and precipitation affect both the patient and the rescue team.
- Evacuation distance—How far the party is from the trailhead affects the number of rescuers needed.
- Rescuers' condition—Assess the number of rescuers available, their state of exhaustion, and their level of experience and training.
- Available equipment—Assess what equipment was lost or damaged in the accident, and what equipment is available from other parties.

Other rescuers, especially the first-aid leader, can help the climb leader by offering their own assessments of the situation.

Step 5. Make a Plan

With the assessment completed, the climb leader next draws together a plan of action for both the immediate rescue and an evacuation if one is needed. The plan identifies the tasks to be done and who will perform them. Input from other rescue team members can ensure that the climb leader considers all crucial factors.

Tasks in a typical rescue may include providing first-aid treatment, operating the raising or lowering system, providing a belay, coordinating the execution of the rescue system, and sending for additional assistance. Some members of the group may be unable to carry out a task—consider sending them back to the trailhead.

Step 6. Requesting Outside Assistance

Outside assistance is usually required for severely injured climbers, complex rescue situations, and long evacuations. Unless it is obvious that the injured climber can self-evacuate, the climb leader should send for outside assistance. It is better to have outside assistance on the way to you, even if it turns out later that it is not needed, than to delay the request for outside assistance until you are sure it is necessary, only to have it urgently needed by the time it arrives. Consider what is best for the patient.

Contact the appropriate outside agency: Know who to contact before the climbing party departs on its outing. In the United States, usually the responsible agency is either the sheriff of the county in which the accident occurred or, if it occurred within a national park, a park service ranger. If an accident does happen and you are unsure who to contact, personnel at 911 dispatch phone centers know how to contact the appropriate agency in an emergency.

Prepare a report: It is essential to communicate concisely and clearly with the outside agency. For each patient, responders need to know "Who, What, Where, When, Injuries, and Plan of Action." No matter how the rescue party plans to deliver the information, first take the time to write a separate, concise report for each injured climber. The accident report filled out by the first-aid leader as part of Step 4, above, is a suitable report format. Append a list of all members in the climbing party, as well as a list of all members of the rescue party if it is different from the climbing party (i.e., climbers from another party may join in the rescue effort), and a map showing the precise location of the rescue party. Add current global positioning system (GPS) coordinates, if they are known, to the map.

Deliver the report: A number of methods are available for delivering the report—radios, wireless phones, and messengers.

Radios and wireless phones get through very quickly, if they *can* get through. Radios require line-of-sight communications with another radio or repeater station. Wireless phones need to be in range of antenna or receiving sites. In the mountains and wilderness, wireless phones and radios may be unreliable. If you are able to make contact by radio or wireless phone, read from the accident report instead of relying on memory. Add the wireless phone number or radio call

24

sign to the report so the responding rescue organization can call you back if necessary.

In many situations, messengers may be your only means of communicating with outside help. If an adequate number of rescuers is available, send two messengers for safety reasons. It is more important to be certain that one of the messengers will reach assistance than to worry about the speed with which they reach assistance. Messengers should deliver their reports to an agency rescue leader; written reports guard against messages becoming garbled. Messengers should be prepared to escort outside rescuers back to the accident scene if that is requested.

Step 7. Carry Out the Rescue and Evacuation

The team is now prepared to carry out the rescue plan. The climb leader assigns a role and task to each rescuer, and then should pull back, observe, and continue to plan and replan. Let the team perform the planned rescue and evacuation. Typical roles for climbers in the rescue team include:

Leader: This is the climb leader. The Leader's role is that of an overseer—watching the rescue and anticipating problems (fig. 24-1d). The Leader's focus of attention is over the entire rescue and evacuation and over all the climbers present. The Leader continually revises the plan.

Safety: The Safety ensures that unsafe conditions do not develop and corrects them if they do. The Safety can halt the rescue at any time. The Safety's focus of attention is still quite wide so as to take in the immediate rescue operation and surroundings. This person inspects anchors, knots, tie-ins, raise/lower systems, and the belay system.

Controller: The Controller directs the operation of the rescue systems and gives the raise/lower commands. The Controller's focus is tighter yet—concentrating on accomplishing the raise or lower.

When the number of rescuers is small, the Leader may have to act as the Safety and Controller. The danger here is in the tightening of the focus of attention—problems may develop without the Leader noticing them.

Belayer: The Belayer operates the rope that provides a belay for the patient and Attendant (fig. 24-1b). The

Belayer's focus is quite narrow, because the task of keeping the belay snug but not under load demands concentration.

Main Line (Raise/Lower): The Main Line sets up and runs the system on the main rope that is used to raise and/or lower the patient and Attendant (fig. 24-1a). Like the Belayer, the Main Line's task demands concentration and a tight focus of attention, concentrating on ensuring that the ropes run smoothly.

Attendant: The Attendant accompanies the patient during the rescue (fig. 24-1e), monitoring the patient's medical condition and assisting the patient during a raise or lower. The Attendant's focus is tightly fixed on the patient's safety.

Helpers: The remaining members of the rescue party are the helpers. Helpers perform tasks such as equipment and rope management, anchor building, patient movement at the start and end of a raise or lower, and other tasks assigned by the Controller. Their focus of attention is on only their current assigned task.

RESCUE FROM TECHNICAL TERRAIN

When an injured climber or stranded hiker is in terrain that is very steep (rock cliffs, icefalls, or steep boulder fields), a rescue team sets up rope rescue systems that use gravity or mechanical advantage to make movement of the patient easier (see Figure 24-1, below).

Safety

Safety is a critical part of the rescue system. Safety issues concerning the rescuers, the patient, and the rope systems need to be examined.

Rescuers

Rescuers wear protective gear such as helmets, eye protection, and belay gloves. In accident situations, a rescuer's focus of attention on the patient or on the assigned task may be so complete that surrounding dangers are ignored unless special effort is made. Rescuers close to the edge of a cliff or icefall should tie in or attach themselves to a rope with a prusik sling. All climbing or scrambling is belayed.

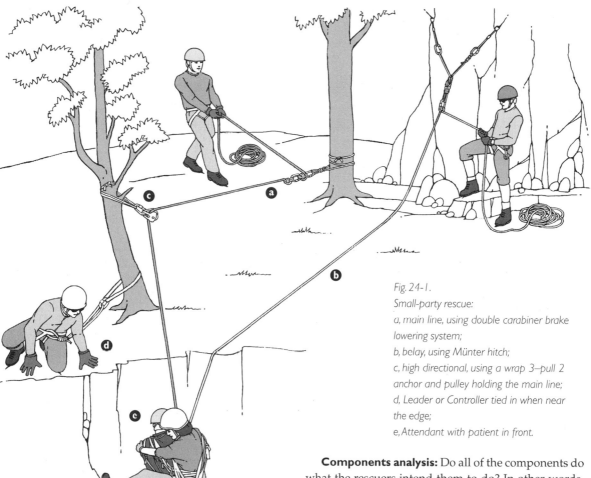

Fig. 24-1.

Small-party rescue:

a, main line, using double carabiner brake lowering system;

b, belay, using Münter hitch;

c, high directional, using a wrap 3–pull 2 anchor and pulley holding the main line;

d, Leader or Controller tied in when near the edge;

e, Attendant with patient in front.

Patient

Patient safety is increased by insuring that the patient has adequate protective gear (helmet, eye protection, warm clothing, secure splints, etc.) and is secured to an anchor at all times.

Systems

System safety depends on the rescuers carefully setting up the systems. Formal rescue organizations subject their rescue systems to the "Three Tests of a Safe Rescue System" (from Rick Lipke's *Technical Rescue Riggers Guide*; see Appendix C, Supplementary Reading, at the back of this book):

Components analysis: Do all of the components do what the rescuers intend them to do? In other words, will the belay system really hold? Will the raising system lift the patient without tremendous strain? Will the anchor hold?

Critical points examination: Are all components backed up by other system components in such a way that failure of no one point (either gear or personnel) would cause a serious accident?

Whistle (hold up) test: If a whistle sounded and every rescuer let go of the system, would the system still protect the patient and rescuers from catastrophe?

A small climbing party suddenly thrust into a rescue situation may not have the time or equipment for such formal and rigorous examination of their systems. However, rescuers always should try to keep the intent of these tests in mind when they are setting up the rescue systems. Clean setups, neat knots, and simple systems allow the rescue team to quickly but thoroughly inspect all systems using the above three tests. The Münter hitch belay (see "Belay Techniques," below) does not meet the whistle test, and special care must be taken to put the belay system in a safe and secure area (out of rockfall danger, for example). This lessens the chance that the belayer might suddenly be forced to let go. The tandem prusik belay (also described in "Belay Techniques," below) is one of the few systems that passes the whistle test.

Anchors for Rescue

In technical rescues, anchors are the most important part of the system. They must be able to bear the weight of two or three climbers, and thus need to be stronger than anchors used for climbing. Well-rooted trees and solid rock formations make excellent anchors. A single wrap 3–pull 2 or wrap 2–pull 1 anchor made from webbing tied to a natural anchor has the strength required for rescue systems. Create a wrap 3–pull 2 anchor by wrapping webbing three times around the natural anchor (fig. 24-2a), tying a ring bend knot (water knot) in the webbing (fig. 24-2b), and then pulling on the two wraps without the knot. Clip them with a carabiner (fig. 24-2c). A wrap 2–pull 1 anchor makes two wraps and pulls the one wrap without the knot.

Climbing protection such as cams and chocks are effective only as part of a multiple anchor system—a single cam or chock should not be used alone. Use a cordelette to distribute the load between multiple anchor points to create an anchor with static equalization. See "Equalizing Multiple Anchors" in Chapter 10, Belaying. Static equalization is preferred over self-equalization because failure of one of the anchors in a self-equalizing setup results in shock-loading the remaining anchors.

On snow and ice, rescuers may need to construct anchors from bollards, pickets, flukes, ice screws, V-threads, and buried objects. Ice and snow climbers should become familiar with these anchors and learn about their strengths and limitations. See "Snow Anchors" in Chapter 16, Snow Travel and Climbing, and "Equipment" in Chapter 18, Alpine Ice Climbing.

Overengineered anchor systems actually decrease safety. Anchors backing up anchors that are backing up

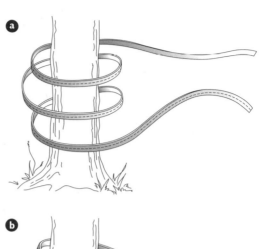

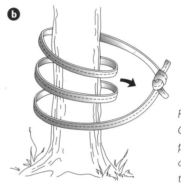

Fig. 24-2.
Constructing a wrap 3–pull 2 anchor system: a, wrap webbing three times around anchor; b, join ends of webbing together with water knot; c, place water knot on front side of anchor and pull on the two wraps not containing the knot, extending them equally and clipping with a locking carabiner.

other anchors can lead to a complex tangle of rope and webbing that no one understands. Keep anchors clean and simple.

Systems for Rescue

On a safe and successful technical rescue, three systems work together: belay, main line (raise/lower), and patient/attendant. In a two-rope rescue system, the main line is the rope that carries all the weight of the patient and the attendant. The belay rope protects the patient and the attendant, but does not normally carry any weight; the belay system backs up the main-line system.

Caution: Be careful about tying additional climbing ropes to the main line and belay ropes to increase the total length of a single raising or lowering system. The stretch in a suddenly loaded 300-foot (100-meter) belay system made with dynamic ropes can be as much as 24 feet (8 meters)—a long way for the patient to fall while on belay.

Climbing ropes are dynamic—they stretch under load, typically 8 percent, or 12 feet (3.7 meters) for a fully extended 150-foot (50-meter) rope. The main line is always under load and always stretched. The belay rope should be under load only in an instance of main-line failure, and thus it is not stretched when the rescue is running smoothly. If the main line has 100 feet (30 meters) of rope extended out tightly from the patient to the belayer and there is a main-line failure, this will cause a fall on the belay line of approximately 8 feet (2.4 meters) due to rope stretch alone as the belay rope becomes loaded.

Organized rescue units use low-stretch ropes for both main line and belay. These units routinely tie additional low-stretch ropes to the main line and belay, and then deal with the joining knots using the knot-passing techniques described later in this chapter.

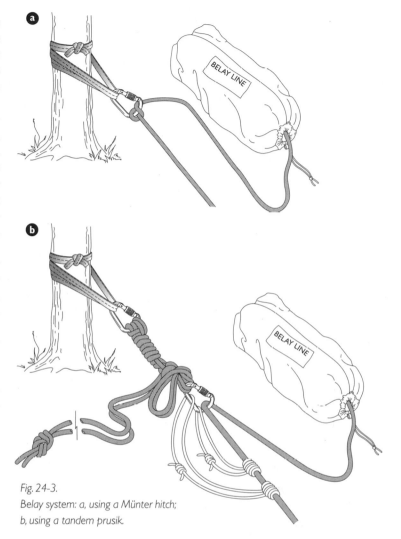

Fig. 24-3.
Belay system: a, using a Münter hitch;
b, using a tandem prusik.

Belay Technique

It is desirable to have an independent belay system for the patient and the attendant (see Figure 24-1b, above). The belay system should never carry a load except when the main line fails. Where the belay and main-line ropes run over sharp edges, it is the belay rope that must be protected from the edge.

Be aware that the belay line will always stretch upon being loaded in the event of a main line failure, and it will possible drop the patient and attendant a surprising distance. For example, with a two-person load potentially causing a 10 percent stretch factor or more, and with 50 meters of rope out, the load could fall 5 meters or more due just to the stretch. This is a special hazard of using dynamic climbing ropes as a rescue belay. Organized rescue operations always use low-stretch rescue ropes, but they must use higher strength systems to deal with the increased shock load.

For a two-person load, a Münter hitch anchored 2 meters or more from the edge, or a tandem prusik

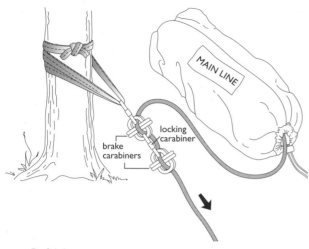

Fig. 24-4.
*Main-line lowering system
using a double carabiner brake.*

belay attached to a load-releasing hitch, provides enough friction to stop the load.

Münter hitch: The Münter hitch is described and illustrated in Chapter 9, Basic Safety System. The Münter hitch should be attached directly to an anchor 2 meters or more from the edge so that the anchor and belay line—not the belayer's body—absorb the forces generated by a rescue-load (two-person) fall (fig. 24-3a). The Münter hitch belay holds best when the free end of the rope passing through the Münter hitch is kept parallel to the climber's end of the rope and not angled to one side. In tests, the dynamic nature of the climbing rope used as the belay line absorbs enough of the shock of a fall to allow a Münter hitch to hold. Enough rope (2 meters or more) must be in the system to provide sufficient stretch to absorb much of the shock load.

Tandem prusik: The tandem prusik belay consists of two 7- or 8-millimeter prusik loops of different size. The short loop is formed from a 1.35-meter length of perlon, and the longer loop is formed from a 1.65-meter length, with ends joined by a double fisherman's knot. Fasten the loops onto the belay line using triple-wrapped prusiks, with the longer loop nearer the attendant/patient load. The loops are then clipped into the load-releasing hitch (LRH) carabiner containing the

tail of the LRH; load-releasing hitches are described below. The other end of the LRH is connected to the belay anchor (fig. 24-3b).

The task of the belayer is to keep the tandem prusiks from grabbing onto the belay line. One hand tends the two prusiks. The other hand manages the rope and checks that 10 to 20 cm of slack (but not more) is present. The belayer keeps this small amount of slack in the system to reduce the chance that the tandem prusiks will inadvertently grab and stop the belay line.

In the event of a main line failure, the belayer releases the prusiks, which will immediately grab the line. The LRH is extended to release any deliberate or inadvertent setup of the belay.

Note that the belay will engage if anything happens to the belayer or if the belay line starts to move so quickly that the belayer can't keep up. This is why the tandem prusik belay is one of the few systems that passes the whistle test.

Main-Line Lower Technique

The best lowering device for a small party without specialized rescue gear is the double carabiner brake system (fig. 24-4). Construct two carabiner brakes (see Figure 11-11 in Chapter 11, Rappelling) and join them with a single locking carabiner, gate up, which eliminates the possibility that the rope could become pinched between a pair of carabiner brakes. For the carabiner brakes themselves, standard symmetrical oval carabiners work best. The front carabiner brake should be made with two brake carabiners (as shown in Figure 11-11b); the rear carabiner brake may have one or two brake carabiners (as shown in Figure 11-11a), depending on the total weight of the load and the steepness of the terrain. Be conservative, but recognize that too much friction in the lowering system may cause problems on low-angle terrain.

Main-Line Raise Technique

For a raising system, rescuers usually use the 3:1 (Z) pulley system (fig. 24-5), the most efficient of the simple raising systems. See Chapter 17, Glacier Travel and Crevasse Rescue. Be careful that haulers do not pull too zealously on the rope. A fast, jerky raise makes it difficult for the patient to negotiate broken terrain and maintain a

24

The high directional is a pulley suspended 4 to 9 feet (1 to 3 meters) off the ground, through which the main-line rope runs (see Figure 24-1c, above.) If a sturdy tree is growing at the cliff's edge, rescuers can wrap webbing around the tree trunk three to five times, preferably above a branch to prevent slippage, and attach a pulley. They then thread the main-line rope through the pulley before tying the patient in.

Note: Never rig the belay rope through a high directional. High directionals could potentially fail, leading to a sudden drop of the patient. This is not acceptable for a belay system.

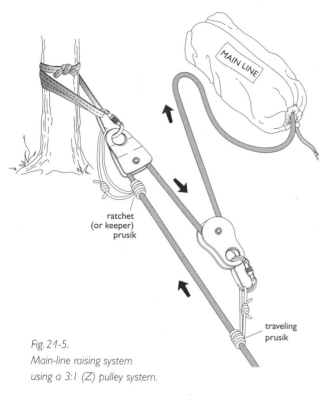

Fig. 24-5.
Main-line raising system
using a 3:1 (Z) pulley system.

stable position. If the rope jams and the haulers keep pulling, the system then applies its powerful three-to-one mechanical advantage to the anchors instead of to raising the injured climber; this may yank out the anchors.

If only a few rescuers are available, a 5:1 pulley system can be constructed by adding to the 3:1 system a triple runner or cordelette that is 15 to 25 feet (5 to 8 meters) long. Clip the triple runner to the anchor carabiner (fig. 24-6a), then clip the triple runner in to the traveling sling and pulley (fig. 24-6b). With this system, a single climber can hoist a partner.

High Directional for Main Line

Moving the patient over the edge of a cliff involves shifting the direction of movement from vertical to horizontal (or vice versa). This transition in direction often poses difficulties and requires the most effort from the rescue team. A high directional can be created that in essence "moves the cliff edge" to several feet directly above the patient, thus eliminating a transition of direction from vertical to horizontal.

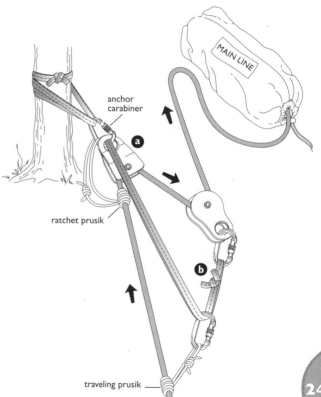

Fig. 24-6.
One-person 5:1 raising system converted from a 3:1 (Z) pulley system: a, add a triple runner or cordelette (15–25 feet long) to the anchor carabiner; b, clip the triple runner or cordelette into the traveling prusik and pulley.

503

Patient and Attendant

If the patient is uninjured or has minor upper-body injuries, the rescuers may decide to raise or lower the patient without an attendant. This puts less stress on the rescue systems. The patient ties in to both the main-line and belay ropes.

If the patient has leg or foot injuries that do not allow the patient to assist in being raised, an attendant may be required. Usually this is the first-aid leader. Both the patient and attendant tie in to the belay and main-line ropes (see Figure 24-1e, above).

Main-line rope: On the main-line rope, the attendant ties in at the very end. Attach the patient to the main line with a prusik knot and clip the prusik loop to the seat harness. Adjust the prusik to place the patient alongside or on the back of the attendant.

Belay rope: On the belay rope, the attendant ties in about 6 feet (2 meters) from the end using a longtail bowline (fig. 24-7), and then ties in the patient with a figure-eight knot at the end of the bowline's tail.

Both the patient and the attendant are now firmly attached to both the rescue and belay systems. As they move together, the attendant's chest should be even with the patient's back, putting the attendant in position to help support and stabilize the patient. In some situations, it may be necessary for the attendant to carry the patient. The attendant needs to be strong enough to carry the patient's weight, especially when the rescue is on lower-angle terrain. For short distances, the coil carry or the nylon-webbing carry can be used.

Coil carry: In the coil carry, a coiled rope is divided into two loops (fig. 24-8a), then the patient's legs are placed through the lower part of the loops (fig. 24-8b). The attendant slips the upper half of the loops over each shoulder (fig. 24-8c). This seat can be padded to help make the patient more comfortable. Tie a short piece of webbing around both loops at the attendant's sternum to keep the coils from slipping off the attendant's shoulders. Run a prusik loop from the main-line lowering rope to the patient's chest harness to take some of the weight off the attendant's shoulders and help keep the patient upright.

Nylon-webbing carry: The nylon-webbing carry employs nylon webbing to support and distribute the patient's weight. Place the webbing around the patient's back and cross it in front of the chest (fig. 24-9a). Bring the ends over the attendant's shoulders (fig. 24-9b), then under the attendant's arms, through the patient's crotch, and around the outside of the patient's thighs (fig. 24-9c). The attendant then secures the ends to his or her seat harness (fig. 24-9d) and the patient grasps the attendant's shoulders (fig. 24-9e). The webbing should be extremely well padded, especially under the patient's thighs and at the attendant's shoulders, to prevent loss of circulation.

Note: For severe injuries (internal injures, head injuries, multiple fractures, etc.), the rescue team should secure the patient in a safe location and wait for an outside rescue team and a rigid litter.

Fig. 24-7.

Longtail bowline should be approximately 5 feet long. Attendant ties in using the bowline, and the patient is connected via a figure-eight knot. (Knots shown are not yet properly dressed.)

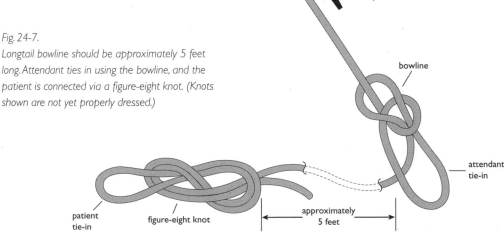

to belay

bowline

attendant
tie-in

patient
tie-in

figure-eight knot

approximately
5 feet

24

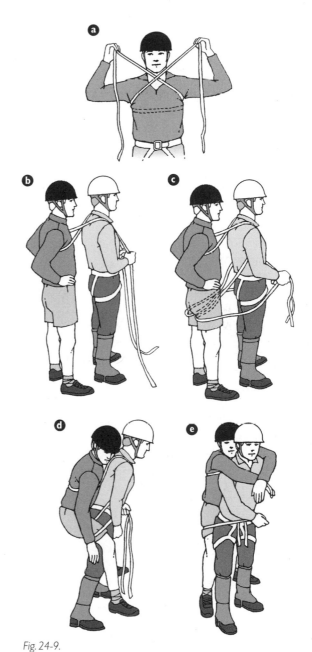

Fig. 24-8.
Coil carry: a, coil the rope, sizing the loops to fit from the patient's armpits to crotch; b, place patient's legs through lower part of loops; c, attendant slips upper part of loops over the shoulders and ties these loops together at the chest with a short piece of webbing.

Fig. 24-9.
Nylon-webbing carry: a, place webbing around patient's back and cross in front of chest; b, place ends over attendant's shoulders; c, bring ends under attendant's arms, through patient's crotch, and around outside of patient's thighs; d, attendant ties together ends of webbing around waist; e, patient puts arms over attendant's shoulders.

24

Knot Passing

In the stress of responding to a rescue situation, rescuers may not detect a knot or tangle until the rescue system is in use. Experienced rescuers anticipate such problems with the rescue system (knot passes, changing from a raise to a lower, etc.) and have ready a hitch and prusik placed on a rope. With a load-releasing hitch (LRH), a rescuer is able to safely rearrange or reconstruct the main-line or belay system. Practice knot passing on belay, raising, and lowering systems before using the LRH in the mountains.

Tying a Load-Releasing Hitch

The load-releasing hitch (LRH) is used with a single prusik to form an easy-to-release hitch that can hold the main line for knot passes or changing from a raise to a lower. It can also be used with two prusiks to form the tandem prusik belay.

Make the LRH from a cordelette of 5.5-millimeter Spectra or 7- or 8-millimeter perlon cord that is 15 to 25 feet (5 to 8 meters) long. The LRH for the tandem prusik belay should be made from 7- or 8-millimeter perlon cord only, not from 5.5-millimeter Spectra. LRHs made with Spectra are only used in main-line knot passes.

Warning: Little is known about the consequences of using Spectra in LRHs used as part of the tandem prusik belay on climbing ropes. When a Spectra LRH is used on low-stretch rescue ropes, the Spectra has the potential of melting during the catch of a fall, where the force of the fall is entirely absorbed by the double prusiks and the LRH. Until more is known, do not use Spectra in the tandem prusik belay on dynamic climbing ropes.

To make the LRH, find the center of the cord and form a loop with strands of equal length. Clip the loop to a locking carabiner, which will be called the LRH carabiner, then use a Münter hitch to attach the rest of the cord to a locking pear-shaped carabiner, which will be called the anchor carabiner (fig. 24-10a). The anchor carabiner must be a locking pear-shaped carabiner or a large rescue carabiner in order to allow the Münter hitch to perform its characteristic flip during use.

To create additional friction, wrap the free end of the cord around the doubled cord between the LRH carabiner and the Münter hitch four to six times (fig. 24-10b). Pass a small bight through the doubled cord below the

wraps (fig. 24-10c). Tie an overhand knot with the bight and the free end of the cord (fig. 24-10d). Pull each strand of the bight tight. Finally, tie an overhand or figure-eight knot at the end of the cord (fig. 24-10e) to prevent the LRH from coming completely undone if it is left unattended (the knot will jam in the Münter hitch).

For the tandem prusik belay, two prusik loops are attached to the belay line (the smaller loop closer on the rope, the longer loop farther away) with triple-wrapped prusiks and then to the LRH carabiner. (See Figure 24-3b, above.)

During changeovers and knot passes, the LRH is fastened to the main line or belay rope with a single triple-wrapped prusik whose single loop is clipped to the LRH carabiner (fig. 24-10f).

To release the prusik(s) attached to the LRH when under a load, untie the loose-end tie-off. Without removing the wraps, "unscrew" (loosen) these wraps using your hand, which feeds the cord through the Münter hitch and lengthens the LRH.

Passing a Main-Line Knot During a Lower

When a knot or tangle in the main-line rope gets within 6 inches (15 centimeters) of a lower rescue system (fig. 24-11a), stop using the system and attach the LRH below the system (fig. 24-11b). Ease the load onto the LRH and remove the old system from the rope (fig. 24-11c), and then reattach the old system on the other side of the knot (fig. 24-11d). Finally, lengthen the LRH to return the load to the rescue system: Untie the loose-end tie-off and, without removing the wraps, "unscrew" (loosen) these wraps using your hand, which then feeds the cord through the Münter hitch and lengthens the LRH (fig. 24-11e). Return the load to the main-line rope and then remove the LRH (fig. 24-11f).

Passing a Main-Line Knot During a Raise

When a knot or tangle gets within 6 inches (15 centimeters) of the traveling prusik, stop the raise and let the ratchet prusik take the load (fig. 24-12a). Untie, then retie the traveling prusik below the knot (fig. 24-12b).

When the knot or tangle gets within 6 inches (15 centimeters) of the rachet prusik, stop the raise and let the rachet prusik hold the load. Add a longer length of webbing to the anchor; attach another pulley and prusik

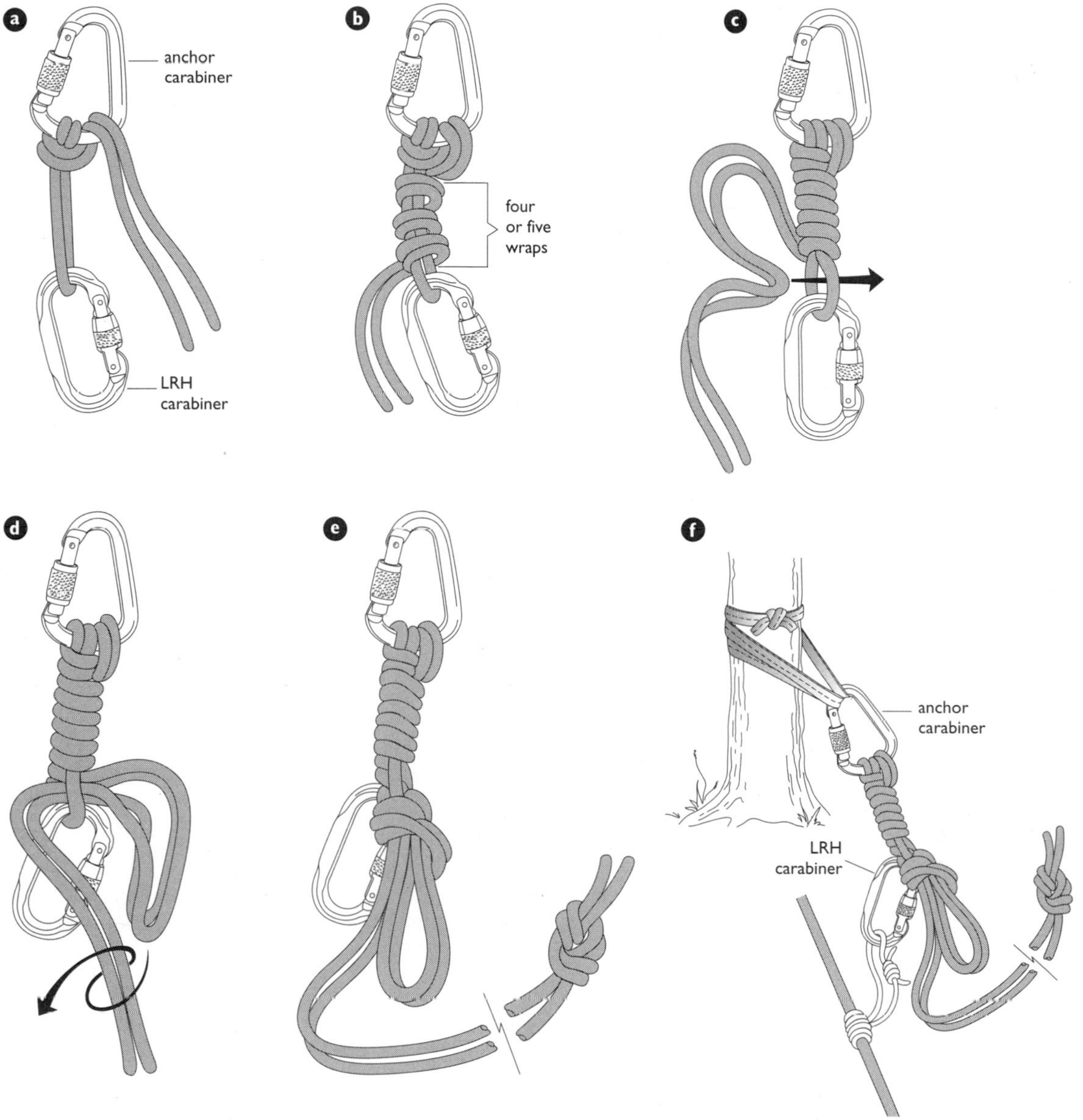

Fig. 24-10.

Tying a load-releasing hitch (LRH): a, clip cord loop to the LRH carabiner, then use a Münter hitch to attach cord to anchor carabiner; b, wrap free end of cord around doubled cord between carabiners; c, insert one bight of the two parallel pieces of cord through the doubled cord strands; d, tie the bight and the free end of cord with an overhand knot; e, tighten all four strands of the bight to form a tight knot and tie off bottom of free end with figure-eight or overhand knot; f, for a changeover or knot pass, attach carabiner with Münter hitch to anchor and connect the LHR carabiner to prusik on main line or belay rope.

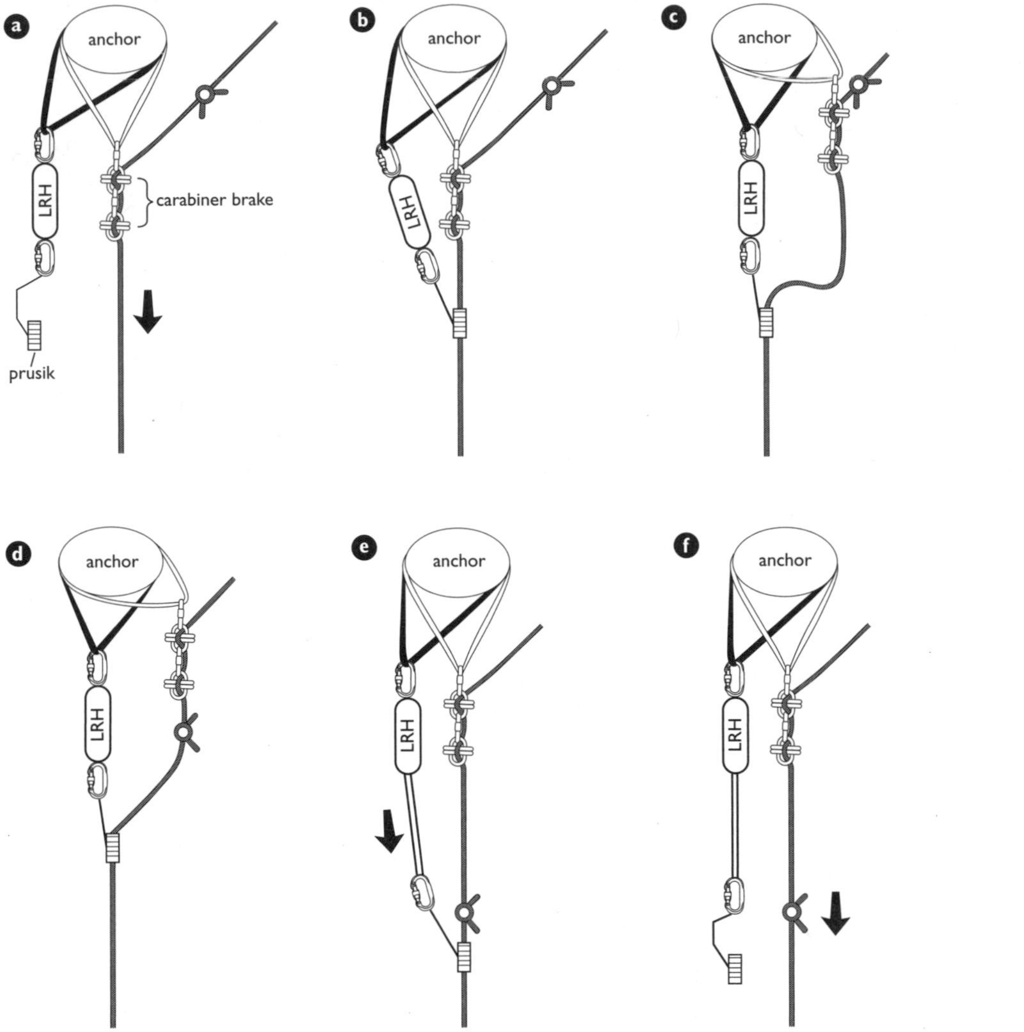

Fig. 24-11.

Passing a main-line knot during a lower: a, when the knot approaches the double carabiner brake, stop using the system; b, attach the LRH and prusik to the main line below the double carabiner brake; c, ease the load onto the LRH and unclip the main line from the double carabiner brake; d, reattach the double carabiner brake to the main line above the knot; e, lengthen the LRH to weight the double carabiner brake; f, remove the LRH and prusik.

(fig. 24-12c). Put this new pulley and new rachet prusik on the rope below the knot (fig. 24-12d). The haulers now pull up slightly to release the rachet prusik. Holding the rachet prusik open, let the rope slip through the original ratchet prusik while the haulers lower the load slowly onto the new ratchet prusik and new pulley.

At this point, the original ratchet prusik and pulley are no longer under tension and are removed (fig. 24-12e). When the knot approaches the traveling pulley, stop the raise and let the new ratchet prusik take the load. Undo, then redo the traveling pulley below the knot (fig. 24-12f).

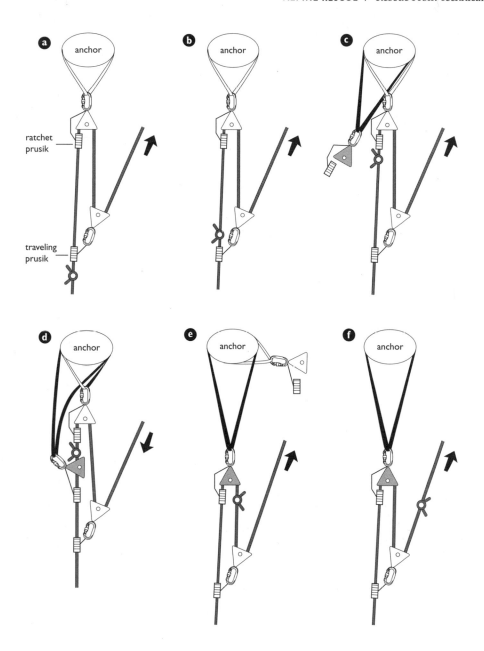

Fig. 24-12.

Passing a main-line knot during a raise: a, when the knot approaches the traveling prusik, stop the system and ease the load onto the ratchet prusik; b, untie the traveling prusik and retie it below the knot; c, when the knot approaches the ratchet prusik, stop the system and allow the ratchet prusik to hold the load, then add a longer anchor webbing with a new pulley and new ratchet prusik; d, tie the new ratchet prusik below the knot and hold the original ratchet prusik open while the main line is lowered until a new ratchet prusik and new pulley hold the load; e, remove the original ratchet prusik and pulley; f, when the knot approaches the traveling prusik's pulley, stop the system, ease the load onto the ratchet prusik, then remove the traveling pulley and reattach it below the knot.

Passing a Knot While Belaying

Passing the knot through the belay system is the same whether you are lowering or raising. The belay line always has some slack in it, which allows you to attach a new belay system. When the knot on the belay line gets within 12 inches (30 centimeters) of the Münter hitch or the tandem prusiks, stop the lower or raise but keep the belay on.

Münter hitch: Add a completely new anchor and belay system on the other side of the knot. Allow just enough slack in the belay rope, if you are raising, to tie the Münter hitch for the new belay. When the new belay system is ready, untie the original Münter hitch and remove its carabiner and anchor webbing.

Tandem prusik belay: Tie two new tandem prusik loops (long and short) onto the belay line with triple-wrapped prusik knots on the other side of the belay line knot and connect to a new locking carabiner on the load-releasing hitch (LRH). Then untie the original loops and remove the loops and the original locking carabiner on the LRH.

EVACUATION

Once the rescue party is off the steep terrain of ice or rock, the hard work of evacuation back to the trailhead begins. Miles of cross-country and trail travel may be necessary. The patient's condition, the distance to be covered, and the rescue party's strength determine whether overland evacuation to the trailhead is feasible. If not, the rescue party may decide to evacuate the patient to an area suitable for helicopter pickup instead or to remain in place and wait until outside assistance arrives.

Snow Evacuations

Snow evacuations can be as simple as placing the patient in a bivy sack or blanket and sliding the patient down the slope. It is particularly urgent to protect the patient from heat loss while on snow. Belay the patient during transport. Rescuers can set up anchors for belays and braking devices using pickets, flukes, bollards, and deadman anchors (see "Roped Snow-Climbing Techniques" in Chapter 16, Snow Travel and Climbing). Note that the boot-ax belay is not strong enough for use in rescues.

Cross-Country and Trail Evacuations

A rescue team can use a number of techniques to move the patient to the trailhead. However, it takes considerable effort to move just a short distance, especially if the trail or path is difficult. These techniques include:

Assisted walk: The patient walks, and a rescuer walks alongside the patient, providing physical support.

Four-hand seat: This technique, useful for only very short distances, requires two carriers who are approximately the same height. The carriers grasp wrists with their palms down (fig. 24-13a). This forms a seat for the patient (fig. 24-13b).

Fig. 24-13.
Four-hand seat carry:
a, two rescuers of
equal height grasp
wrists; b, the patient
sits on this seat and
puts arms around
rescuers' shoulders for
a short-distance carry.

Back carries: Strong climbers may be able carry a person on their back for a short distance if the weight is distributed properly. The coil carry and nylon-webbing carry described in "Systems for Rescue" earlier in this chapter work well. Rescuers should take turns acting as carriers as often as necessary to prevent exhausting any one member of the rescue party. The rucksack carry is another useful type of back carry. In this method, you make slits in the sides of a large backpack so the patient can step into it as though it were a pair of shorts.

Rope litter: Although you can build a rudimentary litter out of a climbing rope or blanket, consider the patient's condition before you attempt to use one. Usually such a litter aggravates existing injuries. If a litter is required, wait for a rigid litter to arrive.

Stream and Boulder-Field Crossings

While the rescue party is traveling cross-country, swift-running streams or jumbled boulder fields occasionally must be crossed. Loss of footing could prove disastrous to both the patient and a rescuer who is doing a back carry.

To cross either a stream or a boulder field, form two lines of rescuers across the obstacle: in the stream from shore to shore, or across the boulder field from one end to the other. These rescuers can act as handholds and supports for the rescuer who is carrying the patient. Alternatively, place the patient in a rudimentary litter and pass the litter hand to hand across the stream or boulder field.

Helicopter Evacuations

Helicopters have revolutionized mountain rescue. When weather permits, they can deliver rescue teams to remote areas and pluck injured climbers from cliffs and glaciers. Helicopters can deliver an injured climber to the hospital in hours, whereas ground transport can take days.

Do not base your rescue plans on an immediate helicopter rescue just because helicopters are used in your area. A helicopter may not be available at the time your climbing party needs help. Bad weather, poor visibility, hot temperatures, or high altitude may limit helicopter operation.

Rescue helicopters load and transport an injured person in one of three ways:
- Land and take the patient aboard.
- Hover while winching the injured climber, safely attached to a steel cable, aboard.
- Dangle the injured climber by a cable fastened to a harness or litter and fly the patient to safety.

The rescue team's role in helicopter rescue is to:
- Help the pilot spot the team by waving brightly colored objects and clothing.
- Indicate wind direction using streamers or by standing with backs to the wind, arms forward.
- Move all loose objects, including natural vegetation such as fallen branches, well away from the landing zone.
- Move the patient and rescuers to an area well away from the landing zone.
- Protect the patient and rescuers from windblown debris.
- Follow the instructions of the helicopter crew chief.

A member of the helicopter crew may be lowered to the ground to assess the patient's condition, evaluate potential landing zones and wind conditions, and radio pertinent information to the pilot. The rescue team must be prepared to assist this crew member, remembering that this person may be a nonclimber and unfamiliar with things such as hidden dangers on glaciers or how to move on steep terrain. The helicopter pilot might then attempt a landing or may decide to hoist the patient if the helicopter is capable of this.

Safety concerns are of the utmost importance when dealing with helicopters. So many things pose a danger: gusts of wind, static electricity buildup on the helicopter, brush or grass fires sparked by the helicopter exhaust, and blowing dust and debris, among others. The downwash and noise of the helicopter are overwhelming; wear eye protection and climbing helmets, and protect your ears if possible. Stay away from the helicopter, do not touch any cables and baskets, and do not move until you are signaled by the helicopter crew chief. If the helicopter lands, approach *only* from the front of the helicopter, and only when instructed to do so.

24

SEARCHES

Infrequently, a climber becomes separated from the climbing party.

If this climber is well equipped and experienced and on easy terrain, it may be best for the party to wait for the person at the trailhead. In this instance, postpone any search until the next morning.

If bad weather, difficult terrain, or medical considerations indicate that the missing climber might need help, start the search immediately. The most effective search method is to return to the point where the missing person was last seen and retrace the party's route. Look for places where the climber might have left the route; try to visualize errors the person might have made. Look for clues, such as footprints in mud, sand, or snow.

Before sending out search teams, the climb leader should discuss meeting times and return times for each of the teams. If radios or wireless phones are available, the teams should agree on scheduled call-in times. As in technical rescues, the safety of the rescuers comes first.

If, after several hours of searching, the searchers find no sign of the missing climber, it is probably time to request outside help.

OUTSIDE RESCUE ASSISTANCE

Organized rescue groups bring to the scene the benefits of extensive training and experience, combined with specialized equipment and techniques, including helicopter rescue. Outside rescue assistance is needed when:

- The technical rescue will take too long
- The patient is too severely injured
- The evacuation will take too long
- The search area is too expansive

Organized rescue groups may be professional, as they are in much of Europe; the famed Swiss Air Rescue Service is the best known. In North America, official responsibility for rescue rests with local government agencies such as the county sheriff's department or the National Park Service. Many sheriff's departments have

officers trained in search and rescue (SAR) techniques, and the larger national parks have skilled climbing rangers whose main job is to assist climbers in trouble and organize searches for lost hikers. Some organized rescue groups are military helicopter units, such as the 304th Rescue Squadron based in Portland, Oregon.

In the United States and Canada, however, most organized mountain rescue groups are volunteer organizations, consisting of local climbers who receive specialized training in high-angle rescue, search techniques, and helicopter operations. Mountain rescue volunteers are usually called in to assist the responsible government agency by providing the necessary number of leaders and support members to successfully complete a rescue.

Searches with Outside Rescue Groups

The science of searching has advanced in recent years, as can be seen in the techniques used during an organized search. Search coordinators from the responsible government agency use mathematical models to predict the behavior of lost subjects. They employ computers to assess probabilities of detection, to assign zones for each party of searchers, and to evaluate urgency factors.

A number of search-and-rescue (SAR) groups, usually volunteer, may work with the search coordinators. Search dogs follow scents; human trackers can spot signs of passage; helicopters cover large areas quickly; trained interviewers (usually police officers) develop personality profiles that help searchers guess the possible behavior of the subject; four-wheel-drive vehicles travel rough roads and wait at exit trailheads; mountain rescue units cover steep terrain.

Once these SAR groups have been called in to take over the search, the best action the original climbing team can do is to stay safe and communicate with the search coordinators. This may mean waiting at the accident site until the SAR group arrives, or it could mean evacuating all team members who are not needed for patient care until the outside rescue group takes over. Each rescue has different needs. The search coordinators will want information that only the climbing team can provide. After an initial briefing, the search coordinators may ask the climbing team to assist in the search effort or may release the team to go home.

Evacuations with Outside Rescue Groups

When an organized mountain rescue team arrives to aid an injured person, the initial rescuers can help by cooperating closely with the new team. These new rescuers will assume responsibility for first-aid treatment and completing the rescue and evacuation.

The new rescue leader will assess the situation, concentrating on the status of the injured climber, and then organize the outside group's team to carry out the rescue. This new rescue leader will look to members of the outside rescue team to perform most of the vital tasks. This team will have trained together and developed the teamwork skills to safely and quickly carry out the rescue.

The original climb leader will remain in charge of the climbing party and be responsible for its safety. However, the climbing party should be prepared to lend a hand if the new rescue leader specifically asks for help.

If this happens, the new rescue leader assumes authority over everyone at the scene. All the rescuers at the scene need to perform their tasks and fulfill their roles to the best of their abilities and training in order for a successful rescue and evacuation to occur.

USING ALL THESE SKILLS

Good leadership and climbing skills help climbers avoid situations where first aid and rescue techniques are needed. Yet, unexpected circumstances can arise that place climbers in jeopardy, so being prepared to help fellow climbers is essential. Learn leadership, first-aid, and rescue skills and keep current in their application through regular review. Make sure to practice the rescue techniques outlined in this chapter—reading by itself does not provide the necessary skills.

Become one of those climbers—confident of leadership, first-aid, and rescue skills—who has the ability to safely rescue and evacuate an injured person in treacherous terrain. Then you will be more fully prepared to explore the freedom of the hills.

24

Next page: *Climbers crossing a glacier with sun cups, a lenticular cloud overhead, on Mount Rainier* (Photo by Mark Kroese)

THE MOUNTAIN ENVIRONMENT

Mountain Geology

Geology is the basis for understanding the form and substance of mountains. Climbers learn from experience that different types of rock affect what different routes are like, ranging from sheer walls to those having cracks and ledges galore. Climbers also discover that some kinds of rocks are nearly always solid, whereas others crumble under pressure. Geology is essential knowledge; climbing success or even your life can depend on that knowledge.

GEOLOGIC PERSPECTIVES

You can gain a better understanding of mountains by examining them on three scales: as an overall landscape, as a single outcrop, and as a close-up view of a single specimen of rock. Each perspective contributes to your overall comprehension of the mountain environment.

Landscape: This wide-angle view examines the mountain as a whole, sometimes from miles away. Observing geology at this scale helps you find a viable route to the summit. Using photos or binoculars, you can look for routes with strong, supporting rock, or identify areas where rock may be weak and unreliable—in other words, places to trust and places to treat with caution. Ridges may follow a layer of resistant rock. Sets of fractures may offer a zigzag route to the summit. Sudden changes in slope may indicate a fault (a fracture along which movement has occurred) or an abrupt change in rock type.

Outcrop: This perspective focuses on specific outcrops from 10 to 100 feet (3 to 30 meters) away. Here you can see features that could help—or hinder—an ascent. For example, a regular pattern of cracks is probably a good bet for chocks, and a resistant dike (fractures that were filled by molten rock) may provide an avenue upward.

Rock specimen: At arm's length from the outcrop or closer, the details of rocks are more apparent. At this scale, you can identify rock types and recognize textures that might be difficult to climb or provide advantageous holds.

HOW MOUNTAINS ARE FORMED

The ultimate landscape view is the whole Earth. When you look at mountain ranges on a global scale, you can see a clear pattern of their occurrence, and this pattern can be explained by plate tectonic processes. According to the theory of plate tectonics, the outermost layer of the Earth (called the lithosphere) is broken into plates that are slowly but constantly moving.

Most mountain ranges are formed by immense forces that squeeze rock masses together or pull them apart. Where tectonic plates move toward each other, their edges (margins) are called convergent. Where tectonic plates pull away from each other, their margins are called divergent. A third type of plate margin, transform margins, move blocks of lithosphere side by side, and mountains are rarely produced in these areas. This section describes the two types of mountain-forming plate margins.

Convergent Plate Margins

Three varieties of convergent margins each produce a somewhat different style of mountains.

Ocean-ocean margins: These occur where two plates of oceanic lithosphere converge (fig. 25-1a). The older, colder slab forms a subduction zone by taking a dive beneath the younger, warmer slab. Deep within the subduction zone, 55 to 60 miles (90 to 100 kilometers) below the Earth's surface, abundant magma (molten rock beneath the surface of the Earth) is formed and rises buoyantly. Over time, much of the magma makes its way to the surface, where a chain of oceanic island volcanoes grows. The island mountains of the Aleutians and Indonesia are two examples.

Ocean-continent margins: Subduction can also occur where oceanic lithosphere is subducted beneath the edge of a continent (fig. 25-1b). This produces a chain of volcanic mountains on land. Three types of volcanoes can be formed. Shield volcanoes, great conical stacks of basalt flows with gentle slopes, such as Belknap Crater in the Cascades Range of central Oregon, are uncommon. Most of the climbing destinations along ocean-continent convergent margins are stratovolcanoes, typically composed of andesite with steep slopes, such as Washington's Mount Rainier and Mount Baker or Mount Fujiyama in Japan. Cinder cones, composed of pyroclastic fragments, are generally only a few hundred feet high. These include the Black Buttes near Bend, Oregon, and Wizard Island in Oregon's Crater Lake.

As tectonic plates move, they cause various stresses—faulting, folding, and uplift—that create mountain structures (see "Mountain Structures" later in this chapter). These movements, as well as erosion, expose deeper layers of the Earth's crust. For example, the schist and gneiss exposed in Washington's North Cascades originated as clay and silt on the seafloor 250 million years ago. During plate convergence, this material was buried as much as 100,000 feet (30,000 meters) beneath the Earth's surface, where it was metamorphosed by heat and pressure into schist and gneiss. Continued plate convergence has now moved these rocks back to the surface in the northern part of the range. To the south, volcanism has buried the metamorphic basement yet again and has built a chain of large stratovolcanoes that extends from British Columbia to northern California.

25

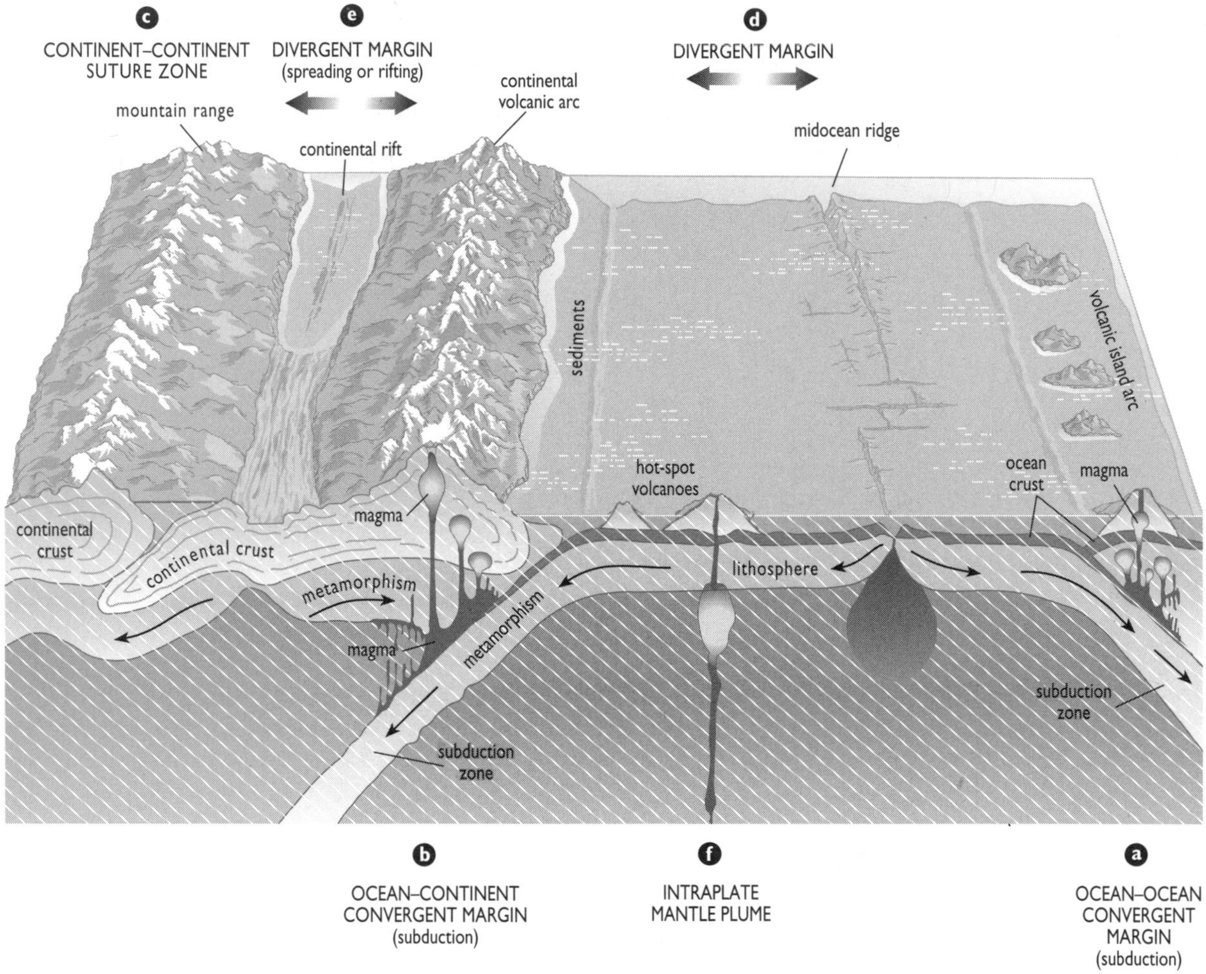

Fig. 25-1.

Characteristic features of various types of convergent and divergent plate margins: a, ocean-ocean convergent margin producing a volcanic island arc; b, ocean-continent convergent margin producing a continental magmatic arc; c, continent-continent convergence zone producing a suture zone mountain range; d, oceanic divergent margin producing a midocean ridge; e, continental divergent margin producing rifts; f, intraplate mantle plume producing a chain of seafloor volcanoes.

Mountain ranges of similar origin include the Andes of South America and the Japanese Alps.

Suture zones: Many of the major mountain ranges of the Earth are found where continental or island arc plates have smashed together as they have converged (fig. 25-1c). For example, the Himalayas have been uplifted by the collision of India and Asia, Europe's Alps were created by Africa's northward push into Europe,

and the Rocky Mountains were uplifted by the collision of numerous microplates that extended the edge of North America hundreds of miles westward over the past 170 million years. In these mountain ranges, faulting may thrust one part of the range over another. These huge thrust-faulted structures are well exposed in the Alps, the Canadian Rockies, and the North Cascades (see Figure 25-3, below).

25

Divergent Plate Margins

Where lithospheric plates diverge, the lithosphere is stretched and ultimately breaks apart, as when taffy is pulled too quickly. The most extensive divergent margins are the submarine mountain ranges of the midoceanic ridges (fig. 25-1d), but these are obviously inaccessible to climbers. Divergent margins also develop within continents (fig. 25-1e), and these definitely produce terrain of interest to mountaineers.

Continental rifts: As the lithospheric plates move apart along continental rifts, vertical faults break the crust into huge block-shaped mountains with nearly vertical faces on one side and more gentle slopes on the other. These form great escarpments, such as the East African Rift Valleys. Some mountains of the western United States, including Utah's Wasatch Range and California's Sierra Nevada, are fault-block ranges associated with stretching (extension) within the North American Plate rather than along its margin (fig. 25-2).

Mountains created by extension generally have less relief (contrasting elevations) than those created by convergent margins, but not always. Mount Whitney, part of the Sierra Nevada, is the highest peak in the contiguous United States at 14,494 feet (4,400 meters); Wheeler Peak of the Snake Range in eastern Nevada rises above 13,000 feet (4,000 meters).

Volcanism also affects the topography of rifted margins. Magma from the upwelling mantle beneath the rift can rise through faults to the surface, where over time it builds up both shield volcanoes and composite cones, such as Africa's Kilimanjaro.

Intraplate "Hot-Spot" Volcanoes

The tallest mountain on Earth is not Mount Everest but, rather, the island of Hawaii, where the summit of Mauna Kea is 30,000 feet (9,000 meters) above the seafloor. Hawaii is part of a chain of volcanic islands and underwater seamounts that extend from the mid-Pacific nearly to Japan. These gigantic islands of basalt are the surface expression of thermal plumes, called hot spots (fig. 25-1f), that rise from the lower mantle toward the overlying lithosphere like a cumulus cloud building toward the stratosphere on a warm summer day. These plumes burn through the moving lithosphere, creating a chain of volcanoes built upward from the seafloor.

Hot spots are also located within the continents—an example is the chain of volcanoes and lava flows (lava is rock that is molten at the surface of the Earth) that extend across the Snake River Plain from near Boise, Idaho, northeast to Yellowstone National Park, where the plume is currently located. Because hot spots

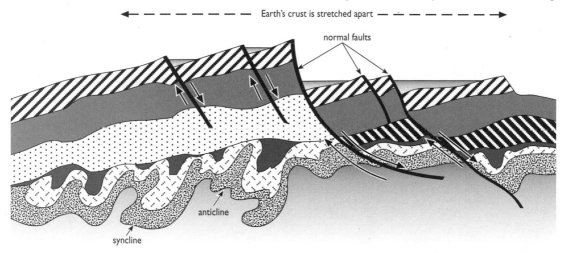

Earth's crust is stretched apart

normal faults

anticline

syncline

Fig. 25-2.

Typical structures of a continental divergent plate margin, such as the Basin and Range of the western United States or the African Rift Valleys. Note steep escarpment formed due to normal faulting.

25

produce mainly shield volcanoes with gentle slopes, technical climbing is rarely required for ascending them, but one of the most interesting traverses in the world is the trail to the summit of Mauna Loa on the island of Hawaii.

MOUNTAIN STRUCTURES

The slowest tectonic plates move at about the same velocity as fingernails grow, and the fastest move at about the same velocity as hair grows—about 2 to 7 inches (5 to 17 centimeters) per year. Such slow movements cannot be seen, but the effect on the surface of the Earth can be profound. Slow as it is, this movement of the tectonic plates stresses rocks, and the results are the varying structures we know as mountains. These stresses move mountains up, down, or from side to side and break them up into pieces. Near the Earth's surface the rock layers are brittle, so they fracture into joints or move along faults. At greater depth, where the temperature and pressure are higher, the rocks tend to bend into folds rather than breaking.

Folds

Most sedimentary rocks are originally deposited in horizontal layers known as beds. However, in mountains such as the Front Range of Colorado, it is common to see beds that dip steeply or are even vertical.

These rocks have been compressed into folds. You can simulate this by laying a napkin flat on a table and pushing its sides together, producing a series of archlike anticlines and troughlike synclines (fig. 25-3). Folds range in size from microscopic to a mile or more high. In some cases, such as the Ridge and Valley Province of the Appalachians, the shape of the entire range is dictated by the underlying fold structure. Folds are best observed by looking at the landscape or outcrop view, rather than at a rock specimen. The patterns of folds create ramps, overhangs, and resistant ridges that can be crucial factors in planning a route to a summit.

Joints and Veins

Joints are cracks that develop when rock masses expand or contract. Contraction joints are formed when hot rock shrinks during cooling. The only common kind of pure contraction jointing is the columnar structure of lava flows. The result is an array of roughly hexagonal columns that are typically 10 feet (3 meters) in height. Exceptionally high columns such as Devils Tower in Wyoming provide spectacular climbing opportunities.

Joints also develop when erosion exposes rocks that were once buried deeply within the Earth, and as the overlying rocks are stripped away, fracturing can result from the once-buried rocks expanding upward. If the expansion joints develop parallel to the exposed surface (as at Half Dome in Yosemite), rocks peel off in

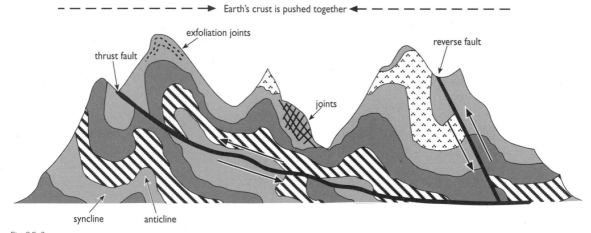

Fig. 25-3.
Typical structures of a continental convergent margin, such as the Alps, Himalayas, and Rocky Mountains.

layers that are called exfoliation joints (as shown in Figure 25-3). Sets of joints commonly occur at angles of 30, 60, or 90 degrees to each other—and these joint angles tend to be persistent as long as the rock type is the same. Recognition of joint patterns is essential for routefinding, especially on vertical faces in granitic rocks, where joints could be your only path to the summit without aid climbing.

Veins are fractures that have been filled by minerals, most commonly quartz or calcite. Veins can have an important effect on the texture of weathered rock surfaces. Quartz veins tend to project out as resistant ridges, whereas softer calcite veins are recessed. On some sheer faces, these can provide the only holds available, so the pattern of fractures determines where you should look for the next hand- or foothold.

Faults

Faults are fractures along which movement has occurred. The discernible movement may be only a fraction of an inch, or the movement can uplift a whole mountain range, such as the east face of the Sierra Nevada. Climbers need to know about faults because they can bring blocks of very different rock together. Fault zones also can consist of very weak, ground-up rock called gouge that may present a hazard to climbers.

Faults are classified according to their relative movement. Normal faults involve vertical movement that occurs when the Earth's crust is stretched to the point of breaking (as shown in Figure 25-2, above), as in the Basin and Range of Nevada, Utah, and California. Vertical movement also occurs along reverse faults and along thrust faults, which are reverse faults with an angle of less than 20 degrees (as shown in Figure 25-3). Here the fault is caused by compression due to the collision of lithospheric plates; examples are the Alps and the Himalayas.

Strike-slip faults (for example, the San Andreas Fault in California) move the lithosphere in a horizontal plane, rather than up and down. This can move mountains from place to place, but does not generally cause uplift.

MOUNTAIN MATERIALS

The rocks that compose mountains are the foundation of the climbing experience. Each type of rock has a different fracture pattern, surface texture, and durability. The strength of rocks, as well as their resistance to erosion and weathering, depends on the minerals of which they are composed. This in turn determines the reliability of holds and your overall climbing strategy for different rock types.

Minerals

Minerals are crystals that are solid and inorganic; they have unique properties by which they can be identified: color, hardness, cleavage (the tendency to split along definite crystalline planes), luster, and crystal shape. Only seven minerals compose most rocks of the Earth's crust. Six of these are silicate minerals: feldspar, quartz, olivine, pyroxene, amphibole, and biotite. These silicates are generally hard and resistant to weathering. Only one common mineral, calcite, is soft and soluble.

TABLE 25-1. CLASSIFICATION OF VOLCANIC AND PLUTONIC ROCKS		
Color/Mineral Content	Volcanic (Extrusive) fine-grained rock erupted as lava or ash; cools quickly; may contain small holes or crystals	Plutonic (Intrusive) coarse-grained rock that cools and crystallizes slowly underground
light-colored; very little iron in rock	rhyolite or dacite (black, glassy = obsidian)	granite or granodiorite
usually gray; moderate iron in rock	andesite	diorite
dark (black to green-black); high iron content	basalt	gabbro or peridotite (rare)

25

Calcite is a carbonate, composed of calcium carbonate (the major ingredient in many antacid tablets). It is resistant and stable in arid climates, but dissolves readily in humid climates—and in acid rain.

Feldspar and quartz are the most resistant to breakdown under the constant assault of weathering. They are also the most abundant rock-forming minerals, composing most granites and sandstones. The other silicates (olivine, pyroxene, amphibole, and biotite) are dark, iron-rich minerals. Pyroxene is commonly found in basalt and gabbro. Amphibole and biotite are familiar as the black specks in granite, granodiorite, and diorite, as well as in many schists and gneisses.

Rocks

Rocks are subdivided into three categories: igneous (crystallized from a melt), sedimentary (deposited as particles, precipitates, or organic matter), and metamorphic (recrystallized by heat and/or pressure).

A mountain climber does not need to be an expert in classifying rocks. However, it is very useful to be able to recognize a few general categories, because different rock types call for very different climbing strategies.

The first thing you need to know is that rocks are like a box of chocolates: You cannot tell what flavor they are until you look inside each one. Weathering or lichens obscure the surface of most rock outcrops. To identify a rock's true color and appearance, look for a fresh surface that has recently broken open. Beneath a brown exterior there may be a black basalt, a white rhyolite, or even a glassy obsidian.

The following sections contain a few glittering generalities about what kinds of climbing are effective on some of the most common rock types.

Igneous Rocks

Igneous rocks (from the Latin *ignis,* meaning "fire") crystallize from magma or lava. Plutonic rocks (named for Pluto, the Roman god of the underworld) form underground from magma; volcanic rocks (named for Vulcan, the Roman god of fire) form from lava that is extruded at the surface (see Table 25-1).

Plutonic rocks: The most common plutonic rocks are the coarse-grained granitoids—granite, granodiorite, and diorite. Granitoids are very durable unless

highly weathered. They tend to have multiple fracture planes that define crack systems toward the summit or chimneys if accentuated by weathering. A good way to check the reliability of protection in granitoid rock is to hit it with a hammer. If it rings, it is good rock; if it makes a dull thud, be careful.

Volcanic rock: There are two types of volcanic rock—lava flows and pyroclastics. Most lavas crystallize rapidly under conditions of supercooling, so they commonly consist mainly of very tiny mineral grains that are invisible without magnification. However, they often include large crystals that formed in magma chambers underground before eruption. The composition of lava flows is essentially the same as their plutonic counterparts, the granitoids—in others words, rhyolite has the same chemical composition and minerals as granite, while andesite matches diorite and basalt matches gabbro. Most lava flows make very good climbing rock. Exceptions are lavas that are full of small cavities formed by gas bubbles and flows that have been chemically altered (alteration zones) by corrosive volcanic gases. This type of lava flow is composed of crumbly rock that is hazardous to climb and can be found on most volcanoes.

Pyroclastics are deposits of volcanic rock fragments produced by explosive eruptions. These include outcrops of ash and pumice that tend to fail unpredictably and therefore should be avoided on climbing routes if possible. Many pyroclastics also show some degree of chemical alteration. Anyone climbing stratovolcanoes from the Aleutians to the Andes should be aware of this potential hazard.

Sedimentary Rocks

Most sedimentary rocks are made of three types of material: fragments (clastics) of preexisting rocks, precipitates from solution (chemical), or organic material. Clastic rocks are classified according to the size of fragments in the rock. Fine-grained rocks, including thinly bedded shales, are the products of deposition in quiet, low-energy environments such as lakes or the seafloor (fig. 25-4). Coarse-grained clastic rocks, including sandstones and conglomerates, are transported and deposited in higher-energy regimes such as stream channels and waves crashing onshore.

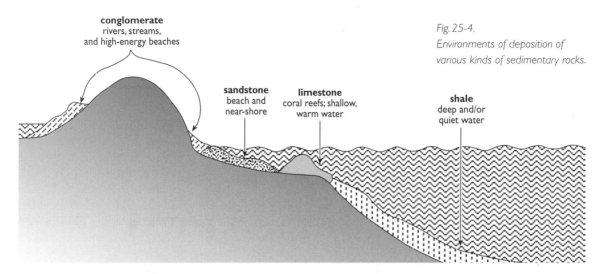

conglomerate
rivers, streams,
and high-energy beaches

sandstone
beach and
near-shore

limestone
coral reefs; shallow,
warm water

shale
deep and/or
quiet water

Fig. 25-4.
Environments of deposition of
various kinds of sedimentary rocks.

Sandstone with silica cement (gritstone) is, for many, the most desirable rock to climb. It has continuous fracture systems, as do granitoids, coupled with high friction from its sandpaperlike surface formed of quartz and feldspar grains. Sandstone outcrops are commonly slabby with many reliable hand- and footholds. Sandstone provides good protection unless it is highly weathered or poorly cemented by the soluble mineral calcite.

Shale is also slabby, but because it is composed chiefly of soft clay, it crumbles just as easily as do altered pyroclastics. The best protection is probably a long, thin blade driven between layers, but nothing should be trusted. Avoid shale if possible, but be aware that it is almost always found as layers between sandstones.

Limestones, composed of chemical precipitates or organic material, are deposited in warm equatorial seas. Routefinding on limestone can be challenging because crack systems are far less continuous than on granitoid rocks. Also, limestone is composed of the soft mineral calcite, so if protection points are stressed during an ascent, as in the event of a leader fall, they can degrade and fail. Where limestone has been below the water table before uplift, it can have many solution cavities, caves, and overhangs that make climbing interesting.

Metamorphic Rocks

Metamorphic rocks are igneous or sedimentary rocks that have been recrystallized by heat and pressure. The most distinctive change is foliation, when minerals are aligned like the grain in wood; foliation is found in slates, phyllites, schists, and gneisses. Foliation is a plane of weakness in the rock, from a rock climber's viewpoint. This weakness dominates in slate, which is fine-grained. If you try to drive a piton parallel to the foliation, you will easily split off a slab of rock that looks like a piece of blackboard. Schist, which has mineral grains coarse enough to be visible, has more resistance to splitting, but protection is still poor if it is placed parallel to the foliation. Most gneisses are similar to granitoids in strength, but you should still be aware of the foliation plane.

There are also several nonfoliated metamorphic rock types, including quartzite, marble, and hornfels. Quartzite, like sandstone, is a climber's favorite. It is slabby with continuous fractures and forms very solid outcrops, but it lacks the friction of sandstone, especially when wet. Note that in the alpine zone, where extensive freezing and thawing occur, quartzite slabs can slough off, but not as easily as sandstone does. Marble is similar to limestone in that it is composed of soft calcite that is easily degraded and soluble in humid climates. It tends to have more continuous fractures than limestone, but expect unusual topography. Hornfels is a baked rock that is formed along the margin of granitoid plutons. It is very hard and brittle. Chocks and cams work well in this rock, but pitons and bolts tend to create splinters.

25

Climbers should be aware of metamorphic changes along fault zones. In the shallow part of faults, movement shatters or grinds rock into gouge. Decomposition can also occur if hot fluids circulate through the fractured rock. Both the gouge and decomposed rock are very weak and are unreliable for protection. Deeper in the fault zone, rocks tend to flow rather than break. This produces mylonites, which have an intense foliation and are generally as unreliable as schist for protection points.

WHERE TO GET GEOLOGIC INFORMATION

The primary provider of geologic maps and information in the United States is the U.S. Geological Survey. The home page of the USGS website *(www.usgs.gov)* is the gateway to a cornucopia of geologic data for the entire world. Check out links to the USGS map finder—a clickable set of maps showing the name and location of all available 7.5-minute topographic maps. The USGS also has a cooperative arrangement with the Microsoft Terra-server that can provide online maps and aerial photos of nearly every part of the United States. Another useful service of the USGS is the national geologic map database *(www.ngmdb.usgs.gov)*. A new venture of the USGS is the Geology in the Parks program, which provides information via a website and brochures in cooperation with the National Park Service *(www.aqd.nps.gov/grd/usgsnps/project/home.hmtl)*. The USGS Cascades Volcano Observatory's "Big List of Volcano and Earth Science–Oriented Websites" *(vulcan.wr.usgs.gov/Servers/earth_servers.html)* is also a good resource.

Other federal agencies that dispense geologic data are the U.S. Forest Service *(www.fs.fed.us)* and the Bureau of Land Management *(www.blm.gov)*.

Other places to go for geologic information are the state geologic surveys, nearly all of which maintain websites with abundant information; links to state geological surveys are listed online *(www.isgs.uiuc.edu/us-map/usa-surveys.html)*.

However, to get a site-specific geologic map or details on the geology of a chosen climbing route, there is no better place than your nearest college geology department. Many have websites, and all have faculty and students who are avid climbers and know exactly what rocks and structures they have seen on different routes.

Better still, start looking carefully and making detailed notes on the geologic features of the routes that you climb. Climbers are indeed practicing geologists, and your personal observations are the best way to learn how to read the rocks.

25

26
CHAPTER

The Cycle of Snow

Understanding the cycle of snow will help climbers anticipate changes in traveling conditions from the bottom of the mountain to the top, from morning to evening, and from day to day. While dramatic changes occur during storms, often more subtle changes, caused by different exposures to sun and wind or gradual aging processes, create significant impediments or enhancements to travel.

Snow crystals form in the atmosphere when water vapor condenses at temperatures below freezing. They form around centers of foreign matter, such as microscopic dust particles, and grow as more atmospheric water vapor condenses onto them. Tiny water droplets also may contribute to snow-crystal growth. The crystals generally are hexagonal, but variations in size and shape are almost limitless, including plates (fig. 26-1a),

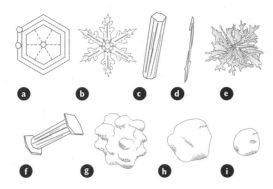

Fig. 26-1.

Snow-crystal forms: a, plates; b, dendrites (stellar crystals); c, columns; d, needles; e, spatial dendrites (combinations of feathery crystals); f, capped columns; g, graupel (soft hail); h, hail (solid ice); i, sleet (icy shell, inside wet).

columns (fig. 26-1c), and needles (fig. 26-1d). The particular shape depends on the air temperature and the amount of water vapor available.

When a snow crystal falls through air masses of different temperatures and with different water-vapor contents, snow crystals may become more complex or combine. In air that has a temperature near freezing, snow crystals stick together to become snowflakes: aggregates of individual crystals. When snow crystals fall through air that contains water droplets, the droplets freeze to the crystals, forming the rounded snow particles called graupel (fig. 26-1g)—soft hail. When snow crystals ascend and descend into alternating layers of above- and below-freezing clouds, layers of glaze and rime build up to form hailstones (fig. 26-1h). Sleet (fig. 26-1i) is a refrozen raindrop or melted snowflakes that have refrozen.

The density of new-fallen snow depends on weather conditions. The general rule is that the higher the temperature, the more dense (heavier and wetter) the snow. However, density varies widely in the range of 20 to 32 degrees Fahrenheit (minus 6 to 0 degrees Celsius). Wind affects snow density, because high winds break up falling crystals into fragments that pack together to form dense, fine-grained snow. The stronger the wind, the denser the snow. The lowest-density snow (lightest and driest) falls under moderately cold and very calm conditions. At extremely low temperatures, new snow is fine and granular, with somewhat higher densities. The very highest densities are associated with graupel or needle crystals falling at temperatures near freezing.

The amount of water (solid or liquid) in layers of snow can indicate its density. Higher water content means that more space is occupied by ice or water and less air is present, causing higher density. In new-fallen snow, water content ranges from 1 to 30 percent, sometimes even higher, with the average for mountain snowfall being 7 to 10 percent.

SURFACE FORMS OF SNOW COVER

Snow and ice undergo endless surface changes as they are affected by wind, air temperature, solar radiation, freeze-and-thaw cycles, and rain. This section describes most of the surface permutations that mountaineers typically encounter. See Table 26-1 below for a summary of the dangers and travel considerations associated with these various forms of snow.

Rime: This type of snow forms right at ground level. It is the dull white, dense deposit formed by water droplets freezing on trees, rocks, and other objects exposed to the wind. Rime deposits build into the oncoming wind. Rime may form large, feathery flakes or a solid incrustation, but it lacks regular crystalline patterns. Typically it is easy to break, forming a weak, crusty surface when it is on top of snow and a poor, unreliable anchor when it is on rock or ice faces.

Hoarfrost: This is another type of snow that forms at ground level. Hoarfrost forms on solid objects by the process of sublimation—the direct conversion of atmospheric water vapor to a solid. Unlike rime, hoarfrost displays distinct crystalline shapes: blades, cups, and scrolls. The crystals appear fragile and feathery, and sparkle brilliantly in sunlight. Deposited on top of snow, hoarfrost is known as surface hoar, generally produced during a cold, clear night. A heavy deposit of surface hoar makes for fast, excellent skiing with fun, crinkly sounds. (For depth hoar, see "Aging of the Snow Cover" later in this chapter.)

Powder snow: A popular term for light, fluffy, new-fallen snow, this is more specifically defined as new snow that has lost some of its cohesion because large temperature differences between the pits and peaks of its feathery dendrite (branching) crystals have caused recrystallization. The changed snow is loose (unco-hesive) and powdery (mostly air). It commonly affords good downhill skiing and may form dry, loose-snow avalanches. Climbing or walking through powder is difficult, and any weight on it readily sinks.

Corn snow: After the advent of melting in early spring, a period of fair weather may lead to the forma-tion of coarse, rounded crystals on the snow surface. The crystals, often called corn snow, are formed when the same surface layer of snow melts and refreezes for several days. When corn snow thaws each morning after the nighttime freeze, it is great for skiing and step-kicking. Later in the day, after thawing has continued, corn snow can become too thick and gooey for easy travel. During the afternoon, the associated meltwater also may lubricate the underlying snow and promote wet, loose-snow avalanches, especially if the snow is stressed by people glissading on it or by the sliding and turning actions of skis, snowboards, and snowmobiles.

Rotten snow: Rotten snow is a spring condition characterized by soft, wet lower layers that offer little support to the firmer layers above. Rotten snow forms when lower layers of depth hoar (see "Aging of the Snow Cover" later in this chapter) become wet and lose what little strength they have. It is a condition that often leads to wet, loose-snow or slab avalanches run-ning clear to the bare ground. Continental climates, such as that of the American Rockies, often produce rotten snow. Maritime climates, such as that of the Pacific coastal ranges, which usually have deep, dense snow covers, are less likely to produce rotten snow condi-tions. In its worst forms, rotten snow will not even sup-port the weight of a skier. Snow that promises good spring skiing in the morning, when there is some strength in the crust, may deteriorate to rotten snow later in the day.

Meltwater crust: This is a snow crust that forms when water that melted on the snow's surface refreezes and bonds snow crystals into a cohesive layer. Sources of heat that cause meltwater crusts include warm air, con-densation at the snow surface, direct sunlight, and rain.

Sun crust is a common variety of meltwater crust that derives its name from the main source of heat for melting. In winter and early spring, the thickness of a sun crust over dry snow usually is determined by the depth of solar heating. Often it is thin enough that skiers and hikers break through, which is very uncomfortable. In later spring and summer when free water is found throughout the snow cover, the thickness—usually less than about 2 inches (5 centimeters)—depends on how cold it becomes at night.

Rain crust is another type of meltwater crust; it forms after rainwater has percolated into the surface layers of snow. The rainwater often follows preferred paths as it percolates through the snow, creating fingerlike features that act as pinning points, holding the crust to the underlying snow after it refreezes. The pinning ac-tion of many rain crusts helps to stabilize the snow against avalanching and makes for strong walking sur-faces, especially in the coastal mountain ranges where heavy winter rainfall is common, even at high eleva-tions. Glazed rain crusts can be extremely slippery and dangerous. Rain nearly always freezes on top of gla-cier ice, even during summer. This makes travel on gla-ciers following a fresh rain particularly hazardous.

Wind slab: After surface snow layers are disturbed by the wind, age-hardening takes place. When fragments of snow crystals broken by the wind come to rest, they are compacted together. Then the wind provides heat, particularly through water-vapor condensation, which causes melting. Even when there is not enough heat to cause melting, the disturbed surface layer warms and then cools when the wind dies, providing additional metamorphic hardening. Traveling usually is fast and easy on hard wind slabs, but the slabs can break in long-running fractures, and if they overlie a weak layer or form a cornice, added stress causes avalanching.

Firnspiegel: The thin layer of clear ice sometimes seen on snow surfaces in spring or summer is called *firnspiegel* (a German word meaning "snow mirror," pronounced FEARN-spee-gull). Under the right con-ditions of sunlight and slope angle, the reflecting of sunlight on firnspiegel produces the brilliant sheen called glacier fire. Firnspiegel forms when solar radia-tion penetrates the snow and causes melting just be-low the surface at the same time that freezing condi-tions prevail at the surface. Once firnspiegel is formed, it acts like a greenhouse, allowing snow beneath to melt

26

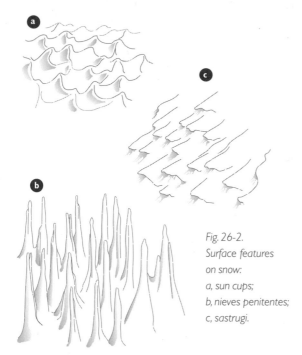

Fig. 26-2.
Surface features
on snow:
a, sun cups;
b, nieves penitentes;
c, sastrugi.

melting can occur with only one-seventh of the heat that is required for evaporation, the hollows melt and deepen faster than the ridges evaporate. The hollows are further deepened by differential melting when dirt in the hollows absorbs solar radiation. The sun cups melt faster on the south (sunny) side in the northern hemisphere, so the whole sun-cup pattern gradually migrates northward across a snowfield.

Warm, moist winds tend to destroy sun cups by causing faster melt at the high points and edges. A prolonged summer storm accompanied by fog, wind, and rain often will erase a sun-cup pattern completely, but the cups start to form again as soon as dry, fair weather returns. While you are skiing over sun cups, you can easily catch an edge, especially if the cups are hard and frozen from nighttime cooling. The unevenness of sun-cupped surfaces makes walking uphill tedious, but traveling downhill is made a little easier by "skating" into each hollow.

Nieves penitentes: When sun cups grow up, they become *nieves penitentes* (nee-EH-vays pen-ih-TEN-tays, from the Spanish for "penitent snow"). Nieves penitentes are the pillars produced when sun-cup hollows become very deep, accentuating the ridges into columns of snow that look like praying statues (fig. 26-2b). They are peculiar to snowfields at high altitudes and low latitudes, where solar radiation and atmospheric conditions conducive to sun cups are intense. The columns often slant toward the midday sun. Nieves penitentes reach their most striking development among the higher peaks of the Andes and the Himalayas, where they may become several feet high and make mountain travel very difficult.

Drain channels: After melting has begun in spring, water runoff forms drainage patterns on snowfields. The actual flow takes place within the snowpack, not on the surface. As snow melts at the surface, the water formed percolates downward until it encounters either impervious layers that deflect its course or highly permeable layers that it can easily follow. Much of the water also reaches the earth beneath. Water that flows within the snow often causes a branching pattern of channels that appear on the surface. This happens because the flowing water accelerates the snow settlement around its channels, which are soon outlined by

while the transparent ice layer at the surface remains frozen. Firnspiegel usually is paper thin and quite breakable. Breaking through firnspiegel while you are traveling causes little discomfort, unlike sun crusts.

Verglas: This is a layer of thin, clear ice formed by water, from either rainfall or snowmelt, freezing on rock. It is most commonly encountered at higher elevations in the spring or summer when a freeze follows a thaw. *Verglas* (a French word meaning "glazed frost" or "glass ice," pronounced vair-GLAH) also may be formed by supercooled raindrops freezing directly as they fall onto exposed objects (freezing rain, also sometimes inaccurately called silver thaw). Verglas forms a very slippery surface and, like black ice on a roadway, it can be difficult to anticipate.

Sun cups: Also called ablation hollows, these can vary in depth from 1 inch to 3 feet or more (fig. 26-2a). Where sunshine is intense and the air is relatively dry, sun cup depths usually increase with increasing elevation and decreasing latitude. On the ridges of each cup, sun-heated water molecules evaporate from the snow surface. In the hollows, water molecules released by solar heating are trapped near the snow surface, forming a liquid layer that promotes further melt. Because

depressions at the surface. The dirt that collects in these depressions absorbs solar radiation, causing differential melting that further deepens them.

On a sloping surface, drain channels flow downhill and form a parallel ridge pattern that can make it a little difficult to turn while you are glissading or skiing. On flat surfaces, drain fields create a dimply-looking surface, similar to sun cups but more rounded. The appearance of dimples or drain channels suggests that a significant amount of water has percolated into the snow cover. If these dimples or channels are frozen, it can be a good sign of stability against avalanches. However, if they are newly formed and still soft with liquid water, snow stability may be compromised by meltwater that has percolated into a susceptible buried layer and weakened it.

Sastrugi and barchans: When it is scoured by wind, the surface of dry snow develops a variety of erosional forms, such as small ripples and irregularities. On high ridges and flat, treeless territory, which are under the full sweep of the wind, these features attain considerable size. Most characteristic are *sastrugi* (sass-TRUE-gee, a Russian word meaning "grooves"), the wavelike forms with sharp prows directed into the prevailing wind (fig. 26-2c). A field of sastrugi—hard, unyielding, and as much as several feet high—can make for tough going.

High winds over featureless snow plains also produce dunes similar to those found in desert sand, with the crescent-shaped dune, or *barchan,* being most common. These stiff, uneven features cause difficult traveling, especially when ice or rocky ground is exposed between each one.

Cornices: These are deposits of snow on the lee edge of a ridge top, pinnacle, or cliff (fig. 26-3). Snow that falls during storms furnishes material for cornice formation. Cornices also are formed or enlarged by snow blown from snowfields that lie to the windward side of the ridge or feature. As a general rule, cornices formed during snowstorms are softer than those produced by wind drift alone. Cornices present a particular hazard because they overhang, forming an unsupported, unstable mass that can break off due to natural causes or human disturbance. It is dangerous to walk on a cornice. In addition, falling cornices are dangerous to those below and also can set off avalanches.

AGING OF THE SNOW COVER

Snow that remains on the ground changes with time. The crystals undergo a process of change—metamorphism—that usually results in smaller, simpler forms and a snowpack that shrinks and settles. Metamorphism begins the moment that snow falls and lasts

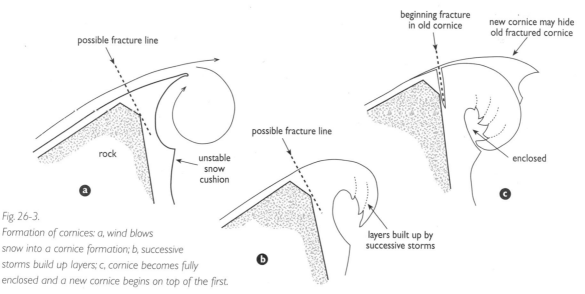

Fig. 26-3.
Formation of cornices: a, wind blows snow into a cornice formation; b, successive storms build up layers; c, cornice becomes fully enclosed and a new cornice begins on top of the first.

529

TABLE 26-1. SNOW CONDITIONS AND THEIR RELATED TRAVEL CONSIDERATIONS AND DANGERS			
Snow Condition	Effects on Travel	Effects on Protection	Dangers
Rime	Breakable; can trap feet or skis	—	—
Hoarfrost	Fun skiing	—	If hoarfrost is buried, potential avalanche danger
Powder snow	Difficult walking, good skiing	Ropes cut through it; ice axes do not hold in it; clogs crampons; deadmen need reinforcing with buried packs, etc.	Potential avalanche danger
Corn snow	Walking on it best in morning; skiing on it best in afternoon	Bollards must be large to hold	When frozen, avalanche potential low; when melted, stability depends on water content and underlying layer strengths
Rotten snow	Difficult traveling	Ropes cut through it; ice axes do not hold in it; deadmen need reinforcing with buried packs, etc.	Potential avalanche danger
Meltwater crust	Breakable; can trap feet if crust thin; good walking if crust thick; skis require edges	May require crampons	Slippery
Wind slab	Good walking	—	Potential avalanche danger, especially on leeward slopes
Firnspiegel	Breakable	—	—
Verglas	Breakable; impedes rock travel	—	Slippery
Sun cups	Uneven but solid walking or skiing	—	Low danger because usually form in old, stable snow
Nieves penitentes	Difficult to negotiate	Ropes catch on them	Low danger because usually form in old, stable snow
Drain channels	Uneven but solid walking or skiing	—	Low danger because usually form in old, stable snow
Sastrugi	Uneven but solid walking or skiing	Ropes catch on them	A sign of wind transport and potential slab formation; ski edges may catch on them

TABLE 26-1. Continued

Cornices	Difficult to negotiate; best to avoid	Ropes cut through them	Can break away underneath or above traveler
Crevasses	Difficult to negotiate; may be hidden by snow; best to avoid	Require rope protection	Easy to fall into, especially if hidden
Seracs	Difficult to negotiate; best to avoid	Ropes catch on them	Very unstable; can break catastrophically
Avalanche paths	Hard surface, good walking	—	Slippery; relatively free from avalanche danger unless portion of slab remains or is recharged by new snow
Avalanche debris	Difficult to negotiate	—	Relatively free from avalanche danger unless portion of slab remains or is recharged by new snow

until it completely melts away. Because the snowpack continually changes over time, mountaineers find it useful to know the recent history of weather and snow conditions in an area, in order to calculate what the snow cover will be like.

One type of metamorphism, the equilibrium growth process, gradually converts the varied original forms of the snow crystals into old snow—homogeneous, rounded grains of ice (fig. 26-4). Both temperature and pressure affect the rate of change. When temperature within the snow is near the freezing point—32 degrees Fahrenheit (0 degrees Celsius)—change is rapid. The colder it gets, the slower the change; it virtually stops below minus 40 degrees Fahrenheit (minus 40 degrees Celsius). Pressure from the weight of new snowfall speeds changes within older layers. Snow that has reached old age—surviving at least one year and with all original snow crystals now converted into grains of ice—is called firn or névé. Any further changes to firn snow lead to formation of glacier ice.

Another type of metamorphism, the kinetic growth process, takes place when water vapor moves from one part of the snowpack to another by vapor diffusion, which deposits ice crystals that are different from those of the original snow. This kinetic growth produces faceted crystals (fig. 26-5). When the process is completed,

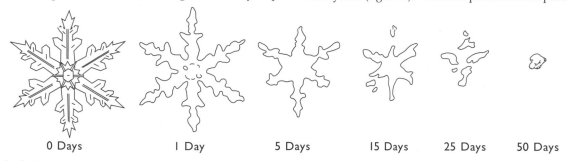

| 0 Days | 1 Day | 5 Days | 15 Days | 25 Days | 50 Days |

Fig. 26-4.
Metamorphism of a snow crystal in the equilibrium growth process. Days indicate time required for shapes to change under average temperature and pressure conditions in a typical seasonal snow cover.

531

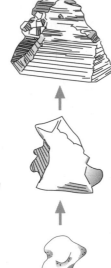

Fig. 26-5.
Metamorphism of a
snow crystal in the
kinetic growth
process.

the crystals often have a scroll or cup shape, appear to be layered, and may grow to considerable size—up to an inch (2.5 centimeters) or so. They form a fragile structure known as depth hoar that loses all strength when crushed and becomes very soft and weak when wet. This weak, unstable snow form is popularly referred to as "sugar snow" when dry and "rotten snow" when wet. The conditions necessary for its formation are a large difference in temperature at different depths in the snow and sufficient air space so that water vapor can diffuse freely. The conditions are most common early in winter when the snowpack is shallow and unconsolidated.

In addition to undergoing metamorphic changes caused by variations in temperature and pressure, snow can age by mechanical means, such as wind. Snow particles broken by wind or other mechanical disturbances undergo a process known as age-hardening for several hours after they are disturbed. This hardening is the reason why it is easier to travel in snow if you follow tracks previously set by feet, skis, snowshoes, or snowmobiles.

Snow's variations in strength are among the widest strength variations found in nature: New snow is about 90 percent air, and the individual, unconnected grains make it a fluffy, weak material that is easy to break apart. In contrast, wind-packed old snow may contain less than 30 percent air, with the small, broken particles forming strong interconnected bonds that can create layers 50,000 times harder than fluffy new snow. The variations between these two extremes and the continual changes in strength caused by changes in temperature, pressure, and wind make for highly variable conditions from place to place and hour to hour.

THE FORMATION OF GLACIERS

Glaciers form for a rather simple reason. Snow that does not melt or evaporate during the course of a year is carried over to the next winter. If snow continues to accumulate year after year, eventually consolidating and beginning a slow downhill movement, it has become a glacier.

Within the old snow—the firn or névé—the metamorphic conversion of snow crystals into grains of ice has been completed. Now the grains of ice are changed into glacier ice in a process called firnification. Firn turns into glacier ice when the air spaces between the grains become sealed off from each other so that the mass becomes airtight (fig. 26-6).

Each spring when the lower snow layers are still at temperatures below freezing, percolating meltwater refreezes when it reaches these lower layers. This refrozen meltwater forms ice layers within the firn. Therefore, by the time compaction and metamorphism have prepared an entire area of firn for conversion to glacier ice, the firn may already contain irregular bodies of ice.

Once glacier ice has formed, metamorphism does not cease. Some of the ice grains continue to grow at the expense of their neighbors, and the average size of the ice crystals increases with age (fig. 26-7). Large glaciers, in which the ice takes centuries to reach the

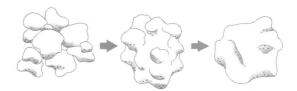

Fig. 26-6.
Rounded snow grains that are pressed and squeezed together form a large glacier ice crystal.

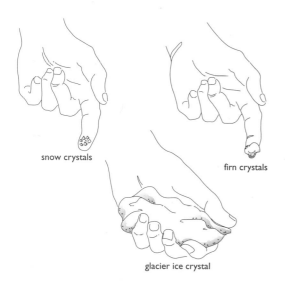

snow crystals

firn crystals

glacier ice crystal

Fig. 26-7.
Ice crystals increase greatly in size as they transform from snowflakes and firn into glacier ice.

glacier's foot, may produce crystals more than 1 foot (30 centimeters) in diameter, gigantic specimens grown from minute snow particles.

To understand how a simple, valley-type alpine glacier is born, picture a mountain in the northern hemisphere that has no glaciers. Now suppose climatic changes occur that cause snow to persist from year to year in a sheltered spot with northern exposure. From the beginning, snow starts to flow toward the valley in the very slow motion called creep. New layers are added each year, the patch of firn snow grows deeper and bigger, and the amount of snow in motion increases. The creeping snow dislodges soil and rock, while melting and refreezing, and the flow of water around and under the snow patch additionally impact the surroundings. This small-scale process of erosion eventually leads to formation of a hollow where the winter snows are deposited in deeper drifts. After the snow deepens beyond 100 feet (30 meters) or so, the increasing pressure of the many upper layers of firn causes the lower layers to begin turning to glacier ice. A glacier is born.

With continued nourishment from heavy winter snows, the glacier flows toward the valley as a stream

of ice. At some point in its descent, the glacier reaches an elevation low enough and warm enough that no new snow accumulates. The glacier ice begins to melt. Eventually the glacier reaches a point, even lower and warmer, at which all ice carried down from above melts each year. This is the lower limit of the glacier.

Glaciers vary from stagnant masses with little motion to vigorously flowing rivers of ice that transport large masses each year from higher to lower elevations. Glaciers in relatively temperate climates flow both by internal deformation and by sliding on their beds. Differences in speed within the glacier are somewhat like those in a river: fastest at the center and surface and slower at the sides and bottom where bedrock creates drag. Small polar glaciers present a striking difference in appearance from their temperate cousins, for they are frozen to their beds and can flow only by internal deformation. The polar glaciers look much like flowing molasses, whereas temperate glaciers are rivers of broken ice.

Crevasses

Crevasses are important features of glaciers. Crevasses are fractures that occur when ice encounters a force greater than it can bear. Near the surface of a glacier, where ice is just beginning to form, the ice is full of tiny flaws and weakly bonded crystals. When it stretches or bends too fast, it can break apart in a brittle manner, like glass. The result is a crevasse.

Crevasses typically are 80 to 100 feet (25 to 30 meters) deep. At depths greater than that, ice layers become stronger, with increasingly large and well-bonded crystals. When stresses try to pull this deeply buried ice apart, overlying pressure further squeezes it together, causing it to flow and deform like thick, gooey honey. In colder glaciers—at high elevations or in polar climates—crevasses can penetrate somewhat deeper because colder ice is more brittle and tends to break more easily.

Temperate glaciers normally have more, and shallower, crevasses than polar glaciers because temperate glaciers usually move faster. When glaciers move very fast, such as over a very precipitous drop, icefall—extensive fracturing—occurs. The numerous crevasses link together, isolating columns of ice called seracs.

26

Ice Avalanches

Ice avalanches can pour from hanging glaciers, ice-falls, and any serac-covered portion of a glacier. Ice avalanches are caused by a combination of glacier movement, temperature, and serac configuration. On warm, low-elevation glaciers, ice avalanches are most common during late summer and early fall when melt-water has accumulated enough to flow underneath the glacier and increase its movement. The avalanche activity of high-elevation glaciers and cold glaciers that are frozen to the bedrock has no such seasonal cycle.

Reports differ on what time of day ice avalanches are most active. Field observers suggest that they are most common during the afternoon. This may be possible in a snow-covered serac field if daytime heating loosens snow enough to avalanche into seracs and cause them to fall, creating an ice avalanche. However, scientists have discovered an increase in activity during the early morning hours when the ice is cold and most brittle. Ice avalanches can occur any time of year and any time of day or night.

THE FORMATION OF SNOW AVALANCHES

Numerous combinations of snow patterns cause avalanches. Every snowstorm deposits a new layer of snow. Even during the same storm, a different type of layer may be deposited each time the wind shifts or the temperature changes. After snow layers are deposited, their character is continually altered by the forces of wind, temperature, sun, and gravity. Each layer is composed of a set of snow crystals that are similar in shape to each other and that are bonded together in similar ways. Because each layer—each set of crystals—is different, each reacts differently to the various forces. Knowing something about these differences can help you understand and avoid avalanches.

Snow avalanches usually are categorized by their release mechanism: loose avalanches (sometimes called loose-snow avalanches) start at a point; slab avalanches begin in blocks. Slab avalanches usually are much larger and involve deeper layers of snow. Loose avalanches can be equally dangerous, however—especially if they are wet and heavy, if they catch victims who are above cliffs or crevasses, or if they trigger slab avalanches or serac falls.

Loose Avalanches

Loose avalanches can occur when new snow builds up on steep slopes and loses its ability to remain on the slope. The snow rolls off the slope, drawing more snow along as it descends. Sun and rain also can weaken the bonds between snow crystals, especially if they are newly deposited, causing individual grains to roll and slide into loose avalanches. Skiing, glissading, and other human activities also can set off loose avalanches by disturbing the snow. Loose avalanches can easily sweep climbers into crevasses and over cliffs, destroy tents, and bury or carry away vital equipment.

Slab Avalanches

Slab avalanches are more difficult to anticipate than loose avalanches because they involve buried layers of snow that often cannot be detected from the surface. Usually a buried weak layer or weak interface is sandwiched between a slab layer and a bed layer (fig. 26-8). The buried weakness is disturbed in a way that causes it to reduce its frictional hold on the overlying slab.

Slab avalanches create an equal or greater amount of havoc to climbers than loose avalanches. Not only can slab avalanches fling people and equipment off slopes or bury them, but the tremendous speed of a slab avalanche and the force of impact have been known to move entire buildings and transport objects and people hundreds of yards downslope. It is difficult to survive an avalanche that is hurtling downslope, and once you

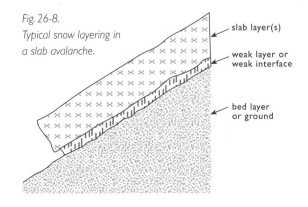

Fig. 26-8.
Typical snow layering in a slab avalanche.

slab layer(s)

weak layer or weak interface

bed layer or ground

26

are buried, the snow hardens, rapidly making it difficult to breath and hampering rescue.

The Buried Weak Layer

Depth hoar and buried surface hoar (hoarfrost) are the most notorious weak layers. They can withstand a significant amount of vertical load but have little or no shear strength; that is, they slide easily along their horizontal interface. They may collapse like a house of cards, or their structure may give way like a row of dominoes. In addition, depth hoar and buried surface hoar can survive weeks to months with little change in their fragile structure.

Surface hoar can form all across the snow cover, persisting most in shaded places that are protected from wind. Buried by subsequent snowfall, it becomes a weak layer that can promote avalanching. It becomes most dangerous if the first storm following hoarfrost formation begins with cool, calm conditions.

Depth hoar matures fastest in the shallow snow of early winter, when the ground is still warm and the air is cold (common in continental regions), but can develop anytime or anywhere there are large differences in temperature at different depths of snow. Weakness begins as soon as temperature and associated vapor-pressure differences cause molecules of water vapor to move onto facets of individual ice crystals instead of into bonds between crystals. This causes a loose, sugarlike collection of ice grains. Therefore, immature depth hoar (solid, faceted shapes) may be just as weak as mature depth hoar (open, cup, and scroll shapes).

Buried graupel (soft hail; see Figure 26-1g, above) is another classic weakness within the snowpack because it can act like ball bearings if disrupted. Other weaknesses that can make it easier for slabs to avalanche include plate-shaped crystals (see Figure 26-1a, above).

Buried weak layers may persist longer over glacier ice than over bare ground. The glacier reduces the amount of geothermal heating available to the snow from the ground, keeping temperatures somewhat cooler and slowing metamorphism. This means that buried weaknesses in seasonal snow underlain by glaciers can persist following storms and well into the summer long after adjacent snowy slopes have stabilized.

The Slab Layer

Once the underpinning of a snowpack is sufficiently weakened, the overlying snow (either a single layer or group of layers) begins to slide. If the overlying snow is cohesive enough to develop some tension as sliding begins—that is, if it sticks together enough to form a slab—it may break in long fractures that propagate across the slope. Lengthy fractures can result in large, heavy blocks that easily pull away from the rest of the slope, such as along the side and bottom of a slope where more stable snow may exist.

Slabs commonly are formed by brittle, wind-deposited snow layers. Wind often deposits snow in pillowlike patterns on the leeward side of ridges, thickest in the middle of the slope (where most of the weight of the slab, and thus the greatest avalanche danger, exists) and thinner on the edges. Wind slabs can maintain their blocky integrity throughout a slide, thrusting powerful masses downslope.

Slabs also are commonly formed by layers of needle-shaped crystals (see Figure 26-1d, above) deposited like a pile of pickup sticks, and by layers of branching crystals with many interlocking arms (see Figure 26-1b and e, above), which often pulverize immediately after release to form fast-moving powder avalanches.

Thick rain crusts often bridge over weakened surfaces and are rarely involved in avalanches until they begin to melt in spring. Sun crusts, on the other hand, usually are thinner and weaker than rain crusts and can be incorporated in a group of slab layers.

If the overlying snow is too warm or too wet compared to the underlying weakness, it may not break, but just deform slightly in response to the change in basal friction, and stay on the slope. However, if the underlying weak layer fails quickly and initial movement is significant, even this wet and pliable slab can avalanche. This scenario occurs commonly during spring when thick layers of old depth hoar are weakened by percolating meltwater. The resulting collapse of the depth hoar can cause a bending motion, like a whip, that overstresses the slab and causes it to fracture and slide. This whiplike effect also can occur in dry snow.

If the overlying snow is fragile and noncohesive—technically not a slab—the failure of a weak layer may

26

simply result in snow grains in the overlying snow collapsing over each other but remaining in place. However, if the weak layer is buried surface hoar or slightly rounded branching or plate crystals, the failure can be so rapid that even the most fragile snow layers can turn into slab avalanches.

The Bed Layer

A bed layer provides the initial sliding surface of avalanches. Common bed layers are the smooth surfaces of old snow, meltwater crust, glaciers, bedrock, or grass. The interface of these smooth surfaces and the snow above can be further weakened if temperature changes promote the formation of depth hoar or if the interface is lubricated by meltwater or percolating rainwater. The bed layer also can be the collapsed fragments of old depth hoar.

Avalanche Triggers

Humans are efficient trigger mechanisms for avalanches. Stomping snowshoers and ascending skiers, especially executing kick-turns, easily disturb layers of depth hoar or buried surface hoar. The sweeping turns and traversing motions of downhill skiers and snowboarders are effective at releasing loose-snow avalanches and fragile but fast-moving soft-slab avalanches. Skiers doing snowplow turns or sliding downhill, snowboarders, and glissaders efficiently release wet loose-snow and wet slab avalanches. It is even possible to initiate an avalanche by traveling below a slope, especially if the buried weakness is surface or depth hoar, because a domino effect can occur as the delicate crystal structure collapses, propagating the failure uphill. The weight and vibration of snowmobiles can set off avalanches in places that nonmotorized travel would not.

Storms also trigger avalanches. Many types of buried layers (such as thin layers of slightly rounded branches and platelike crystals) fail when a force is applied evenly over a broad surface, as occurs when storms deposit layers of new snow. Earthquakes, cornice and serac falls, and other internal and external effects on the snow can cause avalanches at unpredictable times and places.

UNDERSTANDING THE CYCLE OF SNOW

Learning about the terrain and weather preceding a trip can help climbers anticipate snow conditions before leaving home. During a trip, understanding how wind, sun, and precipitation affect snow at different elevations and on different slope aspects will help determine choice of route and use of equipment.

Dense snow can provide good walking surfaces and sound bollards for rope belays, but if the snow is dense enough to have transformed to ice, then the walking can be slippery and carving bollards can be difficult. Fluffy new snow is fun for skiing downhill, but makes uphill travel arduous and provides little or no support for belaying. Combinations of snow layering can promote avalanching.

From the first falling flake to glacier ice or meltwater, the cycle of snow creates a dramatic and ever-evolving environment for climbers.

Mountain Weather

**FORCES THAT CREATE WEATHER ■ THUNDER AND LIGHTNING ■
LOCALIZED WINDS ■ FIELD FORECASTING IN THE MOUNTAINS ■
FREEZING LEVEL AND SNOW LEVEL ■ CREATING YOUR OWN
WEATHER BRIEFINGS ■ APPLYING THE INFORMATION**

**It is no accident that many of the world's grandest monuments and temples—the
pyramids of Egypt and Mexico, for example—mimic mountains. Mountains exude
massive strength and permanence, their summits frequently assailed by storms
that the ancients believed were signals of divine presence and power. Approaching
the summit of such a peak was an act thought to risk the disfavor of the gods.**

Today most climbers believe that a disastrous
encounter with severe weather is the result of insufficient respect for the elements or bad luck, rather than
the work of an angry god. There is no question that a
trip into the mountains can expose people to more dangerous weather than any other environment on Earth.

Refuge can be harder to find, and major peaks can manufacture their own weather. Despite improvements in weather forecasting, knowledge of exactly how the atmosphere works, particularly in mountainous regions, is still incomplete. The wise climber carefully checks weather forecasts and reports before a trip, but also develops an ability to assess the weather in the field.

FORCES THAT CREATE WEATHER

The Sun

The sun does far more than simply illuminate planet Earth. It is the engine that drives the Earth's atmosphere, providing the heat that, along with other factors, creates the temperature variations that are ultimately responsible for wind, rain, snow, thunder, and lightning—everything known as weather.

The key to the sun's impact is that the intensity of the sun's radiation varies across the Earth's surface. Closer to the equator, the sun's heat is more intense. The extremes in temperature between the equator and the poles come as little surprise. However, as large as those differences in air temperature can be, they also lead to air movement, which prevents unrestrained heating or cooling and moderates those temperature extremes.

Air Movement

The horizontal movement of air (what we call wind) is all too familiar to anyone who has pitched a tent in the mountains. However, air also rises and descends, vertical movements that can generate or dissipate clouds. When air cools, it becomes more dense and sinks; the air pressure increases. When air warms, it becomes less dense and rises; the air pressure decreases. These pressure differences, the result of temperature differences, produce moving air—known as wind. Air generally moves from an area of high pressure to one of low pressure (fig. 27-1).

Air moving from high to low pressure carries moisture with it. As that air rises and then cools, the moisture condenses into clouds or fog. This occurs because, as air cools, its capacity to hold water vapor is reduced.

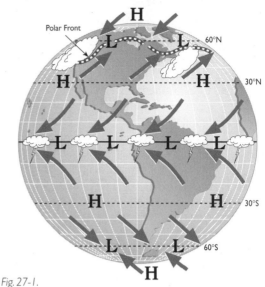

Fig. 27-1.
Air circulation patterns: movement from areas of high pressure to areas of low pressure.

The process of cooling and condensation operates on a large scale in the atmosphere as air moves from high-pressure systems into low-pressure systems, where it is then lifted.

Because polar and arctic air is colder and therefore more dense than air farther south, it sinks. The zone where it sinks and piles up is a region of high pressure. As the air sinks and its pressure increases, its temperature also increases. The effect is similar to what happens to football or rugby players caught at the bottom of a pile: They get squeezed the most, and their temperature (and possibly temperament) heats up. In the atmosphere, this warming within a high-pressure area tends to evaporate the little moisture present. That is why the Arctic receives very little precipitation. Although this sinking motion heats the air enough to evaporate much of the moisture present, it does not heat up enough to transform the poles into the tropics!

The Earth's Rotation

If planet Earth did not rotate, the cold polar air would just continue to slide southward to the equator. Intense solar heating near the equator forces air to rise, creating a region of low pressure that rings the globe. As air within this band rises, it cools, which tends to condense

27

water vapor into liquid water droplets that form clouds. Any satellite photograph shows extensive bands of thundershowers over or near the equator.

However, the air sinking and moving south from the poles and the air rising from the equator do not form a simple loop moving from north to south and back again. The rotation of the Earth on its axis deflects this air. Some of the air rising from the equator descends over the subtropics, creating a region of high pressure. In turn, part of the air moving from these subtropical highs moves north into the air moving south from the poles. The boundary between these two very different air masses is called the polar front. When this boundary does not move, it is called a stationary front. It often serves as a nursery for the development of storms.

Cold Fronts and Warm Fronts

Because of the great contrast in temperatures across the polar front, together with imbalances caused by the rotation of the Earth and differing influences of land, sea, ice, and mountains, some of the cold, dry air from the north slides south. That forces some of the warm air to rise. The zone where cold air is replacing warm air is referred to as a cold front (fig. 27-2a), and the zone where warm air is gradually replacing cooler air is referred to as a warm front (fig. 27-2b); both types of fronts appear as a "wave" or bend on the stationary front. An occluded front combines characteristics of warm and cold fronts and is typically found near the center of a mature low-pressure system.

Both cold and warm fronts are marked by unique clouds, which help the mountaineer distinguish one type of front from the other. Clouds seen ahead of, along, or just behind a cold front include cumulus (fig. 27-3a), altocumulus (fig. 27-3b), cumulonimbus (fig. 27-3c), and stratocumulus (fig. 27-3d). These clouds are puffy, resembling cotton candy. The name *cumulus* refers to their "pile" or "heap" shape. Stratocumulus clouds are sheetlike layers of cumulus clouds; the name *stratus* refers to the "sheetlike" or "layered" characteristics of these clouds.

Clouds seen ahead of or along a warm front include a halo (fig. 27-3e), lenticular (fig. 27-3f), stratus (fig. 27-3g), cirrocumulus (fig. 27-3h), cirrostratus (fig. 27-3i), altostratus (fig. 27-3j), and nimbostratus (fig. 27-3k).

The "wave" or bend that develops along what started out as a stationary front may develop into a low-pressure system, with air circulating counterclockwise around the low (the opposite direction of air moving around a high)—again a consequence of the Earth's rotation and friction.

THUNDER AND LIGHTNING

Thunderstorms can be set off by the collision of different air masses when fronts move through, or by the rapid heating of air when it comes in contact with sun-warmed mountain slopes. Once this air is warmed, it becomes buoyant and tends to rise. If the atmosphere above is cold enough, the air will tend to keep rising, producing what are called air mass thunderstorms. A single lightning bolt can heat the surrounding air up to 50,000 degrees Fahrenheit (approximately 25,000 degrees Celsius). That heating causes the air to expand explosively, generating earsplitting thunder.

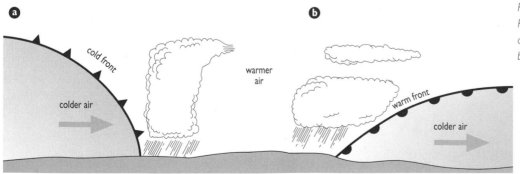

Fig. 27-2.
Fronts:
a, cold front;
b, warm front.

27

CLOUD TYPES SEEN AHEAD OF, ALONG, OR JUST BEHIND A COLD FRONT

a **cumulus**—with continued upward growth, these suggest showers later in the day

b **altocumulus**—high-based clouds often indicating potential for thunder, rain showers

c **cumulonimbus**—cumulus producing rain, snow, or thunder and lightning

d **stratocumulus**—lumpy, layered clouds often following a cold front, suggesting showers

CLOUD TYPES SEEN AHEAD OF OR ALONG A WARM FRONT

e **halo**—commonly seen 24–48 hours ahead of precipitation

f **lenticular**—wavelike clouds over mountains often suggesting precipitation within 48 hours

g **stratus**—layerlike clouds associated with widespread precipitation or ocean air

cirrocumulus **h**

i **cirrostratus**

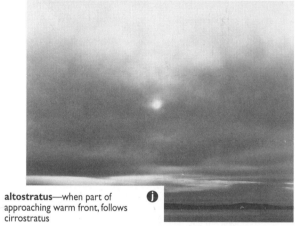

altostratus—when part of approaching warm front, follows cirrostratus **j**

k **nimbostratus**—stratus clouds producing widespread precipitation and low visibility

Fig. 27-3.
Identifying cloud types: a–d, cloud types seen ahead of, along, or just behind a cold front; e–k, cloud types see ahead of or along a warm front.

27

can also produce winds of lethal intensity, capable of leveling entire stretches of forest.

By taking a few precautions, you can avoid most accidents caused by mountain thunderstorms. Begin by obtaining updated weather reports and forecasts before you hit the trail.

Gauge the Movement of a Thunderstorm

How is it possible to gauge the movement of a thunderstorm? It is easy with a watch. Use the Flash to Bang principle. The moment lightning flashes, start counting the seconds. Stop timing once you hear the bang of thunder. Divide the number of seconds by five; the result is the thunderstorm's distance from you in miles. Continue to time lightning and thunder discharges to judge whether the thunderstorm is approaching, remaining in one place, or receding. If the time interval between the lightning and thunder is decreasing, the thunderstorm is approaching; if the interval is increasing, it is moving away.

This technique works because the light from the lightning moves much faster than the sound from the thunder. Although the thunder occurs at virtually the same instant as the lightning, its sound travels to you at only about 1 mile (1.6 kilometers) every 5 seconds, whereas the lightning flash, traveling at 186,000 miles (300,000 kilometers) per second, arrives essentially instantaneously. That is why the lightning is seen before the thunder is heard, unless the thunderstorm is very close—too close.

If a Thunderstorm Approaches

If you are caught out in the open during a thunderstorm, try to seek shelter. Tents are poor protection: Metal tent poles may function as lightning rods; stay

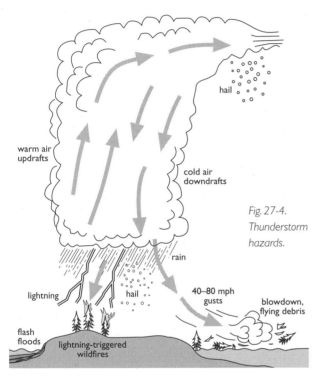

Fig. 27-4. Thunderstorm hazards.

Labels: warm air updrafts, cold air downdrafts, hail, rain, lightning, hail, 40–80 mph gusts, blowdown, flying debris, flash floods, lightning-triggered wildfires

Thunderstorms in the mountains can and do kill (fig. 27-4)—and not just from lightning strikes, although lightning is the biggest killer, claiming an average of 200 lives in the United States alone each year. Lightning can also spark dangerous wildfires, and even a moderate thunderstorm may release up to 125 million gallons (473 million liters) of rainwater. The resulting flash floods can quickly inundate streambeds and small valleys, sweeping away entire campgrounds. The growing popularity of canyoneering, particularly rappelling in deep slot canyons, increases climbers' exposure to flash floods and drowning. Thunderstorms

27

away from poles and wet items inside the tent. Take the following precautions to avoid being struck by lightning.

■ Get away from water, which readily conducts electricity.

■ Seek low ground if you are in an open valley or meadow.

■ If your hair stands on end, move immediately.

■ Avoid standing on ridge tops, at lookout structures, or near or under lone tall trees, especially isolated or diseased trees.

■ If you are in a wooded area, look for a stand of even-sized trees.

■ Do not remain near or on rocky pinnacles or peaks.

■ Do not remain near, touch, or wear metal or graphite equipment, such as ice axes, crampons, climbing devices, and frame packs.

■ Insulate yourself from the ground if possible. Sit on a soft pack or foam pad to protect against step-voltage transfer of the lightning strike through the ground—though ground currents may move through such insulation.

■ Crouch to minimize your profile, and cover your head and ears.

■ Do not lie down—this puts more of your body in contact with the ground, which can conduct more electrical current.

LOCALIZED WINDS

Understanding large-scale wind patterns, both at the Earth's surface and in the upper atmosphere, is important for being able to gauge the weather. However, because mountains, by their very nature, alter wind considerably, understanding localized patterns is crucial to the mountaineer. It can mean the difference between successfully reaching the summit, being tent-bound, or getting blown off the mountain.

Gap Winds

Winds are often channeled through gaps in the terrain, such as major passes or even between two peaks. Wind speeds can easily double as they move through such gaps (fig. 27-5).

You can use this knowledge to your advantage. If possible, gauge the surface wind speeds upwind of a

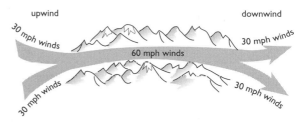

Fig. 27-5.
Wind acceleration through gaps and passes.

gap or pass before you travel into the vicinity of these terrain features. Knowing the upwind velocities, you can be prepared for gap winds that may be twice as strong. Avoid camping near the downwind portion of the gap, and consider selecting climbing routes not exposed to such winds. A major peak can block or slow winds for a few miles downwind.

Valley and Gravity Winds

Sparsely vegetated ground is typically found closer to ridges. Because it heats more rapidly than forest-covered land near valley floors, and because heated air rises, wind is generated that moves up either side of a valley, spilling over adjoining ridge tops. Such uphill breezes, called valley winds, can reach 10 to 15 miles (16 to 24 kilometers) per hour, attaining peak speed during the early afternoon and dying out shortly before sunset.

At night the land cools, and the cool air flows downslope in what is called a gravity wind. Such downslope breezes reach their maximum after midnight, dying out just before sunrise. Camping at the base of a cliff may result in an uncomfortably breezy evening. The more open the slopes between a campsite and the ridge above, the faster the winds will be.

Foehn or Chinook Winds

When winds descend a slope, air temperatures may increase dramatically in what is called a foehn wind or, in the western United States, a chinook. The air heats as it sinks and compresses on the leeward side of the crest, sometimes warming 30 degrees Fahrenheit (17 degrees Celsius) in minutes, melting as much as a foot of snow in a few hours (fig. 27-6). These winds are significant because of their potential speed, the rapid rise

27

543

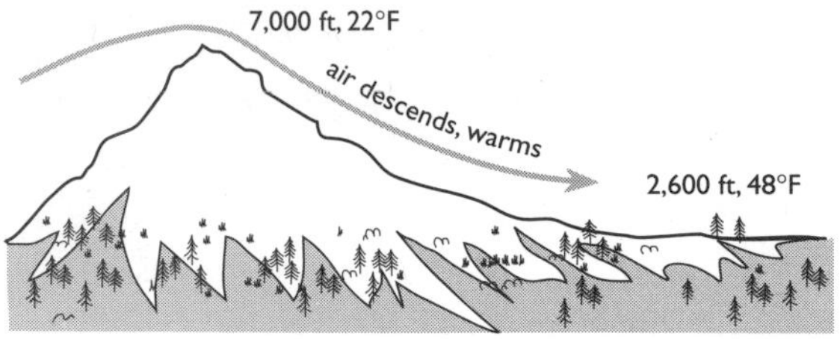

Fig. 27-6.
Foehn (chinook) winds.

in air temperature associated with them, and the potential they create for both rapid melting of snow and flooding. Such winds can increase the risk of avalanches, weaken snow bridges, and lead to sudden rises in stream levels.

Warning signs make it possible to anticipate a potentially dangerous foehn or chinook wind. Expect such a wind, with temperatures warming as much as 6 degrees Fahrenheit per 1,000 feet (3 degrees Celsius per 300 meters) of descent, if these three conditions are met:

1. You are downwind of a major ridge or crest, primarily to the east of mountains.
2. Wind speeds across the crest or ridge exceed 30 miles (48 kilometers) per hour.
3. You observe precipitation above the crest.

Bora Winds

The opposite of a chinook is a bora or, as it is called in Greenland, a *piteraq*. A bora is simply wind consisting of air so cold that its sinking, compressing motion as it flows downslope fails to warm it significantly. Such subzero winds are most common downslope of large glaciers. Their speeds can easily exceed 50 miles (80 kilometers) per hour. A bora can blow away tents, throw you off balance, lower the wind chill to dangerous levels (see Appendix B, Wind Chill Temperature Index), and obscure visibility by blowing snow.

FIELD FORECASTING IN THE MOUNTAINS

The process of gathering and evaluating weather data should not end at the trailhead or at the beginning of the climbing route. Changes in weather—which can

cause weather-related accidents in the mountains—rarely occur without warning. At times the clues can be subtle, and sometimes they are as broad as daylight (see sidebar).

MAJOR INDICATORS OF AN APPROACHING STORM

- Changes in cloud cover
- Changes in air pressure
- Changes in wind direction
- Changes in wind speed

No single one of the four factors shown in the sidebar will tell you all you need to know; you should examine each carefully. The rest of this section gives you some guidelines for evaluating these elements, which can enhance the weather reports and forecasts you obtain before leaving home.

Air-Pressure Clues

A barometer or barometer/altimeter can give excellent warning of an approaching weather system. A barometer measures air pressure directly; a barometer/altimeter measures air pressure and reports elevation. A decrease in air pressure shows on an altimeter as an increase in elevation even when there has not been a change in elevation; an increase in air pressure shows on an altimeter as a decrease in elevation, again, even when there has not been a change in elevation. (See "The Altimeter" in Chapter 5, Navigation.)

Table 27-2 evaluates a developing low-pressure system, but rapidly building high pressure also can have its troublesome effects: principally, strong winds.

FREEZING LEVEL AND SNOW LEVEL

It can be useful to estimate the freezing level and snow level. Such estimates are subject to error because they are based on the average decrease in temperature as altitude increases: 3.5 degrees Fahrenheit per 1,000 feet (2 degrees Celsius per 304 meters) of elevation gain. Still, such estimates are usually better than the alternative: no estimate.

TABLE 27-1. CLOUD-COVER CLUES (REFER TO FIGURE 27-3)

If	Then	Check for
High cirrus clouds forming loose halo around sun/moon (fig. 27-3e)	Precipitation possible within 24 to 48 hours	Lowering, thickening clouds
High cirrus clouds forming tight ring or corona around sun/moon (fig. 27-3e)	Precipitation possible within 24 hours	Lowering, thickening clouds
"Cap" or lenticular clouds forming over peaks (fig. 27-3f)	Precipitation possible within 24 to more than 48 hours; strong winds possible near summits or leeward slopes	Lowering, thickening clouds
Thickening, lowering, layered flat clouds (fig. 27-3j)	Warm or occluded front likely approaching within 12 to 24 hours	Wind shifts; air pressure drops
Breaks in cloud cover closing up (fig. 27-3c and d)	Cold front likely within 12 hours	Wind shifts; air pressure drops

TABLE 27-2. AIR PRESSURE/ALTIMETER CHANGE OVER 3 HOURS

Pressure Decrease	Altimeter Increase	Advised Action
0.02–0.04 inch (0.6–1.2 millibars)	20–40 feet (6–12 meters)	None. Continue to monitor.
0.04–0.06 inch (1.2–1.8 millibars)	40–60 feet (12–18 meters)	Clouds lowering/thickening? If so, begin checking air pressure changes hourly.
0.06–0.08 inch (1.8–2.4 millibars)	60–80 feet (18–24 meters)	Winds ranging from 18–33 knots (21–38 miles per hour) are likely. Consider less-exposed locations; continue monitoring conditions.
More than 0.08 inch (more than 2.4 millibars)	More than 80 feet (more than 24 meters)	Winds of 34 knots (40 miles per hour) or greater are likely. Immediate movement to protected area advised.

TABLE 27-3. WIND DIRECTION/SPEED CLUES (NORTHERN HEMISPHERE)

If	And If	Then
Winds shift direction from E or SE	Low-pressure system approaching; air pressure drops	Lowering, thickening clouds; precipitation possible
Winds shift direction ranging from SW to NW	Cold-front passage; rising pressure	Drying and clearing likely; possible showers on windward slopes, especially along the U.S. or Canadian west coast
Increasing winds from SE or E	Low-pressure system approaching; continued air pressure drop	Acceleration of increase in wind speed
Increasing winds from SW or W	High-pressure system approaching; accelerating air pressure rise	Gusty winds gradually decrease

27

Estimating Freezing Level and Snow Level

To estimate the elevation at which the temperature drops to 32 degrees Fahrenheit, you simply need to know your elevation and the temperature in degrees Fahrenheit:

Your elevation in feet + $\dfrac{\text{(Fahrenheit temperature - 32) x 1,000}}{\text{3.5}}$ = estimated freezing level

For example:

1,000 feet + $\dfrac{\text{(39 degrees - 32) x 1,000}}{\text{3.5}}$ = 1,000 feet + $\dfrac{\text{7,000}}{\text{3.5}}$ = 1,000 feet + 2,000 = 3,000 feet

To estimate the elevation at which the temperature drops to 0 degrees Celsius, you simply need to know your elevation and the temperature in degrees Celsius:

Your elevation in meters + $\dfrac{\text{(camp temperature - 0 degrees Celsius) x 304}}{\text{2}}$ = estimated freezing level

Once you have estimated the freezing level, use the guidelines in Table 27-4 to estimate the snow level.

TABLE 27-4. ESTIMATING THE SNOW LEVEL		
If	**And If**	**Then**
Stratus clouds or fog present	Steady, widespread precipitation	Expect to find the snow level 1,000 feet (304 meters) below the freezing level
Cumulus clouds present or cold front approaching	Locally heavy precipitation, varying from time to time or place to place	Expect to find the snow level as much as 2,000 feet (608 meters) below the freezing level; snow will stick 1,000 feet (304 meters) below the freezing level

CREATING YOUR OWN WEATHER BRIEFINGS

Consider gathering weather information at least one day, and preferably two days, before your planned departure. That gives you a chance to verify the forecasts by observing conditions. If the forecasts are pretty close to what you actually see, you can proceed with your planning with more confidence than if the forecast and observed weather conditions are 180 degrees apart.

Two Days Before the Trip

- Check the overall weather pattern: the positions of highs, lows, and fronts.
- Check the projected weather forecast for the next two days.

One Day Before the Trip

- Check the current weather to evaluate the accuracy of the previous day's forecasts.
- Again, check the overall weather pattern: the positions of highs, lows, and fronts.
- Check the projected weather for the next two days.
- If the possibility of strong winds, thunderstorms, or significant snow or rain is mentioned, plan on checking for updates every 6 to 8 hours. The lead time on such forecasts is short because of the rapid changes that sometimes occur.

On the First Day of the Trip

- Check the current weather to evaluate the accuracy of the previous day's forecasts.

27

- Check the projected weather for the trip's duration.
- Make a go/no go decision based on current forecasts, the track record of earlier forecasts, personal experience, and the demands of the trip.

APPLYING THE INFORMATION

Mountaineers have a rich supply of weather information sources available to them before they depart on a trip. Although information by itself is of limited use, information gathered with a purpose is of great value. That begins with the vital step of obtaining current forecasts for the locale of the climb, followed by careful observation during the outing. Continue to analyze changes in cloud cover, pressure, and wind speed and direction. Consider all such weather information thoroughly when you select approach and climbing routes, camp locations, and start and turnaround times. Constant awareness of your environment and its impact on your plans will create a greater margin of safety during your pursuit of the freedom of the hills.

Next page: *Porters approaching the West Face of Gasherbrum IV, Pakistan* (Photo by Mark Burns)

27

APPENDIX A
Rating Systems

The development of rating systems for climbing began in the late nineteenth and early twentieth centuries in Britain and Germany. In the 1920s, Willo Welzenbach defined a rating system, using roman numerals and the British adjectival system to compare and describe routes in the Alps, which today forms the basis of the UIAA (Union Internationale des Associations d'Alpinisme) system of rating. Rating systems have since proliferated. Ratings used internationally today include no less than seven systems for rock, four for alpine climbing, four for ice, and two for aid climbing. This appendix briefly describes and compares some of these systems.

A rating system is a tool that helps a climber choose a climb that is challenging and within his or her ability. In some circumstances a rating will indicate the amount and type of equipment needed.

Rating climbs is a subjective task, which makes consistency between climbing areas elusive. The rating of climbs assumes good weather and the best equipment available. Variables that affect the rating include the size, strength, and flexibility of the climber and the type of climb (for instance, face, crack, or friction rock climbing).

Ideally a route is rated by consensus in order to reduce personal bias, though climbs often are rated by the first-ascent party. A guidebook author typically does not climb every route in the guidebook and therefore has to rely on the opinions of others. In some cases a route may have been completed only once.

Ratings described as "stiff" indicate that the climb is harder than it is rated, whereas a description of "soft" indicates it is easier than it is rated. Of course, evaluation of a rating system is no more precise than the rating system itself. Whenever you climb in an area for the first time, it's a good idea to start out on recommended or "starred" routes at a level lower than your usual ability until you can evaluate the local ratings and the nature of the rock.

ALPINE CLIMBING

The National Climbing Classification System (NCCS), developed in the United States, assigns grades to describe the overall difficulty of a multipitch alpine climb or long rock climb in terms of time and technical rock difficulty. It takes the following factors into account: length of climb, number of hard pitches, difficulty of hardest pitch, average pitch difficulty, commitment, routefinding problems, and ascent time. The approach and remoteness of a climb might or might not affect the grade given, depending on the guidebook and area. It should be emphasized that with increasing grade, an increasing level of psychological preparation and commitment is necessary. This system assumes a competent party for the level of climbing expected.

Grade I: Normally requires several hours; can be of any technical difficulty.

Grade II: Requires half a day; any technical difficulty.

Grade III: Requires a day to do the technical portion; any technical difficulty.

Grade IV: Requires a full day for the technical portion; the hardest pitch is usually no less than 5.7 (in the Yosemite Decimal System for rating rock climbs; see below).

Grade V: Requires a day and a half; the hardest pitch is usually 5.8 or harder.

Grade VI: A multiday excursion with difficult free climbing and/or aid climbing.

Like other rating systems, the grade is subjective. For example, the Nose on El Capitan in Yosemite is rated Grade VI. Warren Harding and companions took forty-five days for the first ascent, in 1958. John Long, Billy Westbay, and Jim Bridwell made the first one-day ascent in 1975. Hans Florine and Peter Croft cut the time to under 4½ hours in 1992, and Lynn Hill (accompanied by a belayer) led the first free ascent in 1993 and the first one-day free ascent in 1994. The time needed for a climb is as relative as the abilities and technologies of the climbers. The type of climb affects what factors of the given grade are to be emphasized. Proper planning, including study of a route description, are more valuable in estimating your time than the given grade.

ROCK CLIMBING
Free Climbing

In 1937, a modified Welzenbach rating system was introduced in the United States as the Sierra Club System. In the 1950s, this system was modified to more accurately describe rock climbing being done at Tahquitz Rock in California by adding a decimal to the Class 5 rating. This is now known as the Yosemite Decimal System (YDS). This system categorizes terrain according to the techniques and physical difficulties encountered when rock climbing. (See Figure A-1 for a comparison of the YDS with other international rating systems.)

Class 1: Hiking.

Class 2: Simple scrambling, with possible occasional use of the hands.

Class 3: Scrambling; a rope might be carried.

Class 4: Simple climbing, often with exposure. A rope is often used. A fall on Class-4 rock could be fatal. Typically, natural protection can be easily found.

Class 5: Where rock climbing begins in earnest. Climbing involves the use of a rope, belaying, and protection (natural or artificial) to protect the leader from a long fall.

The decimal extension of Class-5 climbing originally was meant to be a closed-end scale of 5.0 to 5.9. Up until 1960 or so, a climb that was the hardest of that era would be rated 5.9. The rising standards in the 1960s, however, led to a need for an open-ended scale. Strict decimal protocol was abandoned, and 5.10 (pronounced "five-ten") was adopted as the next highest level. As the open-ended system let the decimal numbers go up to 5.11, 5.12, and ever higher, not all climbs were rerated, leaving a disparity between the "old-school ratings" and the new ratings.

The YDS numbers reached 5.15 in the first few years of the twenty-first century. The ratings from 5.10 to 5.15 are subdivided into a, b, c, and d levels to more precisely state the difficulty. The most difficult 5.12 climb, for instance, is rated 5.12d. A plus sign or a minus sign is occasionally used as a more approximate way to refine a classification. Sometimes a plus sign will be added to indicate that the pitch is sustained at its particular rating, while a minus sign might indicate that the pitch has only a single move at that level.

The extended numbers of the fifth-class rating system can't be defined precisely, but the following descriptions offer general guidelines:

5.0–5.7: Easy for experienced climbers; where most novices begin.

5.8–5.9: Where most weekend climbers become comfortable; employs the specific skills of rock climbing, such as jamming, liebacks, and mantels.

5.10: A dedicated weekend climber might attain this level.

5.11–5.15: The realm of true experts; demands much training and natural ability and, often, repeated working of a route.

The YDS rates only the hardest move on a pitch and, for multipitch climbs, the hardest pitch on a climb. The YDS gives no indication of overall difficulty, protection, exposure, runout, or strenuousness. Some guidebooks, however, will rate a pitch harder than the hardest move if it is very sustained at a lower level. A guidebook's

UIAA	FRENCH	YOSEMITE DECIMAL SYSTEM	AUSTRALIAN	BRAZILIAN	BRITISH	
I	1	5.2			3a	VD
II	2	5.3	11		3b	
III	3	5.4	12	II	3c	HVD / MS
IV	4	5.5		IIsup	4a	S
V–		5.6	13	III	4b	HS
V	5	5.7	14	IIIsup		VS
V+			15		4c	
VI–		5.8	16	IV		HVS
VI	6a	5.9	17 / 18	IVsup	5a	E1
VI+	6a+	5.10a	19	V		
VII–	6b	5.10b / 5.10c	20 / 21	Vsup / VI	5b	E2
VII	6b+	5.10d	22	VIsup	5c	E3
VII+	6c / 6c+	5.11a / 5.11b	23	VII		E4
VIII–	7a	5.11c	24	VIIsup	6a	
VIII	7a+ / 7b	5.11d / 5.12a	25	VIII / VIIIsup		E5
VIII+	7b+	5.12b	26		6b	E6
IX–	7c	5.12c / 5.12d	27		6c	
IX	7c+	5.13a	28		7a	E7
IX+	8a	5.13b / 5.13c	29 / 30			
X–	8a+		31			
X	8b / 8b+	5.13d	32			
X+	8c	5.14a	33			
XI–	8c+	5.14b / 5.14c				
XI	9a	5.14d				
XI+	9a+	5.15a				
XII–		5.15b				

Fig. A-1.
Rating systems.

introduction should explain any variations on the YDS that may be used.

Because the YDS does not calculate the potential of a fall, but only the difficulty of a move or pitch, a seriousness rating has been developed. This seriousness rating (introduced by James Erickson in 1980) appears in guidebooks in a variety of forms; read the introduction to any guidebook for an explanation of its particular version.

PG-13: Protection is adequate; if it is properly placed, a fall would not be long.

R: Protection is considered inadequate; there is potential for a long fall, and a falling leader would take a real whipper, suffering injuries.

X: Inadequate or no protection; a fall would be very long with serious, perhaps fatal, consequences.

Ratings of the quality of routes are common in guidebooks. If anything, they are even more subjective than the basic climb ratings because they attempt to indicate aesthetics. The number of stars given for a route indicates the quality of the route in the eyes of the guidebook writer. A standard number of stars for the very best climbs has not been established. A climb with no stars does not mean the climb isn't worth doing, nor does a star-spangled listing mean that everyone will like the route.

Aid Climbing

Rating aid moves or aid climbs is different from rating free climbs in that the rating system is not open-ended like the YDS. An aid-climbing rating indicates the difficulty of placing protection and the quality of that protection.

The scale is from A0 to A5 or from C0 to C5. The "A" refers to aid climbs in general, which may utilize pitons, bolts, or chocks. The "C" refers to clean aid climbing, using only chocks, which do not mar the rock. It is sometimes possible to clean-climb a route that is rated with the A0–A5 system. For a climb rated with the C0–C5 system, subsequent climbers are expected to honor the clean style that has been established.

The following rating system is used worldwide except in Australia, which uses M0 to M8; the "M" stands for mechanical:

A0 or C0: Fixed protection is in place.

A1 or C1: Easy aid placements, where virtually every placement is capable of holding a fall. Often climbed "French free," simply grabbing the fixed gear.

A2 or C2: Placements are fairly good, but may be tricky to place. There may be a couple of bad placements between good placements.

A2+ or C2+: Same as A2, though with increased fall potential—perhaps 20 to 30 feet (6 to 10 meters).

A3 or C3: Hard aid. Several hours to lead a pitch, with the potential of 60- to 80-foot (18- to 24-meter) falls, but without danger of grounding or serious injury. Requires active testing of placements.

A3+ or C3+: Same as A3, but with the potential of serious injury in a fall. Tenuous placements.

A4 or C4: Serious aid. Fall potential of 80 to 100 feet (24 to 30 meters), with very bad landings. Placements hold only body weight.

A4+ or C4+: More serious than A4. More time on the route, with increased danger.

A5 or C5: Placements hold only body weight for an entire pitch, with no solid protection such as bolts. A leader fall at the top of an A5 pitch means a 300-foot (90-meter) fall.

A5+: A theoretical grade; A5, but with bad belay anchors. If you fall, you go until you hit the ground.

Aid ratings are always subject to change. What was once a difficult A4 seam may have been beaten out with pitons to the point that it will accept large chocks, rendering it C1. Camming devices and other examples of newer technology can sometimes turn difficult climbs into easy ones. Some climbs once considered A5 might now be rated A2 or A3 by today's standards.

Bouldering

Bouldering—climbing on large rocks, fairly close to the ground—has gained popularity. Though once a game played by alpinists in mountain boots on days too rainy to climb, bouldering has become an all-out pursuit of its own. John Gill created his B-scale to rate boulder problems:

B1: Requires moves at a high level of skill—moves that would be rated 5.12 or 5.13.

B2: Moves as hard as the hardest climbs being done in

standard rock climbing (5.15 as of 2003).

B3: A successful B2 climb that has yet to be repeated. Once repeated, the boulder rating automatically drops to B2.

John Sherman created the open-ended V-scale, which gives permanent ratings to boulder problems (unlike Gill's scale, with its floating ratings). As shown in Figure A-2, Sherman's scale starts at V0- (comparable to 5.8 YDS); it moves up through V0, V0+, V1, V2, and

YOSEMITE DECIMAL SYSTEM	SHERMAN V-SCALE (BOULDERING)
5.8	V0-
5.9	V0
5.10a/b	V0+
5.10c/d	V1
5.11a/b	V2
5.11c/d	V3
5.12-	V4
5.12	V5
5.12+	V6
5.13-	V7
5.13	V8
5.13+	V9
5.14-	V10
5.14	V11
5.14+	V12
5.15-	V13
5.15	V14
5.15+	V15

Fig. A-2.
The Sherman V-scale for rating boulder problems compared with the Yosemite Decimal System for rating rock climbs.

so on, with V14 being comparable to 5.15 YDS. Neither the B nor V scale takes into account the consequences of a rough landing on uneven terrain.

ICE CLIMBING

The variable conditions of snow and ice climbing make rating climbs difficult. The only factors that usually do not vary throughout the season and from year to year are length and steepness. Snow depth, thickness of the ice, and temperature affect the conditions of the route; these factors plus the nature of the ice and its protection possibilities determine a route's difficulty. These rating systems apply mainly to waterfall ice and other ice formed by meltwater (rather than from consolidating snow, as on glaciers).

Commitment Rating

The important factors in this ice-climbing rating system are length of the approach and descent, length of the climb itself, objective hazards, and the nature of the climbing. (The roman-numeral ratings used in this system have no correlation to the numerals used in the grading system for alpine climbs.)

I: A short, easy climb near the road, with no avalanche hazard and a straightforward descent.

II: A route of one or two pitches within a short distance of rescue assistance, with very little objective hazard.

III: A multipitch route at low elevation, or a one-pitch climb with an approach that takes an hour or so. The route requires from a few hours to a long day to complete. Descent may require building rappel anchors, and the route might be prone to avalanche.

IV: A multipitch route at higher elevations; may require several hours of approach on skis or foot. Subject to objective hazards; possibly with a hazardous descent.

V: A long climb in a remote setting, requiring all day to complete the climb itself. Requires many rappels off anchors for the descent. Sustained exposure to avalanche or other objective hazard.

VI: A long ice climb in an alpine setting, with sustained technical climbing. Only elite climbers will complete it in a day. A difficult and involved approach and descent, with objective hazards ever-present, all in a remote area far from the road.

VII: Everything a grade VI has, and more of it. Possibly requires days to approach the climb, and objective hazards render survival as certain as a coin toss. Needless to say, difficult physically and mentally.

Technical Rating

The technical grade rates the single most difficult pitch, taking into account the sustained nature of the climbing, ice thickness, and natural ice features, such as chandeliers, mushrooms, or overhanging bulges. These ratings have been further subdivided, with a plus added to grades of 4 and above if the route is usually more difficult than its stated numerical grade.

1: A frozen lake or streambed (the equivalent of an ice rink).

2: A pitch with short sections of ice up to 80 degrees; lots of opportunity for protection and good anchors.

3: Sustained ice up to 80 degrees; the ice is usually good, with places to rest, but it requires skill at placing pro and setting anchors.

4: A sustained pitch that is vertical or slightly less than vertical; may have special features such as chandeliers and runouts between protection.

5: A long, strenuous pitch—possibly 165 feet (50 meters) of 85- to 90-degree ice with few if any rests between anchors. Or the pitch may be shorter, but on featureless ice. Good skills at placing protection are required.

6: A full 165-foot pitch of dead-vertical ice, possibly of poor quality; requires efficiency of movement and ability to place protection while in awkward stances.

7: A full pitch of thin vertical or overhanging ice of dubious adhesion. An extremely tough pitch, physically and mentally, requiring agility and creativity.

8: Thin, gymnastic, overhanging, and bold. Pure ice climbs at this level are extremely rare.

These ratings usually describe a route in its first-ascent condition. Therefore a route that was rated a 5 on its first ascent might be a 6- in a lean year for ice, but only a 4+ in a year with thick ice. The numerical ice ratings are often prefaced with WI (water ice, or frozen waterfalls); AI (alpine ice); or M (mixed rock and ice). (Historically, mixed climbs were described with the Yosemite Decimal System.)

New England Ice Rating System

This system was developed for the water ice found in New England. It applies to normal winter ascent of a route in moderate weather conditions:

NEI 1: Low-angle water ice of 40 to 50 degrees, or a long moderate snow climb requiring a basic level of technical expertise for safety.

NEI 2: Low-angle water ice with short bulges up to 60 degrees.

NEI 3: Steeper water ice of 50 to 60 degrees, with bulges of 70 to 90 degrees.

NEI 4: Short vertical columns, interspersed with rests, on 50- to 60-degree ice; fairly sustained climbing.

NEI 5: Generally multipitch ice climbing with sustained difficulties and/or strenuous vertical columns, with little rest possible.

NEI 5+: Multipitch routes with a heightened degree of seriousness, long vertical sections, and extremely sustained difficulties; the hardest ice climbing in New England to date.

Mixed Climbing

Jeff Lowe introduced the Modern Mixed Climbing Grade to simplify the rating of the crux on mixed ice and rock routes. It is an open-ended scale with routes rated M1 to M11 or so. A plus sign or a minus sign is added to broaden the range and to prevent grade compression. It is the consensus of top climbers that the M ratings in Europe are inflated by one grade. See Figure A-3 for a comparison of the M grades to YDS ratings.

OTHER MAJOR RATING SYSTEMS

A variety of rating systems are used throughout the world. Figure A-1 compares the principal systems. Apart from the main rating systems described here, there are other rating systems used around the world, which are unique to their own treatment of seriousness

MODERN MIXED GRADE	YOSEMITE DECIMAL SYSTEM
M4	5.8
M5	5.9
M6	5.10
M7	5.11
M8	5.11 + /5.12–
M9	5.12 + /5.13–
M10	5.13 + /5.14–
M11	5.14 + /5.15–

Fig. A-3.

Comparison of the Modern Mixed Climbing Grade for mixed rock and ice climbs with the Yosemite Decimal System for rating rock climbs.

and local weather and conditional phenomena. The Alaska Grade, for example, is a grading system unique to Alaska that takes into account severe storms, cold, altitude, and cornicing, and extends from Grade 1 to 6 (instead of overall commitment ratings I to VII).

When climbing in a new area, be sure to check with local authorities and/or guidebooks and become knowledgeable about any possible local grading systems and their peculiarities.

Rock Climbing

Australian: The Australian system uses open-ended numerics. The Australian number 33, for example, is equivalent to 5.14a in the Yosemite Decimal System.

Brazilian: The rating of climbs in Brazil is composed of two parts. The first part gives the general level of difficulty of the route as a whole, ranging from first to eighth grade (or degree). The second part gives the difficulty of the hardest free move (or sequence of moves without a natural rest), expressed in roman numerals; the designation "sup" (for superior) can be added to a numeral in order to refine the accuracy of the rating. (Figure A-1 shows only the roman numeral portion of

the Brazilian system, which is the part that is most comparable to the other systems shown.)

British: The British system is composed of two elements, an adjectival grade and a technical grade.

The adjectival grade (such as Very Difficult or Hard Severe) describes the overall difficulty of a route, including such factors as exposure, seriousness, strenuousness, protection, and runouts. The list of adjectives to describe increasingly difficult routes became so cumbersome that the British finally ended it at Extremely Severe, and now simply advance the listing with numbers: E1 for Extremely Severe 1; E2 for Extremely Severe 2; and so forth:

Easy	E
Moderate	M
Difficult	D
Very Difficult	VD
Hard Very Difficult	HVD
Mild Severe	MS
Severe	S
Hard Severe	HS
Very Severe	VS
Hard Very Severe	HVS
Extremely Severe 1	E1
Extremely Severe 2	E2
Extremely Severe 3	E3
Etc.	

The technical grade is defined as the hardest move on a particular route. This numeric component of the British system is also open-ended and is subdivided into a, b, and c.

The two grades are linked to each other. For example, the standard adjectival grade for a well-protected 6a, which is not particularly sustained, is E3 (and the combined rating would be expressed as E3 6a). If the route is a bit runout, it would be E4; if it is really runout, it would be E5.

French: In the French open-ended system, ratings of 6 and above are subdivided into a, a+, b, b+, c, and c+. The French rating of 8c is comparable to 5.14a.

UIAA: The UIAA open-ended rating system uses Roman numerals. Beginning with the fifth level (V), the ratings also include pluses and minuses. The UIAA rating of X+ is comparable to 5.14a. German climbers use the UIAA system.

Alpine Climbing/Ice Climbing

The International French Adjectival System (IFAS) is an overall rating of alpine and ice climbs used primarily in the Alps. The system is utilized by several countries, including France, Britain, Germany, Italy, and Spain. It expresses the seriousness of the route, including factors such as length, objective danger, commitment, altitude, runouts, descent, and technical difficulty in terms of terrain.

The system has six categories that are symbolized by the initials of the French adjectives used. It is further refined with the use of plus or minus signs, or the terms "sup" (superior) or "inf" (inferior). The ratings end with an adjective readily understood in English:

F: *Facile* ("easy"). Steep walking routes, rock scrambling, and easy snow slopes. Crevasses possible on glaciers. Rope not always necessary.

PD: *Peu difficile* ("a little difficult"). Rock climbing with some technical difficulty, snow and ice slopes, serious glaciers, and narrow ridges.

AD: *Assez difficile* ("fairly difficult"). Fairly hard climbs, steep rock climbing, and long snow/ice slopes above 50 degrees.

D: *Difficile* ("difficult"). Sustained hard rock and snow/ice climbing.

TD: *Tres difficile* ("very difficult"). Serious technical climbing on all kinds of terrain.

ED: *Extremement difficile* ("extremely difficult"). Extremely serious climbs with long, sustained difficulties of the highest order.

ABO: *Abominable*.

Wind Chill Temperature Index

Wind chill gives us an idea of how the cold, amplified by wind, will affect exposed skin. Wind chill is based on heat-transfer theory. As the wind increases, it draws heat away from exposed skin, speeding up relative cooling time. Therefore, the wind makes exposed skin cool at a faster rate than if there were no wind at all. For example, if the temperature is minus 10 degrees Fahrenheit (minus 23 degrees Celsius) and the wind is blowing at 25 miles per hour (40 kilometers per hour), then the wind chill is minus 37 degrees Fahrenheit (minus 38 degrees Celsius), as shown in Figure B-1. At this temperature and at this wind speed, exposed skin can freeze in 10 minutes.

Keep in mind that the wind chill affects only exposed skin. If you are properly dressed for the mountain environment, implement a layering clothing system, cover your extremities, and wear a balaclava in extreme cold and wind, then you will not encounter the wind chill effect.

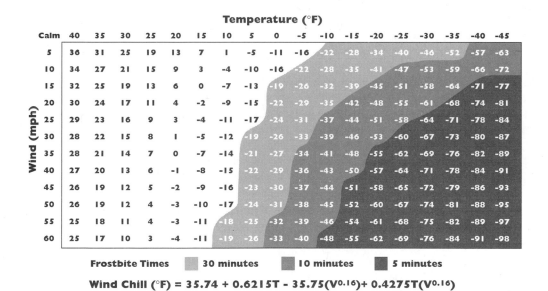

Temperature (°F)

Wind (mph) \ Temp	Calm	40	35	30	25	20	15	10	5	0	-5	-10	-15	-20	-25	-30	-35	-40	-45
5		36	31	25	19	13	7	1	-5	-11	-16	-22	-28	-34	-40	-46	-52	-57	-63
10		34	27	21	15	9	3	-4	-10	-16	-22	-28	-35	-41	-47	-53	-59	-66	-72
15		32	25	19	13	6	0	-7	-13	-19	-26	-32	-39	-45	-51	-58	-64	-71	-77
20		30	24	17	11	4	-2	-9	-15	-22	-29	-35	-42	-48	-55	-61	-68	-74	-81
25		29	23	16	9	3	-4	-11	-17	-24	-31	-37	-44	-51	-58	-64	-71	-78	-84
30		28	22	15	8	1	-5	-12	-19	-26	-33	-39	-46	-53	-60	-67	-73	-80	-87
35		28	21	14	7	0	-7	-14	-21	-27	-34	-41	-48	-55	-62	-69	-76	-82	-89
40		27	20	13	6	-1	-8	-15	-22	-29	-36	-43	-50	-57	-64	-71	-78	-84	-91
45		26	19	12	5	-2	-9	-16	-23	-30	-37	-44	-51	-58	-65	-72	-79	-86	-93
50		26	19	12	4	-3	-10	-17	-24	-31	-38	-45	-52	-60	-67	-74	-81	-88	-95
55		25	18	11	4	-3	-11	-18	-25	-32	-39	-46	-54	-61	-68	-75	-82	-89	-97
60		25	17	10	3	-4	-11	-19	-26	-33	-40	-48	-55	-62	-69	-76	-84	-91	-98

Frostbite Times   ▓ **30 minutes**   ▓ **10 minutes**   ▓ **5 minutes**

Wind Chill (°F) = 35.74 + 0.6215T − 35.75($V^{0.16}$) + 0.4275T($V^{0.16}$)

Where T = Air Temperature (°F) and V = Wind Speed (mph)

Fig. B-1.
Wind chill temperature index (Source: National Oceanographic and Atmospheric Administration, National Weather Service).

APPENDIX C
Supplementary Reading

Chapter 1. First Steps

Csiksezentmihalyi, Mihaly. *Flow: The Psychology of Optimal Experience.* New York: HarperCollins, 1991.

O'Connell, Nicholas. *Beyond Risk: Conversations with Climbers.* Seattle: The Mountaineers Books, 1995.

Rebuffat, Gaston. *Starlight and Storm.* New York: Modern Library, 1999.

Chapter 2. Clothing and Equipment

Carline, Jan D., Martha J. Lentz, and Steven C. Macdonald. *Mountaineering First Aid: A Guide to Accident Response and First Aid Care.* Seattle: The Mountaineers Books, 1996.

Manning, Harvey. *Backpacking One Step at a Time.* New York: Random House, 1986.

Soles, Clyde. *Rock and Ice Gear: Equipment for the Vertical World.* Seattle: The Mountaineers Books, 2000.

Weiss, Hal. *Secrets of Warmth: For Comfort or Survival.* Seattle: The Mountaineers Books, 1998.

Wilkerson, James A., M.D., ed. *Medicine for Mountaineering and Other Wilderness Activities.* 5th ed. Seattle: The Mountaineers Books, 2001.

Chapter 3. Camping and Food

Backer, Howard. "In Search of the Perfect Water Treatment Method." *Wilderness and Environmental Medicine* 11 (2000): 1–4.

Curtis, Rick. *The Backpacker's Field Manual: A Comprehensive Guide to Mastering Backcountry Skills.* New York: Three Rivers Press, 1998.

Fleming, June. *The Well-Fed Backpacker.* New York: Vintage Books, 1986.

Gorman, Stephen. *Winter Camping.* 2d ed. Lebanon, N.H.: Appalachian Mountain Club, 1999.

Howe, Steve, Alan Kesselheim, and Dennis Coello. *Making Camp: A Complete Guide for Hikers, Mountain Bikers, Paddlers and Skiers.* Seattle: The Mountaineers Books, 1997.

Keyes, Linda E., Robert S. Hamilton, and John S. Rose. "Carbon Monoxide Exposure from Cooking in Snow Caves at High Altitude." *Wilderness and Environmental Medicine* 12 (2001): 208–12.

Miller, Dorcas. *Backcountry Cooking: From Pack to Plate in 10 Minutes.* Seattle: The Mountaineers Books, 1998.

Prater, Yvonne, and Ruth D. Mendenhall. *Gorp, Glop and Glue Stew: Favorite Foods from 165 Outdoor Experts.* Seattle: The Mountaineers Books, 1982.

Prichard, Nancy. "Buying a Camp Stove," "Buying a Camp Stove: Cartridge Stoves," "Buying a Camp Stove: Liquid Gas," "Buying a Camp Stove: Before You Buy." Available from *www.gorp.com.*

Tilton, Buck, and Rick Bennett, Ph.D. *Don't Get Sick: The Hidden Dangers of Camping and Hiking.* Seattle: The Mountaineers Books, 2002.

Townsend, Chris. *The Backpacker's Handbook.* 2d ed. New York: McGraw-Hill, 1996.

Chapter 4. Physical Conditioning

Ilg, Steve. *The Outdoor Athlete: Total Training for Outdoor Performance.* Boulder, Colo.: Johnson Books, 1987.

Musnick, David, M.D., and Mark Pierce, A.T.C. *Conditioning for Outdoor Fitness.* Seattle: The Mountaineers Books, 1999.

Schurman, C. W., and D. G. Schurman. *How to Train to Climb Mt. Rainier.* Seattle: Body Results, 2002. Video, 63 minutes. Available from *www.bodyresults.com.*

Twight, Mark, and James Martin. *Extreme Alpinism: Climbing Light, Fast, and High.* Seattle: The Mountaineers Books, 1999.

Chapter 5. Navigation
Burns, Bob, and Mike Burns. *Wilderness Navigation.* Seattle: The Mountaineers Books, 1999.

Canadian Geomagnetic Reference Field. Available at *www.geolab.nrcan.gc.ca/geomag/e_cgrf.html.*

Fleming, June. *Staying Found.* 3d ed. Seattle: The Mountaineers Books, 2001.

Letham, Lawrence. *GPS Made Easy.* Seattle: The Mountaineers Books, 2001.

Renner, Jeff. *Northwest Mountain Weather.* Seattle: The Mountaineers Books, 1992.

USGS. *Magnetic Field of the U.S. Declination Chart.* Denver, Colo.: USGS (P.O. Box 25286, 80225; 888-ASK-USGS).

Chapter 6. Wilderness Travel
Allen, Dan. *Don't Die on the Mountain.* 2d ed. New London, N.H.: Diapensia Press, 1998.

Berger, Karen. *Everyday Wisdom.* Seattle: The Mountaineers Books, 1997.

Fletcher, Colin, and Chip Rawlins. *The Complete Walker IV.* New York: Alfred A. Knopf, 2002.

Herrero, Stephen. *Bear Attacks: Their Causes and Avoidance.* Guilford, Conn.: The Lyons Press, 2002.

Nelson, Dan. *Predators at Risk.* Seattle: The Mountaineers Books, 2000.

Petzoldt, Paul. *The New Wilderness Handbook.* New York: W. W. Norton, 1984.

Schrad, Jerry, and David Moser, eds. *Wilderness Basics.* 2d ed. Seattle: The Mountaineers Books, 1993.

Smith, Dave. *Backcountry Bear Basics.* Seattle: The Mountaineers Books, 1997.

Chapter 7. Leave No Trace
Hampton, Bruce, and David Cole. *Soft Paths: How to Enjoy the Wilderness Without Harming It.* Mechanicsburg, Pa.: Stackpole Books, 1995.

McGivney, Annette. *Leave No Trace: A Guide to the New Wilderness Etiquette.* 2d ed. Seattle: The Mountaineers Books, 2003.

National Outdoor Leadership School. *Leave No Trace, Outdoor Skills and Ethics.* Booklet series specific to geographic regions and outdoor activities. Boulder, Colo.: Leave No Trace, Inc.

Strauss, Robert. *Adventure Trekking: A Handbook for Independent Travelers.* Seattle: The Mountaineers Books, 1995.

Chapter 8. Stewardship and Access
Access Fund, The. *Climbing Management: A Guide to Climbing Issues and the Production of a Climbing Management Plan.* Boulder, Colo.: The Access Fund, 2001.

Attarian, Aram, Ph.D., and Kath Pyke, M.S., comp. *Climbing and Natural Resources Management: An Annotated Bibliography.* Raleigh, N.C.: North Carolina State University; Boulder, Colo.: The Access Fund, 2001. Available at *www.accessfund.org.*

Leave No Trace, Inc. *Skills & Ethics: Rock Climbing.* Boulder, Colo.: Leave No Trace, Inc., 2001. Available at *www.lnt.org.*

Chapter 9. Basic Safety System
Lewis, S. Peter, and Dan Cauthorn. *Climbing: From Gym to Crag.* Seattle: The Mountaineers Books, 2000.

Luebben, Craig. *Knots for Climbers.* Guilford, Conn.: Globe Pequot/Falcon, 2001.

Owen, Peter. *The Book of Climbing Knots.* Guilford, Conn.: The Lyons Press, 2000.

Soles, Clyde. *Rock and Ice Gear: Equipment for the Vertical World.* Seattle: The Mountaineers Books, 2000.

Chapter 10. Belaying
Lewis, S. Peter, and Dan Cauthorn. *Climbing: From Gym to Crag.* Seattle: The Mountaineers Books, 2000.

Long, John. *Climbing Anchors.* Guilford, Conn.: Globe Pequot/Falcon, 1993.

Long, John, and Bob Gaines. *More Climbing Anchors.* Guilford, Conn.: Globe Pequot/Falcon, 1998.

Chapter 11. Rappelling
Lewis, S. Peter, and Dan Cauthorn. *Climbing: From Gym to Crag.* Seattle: The Mountaineers Books, 2000.

Luebben, Craig. *How to Rappel.* Guilford, Conn.: Globe Pequot/Falcon, 2000.

Luebben, Craig. *Knots for Climbers.* Guilford, Conn.: Globe Pequot/Falcon, 2001.

Chapter 12. Alpine Rock-Climbing Technique

Goodard, D., and U. Neumann. *Performance Rock Climbing.* Mechanicsburg, Pa.: Stackpole Books, 1993.

Lewis, S. Peter, and Dan Cauthorn. *Climbing: From Gym to Crag.* Seattle: The Mountaineers Books, 2000.

Long, John. *Sport and Face Climbing.* Evergreen, Colo.: Chockstone Press, 1994.

———. *How to Rock Climb!* 3d ed. Guilford, Conn.: Globe Pequot/Falcon, 2000.

Long, John, and John Middendorf. *Big Walls.* Guilford, Conn.: Globe Pequot/Falcon, 1994.

Loughman, Michael. *Learning to Rock Climb.* San Francisco: Sierra Club Books, 1981.

Chapter 13. Rock Protection and Chapter 14. Leading on Rock

Long, John. *Climbing Anchors.* Guilford, Conn.: Globe Pequot/Falcon, 1993.

Long, John, and Bob Gaines. *More Climbing Anchors.* Guilford, Conn.: Globe Pequot/Falcon, 1998.

Long, John, and Craig Luebben. *Advanced Rock Climbing.* Guilford, Conn.: Globe Pequot/Falcon, 1997.

Chapter 15. Aid Climbing

Long, John, and John Middendorf. *Big Walls.* Guilford, Conn.: Globe Pequot/Falcon, 1994.

McNamara, Chris. *Yosemite Big Walls: SuperTopos.* San Francisco: SuperTopo, 2000.

Robbins, Royal. *Advanced Rock Craft.* Glendale, Calif.: La Siesta Press, 1973.

Chapter 16. Snow Travel and Climbing

Armstrong, Betsy R., and Knox Williams. *The Avalanche Book.* Golden, Colo.: Fulcrum Publishing, 1992.

Atkins, Dale. *Avalanche Rescue Beacons: A Race against Time.* Video, 38 minutes. Boulder, Colo.: People Productions, 1995.

Cliff, Peter. *Ski Mountaineering.* Seattle: Pacific Search Press, 1987.

Daffern, Tony. *Avalanche Safety for Skiers and Climbers.* 2d ed. Seattle: The Mountaineers Books, 2000.

Dostie, Craig. "Ooops on the Range: Beacon Basics for the Primary Search." *Couloir* (November 2001): 84–87.

Fredston, Jill A., and Doug Fesler. *Snow Sense.* Anchorage: Alaska Mountain Safety, 1999.

Fyffe, Allen, and Iain Peter. *The Handbook of Climbing.* London: Pelham Books, 1997.

LaChapelle, E. R. *Secrets of Snow: Visual Clues to Avalanche and Ski Conditions.* Seattle: University of Washington Press, 2001.

Ferguson, Sue, and E. R. LaChapelle. *The ABCs of Avalanche Safety.* 3d ed. Seattle: The Mountaineers Books, 2003.

McClung, David, and Peter Schaerer. *The Avalanche Handbook.* Seattle: The Mountaineers Books, 1993.

Parker, Paul. *Free-Heel Skiing: Telemark and Parallel Techniques for all Conditions.* 3d ed. Seattle: The Mountaineers Books, 2001.

Prater, Gene, and Dave Felkley. *Snowshoeing: From Novice to Master.* 5th ed. Seattle: The Mountaineers Books, 2002.

Soles, Clyde. *Rock and Ice Gear: Equipment for the Vertical World.* Seattle: The Mountaineers Books, 2000.

Tremper, Bruce. *Staying Alive in Avalanche Terrain.* Seattle: The Mountaineers Books, 2001.

Twight, Mark, and James Martin. *Extreme Alpinism: Climbing Light, Fast, and High.* Seattle: The Mountaineers Books, 1999.

Wasatch Interpretive Association. *Winning the Avalanche Game.* Video, 60 minutes. Salt Lake City: Wasatch Interpretive Association, 1993.

Westside Network avalanche forecasts and safety information. Available at *www.avalanche.org.*

Chapter 17. Glacier Travel and Crevasse Rescue

Barry, John. *Snow and Ice Climbing.* Seattle: Cloudcap Press, 1987.

Cinnamon, Jerry. *Climbing Rock and Ice: Learning the Vertical Dance.* Camden, Maine: Rugged Mountain Press, 1994.

Cliff, Peter. *Ski Mountaineering.* Seattle: Pacific Search Press, 1987.

Fawcett, Ron, Jeff Lowe, Paul Nunn, and Alan Rouse. *The Climber's Handbook.* San Francisco: Sierra Club Books, 1987.

Ferguson, Sue. *Glaciers of North America.* Golden, Colo.: Fulcrum Publishing, 1992.

Fyffe, Allen, and Iain Peter. *The Handbook of Climbing.* London: Pelham Books, 1997.

Hambrey, Michael and Jurg Alean. *Glaciers.* Cambridge, England: Cambridge University Press, 1992.

March, Bill. *Modern Snow and Ice Techniques.* Milnthorpe, Cumbria, England: Cicerone Press, 1984.

McMullen, John. *The Basic Essentials of Climbing Ice.* Merrillville, Ind.: ICS Books, 1992.

Powers, Phil. *NOLS Wilderness Mountaineering.* Mechanicsburg, Pa.: Stackpole Books, 1993.

Schubert, Pit. *Modern Alpine Climbing, Equipment, and Techniques.* Trans. G. Steele and M. Vapenikova. Milnthorpe, Cumbria, England: Cicerone Press, 1991.

Selters, Andy. *Glacier Travel and Crevasse Rescue.* Seattle: The Mountaineers Books, 1999.

Shirahata, Shiro. *The Karakoram: Mountains of Pakistan.* Seattle: Cloudcap Press, 1990.

Soles, Clyde. *Rock and Ice Gear: Equipment for the Vertical World.* Seattle: The Mountaineers Books, 2000.

Chapter 18. Alpine Ice Climbing and Chapter 19. Waterfall Ice and Mixed Climbing

Barry, John. *Alpine Climbing.* Seattle: Cloudcap Press, 1988.

Chouinard, Yvon. *Climbing Ice.* San Francisco: Sierra Club Books, 1978.

Cliff, Peter. *Ski Mountaineering.* Seattle: Pacific Search Press, 1987.

Fawcett, Ron, Jeff Lowe, Paul Nunn, and Alan Rouse. *The Climber's Handbook.* San Francisco: Sierra Club Books, 1987.

Fyffe, Allen, and Iain Peter. *The Handbook of Climbing.* London: Pelham Books, 1997.

Harmston, Chris. "Myths, Cautions and Techniques of Ice Screw Placement." Paper presented at International Rescue Symposium, 1999. Available at *www.hi.is/~haraldg/isskrufu_paelingar.html.*

Lowe, Jeff. *The Ice Experience.* Chicago: Contemporary Books, 1979.

———. *Ice World: Techniques and Experiences of Modern Ice Climbing.* Seattle: The Mountaineers Books, 1996.

Luebben, Craig. *How to Ice Climb!* Guilford, Conn.: Globe Pequot/Falcon, 2001.

March, Bill. *Modern Snow and Ice Techniques.* Milnthorpe, Cumbria, England: Cicerone Press, 1984.

Raleigh, Duane. *Ice Tools and Techniques.* Carbondale, Colo.: Primedia, Inc. (publisher of *Climbing* magazine), 1995.

Soles, Clyde. *Rock and Ice Gear: Equipment for the Vertical World.* Seattle: The Mountaineers Books, 2000.

Twight, Mark, and James Martin. *Extreme Alpinism: Climbing Light, Fast, and High.* Seattle: The Mountaineers Books, 1999.

Chapter 20. Expedition Climbing

Bearzi, Michael. "Doing the Mixed Thing." *Climbing,* no. 130 (February-March 1992): 101–3.

Bezruchka, Stephen. *The Pocket Doctor.* 3d ed. Seattle: The Mountaineers Books, 1999.

Clark, Nancy. "Expedition Nutrition: Tips for Menu Planning." *Climbing,* no. 97 (August-September 1986): 66–9.

Fyffe, Allen, and Iain Peter. *The Handbook of Climbing.* London: Pelham Books, 1997.

Houston, Charles, M.D. *Going Higher: Oxygen, Man, and Mountains.* 4th ed. Seattle: The Mountaineers, 1998.

Jenkins, Mark, and Dan Moe. "Adventures in the Refrigerator Zone: 30 Tips for Successful Winter Camping." *Backpacker* (October 1993): 42–3.

Soles, Clyde. *Rock and Ice Gear: Equipment for the Vertical World.* Seattle: The Mountaineers Books, 2000.

Warrell, David, and Sarah Anderson, eds. *The Royal Geographic Society Expedition Medicine.* London: Profile Books, 1998.

Chapter 21. Leadership

American Alpine Club and Alpine Club of Canada. *Accidents in North American Mountaineering.* Annual publication. Distributed by The Mountaineers Books, Seattle.

Bass, Bernard M. and Ralph Melvin Stogdill. *Bass and Stogdill's Handbook of Leadership.* 3d ed. New York: Free Press, 1990.

Graham, John. *Outdoor Leadership: Technique, Common Sense, and Self Confidence.* Seattle: The Mountaineers Books, 1997.

Petzoldt, Paul. *The New Wilderness Handbook.* New York: W. W. Norton, 1984.

Roskelley, John. *Nanda Devi: The Tragic Expedition.* Seattle: The Mountaineers Books, 2000.

Chapter 22. Safety

American Alpine Club and Alpine Club of Canada. *Accidents in North American Mountaineering.* Annual publication. Distributed by The Mountaineers Books, Seattle.

Chapter 23. First Aid

Bergeron, J. David, and Gloria Bizjak. *First Responder.* 6th ed. Englewood Cliffs, N.J.: Brady/Prentice Hall, 2000.

Bezruchka, Stephen. *Altitude Illness: Prevention and Treatment.* Seattle: The Mountaineers Books, 1994.

Carline, Jan D., Martha J. Lentz, and Steven C. Macdonald. *Mountaineering First Aid: A Guide to Accident Response and First Aid Care.* 4th ed. Seattle: The Mountaineers Books, 1996.

Darville, Fred T. Jr. *Mountaineering Medicine: A Wilderness Medical Guide.* 12th ed. Berkeley: Wilderness Press, 1989.

Drummond, Roger. *Ticks and What You Can Do about Them.* Revised ed. Berkeley: Wilderness Press, 1998.

Dubas, Frédéric, and Jacques Valloton, eds. *Color Atlas of Mountain Medicine.* St. Louis: Mosby, 1991.

Forgey, William W. *Wilderness Medicine: Beyond First Aid.* 4th ed. Merrillville, Ind.: ICS Books, 1994.

———, ed. *Wilderness Medical Society Practice Guidelines for Wilderness Emergency Care.* 2d ed. Guilford, Conn.: Globe Pequot/Falcon, 1999.

Fritz, Robert L., M.D., and David H. Perrin, Ph.D. "Cold Exposure Injuries: Prevention and Treatment." *Clinics in Sports Medicine* 8, no. 1 (January 1989): 111–28.

Gentile, Douglas A., John A. Morris, Tod Schmelpfing, Sue M. Bass, and Paul S. Auerbach. "Wilderness Injuries and Illness." *Annals of Emergency Medicine* 21, no. 7 (July 1992).

Hackett, Peter H. *Mountain Sickness: Prevention, Recognition, and Treatment.* 2d ed. Golden, Colo.: The American Alpine Club, 1995.

Hackett, Peter H., M.D., and Robert C. Roach, Ph.D. "High Altitude Illness." *New England Journal of Medicine* 345, no. 2 (July 12, 2001): 107–14.

Houston, Charles. *High Altitude: Illness and Wellness.* Merrillville, Ind.: ICS Books, 1993.

Isaac, Jeff, and Peter Goth. *The Outward Bound Wilderness First-Aid Handbook.* New York: Lyons & Burford, 1991.

Milledge, James, John B. West, and Michael P. Ward. *High Altitude Medicine and Physiology.* 3d ed. Edward Arnold, 2000.

Schimelpfenig, Tod, and Linda Lindsey. *Wilderness First Aid.* 3d ed. (National Outdoor Leadership School.) Mechanicsburg, Pa.: Stackpole Books, 2002.

Steele, Peter, M.D. *Backcountry Medical Guide.* 2d ed. Seattle: The Mountaineers Books, 1999.

Tilton, Buck, M.S., and Tom Burke, M.D. *The Wilderness First Responder.* Guilford, Conn.: Globe Pequot/Falcon, 1998.

Tilton, Buck, M.S., and Frank Hubbell, D. O. *Medicine for the Backcountry.* 3d ed. Guilford, Conn.: Globe Pequot/Falcon, 1999.

Van Tilburg, Christopher, M.D., ed. *First Aid: A Pocket Guide. Quick Information for Mountaineering and Backcountry Use.* 4th ed. Seattle: The Mountaineers Books, 2001.

Warrell, David., and Sarah Anderson, eds. *Expedition Medicine.* 6th ed. Fitzroy Dearborn Publishers, 2003.

Weiss, Eric A. *A Comprehensive Guide to Wilderness and Travel Medicine.* 2d ed. Berkeley: Adventure Medical Kits, 1998.

———. *Wilderness 911: A Step-by-Step Guide for Medical Emergencies and Improvised Care in the Backcountry.* Seattle: The Mountaineers Books, 1998.

Wilkerson, James A., ed. *Medicine for Mountaineering and Other Wilderness Activities.* 5th ed. Seattle: The Mountaineers Books, 2001.

Wilkerson, James A., ed., Cameron C. Bangs, and John S. Hayward. *Hypothermia, Frostbite, and Other Cold Injuries: Prevention, Recognition, and Prehospital Treatment.* Seattle: The Mountaineers Books, 1993.

Chapter 24. Alpine Rescue

Fasulo, David. *Self-Rescue.* Guilford, Conn.: Globe Pequot/Chockstone, 1997.

Lipke, Rick. *Technical Rescue Riggers Guide.* Bellingham, Wash.: Conterra Technical Systems, 1997.

Long, John. *Climbing Anchors.* Guilford, Conn.: Globe Pequot/Falcon, 1993.

Long, John, and Bob Gaines. *More Climbing Anchors.* Guilford, Conn.: Globe Pequot/Falcon, 1998.

May, W. G. *Mountain Search and Rescue Techniques.* Boulder, Colo.: Rocky Mountain Rescue Group, Inc., 1973.

Padgett, Allen, and Bruce Smith. *On Rope.* Huntsville, Ala.: National Speleological Society, 1987.

Setnica, Tim. *Wilderness Search and Rescue.* Boston: Appalachian Mountain Club, 1980.

Chapter 25. Mountain Geology

Hiking the Geology Series (various states). Seattle: The Mountaineers Books, various dates.

McPhee, John. *Assembling California.* New York: Farrar, Straus and Giroux, 1993.

———. *Basin and Range.* New York: Farrar, Straus and Giroux, 1981.

Roadside Geology Series (various states). Missoula, Mont.: Mountain Press, various dates.

Chapter 26. The Cycle of Snow

Benn, Douglas I., and David J. A. Evans. *Glaciers and Glaciation.* New York: John Wiley and Sons, 1998.

Colbeck, S., E. Akitaya, R. Armstrong, H. Gubler, J. Lafeuille, K. Lied, D. McClung, and E. Morris. *The International Classification for Seasonal Snow on the Ground.* Cambridge, England: International Glaciological Society and International Association of Scientific Hydrology, 1992.

Ferguson, Sue. *Glaciers of North America: A Field Guide.* Golden, Colo.: Fulcrum Publishing, 1992.

Gray, D. M., and D. H. Male, eds. *Handbook of Snow.* New York: Pergamon Press, 1981.

Hobbs, P. V. *Ice Physics.* Oxford: Claredon Press, 1974.

LaChapelle, Edward R. *Field Guide to Snow Crystals.* Cambridge, England: International Glaciological Society, 1992.

———. *Secrets of Snow: Visual Clues to Avalanche and Ski Conditions.* Seattle: University of Washington Press in association with the International Glaciological Society (Cambridge, England), 2001.

Paterson, W. S. B. *The Physics of Glaciers.* 3d ed. New York: Pergamon Press, 1994.

Post, Austin, and Edward R. LaChapelle. *Glacier Ice.* Seattle: University of Washington Press in association with the International Glaciological Society (Cambridge, England), 2000.

Chapter 27. Mountain Weather

Renner, Jeff. *Lightning Strikes: Staying Safe under Stormy Skies.* Seattle: The Mountaineers Books, 2002.

———. *Northwest Mountain Weather.* Seattle: The Mountaineers Books, 1992.

Schaefer, Vincent J., and John A. Day. *A Field Guide to the Atmosphere.* Boston: Houghton Mifflin Company, 1991.

Whiteman, David C. *Mountain Meteorology: Fundamentals and Applications.* New York and London: Oxford University Press, 2000.

Williams, Jack. *The Weather Book.* McLean, Va.: USA Today, 1992.

Glossary

2:1 pulley system. Rescue system that nearly doubles the amount of weight that a rescue team could haul without a pulley; also called the single-pulley system.

3:1 pulley system. Rescue system that theoretically triples the amount of weight a rescue team could haul without a pulley; also called the Z-pulley system.

accumulation zone. That portion of a glacier that receives more snow every year than it loses to melting.

acute mountain sickness (AMS). An altitude-related illness.

aid climbing. The technique of using gear to support a climber's weight as he or she climbs.

aiders. *See* **etriers.**

alpine rock climbing. Rock climbing that requires mountaineering skills.

alpine start. Starting before daybreak.

AMS. *See* **acute mountain sickness.**

American technique. Cramponing technique that blends flat-footing and front-pointing in combination on steep snow or ice; also called combination technique.

anchor. The point on the mountain to which the climbing system is attached; there are belay anchors, rappel anchors, and protection in rock, snow, and ice.

approach shoes. Lightweight sticky-soled shoes designed for both trails and moderate rock climbing.

ascender. Mechanical device used to ascend a rope.

autoblock. A self-belay backup used for rappelling.

balance-climbing. Moving up from one position of balance to the next.

bashies. Malleable hardware used in aid climbing; also called heads.

bearing. Line between two points measured in degrees.

belay device. A piece of equipment that applies friction to the rope to arrest a fall.

belaying. Fundamental technique of using a rope to stop a fall if one should occur while climbing.

bergschrund. Giant crevasse found at the upper limit of glacier movement, formed where the moving glacier breaks away from the ice cap or snowfield above.

bight. A 180-degree turn in a rope.

big-wall climbing. Climbing on a large, sheer wall, which usually requires bivouacs and extensive aid climbing.

bivy. From the French *bivouac,* meaning "temporary encampment."

bivy sack. No-frills, weatherproof tube shelter.

bollard. A mound carved out of snow or ice and rigged with rope, webbing, or cord to provide an anchor.

bolt. Permanent piece of artificial protection consisting of a threaded bolt that is placed into a hole drilled into rock.

boot. *See* **mountaineering boot.**

braking hand. The belayer's hand that secures the belay; must stay in contact with the rope at all times.

C-pulley system. *See* **2:1 pulley system.**

cairn. A pile of rocks used as a route marker.

cam. *See* **spring-loaded camming device, Tri-cam.**

camming. Application of torquing or counterpressure with climbing gear.

carabiner. Metal snap-links of various shapes and sizes; indispensable and versatile tool of climbing used for belaying, rappelling, clipping in to safety anchors, securing the rope to points of protection, and numerous other tasks.

CEN. Comitée Européen de Normalisation, the European group responsible for creating and maintaining climbing equipment standards. *See also* **UIAA.**

chimney. A crack wide enough to fit a climber's body and narrow enough to allow for opposing force to be applied to both walls.

chock. Climbers' hardware comprising removable protection.

chock pick. Tool used for removing protection; also known as nut tool.

chockstone. A rock firmly lodged in a crack or between gully walls.

clean climbing. Climbing without permanently marring the rock.

cleaning. Removing protection.

combination technique. *See* **American technique.**

contour lines. Lines on topographic maps that represent constant elevations.

cordelette. A long runner usually made of 7-millimeter to 8-millimeter perlon or small-diameter, high-strength cord.

crag climbing. Technical rock climbing close to roads and civilization that does not require alpine skills.

crampons. A set of metal spikes that attach to boots in order to penetrate hard snow and ice.

crevasse. A chasm that splits a glacier.

crux. The most significant, committing, or difficult section of a pitch or climb.

daisy chain. Sewn sling with sewn loops.

deadman. Any object buried in the snow to serve as an anchor.

dihedral. Where two walls meet in approximately a right-angled inside corner; also called an open book.

dry rope. Rope treated with a coating to make it more water-repellent.

dry tooling. Climbing on rock with ice tools and crampons.

dynamic rope. A rope that stretches under loads.

edging. Climbing technique using either the inside or outside edge of the foot so that the edge of the sole is weighted over the hold.

equalization. Equalizing forces on a multipoint anchor.

etriers. Ladderlike slings that allow an aid climber to step up; also called aiders.

fall factor. The length of the fall divided by the length of the rope between belay device and fallen climber.

feeling hand. The belayer's hand that pays the rope in and out.

fixed line. Ropes anchored in place.

fixed pin. Permanent piton.

flagging. Climbing technique that involves extending a limb to prevent pivoting or "barn-door" effect.

flaking. Uncoiling the rope, one loop at a time, into a neat pile.

flat-footing. *See* **French technique.**

fluke. Metal-plate anchor used in snow and sand.

follower. *See* **second.**

free climbing. Climbing using only physical ability to move over the rock via handholds and footholds, without weighting protection.

French technique. Cramponing technique used on moderately steep snow and ice in which the feet are placed flat against the surface of the snow or ice; also called flat-footing.

front-pointing. Kicking front crampon points into hard snow or ice; also known as German technique.

German technique. *See* **front-pointing.**

glissade. A controlled slide on snow.

HACE. *See* **high-altitude cerebral edema.**

HAPE. *See* **high-altitude pulmonary edema.**

halbmastwurf sicherung. German for "half clove-hitch belay," abbreviated as HMS; another term for the Münter hitch. Carabiners stamped "HMS" accommodate the Münter hitch.

heads. Malleable hardware used in aid climbing; also called bashies.

hex. Hexagonally shaped removable protection.

high-altitude cerebral edema (HACE). An altitude-related illness affecting the brain.

high-altitude pulmonary edema (HAPE). An altitude-related illness affecting the lungs.

hip belay. A method of applying friction to the rope with the belayer's body that does not require a mechanical device; also known as a body belay.

ice ax. Specialized ax used by climbers, generally for snow and ice travel.

icefall. Steep, jumbled section of a glacier.

ice screw. Ice protection that is a tubular, hollow screw.

ice tool. Short ice ax used for steep ice climbing.

jugging. Ascending the climbing rope with mechanical ascenders in aid climbing; also called jumaring.

jumaring. *See* **jugging.**

kernmantle rope. Rope composed of a core of braided or parallel nylon filaments encased in a smooth, woven sheath of nylon; designed specifically for climbing.

Kiwi coil. The preferred tie-in method for two-person glacier travel teams.

leader. The climber who takes the lead on a roped pitch.

Leave No Trace. Principles of minimum impact developed by an organization of the same name.

lieback. A rock-climbing technique that uses hands in opposition to feet to create a counterforce.

load-limiting runner. A presewn runner with a series of weaker bar-tacks that fail at lower impact forces and absorb high loads; also called an energy-absorbing sling.

mantel. A climbing technique that uses hand down-pressure to permit raising of the feet.

matching. Climbing technique in which both hands or feet are placed on the same hold.

moat. Gap between snow and rock.

moraine. Mounds of rock and debris deposited by a glacier.

mountaineering boot. Crampon-compatible, stiff-soled footwear.

Münter hitch. A friction knot used for belaying.

nut. Passive removable protection that is a wedging-type chock.

objective hazard. Physical hazard associated with a climbing route, such as rockfall, exposure, and high altitude.

off-width. A crack that is too wide for a hand jam but too narrow for chimney technique.

open book. *See* **dihedral.**

picket. An aluminum stake used for an anchor in snow.

pitch. The distance between belays on a climb.

piton. A metal spike used as protection.

plunge-stepping. A technique for walking down a snow slope that involves assertively stepping away from the slope and landing solidly on the heel with the leg vertical (but knees not locked), transferring weight to the new position.

posthole. To sink deeply with each step in snow.

protection. Point of attachment that links climbing rope to the terrain; also known as pro.

prusik (noun). A friction knot.

prusik (verb). To ascend a climbing rope using friction knots.

randonée skiing. Ski technique used by climbers using hybrid equipment that allows free-heel ascent and alpine descent and that accommodates climbing boots; also know as alpine touring and ski mountaineering.

rappelling. The technique of descending a rope by using friction to safely control the rate of descent.

rest step. Ascent technique that ends every step with a momentary but complete stop.

rock shoe. Specialized rock-climbing footwear with a sticky rubber sole.

rope drag. Friction that impedes the rope's travel.

runner. Length of webbing or cord used to connect components of the climbing safety system; also called a sling.

running belay. Climbing technique in which all members of the rope team climb at the same time, relying on immediate protection rather than a fixed belay.

scrambling. Unroped, off-trail travel that requires some use of hands.

scree. Loose slope of rock fragments smaller than talus.

second. The climber who follows the leader on a roped pitch; also known as a follower.

self-arrest. Ice-ax technique used to stop a fall on snow.

self-belay. Ice-ax technique in which the ice ax is jammed straight down into the snow and held by the head or head and shaft.

serac. Tower of ice on a glacier.

single-pulley system. *See* **2:1 pulley system.**

ski mountaineering. *See* **randonée skiing.**

skins. Strips of textured material attached to the bottom of skis for traction.

SLCD. *See* **spring-loaded camming device.**

sling. *See* **runner.**

smearing. Rock-climbing technique in which the foot points uphill and the climber maximizes sole contact for friction.

snow-pit. Pit dug into snow in order to observe snow conditions.

sport climbing. Technical rock climbing that relies on fixed protection or a top rope and that does not require mountaineering skills.

spring-loaded camming device (SLCD). Active removable protection that uses spring-loaded cam lobes to create opposing force in a crack.

spring-loaded wedge. A chock that uses a small sliding piece to expand the profile of the chock after it is placed in a crack.

static rope. A rope that does not stretch; used for fixed lines and hauling.

stemming. Climbing technique using counterforce in which one foot presses against one feature while the other foot or an opposing hand pushes against another feature; commonly used to climb chimneys or dihedrals. Also called bridging.

step-kicking. Climbing technique that creates ascending steps in snow.

sun cup. Small hollow in snow or ice that is created by melting and evaporation.

talus. Rock fragments large enough to step on individually.

team arrest. Arrest effected by several members of a rope team on a snow slope.

technical climbing. Climbing in which belays or protection should be used for safety.

topos. Topographic maps or route sketches.

Tri-cam. Removable protection with a lobe-shaped camming wedge; can be set actively or passively.

tube chock. Telescoping protection used for off-width cracks.

UIAA. Union Internationale des Associations d'Alpinisme, the internationally recognized authority in setting standards for climbing equipment.

verglas. The thin, clear coating of ice that forms when rainfall or melting snow freezes on a rock surface.

V-thread anchor. A V-shaped tunnel bored into the ice, with a cord or webbing threaded through the tunnel and tied to form a sling.

V-thread tool. A hooking device used to pull cord or webbing through the drilled tunnel of a V-thread ice anchor.

webolette. Cordelette made of 9/16-inch webbing with a loop sewn into each end.

wired nut. Passive removable protection; also known as a chock or stopper.

Z-pulley system. *See* **3:1 pulley system.**

Index

Boldface numbers indicate pages with illustrations or tables.

OTHER TITLES YOU MIGHT ENJOY FROM THE MOUNTAINEERS BOOKS:

Medicine for Mountaineering & Other Wilderness Activities, *James Wilkerson, M.D.*
A classic since 1967, this book starts where most first-aid manuals stop. Written and edited by a team of climber-physicians, this is the perfect companion to *Mountaineering: The Freedom of the Hills.*

Extreme Alpinism: Climbing Light, Fast, & High,
Mark Twight & Jim Martin
This master class centers on climbing the hardest routes with little gear and the most speed.

Fifty Favorite Climbs: The Ultimate North American Tick List,
Mark Kroese
Fifty elite climbers share their favorite routes—a celebration of contemporary climbing history and the climbers who have shaped it.

Climb! The History of Rock Climbing in Colorado,
Jeff Achey & Dudley Chelton.
25th anniversary edition of a cult classic that profoundly changed the world of rock climbing.

FROM THE MOUNTAINEERS OUTDOOR EXPERT SERIES:

Ice & Mixed Climbing:
Modern Technique, *Will Gadd*
Climbing: Expedition Planning,
Clyde Soles & Phil Powers
Climbing: Training for Peak
Performance, *Clyde Soles*
Climbing: From Gym to Crag,
S. Peter Lewis & Dan Cauthorn

READY TO ROCK? OUR GUIDES CAN TAKE YOU THERE:

Alaska: A Climbing Guide, *Mike Wood & Colby Coombs*
Bugaboo Rock: A Climbing Guide, *Randall Green & Joe Bensen*
Selected Climbs in North Carolina, *Yon Lambert & Harrison Shull*
Selected Climbs in the Northeast: Rock, Alpine, & Ice Routes from the Gunks to Acadia,
 S. Peter Lewis & Dave Horowitz
Selected Climbs in the Cascades: Volumes I & II, *Jim Nelson & Peter Potterfield*

Available at fine bookstores and outdoor stores, by phone at 800-553-4453 or on the Web at *www.mountaineersbooks.org*

THE MOUNTAINEERS BOOKS